AVOT

פרקי אבות

A Comprehensive Commentary on the Ethics of the Fathers

Shlomo P. Toperoff

JASON ARONSON INC.
Northvale, New Jersey
Jerusalem

First Jason Aronson Inc. edition—1997

10 9 8 7 6 5 4 3 2 1

Library of Congress Cataloging-in-Publication Data

Toperoff, Shlomo Pesach.
[Lev avot]
Avot : a comprehensive commentary on the Ethics of the fathers / Shlomo P. Toperoff.
p. cm.
Previously published : Lev avot. [Israel?] : S.P. Toperoff, [1984?].
Contains text of Mishnah Avot with English translation.
Includeds index.
ISBN 0-7657-5970-5
1. Mishnah. Avot—Commentaries. I. Mishnah. Avot. II. Mishnah. Avot. English. III. Title.
BM506.A23T66 1997
296.1'23—dc20

96-46456

Manufactured in the United States of America. Jason Aronson Inc. offers books and cassettes. For information and catalog write to Jason Aronson Inc., 230 Livingston Street, Northvale, New Jersey 07647.

To our beloved children
Joy, Naomi, and Meir David

CONTENTS

Abbreviations

ARN.	Avot De Rabbi Nathan.
A.Z.	Avodah Zarah.
B.B.	Bava Batra.
B.K.	Bava Kama.
B.M.	Bava Metzia
Bek.	Bekhorot.
Ber.	Berakhot.
Bez.	Bezah.
Bik.	Bikkurim.
Cant.	Canticles.
Cant. R.	Canticles Rabbah.
I Chron.	I Chronicles.
II Chron.	II Chronicles.
Deut.	Deuteronomy.
Deut. R.	Deuteronomy Rabbah.
Ec.	Ecclesiastes.
Ec. R.	Ecclesiastes Rabbah.
Edu.	Eduyot.
Er.	Eruvin.
Ex.	Exodus.
Ex. R.	Exodus Rabbah.
Ez.	Ezekiel.
Gen.	Genesis.
Gen. R.	Genesis Rabbah.
Git.	Gittin.
Ha.	Hagigah.
Hag.	Haggai.
Hor.	Horayot.
Hul.	Hullin.
Is.	Isaiah.
Jer.	Jeremiah.
Jos.	Joshua.
Jud.	Judges
I K.	I Kings.
II K.	II Kings.
Ket.	Ketubot.
Kid.	Kiddushin.
Lam.	Lamentations.
Lev.	Leviticus.
Lev. R.	Leviticus Rabbah.
M.K.	Moed Katan.
I Mac.	I Maccabees.
II Mac.	II Maccabees.
Maim.	Maimonides.
Mak.	Makkot.
Mal.	Malakhi.
Meg.	Megillah.
Men.	Menahot.
Ned.	Nedarim.
Neh.	Nehemiah.
Nid.	Niddah.
Nu. R.	Numbers Rabbah.
Pes.	Pesahim.
Prov.	Proverbs.
Ps.	Psalms.
R.H.	Rosh Hashanah.
R.	Rabbi.
Ruth R.	Ruth Rabbah.
I Sam.	I Samuel.
II Sam.	II Samuel.
Sanh.	Sanhedrin.
Shab.	Shabbat.
Shev.	Sheviit.
So.	Sotah.
Suk.	Sukkah.
Ta.	Taanit.
Tem.	Temurah.
Y.	Yerushalmi.
Y.K.	Yom Kippur.
Yev.	Yevamot.
Zekh.	Zekhariah.
Zeph.	Zephania.

Foreword

by Sir Immanuel Jakobovits, Chief Rabbi

The association of Fathers with Ethics in Judaism is hardly coincidental. The origins of our people are traced to the three Patriarchs — Fathers in Hebrew, whilst our destiny lies primarily in the field of ethics, the Messianic consummation of the Jewish purpose 'through justice' and 'through righteousness' in Isaiah's vision of Zion's Redemption.

It is because of the centrality of the ethical tradition in the Jewish heritage bequeathed from generation to generation going back to Sinai that the directives on fundamental human virtues and Jewish imperatives on the discipline of life are codified in the Mishnah simply under the title of 'Chapters of the Fathers'. It is for the same reason that no tractate has attracted a greater profusion of learned commentaries and popular expositions.

The author of this volume now adds to his long and distinguished role as a Spiritual Father in Anglo-Jewry the 'fathering' of the teachings and interpretations enshrined in this work as a valuable bequest to generations of readers who, I am confident, will be enriched and ethically edified by his labours.

The literary output of Anglo-Jewish Rabbis is none-too-prolific, specialising more — as most have done — in the pastoral sphere. Rabbi Toperoff's contribution is therefore all the more welcome, and I hope it will add to both our literary and our ethical treasures.

Immanuel Jakobovits
Chief Rabbi

Preface

Because of its singular popularity in the Synagogue, Bet Hamidrash and the Home, Avot has run into many editions and it has been commented upon by many scholars in diverse lands and languages. It is therefore more than strange that in Britain only a small number of editions written by Anglo-Jewish writers have appeared on the horizon.

It is true that some non-Jewish scholars (W.O.E. Osterley, Charles Taylor and Travers Herford) have written able commentaries but Avot is a product of the Jewish genius and should receive the attention of Jewish minds. Even Travers Herford who made a special study of Pharisaism and maintained that he wrote his commentary for Jewish readers, none-the-less admitted that he had reservations and observed that perhaps he may 'Be deaf to melodies which sing divinely to a Jewish ear'. Moreover, Avot is not only an integral part of the Jewish liturgy in the Synagogue but it is also treated as a 'classic' in the Jewish home.

There are a number of our people, who for a variety of reasons, do not attend Divine Service at Minhah on Shabbat when Avot is read, yet they are intensely interested in the contents of this ethical treatise and read and study it keenly at home. Thus the Synagogue and Home, the two main institutions in Jewish Life, join hands in popularising Avot.

Indeed, my commentary is the outcome of Shiurim I have given in the Synagoge and the Home — in Sunderland, Ryhope Road Synagogue, in Newcastle-upon-Tyne, Leazes Park Road Synagogue and Gosforth and Kenton Synagogue, and since my retirement in Israel, I have given weekly Shiurim on Avot in our home.

I should add that of the few specifically Jewish studies on Avot, that of Dr. J. Hertz is rather sketchy and is a section of a larger work, the excellent edition of 'The Authorised Daily Prayer Book' and that of the Reverend J. Israelstam is also an abridged though important section of the Soncino Talmud which covers sixty two tractates. We should also remember that many of our co-religionists have not the capacity to absorb a purely Hebrew commentary, of which there are a goodly number, and would welcome an English edition.

With these considerations in mind, I have decided to join the small number of Anglo-Jewish writers and issue a 'Jewish' comprehensive commentary containing biographical, historical, exegetical, homiletical and hasidic notes, and I pray that it will find favour in the eyes of God and man.

In this presentation which is provided for the general reader I have introduced a new feature, the inclusion at the end of every Mishnah of a hasidic saying, story or parable, which is relevant to the subject matter of the Mishnah. Hasidic literature is a vital and rich section of our spiritual legacy and I feel that the gems of wisdom enshrined in it should reach a wider public. The extracts are culled from a number of hasidic anthologies, and appear under the heading 'Hasidic Lore'.

I take this opportunity of expressing my indebtedness to my late and distinguished father-in-law, Rabbi Zvi Hirsch Ferber, זצ"ל whose works in general and Higyonei Zvi in particular, have inspired me with a number of new insights which have been woven into the fabric of this work.

My sincere thanks to Chief Rabbi Sir Immanuel Jakobovits for his Foreword, also to the Rev. Joseph Halpern, M.A., and particularly to Sol Greenberg B.A., A.C.A. (N.Z.) who have kindly read the proofs of my manuscript and have offered a number of valued suggestions.

Finally, my personal gratitude to my dear wife who has typed the whole of my manuscript with painstaking care and consummate skill.

July 1984 — Tammuz 5744

Introduction.

Avot is an integral part of the Mishnah. As the Mishnah was the work of a number of Sages, so *Avot* is probably the work of a number of Rabbis including Hillel, R. Akiva and R. Meir. However, it is known that the final redactor was R. Judah Ha-Nasi who lived in the second century of the Common Era. Though it is a section of the Mishnah, *Avot* has some special characteristics which set it apart from the rest of the Mishnah.

Title

The first distinction which strikes one is the title. This tractate has often been referred to simply as *Avot*, 'Fathers', which is its original title. The word Perek is applied to the chapters of every tractate in the Talmud and the usual translation of *Pirkei Avot* is Chapters of the Fathers or Ethics of the Fathers, which is a paraphrase epitomising the contents of the tractate, but is not a translation. That the title *Avot* was known to, and used by, the Rabbis is attested to by the well known saying recorded in the Talmud (B.K. 30a), 'He who would become a saint (pious) should fulfil the words of Nezikin; Rava said, the words of *Avot*'. Both Bahya and Maimonides use this title for our tractate, although the Vitry refers to it by the title Pirkei Avot. The talmudic statement is most instructive. In the first place both R. Judah and Rava suggest that the person who fulfils the words contained in our tractate is saintly or pious. This definition of 'hasid' may have given rise to the English sub-title of *Avot*, namely —The Ethics of the Fathers , for a hasid (Aramaic hasida) is one who regulates his life in accordance with the ethical and moral teachings of Judaism. Secondly, R. Judah reminds us that *Avot* is one of the tractates of Seder Nezikin, one of the Six Orders of the Mishnah, and deals with civil damages. At the outset it seems strange that *Avot* should be included in a section dealing with 'damages'. However, R. Judah wishes to convey a significant message. In addition to the outward mitzvot such as Tefillin, Tzitzit, Tallit and Mezuzah which people can see, God seeks the heart and the mind, so that man does His bidding in a quiet and unostentatious manner. Inner convictions and outward behaviour should agree with each other; one should not have double standards. The Rabbis tersely express this in two words, *Tokho Kevaro*, man should be the same 'within and without'. It should be remembered that Nezikin is not restricted to damages incurred against one's property, goods or money; one may damage a person's reputation by thought or word of mouth. R. Judah and Rava do not differ; they speak the same language but couch it in different terms. The hasid, the saintly person, will observe not only Shabbat and Yom Tov, the outward mitzvot, but will act ethically in his vocation, business and professional life; he will always speak the truth and conduct himself honourably.

We must now consider the meaning of *Avot* in this context. The principal types of work prohibited on the Shabbat are called *Avot Melakhah*, the Fathers of Work. We see, therefore, that the word 'Fathers' is used to designate something which is important. The principal characteristics which govern the Jew in his conduct are delineated for us in our tractate and because of their pre-eminence they are called Fathers, *Avot*. Hoffman in his Seder Nezikin cites the expresssion *Avot Haolam* found in Edu, 1:4, which means 'the Fathers of the World', and the thoughts found in *Avot* have a message for the world. We would take this a step further and suggest that as *Avot Melakhah* are followed by *Toledot*, meaning derivatives, so *Pirkei Avot* is the supreme collection of fatherly sayings and from this tractate flow *Toledot*, all other collections and works of this nature which have inspired and guided our people throughout the ages.

Composition of the tractate.

Though *Pirkei Avot* is a section of the Mishnah, it is in content, arrangement and style, very different from the Mishnah. It contains no Halakhic decisions, nor is it devoted to Aggadah. It is an anthology or compendium of ethical, moralistic and philosophical sayings and aphorisms. *Pirkei Avot* was not handed down to us in its present form; it grew in stature and is composed of a number of strands of thought. Unlike *Pirkei Avot*, other tractates are primarily restricted to one special subject. For instance, Berakhot discusses the different blessings which adorn Jewish life. The tractate Shabbat is devoted mainly to the laws of the Shabbat. Rosh Hashannah deals with the New Year and Yoma with Yom Kippur, whilst Megillah discusses the laws of Purim. Moreover, Shabbat, Rosh Hashannah, Yom Kippur and Purim are observed on certain days or seasons of the year. However, *Avot* governs our relationship to God and man every day of the year. In addition, Shabbat, Rosh Hashannah, Yom Kippur and Purim apply only to the Jew, but ethical behaviour is universal and affects the whole human race. At the root of all Jewish ethics is the established fact recorded in the beginning of the Torah, that every man is created in the image of God. This may account for the interest taken in *Avot* by non-Jewish scholars.

In content and form, *Avot* covers a variety of subjects. Thus in the first chapter advice is directed towards the judge and the manner in which he dispenses justice. 'Be very searching in the examination of witnesses' (1:9)... The last words of chapter one are a fitting climax to the cause of justice, 'Judge the truth and the judgment of peace in your gates' (Zekh. 8:16). Indeed, Maimonides suggests that *Avot* is in the fourth Order, Seder Nezikin, and follows Sanhedrin, so that the functions of the judges which are dealt with in Sanhedrin, should be qualified by ethical considerations relating to the judge's office as delineated in *Avot*. It is not surprising that justice looms large in the first chapter of *Avot*, for justice is considered by many authorities to be the first stage or step in the ladder connecting heaven and earth. Justice is indispensable to society and divine justice must be reflected in human justice. Without justice we retrogress to the jungle. In the scale of human behaviour, the Prophet Micah places justice first. God requires us 'to do justice, to love mercy and to walk humbly with your God' (6:8). It is true that the Rabbis assert that justice must be tempered with mercy, but justice precedes mercy: justice is definitely one of the 'Fathers' of Jewish life.

It is not our intention to catalogue here all the concepts of Judaism restated in epigrammatic form in our tractate. We shall refer only to one more theme which is met with in *Avot* under a variety of headings, namely, wisdom, knowledge and learning. All roads lead to one goal, Torah, which runs through Avot as a golden thread adorning and crowning it with glory. This abiding love for learning and study of Torah is mentioned in the first Mishnah of our tractate. 'Raise up many disciples'. The same theme recurs under different forms again and again. At times the disciple is mentioned, on other occasions it is the teacher who is emphasised, Thus we are told, 'Acquire for yourself a teacher' (1:6, 1:16). So high was scholarship rated that *Avot* devotes nine passages to the distinctive qualities of the disciples of R. Johanan Ben Zakkai (2:10 -2:19). Every chapter contains a goodly number of references specifically devoted to the study of Torah, whilst the sixth chapter fully deserves its title, Kinyan Torah, and is wholly devoted to the acquisition of Torah and is a fitting climax to a tractate which commences with Torah and traces the chain of Jewish tradition from Moses, and Joshua through the Elders and the Prophets to the men of the Great Synagogue and the Rabbis. This line of tradition which begins with the opening words of *Avot* thus takes us till the fall of Jerusalem. Who can deny that the study of Torah deserves the title of 'Father'?

Authorship of Avot

Avot is not the work of one author. It is generally conceded that several collections of sayings were made by a number of Sages. One collection older than *Pirkei Avot* and to which we often refer in our notes is *Avot De Rabbi Nathan*, a more complete version of *Pirkei Avot* and it is found in two versions, however, scholars agree that *Avot* in its original format was edited by R. Judah Ha-Nasi who codified the whole of the Mishnah. We may well ask why did R. Judah edit *Avot?* It is logical to assume that during his lifetime Jews were leaving Palestine because of the Hadrianic persecutions, and R. Judah wished to continue the chain of tradition and transmit in the spirit of the first Mishnah of *Avot*, in one compact form, some of the wise sayings of the Sages, so that Torah would not be forgotten in the Diaspora with which he was in contact.

Why did R. Judah choose to edit primarily the ethical sayings? Because he had himself lived an ethical and saintly life. He was known as Rabbenu Hakadosh, our teacher the holy or saintly one. In addition to his eminence as an outstanding Jewish scholar, he was also familiar with the sciences and had learnt Greek. He was also blessed with wealth and influence for he was Patriarch and the uncrowned ruler of Palestine Jewry. But, above all, he was a dignified and saintly character and eschewed the pleasures of life. This is borne out by one of his sayings 'Whoever chooses the delights of this world will be deprived of the delights of the world to come; whoever renounces the former will receive the latter' (Ta. 7a).

If we revert to the central dictum of B.K. where we learn that he who would become a saint should fulfil the words of *Nezikin* or *Avot*, we readily see the motive which impelled R. Judah to occupy himself with editing and transmitting *Avot*, which is a compilation of saintly and pious thoughts.

Piety may also explain some of the apparent difficulties with which we are faced in *Avot*. For instance, alongside the mention of eminent scholars, we also find in *Avot* some comparatively unknown sages. Furthermore, why should an apostate like Elisha Ben Avuyah be mentioned? However, R. Judah was a unique personality and in his generosity of heart and innate saintliness and kindness (hasid is closely connected with hesed, loving-kindness), he spread his net far and wide and introduced us to obscure personages and included even a heretic.

An extension of this idea presents itself when we examine the language of *Avot* which, in the main, is written in Mishnaic Hebrew with the exception of four statements (1:13, 2:7, 5:25, 5:26) which are in Aramaic, the vernacular of Jews in Palestine and at that time Babylon. In this respect it is interesting to record that R. Judah was averse to Aramaic and forbade it in his home where even his servants were obliged to speak Hebrew (R. H. 26b). When scholars spoke in Aramaic and not in the holy tongue, he chided them (B. K. 82b). However, such was the tolerance and goodness of R. Judah that he incorporated four statements in their original Aramaic although he personally disliked that language.

Avot and the Prayer Book

We suggested above that it was the prayer and wish of R. Judah Ha-Nasi that *Avot* would accompany Jews outside Palestine in the Diaspora and that it would be a source of comfort and inspiration to them. Little did he realise that his dream would come true and that *Avot* would be incorporated into the Siddur and thus reach millions of Jews throughout the world. Our Siddur is not restricted to prayers and songs of praise. It is not purely devotional. It also contains excerpts from the Talmud and post-talmudic literature. However, *Avot* is unique in that it is not excerpted but adopted in toto. Indeed, the sixth chapter was added so that a separate chapter could be read on each of the Sabbaths between Pesah and Shavuot, the period during which *Avot* was originally read.

Today we read *Avot* from the Sabbath after Pesah till the Sabbath before Rosh Hashanah. The reading of *Avot* in the Synagogue during the summer months at Minhah (afternoon service) began in Geonic times (7th-11th centuries). Many reasons have been offered for the introduction of this custom. It is reasonable to assume that its originators wished to bridge the wide gap in time between Minhah and Maariv in summer and ingeniously introduced the reading of *Avot*. This, in turn, led to the study of *Avot* and today shiurim, talks and cultural debates are conducted by many Rabbis in the Synagogue. It is fitting that on Sabbath we regale ourselves not only with tasty dishes but also nourish the *Neshamah Yeseirah* (additional soul) with the spiritual truths which fill the pages of *Avot*. In this manner the healthgiving properties of the sun without are supplemented by the curative and soul stirring philosophy of Perek heard within the Synagogue.

The inclusion of *Avot* in the liturgy has popularised it and it is no exaggeration to say that it is prayerfully read and minutely studied more than any other treatise in the Talmud. If Jews are the People of the Book, *Avot* has become the Book of the People. The broad masses who are not well versed in talmudic law are richly compensated by reading and rereading the exhilarating collection of the sparkling gems and pearls of rabbinic wisdom in *Avot* and so refresh themselves week by week on the Sabbath by drinking avidly from the wells of salvation.

כָּל יִשְׂרָאֵל יֵשׁ לָהֶם חֵלֶק לָעוֹלָם הַבָּא. שֶׁנֶּאֱמַר וְעַמֵּךְ כֻּלָּם צַדִּיקִים לְעוֹלָם יִירְשׁוּ אָרֶץ נֵצֶר מַטָּעַי מַעֲשֵׂה יָדַי לְהִתְפָּאֵר:

Introductory Mishnah

All Israel have a portion in the world to come, as it is said, 'And Thy people shall be all righteous, they shall inherit the land for ever; the branch of My planting, the work of My hands, that I may be glorified' (Is. 60:21).

This introductory Mishnah which is placed at the head of each chapter is not part of *Avot* but is derived from the Talmud, Sanh.99a. Only the first section of the Mishnah is recorded here, but in Sanhedrin it is followed by the second half which reads as follows: And these are the ones that have no portion in the world to come. One who declares that resurrection is not derived from the Torah, that the Torah was not revealed from heaven, the *Epikoras* ...

Kol Yisrael The word *kol* has a two-fold connotation. It can mean all, the whole of the Jewish people, or in a restricted sense the whole, perfect or fully committed Jew. We follow the first interpretation as it agrees with the expression *yesh lachem*, they have; otherwise we should expect *yesh lo*, he has.

The world to come. This expression is open to a number of interpretations. It is generally conceded that it refers to a golden age in the Hereafter when truth, justice and everlasting peace will reign supreme. In this world we are concerned with our physical desires and needs; in the world to come the body does not exist and the joys of heavenly bliss are therefore portrayed to us in figurative language as a state of Paradise. It is therefore called the world to come. as none can experience it in this world; it is stored up for the righteous in the future, or in the Hereafter. It has been said, 'There is no good in this life which does not receive its reward in the world to come and there is no good in the after-life which cannot be deserved in this life'. For a correct appraisal of the term 'the world to come' we cannot improve on the exposition of the Rabbis on Deut. 32:4 which is part of the Burial Service. 'A God of faithfulnes and without iniquity'. 'A God of faithfulness' signifies that just as the Holy One blessed be He rewards the righteous in the world to come for every light precept they have performed in this world, so does He reward the wicked in this world for every light precept they perform. 'Without iniquity', implies that just as He punishes the wicked in the world to come for every slight transgression they commit in this world, so He punishes the righteous in this world for every slight transgression they commit in this world. 'Just and right is He'. It was said that when man departs this life all his deeds are enumerated before him and he is told, 'Thus have you done, in that place on that day'. He, admitting it, says, 'Yes' and he is then told to sign the record and he signs, as it is said (Job 37:7), 'He seals up by the hand of every man'. Not only that, but he even acknowledges the justice of the verdict and says, 'You have judged me lightly, as it is said, (Ps.51:6) 'That you may be justified when you speak and be in the right when you judge' (Ta. 11a). Now that we have briefly interpreted the first part of the Mishnah, we must justify its introduction and see if we can possibly find a logical connection between it and each chapter of the Perek. In the six chapters of our treatise there are concentrated some of the noblest concepts of the Jewish faith. This distilled wisdom of the teachings, aphorisms and sayings, should not estrange the ordinary man who instinctively feels he cannot possibly aspire to reach celestial heights, or follow the ethical behaviour demanded in *Avot*. To encourage this type of person the Mishnah recalls that every Jew has a share in the world to come. Judaism will not tolerate any class distinction; all have a share in the glorious future of our faith. It is therefore fitting that each chapter should be headed by this note of optimism, befriending and inspiring every Jew, whatever his station in life, so that he be worthy of spiritual redemption. Paradoxically, however, there is an element of danger inherent in this philosophy. If every Jew is assured of a portion in the world to come without any initiative on his part, he may resign himself to an existence of idleness and unobservance. To correct this false impression, we must re-interpret 'Kol Yisrael' to mean not only every Jew, but also the whole of Israel. We shall enjoy Jewish survival only if we are united and resolved to work together for the salvation of the Jewish body politic. Every Jew must make some individual contribution to the common weal and help to strengthen the ramparts of the House of Israel. It must be a concerted effort; every Jew counts and every Jew must strive actively to attach himself to the Jewish people. Commenting on Deut. 14:1, 'You shall not cut yourselves', the Rabbis add, 'Do not form yourselves into sections, but be all of you one band' (Sifre).

The Sages often remind us that if a man takes a bundle of reeds, he cannot break them when they are tied together, but if they are taken singly even a child can break them (Nitzavim, Deut. R.). This sentiment of unity is reflected in the first two words of our Mishnah. The word '*kol*' is made up of two letters, kaph and lamed, which stand for Cohen and Levi and these are followed by Yisrael thus forming the three constituent section of the Jewish people. When Jews are joined together by bonds of unity and brotherhood, they conjointly enjoy a share in the world to come. This concept of the oneness of the Jewish people is a very appropriate introduction to Jewish ethics.

Proof text. The ideal of unity is stressed by the Prophet Isaiah. The Hebrew for 'people' can be expressed by one of four words: *am, goy, oomah* or *leom..* Isaiah advisedly uses *am* because it is closely connected with *im* meaning with or together from the root *amam.* When there is a togetherness amongst the people it is best expressed by *am.* Compare Ex. 19:8 '*Vayaanu Kol haam yahdav,*' and all the people answered together'. *Am* is followed by *yahdov,* together. No individual alone can be all righteous as we are reminded by Ecclesiastes. 'There is none righteous upon the earth who does only good and sins not' (7:20). *Kulam* refers to all the Jewish people as one entity; only united can God's people be righteous.

The branch of My planting. The image of the tree with all its parts deriving sustenance from each other, bears testimony to the wholeness and oneness of Jewish life. This is beautifully portrayed by the Rabbis who discuss the function of the vine. 'This people Israel is compared to a vine. The vine shoots represent the members of the community, the grapes resemble the scholars, the leaves the ignorant ..... let the grapes pray for the leaves. But for the leaves, the grapes would not exist' (Hul. 92a). This teaches how interlaced and interdependent the different section of the tree are to one another. As long as the branch is attached to the tree and draws its sap from roots which are deeply embedded in the soil, the branch and its fruit will blossom. However, if it is severed from the stem of the tree, the branch withers and decays, so it is with the Jew. If he is attached to the Torah, the Tree of Life, he lives and flourishes, but as soon as he veers away from the traditional practice and cuts himself off from the source of the Torah, he disintegrates and is lost to his faith.

The work of My hands. Here again we underline the unity and totality of the Jewish people, who, as tools of the Almighty, are undivided by worshipping the one God. The unification of our people brings about the glorification of our God. We should point out that this Mishnah does not reserve a share in the future world for Jews alone. The Rabbis have specifically stated that the pious of all nations have a portion in the world to come (Tosefta Sanh. 12). Maimonides in Mishnah Torah 1, Hilkhot Teshuvah 3:5, states, 'Let them aspire to reach the heights of the righteous of the peoples of the world who shall enjoy a share in the world to come and so bring peace into the minds and hearts of humanity'. Such a peace is not only *Shalom*, but also *Shalem*, which means perfect. This is the peace we all yearn and pray for; it is a peace which will not be human or transitory, but divine and permanent.

Hasidic Lore

The world to come. R. Nahum Tzernobiler asked a wealthy man to contribute a large sum to a charitable cause. The man refused and R. Nahum sold his share in the world to come and used the money for the cause. His hasidim enquired how he could bring himself to make such a sale. The Rabbi answered: I say twice daily in the *Shema*, Love your God with all your heart, with all your soul and with all your possessions. What beside my share in the world to come does a poor man like myself possess? Shall I prove to be a falsifier and refuse to give to God that which I do in truth possess?

PEREK ONE

פרק ראשון

(א) **מֹשֶׁה** קִבֵּל תּוֹרָה מִסִּינַי וּמְסָרָהּ לִיהוֹשֻׁעַ וִיהוֹשֻׁעַ לִזְקֵנִים וּזְקֵנִים לִנְבִיאִים וּנְבִיאִים מְסָרוּהָ לְאַנְשֵׁי כְנֶסֶת הַגְּדוֹלָה. הֵם אָמְרוּ שְׁלֹשָׁה דְבָרִים הֱווּ מְתוּנִים בַּדִּין וְהַעֲמִידוּ תַלְמִידִים הַרְבֵּה וַעֲשׂוּ סְיָג לַתּוֹרָה:

Mishnah One

Moses received the Torah from Sinai and handed it down to Joshua and Joshua to the Elders and the Elders to the Prophets and the Prophets handed it down to the Men of the Great Synagogue. They said three things: Be deliberate in judgment and raise up many disciples and make a fence for the Torah.

Moses received the Torah from Sinai. Many have questioned the absence of the name of God in the first expression. It is patently clear that Moses received the Torah at the hand of God. This was the purpose for Moses ascending Mount Sinai. However, the Mishnah here highlights the fundamental role which Sinai plays in Jewish Life. The existence of God predated Sinai. It is the Sinaitic Revelation that is underlined. For this reason the Mishnah deliberately emphasises that Moses received the Torah from Sinai. This revelation signals the greatest spiritual revolution in the history of the human race in general and Israel in particular. For this reason all Oral Laws revealed to Moses on Sinai are called *Halakhah L'Moshe MiSinai* and enjoy the imprimatur of Divine Law.

The other difficulty in this first expression which calls for interpretation is the word *MiSinai*. Normally we would expect Moses to receive the Torah 'at' Sinai. Some see in the word *MiSinai* (from Sinai) an allusion to the forty days and nights Moses spent with God, as the letter *Mem* is numerically equivalent to forty. More important is it to remember that the Jewish tradition in all its fulness flows directly from Sinai, not only the Written Law but also the Oral Law. The authentic interpretation of the Written Law stems from Sinai. It is well to note that the Mishnah does not state *HaTorah*, the Law, but Torah without the definite article. All learning throughout the ages till the present day has validity only if it is based upon, and is rooted in, the tradition which emanates from Sinai. 'At Sinai' would imply that the Halakhah is static and has no relevance to our day. But such is the elasticity of Halakhah, that Jewish Law provides guidance and direction for every new development that takes place in every age. All questions, *shaalot*, are dealt with exhaustively by the Rabbis in their voluminous Responsa which appear in every age. In this manner tradition is continued and preserved for all time.

Why was the Torah given on Sinai and on no other mountain? The Torah was not given on one of the highest mountains, but on Sinai which is a lowly mountain. It is proper that the ethical treatise *Avot* should commence with the outstanding ethical principle of humility and meekness which Sinai symbolises. Indeed, the first word of the Mishnah also stresses this same quality of modesty.

Moses. In the gallery of portraits depicted in the Torah, Moses stands out in splendid isolation. He is too great to be classified in a few lines. We shall not attempt to dilate on his superhuman qualities as Teacher, Leader and Liberator of his people. His name and fame are immortalised by the Torah with which he is eternally linked. *Torat Moshe*, the Law of Moses, is read in the Synagogue every Shabbat and Yom Tov, in addition to Monday and Thursday mornings, Rosh Hodesh and fast days.

Here the name of Moses is mentioned in connection with the Sinaitic Revelation, a unique religious experience vouchsafed for Moses alone, when he received the Law at the hand of God and transmitted it to the vast multitude of people who had gathered at the foot of Mount Sinai. This soul-stirring spectacle was so world-shattering that in the words of the Sages the maid-servant was enabled to derive what even the Prophets in their prophetic ecstasy could not attain. (Mekhilta on Ex. 15:2).

It is fitting that a treatise devoted to Ethics should commence with Moses, a character whose ethical and moral stature was unsurpassed in the annals of the human race. Moses is presented to us here unadorned, without titles, but simply referred to as Moshe. Compare Nu. 12:3, 'Now the man Moses was very meek, above all the men that were upon the face of the earth'.

Moses received the Torah. Here we have a clear and precise definition of the chain of Jewish tradition, how it was handed down from Moses to Joshua to the Elders and the Prophets. This notion of the cycle of tradition popularised by *Avot* is not new, but is developed in Midrash and Talmud in a number of instances. We shall give a few brief examples to show how the Written and Oral Law formed the basis of the chain of Jewish tradition.

R. Levi Bar Hama said in the name of R. Simeon Bar Lakish: What is the meaning of that which is written 'And I will give you the tables of stone and the Law and Commandments which I have written that you may teach them' (Ex. 24:12). 'Tables of stone', that is, the Ten Commandments; 'Law', that is, the Pentateuch; 'Commandments', that is, Mishnah; 'Which I have written', that is, the Gemara. This verse teaches us that all of them were given to Moses by God on Mount Sinai (Ber. 5a).

R. Johanan said: The Holy One blessed be He only made a covenant with Israel for the sake of the laws given by word of mouth, as it is said, 'For after the tenor (the mouth) of these words I have made a covenant with you and Israel (Ex. 34:27) (Git. 60b).

R. Haggai said in the name of R. Samuel Bar Nahman: Some words were communicated by word of mouth and others communicated in writing, though we know not which of them are more beloved. But from that which is written, 'For after the tenor (mouth) of these words, I have made a covenant with you and with Israel' (Ex. 34:27), it seems that the message communicated by word of mouth is more beloved (Y. Peah 11.6.17a).

The Besht commented on the phrase, ' Our God and the God of our fathers' in the Prayer Book. He said, 'Some persons have faith because their fathers taught them to believe. In one sense this is satisfactory; no philosophical axioms will break their belief. In another sense, it is unsatisfactory, since their belief does not come from personal knowledge. Others come to belief through conviction after research. This is satisfactory in one sense: they know God from inner conviction. In another it is unsatisfactory; if other students demonstrate to them the fallacy of their reasoning, they may become unbelievers. The best believers are those whose beliefs are satisfactory in every way. They believe because of tradition and also through their own reasoning. This is what we mean when we say, 'Our God and the God of our fathers'. The Lord is our Master both because we know He is our God and because our fathers have taught us He is God'.

Moses received the Torah and handed it down. *Kabbalah* and *Masorah* are the two key words of Jewish tradition. Our God-centered Torah flourishes when these two qualities activate each other. Kabbalah (not to be confused with esoteric teaching and mysticism) means receiving, and Masorah transmitting. Jewish tradition is not to be viewed as a museum piece or hidden between the covers of old tomes; it must be received, studied, imbibed and observed, but we cannot halt there. In order that tradition be effective and continuous, it must also be transmitted to our children, the next generation. If Kabbalah is to be meaningful, it must be followed by Masorah — transmission; both are part of the same equation. Kabbalah without Masorah is dangerous for our survival. Masorah without Kabbalah is meaningless, for we cannot possibly pass on any tradition if we do not possess a sound Jewish education. It is interesting that the radio works on the same principle of receiving and transmitting! The waves of the ether receive the voices or sounds and transmit them.

We even find the process of Kabbalah and Masorah in Nature, which has been called the handmaid of God. For example, the clouds receive the moisture from the seas, and transmit refreshing rain. Conversely the soil, fields, trees, plants, flowers and vegetation receive the air, the sun and the rain and transmit wheat, fruit, vegetables, plants and flowers. As the cycle of tradition, so is the cycle of the growth of food which sustains us. As God is in tradition, He is also in Nature. We now see why we place so much faith in tradition; it is part of our natural habitat. We have outlived the unspeakable sufferings foisted upon us in all ages, because we always hark back to our tradition. The greatest of our traditions have withstood the test of time and are as valid today as they were thousands of years ago. The late Chief Rabbi Kook summed up succinctly the relevance of tradition in these words: Let the old be revived, let the new be sanctified.

Masorah. The Masorites were a body of scholars who wrote brief notes to the marginal reading of the old text of the Bible, divided the continuous script into words and chapters and devised the cantillation and the final letters of the alphabet.

Joshua. From early times Joshua seemed to be predestined as a leader. He was the only one of the spies whose name was altered as a title of distinction, and this took place even before the mission to Canaan was undertaken. When Moses asked that a successor should be appointed, God said, 'Take for you Joshua... a man in whom is the spirit' (Nu. 27:18). This is interpreted by the Sifre (52b) as follows: He is able to go against the views of everyone. Joshua rightly earned his rise to power because he faithfully and loyally served his Master Moses at all times.

The Elders. The Elders were a compact body of men who in Egypt were already playing a vital role in the organisation of the Children of Israel. 'Go and gather the Elders of Israel together' (Ex. 3:16, 18; 17:5,6; 18:12; 19:7). The setting up of the seventy Elders was the forerunner of the Sanhedrin of seventy one and is reported in Mishnah Sanh. 1:6.

The Prophets. The Prophets are unique to Judaism. Whereas other religions are founded on the life and death of a prophet whom they deify and worship, Judaism is a monetheistic religion, and we worship only the living eternal God. No Prophet, not even Moses the greatest of Prophets, is worshipped. We are favoured with 'The Prophets', all of whom gave Judaism its spiritual outlook and historic direction.

Basically, the Prophets were messengers and ambassadors of God; they spoke when the spirit of God descended upon them. However, they were simple individuals fired with a love and knowledge of God which they transmitted to mankind in general and to Israel in particular. They were seized with the spirit of God and were fearless in their denunciation of king and commoner alike. Righteousness, social justice to all classes of society, charity and world peace were some of the planks of their charter. Their words, speeches and messages, written in matchless phraseology and poetry, comprise the greater part of *Tanakh*. 'By some power of which we have no knowledge, the Prophets were able to burst through the bonds of their natural environment and perceive things not perceived by others. As genius can defy limitations of circumstance and environment, so can the Prophets, for genius is not a quality of the mind but of the soul' (Isadore Epstein).

Men of the Great Synagogue. The Men of the Great Synagogue were an illustrious body of scribes, priests and selected men (one hundred and twenty) founded by the leaders of the Jews who returned from the Babylonian Captivity. They were primarily a teaching body who followed Ezra (444 B.C.E.). Their name was supposed to be derived from Neh. 9:32. Every gathering for religious purposes was called a Knesset. This being a very special gathering for the reinterpretation of Judaism in the chain of Jewish tradition, it was called 'The Great Knesset' or Assembly.

Their greatness consisted in the fact that they laid the foundations of organised Judaism in the School, the Synagogue and the Home. Thus they composed and edited the Amidah in outline, the Kiddush and Havdalah (Ber. 33a). They also edited the Bible and included in the canon the Books of Esther, Canticles and Ecclesiastes. So effective was their influence that the Rabbis declared, 'They restored the crown of the Torah to its ancient glory' (Yoma 69b). They were the direct successors of Haggai, Zekhariah and Malakhi and thus became the legal depositories of the Mosaic Law.

A remarkable testimony to the trustworthiness of Jewish tradition is afforded by Josephus who writes: 'We Jews yield to the Greek writers as to the eloquence of composition, but we give them no such preference as to the verity of ancient history... Our forefathers... committed the matter to their high priests and to their prophets, and these records have been written all along down to our own times with the greatest accuracy.... The strongest argument of our exact management in this matter is that we have the names of our high priests from father to son set down in our records for the period of two thousand years. If any have transgressed these rules, they are forbidden to present themselves at the altar or to partake of any other of our purifications. This is ... necessarily done, because everyone is not permitted of his own accord to be a writer, nor is there any disagreement in what is written; and only prophets have written the original and earliest accounts of things as they learned them from God Himself by inspiration... For we do not have an innumerable multitude of books, disagreeing from one another as the Greeks have... for during so many ages as have already passed no one has been so bold as either to add anything to them, or to take anything from them or to make any change in them.' (Contra Apion, 1, 5-7).

Be deliberate in judgment. The Judges should be patient and forbearing. They must weigh up the evidence meticulously and come to a just conclusion. The same words especially apply to the protagonists in a lawsuit. It is better to settle their differences between themselves through arbitration rather than face trial in a law court, which is always unpleasant and unpredictable.

Being deliberate in judgment need not necessarily apply only to the parties in a lawsuit. We are apt to judge people too rashly and we are ready, at times, to condemn a person for his actions. The Mishnah advises us to be cautious and not to judge a person lightly; there may be extenuating circumstances which prompted the individual to act as he did. A shallow judment can do an incalculable amount of harm.

The Rabbis wisely declared that just as a man is bound to perform his religious duties conscientiously and earnestly without any selfish motives or false thoughts, even so should he act in all matters concerning his fellow-man. R. Israel Salanter said, 'A hasid is not one who guards his own body and someone else's soul, but one who guards his own soul and someone else's body'.

Din. By emphasising the word '*din*' as Jewish Law, we derive a useful lesson. Too many criticise Jewish Law and find fault with the *din*. We tend to censure God for much of the misery that befalls us. More knowledge, faith and loyalty would correct this false assumption on our part. Be patient with the *din*.

Raise up many disciples. We have always worshipped learning; we are eternal students. An outstanding scholar is called a Talmid Hakham. He may be wise and profound but he still retains the title of student or disciple. Even the dayan — the judge — who is well versed in Jewish Law, can learn from others, and this capacity to learn assists him to arrive at a just decision. In like manner we should all learn from others before arriving at a solution to the problems of life. Throughout the Middle Ages the non-Jewish clergyman was the only person who could read and write whilst the masses were generally abysmally ignorant, whereas Jewish education was the prerogative of all classes of society. 'Raise up' in Hebrew literally means 'make stand'. From Moses till the death of R. Gamliel all pupils stood in their thousands, whilst the teacher sat.

Haamidu. The hiphil (causative) reminds us that the function of talmudic methodology is to help the student to master the intricate discussions in talmudic learning, so that he may ultimately stand on his own feet. So vast and illimitable is the *Yam Hatalmud*, the bottomless depth of talmudic learning, that it is essential to raise many disciples who could learn in depth.

Harbeh qualifies not only the number of disciples but also the intensity of scholarship. Jewish scholarship will flourish and continue only if we adhere to the full implementation of this teaching.

Make a fence for the Torah. The Torah with its distinctive laws and practices has projected the Jewish image in every age. We are a small people, a minority in many countries, united by the indivisibility of Jewish tradition which is handed down from age to age intact, and which has preserved us in the face of untold suffering. Whenever and wherever we break through the fence of Jewish Law, history has testified to the fact that we have exposed ourselves to the alien cultures of a hostile world to which we become assimilated, and this eventually leads to spiritual suicide.

Many commentators stress that the 'fence' is the Oral Law which is, the complement of the Written Law. Make a hedge about the Torah, refers to the decrees and enactments of the Sages. These keep a man far from transgression, as the Torah states: 'Therefore shall you keep what I have given you to keep' (Lev. 18:30) which the Talmud (Yev. 21a) interprets to mean, 'Add protection to what I have already given you as protection' (Maim.).

ARN explains the 'fence' in an original manner. 'Let every man take care that what he says should not be too difficult for any listener to understand. Let him take care to speak of the Torah only at the right time, in the right idiom, in the right place, and under the right circumstances'.

Hasidic Lore

The greatness of Moses.

Once Rabbi David Moshe of Tchortkov said with tears in his eyes: It is written that Moses was meek above all men. How are we to interpret this? He with whom God spoke face to face and whose work was so mighty — how could he think himself less than all others? The reason is this: In those forty days which Moses spent on the heights his body had become pure and luminous like that of the ministering angels. After that time he said to himself: 'Of what importance is it, if I, whose body was purified, give service to God? But if one of Israel who is still clad in his turbid flesh serves God — how much greater is he than I!'.

(ב) שִׁמְעוֹן הַצַּדִּיק הָיָה מִשְּׁיָרֵי כְנֶסֶת הַגְּדוֹלָה. הוּא הָיָה אוֹמֵר עַל שְׁלֹשָׁה דְבָרִים הָעוֹלָם עוֹמֵד עַל הַתּוֹרָה וְעַל הָעֲבוֹדָה וְעַל גְּמִילוּת חֲסָדִים:

Mishnah Two

Simeon the Righteous was one of the last members of the Great Synagogue. He used to say: On three things the world stands; on the Torah, on worship and on acts of lovingkindness.

Simeon the Righteous. There were two High Priests named Simeon who lived before the Maccabean period. The first during and after the reign of Alexander the Great (356-323 B.C.E.) and the second from 219-199 B.C.E. Josephus called the older Simeon 'The Righteous'. Authorities differ as to which Simeon the Mishnah refers. What is certain is, that he plays a vital role in the history of Jewish tradition, for he was the last survivor of the Men of the Great Synagogue and the first of a new line of Rabbis to transmit the Kabbalah which is the essence of Jewish tradition.

According to legend Simeon welcomed Alexander during his travels in Palestine. When Alexander asked that a statue of him be erected in the Temple, the High Priest had to refuse but promised him that all sons born of Priests in that year would be called Alexander.

He used to say. This idiom is often used in Avot to indicate that 'he was in the habit of saying'.

The world stands. Food and drink satisfy one momentarily, but these three things stand and enjoy continuity and permanence.

Torah. This is mistranslated by the word 'law' and is an all-embracing term which includes the study and practice of authentic Jewish teaching from the earliest times to the present day. The study of Torah leads us to the will of God. 'From the very outset God stipulated it as a condition with the works of Creation. If Israel will accept the Torah, well and good, otherwise I shall reduce the universe to chaos again' (A.Z. 3a). The world owes its existence to the Torah as we learn from the following statement. 'Great is the Torah, for if it did not exist heaven and earth would have no future' (Ned. 32b).

The mainspring of the Torah teaches us that the world is built on moral and ethical foundations. The Torah is at all times the source of religious inspiration, and Israel, being a kingdom of priests, is privileged and duty bound to live by the precepts of the Torah in all its fulness. Torah here is preceded by the definite article, for the Torah is indivisible in every age; it is constant and therefore stands for all time.

Avodah - Service. As Torah, so is Avodah, preceded by the definite article. The Service in the Synagogue is virtually the same throughout the world. We all pray in the same Hebrew language which unites us wherever we find ourselves. Every authentic Jewish Service is specifically traditional and this is its distinctive feature. We should stress the meaning of the root *avad*, to work. The Service should not be a mechanical, perfunctory performance. Every member of the congregation should work and strive together to produce a living and vibrant Service to God both in and outside the Synagogue. Originally avodah referred to the Temple ritual and the sacrifices. With the destruction of the Temple, prayer replaced sacrifice and avodah is generally designated as the service of the heart.

Gemilut Hasadim, Acts of lovingkindness. In the Prayer Book, God is depicted as the bestower of Gemilut Hasadim. The Talmud differentiates this from charity. 'In three things is it greater than mere charity. Charity can be given only to the poor, Gemilut Hasadim both to the rich and to the poor. Charity is dispensed only in material gifts, Gemilut Hasadim both in material gifts and through personal guidance. Charity can be given only to the living but Gemilut Hasadim applies both to the living and the dead' (Suk. 49b).

Regarding the Book of Ruth R. Zeira said, 'Here is no discussion of laws of uncleanness and cleanness, the prohibited and permitted. Why then was it written? To teach us how great was the reward for those who practise acts of loving-kindness (Ruth R. 2:14).

Gemilut Hasadim has entered the vocabulary of Jewish communal life in the Diaspora through the establishment of Gemilut Hasadim Societies which have granted worthy Jews loans free of interest, in order that they may rehabilitate themselves in their new surroundings. 'Torah and Avodah are the bricks and stones of which the structure of civilisation is composed; Gemilat Hasadim is the cohesive element, the unseen mortar which binds together the bricks and the stones and prevents the edifice from collapsing'.

It is reported of the Noda Biyehudah that he remonstrated with his community of Prague that they did not practise Gemilut Hasadim. When he was unsuccessful, he temporarily closed the Yeshivah and wandered through the market. His followers were puzzled at his action, but he explained that a table of three legs can be supported even when one leg is broken, but it cannot possibly stand when two legs are broken. The world is a tripod standing on three principles. One leg, Avodah, was broken with the destruction of the Temple and now, with the breakdown of Gemilut Hasadim, Torah itself cannot exist if it is divorced from acts of loving-kindness.

Torah, Avodah and Gemilut Hasadim. In this saying the Patriarchs are reflected. Torah is symbolised by Jacob who studied Torah for fourteen years in the schools of Shem and Ever. Avodah is represented by Isaac who was willing to sacrifice himself to God, and Gemilut Hasadim stands for Abraham who introduced hospitality into a hostile and unfriendly world. This order of the Patriarchs is evident in Lev. 26:42.

We can gauge the significance of Gemilut Hasadim from the following dicta of the Rabbis.

The Torah begins and concludes with acts of loving-kindness. (So. 14a.) There are three traits the possession of which characterise one as a descendant of the Patriarchs, namely, the sense of compassion, the sense of shame and acts of loving-kindness (Yev. 79a, Bez. 32b).

Greater than alms-giving is Gemilut Hasadim, for the former is called sowing, and the latter, reaping. When a man sows he is in doubt whether he will enjoy what he has sown, but what he reaps he will surely enjoy (Suk. 49b). Finally, whereas Torah and Avodah are preceded by the definite article, Gemilut Hasadim is without it. From this we infer that it applies to all, scholar and ignorant, rich and poor, Jew and non-Jew.

Now that we have briefly interpreted Torah, Avodah and Gemilut Hasadim, what need is there to highlight Avodah and Gemilut Hasadim? Do not these come under the general title of Torah? Further, what prompted the author to devise this particular order, placing Torah first, Avodah second and Gemilut Hasadim last? Torah is pre-eminent because it affects us in every period of life. We cannot divorce Torah from our activities and suddenly enthrone it at a Brit Milah, Bar Mitzvah or Wedding. Avodah, prayer, is more limited; it is invoked at definite periods of the day, Shaharit, Minhah and Maariv, when we petition God for our needs and requirements, when we pray for health and sustenance. Torah, which means teaching, is primarily addressed to the student, to every Jew. 'All your children are learned of the Lord', said Isaiah (54:13).

This distinction between study of Torah and prayer is formulated into a rule of Law. Thus, a House of Study may not be converted into a Synagogue, but a Synagogue may be converted into a Bet Hamidrash, a House of Study. Nor was the study of Torah to be considered a mental or intellectual exercise; it was to lead to observance of the Law. The Midrash declares that if there is Torah in a man, he takes care not to become embroiled in transgression or sin. That the study of Torah in itself is of paramount importance is attested to by the fact that the Torah student to this day studies fervently and intently laws which do not obtain at the present time, such as laws regarding the sacrifices. All laws in the Torah, even those which are not applicable to modern life, are invested with sanctity, and are therefore studied with enthusiasm and love.

The study of Torah is followed by Avodah, prayer. We have drawn a distinction between Torah and Avodah, but both belong to the vocabulary of religion. The Bet Hamidrash, the House of Study, and the Bet Hakneset, the Synagogue, are equally unique contributions which Judaism has introduced to the world. 'Prayer proceeds from below to above; in Torah we occupy ourselves by infusing the life from above with that below. From the high peak of divine intelligence, from the source from which the Torah has been drawn, we take seeds of life, draw them down, and implant them deep in our nature' (A.I. Kook).

When we consider acts of loving-kindness, the third constituent, we find that many regard these as purely social, bereft of all religious significance. For this reason Simeon the Righteous includes Gemilut Hasadim in his famous trilogy. In the Jewish mind acts of lovingkindness have their source in God... This three-fold cord cannot be torn asunder; they are closely interlinked and inseparable. We cannot envisage a student of Torah ignoring prayer or failing to perform deeds of lovingkindness. The loyal Jew combines the three qualities in equal measure and in this manner fulfils his duty towards God and man.

One further problem remains to be solved. Simeon the Righteous mentions Gemilut Hasadim and not zedakah, charity, which in the minds of many people appears to be superior. However, the Rabbis explicitly state that Gemilut Hesed is greater than charity. To write out a cheque is commendable and praiseworthy, but it is a simple exercise if one is wealthy. However, helping a person in some tangible way by performing a Gemilut Hesed, may require days and weeks of patient and constructive aid which is often unseen. Charity may be devoid of personal responsibility, but a Gemilut Hesed demands constant attention. The Torah clearly underlines that deeds of lovingkindness are superior to charity. 'If your brother be waxen poor and his means fail with you, then you shall uphold him; as a stranger and a settler shall he live with you' (Lev. 25:35). It is your duty to help him and put him on his feet, so that he regain his self-confidence.

The story is told of a sinner who, after death, came before the heavenly tribunal. The court was about to condemn him, when the defending counsel referred to the acts of lovingkindness he had performed. It appears that during the rainy season, a poor pedlar had his horse and wagon bogged down in the mud. His merchandise was ruined and he became very despondent. This man, however, helped him pull the horse and wagon out of the mire and he also assisted him with a loan so that he could purchase new stock. On hearing this, the court ordered that they put the horse, the wagon and the goods on the scales of justice; but they did not outweigh the sins of the accused man. Then the defending counsel suggested that since the horse and wagon were covered with mud, let the mud also be placed on the scales. This time, the mud tipped the scales and the sinner was eventually saved through a deed of lovingkindness.

We have thus accounted for the order of Torah, Avodah and Gemilut Hasadim; each ingredient has its rightful place in the Jewish world.

Hasidic Lore

Torah. The Besht said that according to Ps. 19:11 the words of the Torah are 'more desirable than gold and sweeter than honey'. Gold is highly delectable but it is unsatisfying, as no man is ever content with the amount of gold he possesses. Honey is exceedingly sweet, but it is unpleasant to the sated man. The Torah, however, is both satisfying and pleasant.

Avodah. The Gerer Rabbi interpreted Ps. 147:10-11 in these words: The Lord does not desire to be served by the animal strength in a man, nor by the bodily might within him. He does not wish a man ever to exert himself or to serve Him with the limbs. He does take pleasure in those who revere Him and who hope for His kindness.

The Lizensker said, 'In the palace a king demands regularity and perfection of service. When he travels, however, he is satisfied with the accommodation available. Likewise, in the Holy Land the Lord demands perfect service from Israel, but in exile He is satisfied with the poorer service we render Him.

Gemilut Hasadim. The Medzibozer commented on the words 'Abounding in lovingkindness and truth' (Ex. 34:6), and said that lovingkindness denoted undeserved giving. How can this be reconciled with truth, which implies deserved reward? The explanation lies in the following: It is the Lord's lovingkindness to reward man according to his true deserts, and in order to do so He aids each man in his efforts to do good and causes opportunities to come to him to achieve it.

(ג) אַנְטִיגְנוֹס אִישׁ סוֹכוֹ קִבֵּל מִשִּׁמְעוֹן הַצַּדִּיק. הוּא הָיָה אוֹמֵר אַל תִּהְיוּ כַּעֲבָדִים הַמְשַׁמְּשִׁים אֶת הָרַב עַל מְנָת לְקַבֵּל פְּרָס אֶלָּא הֱווּ כַּעֲבָדִים הַמְשַׁמְּשִׁים אֶת הָרַב שֶׁלֹּא עַל מְנָת לְקַבֵּל פְּרָס וִיהִי מוֹרָא שָׁמַיִם עֲלֵיכֶם:

Mishnah Three

Antigonos of Sokho received the tradition from Simeon the Righteous. He used to say: Be not like servants who serve the master conditionally, to receive a gift, but be like servants who serve the master without condition of receiving a reward, and let the fear of Heaven be upon you.

Antigonos (3rd century B.C.E.) was the first noted Jew who had a Greek name. ARN informs us that Antigonos had two disciples, Zadok and Boethus and these rejected the master's teaching and lapsed into heresy. From these arose the Sadducees and the Boethusians; both denied the doctrines of the Immortality of the Soul and of the Resurrection of the Dead (Chap. 5).

Sokho. See Jos. 15:35, I Sam. 17:1. Sokho was about sixteen miles southwest of Jerusalem, on the road to Gaza.

A man of Sokho. '*Ish*' is followed by the name of a place and points to a leader or head of the community.

Be not like servants... We are all servants of God our Master.

Moses is introduced to us as *Eved Hashem*, the servant of the Lord.

There is no contradiction between the dictum of Antigonos and the Torah which promises a reward for obedience to the behests of God. Antigonos stresses the need for man to serve God lovingly and voluntarily, to make sacrifices without regard to any possible reward. For example, Cain (Gen. 4:2) was motivated, but Abel served God selflessly and dutifully, therefore God looked on Abel with favour. We all make sacrifices throughout life, but we should not expect or demand a reward. Our service to God should be unsullied and unadulterated by any thoughts of gain. Whether serving God or man, our motives should be pure and unselfish.

Don Isaac Abarbanel (1437-1508) has summed it up in the following words. 'And so the pious Antigonos admonished man that his labours should not constitute the type which hopes for a reward in the future or who has fear of the future punishment which will accrue, but he shall be of that concept which postulates that it is an obligation upon him that he accepts the Almighty and that he does this labour willingly'.

Peras. We should point out that there is a distinction between *Peras*, which means a gift, and *Sechar* which means a reward, and which one may rightly expect for services rendered. *Peras* here refers to divine approval of man's actions, a prize which God bestows on man.

Buchler translates *Peras* by 'maintenance' and gives the Mishnah this interpretation - 'Antigonos warned his audience not to sink to the level of slaves who are not actuated in their work by any attachment to their master, but only by the food awaiting them after their labour has been completed'.

We should add that though Antigonos possessed a hellenised name, his philosophy was grounded in Jewish thought. This emerges from a comparison between the ethical system of ancient Greece and that of Judea. In ancient Greece and Rome everything, including ethics and morals, was subservient to the State which was all-powerful and supreme. In Judaism, however, the State, including the king or ruler, was submissive to God. Every action or deed is rooted in the Creator of heaven and earth. Thus Antigonos correctly concludes his statement with the climactic admonition, 'Let the fear of Heaven be upon you'.

Fear. In religious terminology 'fear' does not mean dread, but that something is full of awe, wonder and the might of God.

Heaven. This is a name for God in rabbinic literaure. The word God is avoided, and a variety of names is used as an alternative. 'Our Father who is in Heaven' is of course Jewish in origin.

Upon you. It is not enough that fear of God be felt and experienced inwardly; we should also show the fear of God outwardly upon us.

Let The Fear of Heaven... This concluding expression is a fitting sequel to the Mishnah. As the hosts of heaven, the sun, moon and stars, fulfil the will of God day and night without any expectation of reward, so should man emulate the hosts of heaven and labour in the service of the Lord without thought of immediate reward. Maimonides asserts that 'Along with worshipping God out of love, do not altogether neglect the element of fear, for the command to fear God is stated in the Torah, as it is said, 'You shall fear the Lord your God' (Deut. 6:13).

Hasidic Lore

The Nature of Service. The Riziner Rabbi said: This is the service man must perform all of his days: to shape matter into form, to refine the flesh, and to let the light penetrate the darkness until the darkness itself shines and there is no longer any division between the two. As it is written: And there was evening and there was morning — one day.

On another occasion he said: One should not boast about serving God. Does the hand boast when it carries out the will of the heart?

Fear of Heaven. The Koretzer was asked, 'How can we pray that a man repents, since we are taught in the Talmud (Ber. 33b) that the fear of heaven is not in heaven's hands? The Rabbi replied, 'All souls are included in the One Soul; hence if a man repents himself, he may give rise to an impulse towards repentance in another soul which he envisages. We know that when one Jew is elevated to a high rank, all Jewish souls are elated. It is because one soul is included in the other; because both are parts of the One Inclusive All-Soul. Hence we pray that the impulse enters within us'.

(ד) יוֹסֵי בֶּן יוֹעֶזֶר אִישׁ צְרֵדָה וְיוֹסֵי בֶּן יוֹחָנָן אִישׁ יְרוּשָׁלַיִם קִבְּלוּ מֵהֶם. יוֹסֵי בֶּן יוֹעֶזֶר אִישׁ צְרֵדָה אוֹמֵר יְהִי בֵיתְךָ בֵּית וַעַד לַחֲכָמִים וֶהֱוֵי מִתְאַבֵּק בַּעֲפַר רַגְלֵיהֶם וֶהֱוֵי שׁוֹתֶה בַצָּמָא אֶת דִּבְרֵיהֶם:

Mishnah Four

Jose Ben Joezer of Zeredah and Jose Ben Johanan of Jerusalem received the tradition from them. Jose Ben Joezer of Zeredah said: Let your house be a place of meeting for the wise and sit in the dust of their feet and drink their words with thirst.

In this Mishnah we are introduced to the *Zugot*, the Pairs. We learn that when two important teachers are named together in the Mishnah as having received the Torah, they constitute a 'Pair' (Ha. 2:2). The first is the President (Nasi) and the other the Vice-President (Av Bet Din) of the Sanhedrin.

There were five Pairs who lived between 170 and 30 B.C.E. This title (Pairs) was used prior to the age of the Tannaim. Jose Ben Joezer was famed for his piety and was singled out as 'The Pious' of the priesthood (Ha. 2:7). In some of his decisions he was lenient and was called 'One who permits'. It is reported that he was crucified by a Syrian general at the instruction of Alcimus the High Priest, the son of his sister (II Mac. 7:16). Both Jose Ben Joezer and Jose Ben Johanan, who flourished at the time of the Maccabean Wars of Independence, were opposed to Hellenism and were the last of the *Eshkholot*, a title given to the outstanding scholars of the early Maccabean period (So. 49a). *Eshkhol* basically means a cluster of grapes.

Jose of Zeredah. Zeredah was the birth-place of Jereboam and was situated in the hill country of Ephraim (I K. 11:26).

Zevi Chajes has an interesting note on this period. It was only from the time of Jose Ben Joezer, a contemporary of the Hasmonians, that controversies began to remain unsettled because the scholars of that time had been exiled to various places as a result of decrees issued by Antiochus Epiphanes. They could not assemble in one place, and consequently could not ascertain the opinion of the court by a majority vote (Students Guide through Talmud, Shachter p. 114).

Let your house be a place of meeting for the wise. The two main institutions of Jewish life are the Synagogue and the home. Many who attend the Synagogue occasionally ignore the claims of the home, which in many respects is even more vital to the survival of Judaism than the Synagogue. Religion is synonymous with life; we visit the Synagogue, but live in the home. The greater number of the Mitzvot are practised in the home. The home is a miniature Temple and sanctuary. The home should not be used merely as a filling and parking station, but should function as an educational precinct where children should be trained and nurtured to walk in the paths of the righteous.

Thus Jose Ben Joezer advises us to make the home a meeting-place of the wise. The teaching of Torah should not be restricted to the school or Bet Hamidrash, but should be consistently pursued in the home, the natural habitat of the family. When the home is the repository of Torah and culture and is a bastion of Jewish learning, when the home is a meeting place of rabbinical scholars, when the home enjoys regular *shiurim* and children hear the voice of Torah — such a home will receive and pass on to the next generation the eternal truths of our Jewish heritage.

Commenting on I Sam. 7:17, the Talmud says of Samuel the Prophet who travelled extensively, that 'wherever he went, his home went with him' (Ned. 38a). Geographically Samuel often left his home, but spiritually he took with him all the great traditions of learning invested in the Jewish home.

Commenting on II Sam. 6:12, 'The Lord blessed the home of Oved Edom.... because of the Ark of God', ARN observes, 'If a house was blessed because of the Ark of God in which were no more than the two tables of the Commandments, how much more will be the blessing when sages and their disciples come into a person's house?'

R. Eliakim Getzel, son of Joseph of Ostroah, lived in a simple room for which he paid rent. The townspeople of Ostroah wanted to build a home for him, but he refused saying, 'I do not wish to possess a permanent home outside the Land of Israel'.

Sit in the dust of their feet. In antiquity the streets were not paved, nor were the floors of the home covered; the teacher alone sat, whilst the diciples squatted on the ground. The expression, 'sitting at the feet of a teacher', has passed into the modern idiom and denotes an unqualified attachment and devotion to the master.

Mitabbak. This word can be compared with the similar root used in Gen. 32:25, where we read the story of Jacob struggling with the angel. One must struggle with oneself in order to comprehend and grasp the teachings and disquisitions of the Talmud.

Drink their words with thirst. Drink slowly and satisfy your quest for knowledge, as one who thirsts for more will eventually plumb the depths of Torah study, which leaves one thirsting for more. The great store of talmudic learning is called *Yam Hatalmud* (sea of learning) and few can penetrate the abyss of the ocean of rabbinic scholarship. In rabbinic literature Torah is often equated with water, *Mayim, zu Torah.* Of R. Akiva it is reported that he was ignorant of Torah until the age of forty. He once stood by the mouth of a well and wondered how the stone was hollowed out. He was told that it was caused by the water flowing upon it continually. R. Akiva pondered — if what is soft wears down the hard stone, all the more shall the words of the Torah which are as hard as iron, penetrate the heart which is flesh and blood, and immediately he commenced to study the Torah. At the end of thirteen years he taught Torah to multitudes.

Drink with thirst. We should also remember that the thirsty person will not choose, or argue as to which drink would quench his thirst. Similarly, one thirsty for Torah will not show any predilection for one branch of learning more than another. Every section of Torah, without discrimination, will satisfy his thirst for knowledge.

In reply to the question why the Mishnah should mention 'drink' rather than food, we know that food must be masticated and digested and in the process it changes its character and form. Not so with drink. It is possible that Jose uses this simile advisedly to teach us that as liquid does not radically change but remains the same in essence, so should our approach be to Torah; it never changes from age to age but is constant, giving life to those who thirst for it.

Hasidic Lore

Thirst for knowledge. Said the Besht: A man ought to be generous in his praise of a good man. But when he wishes to praise himself and remarks, 'Reuben is very wise and no one has succeeded in outwitting him except myself', such praise is unworthy. In this trait, as in others, we must practise discrimination. In love, we must love good and not evil; in fear, we must fear God and not poverty; in praise, we must praise God and not ourselves; in thirst for learning, we must learn Torah and not futile subjects.

(ה) יוֹסֵי בֶּן יוֹחָנָן אִישׁ יְרוּשָׁלַיִם אוֹמֵר יְהִי בֵיתְךָ פָּתוּחַ לָרְוָחָה וְיִהְיוּ עֲנִיִּים בְּנֵי בֵיתֶךָ וְאַל תַּרְבֶּה שִׂיחָה עִם הָאִשָּׁה בְּאִשְׁתּוֹ אָמְרוּ קַל וָחֹמֶר בְּאֵשֶׁת חֲבֵרוֹ. מִכַּאן אָמְרוּ חֲכָמִים כָּל הַמַּרְבֶּה שִׂיחָה עִם הָאִשָּׁה גּוֹרֵם רָעָה לְעַצְמוֹ וּבוֹטֵל מִדִּבְרֵי תוֹרָה וְסוֹפוֹ יוֹרֵשׁ גֵּיהִנֹּם:

Mishnah Five

Jose Ben Johanan of Jerusalem says: Let your house be opened wide and let the poor be members of your household and talk not overmuch with women. He said this in the case of his own wife, all the more in the case of his companion's wife. Hence the wise said that as long as a man talks overmuch with women, he brings evil upon himself and neglects the words of Torah and his end is that he inherits Gehinnom.

The two Joses complement each other, for they both speak about the home but in different circumstances. Jose Ben Joezer lived in a village where the facilities for a full Jewish education were meagre. He therefore suggested that every home should be converted into a miniature Yeshivah where Torah could be disseminated. Jose Ben Johanan lived in Jerusalem, the holy city, which was well equipped with Batei Midrash and Yeshivot. In addition, Jerusalem also had its full quota of poor including a goodly number of itinerant Rabbis, scholars and laymen. In such circumstances it was essential that the great mitzvah of hospitality should be stressed and that the home should be opened wide to welcome the large and varied number of visitors passing through the holy city.

Let your house be opened wide. On the merits of hopitality, we find many examples in rabbinic literature. We shall offer a few.

He who prolongs his stay at the table prolongs his life; perhaps a poor man will come and will be offered food. As long as the Temple existed the altar used to atone for Israel, but now a man's table atones for him by having the poor as his guests (Ber. 55a).

The door which is not opened for charity will be opened to the physician. (Cant. R. 6:11).

When a beggar stands at your door, the Holy One blessed be He stands at his right hand (Lev. R. 34:9).

Greater is the reception of wayfarers than the reception of the Shekhinah (Shab. 127a).

The biblical heroes Job and Abraham are praised for their hospitality. Of Job it is related that he made four doors to his house so that the poor should not be troubled to go round it to find the entrance (ARN 7).

Of the Patriarch Abraham, we are told he planted a tamarisk tree, *(Eshel)* in Beersheba (Gen. 21:33). *Eshel* acquired the meaning 'a lodging place' where Abraham used to receive passers-by, and when they had eaten and drunk he would say, 'Stay the night and bless God' (Gen. R. 54:6). His house, too, was always open to wayfarers. The word *Eshel* is a mnemonic for three Hebrew words, *Akhilah* (eating), *shetiyah* (drinking) and *linah* (lodging).

It is reported of Rav Huna that when he sat down to a meal, he opened the door and exclaimed, 'Whoever is in need let him enter and eat' (Ta. 20b).

'Let your house be opened wide' can also be interpreted to mean that we should not reside a distance from the community to avoid the poor. Live in an open place easily accessible, so that you can discharge your duty to the needy. We are also warned not to treat the poor disrespectfully but to regard them with the same concern and consideration as we would show towards members of our household.

It is possible that the Mishnah is not dealing specifically with almsgiving and charity as we generally understand it. Commenting on the verse, 'You shall surely lend him sufficient for his needs' (Deut. 15:8), the Rabbis remark, 'You are not commanded to enrich him but to give him what he requires, even a horse or a slave. It is told of Hillel that he gave a poor man who had come from a well-to-do family, the one horse with which he used to do his work and the one slave who attended upon him' (Sifre Deut. 98d). In another version it is reported that when Hillel was once unable to provide a poor man with a slave to run in front of the horse, he did so himself (Ket. 67b).

The ethical content of our Mishnah demands of us to treat the poor man according to his former station in life. Restore to him his personality and individuality. Do not offer him the crumbs of your table; let your house be open wide; be magnanimous and offer him the comforts he was accustomed to enjoy in the past. Such help is not merely charity, but zedakah, a form of righteousness which should be the basis of all charity.

Talk not overmuch with women. These words should be understood in the context of the Mishnah and not be isolated. The Mishnah encourages us to open our homes wide and entertain the stranger and wayfarer. However, this should not be extended indiscriminately to women. We must draw a clear line of demarcation between charity and idle chatter which can lead to promiscuity. Furthermore, we are to find time to spend with the poor; this is a mitzvah, but time is precious and should not be frittered away in unnecessary conversation even with one's own wife and certainly not with the wife of one's friend.

The Rabbis were not averse to conversation which is essential and conducive to friendship, but they do frown upon overmuch talk. Who can deny that too much talk can bring in its train mischief, slander and talebearing.

And his end. Lighthearted talk in itself may seem an innocent pastime but in the end it grows upon people. Instead of cultivating the art of good listening, you become a compulsive talker, denying yourself the time to learn Torah; consequently you inherit ignorance and confusion and ultimately succumb to spiritual death.

Gehinnom, literally the valley of Hinnom near Jerusalem. At one period children were burnt alive there and sacrificed to the idol Molokh. Later it was used as a dumping ground for the refuse of the city. Eventually it became symbolic of the punishment inflicted on the wicked.

Hasidic Lore

Hospitality. The Kobriner Rabbi related that in his boyhood a famine had occurred and the poor wandered from village to village to beg for food from the Jewish residents. A number of them came to the home of the Rabbi's mother and she prepared the oven to bake for them. Some of the beggars, growing impatient, began to abuse her with their words and the distressed woman started to cry. Her small son, the future Rabbi, said to his mother, 'Why should you be troubled by their abuse? Does not this help you to aid them with a pure heart and to perform a good deed in perfection of spirit? On the other hand, had the poor praised and blessed you, the good deed would be less praiseworthy since you might have performed it to gain their praises and not entirely in obedience to the Lord's command and for the sake of His service'.

(ו) יְהוֹשֻׁעַ בֶּן פְּרַחְיָה וְנִתַּאי הָאַרְבֵּלִי קִבְּלוּ מֵהֶם. יְהוֹשֻׁעַ בֶּן פְּרַחְיָה אוֹמֵר עֲשֵׂה לְךָ רַב וּקְנֵה לְךָ חָבֵר וֶהֱוֵי דָן אֶת כָּל הָאָדָם לְכַף זְכוּת:

Mishnah Six

Joshua Ben Perahyah and Nittai the Arbelite received the tradition from them. Joshua Ben Perahyah says: Provide for yourself a teacher and get you a companion and judge every man in the scale of merit.

Joshua Ben Perahyah was Nasi (President) of the Sanhedrin at the time of John Hyrcanus (2nd century B.C.E.). During the period when the Pharisees were persecuted by John Hyrcanus, Joshua was deposed and he escaped to Alexandria; but with the return of the Pharisees he was recalled to Jerusalem.

Provide (make) for yourself a teacher. The Rabbis always stressed the need for learning with a teacher rather than learning alone. The teacher was therefore held in high esteem, whilst those who were self-satisfied with their learning but refused to impart it were frowned upon, as reflected in the following extract. 'To what is a scholar likened? To a flask containing aromatic ointment. When it is unstopped the fragrance is diffused, when it is stopped up the fragrance is not diffused' (A.Z. 35b).

The Rabbis also observe that whoever learns Torah and does not teach it, is like a myrtle in the desert (R.H. 23a), and he who teaches Torah to the son of his fellow-man has it ascribed to him as though he had begotten him (Sanh. 19b).

In the early days before education was organised, the parent was the teacher, according to the injunction, 'And you shall teach your children diligently' (Deut. 6:7).

The following story from the Talmud is apposite to our subject. Because there was a drought, the Precentor of the congregation conducted the Service and when he uttered the words, 'He causes the wind to blow', the wind at once blew; and when he uttered the words, 'He causes the rain to fall', the rain fell immediately. Rav said to him, 'What is your exceptional merit?' He replied, 'I am an elementary teacher and I instruct the children of the poor exactly in the same way as I teach the children of the rich. If anyone is unable to pay me a fee, I forgo it. I also have a fish pond and when I find a pupil negligent in his studies I bribe him with some fish so that he comes regularly to learn' (Ta. 24a).

The author of our Mishnah warns us not to hinder the teacher in any manner. The pupil should be receptive and responsive; in this manner he will 'make' and establish the teacher and help him to use to advantage the talents with which God has endowed him.

Get you (acquire) a companion. Commentators point to the different expressions used — 'make' a teacher but 'acquire' or buy a companion. Maimonides explains, 'If necessary a man should buy a devoted friend for himself, as the Rabbis say (Ta. 23a), 'Give me friendship or give me death'. And if a person cannot easily find a friend he must strive with all his heart to do so, even if he has to buy his love and friendship'. A teacher can lay the foundation for your studies. In every walk of life we need a friend to stand at our side, to animate and inspire us. The Rabbis affirm: The Angels are called companions because neither envy nor malevolence divides them and hence they are closely bound to one another; so should it be amongst men (Midrash Rabbah on Cant. 8).

In addition, we should point out that the difference between the two introductory verbs is reflected in the basic distinction between a teacher and a companion. A teacher is appointed, not by the disciples, but by an outside body. If progress is to be maintained the disciple must submit to the will of the teacher. However, a companion is chosen or selected by his opposite number. In the pursuit of a good and loyal friend, one has to spend time and energy and should judiciously search for an appropriate and suitable person. This may involve expense, hence the expression *kenay*, get, acquire or buy, is used.

Adam, man. The Jewish doctrine of man as exemplified in Avot is significant and should not be overlooked. It is not accidental that adam, man, is frequently employed, in Avot; indeed, it is found twenty-six times: 1:15; 2:1; 2:3,3; 2:13; 2:14,14; 2:16; 3:14; 3:16; 3:17; 3:18,18; 3:20; 4:1; 4:3,3; 4:12; 4:20; 4:28; 5:8; 5:13; 6:9,9,9.

The frequent use of adam, man, in Avot teaches us that Jewish ethics are not national, but international. Judaism is universal in outlook and is directed to 'man' who is a citizen of the world. This oneness of man flows naturally from Monotheism, the Oneness of God, which is fundamental to Judaism and is the hall-mark of Jewish thought. In the sight of God all men are equal, for man is created in the image of God. The function of man is reflected in a discussion between R. Akiva and Ben Azzai. 'Love your neighbour as yourself' (Lev. 19:18) is hailed by R. Akiva as a supreme principle in the Torah. Ben Azzai, however, chooses Gen. 5:1, 'This is the book of the generations of man'. To Ben Azzai this verse is more comprehensive because it underlines the Jewish attitude towards man — all men. The universalism of Judaism thus links the Oneness of God with the oneness of man, which must lead to the oneness of humanity.

Judge all men in the scale of merit. People generally expect to be judged by others in the scale of merit but they themselves are not always inclined to act accordingly towards their fellow-man. Friendships are torn asunder and families are divided because we impute evil intentions and wrong motives to others. We are to judge every individual in the scale of merit; how much more should we judge a whole nation favourably and not condemn a people for the failings of certain individuals. Whole Jewish communities are indiscriminately and adversely judged because of the malefactions of a small number of Jews. We should, however, remember that the reverse is also true. We should not malign a whole people but look for a *zekhut*, merit.

A typical example of judging one graciously is furnished by ARN 19. Once a man sent his son to a neighbour to borrow a measure of wheat. Although the son saw the neighbour measuring wheat, he was informed that there was none to spare. The lad reported this to his father who suggested that the wheat was part of the second tithe, which could not be used indiscriminately and requested his son to return and ask for a loan of money. Again, the neighbour who was occupied in counting money, refused to advance the loan intimating that he had no money. On receiving this information, the father surmised that his neighbour was counting trust money.

On meeting each other, the neighbour was curious to learn the reaction of his friend who had refused to lend the wheat or advance a loan of money, in spite of the fact that there were visible reserves of both wheat and money. The father replied, 'I presumed the wheat was of the second tithe and that the money was trust money, over which you had no jurisdiction'. The neighbour said, 'So indeed it was even as you say. You have not turned aside to the right or to the left, but you judged every man in the scale of merit'.

Some translate *kol haadam* to refer to the individual and not to all the people. Judge the whole of man; do not concentrate only on his faults; he may possess some sterling qualities. The Talmud (Shab. 127b) records a number of stories illustrating the meaning of the dictum in our Mishnah.

To understand the term 'scale of merit', let us turn to Kid. 40a-b. 'A man should always regard himself as though he were half guilty and half meritorious. If he performs one precept, happy is he for weighing himself down in the scale of merit. If he commit one transgression, woe to him for weighing himself down in the scale of guilt... on account of a single sin which he commits, much good is lost to him'.

Maimonides sums it up in these words: If there is some person whom you do not know to be either righteous or wicked and you see him doing or saying something which might be interpreted either favourably or unfavourably, interpret his action favourably and do not suspect him of evil. But if the person is well known as a righteous man always doing good and some action of his seems bad (only with difficulty can one justify it), then it is proper to judge favourably since there is at least a remote possibility that the action is a good one, and it is not permitted to suspect such a person of evil.

Hasidic Lore

Judge all men in the scale of merit. The Sidlover Rabbi said, 'When a Rabbi dies, the learned hasid often hesitates to accept the newly elected Rabbi as his teacher; he is told that if he does not care to acknowledge him as his teacher, let him accept him as a companion. Nevertheless the hasid may hesitate because he thinks, 'I may accept him merely as a companion but he may think of himself as my teacher and thus a false situation is created. How shall I seek the companionship of a person who harbours untruthful thoughts? He is told therefore to judge all men in the scale of merit and to believe that though he calls him 'Rabbi', he seeks his friendship as a companion'.

(ז) נִתַּאי הָאַרְבֵּלִי אוֹמֵר הַרְחֵק מִשָּׁכֵן רָע וְאַל תִּתְחַבֵּר לָרָשָׁע וְאַל תִּתְיָאֵשׁ מִן הַפּוּרְעָנוּת:

Mishnah Seven

Nittai the Arbelite says: Keep aloof from a bad neighbour, do not associate with the wicked and do not abandon the belief in retribution.

Nittai is probably a shortened form of Natanya. An Arbelite is a native or resident of Arbel or Arbela, which is in Galilee near Tiberias.

Nittai was the Vice-President of the Sanhedrin over which Joshua (Mishnah 6) presided. In the Palestinian Talmud he is known as Mattai of Ardela. This saying of Nittai seems to suggest that John Hyrcanus had already deserted the Pharisees and joined the Sadducees and that eventually Hyrcanus himself would suffer retribution.

Keep aloof from a bad neighbour. At the outset, we should differentiate between *ra* (evil) and *rasha* (wicked). Ra, evil, deals with thought and intention. Compare Gen. 6:5, 'That every imagination of the thoughts of his heart was only evil (ra) continually'; Ps. 9:17, 'the wicked (rasha) is snared in the work of his own hands' and Ps. 141:4, 'Incline not my heart to any evil things (ra), to be occupied in deeds of wickedness (rasha)'. From this distinction we may deduce that the evil neighbour is even more dangerous than the rasha, the wicked, for the latter is branded by public opinion. He does not hide from his wicked actions, therefore the Mishnah warns us not to associate with such an unsavoury character. But the evil neighbour can camouflage his real intentions with flattering words; he is *shakhen*, physically and geographically near to you, but *(ra)* evil, lurks in his heart. Such a person can mislead many, therefore the Mishnah employs the stronger term — keep far from him for his motives are insincere.

If our assumption be correct, it would give an added meaning to a prayer formulated by R. Judah Ha-Nasi and included in the early morning prayers of our Siddur: May it be Thy will, O Lord my God and the God of my fathers, to save me this day and every day from an evil neighbour. The prayerful and plaintive cry, 'Save me from an evil neighbour', is more powerful and poignant than the Mishnaic expression, 'Keep aloof from an evil neighbour'. In this respect it is worth recording that Judah Ha-Nasi was an intimate friend of the Roman Procurator in Judea. Although the latter placed a number of men at the Rabbi's disposal to protect him, he prayed to God to deliver him from his adversaries and did not rely on human aid alone, 'Keep aloof'... Some maintain that we have here a veiled reference to the founder of Christianity who preached neighbourly love with the ulterior motive of initiating a new religion. Nittai, who lived at this period, foresaw the dangers of the new movement and warned his generation to keep aloof from the new-fangled teachings of their neighbours (Sanh. 107b, So. 47a).

Do not associate with the wicked. The oft repeated saying, 'Woe to the wicked and woe to his neighbour' (Nu. R:18) comes to mind. 'Lest a person say, 'I shall take care not to live in the neighbourhood of an evil person because that would involve constant association, but I shall be allied with him occasionally for purposes of business'.... he is therefore warned not to associate with the wicked, that is, in any kind of association' (Meiri). In this connection we should carefully note the opening words of the Book of Psalms, 'Happy is the man who does not walk in the counsel of the wicked'. The Psalmist does not say 'he should not associate with the wicked'. He goes further and reminds us that we should not even walk in the same path, nor stand on a par with him.

Do not abandon belief in retribution. ARN states, 'Let him who is enjoying good fortune not shrug off the thought of calamity.... and let him who is in the midst of calamity not despair of good fortune'. Maimonides remarks, 'If you sin or see somebody sinning, do not think confidently that God will punish the wicked only in the world to come; do not give up hope of speedy retribution for that sin'. The Book of Proverbs epitomises this teaching in these words: 'Happy is the man that fears always, but he that hardens his heart shall fall into evil' (28:14). He who stands in awe of God in all situations, in fortune or misfortune, puts his trust in the Almighty, but he who hardens his heart will not believe in retribution and so he will automatically sink into evil-doing.

Hasidic Lore

Retribution. The Slonimer Rabbi says, 'Happy is he who reminds himself at all times to fear the Lord and His retribution.

(ח) יְהוּדָה בֶּן טַבַּאי וְשִׁמְעוֹן בֶּן שָׁטַח קִבְּלוּ מֵהֶם. יְהוּדָה בֶּן טַבַּאי אוֹמֵר אַל תַּעַשׂ עַצְמְךָ כְּעוֹרְכֵי הַדַּיָּנִין וּכְשֶׁיִּהְיוּ בַּעֲלֵי הַדִּין עוֹמְדִים לְפָנֶיךָ יִהְיוּ בְעֵינֶיךָ כִּרְשָׁעִים וּכְשֶׁנִּפְטָרִים מִלְּפָנֶיךָ יִהְיוּ בְעֵינֶיךָ כְּזַכָּאִין כְּשֶׁקִּבְּלוּ עֲלֵיהֶם אֶת הַדִּין:

Mishnah Eight

Judah Ben Tabbai and Simeon Ben Shatah received the tradition from them. Judah Ben Tabbai says: Make not yourself as they who prepare the judges, and whilst the litigants are standing before you let them be regarded by you as guilty. But when they are departed from your presence, regard them as innocent, as they have accepted the sentence upon themselves.

Here we have the third of the 'Pairs', but there is a difference of opinion as to which of them is the *Nasi* (President) and which the *Av Bet Din* (Vice-president) (Ha. 16b). If, as seems likely, Judah was the Nasi, it was he who fled to Alexandria because of the persecution of the Pharisees by Alexander Yannai, 126-76 B.C.E.

Simeon Ben Shatah, 104-69 B.C.E. was the brother of Queen Alexandra Salome who succeeded Alexander Yannai, and was responsible for recalling the Pharisees from Alexandria. He it was who re-established the pharisaic teachings of the Law and became known as 'The Restorer of the Law who has given back to the crown of learning its pristine glory' (Kid. 66a). Simeon introduced schools for children. Before his time there were no elementary schools in Judea; children were taught mainly by their fathers.

His honesty and integrity are vouched for by the following story. He lived in very humble surroundings, supporting himself by selling linen goods. His pupils presented him with an ass which they bought from an Arab. After the purchase, they noticed a costly jewel on the neck of the animal and were happy for their master, who could now live more comfortably. Simeon, however, refused to accept the jewel, claiming that the Arab sold the ass alone. When the jewel was returned, the Arab exclaimed, 'Praised be the glory of Simeon Ben Shetah' (Deut. R. 3:5).

Make not yourself as they who prepare the judges. We should stress the word *azmekha*, yourself. Do not set yourself up as an authority; it is the function of the judge to make decisions. To understand this injunction, we go to the Talmud, where we shall learn who is qualified to be a judge. 'We only appoint to a Sanhedrin men of stature possessed of wisdom and imposing appearance, of mature age, masters of the magical arts and acquainted with the seventy languages, so that the Sanhedrin does not have to hear a case through the mouth of an interpreter' (Sanh. 17a). This high level of perfection was somewhat watered down to the following, 'If there are three who know how to speak all the languages, it is an average Sanhedrin; if there are four, it is a learned Sanhedrin' (Tosefta Sanh. 8:1).

Some suggest that this injunction refers to the judges themselves. They are warned not to prejudge their colleagues by using their influence for or against one of the parties to the suit. In this connection we should know that judges were not paid officials. 'He who takes a fee to adjudicate, his verdicts are invalid' (Bek. 4:6). One writer paraphrases this Mishnah in these words, 'Make not yourself like the pleaders before the judges, that is, like those who devise legal arguments in order to justify immorality' (Barth). In Jewish life and thought the judges must not take literally the evidence prepared for them. They must use independent judgment and be strictly impartial. 'Judah Ben Tabbai is not warning against teaching a litigant how to argue deceitfully, for that is altogether wicked; what he warns against is saying to a litigant, 'Do such and such, so that you might win the suit' (Duran).

When they stand before you. R. Akiva explained this statement in a novel manner. When men came before him he said, 'Know before whom you are standing; not before me, Akiva, but before the Creator of the world' (Y. Sanh. 1). The impartiality of the judge is often stressed. Commenting on Lev. 19:15, 'In righteousness shall you judge your neighbour', the Rabbis add, 'You must not allow one litigant to speak as much as he wishes and then say to the other, 'Shorten your speech'. You must not allow one to stand and the other to sit' (Sifra 89a).

Let them be as wicked. Though we were advised above to judge all in the scale of merit (Mishnah 6) which applies to life in a normal state of society, here, in times of judgment, the judge must investigate the truth and carefully scrutinise the evidence; in his eyes they are both guilty. It should be pointed out that the judges were wrapped in their prayer shawls and did not see the suitors; only when they had left did the judges revert to the principle of judging all in the scale of merit. However, this can operate only when the litigants have submitted to the judgment and then they are both innocent and should be treated in a friendly manner.

In Mak. 5b it is reported that Judah ben Tabbai sentenced to death a false witness against whom an alibi had been proved, in order to oppose the view of the Sadducees that such a witness was only to be put to death if the person falsely accused by him had already been executed. When his colleague Simeon Ben Shetah proved his sentence was against the law, Judah was convinced that in future he would not give a decision except in the presence of Simeon Ben Shetah.

Hasidic Lore

God can pardon. R. Joshua the son of R. Shalom of Belz had occasion to pray for the recovery of an irreligious Jew who was dangerously ill. He said, 'It may be true that the patient deserves to die if judged by the rules of strict justice. But it is only the judges of the lower tribunal who have no choice under the law and must sentence the offender according to his acts. The king, however, the chief magistrate of the country, may issue a pardon in disregard of the law. 'Thou, O Lord, art like the King, the Judge of all the earth, and mayest grant a pardon. I implore Thee to exercise Thy right of mercy; as Abraham said, 'The Judge of all the earth need not do justice' (Gen. 18:25). R. Joshua deliberately dropped the question mark implied in this verse.

(ט) שִׁמְעוֹן בֶּן שָׁטַח אוֹמֵר הֱוֵי מַרְבֶּה לַחֲקוֹר אֶת הָעֵדִים וֶהֱוֵי זָהִיר בִּדְבָרֶיךָ שֶׁמָּא מִתּוֹכָם יִלְמְדוּ לְשַׁקֵּר:

Mishnah Nine

Simeon Ben Shetah says, 'Be very searching in the examination of witnesses and be careful in your words, lest through them they will learn to lie'.

Be very searching.... It is reported that the son of Simeon was innocently condemned to death on the false evidence of witnesses. The thorough examination of witnesses is based on Deut. 13:15, *vedarashta vehakarta*, 'Then shall you inquire and make search...' The examination of witnesses in Jewish Law was very different from what obtained in Egypt, Rome and Athens, where torture was the order of the day. The fourth Book of Maccabees gives a list of the horrible instruments of torture used to extract evidence from witnesses — wheels, joint screws, dislocators, rocks and bone crushers, catapults, cauldrons, braziers, thumb screws, iron claws, wedges and branding irons (8:13).

'From Rome the institution of torture passed to Medieval Europe, and was standard practice in England, Scotland, France, Italy, Spain, Germany and elsewhere until the eighteenth century. The Church itself, through the Inquisition, employed torture to extort confessions. Heretics were often tortured by the civil power at the direction of the religious authorities. In Asiatic countries, torture as part of the legal system was wellnigh universal' (Silver).

Judaism, to its eternal glory, never practised torture. There is not a trace of it in the Bible. The Mishnah in Sanh. 40a informs us that 'The Judges used to examine the witnesses with seven searching queries'. We endeavoured to reach the truth through detailed investigation and not through inhumane torture, which was taboo.

Be careful in your words. 'This is a warning to the judges not to say anything in the presence of the litigants or the witnesses which might lead them to perceive how to win the suit' (Duran).

Hasidic Lore

When Elijah comes. The Medzibozer recounted the following: Two men deposited money; one a hundred zuzim and the other two hundred zuzim and later each claimed to have invested two hundred. If there is no proof, the money shall remain unpaid until Elijah comes (B.M. 34a). What can Elijah do about it? Must there not be two witnesses for legal evidence? The answer is that when Elijah comes the inhabitants of the world will become truthful and the man who deposited the lesser amount will testify to the truth.

(י) שְׁמַעְיָה וְאַבְטַלְיוֹן קִבְּלוּ מֵהֶם. שְׁמַעְיָה אוֹמֵר אֱהַב אֶת הַמְּלָאכָה וּשְׂנָא אֶת הָרַבָּנוּת וְאַל תִּתְוַדַּע לָרָשׁוּת:

Mishnah Ten

Shemaiah and Avtalion received the tradition from them. Shemaiah says, Love work, hate lordship and seek no intimacy with the ruling power.

Shemaiah and Avtalion are the fourth 'Pair'. Shemaiah was the President, *Nasi*, and Avtalion the Vice President, *Av Bet Din*. They lived in the middle of the first century B.C.E. They were descendants of Sennacherib (Git. 57b) and became righteous proselytes. They attained great fame and proved to be a brilliant and beloved pair in the chain of Jewish tradition. In addition to possessing outstanding scholarship, they were also famed for their preaching (Pes. 70b). It is reported that Hillel went up from Babylon to hear Torah from their mouths. We also learn from Yoma 71b that as the High Priest came from the Sanctuary all the people followed him, but when they saw Shemaiah and Avtalion they forsook him and went after Shemaiah and Avtalion. Eventually the two Masters visited the High Priest to take their leave of him. He said to them, 'May the descendants of the heathen come in peace'. They answered him, 'May the descendants of the heathen who do the work of Aaron arrive in peace, but the descendants of Aaron who do not do the work of Aaron, they shall not come in peace'.

Love work.... One authority (Ritvah) says that this Mishnah continues with the same theme enunciated above (Mishnayot 8-9) which deal with judges. Love work and you will not fall into the hands of judges. Those who do not work (luftmenschen) borrow money and do not repay; eventually they are brought before the judges. One who loves work will not borrow; if he does, he will repay.

ARN (chapter 11) comments, 'Even Adam did not taste food until he had done work, as it is said, 'The Lord God took the man and put him into the Garden of Eden to till it and keep it' (Gen. 2:15), after which He said, 'Of every tree of the garden you may eat'. Even God did not cause His Shekhinah to alight upon Israel until they had done work, as it is said, 'Let them make for Me a Sanctuary that I may dwell among them' (Ex. 25:8).

If one is unemployed, what should he do? If he has a courtyard or a field in a state of decay , let him busy himself with it, as it is said, 'Six days shall you labour and do all your work' (Ex. 20:9). For what purpose were the words 'And do all your work' added? It is to include a person who has a courtyard or field in a state of decay, that he should go and busy himself with it. A man only dies through idleness; work is a natural occupation'.

In the Bible, Abraham, Moses, David and Amos were introduced to us as shepherds. The Talmud proudly reminds us that Hillel was a woodcutter, Eliezer a farmer, Joshua Ben Hananiah a needdle maker, Akiva a shepherd and Johanan a shoemaker. The dignity of labour was always upheld, as we see from the following maxims culled from the Talmud.

A father is obliged to teach his son a trade.

He who does not teach his son a trade, accustoms him to robbery.

He who lives by his labour is superior to a God-fearing man.

All study of the Torah without work must in the end be futile and lead to sin.

Great is work, for it honours him who performs it.

Idleness leads to immorality.

The famine lasted seven years, yet it never reached the craftsman's door.

Skin a dead animal in the market place and get paid for it, but do not say, 'I am a great man and it is beneath my dignity'.

Finally, we record a story in the Midrash. The Emperor Hadrian was passing along the lanes near Tiberias and saw an old man breaking up the soil to plant trees. He said to him, 'Old man, if you had worked early there would have been no need for you to work so late in your life'. The old man replied, 'I have toiled both early and late, and what was pleasing to the Lord of Heaven has He done with me'. Hadrian asked him how old he was and when the answer was one hundred, Hadrian exclaimed, 'You, a hundred years old, and you stand breaking up the soil to plant trees! Do you expect to eat of their fruit?' He replied, 'If I am worthy I shall eat, but if not, as my fathers laboured for me, so I labour for my children' (Lev. R. 25:5).

One cannot refrain from adding that were the worker today to love work in the Mishnaic sense, it would not only improve production and act as a booster to the economy, but, what is more important, it would make for a healthier relationship between employer and employee and this in turn would create a more dignified and respectful climate in the many social and industrial problems of our day.

Hate lordship. Basically *rabbanut* means leadership, authority and superiority (Pes. 87b). In Ber. 55a we read, 'Rav Judah also said, three things shorten a man's days and years'. The last of the three is 'to give oneself an air of superiority'. R. Hama Bar Hanina said, 'Why did Joseph die before his brothers? Because he gave himself superior airs'. Here the same word *rabbanut* is used.

The Sages have warned against lordship, that is to say, let not a rich man be seduced by his wealth to pursue triumph and power over others, for this would only cause everyone to hate him.... The Sages observed, 'When a man has been appointed the head of a community, they regard him as wicked on high because he will probably demand the kind of authority and awe towards himself which is not for the sake of heaven' (Meiri). Furthermore, 'If you hate lordship you will be in a position to obey the commandment to love work, for he who loves lordship does not engage in work, and the meaning of lordship is love of power. Under no circumstances, however, should a man be withheld from struggling to arrive at the lordship of learning' (Duran).

The secondary meaning of *rabbanut* is 'The office of Rabbi'. We should remember that the Rabbi of the talmudic era and post-talmudic period literally followed this injunction. He hated the rabbinate as a profession. The Rabbis were either craftsmen, engaged in business or in some vocation such as medicine, etc. The professional Rabbi first appeared in the Middle Ages and then only as a judge during the period when we enjoyed autonomy. It was not until the middle of the fourteenth century that the Rabbi became an official of the Jewish Community. In the nineteenth century when the Jews lost their legal jurisdiction over their people, the Rabbi became a teacher and religious leader.

Chief Rabbi A.I. Kook interpreted the first two injunctions of the

Mishnah as follows: Love the work and vocation of the rabbinate but hate the authoritarian aspects of the position, the *yikhus*, the honours, pomp, ceremony, flattery and power often attached to the office of Rabbi. Two outstanding examples of world famous Rabbis who refused to function as Rabbis of a community were the Hafetz Hayyim and the Hazon Ish. A Rabbi who accepted a call to become the spiritual leader of Metz asked that the community record (the *Pinkus*) be brought to him. When this was done, he proceeded to write therein the Ten Commandments. The leaders were astounded and asked the Rabbi to explain his action. He replied, 'My experience in the rabbinate has shown me that the words written in the community record are more readily obeyed than those written in the Torah'.

Seek no intimacy with the ruling power. Some connect *rashut* with *rash*, meaning poverty. Love work and hate mastery; you will then be assured that you will not know poverty. However, the generally accepted translation of *rashut* is 'the ruling power', and may refer here to Rome which was an autocracy. Throughout our martyred history, many influential Jews who have been intimately connected with the ruling power and had given loyal service, have met their doom at the hands of their erstwhile benefactors. Commenting on Prov. 30:15, 'The horse leech has two daughters, Give, give', the Rabbis (A.Z. 17a) add, 'Give, give', refers to apostasy which lures the unwary, and the government which constantly imposes new taxes and duties.

Hasidic Lore

Manna. Rabbi Bunam said, 'Manna still descends daily in quantities sufficient for the minimum needs of each person. In the desert it came to a person without toil; today, however, it is distributed to each one of us, through our physical or mental labour'.

(יא) אַבְטַלְיוֹן אוֹמֵר חֲכָמִים הִזָּהֲרוּ בְּדִבְרֵיכֶם שֶׁמָּא תָחוּבוּ חוֹבַת גָּלוּת וְתִגְלוּ לִמְקוֹם מַיִם הָרָעִים וְיִשְׁתּוּ הַתַּלְמִידִים הַבָּאִים אַחֲרֵיכֶם וְיָמוּתוּ וְנִמְצָא שֵׁם שָׁמַיִם מִתְחַלֵּל:

Mishnah Eleven

Avtalion says: You wise men, be heedful of your words lest you incur the penalty of exile and be exiled to a place of evil waters and the disciples who come after you drink thereof and die and the heavenly name be profaned.

You wise men, be heedful of your words. Some connect *hizaharu* with *zohar*, which means brightness, brilliance. The wise teacher or guide is warned to speak with clarity and simplicity so that the disciple will readily understand what the teacher wishes to impart. The greater the teacher, the greater is his responsibility in choosing and weighing his words to avoid misinterpretation. The Talmud (Meg. 25b) says, 'A man should always be careful in wording his answers, because on the ground of the answer which Aaron made to Moses, the unbelievers were able to deny God, as it says, 'And I cast it into the fire and this calf came out' (Ex. 32:24). This would almost amount to an admission that the calf had divine powers. The Mishnah emphasises the responsibility which devolves on the teacher to be explicit in the choice of his words and avoid any hidden meaning. 'Take care to explain clearly the words that come out of your mouth so that it will be impossible for the listener to interpret heretically what you say. Do not say, 'Why be concerned with the audience? If they do not understand what we said, let them come up and ask what we meant, because it is possible that your words have been uttered in a place where listeners do not want to ask; indeed, they are already inclined to a false interpretation and are pleased with it' (Meiri).

Exile. This word is not to be taken literally as we understand it today. False and heretical teachings place one in exile, that is, outside the limits and boundaries of authentic Judaism.

Evil waters. These are false teachings which lead to a profanation of the Name of God. Commenting on Prov. 5:15, 'Drink waters out of your own cistern and running waters out of your own well', the Rabbis add, 'Do not drink from evil (bad) waters'. The Torah is often equated with *Mayim*

Hayyim, living waters. Heretical teachings are the antithesis of the living and refreshing waters of the Torah and bring spiritual death.

Hasidic Lore

Words from the heart. The Koretzer said, 'We recite in the Shema, 'And these words shall be upon your heart and you shall teach them diligently unto your children'. When these words go forth from your heart they will truly influence your children for good.

Clean waters. The Mezeritzer said, 'The good man who desires to receive the constant inspiration of God's benevolence must be like a conduit laid from a spring on a hilltop to water a field. In this conduit there must be no blemish of the smallest size; it must be laid straight and carefully linked to the spring'.

(יב) הִלֵּל וְשַׁמַּאי קִבְּלוּ מֵהֶם. הִלֵּל אוֹמֵר הֱוֵי מִתַּלְמִידָיו שֶׁל אַהֲרֹן אוֹהֵב שָׁלוֹם וְרוֹדֵף שָׁלוֹם אוֹהֵב אֶת הַבְּרִיּוֹת וּמְקָרְבָן לַתּוֹרָה:

Mishnah Twelve

Hillel and Shammai received the tradition from them. Hillel says: Be of the disciples of Aaron, loving peace and pursuing peace; loving fellow creatures and drawing them near to the Torah.

Hillel and Shammai are the last and most famous of the 'Pairs' who formulated Jewish tradition. Each founded a school, Bet Hillel and Bet Shammai, and they vied with each other in plumbing the depths of Torah instruction. Hillel was a model of patience, gentility and humility. He followed a lenient line in Halakhah. Shammai was impatient, rigid and stern, and followed the strict line in his decisions. Apart from his noble character Hillel was famed for collecting and codifying traditional law. His opinion was accepted without question. It is said that he and all his disciples were familiar with nature-study and knew the language of mountains, valleys, trees and beasts of the field.

Be of the disciples of Aaron loving peace and pursuing peace. Aaron was a lovable personality who endeared himself to every one. Indeed, after his death the people mourned even longer for him than for Moses. The Rabbis ask, 'How is one a lover of peace?' It teaches that a man must love peace to abide in Israel among all individuals, as it is said, 'The law of truth was in his mouth, he walked with Me in peace and uprightness and did turn many away from iniquity' (Mal. 2:6). What is the meaning of 'He did turn many away from iniquity?' When Aaron walked along a street and met a wicked man, he greeted him. The next day when that person wanted to commit a transgression he would say to himself, 'How can I, after performing such an act, lift up my eyes and look at Aaron? I should feel ashamed before him who greeted me'. Consequently he would refrain from doing wrong.

Similarly, when two men were quarrelling with each other, Aaron would visit one of them and say to him, 'My son, see how your friend is behaving; he beats his breast, tears his garment and cries, 'Woe is me; how can I look into the face of my friend? I am ashamed before him since it was I who acted shabbily towards him', and Aaron would continue to sit with him until he had banished all enmity from his heart. Then he would go and repeat exactly the same words to the other one until he had removed all hatred from him, The result was that when the two men met, they embraced and kissed each other' (ARN 12).

We should remember that the gentle Hillel does not ask us to be a replica of Aaron who was a unique personality. If we cannot aspire to the exacting heights of an Aaron, we should endeavor to be one of his disciples and admirers.

Some distinguish between 'love peace' and 'pursue peace'. Love peace in the home where *shalom bayit*, domestic bliss, reigns supreme, thus helping to build and strengthen Jewish family life, the foundation of all Jewish existence. Pursue peace outside the home in your dealings with all people. We are thus encouraged to extend greetings of peace to all. It was said of R. Johanan Ben Zakkai that no one ever saluted him first, not even the heathen in the street (Ber. 17a).

So indispensable is peace that 'we greet and inquire after the welfare of gentiles because of ways of peace' (Shev. 4:3). How must we salute them? As we salute Israelites with the greeting 'Peace be unto you' (Y. Shev. 4:35b). Moreover, we must support the poor of the gentiles with the poor of Israel, we must visit the sick of the gentiles with the sick of Israel, we must bury the dead of the gentiles as we bury the dead of Israel, because of the ways of peace (Git. 61a). Rabbi Hiyya Bar Abba said, 'Gentiles outside the Holy Land are not to be regarded as idolaters, for they are only continuing the customs of their fathers' (Hul. 13b).

The above quotations logically lead us to the second phrase, 'Love creatures'. 'Shalom' is one of the names of God who created all humanity. Aaron loved men because they were created by God. When we love man, we love God, the Creator of all men.

And bring them near to the Torah. The Torah is the elixir of life and our most precious possession. It is therefore our duty and privilege to justify our existence by attracting people to Torah through love, consideration and ways of peace.

The Netziv of Volozhin said that this Mishnah seems to urge us to love not only the devout and scholarly, but even more so those who are distant from the Torah, those who are alienated from Judaism because of extenuating circumstances. Hillel, with his abundant love towards all, pleads with us to extend the hand of friendship to those distant from us and so help them to come closer to the Torah which belongs to all.

Hasidic Lore

Peace. Concerning the words of the prayer: 'He who maketh peace in His high places, may He make peace for us....' Rabbi Pinhas said: We all know that Heaven, *shamayim*, came into being when God made peace between fire, *esh*, and water, *mayim*. And He who could make peace between the utmost extremes, will surely be able to make peace between us.

(יג) הוּא הָיָה אוֹמֵר נְגִיד שְׁמָא אֲבַד שְׁמֵהּ וּדְלָא מוֹסִיף יָסֵף וּדְלָא יַלִּיף קְטָלָא חַיָּב וּדְאִשְׁתַּמֵּשׁ בְּתָגָא חֳלָף:

Mishnah Thirteen

He used to say, A name made great is a name destroyed. He who does not increase shall cease. he who does not learn deserves to die, and he who puts the crown to his own use shall perish.

A name made great.... Names are not mere labels but have a special significance of their own. One Rabbi has suggested that the name of a person affects his character (Ber. 7b). The Torah often mentions the name, following it immediately with an explanatory meaning, as in the names of the children of Jacob (Gen. chapters 29-30). Some names begin or conclude with the Name of God, stressing the kinship between man and God. We are reminded not to take the Name of God in vain nor should we misuse the name given to us by our parents. So ingrained is a good name in Jewish life that we have read into the opening words of Ecc. chapter 7 something which is not there. 'A good name is better than precious oil'. The literal translation of the Hebrew is 'a name (which is added ungrammatically to *tov* thus making 'a good name'), is better than precious ointment.'.

He who is an exhibitionist and is constantly advertising his talents and boasting of his alleged greatness, will eventually lose his good name. He who does not have greatness showered upon him but is self-intoxicated with his own success, will destroy all claims to fame.

He who does not increase, shall cease.... Man should not remain static in learning, observance or deeds; he should always forge ahead. If this is true of the material world, it is certainly true of the spiritual world. Man must not be an *omed*, at a standstill, but a *holekh*, moving forward in the performance of mitzvot and good deeds. One should not be satisfied with the minimum of learning but strive to reach the maximum.

He who does not learn deserves to die.... We are the guardians of the Torah and carry the heavy responsibility of learning and studying the words of the Torah which have preserved us throughout the vicissitudes of our long and martyred existence. On the other hand, if we neglect the study of Torah we commit spiritual suicide. Torah is the quintessence of life; without it we are doomed to stagnate and die. So devastating and far reaching is the neglect of learning that even a patient, humble and meek character as Hillel feels that it is imperative for him to pronounce the death penalty on one who fails to learn.

The same thought is expressed in ARN 27: 'He who does not attend on scholars is guilty of death, and he who attends on them but does not fulfil what he learns from them, is guilty of multiplied death'. So efficacious is learning of Torah that it can rid us of the evil impulse which creates such havoc in the heart of man. God said to Israel, 'My children, I have created the evil impulse and I have created the Torah as an antidote to it; if you occupy yourselves with Torah you will not be delivered into its power' (Kid.

30b). Again, 'If this despicable thing (evil impulse) meets you, drag it along to the house of study' (Ibid). The Rabbis also declare, 'Happy are the Israelites; at the time they are engaged with Torah and beneficent acts, their evil impulse is delivered into their power and they are not delivered into the power of their impulse' (A.Z. 5b).

He who puts the crown to his own use... One who does not study *Torah lishmah*, for its own sake, but uses the Torah for self-advancement and vainglory, does not raise the status of learning but drags it down to the mire. Enlarging on Hillel's statement, the Talmud records, 'He who makes a worldly use of the crown of Torah shall waste away as Belshazzar who, for using the holy vessels which had become common, was uprooted from the world; all the more should he who uses the crown of the Torah be uprooted' (Ned. 62a).

The language of this Mishnah is not Mishnaic Hebrew but Aramaic. As the subject matter here is learning and education, which are of supreme importance for the future of Judaism, Aramaic was chosen as the vehicle of expression. Aramaic was the vernacular of the day and the message would thus reach all Jews.

Hasidic Lore

Names. The surname of R. Levi Isaac as carried in the registers of the authorities, was 'The Compassionate', a name not borne by his father before him. This name came to him in the following manner. When the Imperial decree bade every one to add a surname to his given name, the Jews were tardy in fulfilling this behest. The warden of Berditschev went from house to house to enforce registration. When he came to the zaddik's house (speaking his errand by rote) the zaddik looked above and beyond him and said, not heeding him, 'Follow in the footsteps of the Lord and as He is compassionate, you be compassionate'. But the warden caught on the word, took out his list and entered R. Levi Isaac, surname, 'The Compassionate'.

(יד) הוּא הָיָה אוֹמֵר אִם אֵין אֲנִי לִי מִי לִי וּכְשֶׁאֲנִי לְעַצְמִי מָה אֲנִי וְאִם לֹא עַכְשָׁיו אֵימָתָי:

Mishnah Fourteen

He used to say: If I am not for myself, who is for me? And when I am for myself, what am I? And if not now, when?

If I am not for myself. We are here reminded that self-preservation is a natural instinct. We all pursue our own particular bent to develop our individuality, but this is only part of the truth. Man is a gregarious being and cannot live in isolation. We have never encouraged the hermit or ascetic; it is not only anti-social but also anti-Torah. To develop our individuality may be natural and desirable; but it must be limited. On the other hand, self, without the joys of companionship, friendship and service, makes one morbid, introspective and selfish. We must add to self the care of, and concern for, others. At which point should we develop this interest in others? If not now, when? We should not allow our own natural concern for our well-being to deteriorate into base ingratitude, but raise it to the heights of altruism and selflessness and so become a blessing to humanity.

It should be noted that this Mishnah distinguishes between two different persons. One is referred to by *mi*, who, in the first section of the Mishnah and the other by *ma*, what, at the end of the second section. This leads us to another interpretation. 'If I am not for myself, who will be for me?' Compared with the omniscience and omnipotence of God, man is an insignificant speck of star dust. But as he is invested with the divine image, he is a personality and is alluded to by the word *mi*, who.

Alternatively, 'If I am for myself' and selfishly guard my own material interests to the exclusion of everything that is spiritual, I then descend to the depth of depravity; I lose my individuality and I am considered a mere thing, an abstraction. I am then referred to as *ma*, what, and I am denuded of all spirituality.

The Mesillat Yesharim interprets the Mishnah to refer to the acquisition of knowledge, 'If a man will keep watch over himself, God will help him and deliver him from the evil impulse, but if he fails to do so, God will surely not watch over him, for if he has no compassion on himself, who should have compassion on him? Our Sages say, 'It is forbidden to have compassion on one who has spurned knowledge' (Ber. 33a).

The Mishnah can also apply to the acquiring of *zekhut*, merit, which devolves upon every person. 'I must work out my own salvation, yet how weak are my unaided efforts'. This interpretation is supported by the following extract, 'If I have not acquired merit for myself, who will acquire merit for me, making me worthy of the life of the world to come? I have no father, I have no mother, upon whose merit I can rely' (ARN 27b). We are also warned, 'Let not a man say, my father was a pious man, I shall be saved for his sake'. Abraham could not save Ishmael nor could Jacob save Esau' (Midrash Tehillim 46a).

The words of the Mishnah offer still another lesson — not to rely on one's wealth. If I am not for myself, if even my body does not wholly belong to me (for ultimately one must leave this mortal earth), who is for me? What, in reality, does belong to me? We cannot take with us the wealth, luxuries and comforts of life. This teaches us to be humble, generous and charitable *akhshav*, now. We should not reserve our good deeds only for old age, for we cannot tell what tomorrow can bring, and if not now, when? One must serve God at all times; every moment offers us the opportunity to repent.

In all interpretations the operative word is *akhshav*, the present. We often stress the past and the future, we are proud of our ancient heritage and hopeful of a glorious future, but what of the present? In our sacred Scriptures we often meet with *vayehi*, 'and it was' (in the past), and *vehaya*, 'and it shall be' (in the future), but rarely, if ever, do we find 'and it is', in the present. Yet without a creative present we cannot build a constructive future. Commenting on the words in the Shema, 'These words which I command you today', the Rabbis remark, 'The Commandments shall appear to you every day as if they were new, just given to you on Mount Sinai on this very day' (Sifre). The past re-emerges and activates our thoughts and deeds. Let us not boast only of our Jewish past; we should live our Judaism now, in the present, so that we preserve it for the future. In the words of Franz Rosenzweig, 'The present is not only a bridge for tomorrow, it is a springboard to eternity'.

Hillel adds a new dimension to the word *hayom*, today. He stresses the *akhshav*, this moment, which is even more timely than *hayom*, today. Hillel warns us not to procrastinate; one should perform the mitzvah now, immediately, The Rabbis express the thought in this manner: 'You must not allow this mitzvah to become sour by postponing it' (Mekhilta 21). Do it now in the present; we are certain only of the present, therefore we should use it for the service of God and of mankind.

R. Zevi Ezekiel Michaelson explains this Mishnah as follows: 'If I am not learning for myself only, but teaching others as well, then the pupils who profit from my teaching will be a credit to me; but if I study myself without teaching others, of what profit is my learning? And though its futility may not be clear whilst I live, it will be discovered when I die'.

Hasidic Lore

Former days. Said the Kobriner: Some people say, 'Nowadays it is difficult to serve the Lord. Formerly there were many good and pious folk whose example could be imitated'. This notion is absurd, and I say to them, 'Have you truly endeavoured to seek the Lord without avail? Endeavour to seek Him in the manner of those in former days and you will find him, even as they did'. We may learn from this verse (Ec. 7:10), 'Say not, 'How was it that the former days were better than these?' for it is not out of wisdom that you inquire concerning this'.

(טו) שַׁמַּאי אוֹמֵר עֲשֵׂה תוֹרָתְךָ קֶבַע אֱמוֹר מְעַט וַעֲשֵׂה הַרְבֵּה וֶהֱוֵי מְקַבֵּל אֶת כָּל הָאָדָם בְּסֵבֶר פָּנִים יָפוֹת:

Mishnah Fifteen

Shammai says: Make of your Torah a fixed practice, say little and do much, and receive all men with a cheerful countenance.

We know that at the final judgment, the first question a person will face will be, 'Have you fixed set times for the study of Torah? (Shab. 31a). In ARN 28 it is stated: 'He who makes his study of Torah primary and his worldly occupation secondary, will be made primary in the world to come; but he who makes his worldly occupation primary and his study of Torah secondary, will be made secondary in the world to come'. This means that even if he were not guilty of transgression, since he did not make Torah study a primary duty, though he is worthy to be in paradise, he will there be secondary' (R. Jonah).

Keva, a fixed time. This can be interpreted differently. ARN appears to understand it to mean that we should be consistent; do not be lenient with yourself and severe with others. As you are lenient with yourself, be lenient with others, and as you are severe with yourself, be severe with others. The word *keva* can also refer to the immutability of the Torah, which is fixed for all times and cannot be replaced. Maimonides clearly formulates this truth in the ninth principle of his Thirteen Articles of Faith: I believe with perfect faith that the Law will not be changed and that there will never be another Law from the Creator, blessed be His name.

We would add that *keva* is derived from the same root as the central word of the blessing pronounced when fixing a Mezuzah, *likboa*. We can thus see a close relationship between Torah in general and Mezuzah in particular. The Mezuzah is a fixture; it is not seasonal as Tefilin which are not worn on Shabbat or Festival, or Lulav and Etrog reserved only for Sukkot. The Mezuzah is unique, in that it is the only religious appurtenance which is exhibited in the home and Synagogue throughout each and every day of the year. This is the function of Torah learning and study. Like the Mezuzah, Torah is not seasonal, but is always with us. The Mezuzah is in every habitable room of the home, similarly Torah should not be reserved for certain days of the year, or for the Synagogue alone; the Torah should affect and influence us in every area of life. Again, the Mezuzah is placed outside the door facing the public; the Torah Jew does not restrict his Judaism to the home or Synagogue alone, he takes the Torah with him into the public thoroughfare and endeavours to create a *Kiddush Hashem* in his dealings with all people, including the non-Jewish world.

Say little and do much. ARN illustrates this saying by quoting two biblical characters, one righteous who said little but did much, and the other unrighteous who said much but did little. Abraham welcomed the angels and promised them merely a 'morsel of bread' (Gen. 18:15), but eventually he entertained them with a sumptuous feast consisting of three oxen and a measure of fine meal. On the other hand, Ephron the Hittite promised Abraham the field and the cave therein as a burial possession for Sarah. Ephron actually said, 'I give it to you'. He said much but in the end he did little, for in verse 15 he says, 'A piece of land worth four hundred shekels of silver, what is that between me and you?' In point of fact, four hundred shekels of silver in those early days was a very substantial amount of money, but Ephron minimised it and treated it very lightly. Originally he promised much but did little.

This saying can be interpreted in another vein. Rabbinic learning is so vast that it has been called *Yam Hatalmud*, the ocean of the Talmud. To many, Torah is inexhaustible and unexplorable as the bottomless depth of the ocean. To acquire some knowledge of the illimitable extent of the waters of the Talmud, we should say little but exert ourselves and learn much. Some can master a Rashi or Ramban, others can read or memorise a chapter of the Psalms; each according to his intellectual capacity. In this connection we should stress the second word of our Mishnah, *Toratekha*, your Torah not Hatorah. The Torah in its entirety may be beyond the reach of an average individual, therefore make it your personal Torah, *Toratekha*. Torah study should not create a superior caste. Here we come to the third statement of the Mishnah.

'Receive all men with a cheerful countenance'. Do not make any distinction between the rich and the poor, the learned and the ignorant; receive them all favourably and gladly.

ARN adds: This teaches that if one gave his fellow-man all the good gifts in the world with a downcast face, Scripture accounts it to him as though he had given him naught; but if he received his fellow-man with a cheerful countenance, even though he gives him naught, Scripture accounts it to him as though he had given him all the good gifts in the world.

Duran sums up the teachings of this Mishnah in these words: Shammai is here urging three things corresponding to three human attainments; wisdom, strength and riches. As regards wisdom, he says, 'Make your study of Torah a fixed practice'; as regards riches he says, 'Say little and do much'; as regards strength he says, 'Receive all men with a cheerful countenance', that is, let a person master his anger. 'Who is it that is mighty? He who subdues his evil impulse'. A cheerful countenance is the direct antithesis of arrogance and anger.

The last injunction of Shammai seems to belie the general impression that he was impatient and inflexible. It would appear that we must differentiate between Shammai the Halakhist when he is unbending in his decisions, and Shammai in his approach to the performance of mitzvot, for example the giving of charity. Shammai seems to remind us that even if we cannot afford to donate to every Jewish cause, we should show a cheerful countenance to the charity overseer. This is in accordance with the talmudic maxim: He who gives receives six blessings, but he who is unable to help, and yet smiles, receives eleven blessings (B.B. 9b).

Hasidic Lore

Prayer with Joy. R. Bunam saw a Jew in danger of drowning whilst swimming in the sea near Danzig. He noted that the man was about to abandon the struggle to save himself and he shouted to him, 'Give my greetings to the Leviathan'. Unwittingly the drowning man smiled at this levity thereby he regained his presence of mind and was able to hold himself afloat until friends rescued him. Relating this experience, R. Bunam remarked, 'We may learn from this that prayer with a joyful heart and a cheerful countenance reaches the Lord, but prayers with outcries and lamentations may be wasted'.

(טז) רַבָּן גַּמְלִיאֵל הָיָה אוֹמֵר עֲשֵׂה לְךָ רַב וְהִסְתַּלֵּק מִן הַסָּפֵק וְאַל תַּרְבֶּה לְעַשֵּׂר אֻמָּדוֹת:

Mishnah Sixteen

Rabban Gamliel used to say: Make for yourself a teacher and remove yourself from what is doubtful, and tithe not overmuch by conjecture.

Rabban. This means our teacher or master; it is a title held only by Presidents of the Sanhedrin, Gamliel being the first to be thus honoured. He was the grandson of Hillel and passed on this honorific title to a number of his descendants. Later teachers were called Rabbi in Palestine and Rav or Mar in Babylonia. Gamliel originated a number of legal ordinances with a view to improving the world (Git. 4:1; Yev. 16:7; R.H. 2:5). Gamliel was a prominent member of the Sanhedrin and greatly honoured by the people, on whose behalf he was very active. Typical of his regard for rich and poor alike, and disregarding his own dignity, he ordered that he be taken out (to his burial) in flaxen vestments and thereafter the people followed his lead and were taken out (to burial) in flaxen vestments (M.K. 27b). Gamliel was the first Jewish social reformer; he was interested in the welfare of all sections of society. The name Gamliel is first found in Nu. 1:10. He was also called Gamliel the Elder and indeed acted as an elder statesman.

Make for yourself a teacher. This statement is different from a similar statement in 1:6, where it applied specifically to learning and studying, for which one requires a companion. Here it refers to making decisions either by a judge in the law-court or by any person who is called upon to give a ruling on an issue. In either case, one should not refrain from asking advice; even a highly intellectual person should appoint a master over himself in order to consult when in doubt. Scholarship alone is ineffectual if it is not applied to life; this indeed reflects the life of Gamliel who was both an outstanding scholar and an active spokesman on behalf of his people. This may be the reason why his teaching commences with the appropriate word *asseh* — do, be active.

Remove yourself from what is doubtful. The use of the hitpael, the reflexive, should be noted. We are not advised not to doubt, this would be well-nigh impossible to attain; we all have doubts at times. We are asked, through learning and observance, to endeavour to remove doubts which assail us. The Vitry states: In matters of Halakhah do not persist in doubt; instead provide yourself with a teacher.

We can also interpret it to mean that we should avoid such things that may possibly be forbidden. Saadiah Gaon discourses on the subject of doubt, and he quotes from the Talmud: With the increase of numbers of the disciples of Shammai and Hillel who did not advance far enough in their studies, the controversies increased (Sanh. 88b). Saadiah elaborates this to mean that if students persevere and patiently proceed with their studies to their logical conclusions, they will inevitably dispel all doubts; to master all knowledge initially, is to be like God.

Heschel, on the other hand, avers that, 'There is no word in biblical Hebrew for 'doubt'; there are many expressions for wonder. Just as in dealing with judgments, our starting point is doubt; wonder is the biblical starting point in facing reality. The biblical man's sense for the mind — surpassing grandeur of reality prevented the power of doubt from setting up its own independent dynasty. Doubt is an act in which the mind inspects its own ideas; wonder is an act in which the mind confronts the universe'. As one put it, 'In Torah, first came the doubt then came the knowledge; in Israel, first came the idolators then came the believers in Divine unity. A generation in which there is no improvement of ideals, must perish'.

Tithe not overmuch. Tithing, *maaser*, is the giving of one tenth of one's produce. There are three kinds of tithing; 1. *Maaser Rishon*, the first tithe given to the Levites; 2. *Maaser Sheni*, the second tithe, which is taken to Jerusalem and eaten in the forecourt of the Temple; 3. *Maaser Ani*, the tithe paid to the poor. All these tithes have pentateuchal authority — Lev. 27:30; Nu. 18:21; and Deut. 14:22. Tithing demanded that it was required to set aside one's tithes with exactitude and not by guess-work, as the Rabbis rule that 'if a person gives excessive tithes, his produce is made fit but his tithes are unfit' (Kid. 51a; Er. 50b). Rashi and other authorities do not interpret the word 'tithing' literally, but regard the expression as a figure of speech referring to many areas in life. When we apply this to learning and studying Torah, it fits in with the Mishnah as a whole.

Thus provide yourself with a good teacher in whom you should confide; he will remove your doubts. Do not rely on your own judgment as this may often lead to conjecture. Consult an authoritative scholar and teacher; he will provide you with clear, logical decisions. The same lesson applies to the field of charitable endeavour. One should help all who ask, but one should differentiate between casual alms-giving and a *yored*, a respectable person who has fallen on hard times. In such a case, we do not guess or give by conjecture; he is worthy of our personal consideration and we should respond accordingly.

Hasidic Lore

Joy in holiness. A hasid asked the Kosmirer Rabbi: Would it not be a more virtuous act to distribute for charity the money which your hasidim spend on communal meals and wine? The Kosmirer replied: We find that during each period of seven years we are enjoined to set aside a second tithe for our own enjoyment in Jerusalem, on the first, the second, the fourth and the fifth years; whereas it was required to give the tithe for the poor only on the third and sixth years. Hence it may be deduced that enjoyment in an atmosphere of holiness precedes charity and is of double importance.

(יז) שִׁמְעוֹן בְּנוֹ אוֹמֵר כָּל יָמַי גָּדַלְתִּי בֵּין הַחֲכָמִים וְלֹא מָצָאתִי לַגּוּף טוֹב מִשְּׁתִיקָה. וְלֹא הַמִּדְרָשׁ הוּא הָעִיקָר אֶלָּא הַמַּעֲשֶׂה. וְכָל הַמַּרְבֶּה דְבָרִים מֵבִיא חֵטְא:

Mishnah Seventeen

Simeon his son says: All my days I grew up amongst the wise and have found nothing better for one than silence; not study is the chief thing but action and he who multiplies words brings on sin.

Simeon his son. Commentators naturally infer that this Simeon is the son of Gamliel of the previous Mishnah and he is not called Rabban Simeon because he gave utterance to these words before he was ordained. Travers Herford suggests that Simeon is the son of Hillel.

Silence. Simeon reminds us that when one is in the company of the wise, one should refrain from speaking and remain silent. Man is superior to the animal because of the divine gift of speech, but silence is no less divine. The Torah was given on Mount Sinai amidst silence, 'no bird sang or flew, no ox lowed, no creature spoke, the world was silent and still'. (Ex. R. 29). The stillness of the Revelation introduced the Ten Commandments, but the frantic rantings of all rebels lead to violence, terrorism and war. Silence ennobles one who controls his mouth, as the Rabbis assert: Those who are insulted and do not respond in kind, who hear a reproach and do not retort, who do God's will out of love and accept His punishment — of such does the verse in Jud. 5:31 say, 'His beloved shall have the strength of the sun when it goes out in all its glory' (Git. 36b; Yoma 23a).

Commenting on the words, 'And Aaron was silent' (Lev. 10:3), the Rabbis say: The proper merit of visiting a house of mourning is silence (Ber. 6b). This teaching obtains today, not only in the Jewish home but also internationally in the streets of our cities and towns; in England people memorialise the dead of World War I and II on Armistice Day by standing still wherever they happen to be and by observing the two minutes silence. Similarly in Israel we mourn all who died in the Holocaust and in the battles for our State in silence. Nothing is more effective than this complete halt to all movement and sound. There are occasions when it is preferable to be silent; as it is a mitzvah for a person to speak out in a time when his words will be listened to, it is equally a mitzvah for a person to refrain from speaking if he knows that his words will not be heeded (Yev. 65b). The good God has endowed us with two ears, one mouth and one tongue, and this tongue was addressed by God, who said (to the tongue), 'All the limbs of men are erect, but you are horizontal; they are all outside the body, but you are inside. More than that, I have surrounded you with two walls, one of bone and the other of flesh' (Arakhin 15b).

Even in prayer we are reminded that it is not limited to our speaking to God, but waiting expectantly for a message from God and listening to the promptings of one's conscience and heart. In the Synagogue, the silent Amidah precedes the repetition of the Amidah by the Hazan. It is also recorded that the mystics did not speak from Rosh Hodesh Elul till after Yom Kippur. This is a far cry from the raucous noise which assails our ears and enters every sphere of our life, destroying our nerves and robbing us of quiet contemplation and meditation.

Not study is the chief thing. Silence is not restricted only to the welfare of man, it also pervades learning. One can teach more effectively by example than by words. Better is he who keeps quiet and carries out the precepts of the Torah than he who studies and teaches, but does not practise what he preaches. In the words of Duran: Simeon tells us that study which leads to practice is the best of all because it is practice which comes as a consequence of study and, since the person's objective is practice, it is enough for him to listen and learn the right action from his teachers and hold his peace in their presence.

He who multliplies words brings sin. In the performance of a mitzvah, one robs it of its dignity and nobility if one talks over much. Excessive talking is deprecated, for we know that 'silence is a healing for all ailments' (Meg. 18a). The Book of Proverbs strikes the right note, 'In the multitude of words there wanteth not transgression; but he who refrains his lips is wise (10:19). Again, 'Even a fool, when he holds his peace, is counted wise, and he who shuts his lips is esteemed as a man of understanding' (17:28), whilst Ecclesiasticus (20:6) renders it as follows: One keeps silence and is accounted wise and another is despised for his much talking; one keeps silence having nought to say and another keeps silence for he sees it is a time for silence. One authority suggests that the Mishnah is referring specifically to the Halakhah: A man should not rush into speech in matters of Halakhah; he ought rather to take his time and think of what he is saying; his words should be measured and not hurried.

Hasidic Lore

Silence. The Riziner cited this passage from the Tanakh: An altar of earth you shall make unto Me... and if you will make Me an altar of stone, you shall not build it of hewn stone; for if you lift up your tool upon it, you have polluted it (Ex. 20:21-2). The altar of earth, R. Israel interpreted as the altar of silence, which is more pleasing to God than anything else; but if the altar be constructed of stones these must be unhewn.

Verbosity. The Bershider said: Two things I learnt from my master during my last visit to him; 'The less a person talks, the nearer he is to holiness' and 'Only that good deed is valuable of which no one knows'.

(יח) רַבָּן שִׁמְעוֹן בֶּן גַּמְלִיאֵל אוֹמֵר עַל שְׁלשָׁה דְבָרִים הָעוֹלָם קַיָּם עַל הָאֱמֶת וְעַל הַדִּין וְעַל הַשָּׁלוֹם שֶׁנֶּאֱמַר אֱמֶת וּמִשְׁפַּט שָׁלוֹם שִׁפְטוּ בְּשַׁעֲרֵיכֶם:

Mishnah Eighteen

Rabban Simeon Ben Gamliel says: Upon three things the world is sustained, on truth, on justice and on peace; as it is said, 'Truth and judgment of peace, judge in your gates' (Zekh. 8:16).

Rabban Simeon Ben Gamliel, in addition to his attainments in Torah scholarship which helped to make him the President of the Sanhedrin, was also proficient in medicine and Greek philosophy; about one hundred halakhic decisions in his name are mentioned in the Mishnah and even more in the Tosefta and Baraita. With the exception of three, his decisions were final.

Truth. Truth is the touchstone of all our deeds; God's name is truth (Jer. 10:10) and the Torah is called truth (Ps. 119:142). Our Torah does not portray its characters as paragons of virtue; the heroes of Tanakh are human and capable of committing errors. This is the uniqueness of the

Torah; it does not gloss over the weaknesses of the Patriarchs or of Moses. The Torah tells the truth. However, we know how historians have changed the course of history and the destiny of the Jew through misrepresentation, prejudice and falsehoods.

It is symptomatic of the concern of the Rabbis that children should be taught the truth and that promises made to them should be kept. Thus R. Ezra advised: A man should not promise a child something and then fail to give it to him; this teaches falsehood (Suk. 46b). Moreover, the Rabbis ask: Why does the Hebrew word for falsehood, *sheker*, consist of three consecutive letters of the alphabet, whilst the word for truth, *emet*, consists of letters taken from the beginning, middle and end of the alphabet? Because falsehood is common, truth uncommon. Why does the word for falsehood rest on one point, whilst the word for truth has a firm foundation? To teach that truth stands, but falsehood does not stand (Shab. 104a). Each of the Hebrew letters of *sheker* is insecurely poised on one leg whereas the letters of *emet* are firmly set, each resting on two feet.

The words of the Psalmist (15:2), 'And speaks truth in his heart', are applied to Rav Safra. The story is told that he wanted to sell something to a client, who, when he presented himself, found that Rav Safra was reciting the Shema and so could not speak to the client, who imagined that the silence of Safra was interpreted to mean that he wanted more money, so he offered a higher price. When Safra concluded his prayers, he said, 'You can take the article for the initial offer, because that was the amount I originally had in mind' (Mak. 24a).

Truth and justice naturally flow from each other, for one cannot administer justice unless it is based on truth, and both truth and justice lead to peace. This is the reason for the talmudic statement, 'The three are really one; if judgment is executed, truth is vindicated and peace results' (Y. Ta. 68a).

A typical instance of the inter-relation between truth and justice is afforded by the legend told in Lev. R. 27. Alexander of Macedon visited the King of Katzia and was shown the abundance of gold and silver and the riches of the palace. However, his purpose in coming was to learn about the customs and the administration of justice. During his visit two men arrived in order that the king should arbitrate between them on a point of law. One had purchased a hut and discovered a treasure hidden under the floor. He claimed that he had bought the hut but not the treasure, and insisted on returning it. However, the vendor refused to accept it, fearing that it was stolen property, and contended that he had sold the hut and all it contained. Whilst they were arguing, the king asked the purchaser, 'Have you a son?'. The man replied that he had. The king then addressed the vendor, and asked if he had a daughter, to which he replied in the affirmative. The king then said, 'Go and marry your children and give them the treasure'. Alexander was puzzled by this decision, and when asked by the king what he would do if a similar case was brought before him, Alexander replied, 'I would have beheaded them both and confiscated the treasure'. The king was astonished and asked, 'Does your sun shine as brightly as elsewhere?' 'Yes', he replied. 'Do you have plenty of rain in your country?' 'Certainly'. 'Do you have innocent sheep and lambs?' 'Of course'. 'Then it is only for the sake of those innocent lambs that the sun shines and the rain falls for you', exclaimed the king.

Justice. If an individual lies, he removes himself from the truth, but the truth is there; it is extant. Therefore, according to the Rabbis, perversion of justice has more far-reaching consequences for evil than lying, abstaining from telling the truth or following peace. This may explain why, in some texts, justice comes first and not second in the Mishnah.

The question has been asked, 'If there is truth, is this not sufficient? Why do we need law, *din*?'. However, there are occasions when both litigants are truly under the impression that they are telling the truth. The presiding judge must then declare the final decision in court.

Peace. The uniqueness of peace is underlined by the talmudic teacher Hezekiah who observes, 'Great is peace, for with regard to all the Commandments it is written, 'If you meet your enemies.... if you see the ass of your enemy (Ex. 24)... If a bird's nest chances to be before you (Deut. 22:6) — in other words, if an occasion to fulfil a precept presents itself, you should perform it. However, this is not the case with peace; regarding this we are advised to, 'Seek peace and pursue it' (Ps. 34:15), (Lev. R. 9).

The commentators see no contradiction between our Mishnah and the statement made by Simeon the Righteous in 1:2. The Rabbis suggest that they complement each other. The world stands and is preserved on the Torah of truth and not on new-fangled laws. The Service of the Synagogue flourishes when it is based on the *Din*, the prescribed law of tradition, and acts of loving-kindness should be offered peacefully.

Hasidic Lore

Truth. The Lubliner said to R. Bunam: He who knows his true worth is deserving of everyone's approval. When a man imports goods and pays the duty, the goods are stamped 'approved'. Likewise God's seal is 'truth' and the man who knows his true worth bears God's stamp of approval.

Rabbi Pinhas told his disciples: I have found nothing more difficult than to overcome lying. It took me fourteen years. I broke every bone I had, and at last I found a way out.

He also said: For the sake of truth, I served twenty one years. Seven years to find out what truth is, seven to drive out falsehood, and seven to absorb truth.

Justice. R. Bunam said: The verse, 'Justice, justice shall you pursue' (Deut. 16:20), teaches us that we may use only justifiable methods even in the pursuit of justice. The Lubliner interpreted the verse in this manner: When a man believes that he is wholly just and need not strive further, then justice does not recognise him. He must follow and follow justice and never stand still, and in your own eyes, you must always be like a new-born child that has not yet achieved anything at all — for that is true justice.

Peace. R. Mendel of Kotzk and R. Yizhak of Vorki, who had both been taught by wise R. Bunam, were friends, and their brotherly good will toward each other had never been troubled. But their hasidim had many arguments concerning their teachings and could not reconcile their opinions. Once both zaddikim happened to be in the same city. When they had greeted each other, R. Yizhak said: I have news for you. Our disciples have made peace with one another. But at that the Rabbi of Kotzk grew angry. His eyes flashed and he cried: So the power of deception has gained in strength and Satan is about to blot out the truth from the world!

'What's that you say?' R. Yizhak stammered. The Rabbi of Kotzk continued: Remember what the Midrash tells about the hour when God prepared to create man; how the angels formed two factions. Love said: Let him be created, for he will do works of love. Truth said: Let him not be created for he will practise deception. Justice said: Let him be created, for he will do justice. Peace said: Let him not be created, for he will be all controversy. What did God do? He seized truth and hurled it to earth. Have you ever thought this story over? Is it not strange? Truth, to be sure, lay on the ground and no longer hindered the creation of man. But what did God do with peace, and what answer did He give peace?

The Rabbi of Vorki was silent.

'Look', said the Rabbi of Kotzk. 'Our sages taught us that controversies in the name of Heaven spring from the root of truth. After truth had fallen to earth, peace understood that a peace without truth is a false peace'.

רַבִּי חֲנַנְיָא בֶּן עֲקַשְׁיָא אוֹמֵר. רָצָה הַקָּדוֹשׁ בָּרוּךְ הוּא לְזַכּוֹת אֶת יִשְׂרָאֵל לְפִיכָךְ הִרְבָּה לָהֶם תּוֹרָה וּמִצְוֹת. שֶׁנֶּאֱמַר יְהֹוָה חָפֵץ לְמַעַן צִדְקוֹ יַגְדִּיל תּוֹרָה וְיַאְדִּיר:

Concluding Mishnah

R. Hanania Ben Akashia says: The Holy One blessed be He was pleased to make Israel worthy; therefore He multiplied to them Torah and Mitzvot, as it is said (Is. 42:21), 'It pleased the Lord for His righteousness' sake to magnify the Torah and make it glorious'.

R. Hanania Ben Akashia. Very little is known of this teacher whose saying reproduced here is originally derived from the Talmud (Mak. 3:16). Because of its pleasing message it is attached to each chapter of *Pirkei Avot*, thus popularising the name of Hanania Ben Akashia. Only one Halakhah is ascribed to the Rabbi and it is found in Tosefta Shekalim 3:18 and Soferim 5:4.

This Mishnah is conjoined to each chapter for a specific reason. It teaches us a perennial lesson that Judaism is primarily not a religion of belief, but of action. The mitzvah is a command to do, to be active. Judaism is more a deed than a creed; therefore we have a multiplicity of mitzvot. We have much to do and we are judged by our conduct on earth. It is very commendable to read a chapter of *Avot* every Sabbath between Pesah and Rosh Hashanah, but this is inadequate. Nor do we discharge our duty by studying the contents of the *Perek*. The prayerful reading and intensive study must be buttressed by an express observance and practice of the divine precepts. This is the message of R. Hanania. If we are to merit God's salvation we must introduce the many mitzvot entrusted in our charge, into our everyday life. We must put to practical use the great wisdom enshrined in the many sayings, aphorisms and maxims which fill the pages of our treatise. By application and demonstration, the written word must blossom forth into benevolent and altruistic deeds. In this manner we shall magnify and glorify the Torah in the service of God and man.

Lezakot, to make worthy. Some connect this word with *zakh*, meaning 'pure', and understand the Mishnah to convey the sense of God cleansing and purifying the Jewish people through the instrument of the mitzvah. This fits in with the rabbinic saying that the purpose of the mitzvah is to refine or purge mankind from sin (Gen. R. 44). However, most commentators translate the word *lezakot* to mean, 'to make worthy, to be privileged'. This in turn reminds us of the principle of *zekhut avot*, the merit of the fathers. Whatever the interpretation of *Avot* be, the Patriarchs, the exalted antecedents of a former generation, or our contemporaries, we refer to the imputed righteousness of human beings.

Here, however, we lean on the grace and mercy of God Himself who is pleased, *ratzah*, to shower His love upon every Israelite; it is the express wish of God to bestow merit upon every Jew. If we develop this theme we shall comprehend the true nature of God. He is a personal God interested in the welfare of His people. He is not a God of wrath; He does not take delight in punishing man. On the contrary, it pleases God to crown all Israel with love and reward them for their meritorious deeds. This pact of love and friendship between God and Israel can be realised if we study Torah and observe the mitzvot with which we have been favoured in such profusion. The nations of the world are governed by the Noahite Laws, but Israel was presented with six hundred and thirteen precepts. 'To the nations of the earth He gave few laws, but His love to Israel was particularly manifested by the fulness and completeness of the Torah which is wholly theirs' (Ex. R. 30:9).

He multiplied to them Torah and mitzvot. Israel is a great nation, not because of the size of its land or its people, both of which are exceedingly small. The only greatness we can claim is the great number of mitzvot we possess. These are our main lifestream. We cannot exist without them. Some commentators point to the opening remarks of Rashi on the beginning of Bereshit: R. Isaac said that the Torah should have commenced with Ex. 12 which is the first commandment given to Israel. By commencing with Bereshit God added, for the instruction of His people,

Genesis 1 to Exodus 12, which contain many laws. Indeed, according to Rashi, this section of the Pentateuch comprises a distinct book called Sefer Habrit, The Book of the Covenant. See Rashi on Ex. 24:4 and 7. 'Moses wrote all the words from Bereshit till (but not including) the account of the giving of the Torah'.

Maimonides explains the reason for the multiplicity of the precepts in his Commentary on the Mishnah in Mak. 23b. Maimonides declares, 'It is one of the fundamental principles of faith in Torah that when a man fulfils one of the six hundred and thirteen mitzvot in a fit and proper manner without associating any worldly motive whatsoever, but he does it for its own sake out of love, he merits life of the world to come'. Concerning this, R. Hanania said that as the precepts of the Torah are so numerous, it is impossible for a man, during his lifetime, not to fulfil one mitzvah in a proper manner and with right intention; by performing this precept he reveres his soul. Hence we learn that the large number of mitzvot was a merciful act of God to provide an opportunity for every Jew to perform at least one mitzvah conscientiously and willingly. No one is exempt from God's providential care which extends to all.

The story is related in the ethical treatise 'Menorat Hamaor' that a certain Jew studied and mastered only one single tractate of the Talmud known as 'Hagigah'. He became so proficient in the study of this tractate that he eventually memorised it all. This one mitzvah earned for him the respect and esteem of the whole community. Such is the power of one mitzvah if it is observed in its entirety. This explains the reason for the multiplicity of mitzvot. It is wellnigh impossible to observe all the mitzvot as they do not necessarily apply to any one person individually. However, if we choose one mitzvah and expend all our energies and talents in its full implementation, we are fulfilling our duty.

Mitzvot. An old tradition interprets for us the constitution of the six hundred and thirteen precepts. In the name of R. Abba, we learn that the two hundred and forty eight positive commandments correspond to the number of limbs in the human body, so that every limb calls on the person, as it were, to perform a precept through its medium, and he gains thereby eternal life. The three hundred and sixty five negative commands correspond to the days in the year, so that every day, from morning till night, admonishes man, as it were, not to fritter away the precious hours of the day by a transgression that might well tip the scale of the world to the side of guilt (Tanhuma Yashan).

In addition to dividing the precepts into positive and negative commands, we also have precepts which are rationally explained and others which seemingly are not rationalised by human intellect. The former, Saadiah (892-942) called *sikhliut* from the word *sekhel*, understanding, and the latter he called *shimiut* from the word *shema*, traditional laws heard at Sinai. Saadiah Gaon goes further and enlightens us that in some cases even the traditional unfathomable laws yield to rational interpretation. For instance circumcision, which was considered by some as barbarous, is now recognized even by non-Jewish medical opinion as a prophylactic against certain forms of cancer. Indeed, the development of scientific experimentation has, in many cases, proved the efficacy of religious practice. We shall offer two more examples.

Shehitah, the ritual slaughter of animals, is a divine law and has been practised by Jews for more than three thousand years. For the past fifty years Shehitah has withstood the agitation and opposition of a number of people who have repeatedly pleaded for its abolition on the grounds that it was cruel and inhumane. Much of the opposition emanated from anti-semites and there was a recrudescence of the fight against Shehitah in the wake of the rise of Nazism in Germany. In England a number of attempts were made to whip up a vile and baseless propaganda against Shehitah by neo-fascists. In 1962 a Slaughter of Animals Bill was introduced by Lord Somers, Lord Dowding and Baroness Summerskill. The aim was to forbid Shehitah to Anglo-Jewry. A spirited defence was initiated by Lord Cohen of Birkenhead, a past President of the British Medical Association and a brilliant physician and scientist whose name was respected throughout the world. He spoke with authority and refuted all the claims made by the ill-wishers of Shehitah. With his profound and extensive knowledge he proved irrefutably that Shehitah was humane and even preferable to electric stunning, which was widely practised. In this manner a traditional law, *shimit*, was again vested with *sekhel*, rational and scientific understanding.

A third example is one in which I was personally involved. In 1952 a young Jewish student spent a week-end in Newcastle-upon-Tyne attending a conference of the Federation of Zionist Youth and we were happy to entertain him. We soon learnt that he was attending the University of Leeds, where he took a course on Textiles. I suggested to him that he might one day discover some rational explanation for the law of *Shaatnez* which forbade the conjunction of wool and linen in our garments (Lev. 19:19 and Deut. 22:11). I had almost forgotten our meeting when, eight years later, I received through the post an article on 'Some thoughts on the Law of Shaatnez' by Henry Knobil. We cannot reproduce the entire article, but we can state that his thesis maintains that the basic and primary aim which safeguards the divinely ordained state of nature is that any substance which nature intended to keep apart, should not be brought together. He explained that wool is a chemical representing the animal kingdom, while linen is composed, in the main, of cellulose, a carbohydrate and the very embodiment of the vegetable kingdom. Vegetable and animal fibres must not be mixed together and used in the same garment. Again, the *shimit* became a *sikhlit*..

There is of course a tendency to follow the so-called reasonable laws while denigrating the traditional laws, which seemingly are not founded on reason. In this respect we should be guided by Maimonides who combined a love for tradition and a rational approach towards Torah. Maimonides warns us not to commit the capital blunder of deprecating those laws which are not readily understandable by us. It is our duty to study the Torah and strive hard to fathom its laws. Nevertheless, anything which is incomprehensible to us should not be ignored. The Torah has taught us not to treat irreverently even lifeless things such as trees and stones, because they have been sanctified by God's name (Jos. 7:24-27). If this be true of inanimate objects, how much more should we reverence the commandments which were sanctified by the word of God (Mishnah Torah Meilah).

Every mitzvah was an opportunity to serve God. So popular was the mitzvah in Jewish life that apart from the prescribed mitzvot, our pious parents would raise every possible act for good to the stature of a mitzvah.

The most fascinating aspect of a mitzvah was that it was performed unbegrudgingly. Indeed, the opportunity was seized to perform the mitzvah lovingly, joyously and zealously. This is in striking contrast to the view propagated by those who fail to understand the Jewish spirit and who maliciously maintain that the Law is a burden and a bondage. On the contrary, the Law and the mitzvot were vouchsafed to Israel as a token of divine love, designated to train them in moral holiness in order to make them all the more worthy in the eyes of God. Indeed, "the elaborate system of mitzvot that encompasses the life of the Jew in every area of his existence, provides the most remarkable machinery devised to support the Jew with the moral autonomy, the capacity to govern himself from within, so that he be holy unto the Lord without doing violence to human nature and to the physical and aesthetic senses. Their very multiplicity is the perennial spring whereby the soul is refreshed and renewed in its moral struggle without resorting to austerity and asceticism. No worldliness, no secular pursuits, in fact, need interfere with man's striving after divine holiness. On the contrary, by means of the mitzvot, every action becomes sublimated into a holy action, a religious act. Even joys and earthly pleasures become hallowed and sanctified as the expressed command of the holy will of God, the obedience to which renders man holy' (I. Epstein).

A fascinating account of the number of mitzvot that devolve upon the Jew is portrayed by the Midrash in its interpretation of the verse in Nu. 23:10, 'Who has counted the dust of Jacob?' Introducing the Midrash with the rhetorical question, 'Come and see how many mitzvot the Israelites performed through the dust', the Rabbis explain that before we can partake of a morsel of bread, we perform a goodly number of mitzvot. When the Jew goes out to plough, he performs the mitzvah, 'You shall not plough with an ox and ass together' (Deut. 22:10). When he sows, he fulfils the law, 'You shall not sow your field with two kinds of seed' (Lev. 19:19). When he reaps the harvest he observes the law, 'When you reap your harvest in your field and you have forgotten a sheaf in the field, you shall not go back to take it; it shall be for the stranger or the fatherless and the widow' (Deut. 24:10, Lev. 19:19). When he threshes the corn he fulfils the law 'You shall not muzzle the ox when he treads out the corn' (Deut. 25:4). When he preserves the pile of grain he observes the mitzvah of *Terumah* and the first and second tithing (Nu. 18, Deut. 14:22-24). When he bakes he fulfils the mitzvah of *Hallah* (Nu. 15:20). We thus have ten mitzvot (Yalkut Shimoni on Balak 23).

It is also very significant that the Yalkut highlights the great regard and consideration that Jewish Law demands for the dumb creature. It is decidedly wrong and inhumane to saddle an ox and ass together, for it imposes an unequal weight on the ass. Again, it is merciless to muzzle an ox when it threshes the corn. Incidentally, Jewish Law extends this prohibition to apply to human beings who are employed in the production of food. God's mercies are over all His creatures, man or beast. Also included in the

Scriptural verses is the noble concept of charity; consideration for the poor is well authenticated in the Torah. The Yalkut demonstrates the theory that no mitzvah is isolated. In order to produce bread from the earth, we must be kind to the animal and charitable to those who are in need of help.

The proof text cited is from Is. 42:21. There is an affinity between the verb *hafetz* and the opening word of the Mishnah, *ratzah*. As *ratzah* can be used of the will of God, so *hafetz* too, has religious overtones; compare the expression *heftzei shamayim*, heavenly affairs or religious deeds which, we are told, are equal to the study of the Law (M.K. 9b).

To continue the kinship betwen the verse from Isaiah and the Mishnah, Bacher suggests that the word *tzidko* should be vocalised and read as *tzadko* which means 'to make (Israel) righteous'. This would render the proof text as a corollary to the opening words of the Mishnah. As it pleases the Lord to make Israel worthy, so it pleases the Lord to make Israel righteous through the continuous study of Torah and the performance of mitzvot, *Yagdil Veyadir*, He will magnify and make it glorious.

We note that the two concluding verbs of the text are in the future tense. As the creation of the world is a continuous process with man acting as co-worker with God, so is the exposition and elucidation of Torah a continuous and on-going exercise in the future. Scholars love to delve into and plumb the depths of rabbinic interpretation and look for fresh and new insights in the Written and Oral Law. These novellae have reinvigorated our minds and hearts and inspired us to rise to greater and loftier heights of spirituality. The Torah is an inexhaustible mine of wisdom and learning and never fails to yield rich, cultural treasures to all who labour lovingly in the garden of the Lord. The Torah is not an antique or museum piece; the Torah is a living repository of eternal truths which are to guide us in every age. It pleases the Lord to make the Torah great and glorious in the future and at all times.

To explain the driving force of the mitzvah, R. Alexander expounded the verse, 'You have established equity, you have executed justice and righteousness in Jacob' (Ps. 99:4) with a parable. Two ass-drivers who quarrelled were walking along the same road when the ass of one fell under its burden. The other man was prepared to ignore this and walked on, but he had qualms of conscience and was reminded of the mitzvah in Ex. 23:5, 'If you see the ass of one who hates you lying under its burden, you shall surely release it with him'. He therefore assisted the other man to unload.

In their common effort they could not help speaking to each other. Without realising it, they spoke freely and became reconciled, because each thought well of the other and it was a concerted action. When their task was finished they decided to enter an inn and after partaking of refreshments they renewed their friendship. Thus equity and justice are established through the performance of a mitzvah (Tanhuma Mishpatim).

Hasidic Lore

The importance of the Mitzvah. A young hasid, who was accustomed to devote much time to the study of the Talmud and the tenets of Hasidism, became so involved in his business that he was compelled to forgo his studies. On a holiday visit to the Kotzker Rabbi, he bitterly complained of this.

The Rabbi answered: I will explain to you the passage which is recited at the conclusion of each chapter of *Pirkei Avot*. Hanania Ben Akashia said: The Holy One wished to benefit Israel, therefore He gave them a multitude of Commandments. We may ask: Where is the benefit of being in duty bound to observe many commandments? This is a great hardship. Would it not have been preferable to receive merely a limited number of precepts which we could fulfil correctly? The answer is: The great variety of precepts makes it possible for a Jew in every occupation to obey some of the divine injunctions. The farmer, the planter, the builder of houses and others — each has his particular commandments to fulfil and thereby gain favour in the eyes of the Lord.

The merchant, also, by abstaining from misrepresentations, overcharging, and other business deceptions, will please the Creator. (See Philo, quoted in Hertz 'The Book of Jewish Thoughts' p. 289).

PEREK TWO

Introductory Mishnah. Text, translation and commentary on p. 11.

פרק שני

(א) רַבִּי אוֹמֵר אֵיזוֹ הִיא דֶרֶךְ יְשָׁרָה שֶׁיָּבוֹר לוֹ הָאָדָם כָּל שֶׁהִיא תִּפְאֶרֶת לְעֹשֶׂיהָ וְתִפְאֶרֶת לוֹ מִן הָאָדָם. וֶהֱוֵי זָהִיר בְּמִצְוָה קַלָּה כְּבַחֲמוּרָה שֶׁאֵין אַתָּה יוֹדֵעַ מַתַּן שְׂכָרָן שֶׁל מִצְוֹת. וֶהֱוֵי מְחַשֵּׁב הֶפְסֵד מִצְוָה כְּנֶגֶד שְׂכָרָהּ וּשְׂכַר עֲבֵרָה כְּנֶגֶד הֶפְסֵדָהּ. הִסְתַּכֵּל בִּשְׁלֹשָׁה דְבָרִים וְאֵין אַתָּה בָא לִידֵי עֲבֵרָה. דַּע מַה לְמַעְלָה מִמְּךָ עַיִן רוֹאָה וְאֹזֶן שׁוֹמַעַת וְכָל מַעֲשֶׂיךָ בַּסֵּפֶר נִכְתָּבִים:

Mishnah One

Rabbi says: Which is the right way which a man should choose for himself? Whatever is considered praiseworthy by the one who does it and is also considered praiseworthy by men; and be careful in a light mitzvah as in a weighty one, for you know not how the rewards of the mitzvah are given. And count the loss of a mitzvah against its reward and the reward of a sin against its loss. Reflect on three things and you will not come into the clutches of sin; know what is above you, a seeing eye, a hearing ear, and all your deeds are written in the book.

'Rabbi' (Judah Ha-Nasi) is referred to as Rabbenu (our master), Nasi, the prince, and Hakadosh (the holy), but here and often he is simply referred to as Rabbi, a unique title of distinction. He was the chief redactor and compiler of the Mishnah. He combined great erudition with worldly power. Though wealthy, he denied himself the pleasures of this world, but engaged a number of scribes to help him in editing the Mishnah. He was thus one of the early pioneers and builders of Jewish literature. Marcus Aurelius was one of his disciples and he was a contemporary of the Roman Emperor Antoninus Pius, who was his intimate friend.

An interesting legend recalls that the mother of Rabbi exchanged her son after his birth for Antoninus and so escaped the officers of Hadrian who persecuted her because she had her son circumcised. In this manner, it is said that Antoninus imbibed with his milk a love for Jews and Judaism (Tosafot A.Z. 10b). Some say that Antoninus became a righteous proselyte, while others maintain that Antoninus was one of the pious of the nations of the world. This thought may be reflected in the first statement of the Mishnah.

The Talmud makes a distinction between Adam (man) and Haadam (the man); Adam refers to a Jew, but Haadam may signify a non-Jew (Yev. 61a; B.K. 38a, Tosafot). If we were to follow this interpretation, the first section of the Mishnah would offer advice to mankind in general and stress the importance of the mitzvah to the Jew in particular.

However, most commentators understand the way of life to refer to the Halakhah which guides the Jew in every situation.

Derekh — way. The general tendency today is to search for and extract what is thought to be the best in life, even if it is attained by dishonourable or dubious methods. Rabbi, however, does not ask which is the chief good; he asks which is the right path, the correct course a man should take. Compare Mishnah 13 where, again, the Rabbis ask which is the good way to which a man should cleave. The Book of Psalms commences with a warning that he is happy who does not stand in the path of the sinners. The longest Psalm (119) begins with the positive affirmation, 'Happy are they who are upright in the way, who walk in the Law of the Lord'. The Jew regulates his life according to a defined pattern which we call Halakhah. This is the path, the way along which man walks. The Torah is our way of life; it accompanies us and fashions and moulds our character. Rabbi adds that one should not only do that which is right in his own eyes, but follow that which is pleasing and beautiful in the eyes of other people. Many are apt to reverse this process and do things for effect, even against their inner convictions.

Some take *leoseha* to refer to God, consequently the Mishnah would convey this thought — a man should choose a course of action which will bring glory and honour to his Maker, that is, God. In this manner man will earn the praises of other men, who will desire to emulate his example. If a man's actions are beautiful in the eyes of God, they will also receive the sanction and approbation of mankind. This exposition would therefore include laws relating to man and God, and laws affecting the relationship between man and man. This would comprise the philosophy of Rabbi. He bequeathed to us a literary monument in the form of the Mishnah which many commentators have beautified by their brilliant glosses and annotations. He also lived an exemplary life on earth, giving pleasure and honour to many people.

Be careful in a light mitzvah as in a weighty one. The right approach to the mitzvah is to perform the will of God without any thought of reward. All precepts, minor and major, are expressions of divine approval. Commenting on the text, 'Lest she should walk the even path of life, her ways wander, but she knows it not' (Prov. 5:6), R. Abba Bar Kahana said: Do not sit down and weight the precepts of the Torah; do not say, since this command is an important one I will fulfil it, seeing that its reward is great; and since the other is a minor command, I shall not fulfil it'. How did the Holy One blessed be He respond? He did not reveal to mankind the reward attaching to each precept, in order that they might perform all of them with one and the same zeal, as Scripture says: Her ways wander that you cannot know them.

Unto what is this compared? Unto a king who hired some labourers and brought them into his *pardes* (garden) without disclosing the reward for working there, so that they might not leave undone that for which the reward was small and do only that for which the reward was great. In the evening the king summoned before him each workman in turn. 'Under which tree did you work?' he enquired of one. 'Under this tree', was the reply. 'This is a pepper tree'; said the king, 'the wages for tending it are a gold piece'. 'Under which tree did you work?' he enquired of the second. 'Under this tree' was the reply. 'As it is a white blossom, its wages will be only half a gold piece'. He then called a third and asked him, 'Under which tree did you work?' 'Under that one' he replied. 'It is an olive tree' said the king, 'and its wages are two hundred zuzim'. Then the other workmen said, 'Should you not have told us for which tree the reward was greatest so that we might have tended that one?' The king then replied, 'Had I told you this, how could the whole of my *pardes* have been tended?' So was it that God did not reveal the reward for the performance of His precepts except in the case of two of them — the reward for the highest among the more important ones and for the lowest among the less important (Ex. 20:12 and Deut. 22:7) (Deut. R. 6:2 and Pesikta Rabbati 121b).

In his comments on this Mishnah, Albo compares the mitzvot to medicinal herbs and adds: 'They are not equally valuable because each has a special property which is beneficial to the human body as a whole; similarly with the commandments, every one has its own peculiar property and benefit'.

We would add that in the eyes of God there is no distinction between a light precept and a weighty one. Basically, all the mitzvot are of equal validity. It is we who label some mitzvot as important and others as less important. For instance, some children treat the mitzvah of honouring parents lightly. When, however, tragedy befalls them and they lose a parent, they may realise the significance of the mitzvah. Conversely, some parents treat lightly the mitzvah of affording their children a sound Jewish education, with disastrous results. In the light of this interpretation our Mishnah can be paraphrased in these words: Be warned and mindful that what may seem in your eyes a light and insignificant mitzvah, is in reality of the same calibre as a so-called weighty mitzvah. You cannot tell which is minor and which is major; treat them all alike and the Almighty will reward you.

And count the loss of a mitzvah against its reward and the reward of a sin againt its loss. The righteous person may lose time, energy or money in the performance of a precept, but he gains an inner spiritual happiness which stays with him. The transgressor, however, may enjoy temporal gain but no inward satisfaction; his conscience will trouble him and eventually he will lose more than he has gained. The mitzvah achieves peace of mind, the *averah* (transgression), misery.

Clutches of sin. Literally the hands or power of sin. One should not become embroiled in any unsavoury action, even if it is not brazenly sinful. *Averah* comes from the root *avar*, to cross over. One false step can lead a person to the slippery path of wrong-doing and then one may find it impossible to extricate oneself from the grip and power of sin, or the agents of sin.

Know what is above you. In the first place, we are to reflect on the One above, on God, Who looks down from the celestial heights and protects those who raise their eyes heavenwards in thought and deed. Some underline the word *mimekha*, from you; man can derive divine inspiration from himself. One should examine and appreciate the marvels of nature, the miracle of birth, the potentialities for good vested in the human frame; these should lead to an understanding of God. Others read into these words the meaning of tradition, know what goes before you. We owe much to the previous generations who have handed down to us a rich legacy of learning, education and culture.

A seeing eye, a hearing ear. These are figures of speech; we often meet with anthropomorphic expressions which bring God nearer to us, as the Psalmist said: He who planted the ear, shall He not hear? He who formed the eye, shall He not see? (94:9). A philosopher said that this verse contains the strongest argument for the existence of God.

Others interpret the 'seeing eye' to refer to the seer, the Prophet; the 'hearing ear' to the *Bat Kol*, the heavenly voice, which influences those who have an attentive ear to the message of the Torah; and all deeds are written in the Book of Books, which teaches and guides us. The Book of Proverbs also refers to the same idea that man owes his natural faculties to God and should therefore use them in the service of God. 'The hearing ear and the seeing eye, the Lord has made even both of them' (20:12).

And all your deeds are written in the book. R. Jonah explains: When a man stands before kings, princes or famous people, he is ashamed to do anything in their presence which should not be done, or say anything improper; so a person should always keep in mind that he is, as it were, standing in the presence of the Holy One blessed be He, the King of Kings. Thus he will avoid doing or saying anything inappropriate.

Hasidic Lore

The right course. Commenting on the first section of our Mishnah, R. Schmelke said: Nevertheless, he must not believe that this is the only correct course. He must be prepared to admit that there may be other ways in which people may take pride and act honourably.

ב) רַבָּן גַּמְלִיאֵל בְּנוֹ שֶׁל רַבִּי יְהוּדָה הַנָּשִׂיא אוֹמֵר יָפֶה תַלְמוּד תּוֹרָה עִם דֶּרֶךְ אֶרֶץ שֶׁיְּגִיעַת שְׁנֵיהֶם מַשְׁכַּחַת עָוֹן וְכָל תּוֹרָה שֶׁאֵין עִמָּהּ מְלָאכָה סוֹפָהּ בְּטֵלָה וְגוֹרֶרֶת עָוֹן. וְכָל הָעוֹסְקִים עִם הַצִּבּוּר יִהְיוּ עוֹסְקִים עִמָּהֶם לְשֵׁם שָׁמַיִם שֶׁזְּכוּת אֲבוֹתָם מְסַיַּעְתָּם וְצִדְקָתָם עוֹמֶדֶת לָעַד וְאַתֶּם מַעֲלֶה אֲנִי עֲלֵיכֶם שָׂכָר הַרְבֵּה כְּאִלּוּ עֲשִׂיתֶם:

Mishnah Two

R. Gamliel the son of Judah Ha-Nasi says: Splendid is the study of the Torah when combined with a worldly occupation, for labour in them both makes sin forgotten, and the study of the Torah which is not combined with work falls into neglect in the end and becomes the cause of sin; and let all those who labour on behalf of the community labour with them for the sake of Heaven; for the merit of their fathers upholds them and their righteousness endures for ever. And as for you, I lay upon you a plentiful reward as though you had accomplished it.

R. Gamliel. On his death bed R. Judah Ha-Nasi left instructions that his son Simeon be called *Hakham*, wise, and his son Gamliel be called *Nasi*, Patriarch. The Talmud (Ket. 103b) explains that though Simeon was wiser than his brother, the title *Nasi* was conferred on Gamliel because 'he worthily represented his ancestors in his fear of sin'. Compare Avot 3:11. Gamliel is the last Nasi whose name is mentioned in the Mishnah.

Derekh Eretz. Literally this means the 'way of the world'. A trade, vocation or business is usually rendered a worldly occupation. It is possible that we here contrast the Torah which is heavenly, with work which is mundane. The ministering angels live in heaven, they do not toil; but we who are on earth and must subsist through work are asked to synthesize the heavenly with the earthly, that is, to pursue our worldly occupations with honesty and integrity in accordance with the spirit of the Torah. Indeed, when we leave this mortal earth and ascend to heaven, the first question addressed to us is, 'Have you dealt honourably in business?' The dignity of labour is often stressed by the Rabbis and here they spell it out clearly and state that study of the Law alone without the means of a livelihood can lead to sin and tempt one to steal in order to satisfy one's hunger. Compare Kid. 29a, 'He who does not teach his son a trade, teaches him to be a thief'.

Another translation of *derekh eretz* is 'good manners', the norms of society. Scholarship and book learning alone are inadequate. A person should not be divorced from refinement, good breeding and the social graces. It is this blending of Torah and *derekh eretz* which prompted S.R. Hirsch to use this phrase as his battle cry and motto in his fight against Reform Judaism in Germany. In Hirsch's words: We must build seminaries for teachers to instruct the children of Israel in Torah and *derekh eretz* which, if acquired together, will bring healing to all our plagues. Above all, we need schools for Torah and *derekh eretz* for the education of our youth, for we know most assuredly that any city or settlement which is without such a school, shall not be saved from the strife of the times.

It should be noted that the Talmud contains two small tractates called Derekh Eretz Rabba and Derekh Eretz Zuta which offer sound advice on a variety of topics concerned mainly with social and personal conduct.

Those who labour on behalf of the community. We are here referring to the body of communal leaders and workers who, with disinterested love and pure religious motives, have striven and laboured for the formation and preservation of the different congregations throughout the world, which constitute the community of Israel. A special prayer is devoted to them and is recited every Shabbat morning in our Synagogues, 'And all who occupy themselves in faithfulness with the wants of the congregation, may God give them their recompense'. 'In faithfulness' is almost synonymous with the 'Name of Heaven'.

Imahem, with them. The true communal leader will co-operate with the spiritual leader and follow the programme of the Bet Din under whose aegis the Synagogue is incorporated; in this manner he will enjoy the *zekhut*, the merit of the fathers, who will come to his aid.

The merit of their fathers. This refers to the Patriarchs Abraham, Isaac and Jacob whose righteousness lasts for ever. This concept enjoys biblical sanction. Commenting on the Decalogue (Ex. 20:5-6) the Rabbis distinguish between the words, 'visiting the iniquities of the fathers.... unto the third and fourth generations' and 'showing mercy unto thousands of them that love Me'. They interpret 'unto thousands' to mean that the period of divine favour extends to five hundred times as long as that of punishment (So. 11a).

In Ber. 10b and Yalkut on 2 K. 20:12, R. Johanan says: He who relies entirely on his own virtue is made dependent on the virtue of others, and he who depends on the virtue of others has his request granted by reason of his own virtue. For example, Moses interceded for Israel in the sin of the golden calf; Moses' request was granted, not for the sake of the Patriarchs, but because God was assured that Moses himself was worthy of having his request granted (cf. Ps. 106:23). Hezekiah, however, invoked God's help because of his own merit. He said: I beseech Thee, O Lord, remember how I have walked before Thee in truth with an undivided heart and have done what is good in Thine eyes (2 K. 20:3). His request was also granted, not because of his own virtue, but because of the virtue of others (2K. 19:34). From this we deduce that when those who do communal service perform their task without any ulterior motive, the merit of the Fathers will stand them in good stead and they will reap ample reward from our Father in Heaven.

Hasidic Lore

Derekh Eretz. R. Uri Strelisker said: We are taught by our Sages that the study of the Torah is good with 'the way of the earth'. We find that for all our necessities we must thank the earth. Without the earth we have neither food nor clothing. Yet we tread upon her, dig her, spit upon her, and the earth accepts every abuse without complaint. The student of the Torah should adopt these 'ways of the earth'. No matter how greatly his opinion is sought and esteemed, he should consider himself lowly and should accept debasement from anyone without complaint or anger.

Merit. The Besht said: No two persons have the same abilities. Each man should work in the service of God according to his own talents. If one man tries to imitate another, he merely loses his opportunity to do good through his own merit, and he cannot accomplish anything by imitation of the other's service.

(ג) הֱוּו זְהִירִין בָּרָשׁוּת שֶׁאֵין מְקָרְבִין לוֹ לְאָדָם אֶלָּא לְצוֹרֶךְ עַצְמָן נִרְאִין כְּאוֹהֲבִין בִּשְׁעַת הֲנָאָתָן וְאֵין עוֹמְדִין לוֹ לְאָדָם בִּשְׁעַת דָּחְקוֹ:

Mishnah Three

Be cautious with the ruling power, for they do not befriend a person except for their own needs. They seem like friends when it is to their advantage, but they do not stand by man in the hour of his need.

On *Rashut* see Perek 1, Mishnah 10.

Rabban Gamliel had experience of the Roman government, because his father Judah was friendly with the Emperor Antoninus Pius. Many commentators warn the Jew not to be misled by the flattery and cajolery of government officials. This is very true of governments today. Even those who appear to be favourably disposed to the Jew do not always stand by him in the hour of need or distress. The story is told of a certain king who promoted one of his officers. The king would rise up before him and kiss him on his neck. In the end the king slew him and said that he used to kiss the spot where his sword would have to land. People say, 'Do not think that the lion is smiling when he bares his teeth; it is only to devour. Human monarchs are like lions in the animal kingdom'.

Rabban Gamliel had this in mind — when you have dealings with the ruling powers for communal purposes.... beware of their smiling faces and honeyed words. Let them not seduce you into revealing to them the secrets in your heart (Duran).

Some connect *rashut* with *reshut*, meaning that which is permitted. Be cautious even of that which is allowed. For example, drink in small doses can act as a tonic but if indulged in to excess it will not help you in the hour of your distress, but bring about your downfall.

Hasidic Lore

To serve is better than to rule. The advice of the Mishnah to be on one's guard against the ruling power probably inspired the Amshinover Rabbi to say that when a man enters a society of inferiors, he should be advised to serve rather than to rule.

(ד) הוּא הָיָה אוֹמֵר עֲשֵׂה רְצוֹנוֹ כִּרְצוֹנְךָ כְּדֵי שֶׁיַּעֲשֶׂה רְצוֹנְךָ כִּרְצוֹנוֹ. בַּטֵּל רְצוֹנְךָ מִפְּנֵי רְצוֹנוֹ כְּדֵי שֶׁיְּבַטֵּל רְצוֹן אֲחֵרִים מִפְּנֵי רְצוֹנֶךָ:

Mishnah Four

He used to say: Do His will as if it were your will, so that He may do your will as if it was His will. Nullify your will before His will, so that He may nullify the will of others before your will.

Do His will. In the first place we should emphasise the initial word of the Mishnah. Do, perform, act, on the will of God. We too often live in a world of pious wishes and hopes which are left unfulfilled. We should conclude the wish by active participation in the mitzvah which is the will of God. Furthermore, as you perform your own wish with enthusiasm and zest, so perform the will of God gladly and ungrudgingly.

In the world of prayer, *Yehi ratzon milfanekha* plays a significant role. It introduces many a prayer and forms the conclusion of every Amidah. The usual English translation of this prayer is 'May it be Thy Will', yet the Hebrew is not *retzonkha*, Thy will, but *ratzon*, will, and it has been suggested that *ratzon* does not refer to God but to man, and the prayer could be freely translated thus: May the will of man be derived from the presence of God's Shekhinah. This would help us to understand our Mishnah: Do His will as though it were your will, as though you had no will of your own, only His will. Then He will also perform your will, your particular will. Your wishes will not be merely part of what He does in order to sustain the universe as a whole including righteous and sinners alike. What you wish to carry out will become part of His will to satisfy your individual request even if, because of the sins of the generation, it may have been necessary to visit you with misfortune, He will carry out your individual desire and protect you from that evil which should have befallen you (Duran).

The Minhat Shabbat makes a distinction between *ratzon* and *hafetz*. *Hafetz* seems to presuppose some benefit, material or otherwise (Gen. 34:19, Is. 58:3) whilst *ratzon* postulates a disinterested wish without any thought of personal reward (Lev. 1:3, Ps. 147:11). From this we learn that he who performs a mitzvah because of a command of the Torah, comes under the category of *hafetz* which is commendable; but greater still is he who performs the mitzvah intuitively and willingly; he truly performs the will of God.

Hasidic Lore

All roads lead to God. R. Bunam said: Two merchants go to the Leipzig fair. One takes a direct route and the other an indirect route, but both reach the same destination. Likewise the aim of service to God is to attain holiness and to arrive at the point where we make God's will our own. Hence, as long as we reach this point, it makes no difference how long we have served the Lord. One may die young or in the prime of life and become just as holy as one who has died in old age. We are taught in the Talmud that it is the same whether a man does much or little, as long as he has aimed to do God's will (Ber. 5b, Shevuot 15a).

(ה) הִלֵּל אוֹמֵר אַל תִּפְרוֹשׁ מִן הַצִּבּוּר. וְאַל תַּאֲמִין בְּעַצְמְךָ עַד יוֹם מוֹתְךָ. וְאַל תָּדִין אֶת חֲבֵרְךָ עַד שֶׁתַּגִּיעַ לִמְקוֹמוֹ. וְאַל תֹּאמַר דָּבָר שֶׁאִי אֶפְשַׁר לִשְׁמוֹעַ שֶׁסּוֹפוֹ לְהִשָּׁמַע וְאַל תֹּאמַר לִכְשֶׁאֶפְנֶה אֶשְׁנֶה שֶׁמָּא לֹא תִפָּנֶה:

Mishnah Five

Hillel says: Do not withdraw from the community, put no trust in yourself until the day of your death and do not judge your associate until you have reached his place. Say not of a word which is impossible to understand that it will be understood in the end, and say not, when I have leisure I will study, perhaps you will have no leisure.

With this Mishnah Hillel continues from 1:14 with a number of proverbial sayings.

Do not withdraw from the community. We should not stand aloof but share actively in the successes or misfortunes of the community. 'He who does not join the community in time of danger and trouble, will never enjoy the Divine blessing' (Ta. 11a).

In English literature John Milton speaks of 'cloistered virtue'; in Judaism this is unthinkable. The human being is gregarious by nature and should associate freely with his fellow-men. This is inherent in the Hebrew word *tzibur*, used here for community. This word is a mnemonic. The first letter *zadi* stands for *tzadikim*, righteous; the second letter *bet* for *beynonim*, mediocre; and the last two letters, *vav* and *resh*, for *urshaim*, and the wicked. The Jewish congregation is an amalgam of all types of people. Indeed, at the Seder table on Pesah, the *rasha* — the wicked son — is so called because he 'excludes himself from the general community'. He segregates himself from active participation, but we include him in the Seder service; such is the universal and democratic approach to life in Judaism.

We are reminded that praying with a congregation is more praiseworthy than praying alone. Our prayers are in the first person plural, we do not pray selfishly for ourselves, but for the community, for mankind.

Nor should we restrict the word *tzibur* to refer to the Synagogue alone. Hillel's maxim surely goes beyond congregational life. In all our strivings we should be closely attached to the general community and its well-being. We have obligations and responsibilities towards the sick and the helpless, the poor and the needy. Every Jew must play his rightful part and not dissociate himself from any aspect of communal service, religious, cultural, moral, social and domestic.

Put no trust in yourself.... Such is the fickleness of human nature that one cannot foresee the future; death alone is certain. The Talmud (Shab. 147b) informs us that Eleazar Ben Arakh forgot his learning when he isolated himself from his former colleagues, whilst John Hyrcanus, after acting as High Priest for eighty years, became a heretic (Ber. 29a). Some emphasise the word *atzmekha*, yourself; do not place too much confidence in yourself alone without consulting others. No one should be entirely independent; from birth we are subordinate to our elders and at death we are all dependent on the Hevra Kadisha, who perform the final rites.

Do not judge your associate.... Do not condemn or criticise anyone until you are in his position; you must ask yourself how you would react under similar circumstances. The Meiri interprets it as follows: - If you find him fastidious in conduct and full of extraordinary virtues, do not conclude on your own that these constitute his real nature until you get to the place where he dwells. Then note his behaviour there; is he consistent or not? Then you will be in a position to judge him. Many are the mediocre individuals who show their true colours in one place and elsewhere put on a facade of saintliness which is not native to them.

Say not of a word which is impossible to understand... Your words should not have a double meaning, nor should they be capable of being misconstrued. Clarity of thought and expression is vital at the outset. Alternatively, we can explain these words to mean — do not say of a thing which you do not understand, 'I will learn it later'. It is one's duty to master the thought now and not commence with a doubt.

Say not when I have leisure I will study. A Sage once commented: Time past is gone and vanished; time present is like a fleeting shadow; time future, who knows if you will ever reach it? Not only should a person not neglect study because of the pursuit of pleasure, he should not disregard it even for his occupation. If you are indifferent to study because of your livelihood you will find yourself adding one task to another, and you will be the loser on every score (Meiri).

Hasidic Lore

A united community. Hillel said: Do not separate yourself from the community. From this we infer that we should be united through Torah. On this theme of unity the Sochatzover Rabbi said: In our present exile, as in the Babylonian, the Israelites are scattered among the nations, whereas in Egypt they dwelt together in Goshen. The reason is that before we received the Torah there was no force sufficiently strong to bind Israelites together as a particular people, and therefore the Creator decreed that they should sojourn in the same territory. Today, however, our study of the Torah serves to unify us in our dispersion.

(ו) הוּא הָיָה אוֹמֵר אֵין בּוּר יְרֵא חֵטְא וְלֹא עַם הָאָרֶץ חָסִיד וְלֹא הַבַּיְשָׁן לָמֵד וְלֹא הַקַּפְּדָן מְלַמֵּד וְלֹא כָּל הַמַּרְבֶּה בִסְחוֹרָה מַחְכִּים. וּבְמָקוֹם שֶׁאֵין אֲנָשִׁים הִשְׁתַּדֵּל לִהְיוֹת אִישׁ:

Mishnah Six

He used to say: A boor is not a fearer of sin, the *am-haaretz* cannot be pious, a shamefaced man cannot learn, the short-tempered cannot teach; one who is engaged much in business will not grow wise, and in a place where there are no men, strive to be a man.

Bor, boor. This word is connected with the term *sde bor*, an uncultivated field; hence a *bor* is one who is uncultured; he cannot reap what he has not sown. To fear sin is to dread its shame, but as the ignorant man has no shame, he cannot be a sin-fearing person. On Yom Kippur we pray, not for the fear of punishment, but for the fear of sin.

Am haaretz and **hasid.** Authorities differ as to the precise meaning of *am haaretz*, but as it follows the boor, it obviously means an ignorant person or one who disregards the Halakhah with its religious and moral discipline. On the other hand, the hasid is considered to be a pious and saintly person showing *hesed*, kindness and love to all, even the wicked. The *am haaretz* is not devoid of all qualities; he may possess common-place virtues, but he cannot rise to the lofty heights of spirituality and idealism. The *am haaretz* is interested in mundane matters; he is rooted to the earth. The hasid understands the meaning of *devekut*, attachment to and reverence for God. The hasid is preoccupied with prayer and is in communion with God beyond the prescribed times of fixed prayer. Indeed, he offers up private and spontaneous prayers which an *am haaretz* is incapable of doing. Thus it will be readily seen that they are on different levels. The *am haaretz* has neither the knowledge nor the intuition to develop the potentialities required for Hasidut.

The shamefaced cannot learn. We read in Prov. 30:32 'If you have done foolishly in lifting up yourself or if you have planned devices, lay your hand upon your mouth.' This means that he who is ready to play the fool for the sake of learning Torah will in the end be lifted up, but he who refuses to ask questions will in the end be asked about some Halakhah and he will have to lay his hand on his mouth because he will not know the answer.

'Bashfulness is a virtue in every respect except in the course of study, as it is said, 'When I speak of Thy testimonies in the presence of kings, I am not ashamed' (Ps. 119:46). When David fled from Saul and appeared before the heathen kings, he was never ashamed to speak of the Torah and the commandments even if they were to mock and ridicule him when he spoke, for bashfulness is not a good thing in study... This is the meaning of the maxim: 'Ask like a fool and save like the generous,' that is to say, just as the generous do not scatter their wealth but also do not keep it to themselves — instead they give it gladly and graciously where it will do more good — so in the case of wisdom, one should engage in it with the proper people and at the proper time.... but a person should ask every kind of question and not be ashamed to do so, in order that he may learn' (R. Jonah).

The short-tempered cannot teach. Hillel, being a meek and sympathetic pedagogue, would naturally not favour an angry and passionate teacher, because such an instructor might instil fear into the heart of a timid pupil and this would stifle his quest for knowledge.

One who engages much in business. Some business men imagine that if they contribute towards the academies of learning they have fulfilled their duty, but learning Torah devolves upon every Jew including the business man, who should set aside fixed times for learning. The love of money distracts man from the performance of religious duties, for under the pressure of his mighty business he will omit prayers and forget many a mitzvah; that he will neglect the study of Torah is obvious. Commenting on the verse in the Torah, 'It is not beyond the sea' (Deut. 30:13), our Sages observed that the knowledge of the Torah is not to be found amongst those who cross the sea to engage in commerce (Er. 55a).

In a place where there is no man, strive to be a man. If you live in a community where no man assumes leadership, stand up and be counted and shoulder responsibility. If Noah and Abraham had followed the multitude and failed to take decisive action, the result would have been disastrous.

Alternatively, one could read into this maxim the lesson not to adopt a double standard in life. Some are ostensibly pious and observant in the presence of other people, but in their privacy they remove the mask of religion; this is hypocritical. Be a man and practise your faith consistently even when you are alone.

Still another interpretation can be read into this saying. Too often one gives a donation to charity only when it is publicised in the press or displayed in the presence of a multitude of people. Hillel reminds us that it is preferable to be a man in a place where none is present and offer one's service or donate a contribution quietly and unostentatiously.

The verb *hishtadel* reminds us of the *shtadlan*, the intercessor, who played a significant role in Jewish history. Throughout our martyred existence, the *shtadlan* was the representative or spokesman who pleaded our cause before kings, rulers and governments and interceded on our behalf whenever the occasion demanded. We salute the body of *shtadlanim* who, in every age and clime, raised their voices courageously and took up the cudgels on behalf of our distressed and persecuted co-religionists.

Hasidic Lore

A real hasid. The mitnaged, R. Zalman Pozner, said to the Vorker Rabbi: The Talmud (A.Z. 20b) enumerates the many degrees of scholarship through which a man must advance before he attains the degree of Hasidut. Yet your people call themselves hasidim as soon as they visit a Rebbe.

The Vorker replied: When a man loves Zion, he calls himself an Israelite even though he has not yet settled in Israel as he desires.

When the Kotzker heard this, he remarked: I do not agree with the Vorker Rabbi. A man should not style himself a hasid unless he truly is one. It is correct that a few chosen persons may attain the degree of Hasidut without undergoing the preliminary steps but when a multitude claims to do so, their pretensions are false and it becomes imperative to return to the established manner of attaining by discipline and study, the state of Hasidut.

(ז) אַף הוּא רָאָה גֻּלְגּוֹלֶת אַחַת שֶׁצָּפָה עַל פְּנֵי הַמָּיִם. אָמַר לָהּ עַל דְּאַטֵּפְתְּ אַטְפוּךְ וְסוֹף מְטַיְּפָיִךְ יְטוּפוּן:

Mishnah Seven

He also saw a skull floating on the surface of the waters; he said to it, 'Because you drowned others, they have drowned you, and in the end they that drowned you shall themselves be drowned.

This Mishnah teaches the lesson of retributive justice. 'With what measure a man measures, is it measured unto him' (Sanh. 100a, So. 9b).

Rashi in Suk. 53a explains that the skull had been severed from the body and the victim was a robber who was murdered by other brigands. 'Measure for measure' does not justify individual feuds. 'When an injured party takes the law into his own hands, the exacting of measure for measure is not justice, but evil revenge. When the law punishes in this manner, it is following in the path of divine justice. Hebraic tradition foretells that all measures may change, but 'measure for measure' will remain for all times' (Schonfeld).

Also.... Some interpret the first word of the Mishnah to refer to the story related in the end of Hul. 142a where we read of the fate of Huspit Hameturgeman, an eloquent orator who was martyred by the Roman authorities and whose tongue lay in the dust. When Elisha Ben Avuya saw this, he exclaimed, 'How is it that a tongue that uttered such wonderful sayings, should be rotting in the ground?' On account of this experience, his faith was shaken and he was henceforth called *Aher*, another one, because he became an infidel. Hillel *also* saw a skull severed from the body, but his faith was unshaken; on the contrary, it proved the justice of God.

Gulgolet, skull or head. This may refer to the insincere, unprincipled leader or teacher who flows with the stream and who corrupts others through his bad leadership.

In the end. Some culprits are not brought to justice and so escape punishment. However, we are reminded that, ultimately the criminal will meet his doom; if not in this world, in the world to come.

Maimonides comments on this Mishnah in these words: 'This is something borne out by experience at all times and in all places. Whoever does evil and introduces violence and corruption, is himself a victim of the harm caused by those very evils he introduces... 'For the work of a man will He requite unto him and cause every man to find according to his ways' (Job 34:11).

Hasidic Lore

Measure for measure. A contractor was accustomed to visit R. Sussya of Anipol and to present him with gifts in return for his blessings. Once he did not find the Rabbi at home and learned that the latter had left to visit his Rabbi, the Mezeritzer. The contractor deliberated for a moment and resolved to discontinue his visits to the disciple, but go to the master instead. Henceforth, however, the prosperity which had until now attended him dwindled away and he suffered severe losses. Again he visited R. Sussya and asked him' Why have I become unsuccessful ever since I began to visit the Mezeritzer, whom you yourself acknowledge as your superior?' R. Sussya answered: As long as you gave your support to any good man without calculating the degree of his goodness, the Lord likewise granted you a portion out of His abundance without calculating your just deserts. But since you began to look about for a better man to whom you might offer your tithe, the Lord in His turn also looked for a man better than yourself, whom He might endow with His riches. This is measure for measure.

(ח) הוּא הָיָה אוֹמֵר מַרְבֶּה בָשָׂר מַרְבֶּה רִמָּה. מַרְבֶּה נְכָסִים מַרְבֶּה דְאָגָה. מַרְבֶּה נָשִׁים מַרְבֶּה כְשָׁפִים. מַרְבֶּה שְׁפָחוֹת מַרְבֶּה זִמָּה. מַרְבֶּה עֲבָדִים מַרְבֶּה גָזֵל. מַרְבֶּה תוֹרָה מַרְבֶּה חַיִּים. מַרְבֶּה יְשִׁיבָה מַרְבֶּה חָכְמָה. מַרְבֶּה עֵצָה מַרְבֶּה תְבוּנָה. מַרְבֶּה צְדָקָה מַרְבֶּה שָׁלוֹם. קָנָה שֵׁם טוֹב קָנָה לְעַצְמוֹ. קָנָה לוֹ דִּבְרֵי תוֹרָה קָנָה לוֹ חַיֵּי הָעוֹלָם הַבָּא:

Mishnah Eight

He used to say: The more flesh, the more worms; the more property, the more anxiety; the more women, the more witchcraft; the more maidservants, the more lewdness; the more men-servants, the more robbery. The more Torah, the more life; the more (he attends) Yeshivah, the more wisdom; the more counsel, the more understanding; the more charity, the more peace. He who has acquired a good name, has acquired it for himself; he who has acquired for himself words of Torah, has acquired for himself life in the world to come.

We should note the order of the Mishnah. We have here a progression of ideas which manifest themselves in the habits of the worldly man who is contrasted with the spiritual man. The worldly man who is primarily interested in food (meat in ancient times was considered a luxury), will increase his property and possessions to maintain his high standard of living. This in turn will lead to a riotous indulgence in more women, who will demand more maids and, as the household grows larger, one needs more men-servants.

In contrast to this wild style of life, Hillel suggests more Torah education. To acquire this we need more Yeshivot to cater for every section of the community. This requires organisational ability and counselling, and to effect this, we need much charity. Such a life will bring peace of mind and earn for one a good name which excels everything, and acquires for one a portion in the world to come.

The more flesh.... It is generally conceded that we consume far too much food, and dieting has been prescribed by many doctors. The stubborn and rebellious son (Deut. 21:18) is a 'glutton and a drunkard'.

Some connect 'more flesh' with immodesty in dress.

The more property, the more anxiety. The acquisition of wealth often brings anxiety and worry. Compare Prov. 23:4: Weary not yourself to be rich; cease from your own wisdom. Will you set your eyes upon it? It is gone; for riches certainly make themselves wings, like an eagle that flies towards heaven.

The more women the more witchcraft. 'Wives in their jealous rivalry for their husband's attention will resort to seeking charms from witches, whose occupation will prosper and spread' (Soncino Talmud).

On *witchcraft* see Hertz Pentateuch on Ex. 22:17.

The more maid-servants, the more lewdness. With an abundance of servants the women become idle and 'idleness leads to lewdness and mental instability' (Ket. 5:5).

The more servants, the more robbery. One might possibly supervise one or two servants but it is virtually impossible to oversee a large number of servants.

The more Torah, the more life. Compare Prov. 2:1-2. 'My son, forget not my Torah, but let your heart keep my commandments; for length of days and years of life and peace will they add to you'.

Torah is synonymous with life, see note on 6:7. Jewish life in ancient times was highly centralised in the Holy Land, where the Temple in Jerusalem was the rallying point of Jews. Sacrifices were offered up in the Temple; the Sanhedrin held its sessions only in the Temple and three times a year every male was enjoined to make a pilgrimage to the Temple. With the destruction of the First and Second Temples, Jewish life almost came to a standstill, and the Jewish people were exiled from their land. These traumatic experiences would have destroyed any other nation, but such is the uniqueness of our people, that though they were deprived of their spiritual centre, exiled from their land, pilloried and persecuted in every country, they still lived a Jewish life; in fact, they flourished in a number of lands.

How do we account for this miraculous survival of the Jewish people? In all the vicissitudes of their changed fortunes, the Jewish people took with them the Torah. The Torah was the life-force which gave momentum to their continued existence. The Torah regenerated them and salvaged them from total assimilation and extinction.

Even at the Brit Milah the Jewish male infant is initiated into the covenant of Abraham with the Hebraic motto, 'In your blood, live' (Ez. 16:6). With the Psalmist, the Jew exclaims, 'I will not die, but live, and recount the works of the Lord' (118:17).

We should underline the word 'more'. We cannot restrict Torah to a few customs and religious practices. A Brit Milah alone does not create a Jew, nor does a Bar-Mitzvah or Bat-Mitzvah equip a young boy or girl with the weapons of the Jewish spirit. The more we regulate Jewish life according to Torah ideology, the more likely shall we be in a position to attain a greater and richer measure of sustained Jewish life.

Yeshivah. This is an academy of learning. The word is connected with the root *yashav*, to sit or dwell. It is an establishment where young men, not only sit at the feet of their teachers imbibing Torah knowledge, but also dwell in corporate worship and brotherhood, and so constitute a full-fledged community. Communal learning has always been a recognised facet of Jewish life. Indeed, according to one tradition, the Yeshivah existed in the days of the Patriarchs and was first established by Shem, the son of Noah. Shem was later joined by Ever and the institution became known as the Yeshivah of Shem V'Ever. We are told that Jacob the Patriarch was a student there.

Compared with the Yeshivah, the University is a comparatively new institution.

It has been suggested that the first Medical School in Salerno (9th to 10th century) may have recruited some students from the Yeshivah, where they learned Torah for its own sake, *lishmah*, whereas the University was motivated to produce professional men equipped with degrees. And in early times the University was open only to the aristocracy and nobility, while the Yeshivah was always open to all classes, to rich and poor alike. The Yeshivah predated the extra-mural extention-courses of the modern University by many centuries. At the outset it conducted refresher courses for the masses, thus introducing adult education to all during the months of Adar and Elul, the period when agricultural work was at a standstill. These were called Kallah months, and it is interesting that till this day we pray every Shabbat morning 'for the heads of the academies and the heads of the colleges' in the *Yekum Purkon* prayer.

The more Yeshivah, the more wisdom. This maxim applies both to pupils and masters. The longer a pupil stays at a Yeshivah, the more wisdom he acquires. The teacher, too, remaining at the academy, becomes more profound as he cannot repeat himself and must rise to new and higher levels of scholarship. Concerning the teacher the Talmud rightly remarks, 'much have I learned from my masters, more from my colleagues and from my disciples, most of all' (Ta. 7a).

Hakhmah. As a body of men, the Rabbis are often referred to as Hakhamim, wise men, but here we meet the noun 'wisdom' (hakhmah) for the first time in this tractate, and it is therefore important to establish the correct connotation of the word and not confuse it with cleverness, smartness or cunning, all of which may impinge on deceit and fraud.

Wisdom as employed by the Mishnah is far superior to any form of cleverness. It is more noble and pure than smartness. Whilst cleverness is not always related to good conduct, wisdom can lead to righteousness. In a letter sent by Maimonides to his son, the Master distinguishes, in a novel manner, between true wisdom and mere cleverness. He writes, 'Cleverness may serve its own profit, concentrate on its own fame, staying cold and heartless in the face of another's want. Wisdom of the heart brings happiness to our fellow-man, wiping tears off his face and lending strength to his efforts. The moon shines but she lacks warmth, her light may be brilliant and cold; this may be compared to cleverness without human sympathy. Wisdom, however, is like the majestic sun — the sun of kindness with health on its wings'.

He who has acquired a good name, has acquired it for himself. Whilst one leaves his possessions behind, a good name accompanies him to and beyond the grave. When Monobaz, King of Adiabene (1st Century C.E., a convert to Judaism) distributed his wealth to the poor, he said, 'My fathers stored up treasures for others to enjoy; I have stored up treasures for myself' (B.B. 11a).

Others interpret the word *leatzmo*, for himself, to mean that one should acquire a good name in a humble manner and not boast of it; he should reserve it 'for himself', quietly and unobtrusively.

He who has acquired for himself words of Torah. As with a good name, so with Torah. It is not passed on automatically; one must acquire it anew. The word *lo*, for himself, should be emphasised. He will master Torah through his own effort; he must strenuously strive to fill his mind with Torah knowledge.

Hasidic Lore

Life with Torah. In the Morning Service there are two blessings, one on the restoration of the soul after its night-rest, and one on the teaching to us of the Torah by the Lord. R. Bunam declared that we should first recite the Blessing of the Restoration of Life (consciousness). We entrusted our Life-Soul unto God and have received it back refreshed by repose: it is fitting that our first thought should be to thank the Guardian on High Who has shielded our soul.

The Gerer Rabbi, however, said that the Blessing, the teaching of Torah, should be recited first, inasmuch as life without Torah is merely earthly and worthless.

(ט) רַבָּן יוֹחָנָן בֶּן זַכַּאי קִבֵּל מֵהִלֵּל וּמִשַּׁמַּאי. הוּא הָיָה אוֹמֵר אִם לָמַדְתָּ תּוֹרָה הַרְבֵּה אַל תַּחֲזִיק טוֹבָה לְעַצְמְךָ כִּי לְכָךְ נוֹצָרְתָּ:

Mishnah Nine

R. Johanan Ben Zakkai, received the tradition from Hillel and Shammai. He used to say, If you have learnt much Torah, do not ascribe any merit to yourself, because for that you were created.

R. Johanan Ben Zakkai descended from the House of Hillel and survived the fall of Jerusalem in 70 C.E. He salvaged Judaism at a critical period in Jewish history. With the destruction of the Temple which was the crown and glory of Jewish life, our people became despondent and frustrated. At that psychological hour, Johanan fearlessly and courageously escaped in a coffin from Jerusalem whilst it was being besieged by the Roman General Vespasian, and was allowed to proceed to Javneh where he established the 'Vineyard' which henceforth became the centre of Jewish learning. In this manner Johanan regenerated Jewish life with new hope and vigour. Indeed, the Sanhedrin was transplanted from Jerusalem to Javneh and he presided over it, thus continuing the traditions of his Master, and with vision and foresight was responsible for creating a new era of Jewish learning.

A true disciple of Hillel, Johanan was a man of peace, as reflected in his comment on Deut. 27:6, 'Of unhewn stones shall you build the altar of the Lord your God'. Johanan affirmed, 'The sword is a symbol of punishment whilst the altar is a symbol of atonement. If God says of the altar stones, 'You shall not wield iron upon them', how safe from punishment is he who promotes peace between man and man, man and wife, city and city, nation and nation and empire and empire' (Mekhilta 74a).

He received the tradition from Hillel and Shammai. R. Johanan imbibed the best of both schools. He followed the strictness of Shammai, but counteracted this by being naturally kind and approachable; we know that he shared his food with his students. Though he followed both Hillel and Shammai, he was possessed of an independent mind. This would explain why, after having received the tradition, the Mishnah states 'He used to say'.

If you have learned much Torah. One cannot master the whole Torah, for it is 'longer than the earth and broader than the sea' (Job 11:9), but we should aspire to learn much Torah.

Do not ascribe merit unto yourself. If a person is blessed with much Torah knowledge, he should treat it as his natural bent and should not imagine that he is superior to those not so learned. God endowed him with the capacity to learn; this should humble him and inspire him to pass on his knowledge to others. 'The man of understanding will, upon reflection, realise that there is no justification for pride or vainglory, even if he was privileged to become very learned. He who has acquired more knowledge than the average person, has accomplished nothing more than what his nature impelled him to do' (Mesillat Yesharim).

For this purpose you were created. One cannot tell at birth what profession or vocation he will pursue. Not so with Torah; already at birth one commences to imbibe Torah — for this purpose man is created.

Learning is pre-eminent over all other activities in Jewish life. In this respect Jews were unique in antiquity, for they had a passion for learning in which all were invited to participate. In the later period of Greek civilisation learning was the prerogative of certain individuals, and in Rome learning was not an essential ingredient in the curriculum of the State. In Judea alone, learning was included in the programme of the day and people vied with each other to master more and more learning.

Hasidic Lore

Learning. A hasid asked the Gerer Rabbi why he still visits the Kotzker Rabbi although he himself is more renowned. The Rabbi replied, 'As long as a man finds there is someone from whom he can learn, he should not teach others'.

(י) חֲמִשָּׁה תַלְמִידִים הָיוּ לוֹ לְרַבָּן יוֹחָנָן בֶּן זַכַּאי. וְאֵלּוּ הֵן רַבִּי אֱלִיעֶזֶר בֶּן הוֹרְקְנוֹס וְרַבִּי יְהוֹשֻׁעַ בֶּן חֲנַנְיָא וְרַבִּי יוֹסֵי הַכֹּהֵן וְרַבִּי שִׁמְעוֹן בֶּן נְתַנְאֵל וְרַבִּי אֶלְעָזָר בֶּן עֲרָךְ:

Mishnah Ten

R. Johanan Ben Zakkai had five disciples and they are: R. Eliezer Ben Hyrcanus, R. Joshua Ben Hanania, R. Jose the Priest, R. Simeon Ben Nethanel and R. Eleazar Ben Arakh.

R. Johanan had many disciples; the five mentioned here were outstanding.

R. Eliezer was a colleague of Gamliel II, whose sister he married. Rather late in life, he left his regular work against the wish of his father and devoted himself to the study of Torah. It was he, together with Joshua Ben Hanania, who smuggled the master out of Jerusalem. He established his own school in Lydda.

R. Joshua Ben Hanania was a Levite who served in the Temple as a chorister. His pious mother introduced him to the Synagogue almost from birth by carrying him there in his cradle, so that he should hear the sound of prayer and study. He earned his livelihood as a needle-maker and a charcoal-burner. He was also skilled in science and astronomy. His great learning, wit and wisdom, brought him to the court of Hadrian. When Jews began to revolt against the tyranny of Hadrian, Joshua intervened and pacified the people and so earned the title of 'The Peacemaker'.

R. Jose the Priest valued friendship. On the occasion of the death of the son of R. Johanan, Jose consoled his master by reminding him that when Aaron the High Priest lost two sons in one day, he continued his services in the Tabernacle. Jose was devoted to mystical studies.

R. Simeon Ben Nethanel belonged to a noble and priestly family and was particularly praised for his piety and fear of sin. He felt that it was the duty of man to scrutinise and examine his actions every day. He advised that people should be scrupulously honest in the payment of their debts.

R. Eleazar Ben Arakh was particularly interested in the mystical interpretation of Scripture. However, he later left his pupils and transferred to Emmaus, which boasted of a good climate. As a result of this, he was no longer in touch with the scholars of his period and he forgot his learning. According to the Talmud (Shab. 147b) the scholars prayed for him and his learning returned. Because of this, R. Ņehorai warned, 'Be exiled to a place of Torah and say not that it will follow you... and do not rely on your own understanding' (Ibid.).

Hasidic Lore

Faith. Further to the note above regarding Eleazar Ben Arakh and his forgetting of Torah, the following extract by the Besht is apposite: We read in the Talmud (R.H. 21a) that forty-nine doors of understanding out of fifty were opened to Moses. But since man aspires always to know more, how did Moses continue? The answer is that when he found the fiftieth door closed to him as unapproachable to the human mind, he substituted faith and meditated again upon those phases of knowledge open to him.

In this manner, every man should discipline his mind. He should study and reflect to the utmost of his ability. When he has reached a point where he is unable to comprehend further, he may substitute faith and return to the learning within his grasp. Beyond a certain degree of research, both the sage and the ignorant man are alike. It may be that some will apply to you the verse, 'The simpleton believes every word (Prov. 14:15), but you may remind the scoffers of another verse, 'The Lord preserves the simple' (Ps. 116:6).

(יא) הוּא הָיָה מוֹנֶה שִׁבְחָן. רַבִּי אֱלִיעֶזֶר בֶּן הוֹרְקְנוֹס בּוֹר סוּד שֶׁאֵינוֹ מְאַבֵּד טִפָּה. רַבִּי יְהוֹשֻׁעַ בֶּן חֲנַנְיָא אַשְׁרֵי יוֹלַדְתּוֹ. רַבִּי יוֹסֵי הַכֹּהֵן חָסִיד. רַבִּי שִׁמְעוֹן בֶּן נְתַנְאֵל יְרֵא חֵטְא. וְרַבִּי אֶלְעָזָר בֶּן עֲרָךְ כְּמַעְיָן הַמִּתְגַּבֵּר:

Mishnah Eleven

He used to recount their praise; R. Eliezer Ben Hyrcanus is a plastered cistern that does not lose a drop. R. Joshua Ben Hananiah, happy is she who bore him. R. Jose the Priest is a pious man; R. Simeon Ben Nethanel is one who fears sin, and R. Eleazar Ben Arakh is like a spring that gathers force.

He used to recount their praise. In the first instance, we should emphasise the initial word *hu*, meaning he. The master recounts the praises of his disciples who were too modest to speak of their own individual accomplishments. The master also advisedly uses the word *manah* and not *saper*, which also means to count. *Manah* points to the counting of individual qualities. The *minyan*, the religious quorum, is derived from this root; every individual counts towards the minyan. Compare also Ps. 90:12, 'Teach us to number, *limnot*, our days'; each day is vital and should be counted for its own sake. However, the word *saper* from which we get *mispar*, number, can indicate a multitude, especially with the negative (Gen. 16:10 and 41:49), *ein mispar* meaning without number, or innumerable.

A plastered cistern. Hyrcanus was a fountain of learning. As a cemented cistern will effectively retain its waters, so Hyrcanus with his retentive memory, never forgot what he learned. In antiquity books were very rare and expensive, consequently the memory became the instrument of literary education and this affected the whole community. Indeed, the Rabbis even recommended certain foods to act as an aid to the memory. Today, with printing and a multiplicity of books for every conceivable subject, the memory is often stunted as we rely on the printed word.

Happy is she who bore him. The word *ashrei* does not denote a physical but an exalted and spiritual happiness. Similarly, the Book of Psalms opens appropriately with this word. The maxim in the Mishnah postulates the sacred mission of the Jewish mother, who is often extolled in rabbinic literature. This quality of the blessed mother is singled out here because Joshua's mother was directly responsible for his piety. It is possible that Rabban Johanan gave utterance to this eulogy of the Jewish mother because, during the period when his own mother was pregnant with him, his father died, and when she gave birth to him, she too died; he was thus denied the privilege of exhibiting filial piety and so seized this opportunity of praising the Jewish mother.

It is significant that on Rosh Hashanah, the commencement of the most important period in the Jewish year, we read in the Torah and the Scriptural portion, chapters that speak of three great mothers whose prayers were answered and who gave birth to Isaac, Joseph and Samuel. This tradition was based on the Talmud (R.H. 11a) which states: It was on Rosh Hashanah that God decreed that our mothers Sarah, Rachel and Hannah should give birth to their sons. Happy were those mothers who gave birth to such illustrious progeny.

Hasid, pious. Generally this word includes saintliness of character, but since the eighteenth century the word has received a new impetus. To many people, religion is a perfunctory experience, a habit-forming exercise. Hasidism has veered away from the cold formalistic mode of worship and has introduced a more intense and passionate approach to Judaism in general and worship in particular. See above 2:6.

Sin. In the minds of many people, sin is connected with acts directed against religion, but in Judaism every action which violates justice, the moral or social order, is a sin against man and God. Because of our proneness to sin which affects all of us, we fear its consequences. Very early in the Bible we are warned that 'Sin crouches at the door and unto you is its desire, but you shall rule over it' (Gen. 4:7). The door to sin should be kept closed, so that the evil impulse which is often clothed in an attractive garb, be resisted. It is worth noting that in the Jewish view, sin is not implanted within man, it crouches at the door. We do not believe in original sin; we can arrest the evil designs of sin by fearing it. Happy is the person who, by avoiding sin, can raise himself to the posture of being a fearer of Heaven, which is the most exalted form of religious experience.

Like a spring that gathers force. As the melting snow and torrential rain help the spring to overflow, so the penetrating mind of Eleazar Ben Arakh was bursting with new ideas and ever-sustained vigour.

Hasidic Lore

Fear of sin. The Koretzer said: The true fear of God is through fear of sin, but not through the fear of punishment. As it is written, 'And they said unto Moses, 'Speak you with us and we will hear; but let not God speak with us, lest we die' (Ex. 22:18-19). And Moses said unto the people, 'Fear not, for God is come to prove you, and that His fear may be before you, that you sin not'. Moses said, 'Fear not Him because you are afraid of dying. Let His fear be before you, so that you may be afraid of sin'.

(יב) הוּא הָיָה אוֹמֵר אִם יִהְיוּ כָּל חַכְמֵי יִשְׂרָאֵל בְּכַף מֹאזְנַיִם וְרַבִּי אֱלִיעֶזֶר בֶּן הוֹרְקְנוֹס בְּכַף שְׁנִיָּה מַכְרִיעַ אֶת כֻּלָּם. אַבָּא שָׁאוּל אוֹמֵר מִשְּׁמוֹ אִם יִהְיוּ כָּל חַכְמֵי יִשְׂרָאֵל בְּכַף מֹאזְנַיִם וְרַבִּי אֱלִיעֶזֶר בֶּן הוֹרְקְנוֹס אַף עִמָּהֶם וְרַבִּי אֶלְעָזָר בֶּן עֲרָךְ בְּכַף שְׁנִיָּה מַכְרִיעַ אֶת כֻּלָּם:

Mishnah Twelve

He used to say: If all the wise of Israel were in one scale of the balance and Eliezer Ben Hyrcanus in the second scale, he would outweigh them all. Abba Saul said in his name: If all the wise of Israel were in one scale of the balance and Eliezer Ben Hyrcanus with them and Eleazar Ben Arakh in the second scale, he would outweigh them all.

Abba Saul. Abba, father, is a title of honour. The teacher of Abba Saul is not specifically mentioned in the Talmud, but it is reasonable to suggest that he might well have been Johanan Ben Zakkai, in whose name we speak here. Of the five disciples of Johanan, two were pre-eminent, and they were Eliezer Ben Hyrcanus and Eleazar Ben Arakh; each of these followed a different line of thought, which we can ascertain from the manner of their presentation.

Eliezer Ben Hyrcanus is portrayed to us as a plastered cistern that does not lose a drop. This, we have said, betokens a retentive memory. Undoubtedly, this is a great asset to a scholar. Blessed is he who has a phenomenal memory and has the ability to amass a wealth of material in his brain and not allow a detail to be forgotten. Such a person has the capacity to collect from all sources and, like a sponge, absorb them all and preserve them. This description of Eliezer's mind is attested to by the Talmud (Suk. 28a) where we read that Eliezer's colleagues asked him, 'Are your words only reproductions of what you heard?' and Eliezer answered, 'Do you wish to force me to say something which I have not heard from my teacher?... All my life I have never said a thing which I did not hear from my teachers'. In the same passage from the Talmud we learn that the master Johanan, too, never said anything he had not heard from his teacher. In fact, the Talmud explicitly states that Eliezer, in this respect, was a replica of his master whom he followed implicitly. It is therefore no surprise to learn that in Johanan's view, Eliezer outweighed the other disciples, for he was a loyal and faithful student who patterned his life on that of his master.

Abba Saul, however, considered that Eleazar Ben Arakh was far superior to any of his colleagues. Regarding Abba Saul, the description 'an ever-flowing spring that gathers force', implies that Eleazar had an original mind; he was possessed of a brilliant and analytical brain and enjoyed a profound and acute understanding of everything. To Abba Saul, a cemented cistern conserves that which is within, but does not produce originality of thought, whereas an ever-flowing stream could produce creative and startling ideas and theories. Jewish scholarship is in need of both streams of thought. There is no division between Johanan and Abba Saul; they complement each other. In rabbinic terminology, they both speak in the name of the living God.

Hasidic Lore

Originality. Regarding originality of mind referred to above, we record the following note of a hasidic teacher. After R. Noah's succession as Rabbi of Lekhivitz, some hasidim enquired of him, 'Why do you not conduct yourself like your father, the late Rabbi?' 'I do conduct myself like him' retorted R. Noah. 'He did not imitate anybody and I likewise do not imitate any person.'

(יג) אָמַר לָהֶם צְאוּ וּרְאוּ אֵיזוֹ הִיא דֶּרֶךְ טוֹבָה שֶׁיִּדְבַּק בָּהּ הָאָדָם. רַבִּי אֱלִיעֶזֶר אוֹמֵר עַיִן טוֹבָה. רַבִּי יְהוֹשֻׁעַ אוֹמֵר חָבֵר טוֹב. רַבִּי יוֹסֵי אוֹמֵר שָׁכֵן טוֹב. רַבִּי שִׁמְעוֹן אוֹמֵר הָרוֹאֶה אֶת הַנּוֹלָד. רַבִּי אֶלְעָזָר אוֹמֵר לֵב טוֹב. אָמַר לָהֶם רוֹאֶה אֲנִי אֶת דִּבְרֵי אֶלְעָזָר בֶּן עֲרָךְ מִדִּבְרֵיכֶם שֶׁבִּכְלַל דְּבָרָיו דִּבְרֵיכֶם:

Mishnah Thirteen

He said to them: Go out and see which is the good way to which a man should cleave. R. Eliezer said, A good eye; R. Joshua said, A good friend; R. Jose said, A good neighbour; R. Simeon said, One who foresees the event. R. Eleazar said, A good heart. He said to them, 'I approve the words of Eleazar Ben Arakh more than your words, for in his words yours are included'.

Go out and see. After having assessed the relative merits of his distinguished disciples, Rabban Johanan seems to suggest that the time has arrived when they should leave the confined space of the academy and the four ells of Halakhah, and go out into the open world and see how people live; they could then apply their learning to help and guide others. The master was naturally inquisitive to know which particular characteristic each would underline.

A good eye. This makes one content with one's portion; we should not begrudge what others possess. A good eye makes a person beloved to all mankind because he will see only good in people. The eyes are the windows of the soul and should be utilised to see the beauty, wonder and marvels of God's world. The Psalmist bemoans those that have eyes and see not. The Prophets were great because they saw with their eyes; they had visions and looked into the future; thus they were called 'seers'. Some have gentle and sensitive eyes; these are usually kind, generous and understanding people. Others have cruel and piercing eyes, which betoken a jealous and envious disposition. Man was created with two eyes, so that with one he may see God's greatness and with the other his own lowliness, and Maimonides reminds us that man's eyes are in front, and not behind him. We must look ahead and not bemoan the past.

Some maintain that the 'eyes' are the leaders of the community. Commenting on the prayer, 'Enlighten our eyes in Thy law and let our hearts cling to Thy commandments', a wit once said that if the eyes, the leaders, are sincere in their love for Torah, then the hearts of the people are brought closer to the mitzvot and cling to them.

A good friend. R. Joshua does not emphasise the necessity of acquiring a good friend, which is taken for granted; he is here suggesting that the person himself should be a good friend to others. A millionaire without trusted friends is virtually a miserable pauper, but a poor man with loyal friends is spiritually rich. Some of the classical examples of true friendship found in Tanakh are David and Jonathan, and Ruth and Naomi. A trusted friend is one who is a sincere confidant; he will acknowledge the faults as well as the good qualities. Friendship is a man's greatest gift. 'Some friends are like a sundial, useless when the sun sets; others are like the shadow, they follow us when our sun shines'.

The word *haver*, which we translate friend, is also a title for a scholar who is less learned than a *talmid hakham*. It can also refer to a member of a religious or charitable association, especially a member of an order for the observance of the levitical laws in daily conduct.

A good neighbour. Good neighbourliness is a cardinal principle of the Torah. Thus in the great moral and ethical code of Lev. chapter nineteen, we are told to love our neighbour as ourselves because 'he is like you'. Armed with this noble maxim, we have become trained and schooled in the art of good neighbourliness. An excellent example of this regard for our neighbours, even the heathen, is furnished by the Talmud where we learn that the poor of the heathen are not prevented from gathering the gleanings, forgotten sheaves and the corners of the field, to avoid ill-feeling. This is elaborated by the Rabbis who declare that we should suppport the poor of the heathen along with the poor of Israel and visit the sick of the heathen along with the sick of Israel, and bury the poor of the heathen along with the dead of Israel in the interest of peace (Git. 61a). This is summed up by one teacher (Abbaye) who stated that man should seek to be at peace with all men, not excluding the gentile, and so win favour with God and man. Neighbourliness suggests proximity, and the Book of Proverbs correctly reminds us, 'Better a neighbour that is near than a brother far off' (27:10). International peace and understanding must be preceded by good neighbourliness.

One who foresees the event. R. Simeon adopts an independent view; while others stress fellowship, he is interested in the individual. He was haunted by the dangers of sin and his clue to a good life consisted in forecasting the result of an action and, if possible, ascertaining where it would lead to. Simeon advises that we should actively and judiciously plan for the future and, with foresight, avoid the pitfalls and temptations which bestrew the path of life.

We should point out that the Mishnah advisedly states 'He who sees' and not 'He who knows'. God alone knows the future. Man, with his finite mind, cannot delve into the future. He may intuitively foresee the future and read into his visions certain preconceived notions upon which he feels confident to act, but he cannot definitely know what the future will bring.

A good heart. The heart is the seat of all moral and spiritual functions; it is the central organ which conditions all man's activities. 'Above all that you guard, keep your heart, for out of it are the issues of life' (Prov. 4:23). We all know how to distinguish between a mean or hard-hearted person and one who is noble-hearted. The former speaks unkindly and uncharitably of others, whilst the latter exhibits generosity and gentility. As with the social graces, so with prayer and the performance of mitzvot. The Rabbis stated categorically, 'Whether he does much or little (they are equally worthy) provided he directs his heart to heaven' (Men. 13:11). It is the motive behind the prayer or the mitzvah that counts. 'He who best knows how to purify his heart is near to God and is most beloved of Him.... the Merciful One desires the heart' (Sanh. 106b). The Mesillat Yesharim observes that God is not satisfied with deeds performed merely in the spirit of obedience to a command; He desires the heart to be pure and thus attain to true worship. The heart is king and guide to the organs of the body. Little wonder that the Shema commences with the words, 'And you shall love God with all your heart, with all your soul and with all your might'.

To understand the full import of the 'heart' in Jewish life, we direct our attention to the building of the Tabernacle described in Ex. 35. Above we referred to the 'heart' being the seat of the emotions; here we see that the heart is also the seat of the intellect. In Exodus the word 'heart' occurs several times in association with different words, as *hakham lev*, wise hearted, *nediv lev*, willing heart, and 'every one whose heart stirred him up'.

It is well to remember that the designation 'wise-hearted' is not restricted to Bezalel, the chief architect of the Tabernacle. The women who sewed and spun the materials for the Tabernacle are also referred to as wise-hearted. We see, therefore, that the word *lev*, heart, is all-embracing and covers a variety of situations. We should therefore not be altogether surprised that R. Johanan was impelled to confirm the view of R. Eleazar Ben Arakh, who declared that the secret of the good way to which a person should cleave, was that he possessed a good heart. Whereas others refer to single qualities of mind, Eleazar mentions a general and positive principle from which flow many other qualities.

Hasidic Lore

The inhospitable shohet. Several hasidim of Kolomeya complained to the Sadagurer Rabbi that the shohet in their community was a miserly and inhospitable person. The Rabbi exclaimed, 'And do you eat meat from his shehitah?' This question was equivalent to a prohibition and henceforth no one purchased meat. The shohet came to the Rabbi and asked, 'Where do you find that a shohet must be hospitable?' The Rabbi replied that we find in the Talmud that some people are born with a passion for shedding blood. One becomes a murderer, a second a soldier, and the third a shohet (Shab. 156a). The question arises, 'Why do we make use of the meat from an animal killed by a man who is a potential murderer? The whole shehitah legislation has been formulated in order to prevent brutal treatment of the animal, and what is more brutal than to let it perish at the hands of a near-murderer? The answer is that a shohet should have a good heart — notwithstanding his love for the shedding of animal blood; he then may be trusted to avoid brutality in shedding this blood. Thus if a shohet is kind to his fellow-man, he may be trusted to slaughter animals in a mild manner. But if he is unkind, he is in truth a near-murderer who cannot be trusted to observe the humane methods of slaying animals prescribed by law'.

(יד) אָמַר לָהֶם צְאוּ וּרְאוּ אֵיזוֹ הִיא דֶּרֶךְ רָעָה שֶׁיִּתְרַחֵק מִמֶּנָּה הָאָדָם. רַבִּי אֱלִיעֶזֶר אוֹמֵר עַיִן רָעָה. רַבִּי יְהוֹשֻׁעַ אוֹמֵר חָבֵר רָע. רַבִּי יוֹסֵי אוֹמֵר שָׁכֵן רָע. רַבִּי שִׁמְעוֹן אוֹמֵר הַלֹּוֶה וְאֵינוֹ מְשַׁלֵּם אֶחָד הַלֹּוֶה מִן הָאָדָם כְּלֹוֶה מִן הַמָּקוֹם שֶׁנֶּאֱמַר לֹוֶה רָשָׁע וְלֹא יְשַׁלֵּם וְצַדִּיק חוֹנֵן וְנוֹתֵן. רַבִּי אֶלְעָזָר אוֹמֵר לֵב רָע. אָמַר לָהֶם רוֹאֶה אֲנִי אֶת דִּבְרֵי אֶלְעָזָר בֶּן עֲרָךְ מִדִּבְרֵיכֶם שֶׁבִּכְלַל דְּבָרָיו דִּבְרֵיכֶם:

Mishnah Fourteen

He said to them: Go out and see which is the evil way that a man should shun. R. Eliezer said, An evil eye; R. Joshua said, A bad friend; R. Jose said, A bad neighbour; R. Simeon said, He who borrows and does not repay — it is the same whether he borrows from man or from the Omnipresent — as it is said, 'The wicked borrows and does not pay, but the righteous deals graciously and gives' (Ps. 37:21); R. Eleazar said, A bad heart. He then said to them, I approve the words of Eleazar the son of Arakh more than your words, for in his words yours are included.

Some have questioned the relevance of this Mishnah. They claim that the evil way of life is merely the antithesis of the good and it is superfluous to state the negative position. But in reality this is not so; the opposite of good is not necessarily evil. It would be wrong to accuse one who is uncharitable as being a wicked person. This in itself is uncharitable. Saintliness is a great virtue, but one who does not cultivate it could hardly be described as evil.

Evil eye. This may refer to one who is possessed of an insatiable lust for wealth or power. The story is told of Alexander of Macedon that he appeared at the gates of Paradise and demanded admission, but he was told that only the righteous could enter (Ps. 118:20). He maintained that as he was king, he deserved recognition. He was then given an eye socket with an open eye. This was placed on one scale and on the other scale was gold and silver; but the scale with the eye overbalanced. He piled more gold on the scale, but the eye was still heavier. Alexander was puzzled and he asked his wise men for an explanation. They told him that this eye is never satisfied and advised him to close the eye and put earth on it; immediately the scales balanced (Tamid 32b).

The term 'evil eye' has another and different connotation. This corroborates what we have said, that this is not a simple negation of the previous Mishnah. An evil eye is a manifestation of a power which arouses the envy of one against another, individually or collectively. Because of a famine in Canaan, Jacob sent his sons to Egypt to buy grain, and Rashi points out that they hid themselves in the crowd so that the people should not recognise them. They were not to show themselves as a compact group at one entrance to the city, but each one should enter separately by a different gate in order that the evil eye should not have power over them; that is, they should not attract the envious attention of the people (Rashi on Gen. 42:5).

It has been said that children especially are susceptible to the influence of the evil eye. A beautiful child may sometimes arouse feelings of jealousy in the eyes of a mother who may be childless.

On a national scale, Anti-Semitism, the scourge which has visited us almost from the dawn of civilisation, may too result from the evil eye. Our laws and customs are different and we are scattered among the nations of the universe; consequently we have attracted the suspicion and hatred of the non-Jewish world who have cast their spiteful and evil glances upon us, demanding that we sacrifice our peculiar identity and assimilate with the rest of the world.

A bad friend. A bad companion can destroy parental love and undermine the influence of a good home-life. Juvenile delinquency, the bane of youth, is the outcome of bad friendship. As goodness lives and thrives in the service of others, so vice is not isolated but spreads through contacts with gangs of idle and mischievous young men and women. In the early morning service of the Siddur we offer up the prayer, 'Keep us far from a bad man and a bad friend'.

A bad neighbour. A bad neighbour can embroil a whole neighbourhood. In the international sphere war is brought about because nations refuse to cultivate good neighbourliness with one another.

He who borrows and does not repay. This is opposed to the 'foresight' of the previous Mishnah. Initially it may seem a strange contrast, but on examination we can envisage the truth of this statement. He who does not exercise foresight in everything, will not avoid evil. For instance, he who borrows with foresight devises a plan whereby it will be possible for him to repay the loan. If he deliberately fails to make such an arrangement and has no intention to repay, he is virtually a thief.

It is the same whether he borrows from man or God. A great principle of faith is enunciated here. Borrowing is not limited to money; we borrow every moment of our lives. Already at birth, the babe borrows from its mother who sustains it with food. As we grow, we are continuously borrowing from our parents, teachers and friends. We borrow from each other not only the material and physical needs which help us to survive; we also borrow intellectually from the past, ideas, thoughts and philosophies which train us to play our rightful part in society. The greater we are, the more we borrow. How much better are we equipped today! Ben Zoma reminds us, 'What difficulties Adam must have encountered before he produced a morsel of bread or a garment, whilst I rise to find all these things prepared before me' (Ber. 58a). In the technological and intellectual fields, we are blessed with a rich legacy of the past on which we can build; we draw freely from antiquity and borrow incessantly from the innumerable books that are at our disposal. Do we attempt to repay?

The Rabbis observe that when one quotes a teaching, it should be recorded in the name of the teacher, *beshem amro*. In this manner we repay the author and thereby bring redemption to the world. In other words, the Rabbis convey the lesson that those who have the foresight to acknowledge the debt they owe to man, may also acknowledge the debt they owe to God, the source of all. We cannot possibly express the inestimable debt we owe to God from Whom we borrow air, sun, rain, produce, plants, flowers and animal-food. Indeed, we are indebted to God for health, happiness and years. Do we not live on borrowed time? The pious and just will render thanks and gratitude to the Almighty and acknowledge the bountiful and gracious gifts He continually showers upon them.

Makom, place. This word was originally used to designate Jerusalem or the Temple as being the place where God's spirit dwelt; it then came to be used as an appellative for God. 'The term is mainly indicative of God's ubiquity in the world and is best translated by 'Omnipresent' (Shechter).

A bad heart. A bad heart is associated with the evil impulse; compare Gen. 6:5 '...every imagination of the thoughts of his heart was only evil continually'. Ibn Gabirol states, 'Of what avail is the open eye if the heart is blind'. One often reads in Tanakh that the evil heart is associated with callousness — 'the stubbornness of the heart'; 'the hardness of the heart' (Deut. 29:18), (Lam. 3:65); 'brazen-faced and stiff-hearted' (Ex. 2:4); 'uncircumsized in the heart' (Jer. 9:25) and 'the heart (of the godless) is like fat' (Ps. 119:70).

Heart failure is not only a very common physical disease, it is also a dreaded spiritual disease which at times affects many of us. Even when Israel stood at Mount Sinai and witnessed the great and unique spectacle of the Revelation, it is questionable if their hearts truly prompted them to exclaim in unison, 'We will do and obey'. According to R. Meir, at that moment their hearts were directed towards idolatry (Mekhilta Mishpatim 13).

Hasidic Lore

The impulse of the heart. Rabbi Ber of Radishitz asked the Lubliner to teach him the best way of serving the Lord. The Lubliner replied: The best way is the one to which your heart is drawn. Labour in it with your whole strength.

The pure heart. R. Elimelekh of Lizhensk said to his disciples: There is not a single mitzvah which we fulfil perfectly... except circumcision and the Torah we study in our childhood, for these two acts are not infringed upon by 'alien thought' (Midrash Tehillim 6:1).

(טו) הֵם אָמְרוּ שְׁלֹשָׁה דְבָרִים. רַבִּי אֱלִיעֶזֶר אוֹמֵר יְהִי כְבוֹד חֲבֵרְךָ חָבִיב עָלֶיךָ כְּשֶׁלָּךְ וְאַל תְּהִי נוֹחַ לִכְעוֹס וְשׁוּב יוֹם אֶחָד לִפְנֵי מִיתָתְךָ וֶהֱוֵי מִתְחַמֵּם כְּנֶגֶד אוּרָן שֶׁל חֲכָמִים וֶהֱוֵי זָהִיר בְּגַחַלְתָּן שֶׁלֹּא תִכָּוֶה שֶׁנְּשִׁיכָתָן נְשִׁיכַת שׁוּעָל וַעֲקִיצָתָן עֲקִיצַת עַקְרָב וּלְחִישָׁתָן לְחִישַׁת שָׂרָף וְכָל דִּבְרֵיהֶם כְּגַחֲלֵי אֵשׁ:

Mishnah Fifteen

They (each) said three things. Eliezer said: Let the honour of your friend be as dear to you as your own. Be not easily angered and repent a day before your death and warm yourself at the fire of the wise: but beware of their glowing coals lest you be scorched. For their bite is the bite of a fox and their sting the sting of a scorpion and their hiss the hiss of a serpent; and all their words are like coals of fire.

Let the honour of your friend... It is possible that Eliezer is reciprocating the respect and honour his master Johanan exhibited towards him and his four colleagues. Eliezer is confirming the truth that self-love and self-glorification can have serious repercussions, but self-respect which the master showed in full measure begets honour and deferential regard. We are advised not to remain impersonal when a fellow human being is insulted or wronged. If we are true to the fundamental tenet, 'Love your neighbour as yourself', we should uphold his esteem and dignity.

Be not easily angered. Some feel that this qualifies the first maxim. In rising to the aid of your friend, do not easily be provoked; plead his cause in a dignified manner. The classic example of controlling one's anger is reflected in the story told of two men who made a wager of four hundred zuz with each other that he who would anger Hillel would win the money. It was on a Sabbath eve, close to the entry of the Sabbath, that a man presented himself before Hillel and posed this question, 'Why are the eyes of the Tadmorites bleary?' Hillel replied that they made their homes on the desert sands and the winds blew into their eyes. Seemingly satisfied, the questioner left; but after a short while returned and asked another question. 'Why are the Africans' feet flat?' Unperturbed, Hillel answered that they dwelt by the watery marshes and always walked in water. The man went away, only to return once again. This time he asked, 'Why are the heads of the Babylonians long?' Unruffled, Hillel replied that as there are no skilled midwives there when the infant is born, slaves and maid-servants tend it on their laps and so the heads of the Babylonians are long. However, here there are skilful midwives and when the infant is born, it is taken care of in a cradle and its head is rubbed and so the heads of the Palestinians are round. The questioner then exclaimed that he had lost four hundred zuz. Hillel said to him, 'Better that you lose four hundred zuz because of Hillel, than that Hillel lose his temper' (ARN).

We should note that we are not advised to shun anger completely; every quality God has planted within us is good, therefore anger should be utilised judiciously and carefully. It is recorded of one Rabbi that when he became irritated, he would consult the Shulkhan Arukh on some point of law, and in the process his rage would subside. Finally, Resh Lakish warns us that regarding a man who becomes angry, if he is a sage his wisdom departs from him; if he is a Prophet, his prophecy departs from him (Pes. 66b).

Repent one day before death. Man should repent every day of his life, because he does not know on which day he might die (Shab. 15a). In this connection commentators point to Ec. 9:8, 'Let your garments always be clean'. R. Johanan illustrates this verse by a parable of a king who invited his servants to a banquet, without specifying the hour. The wise servants were appropriately dressed when the call came, but the foolish ones were unprepared. The Jew is asked to repent every day, to be prepared to meet his Maker. Sin soils the soul; repentance purifies and renders it white. Repentance is always possible, no matter how far one has strayed from the path of life. An unpardonable sin is a misnomer in the Jewish vocabulary. The essence of repentance is a renewal or return of a personal relationship between God and man. This can take place every day, for God is near to those who call upon Him in truth.

Warm yourself at the fire of the wise. He who wishes to warm himself, will stand at a reasonable distance from the fire and not get too close to it. The words of the Torah are compared to a divine fire (Deut. 33:2). If a person arouses within himself the flaming passion of Jewish law and observance, he can rise to great heights of enthusiasm. However, he who tampers with the glowing coals by casting aside God's laws, can scorch himself and even set his home on fire. Those who have fouled their nest and interfered with the living fire of Judaism, have found that it often acts as a boomerang, burning them and finally robbing them of their Jewish heritage.

Bite of a fox. Some are bitten with the bite of a fox whose crooked teeth get entangled and lacerate the flesh. Many imagine that they can bite into Jewish law with impunity and nothing of serious import will ensue. But they soon realise that they cannot extricate themselves from the dangerous inroads they have made into Jewish Law, and in the process they have cut deep incisions into Jewish life. As the scorpion and the serpent emit poison from their bodies, so too, those who play with fire will poison the Jewish body politic.

Hasidic Lore

Repentance. Many are the sayings on 'Repentance'. We have chosen one which is close in spirit to our Mishnah, which contains references to honour and learning. The Bratzlaver affirmed that there are many scholars who not only fail to repent, but who even quarrel with men of justice. This is because their learning has been acquired in order to attain undeserved honours and the authority and ability to provoke and undermine others. Their learning sharpens their wit and they use it for unworthy purposes. We read in Hosea 14:10, 'For the ways of the Lord are right, and the just do walk in them, but transgressors do stumble therein'. Hence, though learning is good, it may be employed for self-destruction.

(טז) רַבִּי יְהוֹשֻׁעַ אוֹמֵר עַיִן הָרַע וְיֵצֶר הָרָע וְשִׂנְאַת הַבְּרִיּוֹת מוֹצִיאִין אֶת הָאָדָם מִן הָעוֹלָם:

Mishnah Sixteen

R. Joshua says: The evil eye and the evil inclination and hatred of mankind put a man out of the world.

The evil eye. If you see only the evil in your neighbour, you will eventually hate him and make life intolerable for him and so put him out of the world. Rather should one search for and concentrate on the good characteristics of a fellow man.

The evil inclination. This plays an important role in Jewish theology;

its purpose and function are described in the following terms: The evil inclination persuades man to sin in this world and bears witness against him in the future world (Suk. 52b). The evil impulse also acts as the angel of death: He entices man to sin and kills him (Ex. R. 30). R. Simeon Ben Lakish says: The inclination of man assails him every day, endeavouring to kill him, and if God would not support him, man could not resist it (Ibid.). On the other hand, man is bidden to tame his evil inclination and utilise it for a good purpose. In this manner we interpret the words of the Shema, 'And you shall love the Lord with all your heart, with all your soul and with all your might' (Deut. 6:5). How should we love God? 'Love God with all your desires even with your evil inclination, that is to say, make your earthly passions and mundane desires instrumental in the service of God, so that there may be no corner in your heart divided against God' (Sifre 73a; Ber. 61b).

Hatred of mankind. The three ominous characteristics of the Mishnah are links in a chain of progressive evil. The evil or begrudging eye is never content; it is a manifestation of self-love, which in turn is spurred on by the evil inclination into absolute hatred of others. Naturally, people will not associate with those who are stricken with hatred. This withdrawal of man from society isolates him and leads to his downfall. The seeds of hatred are self-destructive. We should note that *beriot* literally means creatures; this is not restricted to the Jew, but encompasses all mankind. We are commanded not to hate, 'You shall not hate your brother in your heart' (Lev. 19:17). This signifies that you shall not hate him because he is your brother.

The worst form of hatred is causeless hatred, which the Rabbis claim was responsible for the destruction of the Temple. R. Nehemiah said that causeless hatred (sinat hinam) destroys the happy relationship between wife and husband so radically, that the children they produce are born prematurely (Shab. 32b). In this connection one cannot refrain from quoting the famous quip of Chief Rabbi Kook to the effect that causeless hatred should be superseded by causeless love; this too should embrace the whole of mankind.

Hasidic Lore

Hatred. The Kotzker Rabbi said: Do not hate the Jew who has wronged you. He has offended you through the evil elements within him, but it may be that his good elements are greater than the goodness within yourself.

(יז) רַבִּי יוֹסֵי אוֹמֵר יְהִי מָמוֹן חֲבֵרְךָ חָבִיב עָלֶיךָ כְּשֶׁלָּךְ וְהַתְקֵן עַצְמְךָ לִלְמוֹד תּוֹרָה שֶׁאֵינָהּ יְרוּשָׁה לָךְ וְכָל מַעֲשֶׂיךָ יִהְיוּ לְשֵׁם שָׁמָיִם:

Mishnah Seventeen

R. Jose says: Let your fellow's property be as dear to you as your own; make yourself fit for the study of Torah, for it is not yours by inheritance. Let all your actions be for the sake of Heaven.

Let your fellow's property be as dear to you as your own. R. Jose was called pious by his master, and his own personal choice for the good life was neighbourliness. Here Jose is true to his philosophy and he elaborates his thesis. He rules that being a good neighbour does not imply only politeness and courteousness, but something far more practical and self-sacrificing. It means that he must be ready to respect the possessions and property of a neighbour with the same love, care and concern that he lavishes on his own wealth. Furthermore, we read into this maxim the right and privilege of every person to possess and enjoy the amenitities of his own private property. Judaism has built a social and economic order which is not akin to either capitalism or communism. The Jewish view is that all wealth belongs to God and man cannot enslave his neighbour, nor dare he confiscate his property. The possessions of every individual must be respected; we should cherish them and hold them as dearly as our own.

Make yourself fit for the study of Torah. The first rule deals with the materialistic side of life, the second rule deals with the spiritual angle, the primacy of Torah, which is fundamentally contrasted with the mundane possessions we acquire. The latter may be inherited from a parent or relative without any personal effort on our part. The study of Torah, however, cannot be bequeathed; it is not inherited. We can acquire learning only through personal exertion; it is necessary to bestir ourselves and even suffer privations in order to master the Torah. For this reason R. Jose advisedly employs the word *atzmekha*, yourself. If you wish to become well versed in the Torah, you cannot rely on others alone; you, yourself, must toil and strive to acquire the Torah ideology which is the secret of life. Moses himself may have nurtured the thought that his sons would succeed him in teaching Torah, but God said to him, 'Take you Joshua' (Nu. 27:18). Even if your antecedents are great scholars and outstanding leaders, you will not automatically inherit their learning or leadership, unless you meditate in the Torah day and night and qualify to act as a leader.

Let all your actions be for the sake of Heaven. The centrality of Torah in the second rule is followed by actions and deeds, *maasekha*, your actions. This agrees with the talmudic principle, 'Great is learning for it leads to action'. Learning may even overcome the evil inclination, as the Talmud advises, 'If that ugly one (the evil inclination) meets you, drag it to the house of learning' (Kid. 30b). If all our actions are motivated with heavenly thoughts, we may begin to recognise God, as we read in Prov. 3:6, 'In all your ways acknowledge Him and He will direct your paths'.

This section of the Mishnah deeply impressed Maimonides who, in his 'Shemoneh Perakim writes: The Sages of blessed memory, too, have summed up this idea of God in so few words and so concisely, at the same time elucidating the whole matter with such complete thoroughness, that when one considers the brevity with which they express this great and mighty thought in its entirety, about which others have written whole books and yet without adequately explaining it, one truly recognises that the Rabbis undoubtedly spoke through divine inspiration. This saying is found among their precepts and is 'Let all your deeds be done in the name of Heaven'.

We would underline the word 'Heaven' in this saying. It is instructive to contrast Heaven with earth. On earth the contours of no two countries are exactly alike, they all differ in shape, size and climate. They have diverse laws and customs and are ruled by different governments. However, to the naked eye, the heavens are the same wherever one finds oneself. Furthermore, the sun, moon and stars all do the bidding of the Almighty and appear with precise regularity. There is no division amongst them; they implicitly obey the divine command every day for thousands of years. What a salutary lesson for man! Let all your actions on earth lead to the same goal of peace and unity as in Heaven. This thought is expressed in a free translation of the concluding words of the *Kaddish*, '*Oseh shalom bimromav.....*' God enjoys peace in the Heavens above; all the heavenly hosts minister to Him loyally and steadfastly. It is our daily prayer that the Almighty in His mercy will bring about a similar unity of purpose and lasting peace to our terrestrial sphere below so that we, too, may enjoy amity, accord and a durable peace.

Hasidic Lore

Torah study. The Medzibozer quoted a maxim of this Mishnah, 'Make yourself fit for the study of Torah, since the knowledge of it is not an inheritance of yours'. How does this saying harmonise with the verse: My words which I have put in your mouth shall not depart out of your mouth, nor out of the mouth of your seed' (Is. 59:21)? Does not this verse indicate that the words shall be inherited by our offspring? The answer is that the desire to learn Torah is often inherited, but it is fitting that each man should not merely repeat what others have said, but that he should originate new thoughts in the Torah; for this task a man must qualify.

Heaven. R. Yerahmiel said: Let no one be hesitant to serve the Lord because the way seems too high for him. At first, every way is as high as the Heavens above; yet, after labouring to achieve your aspiration, it will become near to you. Then you will be shown new ways beyond the skies, to which again you should aspire. Begin in a modest way; maintain an earnest effort to reach higher and higher realms, and before your demise you will have attained undreamed of heights of perfection.

(יח) רַבִּי שִׁמְעוֹן אוֹמֵר הֱוֵי זָהִיר בִּקְרִיאַת שְׁמַע וּבִתְפִלָּה. וּכְשֶׁאַתָּה מִתְפַּלֵּל אַל תַּעַשׂ תְּפִלָּתְךָ קֶבַע אֶלָּא רַחֲמִים וְתַחֲנוּנִים לִפְנֵי הַמָּקוֹם שֶׁנֶּאֱמַר כִּי חַנּוּן וְרַחוּם הוּא אֶרֶךְ אַפַּיִם וְרַב חֶסֶד וְנִחָם עַל הָרָעָה. וְאַל תְּהִי רָשָׁע בִּפְנֵי עַצְמֶךָ:

Mishnah Eighteen

R. Simeon says: Be careful in the reading of the Shema and the Amidah; when you pray, do not make your prayer a fixed form but (an appeal for) mercy and grace before God, as it is said, 'For He is gracious and merciful, longsuffering and abounding in mercy and repents Him of the evil' (Joel 2:13), and be not wicked in your own esteem.

The main burden of this Mishnah is the correct approach towards prayer which has been called 'an ascent of the mind to God'. Prayer is a natural outpouring of the heart of man. From the dawn of civilisation, man has groped and searched for a way to commune with, petition, and adore the Master of the Universe whom man worships with awe, wonder and mystery. Prayer has replaced sacrifice in the Temple, and as sacrifice was offered at certain times in the day, so our Rabbis attached importance to the hour of prayer. Thus the very first question discussed in the Talmud was: At what hour do we recite the Shema? (Ber. 1:1). For this reason our Mishnah opens with the warning to be careful to read the Shema at the prescribed time. It is also understandable why the Mishnah specifically mentions the Shema and the Amidah as the two representative prayers of our liturgy, for they are the twin pillars upon which the superstructure of the Prayer-Book is built and they act as a bridge connecting heaven and earth in the same manner as the ladder of Jacob joined heaven to earth.

Shema. The first six words which form the introduction to the three sections of this prayer, accompany the Jew from the cradle to the grave. They are the first words which a child lisps and the last words as man gasps his final breath. Every day commences and concludes with the Shema. Apart from its inclusion in the statutory services morning and evening, the Shema is recited when the Torah Scroll is taken out of the Ark, in the *Kedushah* of the Musaph Amidah on Shabbat and Festivals and at the conclusion of the Yom Kippur Service. The agonizing cry which falls from the lips of countless martyrs in Jewish history is the Shema, the confession of faith in the justice of God. We should remember that the Shema is a very ancient prayer (Deut. 6:4) which underlines the monotheistic concept of God and, according to tradition, was uttered by the sons of Jacob when the Patriarch expired.

Tefillah. The Synagogue has a variety of names, one of which is *Bet Hatefillah*, the House of Prayer, and the Prayer Book is known as *Seder Tefillah*, order of prayer, but the word Tefillah when alone, refers to the Amidah, the standing prayer; it is also known as *Shemoneh Esrei*, the eighteen blessings (subsequently extended to nineteen). Indeed, the Amidah is the main prayer of the daily morning, afternoon and evening Services. It is the backbone of our liturgy, preceded and followed by additional prayers. As the Shema is old, so is the Amidah; it was first introduced by the Men of the Great Synagogue in the fourth century B.C.E. It was added to and edited by Rabban Gamliel II, after the destruction of the Second Temple (Ber. 4:3).

Mitpalel. The root of the word is *palel*, which means to judge oneself. As the judge must be impartial and honest, so the person who prays should not attempt to bribe God by petitioning Him; man should submit his human will to the will of God. It is a great ethical concept to do justice to ourselves when we pray. This may be one reason why we include the subject of prayer in our collection of ethical sayings. Moreover, prayer is a great leveller; God does not distinguish between rich and poor, scholarly and ignorant. The story is told of an ignorant Jew who had forgotten how to pray, but was irresistibly drawn to the Synagogue on Rosh Hashanah. All he remembered from his youth were the first four letters of the Hebrew alphabet and so he muttered them again and again. We are told that God accepted his prayer because he recited the letters sincerely, and with a contrite heart.

Do not make your prayer a fixed form. Prayer should not become a mechanical exercise, but an active and voluntary entreaty issuing from the heart. The Talmud (Ber. 29b) fully discusses the meaning of *keva*, fixed, used here. It can refer to those who pray in a perfunctory manner; it can signify anyone who is not able to add something new. R. Zera admitted that he was able to compose new material, but he was afraid that he might become confused. Spontaneity in prayer developed into a fixed form.

'The number of prayers has not been prescribed by the Torah, nor has the wording of this prayer been fixed by the Torah, nor has any time been determined for it by the Torah.... a person should, according to his ability, offer up supplication and pray daily.... so the practice obtained from Moses our Teacher to Ezra. After the Jews had been exiled by the wicked Nebukhadnezzar, they mingled with the Persians and Greeks and other nations.... no one was able in his speech to express himself adequately in a single language, without making mistakes. When Ezra and his Bet Din perceived the situation, they arose and instituted eighteen consecutive blessings.... for this reason they ordained that all the blessings and prayers should be orderly in the mouth of all Israel, so that the subject of each blessing should be prepared even for those defective in speech' (Mishnah Torah, Laws of Prayer, chapter 1, Halakhot 1-5, Maim.). From this extract we learn that spontaneity in prayer was the norm in biblical times and it was superseded by a fixed formula through our exile. Another essential ingredient in prayer is *kavannah*, an intense concentration and devotion to prayer. This *kavannah* is more evident in spontaneous prayer and more often absent in fixed prayer, which comes trippingly off the tongue.

Elsewhere (1:15) we connected the word *keva* with the mezuzah blessing (likboa). We would therefore add another dimension to the meaning of *keva* vis-a-vis the mezuzah. The mezuzah is a fixture and does not need to be examined for long periods of time. Prayer is very different; prayer needs *kavannah*, continuous personal examination and heart-felt devotion. Therefore the Mishnah advises, 'Do not make a fixed form of prayer'. Torah in general is fixed and unchangeable like the mezuzah, but prayer is in a different category and should not be compared with the mezuzah. R. Jacob Ben Asher quotes his father, the Rosh (1250-1327), who declared, 'One should be careful not to recite a Tefillah as a free-will offering, unless he introduces a fresh insight. One also has to appraise one's own self as being in an alert and watchful state and judge that he is able to concentrate upon his prayer from beginning to end' (Tur Orah Hayyim, chapter 107).

The proof text from Joel mentioned in the Mishnah suggests that the fixed form of prayer may be impersonal and lack an emotional appeal. We should rather imitate the Almighty and impregnate our prayers with grace, compassion and mercy. In this manner, our prayers will become a moving and ecstatic experience.

Be not wicked in your own esteem. This rule seems to be out of place in a Mishnah dealing with prayer. As we have explained, prayer is the vehicle of expression whereby a man communes with God and this offers him peace of mind; leaning on God, man unburdens himself. The wicked man, however, crowds God out of his existence, he cannot pray, he isolates himself and denies the saving grace of repentance which every Jew can enjoy. Self-criticism can be healthy, but self-hatred — being wicked in one's own esteem — is an unhealthy and devastating philosophy. The ideal set by the Rabbis is as follows: Let a man look upon himself as if he were half righteous and half wicked. When he performs a good deed, he has placed himself and the whole world on the balance of merit. But when he regards himself as wicked, he despairs of doing any good, so he grows more and more wicked (Kid. 40b).

Hasidic Lore

Reciting prayer. The Riziner Rabbi said that those who pray in great haste, swallowing their words, do so because of their great anxiety and eagerness to worship the Almighty. Those people who recite their prayers slowly, deliberately lingering lovingly over every word, do so because they love their prayers so much, that they do not wish to conclude their prayers too quickly.

(יט) רַבִּי אֶלְעָזָר אוֹמֵר הֱוֵי שָׁקוּד לִלְמוֹד תּוֹרָה וְדַע מַה שֶּׁתָּשִׁיב לְאֶפִּיקוֹרוֹס וְדַע לִפְנֵי מִי אַתָּה עָמֵל וּמִי הוּא בַּעַל מְלַאכְתְּךָ שֶׁיְּשַׁלֶּם לְךָ שְׂכַר פְּעֻלָּתֶךָ:

Mishnah Nineteen

R. Eleazar says: Be eager to learn Torah and know what answer to give to the unbeliever; know also before whom you toil and who is the Employer of your work, to give you the reward of your work.

Shakud. The root of this word means 'to be watchful, studious and energetic'. The word can be interpreted either in the sense of Jer. 1:12, 'For I am watchful over My word to perform it', meaning quick and energetic, or it can signify regularity and conformity with the teaching of the Wise, as in Prov. 8:34, 'Watching daily at my gates'. Similarly, a *shakdan* is an industrious and scrupulously honest student who reaches a very high level of scholarship. The meaning of the Mishnah is therefore clear and decisive; it emphasises the primacy of the Torah on all levels, but it goes beyond this when it underlines the second clause. When the Jew is thoroughly versed and immersed in every branch of Jewish knowledge and he is loyal to the observance of the precepts, he can qualify to be a Defender of the Faith, and with courage and conviction he will answer the unbeliever. It has been suggested that R. Eleazar's advocacy of eagerness and enthusiasm in the study of Torah was due to the lesson he had learnt from his own experience, when after the death of his master R. Johanan Ben Zakkai, he refused to join his fellow disciples and decided to reside in Emmaus because it was a pleasant resort, and in the course of a short period of time he forgot his learning.

Epicuros. This term was originally used to designate a follower of Epicuros, 342 B.C.E., whose philosophy was that happiness and the pursuit of pleasure were the aim and goal in life. Later the word was applied by the Rabbis to designate an unbeliever, freethinker or heretic. In the Talmud (Sanh. 99b) a number of explanations are given for *epicuros*. It can refer to one who despises scholarship, or one who interprets the Torah slanderously. In Sanh. 38b, a debate is permitted only with a gentile non-believer. Rashi observes that discussion with a Jewish non-believer is inadvisable, since he is deliberate in his negation of Torah ideology and will not be easily dissuaded. Maimonides derives the word from the Hebrew *hefkar* meaning free, ownerless, and he defines an epicuros as one who refuses to obey the Law, whilst Shechter remarks, 'It implies rather a frivolous treatment of the word of Scripture and Tradition.'

Da ma shetashiv, know what to answer. These three Hebrew words have become a proverbial saying in Jewish life and are addressed to every Jew. Know, not superficially or shallowly, some of the beliefs and practices of the Jewish faith, but make an intensive and profound study of Judaism. The literal translation of these words is not 'know how to answer', but more correctly, 'know what you shall answer'. You must satisfy yourself that your knowledge is deep-seated, not lacking in depth or sincerity.

Know before whom you toil. The reward is according to the labor or toil. The word *amal*, to toil, means to take pains in effecting the work undertaken and is especially applied to those who study the Law. It is interesting to compare the expression here with the prayer uttered by Nehunya Ben Hakkanah who, on leaving the Synagogue, thanked God that his portion was with those who sit in the House of Study. 'I and they (idlers) labour, *amal*, but I labour and receive a reward, whereas they labour and receive no reward' (Ber. 28b).

Employer. We are all servants and not slaves of God, the Employer, whom we serve as our Master. It is ironical that some tend to denigrate the working man, the *baal melakhah*. We have elsewhere referred to the dignity of labour in Jewish thought and the high regard in which it is held. Here, God Himself bears the honourable title *Baal Melakhah*, the Master of work or Employer.

Hasidic Lore

Know how to answer the unbeliever. The Belzer Rabbi said: We find that Pharaoh's magicians were able to perform, by their secret arts, the miracles of turning water into blood and of bringing up frogs. The other miracles, they were unable to duplicate. The question arises, 'Why did the Lord cause Moses to perform miracles that could be duplicated by magic? Could He not have enjoined that all the ten plagues be beyond imitation?' The answer is as follows, 'The Lord knew that in later times unbelievers might arise and contend that the Egyptian soothsayers were possessed of little sagacity and hence Moses was able to deceive them. We, however, would not have been victims of this chicanery'. Then, we believers might retort, 'If you are wiser than the Egyptian sages, accomplish at least as much as they. Turn water into blood and bring up frogs. If you cannot do this, you must admit their superiority and at the same time recognise that they acknowledge the divine power resident in the acts of Moses'.

רַבִּי טַרְפוֹן אוֹמֵר הַיּוֹם קָצֵר וְהַמְּלָאכָה מְרֻבָּה וְהַפּוֹעֲלִים עֲצֵלִים וְהַשָּׂכָר הַרְבֵּה וּבַעַל הַבַּיִת דּוֹחֵק:

Mishnah Twenty

R. Tarfon says: The day is short and the work is plentiful, the labourers are sluggish and the reward is much and the Master of the house is urgent.

R. Tarfon a priest was known as 'The teacher of Israel' because of his erudition. He combined wealth with humility and kindness, and was famed for his charitable deeds. He was a contemporary of R. Akiva.

The day is short. The day is our unit of time. We measure life by days, 'Teach us to number our days' (Ps. 90:12), and when the Psalmist mentions that the span of life is seventy he introduces the statement with the words, 'The days of our years are three score and ten' (90:10); he counts the years by 'days'. The question has been posed, if a day consists of twenty four hours and all days are of similar duration, how is it possible to envisage a short or a long day? It is a trite remark that the busy person will find the time to pursue an infinite variety of tasks, whereas the lazy person finds the day too short to accomplish anything of worth.

The work is plentiful. In reality, the work is not much, but as we tend to postpone the task, study or mitzvah at hand, we find ourselves overpowered by the manifold duties that demand our attention. If we divided our days into well defined compartments, we should find ample time to satisfy all our needs, material and spiritual.

The workers are sluggish. People are lazy for a variety of reasons. One person is indolent because he feels that there is plenty of time to fulfil the task; another finds that his duty seems either too simple or too difficult; again, others are lazy because either the wages are insufficient or because there is no supervision. R. Tarfon replies by reminding us that time is short and precious and the reward is much and we are always supervised by God.

Referring to the sluggard, Solomon said: I went by the field of the slothful, and by the vineyard of the man void of understanding; and, lo, it was all grown over with thistles, the face thereof was covered with nettles, and the stone wall thereof was broken down. Then I beheld, and considered well; I saw, and received instruction. Yet a little sleep, a little slumber, a litle folding of the hands to sleep.... (Prov. 24:30-33).

The Yalkut Shimoni, on the above verses, elaborates in the following words: The phrase 'it was all grown over with thistles' is a figurative description of the state of mind of the man who cannot understand the meaning of a *parshah* in the Torah. 'Nettles had covered the face thereof' implies that the man who has made no effort to know the law will render unclean that which is clean, and clean that which is unclean, and thus break down the 'fence' set up by the Sages..... The evil which befalls the sluggard comes, not at once, but gradually and unawares; he is drawn into one evil after another until he finds himself steeped in wrong-doing. He begins by not exerting himself sufficiently; he then fails to give enough effort to the teaching of the Torah. If the evil consequences were to stop at this point, they would be bad enough; but they grow worse because as he attempts to elucidate any portion or chapter, he is bound to misinterpret the words of the Torah, to pervert the truth, to transgress the ordinances and to break down the 'fences', so that in the end he suffers the destruction which is the punishment awaiting him who breaks down the 'fences'.

The reward is much. The knowledge of Torah is its own reward when it is acquired by diligent work; the more penetrating our learning is, the greater the reward.

The Master of the house. God is known by a variety of names. This title, the Master of the house, is a popular description of God found in the Aggadah according to Marmorstein, who offers several examples; we shall quote one. R. Helbo portrays the relation of God to Israel in the parable of the orphan and the master of the house. The orphan was supplied with everything by the master, but the orphan boasted that he had deserved all by his own work and in lieu of his wages. The master of the house said, 'Truly all that you enjoyed is for the pail of water you have drawn and for the piece of wood you have hewn, but your real wages are kept by me'. God is the Master of the house, Israel the orphan, the goods of this world for the suffering, but real reward is kept for the world to come (Deut. R. 3:7). Man, who should imitate God, must also act as a true master of the house and guide and direct the members of the family to lead righteous lives.

Hasidic Lore

The world to come. On a frosty winter night a man reached the little town of Lekhivitz, where R. Phineas (later of Frankfurt) presided over the community. The traveller, frost-bitten and disconsolate, looked about him for a house of rest and comfort. He saw from afar, a little dwelling and a room alight within — the house of the Rabbi. He knocked at the window and begged for leave to warm himself before the fire.... R. Phineas opened the door for the unknown guest, gave him food and drink and agreeable lodging. The man secretly thought, 'What a world of good and evil fortunes — the Rabbi dwells in peace and security, whilst I must journey wearily in search for bread'. The next morning he enquired of the Rabbi, 'Since I am a poor labourer and suffer hardships in this world, am I certain of a share in the world to come?'

The Rabbi replied: Your horse has the better title than yourself to share in the world to come, if we follow your way of thinking. At this moment you are taking your ease before a comfortable fire, whereas your horse, God's creature like yourself and even a harder worker than you, stands out of doors in the cold, ready to carry you wherever you choose without complaining.

(כא) הוּא הָיָה אוֹמֵר לֹא עָלֶיךָ הַמְּלָאכָה לִגְמוֹר וְלֹא אַתָּה בֶן חוֹרִין לְהִבָּטֵל מִמֶּנָּה. אִם לָמַדְתָּ תּוֹרָה הַרְבֵּה נוֹתְנִין לְךָ שָׂכָר הַרְבֵּה. וְנֶאֱמָן הוּא בַּעַל מְלַאכְתְּךָ שֶׁיְּשַׁלֶּם לְךָ שְׂכַר פְּעֻלָּתֶךָ וְדַע שֶׁמַּתַּן שְׂכָרָן שֶׁל צַדִּיקִים לֶעָתִיד לָבֹא:

Mishnah Twenty One

He used to say: It is not your duty to complete the work but neither are you free to desist from it; if you have studied much Torah, much reward will be given to you; and faithful is your Employer to pay you the reward of your labour; and know that the grant of reward unto the righteous will be in the time to come.

It is not your duty to complete the work.

When we are faced with a seemingly intractable problem, we often refuse to tackle it. How to approach a formidable assignment is explained by the Rabbis in a parable. In the estate of a certain king there was a huge pit, and the king directed that workmen should fill it. Many applied to undertake the work; some labourers, on beholding the enormous chasm, desisted from beginning what they thought was an impossible task; others were more sensible; they were pleased to have employment and were ready to accept a fair day's wage for a day's faithful work.

Some of us treat life and its manifold problems as a yawning chasm, and we refuse to face up to the tasks ahead of us; we are overpowered and lose courage. R. Tarfon's philosophy is very healthy and timely. It is not our duty to complete the work, but we must not free ourselves from actively participating in it. We must not shirk the personal responsibility which devolves upon each of us. If this is true of the physical world about us, it is also true of the spiritual treasures handed down to us from generation to generation. The Talmud, with its commentaries and super-commentaries, has been compared to the oceans, which are unfathomable. Few, if any, can master all the intricacies and subtleties of the vast mass of Jewish Law and Tradition; but we must rededicate our energies every day, even if the task is not completed. Life, in all its varied stages, is an unfinished symphony. No individual can complete the work; this we leave to our children, and they to their children, ad infinitum. Even the great Moses was unable to complete his mission in life and enter the land of Canaan. He could only see it from a distance; his dream was not realised.

The reward of the righteous. The Mishnah uses two words in connection with reward. One is *notenim*, giving, and the other is *meshalmim*, paying. In addition to the monetary reward, *meshalmim*, we also receive a spiritual bonus, *notenim*, in the form of peace of mind and inner satisfaction, so that through learning much Torah and imparting it to others, we are helping to preserve Torah for all times. For this reason the righteous receive *mattan sakhar*, a divine gift (*mattan* is connected with *mattanah*, a gift). Such a present or reward is based on faith, which explains the expression, 'Faithful is your Employer to give the righteous their proper deserts; if not here, in the Hereafter, in the Messianic Era'.

Hasidic Lore

Work. Said R. Yerahmiel: It is written (Ex. 23:25), 'And you shall serve the Lord your God, and He will bless your bread'. It may be asked why the verse begins in the plural and ends in the singular. The answer is that each one who labours that another person may likewise serve the Lord, shall be blessed.

Concluding Mishnah. Text, translation and commentary, see Page 71.

PEREK THREE

Introductory Mishnah. Text, translation and commentary on p. 11.

פרק שלישי

(א) **עֲקַבְיָא** בֶּן מַהֲלַלְאֵל אוֹמֵר הִסְתַּכֵּל בִּשְׁלֹשָׁה דְבָרִים וְאֵין אַתָּה בָא לִידֵי עֲבֵירָה. דַּע מֵאַיִן בָּאתָ וּלְאָן אַתָּה הוֹלֵךְ וְלִפְנֵי מִי אַתָּה עָתִיד לִתֵּן דִּין וְחֶשְׁבּוֹן. מֵאַיִן בָּאתָ מִטִּפָּה סְרוּחָה. וּלְאָן אַתָּה הוֹלֵךְ לִמְקוֹם עָפָר רִמָּה וְתוֹלֵעָה. וְלִפְנֵי מִי אַתָּה עָתִיד לִתֵּן דִּין וְחֶשְׁבּוֹן לִפְנֵי מֶלֶךְ מַלְכֵי הַמְּלָכִים הַקָּדוֹשׁ בָּרוּךְ הוּא:

Mishnah One

Akavya Ben Mahalalel says: Reflect on three things and you will not come within the power of sin. Know whence you came and whither you are going and before whom you will in the future have to give an account and reckoning. Whence you came - from a putrefying drop; whither you are going - to a place of dust, worms and maggots; and before whom you will in the future have to give an account and reckoning — before the King of the King of Kings, the Holy One blessed be He.

Akavya Ben Mahalalel was probably the oldest contemporary of Rabban Johanan Ben Zakkai (middle of the first century). On his death bed Johanan Ben Zakkai also described God as the King of Kings, the Holy One blessed be He (Ber. 28 b). Akavya emphasised personal merit. Shortly before he passed away, he advised his son, 'Your own deeds will cause you to be near, and your own deeds will cause you to be far'; in other words, your own deeds will bring you near to men, and your own deeds will drive you away from them.

Reflect on three things. The three rules should be examined as one entity; to consider one without the other would be ineffective. Each one is buttressed by the other and together they become comprehensible.

The power of sin. Literally the hands of sin. As a handle of a vessel is outside the vessel, so the hand of sin is exposed. When a person reflects on these three rules, he will not even be in touch with the hand of sin. We make a clear distinction between a technical error (the hand of sin) and a habitual criminal in the grip of the evil impulse, who cannot extricate himself. The latter is enslaved to and ruled by sin. We are warned not to fall into the clutches of sin. This introduction to Akavya's maxim runs through the whole gamut of Jewish life from conception (a putrefying drop) until the grave (a place of worms). This is summed up in one word, Halakhah, which should accompany us from birth to death.

Know whence you came. One cannot improve on Luzatto's ethical presentation of our Mishnah in his Mesillat Yesharim: These thoughts counteract pride and make for humility. If a man were to bear in mind the ignoble nature of his origin, he would understand the worthless character of his bodily substance and he would realise why he should not be proud, but rather ashamed and abashed. He will return to dust; surely then would his pride be humbled and his arrogance forgotten.

If we always recalled our immediate past and gratefully acknowledged the miracle of our individual origin and existence, it would also help us to acknowledge the miracle of our collective survival.

This leads us to the historical interpretation of the words 'Know whence you came'. We are a people of history, links in an endless chain of tradition. We cannot detach ourselves from the past with its sublime teachings and eternal truths. In our prayers we constantly remember the Patriarchs, the founders of our People and our Faith. Compare Is. 51: 1-2: Look unto the rock whence you were hewn and to the hole of the pit whence you were digged. Look unto Abraham your father and unto Sarah who bore you.

Whither you are going. Whilst it is commendable to remember the past with its firm and impregnable foundations on which Judaism is built, it is no less vital to be aware of the present. Every Jew should ask himself, What is he doing now to preserve Judaism for the future? Where are you going, are you merely drifting, or planning now for tomorrow so that others may emulate your example and be inspired to traverse the path of rectitude? What is your goal and destiny in life? The Dubner Maggid tells the story of a wagon driver who lost his way on a cold and wet winter night. In the morning he realised that he had taken the wrong road and wept because the wheels of his wagon had left an impression in the thick mud and would mislead others to drive off the beaten track.

Before whom you will in the future..... After dealing with the two visible reactions wherefrom and whereto, Akavya details the wherein, the invisible act of God in which He judges man when he stands before Him in the Hereafter. Büchler rightly point out that 'Stress is laid, not on the alleged terror of the reckoning, but upon the person of the Judge, who sees the most secret action of man and whose attention nothing escapes, and that is why the scholar describes His power and not the method of His judgment or punishment'.

Account and reckoning. Life should be so conducted that we should be prepared to give an account of all our actions before God and man. A spiritual reckoning is called *heshbon hanefesh,* which is unfortunately lacking amongst many. This plays an important role in Jewish life and involves self-scrutiny and self-evaluation, which every person should practise throughout his life. Those who regularly adopt this course are commended by God and are called 'men with a reckoning' (Zohar Nu. 178). One writer commenting on Nu. 21:27, 'Therefore the *moshelim* shall say 'Come to *Heshbon*', translates the verse as follows: Those that rule over their impulses shall say, 'Come, let us render an account of life' (Mesillat Yesharim).

The story is told of a certain Sage who went to a physician noted for his wisdom and his saintly character, and asked him for a prescription for healing the ills of the soul since he was spiritually sick. The physician answered: Take roots of humility together with leaves of hope and expectation and add to them twigs of Torah with roses of wisdom and place them all in the mortar of repentance, and grind them well with wisdom and love and pour in some reverence too. Then place it in a pot and light under it the fire of thankfulness and when it is cooked, wrap it in a cloth of prudence and shake it through the sieve of truth and faith and drink it in the cup of the will, never to revert to that evil behaviour, and then you will be cured (Shevilei Emunah).

Heshbon. *Heshbon* can also mean a business account. Honesty and integrity are often stressed in the Torah. Here we are warned that our financial transactions must conform to the *din.* The first question man is asked in the Hereafter is, 'Have you dealt honourably in business?' (Shab. 31 a).

The central thought and logical order of Akavya's teaching is summed up in one word, - as can be seen from the following comment on Ec. 12:1: Remember your Creator, *Borekha*. R. Akiva interprets this word in three ways: Remember your source,*beerekha*, your grave, *borkha*, and your Creator, *Borekha* (Ec. R. 12:1).

A putrefying drop. This teaches the equality of man. The royal prince and the unknown pauper stem from the same amoeba.

Place of dust. Man emerges from and returns to the dust. The word *makom*, place, should not be overlooked. Man finds his eternal rest in a place of dust. Man's remains should not be cremated and cast to the winds or collected in a casket. They should be buried in a 'place' of earth, *afar*, and worms.

The Holy One blessed be He. Marmorstein is of the opinion that this title of God 'is a later addition to distinguish between God and the Roman or another Emperor who aspired to this honoured and ancient title.

Hasidic Lore

Fear of God. Said the Koretzer: When a man injures or abuses you, it does not lie within your rights to revenge yourself. It is as if a man stood in the presence of a king, and another smote him on the cheek. The only course open to him is to keep silent. The king witnessed the blow, and, if he believes the man deserved it at the hands of his neighbour, the injured person cannot go counter to the king's wish. If the king, however, believes the blow was undeserved, he will surely punish the offender. In the same manner remember that you are always in the presence of the King of Kings. He will inflict punishment upon your adversary if you are undeservedly abused by him.

A thinker asked the Besht: Why are we enjoined to fear the King of Kings when it is known that we stand in fear of a mortal king without any command? The master replied: The fear we have of a mortal king is but an outer fear; a fear of lacking or losing a material thing. After the loss has occurred, we are no longer in fear of him. Such a fear is common to men and beasts. We, however, are enjoined to have an inner fear of the Lord: a fear of lacking proper attachment to God. Such a fear is terminated only by our death. 'A man without inner fear is spiritually dead'.

(ב) רַבִּי חֲנִינָא סְגַן הַכֹּהֲנִים אוֹמֵר הֱוֵי מִתְפַּלֵּל בִּשְׁלוֹמָהּ שֶׁל מַלְכוּת שֶׁאִלְמָלֵא מוֹרָאָהּ אִישׁ אֶת רֵעֵהוּ חַיִּים בְּלָעוֹ:

Mishnah Two.

R. Hanina, the Vice-High Priest, says: Pray for the welfare of the government because were it not for the fear thereof, men would swallow each other alive.

R. Hanina was born about 20 C. E and is believed to have survived the fall of Jerusalem.

Segan. Next in rank to the High Priest. Schurer says that he was the captain of the Temple whose duty it was to superintend arrangements for keeping order in and around the Temple. He was also present at all important functions in which the High Priest participated. Today we have an echo of one of these functions; the person standing at the reading desk when the cantillation of the Torah takes place, is called *Segan* (Yoma 7:1, So. 7:7-8).

Pray for the welfare of the government. Travers Herford restricts the meaning of the word *malkhut*, translated as government, and states that it refers to the Roman government, but this injunction to pray for the welfare of the government did not originate in the Mishnaic period. The Prophet Jeremiah clearly asks us 'to seek the peace of the city whither I have caused you to be carried away captive and pray unto the Lord for it, for in the peace thereof shall you have peace' (29:7). In Ezra (6:10) we are enjoined to pray for the life of the king and of his sons. The loyalty of the Jew to every government has been attested to by history. In the words of R. Jonah, 'A man should pray for the welfare of the whole world and share in the grief of others..... no man ought to offer up supplications and prayers for his own needs only. He should pray on behalf of all men that they enjoy well-being; and in the peace of the government there is peace for the world'. We have always acted on this advice and we offer a prayer for the government of our adopted country during the Service on Sabbaths and Festivals.

The introductory word 'pray' needs clarification. Prayer is not normally an integral part of the political vocabulary; loyalty or allegiance would be expected, yet Hanina asks us to 'pray' for the government. The Tanna of the

Mishnah is probably comparing *malkhut haaretz*, the kingdom on earth, with *malkhut shamayim*, the kingdom in heaven. The heavenly hosts fear and respect the Almighty and are at peace with each other. They do not attempt to swallow up one another. Man on earth does swallow his neighbour, both in the battle-field and on the home front, as it is written: Let us swallow them up alive as the grave (Prov. 1:12). If a prayerful attitude could be infused into the councils of men and the governments of countries, it might bring about a change of heart. We need to implant a bit of heaven into the souls of the political leaders of mankind. We should add that this prayerful wish that the heavenly and earthly governments should merge, does not detract in any way from our absolute recognition and respect for the law of the country. In civil law we are guided by the talmudic dictum of Samuel, *dina d'malkhuta dina*, the law of the country is binding upon us.(B.K. 113b). Graetz observes that Judaism owes to Jeremiah and Samuel the probability of its existence in foreign countries. For instance, evasion of taxation as imposed by any government, is denounced as equivalent to murder, idolatry, incest and profanation of the Sabbath (B. K. 113 a, Ned. 28a).

The correct approach to the government of the day is explicitly given in a remarkable Midrash on Gen. 8:16; quoting the verse in Ec. 8:12. The Tanhuma affirms: The Holy One said unto Israel, 'I adjure you that even though the (Roman) government decrees against you harsh decrees, you shall not rebel against it for anything it decrees, but keep the king's command. However, if it decrees against you to abandon the Torah and the Commandments and deny God, then do not obey it but say unto it, 'I keep the king's laws only in those matters which are necessary for the government'. This statement should be qualified by one overall consideration, that the government in question does not make life for the Jew intolerable. The welfare of the government should include the welfare of all minorities under its aegis.

Hasidic Lore

Loyalty to the state. In his admonitions on Prayer, the Bratzlaver includes and underlines the Scriptural advice to 'Pray for the welfare of the city in which you live'. To strengthen this thought, he adds, 'If you are not at peace with the world, your prayer will not be heard'.

(ג) רַבִּי חֲנַנְיָא בֶּן תְּרַדְיוֹן אוֹמֵר שְׁנַיִם שֶׁיּוֹשְׁבִין וְאֵין בֵּינֵיהֶם דִּבְרֵי תוֹרָה הֲרֵי זֶה מוֹשַׁב לֵצִים. שֶׁנֶּאֱמַר וּבְמוֹשַׁב לֵצִים לֹא יָשָׁב. אֲבָל שְׁנַיִם שֶׁיּוֹשְׁבִין וְיֵשׁ בֵּינֵיהֶם דִּבְרֵי תוֹרָה שְׁכִינָה שְׁרוּיָה בֵּינֵיהֶם. שֶׁנֶּאֱמַר אָז נִדְבְּרוּ יִרְאֵי יְהֹוָה אִישׁ אֶל רֵעֵהוּ וַיַּקְשֵׁב יְהֹוָה וַיִּשְׁמָע וַיִּכָּתֵב סֵפֶר זִכָּרוֹן לְפָנָיו לְיִרְאֵי יְהֹוָה וּלְחֹשְׁבֵי שְׁמוֹ. אֵין לִי אֶלָּא שְׁנַיִם מִנַּיִן אֲפִילוּ אֶחָד שֶׁיּוֹשֵׁב וְעוֹסֵק בַּתּוֹרָה שֶׁהַקָּדוֹשׁ בָּרוּךְ הוּא קוֹבֵעַ לוֹ שָׂכָר שֶׁנֶּאֱמַר יֵשֵׁב בָּדָד וְיִדֹּם כִּי נָטַל עָלָיו:

Mishnah Three

R. Hananya Ben Teradyon says: When two sit together and there are no words of Torah between them, it is a session of scorners, as it is said, 'Nor do they sit in the seat of the scornful' (Ps. 1:1). But when two sit together and there are between them words of Torah, the Shekhinah rests between them, as it is said, 'They who feared the Lord spoke one to another and the Lord hearkened and heard and there was written a book of remembrance before Him for them who feared the Lord and thought upon His name' (Mal. 3:15). Now I know it is so for two; how do we know that even when one sits studying the Torah, the Holy One blessed be He fixes a reward for him? As it is said, 'Let him sit alone and be silent, for he has taken (the reward) upon him' (Lam. 3:28).

R. Hananya Ben Teradyon was one of the martyrs about whom we read in the Yom Kippur liturgy. His execution is described in A.Z. 18b. He left a wife and four children, and his daughter Beruriah became the wife of R. Meir.

When two sit together and there are no words of Torah between them. Learning is so highly exalted amongst us that we introduce Torah even in our every day conversation; at all times we should maintain a high level of conversation. The Rabbis have coined a special term for this, *sihat hullin*, ordinary talk; this was of such a degree that it required study (A.Z. 19b). In support of this the Talmud quotes Ps. 1:3, 'Whose leaf does not wither and whatsoever he does shall prosper'. The table talk of the learned is here compared to the leaves, the least productive item of the tree. However, the art of conversation is also part of the Tree of

Life and was encouraged especially when it was interspersed with *divrei Torah*, words of Torah. This does not mean that we should exhibit an air of intellectual superiority and exclude the unlearned from our company. The *Sefer Hasidim* rules that if we have a guest we should not speak to him about learned matters if he is unable to participate. We should add that *divrei Torah* might also include a discussion on ways and means of strenthening the work of the Synagogue and its ancillary institutions. Indeed, if the conversation veers round any aspect of Torah ideology, it would certainly not be classed as the 'seat of the scornful', which is the direct antithesis of cultured and refined conversation.

The scornful. The proof-text is derived from the first chapter of the Book of Psalms and it should be noted that it refers to three types of people, the wicked, the sinful and the scornful, and the last is considered the most despicable because the scoffer takes a sadistic delight in ridiculing and undermining the religious observer. The Rabbis were critical of the scoffer, and one teacher remarks, 'He who scoffs at the Commandments will end in *Gehinnom*, hell' (A. Z. 18b).

When there are words of Torah the Shekhinah rests..... Torah unites two people and each contributes to the elucidation of the problem which is being discussed. 'Two are better than one because they have a good reward for their labour' (Ec. 4:9). The word *Shekhinah* is derived from a root meaning to dwell, and is a name applied to God. Marmorstein suggests that it is possible that the people, after the destruction of the Temple, popularised this name in order to indicate that in spite of the loss of the Temple and the Land, the Divine Presence still existed in Israel. Compare the talmudic maxim, 'There are four classes of men who will never receive the face of the *Shekhinah*, scoffers, liars, hypocrites and calumniators' (Sanh. 103a).

The proof-text advanced by the Mishnah commences with the word *nidberu* in the *niphal* conjugation and is used in a reciprocal sense; they spoke one with another. This emphasises an important principle; that in a discussion on Torah two people should treat each other with equal respect and mutual consideration. *Ish el reyehu*, each looks on the other as a friend, though they may disagree on a point of law. This leads us to another interpretation of the word *nidberu*, the root of which is *daber* and signifies a reproof whilst *amar* is used of gentle speech. Those who fear God and discuss a halachic problem or participate in a talmudic dissertation, cannot treat the subject in a casual or dispassionate manner. The subject matter is dear to them and of great importance, and in the course of discussion they may raise voices and employ every dialectical method to prove their thesis. This demands daber. Emphatic words are more effective than restrained speech, *amar*.

The Lord hearkened and heard. We, who imitate God, learn a vital lesson from the juxtaposition of the two verbs, one of which may seem superfluous. *Kashav* means to incline, attend. In a discussion on Torah we should, in the first place, apply our minds to give our undivided attention; we are then ready to listen. If we turn to the story of the Shunamite woman in II Kings 4:31, we read that when Gehazi places the staff on the mouth of the child, there was neither voice nor response, *ein kol v'ein kashev;* there was no movement of limb. If we are not attentive and do not respond to Torah in our discussion, we are unable to hear what others are attempting to convey; *kashev* must therefore precede *shama* in order that the discussion be effective. God first hearkened and then listened; we should emulate His example.

When one sits studying the Torah. We have commended the study of Torah with a partner, but we should not infer from this that it is wrong to study Torah alone. Man is never completely alone, God is always at his side. The proof-text is taken from the Book of Lamentations. 'Be silent' suggests that the person here does not plan or act with evil intent; he will not speak slanderously or mischievously, but will quietly sit and meditate on the Torah and thus earn the reward of God.

Hasidic Lore

Conversation. The Bratzlaver said: Every man should frequently converse with his friend on the subject of the fear of the Lord. Each man possesses good qualities which the other lacks. Through such conversation, both receive the benefit of the other's judgment. Often this influence may be transmitted in ordinary conversation.

(ד) רַבִּי שִׁמְעוֹן אוֹמֵר שְׁלֹשָׁה שֶׁאָכְלוּ עַל שֻׁלְחָן אֶחָד וְלֹא אָמְרוּ עָלָיו דִּבְרֵי תוֹרָה כְּאִלּוּ אָכְלוּ מִזִּבְחֵי מֵתִים. שֶׁנֶּאֱמַר כִּי כָּל שֻׁלְחָנוֹת מָלְאוּ קִיא צוֹאָה בְּלִי מָקוֹם. אֲבָל שְׁלֹשָׁה שֶׁאָכְלוּ עַל שֻׁלְחָן אֶחָד וְאָמְרוּ עָלָיו דִּבְרֵי תוֹרָה כְּאִלּוּ אָכְלוּ מִשֻּׁלְחָנוֹ שֶׁל מָקוֹם. שֶׁנֶּאֱמַר וַיְדַבֵּר אֵלַי זֶה הַשֻּׁלְחָן אֲשֶׁר לִפְנֵי יְהֹוָה׃

Mishnah Four.

R. Simeon says: Three who have eaten at one table and have not said over it words of Torah are as if they had eaten of sacrifices of the dead, as it is said, 'For all tables are full of filthy vomit and no place is clean' (Is. 28:8). But three who have eaten at one table and have said over it words of Torah are as if they had eaten from the table of God, as it is said, 'And he said unto me, 'This is the table that is before the Lord' (Ez. 41:22).

R. Simeon Bar Yohai, see 3:9 and 4:14.

Three who have eaten.... This Mishnah introduces us to the correct approach to the family meal in the home. Every aspect of Jewish life is regulated by law and custom. We cannot envisage two people sitting at a meal without having invited a third person to share the meal with them. Hence three is the minimum number for a mezuman, the religious quorum for the appropriate introduction for the Grace after Meals. The number three may also apply to every person who is compounded of three constituent affiliations, father, mother and soul (representing God). These three elements should always be nourished; but if there are no words of Torah, the soul is famished and only the physical side of man is sustained.

Who have eaten. To explain the use of the past tense and not the present, we go to the Talmud (Ta. 5b) where R. Johanan informs us that one should not converse whilst eating because the windpipe might open before the gullet and so endanger life. As it is incorrect and even dangerous to speak during the consumption of food, one should speak words of Torah after the course, hence 'three who have eaten'.

At one table. We treat the table as an altar and so invest the meal with sanctity, and accompany the meal with words of Torah. The inclusion of the word 'one' may seem superfluous, as people normaly eat at one table.

However, when guests or friends, some of whom may come from great distances, sit at a table, partake of kasher food and listen to words of Torah, the table and the company become united as one homogeneous entity. Furthermore, some may have a preference for certain dishes, so that gastronomically they may be divided, but if they hear words of Torah and recite Grace together, they are spiritually unitable and the table is one.

Sacrifices of the dead. Judaism is a religion of joy and happiness, but in the house of mourning study of Torah is forbidden for its own sake. If, therefore, people eat and do not study Torah, it is compared to a meal of mourners, a sacrifice of the dead. Some interpret the 'dead' to refer to idols; compare Ps. 106:28, 'They joined themselves also to Baal Peor (the heathen deity worshipped in Peor - Nu. 23:28) and ate the sacrifice of the dead'. Among pagan and heathen nations, food was placed in the tomb for the dead. Our offering is made to the living; as long as the Temple existed, atonement was made through the Altar. Today we achieve atonement through the table by feeding the poor and needy.

The proof text from Is. 28:8 should be interpreted in its proper context. The previous verse (seven) has a pointed reference to the evils of drink, which was indulged in especially at the end of the vintage season which took place at the time of Sukkot, compare I Sam. 1:13 and Amos 2:8. Drunkenness leads to vomiting and filthy behaviour, hence the strong language of Isaiah.

Bli makom. no place is clean.

Normally food becomes waste matter after it is comsumed, but without Torah the food is considered as waste before it is eaten. This is not its proper place. We can also translate the phrase to mean 'without Godliness'.

This is the table. Ezekiel does not name any other object in the Holy Place besides 'the table'. Indeed, the home is hallowed through the table. We wash our hands (cleanliness is next to Godliness) and we recite the *motzi* blessing, and acknowledge that God is the source of every thing at the table. The food is prepared in accordance with the laws of kashrut, an indispensable adjunct of Jewish life. At the table we recite Kiddush, sing zemirot and invest the meal with gladness and joy; we discuss Jewish learning, thereby introducing Torah outside the Synagogue and Bet Hamidrash, and we recite Grace and underline the importance of gratitude.

At the table we also recite Havdalah, thus concluding the Sabbath and Festival with prayers of sanctification and differentiation. At the table we welcome guests including the mendicant wayfarers who are treated as members of the family, thus upholding the great ideal of *hakhnasat orhim*, hospitality, which, in the words of the Rabbis, is equal to the presence of the Shekhinah. When the table plays its rightful part, it transforms the home into a veritable Temple.

As we have dealt with the table, a few rules on table etiquette, culled from rabbinic literature, would not be out of place.

A guest should not bring with him another uninvited guest.

One should not give food to children without the permission of the host.

A guest should not outstay his welcome.

The host precedes the guest to the house; when leaving, the host follows the guest through the door.

R. Akiva invited students to his home to teach them how to conduct themselves correctly.

Not to lick the fingers nor pick up a large piece of meat and eat it, but to cut it up into small pieces.

Not to wipe a plate with a piece of bread.

Not to eat greedily so that every particle of food is consumed.

Not to belch as this is considered unmannerly.

When sneezing, turn aside; when yawning, cover the mouth with the hands.

After drinking from a glass, it should not be offered to another person.

Not to gulp an entire glass of liquid at one time.

Hasidic Lore

Eating habits. The Bratzlaver said: One who eats more than he needs is worse than an animal. Overeating is the cause of many maladies. When one eats with the motive of gaining bodily strength to serve the Lord, his food becomes incense before God. A man should eat slowly and with etiquette even if he is alone at the table.

The table. On the day of the new moon in the month he was to die, the Rabbi of Apt discussed at his table the death of the righteous man. When he said grace he rose and began to walk back and forth in the room. His face glowed. Then he stopped by the table and said, 'Table, pure table, you will testify in my behalf that I have properly eaten and taught at your board'. Later he bade that his coffin be made from the wood of the table.

(ה) רַבִּי חֲנִינָא בֶּן חֲכִינַאי אוֹמֵר הַנֵּעוֹר בַּלַּיְלָה וְהַמְהַלֵּךְ בַּדֶּרֶךְ יְחִידִי וּמְפַנֶּה לִבּוֹ לְבַטָּלָה הֲרֵי זֶה מִתְחַיֵּב בְּנַפְשׁוֹ:

Mishnah Five.

R. Hanina Ben Hakhinai says: He who is awake in the night and he walks on the way alone and turns his heart to idle matters, he is mortally guilty.

R. Hanina (80-135 C.E.) was a disciple of R. Akiva and was associated with R. Simeon Bar Yohai. He was a master of many languages.

Awake in the night. From a physical angle, the Mishnah warns us against the dangers of insomnia. Sleep is nature's way of reserving our strength. 'God gives His beloved sleep' (Ps. 127:2) and the Talmud states that the night is made for sleep. Incidentally, R. Nahman of Bratzlav advises the sleepless Jew to ponder on our belief in the resurrection of the dead. On the other hand, our Torah literature abounds in aphorisms and sayings encouraging us to study at night. Some, therefore, join the first two clauses. There is nothing inherently wrong in staying awake at night; this is the right time for studying Torah. The danger arises when one idles the evening away and allows the precious hours to slip by without constructive study of Torah. Such a person forfeits his spiritual life; he renders himself guilty of stunting the growth of his soul. If we follow this line of thought, it would complement the previous Mishnah; one should study Torah not only at the table, but also alone at night, whether at home or in the street. Do we not read in the Shema, 'And you shall speak (words of Torah) when you sit in your house and walk by the way?'

We can deduce an entirely different interpretation of the Mishnah if we understand the word *yehidi*, alone, in the sense of selfishness. He who walks on the road of life *yehidi*, thinking only of himself, furthering his own interests to the exclusion of others, forfeits his life. He may be awake at night, but he plans and contrives for his own advancement and ignores others who need guidance and assistance. Such utter selfishness is often allied to vanity, for this person is smugly satisfied with himself and completely disinterested in his community or people. The egoist who walks alone isolates himself and is of no benefit to society; he is oblivious to the needs and wants of his fellow man. The Torah consistently issues the clarion call that we should not walk alone but accompany others, share their problems, and experience their pains and anxieties. Above all, walk with God, 'In all your ways, know Him' (Prov. 3:6).

Yet another interpretation of *yehidi* presents itself when we realise that some observe the laws and customs of our Faith superficially, whilst at home when they are under the surveillance of parents and family for whom they have a certain regard. However, when they leave home and travel *baderekh*, on the road of life, or leave home to get married, they are unseen by parents and remove the thin veneer of religiosity and respectability. At home they ostensibly eat kasher food and attend Synagogue but, when alone, they cast aside their tenuous attachment to Judaism and abrogate many of the laws and customs and unashamedly eat forbidden food and wean themselves away from Synagogue and destroy their souls. The Psalmist warns us against this hypocritical tendency, 'Happy are they who are upright in the way, who walk in the law of the Lord' (119:1). Happy are they who observe the word of God consistently.

Hasidic Lore

The ego. The Zlotzover Maggid commented upon the words, 'I stand between God and you' (Deut. 5:5). He said: A person who thinks of his own importance and of his own ego, entertains an idea which stands between the Lord and himself, he places a barrier, a hedge, between the Godhead and him. The word 'I', only God can utter.

(ו) רַבִּי נְחוּנְיָא בֶּן הַקָּנָה אוֹמֵר כָּל הַמְקַבֵּל עָלָיו עוֹל תּוֹרָה מַעֲבִירִין מִמֶּנּוּ עוֹל מַלְכוּת וְעוֹל דֶּרֶךְ אֶרֶץ. וְכָל הַפּוֹרֵק מִמֶּנּוּ עוֹל תּוֹרָה נוֹתְנִין עָלָיו עוֹל מַלְכוּת וְעוֹל דֶּרֶךְ אֶרֶץ׃

Mishnah Six.

R. Nehunya Ben Ha-Kanah said: Everyone who receives on himself the yoke of Torah, has removed from him the yoke of the kingdom and the yoke of worldly care, but everyone who breaks off from himself the yoke of Torah, there are laid upon him the yoke of the kingdom and the yoke of worldly care.

R. Nehunya lived in the first and second century and survived the fall of Jerusalem. He was a contemporary of R. Johanan Ben Zakkai and the teacher of R. Ishmael Ben Elisha. Despite his wealth, he was noted for his humility and patience. According to Meg. 28a, he attained a ripe old age. He is considered to be the author of a number of short prayers including *Ana bekhoah* which is read during the Friday evening Service.

The yoke of the Torah. The yoke of the animal is placed upon it, not only for service, but also for the purpose of directing it. Similarly with the yoke of the Torah. If one willingly accepts the authority of the Torah, it is no longer a burden but an obligation and responsibility, and it directs the Jew to walk the earth with pride and honour.The Rabbis express this thought beautifully by noting that in biblical days when the portable Ark was carried by the Levites, it was no burden; 'The Ark carried its carriers' (So. 35a). Such is the yoke of the Torah that it carries those who uphold it.

In our Mishnah, however, the yoke of the Torah has an exclusive meaning because it is followed and qualified by the yoke of the kingdom, here the government of Rome which imposed taxes and burdens upon the Jewish people. Büchler deals fully with our Mishnah and says that Nehunya 'advised his colleagues and his disciples to devote themselves wholly to the study of Torah, and to take upon themselves the yoke, the obligation to consecrate their lives to it, as that would relieve them from all the impositions of the Roman administration'. He quotes Maimonides who affirms that the congregation paid the taxes of the scholars who lived and taught in their midst. If this be correct, it would also explain the term 'the yoke of worldly care' in a similar vein. Accepting the yoke of the Torah would remove from the scholar the anxiety of earning a livelihood, for the latter would interfere with his studies and research work.

Everyone who breaks off from himself the yoke of Torah..... The expression *porek ol* has been interpreted in a number of ways. For our purpose we go to the liturgy on Yom Kippur when, during the reading of the *al het*, the list of confessions, we recite, 'For the sin we have committed against Thee by breaking or casting off the yoke'. We can interpret this *al het* to refer to the three types of yoke enumerated in the Mishnah — the yoke of Torah, of the kingdom and of worldly care. A person who will not submit to the Yoke of Torah and refuses to accept its discipline, will be completely dominated by the problems of the government of the day and the means to procure a livelihood. He will become thoroughly assimilated to his surroundings and crowd out from his life every vestige of Jewishness.

Hasidic Lore

The yoke of the people. As the Maggid of Koznitz, sick unto death in the last year before his demise stood and prayed before the Ark on the eve of Yom Kippur, he was silent before he recited the words, 'I forgive'. He then addressed God saying: Lord of the Universe, Thou alone knowest how great is Thy glory, and Thou alone knowest how great is the weakness of my body. And Thou knowest this also, that I have stood before this Ark in prayer this entire month, day after day, not on my behalf but for Thy people Israel. Therefore, I beseech Thee, if it has been easy for me to take upon myself the yoke of Thy people and to perform this service with my suffering body, how can it be burdensome for Thee, unto Whom is omnipotence, to speak two words? Thereupon, in a moment, his countenance was overwhelmed with joy and he cried in a mighty voice, 'He has answered my prayers' and said, 'I have forgiven' (salahti kidvorekha).

(ז) רַבִּי חֲלַפְתָּא בֶּן דּוֹסָא אִישׁ כְּפַר חֲנַנְיָא אוֹמֵר עֲשָׂרָה שֶׁיּוֹשְׁבִין וְעוֹסְקִין בַּתּוֹרָה שְׁכִינָה שְׁרוּיָה בֵינֵיהֶם. שֶׁנֶּאֱמַר אֱלֹהִים נִצָּב בַּעֲדַת אֵל. וּמִנַּיִן אֲפִילוּ חֲמִשָּׁה שֶׁנֶּאֱמַר וַאֲגֻדָּתוֹ עַל אֶרֶץ יְסָדָהּ. וּמִנַּיִן אֲפִילוּ שְׁלשָׁה שֶׁנֶּאֱמַר בְּקֶרֶב אֱלֹהִים יִשְׁפּוֹט. וּמִנַּיִן אֲפִילוּ שְׁנַיִם שֶׁנֶּאֱמַר אָז נִדְבְּרוּ יִרְאֵי יְהוָֹה אִישׁ אֶל רֵעֵהוּ וַיַּקְשֵׁב יְהוָֹה וַיִּשְׁמָע. וּמִנַּיִן אֲפִילוּ אֶחָד שֶׁנֶּאֱמַר בְּכָל הַמָּקוֹם אֲשֶׁר אַזְכִּיר אֶת שְׁמִי אָבֹא אֵלֶיךָ וּבֵרַכְתִּיךָ:

Mishnah Seven.

R. Halafta Ben Dosa of Kfar Hananya says: When ten sit together and are occupied with Torah, the Shekhinah rests amongst them, as it is said, 'God stands in the congregation of the godly' (Ps. 82:1). How do we know that the same is true of five? As it is said, 'And His band He has established on the earth' (Amos 9:6). And how do we know that the same is true of three? As it is said, 'In the midst of the judges, He judges' (Ps. 82:1). How do we know that the same is true of two? As it is said, 'Then they who feared the Lord spoke one to another and the Lord hearkened and heard' (Mal. 3:16). And how do we know that the same is true of one? As it is said, 'In every place where I record My name I will come to you and bless you' (Ex. 20:24).

R. Halafta (2nd. century) was probably a disciple of R. Meir and the Halafta family was of Babylonian extraction.

The village of Hananya was in the district of Galilee; this may explain his concern for a minyan for the village was sparsely inhabited, whereas the study of Torah is obligatory to everyone.

Ten who sit.... These constitute a religious quorum for public worship called *edah*. The Talmud (Sanh. 2a) asks how we know that a congregation consists of not less than ten adult males. It is written, 'How long shall I bear with this evil congregation (edah)'? Excluding Joshua and Caleb, we have ten. See Nu. 14:27 where we read the story of the Twelve Spies; compare also (Meg. 23 b.).

Five. The numbers ten, three, two and one are clearly alluded to in the proof texts mentioned in the Ṃishnah. However, regarding number five, the text from Amos 9:6 does present some apparent difficulty. The word *agudah* is variously translated as vault, or band, something tied together. There is, however, no specific reference to number five. To avoid this difficulty commmentators refer to another version which reverses the texts for five, and three, applying Ps. 82 to five, and Amos 9 to three. Thus we know that monetary cases are adjudicated by three judges; together with the two litigants, we have five. On the other hand, we have Scriptural authority that *agudah* can mean a bundle of three (Ex. 2:2), 'A bundle of hyssop' which consists of three stalks (Mishnah Parah 11:9). Agudah is also used for the binding of the palm branch, myrtlé and willow twigs on Sukkot (Lev. 23:40).

We venture to suggest that the verses in our Mishnah should be retained in their original order. It is possible that Halafta chose numbers ten, five, three, two and one, because he thought of the fingers of the hand. The finger has a sanctity and individuality of its own. The Ten Commandments were written with the 'finger of God' (Ex. 31:18). The number ten, which comprises the fingers of both hands, signifies the highest sanctity in Jewish worship. Halafta therefore commences with ten, *eser*, which is connected with *sar*, a prince. The minyan is a princely figure, the religious quorum for public service is ten. He next proceeds with the figure five, the number of fingers on one hand, and adduces the text from Amos 9:6 which contains the word *agudah*. Closely allied to the word *agudah* is *agudal*, meaning 'thumb'. The root of *agudah* is *agad*, meaning to tie; grammatically it may be inaccurate to connect *agudal* with the same root, but the function of the thumb is to tie down what the hand contains, clasping all five fingers together. This is the meaning of Amos 9:6, 'He founded His vault upon the earth'. Thus, *agudah* implies the tying together of the heaven and earth firmly and securely. We may ask how did God establish His *agudah* on earth.? His upper chambers in the heavens are unseen to the naked eye, but the thumb is firmly established on earth where it performs a unique and most original function. Through the thumb we can detect crime. Such is the finger of God that no two thumbs are identical, an exercise which is utilised in modern criminology. Maimonides does not explicitly make any reference to the thumb, but in explaining the word *agudah* he observes that this word indicates that a number of things are clutched together by the fingers (five) of one hand.

The verses explaining two people and one person are self-explanatory. 'They spoke one to another' refers to two people; 'I will come to you and bless you', refers to one person.

Hasidic Lore

Learn a little. A young man was asked by the Gerer Rabbi if he had learned Torah. 'Just a little', replied the youth. 'That is all anyone has ever learned of the Torah', was the Rabbi's answer.

(ח) רַבִּי אֶלְעָזָר אִישׁ בַּרְתּוֹתָא אוֹמֵר תֶּן לוֹ מִשֶּׁלוֹ שֶׁאַתָּה וְשֶׁלְּךָ שֶׁלוֹ. וְכֵן בְּדָוִד הוּא אוֹמֵר כִּי מִמְּךָ הַכֹּל וּמִיָּדְךָ נָתַנּוּ לָךְ:

Mishnah Eight.

R. Eleazar, a man of Bertota says: Give unto Him of that which is His for you and what you have, are His. So it is in the case of David, who said, 'For, all things come of Thee and of Thine own we have given Thee' (I Chron. 29:14).

R. Eleazar of Bertota, in Upper Gálilee, practised what he preached. His maxim permeated every fibre of his body and he was prepared to give back in charity everything he possessed. The story is told in Ta. 24a that whilst he was in the process of making purchases for his daughter's marriage, he saw the charity collectors. They tried to avoid him, for he had already donated much for charity. Eleazar,however, hurried over to them and enquired as to the nature of their mission. When he heard that they were collecting to enable an orphaned couple to be married, he handed over to them all the money he possessed, declaring 'Their need is greater than that of my daughter'.

Give unto Him. The previous Mishnayot stress the significance of study and learning in every area of life, even during meals and in conversation. It would appear that this Mishnah is a digression and underlines the call for charity; this is not so. Money is only one of the many blessings showered upon us from above. Nor should we be so preoccupied with the acquisition of wealth that we find no time for the study of Torah. One of the most precious commodities put into our charge is time, and the application of it. 'Give unto Him that which is His'; we are asked to sacrifice time for God, for Sabbaths and Festivals, time for Torah study and observance, and time for helping those less fortunate than ourselves. We should emphasise the first letter of *mishelo*, of that which is His. We should willingly give part of our time, skill, talent, and energy. We discourage asceticism; we are asked to return to God only a fraction of our time, *Mishelo*, not all of it. We are to make sacrifices in every sphere of life, not only in the realms of money and possessions. Indeed, the word *tsedakah*, charity, is not mentioned in our Mishanh.

The language of the Mishnah strikes one as being both simple in style and noble in purpose. This remarkable combination manifests itself in both the saying and the proof-text. A minimum of words appears to embrace a world of thought.

Hasidic Lore

A partner with God. The Apter Rabbi told this story: I chanced to stay at a village inn and noticed that the innkeeper used two boxes for cash; whatever money he received he divided equally between them. I was curious to know the reason for this and, making known my identity, I asked the innkeeper. He replied that he had lost all his money in an unlucky venture and could not afford to keep his inn. His wife advised him to look for a partner and he went to the city to do so. Passing through the forest, he suddenly conceived the idea to implore the Lord to enter into partnership with him, in which case he would donate half of his earnings to charity. After offering a prayer, he suddenly found a large sum of money, and regarded this as an indication that his prayer was answered. Thereafter he faithfully observed the contract he made with the Almighty, and prospered. I praised the innkeeper's simple trust in the Lord and pronounced a blessing over him.

(ט) רַבִּי יַעֲקֹב אוֹמֵר הַמְהַלֵּךְ בַּדֶּרֶךְ וְשׁוֹנֶה וּמַפְסִיק מִמִּשְׁנָתוֹ וְאוֹמֵר מַה נָּאֶה אִילָן זֶה מַה נָּאֶה נִיר זֶה מַעֲלֶה עָלָיו הַכָּתוּב כְּאִלּוּ מִתְחַיֵּב בְּנַפְשׁוֹ:

Mishnah Nine.

R. Jacob says: He who is walking by the way and studying, and breaks off his study and says, 'How beautiful is this tree, how beautiful is this fallow field'; him Scripture regards as if he has forfeited his life.

R. Jacob of Kurshai (latter half of the 2nd century), was the teacher of R. Judah the Prince. In Hor. 13b we read an interesting story relating how Jacob Kurshai saved R. Simeon Ben Gamliel in a delicate situation which might have resulted in his deposition from the office of Nasi. Some are of the opinion that Kurshai was the grandson of Elisha Ben Avuya.

In the previous Mishnah we made a brief reference to the importance of time, which belongs to God. Here, too, we shall consider the meaning of time vis-a-vis the study of Torah. Here, too, time is sacrosanct; the study of Torah demands our undivided attention. We are not to be distracted even by the beauty of nature, which is God's handiwork. Every thing has its time; the Jewish student knows that prayer and Torah-study have fixed times which should not be interrupted. The term at a Yeshivah or school is called *zeman*, time. The Rabbis have coined a phrase to denote loss of time during hours of study - *bittul Torah* or *bittul zeman*, that is rendering time null and void and eventually disregarding the study of Torah. If we follow this interpretation, the Mishnah will be more meaningful.

The Jewish approach to natural beauty is well documented. Even the child knows that a special *berakhah* (blessing) is designated on seeing beautiful trees, animals, the rainbow, or the sea. God is beheld in every flower and plant, but nature must not be substituted for the love of Torah which, more than anything, brings us closer to God. If, therefore, we set aside an intensive study of Torah for a momentary aesthetic delight, it is as though we have endangered our spiritual future. We should not overlook the word *keilu*, as though. We are not mortally guilty, but such action can be compared to one who forfeits his spiritual life. This softens the apparent harshness of the statement.

Tree. An entirely different interpretation presents itself if we metaphorically understand the word 'tree' to refer to a great teacher. This is not unknown in rabbinic exposition. Commenting on the words 'are there trees therein' (Nu. 13:20) Rashi, basing himself on B.B.15a paraphrases it as follows, 'Is there a righteous man among them?' thus equating 'tree' with a worthy person.

We are aware that certain individuals enjoy the characteristics which are vested in unusual names, such as *Kalba Shavua* (a person, hungry as a dog, *Kalba*, who is fully fed - see Git. 56a) and Ben Tzitzis, both known to posterity for a particular trait which each exhibited in full measure, one for his consistent hospitality, and the other for dragging his Fringes after him. Similarly, here *ilan*, tree, may refer to R. Simeon Bar Yohai who escaped from the Roman authorities and took refuge in a cave. He stayed there for thirteen years studying and writing, and lived on the fruit of a carob tree which miraculously appeared outside the cave. As a result of his persistent study, many of the mysteries of the Torah were clarified and he is reputed to have produced the Zohar, a mystical commentary on the Torah. If this be a correct supposition, we can re-interpret the Mishnah of R. Jacob to convey a significant lesson. He who is suddenly *mafsik*, that is, he interrupts his normal activities and decides to pattern his life on that of the saintly Bar Yohai by removing himself from the public gaze and starting to live the life of a hermit - such a course is dangerous and unhealthy. We cannot aspire to the heights of a Simeon Bar Yohai; such spiritual giants are rare and unique. The average Jew should avoid all forms of asceticism. We live by our mitzvot and these are performed within the stream of life to the betterment of society and the human race. God planted the first tree, and this was a 'tree of life in the midst of the garden' (Gen. 2:9). The Jewish tree must flourish and blossom in the midst of the garden of civilised life.

Parallel with *ilan*, tree, we have *nir*, which according to Jastrow means 'a piece of land uncropped, growing wild'. If *ilan* refers to Yohai, *nir* can well apply to the cave in which Yohai hid. The secondary meaning of *nir* which Jastrow gives as 'yoke of servitude' also fits in with the life of Yohai who accepted the yoke of servitude spent in the service of God whilst he lived in the cave.

Hasidic Lore

Nature. The thought embodied in the words of our Mishnah seems to be reflected in a saying of the Koretzer Rabbi, who observes that man was created last for this reason: If he is deserving, he shall find all nature at his service; if he is undeserving, he shall find all nature arrayed against him.

(י) רַבִּי דוֹסְתָּאִי בַּר רַבִּי יַנַּאי מִשּׁוּם רַבִּי מֵאִיר אוֹמֵר כָּל הַשּׁוֹכֵחַ דָּבָר אֶחָד מִמִּשְׁנָתוֹ מַעֲלֶה עָלָיו הַכָּתוּב כְּאִלּוּ מִתְחַיֵּב בְּנַפְשׁוֹ. שֶׁנֶּאֱמַר רַק הִשָּׁמֶר לְךָ וּשְׁמוֹר נַפְשְׁךָ מְאֹד פֶּן תִּשְׁכַּח אֶת הַדְּבָרִים אֲשֶׁר רָאוּ עֵינֶיךָ. יָכוֹל אֲפִילוּ תָּקְפָה עָלָיו מִשְׁנָתוֹ תַּלְמוּד לוֹמַר וּפֶן יָסוּרוּ מִלְּבָבְךָ כֹּל יְמֵי חַיֶּיךָ הָא אֵינוֹ מִתְחַיֵּב בְּנַפְשׁוֹ עַד שֶׁיֵּשֵׁב וִיסִירֵם מִלִּבּוֹ:

Mishnah Ten.

R. Dostai Bar Jannai in the name of R. Meir says: If one forgets a single word of his study, Scripture regards him as if he had forfeited his life, as it is said, 'Only take heed of yourself and keep your soul diligently, lest you forget the things which your eyes have seen' (Deut. 4:9). One might suppose that this applies even when his study has been too hard for him; Scripture refutes this when it says, 'And lest they depart from your heart all the days of your life' (ibid). Thus a person's guilt is not established until he deliberately and of set purpose removes (those lessons) from his heart.

R. Dostai's name is of Greek origin. He lived about 160 C.E. and handed down sayings by Rabbis Meir, Jose and Eleazar. His temperament can be gauged from the question asked in his name, 'Why are the thermal springs of Tiberias not found in Jerusalem? So that the Festival Pilgrims should not say, 'Had we merely ascended in order to bathe in the thermal springs of Tiberias, it would have sufficed us, with the result that the pilgrimage would not be for its own sake' (Pes. 8b). Here we have a further lesson on the proper approach to the study of Torah. Our attention has been directed against any distraction, for it can affect our spiritual future adversely.

Here we are warned against another danger, forgetfulness, which too, can prove fatal to our spiritual growth. The general tenor of the Mishnah seems to be that forgetfulness may be an inherent weakness in many people.

Furthermore not everyone is mentally equipped to master fully a difficult dissertation, and this too may encourage forgetfulness. In both instances forgetfulness is understandable and excusable. What however the Tanna sets his face against is the unpardonable crime of deliberately forgetting one's learning; this is a capital offence.

If one forgets. Before the age of printing our forbears relied solely on their memory; if the Torah was to be observed, they had to memorise the traditions handed down to them. In this context, the maxim of R. Dostai has added weight, for the message of the Mishnah is meaningful in every age. Jewish tradition is rooted in the memory; if we are to survive, we must not forget our past. We rob from our treasured heritage if we forget Shabbat and Festival. If we ignore the sacrifices our parents made on our behalf and the many kindnesses they showered upon us, we become hard-hearted, cruel and rebellious, and eventually a danger to society.

The most ominous feature of forgetfulness is amnesia, when the victim is oblivious to the past and has no moorings. During World War II, many Jewish children were rescued from the Holocaust and placed in Christian hostels and homes. After the war, Dayan Grunfeld visited the evacuation camps that housed many of these young people. He was puzzled to know which children were Jewish and was suddenly inspired to mingle amongst them and repeat several times the words *Shema Yisrael.* A number of the youngsters who had suffered from spiritual amnesia heard this plaintive cry from the distant past and they seemed to become aroused through the latent feelings embedded deep down in the recesses of their hearts, and they spontaneously responded by presenting themselves to the Rabbi. The Mishnah records that if a person forgets one word of learning he may forfeit his spiritual life, but the reverse is equally true. The solitary word *Shema* may reactivate the spiritual links which lie dormant in the subconscious mind and may trigger off a chain of events which would recover the loss of memory. So powerful is the potential quality of the one word of learning, that whilst the loss of it can have disastrous results, the vocal image of one word of the spiritual vocabulary of Judaism can produce miraculous results.

The proof text from Deuteronomy is well chosen; it forcibly urges us, physically and spiritually, not to forget the unique spectacle of the Sinaitic Revelation which our ancestors saw with their own eyes, as one united people. The influence of this Revelation is to be with us in every age, all the days of our life. In the words of S. R. Hirsch , 'As you must guard against non-Jewish influences from outside, so, above all, guard your own inner self against the flattering suggestions of sensuality and selfishness.... take care above all that your inner self does not allow itself to forget the facts which your eyes saw'.

Hasidic Lore

Forgetfulness. 1) The Lizensker Rabbi was asked by a student how to prevent forgetfulness. The Rabbi replied: Repent, the Talmud tells us that repentance reaches to the Throne of Glory (Yoma 86a) and we recite in the New Year's prayer, 'There is no forgetfulness before Thy Throne of Glory'. 2). A learned man from Lithuania who was proud of his knowledge, was in the habit of interrupting the sermons of R. Levi Yitzhak of Berditchev with all manner of hair-splitting objections. Time after time the Zaddik invited him to visit him at his home for discussions of this kind, but the Lithuanian absented himself and continued to appear in the House of Prayer, and interrupted the Rabbi again and again. R. Barukh was told of this. 'If he comes to me', he said, 'He will not be in a position to say anything at all'.

These words were reported to the learned man. 'What is the Rabbi specially versed in?' he asked. 'In the Book of Splendour (Zohar)', was the answer. So he selected a difficult passage in the Book of Splendour and went to Mezbizh to ask R. Barukh about it. When he came into the room, he saw the Book of Splendour lying on the desk and opened to the very passage he had in mind. 'What an odd coincidence' he thought to himself, and immediately began to cast about for another difficult passage that might serve to embarrass the Rabbi. But the zaddik anticipated him. 'Are you well versed in the Talmud?' he asked. 'Certainly I am well versed in it', the other replied and laughed. 'In the Talmud', said R. Barukh, 'It is said that when the child is in the mother's womb a light is kindled above his head and he learns the entire Torah, but - when his appointed time to issue forth into the air of earth has arrived - an angel strikes him on the mouth and thereupon he forgets everything. How are we to interpret this? Why should he learn everything only to forget it?' The Lithuanian was silent. R. Barukh continued, 'I shall answer the question myself. At first glance it is not clear why God created forgetfulness. But the meaning of it is this; if there were no forgetting, man would incessantly think of his death. He would build no house, he would launch on no enterprise. That is why God planted forgetfulness in him. So one angel is ordered to teach the child in such a way that it will not forget anything, and the second angel is ordered to strike him on the mouth and make him forget. But occasionally he fails to do this, and then I replace him. And now it is your turn. Recite the whole passage to me'. The man from Lithunania tried to speak, but he stammered and could not utter a single word. He left the Rabbi's house and had forgotten everything. He was an ignorant man. After that he became a servant in the House of Prayer in Berditchev.

(יא) רַבִּי חֲנִינָא בֶּן דּוֹסָא אוֹמֵר כֹּל שֶׁיִּרְאַת חֶטְאוֹ קוֹדֶמֶת לְחָכְמָתוֹ חָכְמָתוֹ מִתְקַיֶּמֶת. וְכֹל שֶׁחָכְמָתוֹ קוֹדֶמֶת לְיִרְאַת חֶטְאוֹ אֵין חָכְמָתוֹ מִתְקַיֶּמֶת:

Mishnah Eleven.

R. Hanina Ben Dosa says: Every one whose fear of sin precedes his wisdom, his wisdom endures; and every one whose wisdom precedes his fear of sin, his wisdom does not endure.

R. Hanina Ben Dosa was a pupil of R. Johanan Ben Zakkai (first century). He was famed not so much for his scholarship, as for his saintliness. He belonged to a school of hasidim who, through prayer, could produce miracles. Thus he was instrumental in curing the son of R. Johanan of a serious illness (Ber. 34b). Similarly, he cured the sick son of R. Gamliel II, and when questioned if he was a prophet, he humbly replied that he was neither a prophet nor the son of a prophet, but experience had taught him that whenever his prayers flowed freely they were granted, otherwise they were rejected.

Fear of sin. This is related more to the sense of awe and wonderment of God than to the fear of punishment. A loving child will hold his parents in such high esteem, that he will be apprehensive to hurt them. Similarly, the loyal Jew will love God and fear to sin against His commandments. Bahya warns us not to think of the smallness of sin, but of the greatness of Him against whom we sin. Judaism teaches that repentance can wipe out all sins.

Wisdom. From time immemorial Judaism has extolled wisdom. Indeed, a section of the Bible is called 'The Wisdom Literature' and includes the books of Job, Proverbs and Ecclesiastes. Outside the canon of the Bible we also have The Wisdom of Solomon and The Wisdom of Ben Sira; thus wisdom is rooted in the Torah.

It is generally conceded that wisdom is pursued by many people today. We possess a plethora of schools, colleges and univerities, but too often the wisdom acquired is divorced from the fear of sin, resulting in angry and rebellious students who are ready to overthrow the Establishment. In the field of science and technology wisdom, without the fear of sin, has produced deadly weapons which threaten to annihilate whole continents. R. Hanina's profound maxim is very timely for our age. Wisdom built on the rock foundations of fear of sin will endure and save civilisation, but wisdom not preceded by fear of sin will eventually destroy the world.

Maimonides sensed this truth when he wrote in his 'Guide to the Perplexed': The intellect which emanated from God to us, is the link that joins us to God. You have it in your power to strengthen that bond if you choose to do so, or to weaken it gradually till it breaks if you prefer this. It will only become strong if you employ it in the Love of God,and seek that love. It will be weakened when you direct your thoughts to other things.

'The beginning of wisdom is the fear of God' (Ps. 111:10). Little wonder that the infant was taught to recite these words every morning. This was to be the guiding principle throughout life.

Hasidic Lore

The God-fearing man. The Yud said in comment on the verse, 'The fear of the Lord is the beginning of wisdom': I came to fear the Lord through my study of the Torah; but my friend R. David of Lelov came to study the Torah through his fear of God. He is, therefore, greater than I am.

Two kinds of fear. The Rabbi of Kotzk was asked, 'When they stood on Mount Sinai, the people said to Moses, 'Speak you with us and we will hear; but let not God speak with us, lest we die'. And Moses answered, 'Fear not'. He went on to say that God had come 'that His fear may be before you, that you sin not'. Is that not a contradiction?'

R. Mendel said: 'Fear not' - that means that this fear of yours, the fear of death, is not the fear which God wants of you. He wishes you to fear Him, he wants you to fear His remoteness, and not to fall into sin which removes you from Him.

(יב) הוּא הָיָה אוֹמֵר כֹּל שֶׁמַּעֲשָׂיו מְרֻבִּין מֵחָכְמָתוֹ חָכְמָתוֹ מִתְקַיֶּמֶת. וְכֹל שֶׁחָכְמָתוֹ מְרֻבָּה מִמַּעֲשָׂיו אֵין חָכְמָתוֹ מִתְקַיֶּמֶת:

Mishnah Twelve.

He used to say: Everyone whose deeds are more than his wisdom, his wisdom endures; and everyone whose wisdom is more than his deeds, his wisdom does not endure.

R. Hanina established the premise that wisdom should be preceded by fear of sin. Here he advances this thesis a step further and suggests that it should be followed by deeds and actions. Wisdom is not an end in itself, but a means to an end; wisdom should lead to action. Judaism is not only a religion but also a way of life, a civilisation which demands activity and the performance of good deeds. We are guided by the Halakhah, the essence of Jewish Law, but we live by *Halakhah Lemaaseh*, putting into practice what we teach. Wisdom is commendable but it will not endure and may even cause harm if it is not chanelled into positive action. For this reason, God has endowed us with six hundred and thirteen mitzvot, comprising *aseh*, positive, and *lo taaseh*, prohibited deeds. It is interesting that those for whom miracles are performed, are called *anshei maaseh*, men of deed. The miracle does not proceed from itself; it is the result of deeds of goodness and saintliness of character. In conjunction with good deeds, wisdom can perform miracles; but if the wisdom is merely an exhibition of intellectualism divorced of any religious appeal, it cannot endure because it is purposeless and hypocritical.

R. Simeon Ben Eleazer expounds our Mishnah with a parable: He whose works exceed his wisdom, to what may he be compared? To one who rides a horse with a bit in its mouth; he can direct the horse wherever he wishes. But one whose wisdom exceeds his works is like a person who rides a horse without a bit in its mouth. When he rides the animal, he falls off and breaks his neck (ARN).

The Vitry interprets the Mishnah in these words: He whose wisdom exceeds his works is one who does not fulfil what he learns, therefore his knowledge of the Torah will not be maintained, for through lack of practice he gradually forgets. According to Sanh. 99a, 'He who studies but does not practise is like a man who sows but does not reap, like a woman who gives birth to children and buries them'.

'He whose works exceed his wisdom is one who sets up many fences and hedges about the Torah and strives to act even beyond the demands of law - his wisdom will endure, for he will never fall into transgression'.

Hasidic Lore

The essence of doing. The Kotzker refers to three types of people. One before performing a deed says, 'I shall do it soon', he has a poor character. Another says, 'I am ready to do it now', his character is of average quality. The third says, 'I am doing it', His character is praiseworthy.

(יג) הוּא הָיָה אוֹמֵר כֹּל שֶׁרוּחַ הַבְּרִיּוֹת נוֹחָה הֵימֶנּוּ רוּחַ הַמָּקוֹם נוֹחָה הֵימֶנּוּ וְכֹל שֶׁאֵין רוּחַ הַבְּרִיּוֹת נוֹחָה הֵימֶנּוּ אֵין רוּחַ הַמָּקוֹם נוֹחָה הֵימֶנּוּ:

Mishnah Thirteen.

He used to say: Anyone from whom the spirit of his fellow creatures derives satisfaction, from him the spirit of the All-Present derives satisfaction, but anyone from whom the spirit of his fellow creatures derives no satisfaction, from him the spirit of the All-Present derives no satisfaction.

This Mishnah is the last of three in the name of R. Hanina Ben Dosa who loved all creatures and was himself beloved by all. This maxim truly reflects his approach to God and man. Some have misread the message conveyed by Hanina. It should be noted that he did not say, 'Whom his fellow creatures like', but 'In whom the spirit of his fellow creatures derives satisfaction'. Fulsome flattery and praise can ring insincere, whilst the quiet and inward spirit can be the hallmark of true friendship. The question has often been asked, what constitutes a good Jew? In order to test the sincerity and loyalty of a religious person, investigate his business or professional dealings. If he is a man of integrity and is scrupulously honest in his relations with man, he will also be honourable and whole-hearted in his relations with God and serve as a shining example to his fellow man. If, however, he is suspected of malpractices in his day to day dealings with man, his so-called outward parade of religious affiliations is suspect; he is devoid of true religion. Honesty and sincerity are indivisible. One cannot measure religion with a different yardstick from that used for man.

The nearest approximation to the whole-hearted Jew is delineated for us in the Talmud: Abbaye explained the words 'And you shall love the Lord your God', to mean that the name of Heaven be beloved because of you. If someone studies Scripture and Mishnah and attends on the disciples of the wise, is honest in business and speaks pleasantly to others, what do people then say concerning him? 'Happy is the father who taught him Torah, happy the teacher who taught him Torah; woe unto people who have not studied the Torah, for this man has studied the Torah — look how fine his ways are, how righteous his deeds..... but if someone studies Scripture and Mishnah, attends on the disciples of the wise, but is dishonest in business and discourteous in his relations with people, what do they say about him? Woe to him who studied the Torah, woe to his father who taught him Torah, woe to his teacher who taught him Torah. This man studied the Torah; look how corrupt are his deeds, how ugly his ways' (Yoma 86a). The highest goal for man to attain is 'to find grace and good favour in the sight of God and man' (Prov. 3:4).

It should be remembered that the Mishnah does not speak of him with whom all men are pleased.The Rabbis are realists; no man can be pleasing to all mankind. This truth is borne out by the praise showered upon Mordekhai, of whom it is said, 'And acceptable to most of his brethren' (Es. 10:3), but not to all his brethren.

The spirit of his fellow creature (man). It would seem that according to the wording of this Mishnah the 'spirit of man' has precedence over that of the All-Present. In this respect our Mishnah goes beyond the Decalogue, in which our duties to God and man run along parallel lines and are therefore on a par, whereas 'the spirit of man' appears first. However, this expression is not considered a part of social ethics; it is a vital manifestation of God's Law. We should remember that the golden rule, 'You shall love your neighbour as yourself' is immediately followed by 'I am the Lord'. God rules over all our destinies. This may explain why the Mishnah designates God as *Ha-Makom*, The Place. In all places and situations, God reigns supreme. Every action and deed of man, even his love for man, does not precede, but is founded on, the will of the All-Present.

Hasidic Lore

The ideal of holiness. R. Mendel of Kotzk paraphrased the verse, 'You shall be holy unto Me', (Lev. 70:26) to mean that the ideal of holiness should not produce an inhuman type of person. R. Mendel said, 'Be holy, but at the same time, be a *mensch*, a human being.

(יד) רַבִּי דוֹסָא בֶּן הָרְכִּינַס אוֹמֵר שֵׁנָה שֶׁל שַׁחֲרִית וְיַיִן שֶׁל צָהֳרַיִם וְשִׂיחַת הַיְלָדִים וִישִׁיבַת בָּתֵּי כְנֵסִיּוֹת שֶׁל עַמֵּי הָאָרֶץ מוֹצִיאִין אֶת הָאָדָם מִן הָעוֹלָם:

Mishnah Fourteen.

R. Dosa Ben Horkinas says: Morning sleep, midday wine, children's talk and sitting in the assemblies of the ignorant, remove a man from the world.

R. Dosa Ben Horkinas was a contemporary of Johanan Ben Zakkai; he lived between 10 C.E. and 90 C.E. and both names are of Greek origin. In the Talmud (Yev. 16a) he is referred to as a great scholar. He was an admirer of R. Akiva whose name, he said, was known from one end of the world to the other.

The terse language of the Mishnah castigates over-sleeping, over-drinking, over-babbling and an overdose of ignorance.

Morning sleep. As God created the world with design and order, so should we plan every day with order. The night is reserved for sleep; the day is initiated, not with sleep, but with *Tefillat Shaharit*, morning prayer. King Solomon testifies that it is the idler who sleeps in the morning, 'The door is turning upon its hinges and the sluggard is still upon his bed' (Prov. 26:14). Heading the individual blessings in the early morning prayers, we recite the words 'to distinguish between day and night'. Night and day are distinct seasons of time and not to be confused; each has its specific task and function.

Midday wine. We are conscious of the evils of intoxicating drink. ARN reminds us that when a man drinks wine at midday, he thereby neglects the study of Torah, as it is said, 'Woe to you O land, when your king is a boy and your princes feast in the morning (Ec. 10:16). It also states, 'Happy are you, O land, when your king is a free man and your princes eat in due season, in strength and not in drunkenness' (Ibid verse 17). It is interesting to record the testimony of a writer who observes that, 'Jewish wine-songs were of an altogether different type; they were merry, but contained not one syllable of licentiousness. Drunkenness was never a prevalent vice amongst Jews. Even in the Targum Sheni, Vashti boasts, 'My ancestor Belshazar drank as much wine as a thousand persons and it never made him indecent in his talk' (I. Abrahams).

Children's talk. When we speak to infants we endeavour to descend to their level, but such talk to adults is unwarranted.

Assemblies of the ignorant. The Synagogue stands for prayer and study of Torah; Judaism never tolerated illiteracy. The first school was housed in a Synagogue; the number of pupils increased to such an extent, that larger premises had to be acquired, and in this manner the Jewish school was established.

'The conversation of the *am-haaretz* is seductive, for he speaks only about daily happenings ..... Neglect of Torah for one hour brings on neglect for another hour, and finally a person departs from the world without any knowledge of Torah. Moreover, a person is attracted to the *am haaretz* by his eating and drinking habits and his frivolity' (Duran).

Some, understand the term *Batei Kneisiyot* here to refer, not to a Synagogue, but a form of club or social gathering. 'In these clubs social topics were discussed and mischievous tittle-tattle indulged in over glasses of wine, to the accompaniment of games of dice, throwing darts and pigeon-racing' (I. Epstein).

Some authorities understand this Mishnah to be a regimen of the whole of life. If we allow our youth, *Shaharit*, to slip away through inactivity and sleep, and later on in the middle forties (midday) we indulge in drink, and conclude in childish talk, we rebel against the Synagogue and all it stands for. We should make a clear distinction between qualitative and quantitative time.

Hasidic Lore

Sleep. R. Sussya said: Even sleep has its purpose. The man who wishes to progress in his service, always forging ahead from holiness to holiness, must first put aside his life-work in order to receive a new spirit whereby a new revelation may come upon him. And therein lies the secret of sleep, yea, even sleep has its service.

Said the Koretzer: Morning sleep is sweet, for the brain is then vacated of thoughts in order to make room for new ones.

It should be noted that our Mishnah specifically deals with *shenah shel Shaharit,* sleep indulged in during the period of morning prayers.

(טו) רַבִּי אֶלְעָזָר הַמּוֹדָעִי אוֹמֵר הַמְחַלֵּל אֶת הַקֳּדָשִׁים וְהַמְבַזֶּה אֶת הַמּוֹעֲדוֹת וְהַמַּלְבִּין פְּנֵי חֲבֵרוֹ בָּרַבִּים וְהַמֵּפֵר בְּרִיתוֹ שֶׁל אַבְרָהָם אָבִינוּ וְהַמְגַלֶּה פָנִים בַּתּוֹרָה שֶׁלֹּא כַהֲלָכָה אַף עַל פִּי שֶׁיֵּשׁ בְּיָדוֹ תּוֹרָה וּמַעֲשִׂים טוֹבִים אֵין לוֹ חֵלֶק לָעוֹלָם הַבָּא:

Mishnah Fifteen.

R. Eleazar of Modiin says: He who profanes holy things and despises the Festivals and puts to shame his fellow in public and makes void the covenant of Abraham our father and gives interpretations of Torah which are not according to Halakhah, even though he possesses Torah and good deeds, he has no portion in the world to come.

R. Eleazar of Modiin (first and second century) was a recognised exponent of aggadic interpretation, as is evident from a statement made by Gamliel II who admitted that 'The Modai's views are still indispensable' (Shab. 55b). He was implicated in the Bar-Kokhba revolt and died in the besieged city of Betar (135 C.E.). Modiin was the home of the Maccabees and was situated several miles from Lydda.

It would appear that the main thought connecting the different stages of Jewish life as outlined in the Mishnah is the absolute and clear distinction between the holy and profane, the sacred and the secular. The Halakhah is our authority and discipline, and the moment we tamper with it and lean on our fallible understanding, we enter the realms of speculation and heresy. 'The transgressions spoken of in our Mishnah, are not such as a man is led to by an overpowering evil impulse ..... the transgressions spoken of arise from a tendency towards false teaching. The individual pretends to know the secret meanings of the Torah; he then puts them forth, although they are not in accordance with the Halakhah' (Meiri).

The holy things. The root meaning of the word 'holy', is separation.

We introduce a measure of holiness when we separate ourselves from that which is forbidden, whether it be trefah foods, illicit sexual behaviour, or any ungodly act. We must draw a clear line of demarcation between the holy and the profane.

One authority (Aknin) interprets *Kadashim* as referring specifically to an incident recorded in I Sam. 2:15, where we read of the unsavoury exploits of the sons of Eli the High Priest, who took advantage of the priestly rights vested in them and so 'profaned the holy things'. As a result of their offensive behaviour the Bible observes, 'The sin of the young men was very great before the Lord' (ibid 2:17).

Despises the Festivals. The terminology used here is psychologically true of the modern Jew who is lax in his observance. One who disregards the Festivals, despises them, whereas one who disregards the Sabbath is equally divided between 'service for God and service for man', '*hetzyo la-Shem vehetzyo lakhem.* The irreligious will not subscribe to the first half of this saying, but will enjoy the social aspects of the Sabbath. He will meet his family, relatives and friends in a convivial atmosphere: he will *not* despise the Sabbath.

The Festivals, however, are in a different category. The non-observant cannot appreciate the religious and historical significance of the Festivals, all of which are of longer duration than the Sabbath, particularly in the Diaspora. They resent the prohibition of work imposed upon them for several days, and consequently despise the Festivals. The author of the Mishnah, with prophetic insight, warns us that to despise the Festivals is tantamount to heresy. Those observant Jews who love the Sabbath but are very critical of the second days of the Festivals, *Yom Tov sheni shel galiut,* should ponder on the message of R. Eleazar. The words of the Mishnah are a clarion call not to despise the *Yamim Tovim* under any circumstances, but to treat them as 'Good Days'.

Shame his fellow in public. The Talmud teaches that if a person disgraces his fellow man in public, it is as though he sheds blood. 'The blush subsides and whiteness takes its place'. This explains the word *malbin,* which means to make white (B.M. 58b). Compare also So. 10b, 'Rather throw yourself into a fiery furnace than put your fellow man to the blush'.

'There are touching instances of the self-denial of great men in shielding even unknown offenders against disgrace. A beautiful series of typical anecdotes and Bible interpretations dealing with this subject is traced from R. Meir to Samuel the Little, from him to Hillel, then through Shekhania Ben Yehiel (Ezra 10:2) and Joshua back to Moses himself' (M. Lazarus).

Makes void the covenant of Abraham. Maimonides says that this refers to him who tries to remove all signs of his circumcision; compare Y. Sanh. XI, page 27c. It is interesting to record that vitamin K (the coagulating element in blood) in a baby's blood increases after birth, reaching its climax on the eighth day, after birth (Gen 17:12) when circumcision is due to take place.

Megaleh panim ba-Torah. This expression is fully discussed in Sanh. 99a.b. and is translated as, 'He who acts impudently or insolently against the Torah'. The Rabbis say that this refers to one who insults a scholar or neighbour to his face; such a person is contemptuous towards the Torah and publicly brings the Torah into disrepute by denying its authoritative interpretation.

Hasidic Lore

The second days of the Festivals. The Alexanderer Rabbi said: The Psalmist commands us to 'Bind the feast with cords' (118:27). This can be compared to the tailor whose work is in vain if he fails to knot the threads. Similarly, unless we strive to secure the lessons learned during the Festivals in our minds, the Rabbi's work is in vain.

The Koznitzer Maggid told the 'Yud' that he felt a greater sense of holiness on the second days of the Festivals than on the first days, and asked him to explain the reason. The 'Yud' replied: When a bride has displeased her bridegroom, she seeks reconciliation with him by proving that she desires his companionship intensely and is loath for him to leave her presence. Consequently, the bridegroom's love is strengthened. Exile is a symbol of God's wrath against Israel. Hence, when Jews in exile devote an extra day to God and keep it holy, they effect a reconciliation between the 'Bride of Israel' and the 'Holy Bridegroom', thereby gaining a stronger manifestation of God's love for Israel.

(טז) רַבִּי יִשְׁמָעֵאל אוֹמֵר הֱוֵי קַל לְרֹאשׁ וְנוֹחַ לְתִשְׁחוֹרֶת וֶהֱוֵי מְקַבֵּל אֶת כָּל הָאָדָם בְּשִׂמְחָה:

Mishnah Sixteen.

R. Ishmael said: Be submissive to a superior and easy (of manner) to the young and receive all men with cheerfulness.

R. Ishmael (60-140 C.E.) had a colourful career. The story is told (Git. 58a) that R. Joshua Ben Hanania was informed that a Jewish child was in a prison in Rome. The child had beautiful eyes, a striking face and curly hair. R. Joshua stood at the door of the prison and quoted a verse from the Torah. Immediately, the child capped it with another verse. On hearing this, R. Joshua swore that he would not leave Rome before he ransomed the child who, he said, would become a great teacher in Israel. This child grew up to become R. Ishmael Ben Elisha, who was an outstanding scholar both in Halakhah and Aggadah. His name is popularised by the inclusion in the Prayer Book of his Principles of Logic, which were adapted from Hillel's Seven Hermeneutical Rules and increased to thirteen principles, by which the Torah is expounded.

The question arises whether the first two expressions are to be treated as variants of the same principle, or as two completely different injunctions. However we interpret them, they are both qualified by the last section of the Mishnah.

Be submissive to a superior. Initially, one is tempted to interpret *Rosh* as Head of the Universe, God. The first expression would therefore mean - be submissive to the Almighty; we mortals of flesh and blood are often too critical of God's rule over the world. Be flexible in your approach to the Creator. This homiletical interpretation is strengthened by a verse in Psalm (119:160), *Rosh devarekha emet*, 'The beginning of Thy word is truth'. Here the word *Rosh* points to God and His Torah; we are asked to be pliable both to God and His Torah.

However, most commentators understand *rosh* to be an earthly ruler or head teacher. Authority is essential and discipline must be maintained in all walks of life. Be submissive to the leader or the government or the city of your domicile. Recognise the superior position of the person in charge, whether he be a political leader or a pedagogue. If we accept this interpretation, the second injunction follows in logical sequence. For this reason we have translated *tishhoret* as youth, following Maimonides who traces the word to *shahor*, black, signifying a young person, not yet grey. We are advised to be at ease with a young leader or teacher. Some people resent a leader or teacher who is younger than they are and therefore do not respect him, but it would be wrong to treat him with frivolity or familiarity because of his young age. A teacher will be succesful if he earns the loyalty of those under his charge.

Others take *tishhoret* to mean compulsory service. 'In all matters, when in the presence of the powerful, he should be submissive and not vaunt himself in give and take with them. The ethical philosophers declare, 'It is risky lording it over lords' (Meiri).

Yet another interpretation would understand *rosh* in the same sense as Rosh Hashanah which is the beginning of a new year. Thus in our Mishnah we are asked to respond to the teacher of Torah at the beginning of life and not postpone it until old age. This would be qualified by the second clause and *tishhoret* might then be connected with *shahar*, a shortened form for *Shaharit*, morning, the early part of the day or the early years of life. In this connection we are reminded of the talmudic maxim, 'Happy is our youth which does not put our old age to shame' (Suk. 53a).

Receive all men with cheerfulness. It is unfortunate that some of our young people are introduced to Jewish practice only in the cemetery at a Burial Service or the consecration of a tombstone. Beyond this, they are outside the pale of Jewish life. These people re-echo the plaintive cry of the Prophet who witnessed the destruction of the Temple and the fall of Jerusalem, when he stated, 'The ways of Zion are mournful' (Lam. 1:4). Judaism is a religion of optimism and cheerfulness. Those who have actively lived as bnei Torah will testify that cheerfulness is the dominant note in our Faith. The mitzvah, which is our guide line, is not a strict rigid command but a *simhah shel mitzvah* a joyous and happy command. Indeed, we are told that the joy with which a deed is performed is more precious than the deed itself. The Rabbis warn us that the *Shekhinah*, God's presence, does not rest on him who is sad and morose. The Sabbath is not a gloomy day, but an *oneg*, a delight; nor are Festivals an encumbrance - 'You shall rejoice in your Festivals' (Deut. 16:14) is a positive command. The Psalmist declares,

'Serve the Lord with gladness' (100:2) and this cheerfulness is to be extended to all the members of the community, the orphan, the widow and the stranger (Deut. 16:4).

In the last century the Hasidic movement captured the imagination of the masses, many of whom were poor and downtrodden. These hapless people were drawn closer to Judaism through the joys of religion.

It is interesting to compare Ishmael's last injunction with a similar maxim by Shammai, 'Receive all men with a cheerful countenance' (1:15). We feel that Ishmael treated the subject with broader vision. It is possible that a cheerful countenance may be merely an outward exhibition which might conceal an inner envy or jealousy. R. Ishmael does not restrict the cheerfulness to the countenance alone, but advises that we should receive all men, of every station in life, with an inner sincere cheerfulness which emanates from the heart and radiates joy.

Hasidic Lore

Cheerfulness. R. Nahman of Bratzlav said: God dislikes melancholy and depressed spirits; it is the duty of the cheerful person to endeavour to bring to those in sadness, a portion of His mood.

(יז) רַבִּי עֲקִיבָא אוֹמֵר שְׂחוֹק וְקַלּוּת רֹאשׁ מַרְגִּילִין אֶת הָאָדָם לְעֶרְוָה. מַסּוֹרֶת סְיָג לַתּוֹרָה מַעְשְׂרוֹת סְיָג לָעוֹשֶׁר נְדָרִים סְיָג לַפְּרִישׁוּת סְיָג לַחָכְמָה שְׁתִיקָה:

Mishnah Seventeen.

R. Akiva said: Laughter and light-headedness lead a man on to lewdness; tradition is a fence to the Torah; tithes a fence to wealth; vows a fence for abstinence; a fence to wisdom is silence.

R. Akiva Ben Joseph (50-132 C.E.) commenced as an ignorant shepherd, but made a meteoric rise which took him to the highest pinnacle of rabbinic scholarship. Indeed, he has been called the father of rabbinic Judaism. Through collecting, compiling and arranging material from talmudic literature, he was primarily responsible for laying the foundations for the Mishnah and for the future of rabbinic Judaism. From Akiva's school came some of the greatest teachers of tannaitic literature. He fought with Bar-Kokhba in the revolution against Hadrian and died a martyr, and his name is prominently mentioned amongst the 'Ten Martyrs', recited in the Synagogue on Yom Kippur and Tisha b'Av. Akiva also fought for the inclusion of the Books of Ecclesiastes and Canticles in the canon of the Bible. To Akiva the Book of Canticles was most holy.

Laughter. We have translated *sehok*, the first word of the Mishnah, as laughter which, in itself, is healthy and even godly - as mother Sarah declared, 'God has made for me laughter' (Gen. 21:6). Laughter or merriment has even earned for some a portion in the world to come, as we learn from the Talmud (Ta. 22a) where Elijah told R. Berokah that two men would have a share in the world to come. Inquisitive to know the reason, R. Berokah asked the two men what their occupation was, and they replied that they were merrymakers; when they saw a man who was downcast, they cheered him up. This interpretation would logically follow the last clause of the previous Mishnah.

Commentators, however, make a special point of joining laughter together with light-headedness. Laughter alone is commendable, but when allied to light-headedness it becomes frivolous and dangerous. Light-headedness is the direct opposite of *Yirat Hashem*, the fear of God, and 'he who bears in mind that the *Shekhinah* hovers over him, will conduct himself with seriousness' (Duran). Laughter in moderation, at the right place and time, is good; in excess at the wrong place and time, it can lead to levity and prove disastrous.

Tradition. The Masorah or tradition is the name given to the notes added in the margin of the Tanakh and testify to the correctness of the text, which is not to be tampered with. The Masorites were nameless scribes who copied the Torah with punctilious care and loving devotion. Their concern was extended to every letter; they were also responsible for the spelling, the accentuation and the musical notation or cantillation. Their painstaking task was a scientific reconstruction of the text based on 'tradition' which was handed down, *masar*, from generation to generation. Thus the Masorah was a fence, hedging around the sacred text and avoiding the interpolation of any foreign matter.

Tithing. This is the first form of taxation on earth. 'The heavens are the heavens of the Lord; but the earth has He given to the children of men' (Ps. 115.16). We give no tithes for the benefits we derive from the heavenly hosts, but we are expected to give tithes for the produce of the earth which is assigned to man. Tithing does not make one poor; on the contrary, it is a fence which protects our wealth. Commenting on the verse in Deut. 14:22, 'You shall surely tithe', *aseyr teaseyr,* by a play on the words the Rabbis paraphrase the expression to read, *aseyr bishvil shetitasheyr*', which means 'Tithe in order that you may become wealthy' (Shab. 119a). Nor does the giving of charity make one poor — again the Rabbis advise 'charity' salts that is, preserves one's wealth' (Ket. 66b).

The Midrash describes tithing by the following parable. There was once a man who made his living from a field that produced a thousand measures. Of these, he used to give one hundred measures as tithes. Before his death, he instructed his son to continue the practice of tithing, but the son ignored his father's advice. As a result, the field produced less and less every year until it produced no more than one tenth of what it had been accustomed to yield. The man's relations explained to him that until now he was the owner, and God was the priest; now God was the owner and he was the priest and he received only one tenth.

Vows. Vows are a fence for abstinence. *Perishut* means separation and is akin to *Perushim,* the Pharisees, who separated themselves from every form of defilement in thought or deed. The vow is a fence to abstinence, for a vow to behave correctly in every area of life presupposes a separation from evil conduct in all its various forms. 'When a man makes vows and keeps them, he succeeds in developing the ability of self-restraint; this habit grows stronger in him, so that it becomes simpler for him to refrain from doing any thing which defiles' (Maim). The Torah does not encourage vows; the person who trains himself to control his evil impulse will eventually dispense with vows.

Silence, See 1:17. In the Shabbat morning liturgy *Shokhen Ad* we read the following words of praise to God: By the mouth of the upright Thou shalt be praised, by the words of the righteous Thou shalt be blessed, by the tongue of the loving ones Thou shalt be extolled and in the midst of the holy, Thou shalt be hallowed.

In this prayer we detect a progression of four stages of praise to God. The first step in the ladder of piety is expressed by the mouth of the upright. This is followed by the words of the righteous and is succeeded by the tongue of the faithful. The highest rung of the ladder is reached not by the mouth, nor by the words, nor even by the tongue, but 'within the holy'. The highest form of worship is expressed through silence, which is unseen and unheard; this leads to holiness.

In the sphere of education (wisdom) R. Jonah offers this advice to the students: A person should not speak in the presence of someone superior to him in wisdom. For example, when a person studies in the presence of his master and a certain interpretation strikes him as the correct one, let him not immediately think that this must be the interpretation. He should not interrupt before his teacher has finished speaking. If he acts impatiently, he will miss what his teacher is saying and not learn the views of the ancient Sages - for his attention will be distracted and he will not learn what these views are. Moreover, his own views cannot be clear until he has first heard what the ancients have said and then weighed in his mind which view is the more correct. That is why silence on the part of the student in the presence of his teacher or of anyone more learned than he in wisdom, is a fence.

Hasidic Lore

Silence. The Rozdoler Rabbi was accustomed to aid his opponents and to forbear with those who abused him. Once his wife asked him why he did not take steps to punish them, in order to halt their calumny. He replied, 'You have seen the crowds which come to me with their donations. The reason why multitudes go to the Zaddik is because he is the foundation of the world (Prov. 10:25) and they endeavour to strengthen the foundation. But I am not a Zaddik. Why, then, do they come to me? The reason is that when there is no Zaddik to uphold the world, another will suffice, namely the one who hears abuse and remains silent. In this manner the Talmud (Hul. 89a) explains the words, 'He suspended the earth on no word' (Job. 26:7). Because of this, I am entitled to receive the approval and support of the people.

(יח) הוּא הָיָה אוֹמֵר חָבִיב אָדָם שֶׁנִּבְרָא בְצֶלֶם (אֱלֹהִים). חִבָּה יְתֵרָה נוֹדַעַת לוֹ שֶׁנִּבְרָא בְּצֶלֶם (אֱלֹהִים) שֶׁנֶּאֱמַר כִּי בְּצֶלֶם אֱלֹהִים עָשָׂה אֶת הָאָדָם. חֲבִיבִין יִשְׂרָאֵל שֶׁנִּקְרְאוּ בָנִים לַמָּקוֹם חִבָּה יְתֵרָה נוֹדַעַת לָהֶם שֶׁנִּקְרְאוּ בָנִים לַמָּקוֹם. שֶׁנֶּאֱמַר בָּנִים אַתֶּם לַיהוָה אֱלֹהֵיכֶם. חֲבִיבִין יִשְׂרָאֵל שֶׁנִּתַּן לָהֶם כְּלִי חֶמְדָּה חִבָּה יְתֵרָה נוֹדַעַת לָהֶם שֶׁנִּתַּן לָהֶם כְּלִי חֶמְדָּה שֶׁבּוֹ נִבְרָא הָעוֹלָם. שֶׁנֶּאֱמַר כִּי לֶקַח טוֹב נָתַתִּי לָכֶם תּוֹרָתִי אַל תַּעֲזֹבוּ:

Mishnah Eighteen.

He used to say: Beloved is man for he was created in the image of God: but it was by a special love that it was made known to him that he was created in the image of God, as it is said, 'For in the image of God made He man' (Gen. 9:6). Beloved are Israel, for they were called children of the All-Present, as it is said, 'You are the children unto the Lord your God' (Deut. 14:1). Beloved are Israel for unto them was given the desirable instrument, but it was by a special love that it was made known to them that that desirable instrument was theirs, through which the world was created, as it is said, 'For I give you good doctrine , forsake not My Law' (Prov. 4:2).

Man. 'The loving God' would be a fitting title for our Mishnah which stresses a three-dimensional love of God, towards man in general, Israel in particular, and a group within Israel who, by keeping the Torah, become the true possessors of the precious instrument from which the world was created.

God loves man, irrespective of creed, race or colour. Every man is possessed of an individuality and personality of his own. 'God displayed a special love towards man by the fact that He made it known to him that he was created in His image. The greatness of the blessing then did not lie in the fact that man was created in the image of God, but in the fact that his notion of likeness to God was firmly fixed in man's consciousness' (Albeck).

Israel All men are equal in the sight of God, but Israel is chosen as His special love. This concept that we are the chosen people, which is often found in the Torah, has placed upon us special duties and responsibilities. 'The reason for your being chosen lay in your nature and His relationship to your forefathers. He found your nature worthy of His love, He found the mental and moral qualities in your nature that are necessary for man to get near to God. He found Himself attracted to you and, at the same time, He had to redeem the oath which He had sworn to your forefathers equally because of their spiritual and moral worthiness'(Hirsch).

The same concept is woven into our prayers in the Friday night Kiddush, and in the liturgy of the High Holy Days and the Festivals where we meet the familiar words *Ata vehartanu*, 'Thou hast chosen us from all the peoples, Thou hast loved us and taken pleasure in us and exalted us above all nations'. We should however remember that we must become inspired and worthy to accept this challenge.

The proof text from Deut. 14:1 is aptly chosen. We are as close to God as children are to their parents. Good children will suffer privations if necessary, and make sacrifices to be worthy of their parents, whose love they reciprocate. Similarly, we as children of God, should be loyal to our Father in Heaven who has chosen us from amongst all the other peoples.

A desirable instument. The word *Keli* is translated as a vessel, a container, an instrument or a tool. The Torah is a treasure house containing divine wisdom; it is an instrument or tool which is the raison d'etre of our existence and the guide-line on which we pattern our life.

Hemdah, which we translate as desirable, is connected with the root meaning 'covet'. The tenth commandment warns us not to covet the material possesions of our neighbour, but the spiritual wealth in the Torah is to be coveted. The mitzvot are 'more desirable than gold, than much fine gold, also sweeter than honey and the honeycomb' (Ps. 19:11). The superior element in Israel consisting of staunch advocates of Torah and faithful observers of its precepts, is the most desirable instrument in the hands of God because these people are partners with Him, recreating the world with a distinctive love which links the Jew to God and God to Israel.

Hasidic Lore

Who may be called man? Concerning the words in the Scriptures, 'When any man of you brings an offering to the Lord...' (Lev. 1:2) the Rabbi of Rizin said, 'Only he who brings himself to the Lord as an offering, may be called man'.

Love of God, Torah and Israel. The Besht was asked, 'What is the chief point in service to the Lord, if it be true as you teach, that fasting and self-chastisement are sinful?' The Besht answered, 'The main thing is to encompass oneself in the love of God, the love of Israel and the love of Torah. A man may attain this if he secures enough nourishment to preserve his health and if he makes use of his strength to battle against evil inclinations.

(יט) הַכֹּל צָפוּי וְהָרְשׁוּת נְתוּנָה וּבְטוּב הָעוֹלָם נָדוֹן וְהַכֹּל לְפִי רוֹב הַמַּעֲשֶׂה:

Mishnah Nineteen.

Everything is foreseen but free will is given and the world is judged by goodness and everything is according to the preponderance of action.

This Mishnah emphasises the foresight of God whose knowledge of man is infinite and unlimited. Whereas man's mind is finite and restricted to time and space, God encompasses past, present and future. Language through grammar has tenses; God has no tenses. So vital is this concept of predestination in Judaism that Maimonides included it in his thirteen Articles of Faith. Number ten reads, 'I firmly believe that the Creator, blessed be His Name, knows all the actions of men and all their thoughts, as it is said, 'He that fashions the hearts of them all, He that considers all their works' (Ps. 33:15).

The poetic counterpart of Maimonides' Creed is the popular hymn *Yigdal* which refers to the same principle in these words, 'He watches and knows our secret thoughts, He beholds the end of a thing in the beginning'. Both Maimonides' Principles and *Yigdal* are an integral part of our daily Prayer Book.

We shall also briefly refer to the descriptions of God's foreknowledge, one in Ps. 139:1-2, 'You know my sitting down and rising up, You understand my thoughts afar off .....' The other is found in the Musaph Amidah of the Rosh Hashanah Liturgy commencing with the words *Ata zokher* where we find God's omniscience fully and beautifully expressed.

But free will is given. If God's foreknowledge is well attested both in Tanakh and Siddur, how do we reconcile this with man's free-will which is no less enjoined in our Torah? Moses, in one of his last utterences, warns us 'I call heaven and earth to witness against you this day that I have set before you life and death, the blessing and the curse; therefore choose life that you may live, you and your seed' (Deut. 30:19). Man is not a puppet or an automaton; he is blessed with free-will to choose between right and wrong, good and evil. The freedom of man is best expressed in this dictum of the Rabbis, 'He who wishes to purify himself is assisted by Heaven to do so, whilst he who wishes to defile himself will find the means open to him' (Yoma 38b). Obviously, the authentic Jew will, through the performance of mitzvot, choose the course of purity and so fulfil the will of God. Should he, however, choose the path of defilement, he may bring misery and destruction upon himself and his family. Man is a free agent and must decide for himself, aided by his parents, teachers and friends. This concept of free-will distinguishes Judaism from Christianity which teaches 'original sin' and demands that man must submit himself wholly to the founder of his religion, otherwise he will not be saved. The Jew is free to commune directly with his God without the aid of an intermediary.

Jewish philosphers throughout the ages have grappled with the apparent contradiction between God's foresight and man's absolute free-will. We should remember the words of Isaiah, 'My thoughts are not your thoughts, neither are your ways My ways, says the Lord' (55:8). Man is on a different level; he is endowed with free-will which the Almighty has graciously bestowed upon him.

And the world is judged by goodness. God does not rule by strict justice alone, but also by mercy and goodness. At the beginning of the Creation God brought light into the world, 'And He saw that it was good'. Out of the chaos of primeval darkness God introduced light, goodness and mercy. It is our privilege and duty to imitate God and judge the world in goodness and maintain and preserve it in mercy. 'Even the wicked are judged by Him mercifully, as it is said, 'The Lord is good to all' (Ps. 145:9) and the wicked are part of the handiwork of the Holy One blessed be He' (Jonah). Furthermore, 'The Lord created the evil impulse, but He created Torah and repentance as its remedy, and the world is judged in mercy in that the sinners' repentance is found acceptable and this is a merciful act of the Lord towards His creatures' (Meiri).

Everything is according to the preponderance of action. We are apt to judge man too critically and rashly. We emphasise the faults and weaknesses and overlook the greater services he has rendered to society; we should minimise the few defects in his conduct. Maimonides explains this phrase as follows: The good qualities a man acquires are not the product of a single great act, but of the recurrence of many good works; only in this manner is virtue firmly acquired. For example, a charitable nature is not gained when a person gives one needy individual a thousand gold pieces on one occasion ... but when a person distributes a thousand gold pieces on a thousand occasions he does acquire a charitable nature. Being charitable once, represents no more than that this individual has been suddenly stirred to perform one good deed; thereafter it may leave him.

A completely different interpretation comes to the surface if we understand the last clause of this Mishnah to qualify the preceding one. The world is judged by goodness, but this goodness must not be restricted to 'the mind or heart'; goodness should be channelled into action. Man can entertain lofty ideals, he may nourish excellent thoughts, but they are meaningless if they are not actuated. Good thoughts and admirable intentions should be developed into purposeful deeds.

Yet another interpretation can be deduced from the Mishnah as a whole. Here God's foreknowledge is contrasted with man's free-will. It is possible that God has hidden from man some of the findings and discoveries latent in the world of nature, in order to arouse the curiosity of man and challenge him to action. Man's free-will, with which God has endowed him, thus assists him to achieve new insights and more exalted horizons for the betterment of the human race.

Finally, we should add a word about the author of the Mishnah, R. Akiva. This Mishnah contains one of the great paradoxes of Jewish religious philosophy. It also mirrors the life of its author who, too, was seemingly a great paradox. Who can comprehend the meteoric rise of the ignorant shepherd who became one of the greatest giants of Jewish Law? Akiva's life and martyred death was one long reconciliation between the passing and changing phases of temporal life and the recognition of, and abiding attachment to, the eternal verities of authentic Judaism.

Hasidic Lore

Freedom of will.

1). The Medzibozer commented on the verse, 'And the Lord said unto Moses, 'Write this for a memorial in the Book and rehearse it in the ears of Joshua, and I will utterly blot out the remembrance of Amalek from under the heaven' (Ex. 7:14). He said, 'The Lord informed Moses of the future fate of Amalek and of His decree to blot out in the future all remembrance of that nation. This occurred when Haman the Amalakite was slain. Yet it was not the Lord's will to mention expressly the time of his extinction, since Mordekhai and the Jews would have had no occasion to implore the Lord to save them and to repent with sincerity. Therefore it is merely hinted in the Written Torah and whispered in the ears of Joshua. Were the people to know the future, there would be no free-will in their service of the Lord.

2). The author of 'Keli Yakar' explains why, after the creation of man, there are not written the words, 'And God saw that it was good' (Gen. 1:25) as in the case of the cattle. All other creatures received their final nature at the time of Creation, but man was endowed with the faculty of free-will or self-improvement. Hence it was impossible to declare concerning him that he was good at the time of Creation. It was fitting to discover first what he would make of himself.

(כ) הוּא הָיָה אוֹמֵר הַכֹּל נָתוּן בָּעֵרָבוֹן וּמְצוּדָה פְרוּסָה עַל כָּל הַחַיִּים הֶחָנוּת פְּתוּחָה וְהַחֶנְוָנִי מַקִּיף וְהַפִּנְקָס פָּתוּחַ וְהַיָּד כּוֹתֶבֶת וְכָל הָרוֹצֶה לִלְווֹת יָבֹא וְיִלְוֶה וְהַגַּבָּאִין מַחֲזִירִין תָּדִיר בְּכָל יוֹם וְנִפְרָעִין מִן הָאָדָם מִדַּעְתּוֹ וְשֶׁלֹּא מִדַּעְתּוֹ וְיֵשׁ לָהֶם עַל מַה שֶּׁיִּסְמוֹכוּ וְהַדִּין דִּין אֱמֶת וְהַכֹּל מְתֻקָּן לִסְעוּדָה:

Mishnah Twenty.

He used to say: Everything is given in pledge and a net is spread over all the living. The shop is open and the shopkeeper gives credit, and the ledger is open and the hand writes and whoever wishes to borrow may come and borrow and the collectors make the rounds continually every day and exact payment of man with or without his knowledge and they have whereon to rely and the judgment is a judgment of truth and every thing is prepared for the feast.

The author is again R. Akiva, who opens the Mishnah with the initial and significant principle of communal responsibility and divine justice. What follows is an analogy or simile in metaphorical language elaborating his thesis. It is interesting to note that Akiva, the religious philosopher of the previous Mishnah, here speaks with the voice of the man of the world and employs the terminology of commerce to expound his teaching. No one can accuse Akiva of living in the clouds or exclusively adopting abstruse or theological concepts.

Pledge. At the time of the giving of the Law at Sinai, God asked Israel what pledges or guarantees they would offer to heed the Torah, and they answered they were ready to pledge their children. This has always been the motivating factor which has preserved the Jewish people. We cannot thrive in splendid isolation, we can maintain our peculiar identity only when we pledge each other to work for the common weal; in the words of the Rabbis, *Kol Yisrael aravin ze leze* - all Jews are accountable to each other. Man is a responsible being and he cannot shelve this trust which he owes to his family, his people and his God; for a net is spread over the whole of life. If we allow this net, *the yezer hara*, the evil impulse, to close in upon us it will spell doom, disaster and death. 'Some men are caught by the net, that is to say they are trapped by the bait, put in the net. These are the fools who have been ensnared by the vanities of the world ..... but the wise, the men of intelligence, know that the bait inside the net was not placed there without purpose but to deceive human beings; so they circumvent the net and never fall into it' (Aknin).

The shop is open. *Hanut* is derived from *hana*, to pitch one's tent. The first shop was a tent, a moveable structure. Here Akiva compares the world to a vast shop. Indeed, it is more than a shop; it is a huge supermarket which has every possible commodity one can imagine. The shopkeeper, God Almighty, gives credit; God is merciful and kind. Naturally the ledger is open and the hand writes, the customer may borrow and take from the shelves whatever he wishes.

We live in a wonderful world full of the good things of life. We breathe freely God's air, we enjoy the health-giving rays of the sun and the refreshing rains in their due season which help to produce the crops and the food we need. The world-shop has a plentiful supply for all; no one should go hungry. Many are guilty of shoplifting, for they refuse to pay for what they receive. We enjoy God's bounty every day but we do not acknowledge that everything emanates from God. This is the underlying reason for the recital of the berakhot,blessings, for everything we consume. We always borrow from God but fail to repay or acknowledge our debt with gratitude. Hence, the collectors make the rounds and exact payment. Some react favourably to the collectors; their conscience warns and guides them to conduct themselves correctly and uprightly. Others, however, ignore the collectors; they stifle their conscience and cheat, defraud and deal treacherously with their fellow-man. Such is the long-suffering attributed to God that man, through his free-will, is allowed to hold on to that which does not properly belong to him. But eventually payment is exacted; we cannot altogether escape the retributive punishment which we deserve.

The judgment is a judgment of truth. We can rely on God's judgment which is truth, the seal of the Almighty. Man, however, has double standards. He may judge others harshly, but he very rarely acknowledges his own guilt; his punishment, he declares, is always undeserved. In this connection the rabbinic interpretation of Deut. 16:20 is apt, 'Justice, justice, shall you pursue'. To explain the repetition of the word 'justice,' the Rabbis declare that the first justice is a call to be just to others, the second is a warning to be just to oneself. *Bamidah sheadam moded modedim bo* (So. 1:7), 'The measure with which man measures, will be measured out to him'. In other words, if a man is kindly disposed towards others, he, too, will be treated with consideration; if on the other hand, he deals with people sternly and strictly, he too will be treated in a harsh and rigorous manner.

All is ready for the feast R. Meshullam Bar Kalonymus of Rome interpreted the word 'feast' as 'the day of death' ...... Why is death called a day of feast? To teach that when men are invited to a feast they all enter through one doorway, but when they sit down they do not take their seats haphazardly, but each according to his station and dignity. Similarly, it is the fate of every man to depart from this world, of the righteous and the wicked, but only in accordance with his work does each person receive what is his due (Vitry).

Death is not to be dreaded nor should the subject of death make us morbid. In Judaism we have no mention of hell-fire or eternal damnation. Death is merely a transition from the physical world which is temporal, to a future world which is timeless. Jewish belief stresses that *olam haba*, the future world, is one of bliss and happiness. The Midrash corroborates this view when it comments on the words 'very good' (Gen. 1:31) as applying to death, thus equating death with goodness. Our Mishnah follows this thought by adding, 'All is made ready for the feast'.

Hasidic Lore

Everything is pre-ordained. Hasidim are not curious inquirers into first and last things — to them both life and death are fulfilment. What is the destiny of the plant that springs from the soil? To grow and to wither. It is the law and the will of God, and therewith man must likewise rest content without inquiry into the Why and the Wherefore. Let him rejoice at being called into life, and return to the fountain-head of his being when the call to him goes forth.

(כא) רַבִּי אֶלְעָזָר בֶּן עֲזַרְיָה אוֹמֵר אִם אֵין תּוֹרָה אֵין דֶּרֶךְ אֶרֶץ. אִם אֵין דֶּרֶךְ אֶרֶץ אֵין תּוֹרָה. אִם אֵין חָכְמָה אֵין יִרְאָה. אִם אֵין יִרְאָה אֵין חָכְמָה. אִם אֵין דַּעַת אֵין בִּינָה. אִם אֵין בִּינָה אֵין דַּעַת. אִם אֵין קֶמַח אֵין תּוֹרָה. אִם אֵין תּוֹרָה אֵין קֶמַח:

Mishnah Twenty One.

R. Eleazar Ben Azariah says: If there is no Torah, there are no manners; if there are no manners, there is no Torah. If there is no wisdom, there is no fear; if there is no fear, there is no wisdom. If there is no knowledge, there is no understanding; if there is no understanding, there is no knowledge. If there is no meal, there is no Torah; if there is no Torah, there is no meal.

R. Eleazar Ben Azariah (first century teacher) was one of the notables of the Academy of Javneh. He was descended from Ezra the Scribe. R. Judah the Prince listed the merits of Eleazar and called him a 'spice pedlar's basket'. When people ask him if he has good oil, ointment or balsam, they ascertain that he has everything. He answers questions on Scripture, Mishnah, Halakhah and Aggadah (ARN chapter 18). His name is popularised through his statement recorded in Mishnah Ber. 1:15 and repeated in the

Haggadah on the Seder night of Pesah, from which we learn that he succeeded R. Gamliel, who was deposed, and became President of the Academy of Javneh at the early age of seventeen or eighteen; such was the brilliance of Eleazar. Here we append some of the famous sayings attributed to him.

Yom Kippur will not atone for sins between man and his neighbour, unless he has appeased him first (Yoma 85 b).

A Sanhedrin which puts to death one man in seventy years is called a tyrannical court (Mak. 1:10).

One should not say, ' I have no desire to eat pig', but he must say, 'Yes, I would like to eat pig, but what can I do? My Father who is in Heaven has forbidden it' (Sifra Kedoshim chapter 9).

We can gauge how wise he was for when he died it was said of him, 'With his death, the crown of wisdom is no more' (So. 49b).

Torah. Torah is the highest possible authority which guides us in all our actions. See note on 2:2.

Derekh eretz. This is often translated as manners, or correct conduct. 'Manners maketh man', says the essayist. In former days, a man of manners was a member of the nobility, one who possessed a university education. In Judaism we possess no class distinction nor do we recognise intellectual snobbery; the poor, too, were learned in the Torah and they behaved with *derekh eretz*. Manners are not only a social grace, they are rooted in Torah. Without Torah, manners are incomplete and change with every age and in every country. Torah, however, is immutable and timeless; so is *derekh eretz* unchangeable. We cannot divorce *derekh eretz* from Torah. It enjoyed the same binding force as Jewish Law, and is not to be treated as a passing phase of society. The Rabbis remind us that *derekh eretz kadmah l'Torah*, derekh eretz even preceded the Torah.

The Hidushei Harim explains that as every book has an introduction, *hakdamah*, so *derekh eretz* is the introduction to the Torah. As one cannot envisage an introduction without the essence of a book following, so we cannot tolerate *derekh eretz* without the Torah. The introduction cannot replace the book. On the other hand, he who discards the Torah cannot possess *derekh eretz*, for they are both parts of one entity. However, if you reside in a community where there is no Torah, do not overplay your gentility or accept the status quo. In such circumstances, do not be a passive onlooker, but become militant and wage war against the absence of Torah learning.

Where there is no wisdom, there is no fear. *Hakhmah*, wisdom, must be grounded in religious practice and fear of God, otherwise wisdom is denigrated to materialism and secularism, which can lead to destruction and war. The race among the super-powers to build vast arsenals of atomic weapons, is taking place before our very eyes. The wisdom of modern scientific technology has brought many benefits to our age, but without fear of God scientific know-how can unleash forces which could completely annihilate the whole of mankind. For this reason we teach the child to include in his morning prayers the verse from Prov. 9:10, 'The beginning of wisdom is the fear of God'.

Hakhmah, wisdom and intellectualism, and *yirah*, fear of God, piety and emotionalism, merge together throughout the whole gamut of Jewish history. In the Bible the priests, who stand for piety, work together with the prophets, who taught wisdom. In the Talmud two strands of thought mingle freely. The Halakhah, wisdom and logic of Jewish Law, runs parallel with Aggadah, the emotionalism of folk-lore. In the Middle Ages, we enjoyed the fruits of Jewish philosophy together with the flowering of Jewish poetry. In the same way Hasidism, which stresses prayer and piety, was a counterbalance to talmudic erudition and *pilpul*, plumbing the depths of rabbinic wisdom.

All this is reflected in the perfomance of the mitzvah of Tefillin. The head Tefillin is placed over above the brain, the seat of wisdom. The hand Tefillin is laid opposite the heart, the seat of the emotions. But according to Jewish Law, both hand and head Tefillin constitute one operation; here *hakhmah* and *yirah* are united. It should be remembered, however, that the *rosh*, (head Tefillin) is always exposed. We are proud of Jewish intellect and endeavour to impart it to others; but the *yad* (the hand Tefillin) is covered as we do not publicly exhibit our heartfelt emotions of kindness, mercy and charity. All virtuous deeds should be performed quietly and unostentatiously in order to avoid embarrassment. When Jewish intellect is wedded to the fear of God and piety, the union will bring blessing and peace of mind.

If there is no knowlege, there is no understanding. *Binah*, understanding or perception, is a divine quality of mind with which we are born. *Daat*, knowledge, we acquire through education. Thus we pray, 'Favour us with knowledge, understanding .....' We should be careful to acquire the right type of knowledge, which should be built on the understanding with which God has favoured us at birth.

If there is no meal, there is no Torah. Here, again, food is coupled with Torah. We should not cultivate one at the expense of the other. In the additional Sabbath morning service we pray for health of body and a higher enlightenment; health comes before Torah. Similarly in Deut. 4:15 we read, 'Only guard yourself and guard your soul exceedingly'. Here, too, the claims of the body precede those of the soul, the spiritual life. Indeed, the Rabbis warn us 'not to reside in a comunity where there is no physician' (Sanh. 17b).

On the other hand, the Torah explicitly states that man does not live by bread alone. It is true that food preserves us, but Jewish history has furnished us with examples of the superiority of the spiritual over the material, as in the days of the Maccabees, the Spanish Inquisition and throughout the ages when Jews chose to be martyrs rather than eat swine's meat. The soul took precedence over the flesh. Authentic Judaism blended body and mind together. We never denied ourselves the legitimate pleasures of the body, nor did we encourage a life of monasticism or asceticism.

If there is no meal. This can be interpreted in the words of the Torah which reminds us, 'If you will walk in My statutes, I will give your rains in their season and the earth shall produce its produce ..... But if you will not listen to Me, you will sow in vain ...' (Lev. 26:3, 14).
Zevulun (merchant) and Issachar (student) must help and complement each other. If we are to produce a line of specialists in Halakhah and Torah learning, we must provide Yeshivot and Torah institutions with the requisite food they need.

This saying of the Mishnah is also directed against profiteers who unjustifiably raise the market prices and so deprive the poor of the necessities of life (Meg. 17b). The ninth blessing of the Amidah, the Blessing of the Years, also indirectly rails against the price racketeers. The prices should be strictly controlled by the *Bet Din*, but as they are debarred from the right to enforce the law, we implore the Almighty to bless the year with good produce. This paragraph is followed by 'Sound the great horn for our freedom', and this in turn is followed by 'Restore our judges as at first', a plea that our judges will judge with honesty and integrity and save the poor from being robbed of their rightful share. If there is insufficient food, we must not censure God who fills the world with His bounty.

There is a plentiful supply of food for all; no one need go hungry. If there is no food, if we abominably destroy good food by dumping it into the sea, or destroy it because 'There is no Torah', we are aiding the godless profiteers who control price rings and we enrich them at the expense of the public. (Compare Amos chapter 8; B.B. 90a; Hoshen Mishpat 231 and Orah Hayim 694).

Finally *kemah,* food, can refer to a livelihood, and this would tally with one of the meanings of *derekh eretz* which, as we have stated above, may also mean a trade, vocation or worldly occupation. If we adopt this interpretation the Mishnah would convey, in its initial and final maxims, the same lesson regarding the relative merits of the study of Torah and the pursuit of work. Judaism is a practical religion and recognises the need to merge both the study of Torah and the earning of a livehood. One should not outstrip the other, they should run along parallel lines; the Tannaim and Amoraim combined the two together. *Im ein kemah,* if there is no livelihood, *ein Torah,* we have not the energy or the stamina to transmit Torah. *Im ein Torah,* if there is no Torah, *ein kemach,* there is no blessing in the food we acquire.

Hasidic Lore

Charity - the food of God. The Trisker Maggid said: It is written, 'My food which is presented unto Me for offerings' (Nu. 28:2). This means, 'Your offerings to charity constitute My food which you should present unto Me'.

(כב) הוּא הָיָה אוֹמֵר כֹּל שֶׁחָכְמָתוֹ מְרֻבָּה מִמַּעֲשָׂיו לְמָה הוּא דוֹמֶה לְאִילָן שֶׁעֲנָפָיו מְרֻבִּין וְשָׁרָשָׁיו מוּעָטִין וְהָרוּחַ בָּאָה וְעוֹקַרְתּוֹ וְהוֹפַכְתּוֹ עַל פָּנָיו שֶׁנֶּאֱמַר וְהָיָה כְּעַרְעָר בָּעֲרָבָה וְלֹא יִרְאֶה כִּי יָבֹא טוֹב וְשָׁכַן חֲרֵרִים בַּמִּדְבָּר אֶרֶץ מְלֵחָה וְלֹא תֵשֵׁב. אֲבָל כֹּל שֶׁמַּעֲשָׂיו מְרֻבִּין מֵחָכְמָתוֹ לְמָה הוּא דוֹמֶה לְאִילָן שֶׁעֲנָפָיו מוּעָטִין וְשָׁרָשָׁיו מְרֻבִּין שֶׁאֲפִילוּ כָּל הָרוּחוֹת שֶׁבָּעוֹלָם בָּאוֹת וְנוֹשְׁבוֹת בּוֹ אֵין מְזִיזִין אוֹתוֹ מִמְּקוֹמוֹ. שֶׁנֶּאֱמַר וְהָיָה כְּעֵץ שָׁתוּל עַל מַיִם וְעַל יוּבַל יְשַׁלַּח שָׁרָשָׁיו וְלֹא יִרְאֶה כִּי יָבֹא חֹם וְהָיָה עָלֵהוּ רַעֲנָן וּבִשְׁנַת בַּצֹּרֶת לֹא יִדְאָג וְלֹא יָמִישׁ מֵעֲשׂוֹת פֶּרִי:

Mishnah TwentyTwo.

He used to say: He whose wisdom exceeds his works, what is he like? A tree whose branches are many and its roots are few and the wind comes and uproots it and overturns it on its face, as it is said, 'And he shall be like a tamarisk in the desert and shall not see when good comes and shall inhabit the parched place in the wildnerness, a land that is salt and not inhabited' (Jer. 17:6). But he whose works exceed his wisdom, what is he like? A tree whose branches are few and its roots many, so that even if all the winds that are in the world come and blow upon it they do not stir it from its place, as it is said, 'He shall be like a tree planted by the waters and that sends forth its roots by the river; and it shall not see when heat comes but its leaf shall be green, and in the year of the drought shall not be troubled nor cease from yielding fruit' (Jer. 17:8).

In this Mishnah the author elaborates on the theme of wisdom, which is sharply constrasted with works or deeds.

Wisdom. Ignorance and illiteracy were always frowned upon by the Rabbis who consistently encourage us to cultivate wisdom and knowledge. This is well illustrated in epigrammatic form in the following aphorism. 'If you lack knowledge, what have you got? If you have knowledge, what do you lack?' (Cant. R. 4:3).

Works (maasim). At the *Brit Milah* the child is initiated into the Jewish religion with the repetition of the familiar words, 'Even as this child has entered into the covenant, so may he enter into the Law, the nuptial canopy and into good deeds'. Even at birth, we express the prayer and wish that the child will practise good deeds. The Talmud relates that an edict was issued by the Roman government punishing with death Jews who engaged in the study of Torah. Two Sages flouted the edict and were imprisoned. Before the trial one said to the other, 'Happy are you, for you are to be condemned only on one charge, but there are five indictments against me'. The other replied, 'Your lot is happier than mine, because during your lifetime you occupied yourself with the study of the Law as well as practising good deeds, whereas I only studied the Law (A.Z. 17b). In other words, I have no works to my credit and I feel my weakness and unworthiness. Wisdom and good deeds together are enjoined on the Jew. Happy is he who allows both in equal measure to penetrate and influence him for good. The Mishnah sounds a warning against fostering wisdom at the expense and exclusion of deeds. The gap between brain and soul, materialism and spirituality, widens with every age. The result is that the students who represent the intelligentsia are often rebellious; seats of modern learning have produced many drop-outs and undesirable characters.

Eleazar very strikingly compares this attitude of mind with the tree which has many branches and ostensibly appears to be very productive, but which has few roots and so will eventually rot and wither. The tree has always played a prominent part in biblical and rabbinic imagery. Judaism will live and flourish if it is a Tree of Life, *Etz Hayyim*. When the Jewish family is deeply rooted in tradition - when its roots spread far and wide and it is in close touch with Jewish Law and Custom - it can withstand the cold, bleak winds of irreligion and anarchy. However, if the roots are few, if our association with the fundamentals and principles of Judaism are tenuous, if the design of Jewish living is vague and we do not practise any of the mitzvot, then we expose ourselves to the winds of change and eventually commit spiritual suicide, intermarry and opt out of Judaism.

In order to appreciate the force of the proof-texts from Jer. 17:6 and 8, it is advisable to read verse 5, 'Thus says the Lord, 'Cursed is the man that trusts in man and makes flesh his arm, and whose heart departs from the Lord'. Similarly, we should read the introductory verse 7 to the second proof-text, 'Blessed be the man that trusts in the Lord and whose trust the Lord is'.

It is obvious from the Mishnah that the tree which is well rooted is preferable to the tree that boasts of many branches. This has the sanction of both the Tanakh and Midrash. Thus Israel 'Will cast forth his roots as Lebanon' (Hosea 14:6). In Midrashic poetry the deep-striking roots of the tree are symbolised by the words of Torah. Commenting on Ec. 12:11, 'As nails well fastened, so are the words of the masters of collections', the Rabbis add, 'As the roots of a tree spread in all directions, so do the words of the wise penetrate the whole body' (Nu. R. 14:4).

Hasidic Lore

Good deeds. The Mezeritzer Maggid said: A man's kind deeds are utilised by the Lord as seed for the planting of trees in the Garden of Eden; thus each man creates his own paradise. The reverse is true when he commits transgressions.

(כג) רַבִּי אֱלְעָזָר בֶּן חִסְמָא אוֹמֵר קִנִּין וּפִתְחֵי נִדָּה הֵן הֵן גוּפֵי הֲלָכוֹת תְּקוּפוֹת וְגִימַטְרִיָּאוֹת פַּרְפְּרָיוֹת לַחָכְמָה:

Mishnah Twenty Three.

R. Eleazar Hisma says: Offerings of birds and purifications of women, these indeed are the essential Halakhot; astronomy and gematria are the after-courses of wisdom.

R. Eleazar was known by the name of *Hisma*, tongue - tied. According to Lev. R. 23, he was invited to officiate at a Synagogue Service, but he refused because he felt incompetent to do so. Eventually his teacher Akiva prompted him; thereafter he was referred to as 'tongue-tied'. Hisma was an outstanding Jewish scholar, but was also a student of astronomy and geometry. He was therefore entitled to compare secular learning with Halakhah in which he was pre-eminent; however, he treated his other academic studies as after-courses.

Kinnim is the name of the Mishnah in the order of *Kadashim*, dealing with young birds brought as sacrifices after childbirth.

Niddah is a Tractate in the order of *Taharot* discussing the laws of uncleanness and purification of women.

R. Eleazar undrlines the significance of the marriage laws, pre and post-natal. He reminds us that marital purity is the very foundation on which Jewish family life should be built. The alarming increase of divorce, indulgence in abortion, and sexual promiscuity - all these vices of the so-called new morality - could be arrested and averted if only we followed the advice of R. Eleazar Hisma with his emphasis on the old morality which is based on the twin orders of *Kadashim* and *Taharot*, on holiness and purity.

They are the essential Halakhot. The word *hein* is repeated to enforce the teaching of *Taharat Hamishpahah*, family purity, with special emphasis. Our modern detractors delight in denigrating the *Halakhah* regarding the Jewish woman. On the contrary, R. Eleazar raises the status of woman to the highest degree possible and labelled it the inner Halakhah.

Astronomy This science has always been popular amongst Jews, one of the reasons being that it is indispensable for the fixing of the Calendar (Shab. 75a). This is often given as an interpretation of Deut. 4:6, 'This is your wisdom and understanding in the eyes of the nations'. The calendar is our guide for the Sabbaths and Festivals of the Jewish year; we not only mark time, but sanctify time. Thus *Mekadesh Yisrael Vehazmanim*, hallowing Israel and the seasons, often occurs in the Festival Liturgy. We can gauge the importance of astronomy in talmudic times because we are told that Samuel (died 254) claimed to have had as exact a knowledge of the heavenly spheres as of the streets of his own city Nehardea (Ber. 58b).

In the post-talmudic era, astronomical tables were formulated by a number of Jews; the earliest treatise on astronomy in Hebrew appeared in Marseilles in 1134. Discussions on astronomy appear in the writings of Yehudah Halevi, Abraham Ibn Ezra and Maimonides. A new system of astronomy is found in 'The Wars of the Lord' by R. Levi Ben Gerson (1288-1344). Echoes of astronomy are recalled in the Prayer Book which records the Service of the Sanctification of the Moon and in the Synagogue on every Sabbath before the New Moon we announce the *Molad*, literally the birth, which is the moment of the conjunction of the sun and the moon. It is interesting to remember that in the curriculum of the Spanish schools in the twelfth century, astronomy was included.

Gematria. This Hebrew word is of Greek origin. Gematria is a popular form of homiletical interpretation of the text of the Torah employed by the

Rabbis, and deals mainly with numbers. The Hebrew alphabet is also numerical, each letter representing a number. The Rabbis, in their love for the Torah, derive lessons from every word and letter through the system *of Gematria*, the science of numbers (Numerology).

We append below several examples:

In Gen. 14:14 we read, 'The trained men in his house, three hundred and eighteen men'. According to the Talmud (Ned. 32a) these were really one person, Eliezer the faithful servant of Abraham. The numerical value of the Hebrew letters of the name Eliezer amounts to 318.

The first letter of each of the first six verses of Deut. 32, the farewell song of Moses, are Hei, Yod, Khaf, Hei, Shin, Hei. These letters add up to 345, the numerical value of the name of Moses, Mem, shin, Hei. This conveys the idea that the lessons enshrined in these verses sum up the philosophy of Moses prior to his death.

The Sidrah *Naso* is the longest in the Torah, containing one hundred and seventy six verses. Ps. 119 is the longest in the Psalter one hundred and seventy six verses and Bava Batra the longest tractate in the Talmud comprises one hundred and seventy six pages.

In Nu. 17:25 Korah uses the term *Meri* to describe his followers. *Meri*, in Hebrew, has the numerical value of two hundred and fifty, and in Nu. 16:2 we read, 'They rose up ... 250 men'.

Deut. 5:2 informs us that God made a covenant with us. *Karat* in Hebrew means 'To cut' and equals the numerical value of six hundred and twenty. This refers to the six hundred and twenty letters in the Ten Commandments which were cut in stone by God. It can also refer to the six hundred and twenty main commandments compounded of the 613 mitzvot plus the seven Noahide Laws.

In Deut. 6:7 we read, 'And you shall speak of them'. The word *bam*, of them, consists of two letters, Bet for *Bereshit*, Genesis, representing the Written Law, and, *Mem*, the first letter of the Oral Law, *Mei-eimasei*, the first word of the tractate Berakhot, which is the first section of the Talmud.

The most fascinating example is found in the following extract. (Jewish curiosities Hausdorff) 'Where in the Tanakh is there a reference to Prohibition in America? The answer is found in Lev. 10:9, 'Wine and strong drink do not drink'. This, however, could apply to any country prohibiting strong drink, but the numerical value of the letters of Lev. 10:9 equals six hundred and eighty. In the year 680 of the fifth millenium (5680) corresponding to 1920, the Volstead Act ordering prohibition to become law in the U.S.A. was passed.

Periphriyot. This word has its origin in the Greek and Latin root, from which is derived the English word periphery, on the border or fringe. The Hebrew word is translated as dessert or sweet and is served as the final course of a meal. Similarly, astronomy and gematria are not to be compared to the main meal, but to the after-courses, or the sweet. R. Eleazar warns us that these external sciences are merely peripheral appetisers, not to be confused with the body of the meal which is likened to family purity, which is indispensable, whereas astronomy and gematria are incidental.

Hasidic Lore

Marriage R. Isaiah Kalman Halberstadt said: We read in the Talmud (Ta. 30b). 'Said Simeon Ben Gamliel, 'There were no holidays in Israel like Yom Kippur and the fifteenth day of Av'. On the latter (Midsummer day) the maidens were privileged to make an offer of marriage. They would arrange an open-air dance in the vineyards; all were dressed in pure white garments and when the youths would approach, the maidens would divide into three groups. The handsome girls would say, 'Observe our beauty, for it is fitting that a wife should be of comely appearance'. Those of noble family would say, 'Observe our high-born lineage for this foretells good children'. Those of unprepossessing countenance would say, 'Take unto yourselves wives for the sake of obeying the will of God and adorn us with gold'.

The phrases of the handsome maidens and the last words spoken by the unhandsome ones may seem to be frivolous; but they will not appear thus on closer scrutiny and explanation.

When a man wishes to donate a Scroll of the Torah, he usually desires to do so in a generous fashion. He may spend additional money to obtain excellent parchment and fine script. This may be accounted 'beauty of the body'. Or he may seek for a Scroll written by a man of rare piety and holiness. This may be interpreted as 'beauty of lineage' since the value of the Scroll lies in its distinguished associations. Or he may strive to obtain a beautiful coverlet or a fine pair of holders or decorative adornments for the Scroll. This may be explained as 'beauty of the exterior'. In each instance the man endeavours to perform the mitzvah in a beautiful manner.

So it is with the maidens. The first group says, 'When you intend to perform the mitzvah of taking a wife to yourself in a fitting manner, consider beauty of the body'. The second group says, 'Consider the beauty of noble descent '. The third group says, 'We have neither beauty of body nor noble descent, but if you wish to marry solely for the sake of the mitzvah and not for ulterior motives, then demonstrate this by marrying us. As for the beauty you may wish to add to the mitzvah, it will be sufficient to adorn us in costly garments and jewels'.

Concluding Mishnah. Text, translation and commentary, see page 71.

PEREK FOUR

Introductory Mishnah. Text, translation and commentary on p. 11.

פרק רביעי

(א) **בֶּן** זוֹמָא אוֹמֵר אֵיזֶהוּ חָכָם הַלּוֹמֵד מִכָּל אָדָם שֶׁנֶּאֱמַר מִכָּל מְלַמְּדַי הִשְׂכַּלְתִּי כִּי עֵדְוֹתֶיךָ שִׂיחָה לִּי. אֵיזֶהוּ גִבּוֹר הַכּוֹבֵשׁ אֶת יִצְרוֹ שֶׁנֶּאֱמַר טוֹב אֶרֶךְ אַפַּיִם מִגִּבּוֹר וּמוֹשֵׁל בְּרוּחוֹ מִלּוֹכֵד עִיר. אֵיזֶהוּ עָשִׁיר הַשָּׂמֵחַ בְּחֶלְקוֹ שֶׁנֶּאֱמַר יְגִיעַ כַּפֶּיךָ כִּי תֹאכֵל אַשְׁרֶיךָ וְטוֹב לָךְ אַשְׁרֶיךָ בָּעוֹלָם הַזֶּה וְטוֹב לָךְ לָעוֹלָם הַבָּא. אֵיזֶהוּ מְכֻבָּד הַמְכַבֵּד אֶת הַבְּרִיּוֹת שֶׁנֶּאֱמַר כִּי מְכַבְּדַי אֲכַבֵּד וּבֹזַי יֵקָלּוּ:

Mishnah One.,

Ben Zoma says: Who is wise? He who learns from all people, as it is said. 'I have more understanding than all my teachers; for Thy testimonies are my meditation' (Ps. 119:99). Who is strong? He who subdues his evil impulse, as it is said, 'He that is slow to anger is better than the mighty, and he who rules his spirit than he who takes a city' (Prov. 16:32). Who is rich? He who rejoices in his portion, as it is said, 'When you eat of the labour of your hands, happy are you and it shall be well with you; (Ps. 128:2): happy are you in this world and it shall be well with you in the world to come'. Who is honoured? He who honours mankind, as it is said. 'For them who honour Me will I honour, and they who despise Me shall be lightly esteemed' (I Sam. 2:30).

Ben Zoma. His standing in rabbinic circles can be gauged from the statement that whoever saw Ben Zoma in a dream was assured of attaining ripe scholarship (Ber. 57b). He was permitted to give decisions in the presence of the Sages in the Sanhedrin at Javneh, and was recognised as a popular expounder of Tanakh. Ben Zoma was one of the four Sages who entered the *Pardes* (paradise or esoteric knowledge) and became demented (Ha. 14b). According to some his full name, Shimon Ben Zoma, is not mentioned here on account of his early death. Others are of the opinion that Ben Zoma was so called in reverential praise of his father; compare 'Divrei Kohelet Ben David' (Ecc. 1:1).

The fourth chapter commences with four rhetorical questions dealing with wisdom, might, wealth and honour. Ben Zoma specifically asks these questions because they are all open to misinterpretation. He does not present us with a simple statement of fact; he wishes to arouse our curiosity so that we might ponder on the correct meaning and understanding of these four sign-posts on the road of life.

Asking questions is a familiar form of exposition which is successfully employed during the reading of the Hagadah on the Seder Night, when the 'four questions' enliven the mind of the child. Here the questions of the Mishnah are addressed to the adult population to stimulate discussion on four characteristic qualities which, unfortunately, are misguidedly adapted to serve the ends of rapacious individuals who strive to use their wisdom, strength, wealth, and honour, to gain mastery over others, and not themselves. We should judge ourselves introspectively and examine our motives. Ben Zoma asks us to view these four subjects in their correct perspective. We shall briefly analyse each of them.

Who is wise? A wise man learns from all people, but not all people are alike in their personal predilections. The wise man not only listens to a variety of opinions, but also learns to accept the good and discard the evil. One should not rely entirely on one's own judgment; it is preferable to discuss and learn from others. This explains why we call a great scholar a Talmid Hakham; he always remains a disciple. Proof that wisdom is the result of learning from all is attested to by the verse from Ps. 119:99, 'I have got understanding from all my teachers'; we learn from many teachers. It is a recognised fact that the average Yeshivah student will spend some time at a number of Yeshivot and sit at the feet of different scholars and learn from all of them. 'For Thy testimonies are my meditation' (ibid); learn from every man but remember that the authentic Jew must be fully conversant with all the mitzvot. This also makes for true humility.

Who is mighty? Jewish thought teaches us that the mighty man is not he who boasts of his brawn and muscle, but he who masters and controls his evil impulse. We are not asked to destroy the evil impulse, for God planted it within man.Without it, we would not marry or work to sustain ourselves and our dependants. It is, however, our constant duty to limit and control the evil inclination which is dormant within us.

It would be instructive to connect the use of the word *kavash*, subdue, in this Mishnah, with the same word first mentioned in the Torah (Gen. 1:28) where mankind is commanded to subdue the earth. We are to become the masters of all the herbs and minerals found in the bowels of the earth. We have suffered much in this age because many of our young people have not subdued the earth, but have submitted to drugs which have become their masters. This is the result of the work of the evil impulse. In times of war the mighty rely on costly and deadly weapons, and it often happens that the victors gain only a pyrrhic victory and lose more than the vanquished. On the home front, however, we need no weapons; real might is shown, not by active conquest of others, but by self-conquest and quiet restraint. This is borne out by the proof text from which we learn that ruling over one's spirit is a greater achievement than conquering a city, which involves suffering and bloodshed.

Yitzro, his impulse. M. Lazarus points out that *yetzer* here is not equivalent to sensuality. Whereas the conqueror of the *yetzer* is he who is 'slow to anger', it is plain that the opposition to the spiritual does not enter into the question, and the Scriptural quotation refers distinctly to the control of the passions, that is, only to the inner spiritual liberty of man. As little as *yetzer tov* means the purely spiritual, so little does *yetzer ra* stand for sensuality.

Who is rich? The great teacher Jacob Anatoli (thirteenth century) said, 'If a man cannot get what he wants, he ought to want what he can get'. The legitimate acquisition of the needs of life is recognised by the Torah. Ben Zoma does not say that man should be satisfied with his portion, but he should rejoice in his portion. This philosophy of being happy with one's peace of mind stresses the great attribute of thankfulness which is pathetically lacking today. In addition to being happy and grateful for what God grants us, we are to remember that every human being, whatever his station in life, is entitled to his allotted portion. The avaricious and over-ambitious are unhappy in their own fortune and endeavour to rob others of their God-given portion. Moreover, the greedy person may acquire his wealth by dishonest or foul means, transgressing the mitzvot and the laws of God.

Contentment does not apply only to the material things of life, but also to our spiritual and moral improvement. We should always forge ahead and aim for spiritual and material advancement, but at every stage we should rejoice in our portion. This limitation of our cravings and desires will help us to realise what we really are. The Hafez Hayyim said, 'When I am called before the heavenly tribunal to give an account of my life, I shall not be called upon to explain why I was not another Moses, but why I was not myself'.

We close this section with two more thoughts on the subject of wealth. In the first place we should note that in addition to Ben Zoma, R. Meir also asked the same question, 'Who is rich?'. His answer was, 'The rich man is he who has pleasure in his wealth' (Shab. 25b). He who hoards his wealth and does not share it with others, cannot enjoy it. Secondly, the philosophy of wealth is read into the Hebrew word for a rich man, *ashir*, which consists of the letters *ayin*, *shin*, *yod*, *resh*. These letters initial the words *ainayim*, eyes; *shinayim*, teeth, *yadayim*, hands and *raglayim*, feet. One who is blessed with the use of these limbs is indeed a rich person.

Who is honoured? After wisdom, might and wealth, a man imagines he possesses everything and may therefore demand honour from others. The Mishnah, therefore, warns us that honour cannot be bought, but must be earned. On the whole, people react favourably to the respectful person who is treated with deference by others. So it is with our relationship to God. Those who honour God, are themselves honoured. The Mesillat Yesharim writes: A man must act respectfully to his neighbour who, he understands, is his superior, be it in a single respect only (Pes. 113b) ..... As it is characteristic of the wicked to show contempt, so is it characteristic of the righteous to show respect, for honour always abides with them, it never departs from them, as we read in Is. 24:23, 'Before His elders shall be glory'.

Our Mishnah, in greater part, is based on Jer. 9:22, 'Let not a wise man boast of his wisdom, neither let the mighty man boast of his might, let not a rich man boast of his riches'. There is a slight discrepancy between the wording of Jeremiah and that of our Mishnah. Of the three terms wise, mighty and rich, only 'mighty' is preceded by the definite article - this cannot be accidental. In terms of physical strength, the mighty person could easily overthrow the wise man and rob a rich man of his wealth, but in the spirit of verse 23, Jeremiah reminds us that the mighty is none other than the Almighty, as we read in the daily Amidah, '*HaEl Hagadol Hagibor* ..... the great the mighty God (Jer. 32:18).

R. Nehunya Ben Ha-Kanah was asked to what he attributed his longevity and he answered, 'I have never obtained honour at the expense of the humiliation of my fellow, and I have never been guilty of cursing my colleague in secret' (Meg. 28a). Jewish law furnishes us with another example. The Torah imposed a five-fold fine on a thief who stole and sold an ox, but only a four-fold fine on a thief who stole and sold a sheep. R. Johanan Ben Zakkai explained, 'How great is the honour of a human being. He who had to carry the sheep on his shoulders, being humiliated, paid only four-fold, but he who only led the ox, paid five-fold' (B.K.79b).

Hasidic Lore

Learn from all. They asked R. Mikhal, 'In the Sayings of the Fathers we read, 'Who is wise?'. He who learns from all men, as it is said, 'From all my teachers have I gotten understanding'. Then why does it not say, 'He who learns from every teacher?'

R. Mikhal explained: The master who pronounced these words is intent on having it clear that we can learn not only from those whose occupation it is to teach, but from every man. Even from one who is ignorant, or from one who is wicked, you can gain understanding how to conduct your life.

The words in the Scriptures, 'But you that cleave unto the Lord your God are alive every one of you this day' (Deut. 4:4) are expounded as follows, 'Cleave to His qualities', but this must be properly understood. Emanating from God are ten qualities and these come in twos which oppose each other like two colours, one of which is apparently in direct contrast to the other. But seen with the true inner eye, they all form one simple unity. It is the task of man to make them appear a unity to the true outer eye as well. Perhaps one man finds it difficult to be merciful because his way is to be rigorous, and another finds it difficult to be rigorous because his way is merciful.

But he who binds the rigour within him to its root, to the rigour of God, and the mercy which is in him to its root, to the mercy of God, and so on in all things, such a man will unite the ten qualities within himself, and he himself will become the unity they represent, for he cleaves to the Lord of the world. Such a man has become wax into which both judgment and mercy can set their seal.

Honour. R. Isaac Vorky said, 'A Jew has to treat his fellow with the utmost respect and should not lean on him for support, for every Jew is like a holy book'. One of his disciples asked, 'But according to the Law, is it not permitted to place one book on the top of another?' The Rabbi answered, 'Yes, but you have to regard yourself as an ordinary mortal'.

(ב) בֶּן עַזַּאי אוֹמֵר הֱוֵי רָץ לְמִצְוָה קַלָּה וּבוֹרֵחַ מִן הָעֲבֵרָה שֶׁמִּצְוָה גוֹרֶרֶת מִצְוָה וַעֲבֵרָה גוֹרֶרֶת עֲבֵרָה שֶׁשְּׂכַר מִצְוָה מִצְוָה וּשְׂכַר עֲבֵרָה עֲבֵרָה:

Mishnah Two

Ben Azzai says: Run to do a light mitzvah and flee from sin, for mitzvah leads to mitzvah and sin to sin; for the reward of a mitzvah is a mitzvah and the reward of sin is sin.

Ben Azzai is Simeon Ben Azzai. He was one of the four who entered the *Pardes*, paradise, and died as a result. It is reported that Ben Azzai was betrothed to the daughter of R. Akiva, but did not marry her. From that period, he devoted himself wholly to the study of Torah. The Mishnah (So. 9:15) records that at the death of Ben Azzai, the last industrious man passed away. Whereas R. Akiva stressed that 'You shall love your neighbour as yourself' (Lev. 19:18) is the great principle of Torah, Ben Azzai pointed to Gen. 6:1, 'This is the book of the generations of man', which to him was the root principle underlying the concept of the brotherhood of all mankind.

Mitzvah. The key to this Mishnah is the basic meaning of mitzvah which, as the word *Torah*, is untranslatable. The mitzvah is generally designated to mean a commandment, but to the average reader a commandment refers to one of the Ten Commandments which, incidentally, are not known as *Aseret Hamitzvot*, Ten Mitzvot, but *Aseret Hadibrot*, Ten Words. Because the mitzvah is all-embracing and has many nuances, we prefer the word mitzvah rather than commandment.

However, we can define it as God's will. The mitzvah brings God down to earth and raises man to heaven and it is introduced where and when both meet. When we perform a mitzvah, an angel escorts us. A mitzvah is a spiritual exercise which ennobles us in all pursuits of life. Every mitzvah is good, pious, righteous and holy. 'The mitzvot have been given for the sole purpose of refining our human nature' (Gen. R. 44:1). The mitzvah is a purifying agent and so introduces purity and sanctity into our every-day life. Thus, when we recite a blessing, we say '*Asher kidshanu bemitzvotav*', 'He sanctified us with His commandments'.

Our moralists, referring to the reasons for the mitzvot, used the expression '*Taamei Hamitzvot*', *taam* meaning taste or flavour. The mitzvot give an added flavour to the humdrum monotony of life; they add zest, fragrance and poetry to the ordinary routine of existence. The mitzvah is an act of inspiration and can affect us at all times. Indeed, it has been said that there is no end to the mysteries of the mitzvah, and if a man lives a thousand years, he would not exhaust the meaning of one single mitzvah in all its depth. Little wonder that even such a rationalist as Ahad Ha-am testified 'more than the Jew has kept the mitzvah, has the mitzvah kept the Jew'. Moreover, the mitzvah is unique to Judaism. The Christian use of the word 'sin' means more than *averah;* original sin is an essential ingredient of Christian theology. We are more *mitzvah*-minded than *averah*-minded. It is true that we emphasise the evil of sin on *Yom Kippur*, but we should remember that *het*, the Hebrew word for sin, basically means 'missing the mark'. Every person can correct this; he needs no intermediary; God is near to all who call upon Him. Similarly, *averah* means 'to pass over, to be out of step'. This, too, can be rectified by the saving grace of repentance.

Run to do a light mitzvah, and flee from sin. The verbs 'to run' and 'to flee' are used advisedly. A mitzvah can bring only goodness. An opportunity for good which is not seized, is an opportunity lost. We should not allow a mitzvah to slip from our grasp, but run to do good and flee from an *averah*. Those who have any experience of social work know that the habitual criminal is one who is not apprehended when he committed the first *averah*. Such a person is automatically drawn into the vortex of sin and will find it very difficult to extricate himself from its deadly grip. The word *goreret* (leads to) is onomatopoetic and self-expressive. One mitzvah urges us to perform another mitzvah; the mitzvah is infectious for good. Similarly, the *averah* is infectious for evil and drags the evil-doer into the mire. This reflects the psychological truth of the rabbinic maxim, 'He who comes to purify himself will be assisted; he who comes to defile himself will find the doors open' (Yoma 38b). This is the price we pay for freedom of will.

The reward of a mitzvah is a mitzvah and the reward of sin is sin. We are not rewarded on this earth; a good deed must not be motivated. The uniqueness of a mitzvah is that it is not publicised and therefore differs from the ceremony or symbol which may be ostentatious. The mitzvah is a quiet, unobtrusive act, without the pursuit of material reward. The spiritual reward is the performance of yet another mitzvah. Conversely, the reward of an *averah* is another *averah*. Some object to the word 'reward' and suggest that 'punishment' would be more appropriate, but the evil-doer does enjoy a temporary reward for his nefarious acts; it is this momentary reward which tempts him to continue to transgress.

Hasidic Lore

One mitzvah draws another mitzvah.

The Apter Rabbi related the following story. A Jew once came to buy grain in a village owned by a Countess who, on meeting the Jew of handsome appearance, fell in love with him. She persuaded him to divorce his wife, be converted to Christianity, and marry her. Consequently, he received the title of Count.

A few years later, whilst the nobility were assembled in the capital to sit in the Seym (public senate), one nobleman reported that a Christian girl belonging to his town had disappeared, and he accused the Jews of having murdered her for ritual purposes. Others added similar tales and affirmed that Christian blood was in constant demand at the ceremonies of the Jews. The king became enraged and issued an edict that all Jews should be banished from Poland. According to the Polish Constitution, every edict had to be signed by each member of the Seym; if there was one dissenter, the edict would be nullified.

The former Jew, the Count, placed his veto on the decree, stating that the 'blood accusation' was entirely without foundation in fact, notwithstanding the manifold repetitions of the accusation throughout the centuries, and despite the fact that the alleged victims had been canonised by Popes. The edict was destroyed and the king reprimanded the nobleman who had levelled the accusation. Since one mitzvah, when performed, draws another mitzvah in its train, it transpired that the Jewish Count repented of his life as a Christian. He consulted a Rabbi, escaped to Amsterdam, and commenced to lead a Jewish life anew. Soon after this occurred, the Countess died. The penitent later remarried his former Jewish wife and henceforth remained a pious and loyal Jew.

(ג) הוּא הָיָה אוֹמֵר אַל תְּהִי בָז לְכָל אָדָם וְאַל תְּהִי מַפְלִיג לְכָל דָּבָר שֶׁאֵין לְךָ אָדָם שֶׁאֵין לוֹ שָׁעָה וְאֵין לְךָ דָבָר שֶׁאֵין לוֹ מָקוֹם:

Mishnah Three.

He used to say: Do not despise any man and carp not at anything, for there is no man who has not his hour, and no thing which has not its place.

Do not despise any man. Respect the personality of every individual because he is created in the image of God. If you despise any man, you despise God; be therefore tolerant even if you disagree with your fellow-man. If, as we are told, no two blades of grass are exactly identical, we cannot expect all people to think alike. In this connection one should remember the mature wisdom of the Rabbis who observe that as no two faces are absolutely alike, so no two minds are exactly alike (Ber. 58a). There is an infinite variety in the universe which is ruled by one God; do not, therefore, despise the whole person even if you should discover an objectionable trait in his character. Be patient and you may yet discover that he possesses an admirable quality. Great men are not always endowed with great ideals. The truly great will not despise the lowly and unsuccessful person but will recognise and respect even the unlearned if he possesses sincerity of purpose.

Thus it is related of R. Finkel of Slobodka, a pupil of Israel Salanter, that he once recited the Kaddish in the Synagogue incorrectly. The congregants were taken aback and later questioned him. He replied that he did not wish to embarrass an elderly gentleman who was unable to pronounce the words of the Kaddish correctly so he also mispronounced the words not to put the old man to shame.

We must not despise any person, but we are permitted to criticise and even reprove him; indeed, this is a positive commandment in the Torah. In the same verse which bids us not to hate our brother in our heart, we are enjoined, 'You shall surely reprove your neighbour and not bear sin against him' (Lev. 19:17). Reprove him, but treat him as a fellow-citizen, as a neighbour, who is entitled to equal status; despising him would be sinful.

The key word here is 'despise'; anything despicable is vile and objectionable. To gauge the difference in character between Jacob and Esau, we need to emphasise one word in the narrative, (Gen. 25:34), *vayivez*, Esau despised the birthright. This word has the same root as *vaz* in our Mishnah and characterises Esau as unworthy to inherit the birthright, which had no significance to him.

Unlike Esau, Joseph, who had good reason to treat his brothers with contempt for having thrown him into a pit and sold him to Egypt, when the opportunity presented itself to wreak vengeance upon them, he pacified them with the words, 'Do not grieve that you sold me; God sent me for a preservation' (Gen. 45:5). Similarly, David, who fled from the enmity of King Saul, subsequently found him in a cave. Instead of taking retributive action, 'David arose and cut off the skirt of Saul's robe privily' (I Sam. 24:5). The Rabbis explain that for repaying evil intention with kindness, both Joseph and David were raised to the exalted position of the monarchy. Throughout our martyred history we have lost many Jews who have despised their ancient heritage and have become assimilated to other religions. However, large numbers of Jews have sacrificed their lives for the sanctification of the Name of God and martyred themselves rather than despise the noble faith into which they were born.

Finally, we should note the language used by Ben Azzai. He does not say, 'You shall not despise'; this would be too harsh a command. He prefaces his dictum with the word *al*, which expresses an entreaty, pleading that one should not despise any man. Ben Azzai's words ring down throughout the corridors of time, cautioning his people not to hate any person, for hatred begets hatred.

There is no man who has not his hour. However difficult the road of life we pursue may be, we must never capitulate; the struggle may be strong and arduous, but if we are patient, our hour will come. We should attempt to rise above our misfortunes and respond to every opportunity that avails itself. What is true of the individual is equally true of a nation. As a people, we are predestined for suffering; we have been the butt and target of every country in the world. However, hope springs eternal in the human breast, and Judaism is a religion of optimism. In spite of our setbacks, we must perseveve in our just struggle for existence; our hour and place are reserved for us and must be realised. We shall yet enjoy our rightful place in the comity of nations, if we are convinced of the justice of our cause.

Hasidic Lore

The hour. A man visited the Lekhivitzer and asked him to teach him humility. As he was speaking, the clock struck the hour. The Rabbi commented, 'From the sound of the clock striking the hour, we can receive ample instruction regarding the submission of the heart. We should all ponder on the thought that another hour of life has departed; have we accomplished any improvement of our soul.?

Place. The Gerer said, 'Each one of us should know his place. We cannot make a myrtle into a lulav; however,we can attach ourselves unto one who is known to be of more consequence. We are then irresistably drawn to him, even as the myrtle is to the lulav'.

Rabbi Abraham was asked: Our Sages say, 'And there is not a thing that has not its place'. And so man too has his own place. Then why do people sometimes feel so crowded? He replied: Because each wants to occupy the place of the other.

(ד) רַבִּי לְוִיטַס אִישׁ יַבְנֶה אוֹמֵר מְאֹד מְאֹד הֱוֵי שְׁפַל רוּחַ שֶׁתִּקְוַת אֱנוֹשׁ רִמָּה:

Mishnah Four.

R. Levitas of Javneh says: Be exceedingly lowly of spirit, for the hope of man is worms.

R. Levitas is comparatively unknown except for this one reference in the 'Ethics' and Pirkei d'R. Eliezer (Chapters 23 and 52). See also ARN 74. It is due to the magnanimity and breadth of vision of the editor of 'Ethics', R. Judah the Prince, that this Mishnah was included, and we are grateful to him for popularising the basic virtue of Jewish ethics.

Be exceedingly lowly of spirit. Here we have a paraphrase of the noble concept of humility, which includes all qualities. The greater the man, the more lowly of spirit will he be. The source of humility is found in the Torah; indeed, in the opening words of the Torah, 'In the beginning God created .....' (Gen. 1:1). It would have been appropriate for the Torah to commence with the name of God, but the Almighty in His humility preferred the Torah to begin with the words *bereshit bara. We mortals should imitate God and withhold our identity in all our undertakings. The same lowliness of spirit manifests itself in our prayers. The first elementary prayer which we teach our children is, Modeh ani lefanekha,* I give thanks unto Thee. Thanks are expressed first, the person is in the second place and God is mentioned last. Similarly, in the recognised formula of all our Berakhot (Blessings), we recite *Baruch Ata Hashem*, Blessed art Thou O Lord; the blessing begins with the word 'Blessed', and not *Hashem*.

When we approach the universe with humility we perceive the illimitable expanse of the heavens, sun, moon, stars and planets with a sense of awe, and are consequently aware of our own insignificance. We are humbled in the presence of the *Shekhinah*. The Talmud asks, 'Why are the words of the Torah likened unto water? .... to indicate that as the water leaves the high places and flows to lower regions, so the words of Torah depart from him who is haughty, and remain with him who is humble (Ta. 7a). Rav Hoshaiah said, 'Why are the words of the Torah likened unto these three liquids, water, wine and milk? To indicate to you that as these three liquids can be preserved in only the cheapest kind of vessels, so will the words of the Torah be preserved only in him who is lowly (Ta. 7a).

The Mesillat Yesharim speaks of humility of thought and humility of action, and the author (H.M. Luzatto) divides the subject into five parts dealing with humility in one's bearing, in enduring insults, in hating to exercise authority, in shunning applause and in honouring every person. From this we see how humility pervades every area of life, and can strengthen both the individual and the nation.

In this connection we should be cautious not to equate humility with timidity or helplessness. True humility derives, not from weakness, but from strength of character. The great Hillel whose patience, forbearance and absence of anger made him truly humble, is a famous example of this characteristic. The exemplar of humility is Moses, who is explicitly referred to as 'exceedingly humble' (Nu. 12:3). Here the word *anav*, humble, is used and is akin to *ani*, poor. As The poor are subjected to and dependent on others for a livelihood, so are we all poor and reliant on God, the source of every thing. We can sum up the all-encompassing virtue of humility with the quotation from the Tanna debei Eliyahu: Let every man be humble with his parents, teachers, wife and children, with his kinsfolk near and far, even with the heathen, and so become beloved on high and desirable below.

M'od m'od. It is unusual to find the repetition of the word *m'od*, which is a noun meaning muchness, abundance or might. Commenting on the words in the Shema, 'And you shall love the Lord your God *bekhol meodekha*, with all your might, the Rabbis interpret these words as meaning 'with all your wealth' (Ber. 57a). Too often we find that the wealthy, those in power and authority, become conceited and vain, unrestrained by the absence of lowliness of spirit. Such people can destroy not only their families, but even a nation. Rabbi Levitas therefore emphasises the word *m'od;* if we are overcome with our own self-importance or power, a greater measure of humility is necessary to minimise our vanity, and we must realise that whatever our ambitions may be, one factor is inescapable - the end of every mortal is the grave; this thought should have a sobering effect on our lives.

In 'Judaism and Christianity' edited by W.O.E. Oesterly, a non-Jewish writer, reminds us that the concept of humility did not originate in Christendom, but in Judaism, and he quotes the famous verse in Micah 6:8, 'Walk humbly with your God'. Christianity adopted the assurance that humility is a virtue from Judaism. This is all the more significant since Christianity, in following the Jewish concept of humility, turns its back not only on the Roman, but as far as Teutonic Christianity is concerned, on its Teutonic past also; for it is an unquestionable fact that Teutonic society was a society built on personal pride' (Vol 2, page 227).

Hasidic Lore

Scholars and humility. Once R. Jacob Yitzhak Lubliner was confident of the advent of the Redeemer before the end of the year. However, when the year came to an end and redemption was still absent the Rabbi said to his favourite disciple the Yud, 'The common people have turned from their evil ways, on their part there is no hindrance to the redemption. It is the scholar that bars the way; he cannot attain to humility and, therefore, not to repentance'.

(ה) רַבִּי יוֹחָנָן בֶּן בְּרוֹקָה אוֹמֵר כָּל הַמְחַלֵּל שֵׁם שָׁמַיִם בַּסֵּתֶר נִפְרָעִין מִמֶּנּוּ בְּגָלוּי אֶחָד שׁוֹגֵג וְאֶחָד מֵזִיד בְּחִלּוּל הַשֵּׁם:

Mishnah Five.

R. Johanan Ben Berokah says: Anyone who profanes the Name of Heaven in secret is punished in public, whether one acts inadvertently or wilfully it is one, regarding the profanation of the Name.

R. Johanan Ben Berokah was a pupil of R. Joshua Ben Hananiah and a colleague of R. Eleazar Hisma. He championed women's rights and sympathised with the Sotah (a woman suspected of faithlessness, Nu. 5:12) who, he said, should not be humiliated (Sifre Naso).

Anyone who profanes the Name of Heaven. In our duties towards God we are constantly reminded to uphold the sanctity and dignity of the Name (Kiddush Hashem). We are to be conscious of our daily conduct which should be exemplary. If we tarnish the fair name of Judaism we commit a *Hillul Hashem*, a Profanation of the Name of God; indeed, it is a greater sin than idolatry (Sanh. 106a). The full implication of this grievous sin is recorded in Lev. 19:12 where we read, 'You shall not swear by My Name falsely, so that you profane not the Name of your God, I am the Lord'. Again, in Lev. 22.32 we read, 'And you shall not profane My holy Name, but I will be hallowed among the Children of Israel'. These two texts should be studied together with the third Commandment, 'You shall not take the Name of the Lord your God in vain, for the Lord will not hold him guiltless who takes His Name in vain' (Ex. 20:7).

The Name of God is sacrosanct and is to be used sparingly and respectfully in the study of the Torah, in prayers, or when required to do so in a court of law to emphasise the truth, It is unfortunate that the masses do not grasp the full meaning of *Hillul Ha-Shem*. The Name of God is used flippantly in ordinary conversation and every-day language, robbing it of its sanctity and making it *hullin*, ordinary, the antithesis of *kodesh*, holy.

The sacred Scriptures are taught and studied as literature, thus depriving them of faith and grace. One shudders at the thought that many perjure themselves in courts of law whilst swearing falsely by the Name of God; these are acts of *Hillul Ha-Shem*. Such is the force of *Hillul Ha-Shem* that it has entered into almost every area of life. Wherever and whenever the Name of God is desecrated, the people of Israel have suffered. The misdeeds of an individual Jew, the malpractices of one member of the Jewish race, have brought shame and disgrace on the House of Israel. Every Jew holds the honour of his people in his hand and it is his duty and privilege to be particularly sensitive to the good name, not only of the Jewish people, but of the Jewish God. The Rabbis treated *Hillul Ha-Shem* with such seriousness that they suggested, 'Better that a letter of the sacred Torah be blotted out, than that the divine Name be profaned' (Yoma 86a).

In secret. He who commits a *Hillul Ha-Shem* in secret is particularly objectionable for we cannot escape from the gaze of the Almighty. This can also betoken a measure of hypocrisy, for some people parade their religiosity openly and ostentatiously, whilst secretly desecrating the authority of God and in various ways bring about a *Hillul Ha-Shem*. 'If the transgressor is a scholar. people will follow his example; he will be punished in broad daylight so that his hypocrisy will be publicised abroad. Because of him people will treat the words of the Torah with contumely; that is why in regard to profaning the Name, the unwitting suffers the same penalty as the witting' (Vitry). The gravity of the offence is summed up by the Meiri in the following manner: The penalty for profaning the Name is so extreme because in this instance a man sins, not because he is overpowered by the evil impulse, but because he wishes to throw off the yoke and treat the Torah and Commandments with contempt and thus he denies the Omniscience and Providence of God'

Hasidic Lore

The Name of God. The Sassover said: Why do we find that in many Prayer Books the Name of God is represented by the duplication of the letter 'Yud'.The explanation is to be found in the fact that thereby we have a demonstration of the principle that if Jews are united the Name of God is fashioned, and no erasure can be made in it even if it is written by mistake in a wrong place. It is different, however, if Jews are disunited and each one stands separated and apart. They do not then create the Name of God, and if they do not stand in their right position it is permissible to erase them .

(ו) רַבִּי יִשְׁמָעֵאל בְּנוֹ אוֹמֵר הַלּוֹמֵד עַל מְנָת לְלַמֵּד מַסְפִּיקִין בְּיָדוֹ לִלְמוֹד וּלְלַמֵּד
וְהַלּוֹמֵד עַל מְנָת לַעֲשׂוֹת מַסְפִּיקִין בְּיָדוֹ לִלְמוֹד וּלְלַמֵּד לִשְׁמוֹר וְלַעֲשׂוֹת:

Mishnah Six.

R. Ishmael his son says: If one learns in order to teach, it is granted to him to learn and to teach; but if one learns in order to practise, it is granted to him to learn and to teach, to observe and to practise.

R. Ishmael was a colleague of the President Simeon Ben Gamliel and Joshua Ben Korha. In the Mishnah he is mentioned only three times, Sanh. 11:1, B.K.10:2 and above. We also meet him in the Tosefta and Baraita.

This Mishnah enumerates the progression of three ideals, each one leading to the other for its fulfilment. They are learning, teaching and practising. Learning, which is the foundation of all Jewish life, is not an end in itself but the means to help and guide others to observe and practise. To one who learns Torah but does not teach, the words in Nu. 15:31, 'He has despised the word of the Lord' apply (Sanh. 99a). The Rabbis often remind us that learning is of paramount importance. If a person does not learn one day, he is removed from Torah, and Torah is removed from him a distance of one day. Therefore he is estranged from Torah a distance of two days. If he refrains from learning for two days, and the Torah is removed from him for two days, this makes a distance of four days. In general, learning is of two kinds, human and divine. Human learning is transient; the findings of science in one age are superseded by the scientific data of another age because the human mind is transitory. Not so with divine learning, which is constant and eternal. Isaiah declares, 'The grass withers, the flower fades, but the word of our God shall stand for ever' (40:8).

Throughout the Middle Ages Jews were forbidden entry to the University and were confined in ghettoes, where they were nourished and sustained by the word of God which was their only source of learning, but in spite of the inhuman restrictions forced upon them, they flourished. With emancipation and the opening of the University to the Jew, human learning, to the exclusion of divine learning, held sway. We are now witnessing the dire results of emancipation, which has been the cause of assimilation and defection from Judaism. The Yeshivah University, which combines the best of both worlds, is the ideal for which we must strive. On Jewish teaching see 1:6.

He who learns in order to practise. To understand the full import of the last words of our Mishnah, we shall briefly analyse the first Mishnah of 'Peah' with which we are very familiar because it is included in the early morning prayers of the Siddur. The Mishnah enumerates a number of *mitzvot maasiyot*, practical deeds such as honouring parents, charity, visiting the sick, dowering the bride, etc. which all come under the category of *laasot*, to do, practise. The climax, which is revealing, announces that learning of the Torah surpasses them all, or leads to them all. The translation is misleading and would appear to contradict our Mishnah which emphasises that practising is the goal of all learning. However, if we translate the word *keneged* as opposite, which is the literal meaning of the word, we get closer to the correct interpretation. *Talmud Torah keneged kullam means that accompanying or opposite each of the practical mitzvot singled out, Torah must be an essential adjunct. A deed without learning is as unworthy as learning without the deed. Both are interdependent and complement each other, and this combination applies to every mitzvah.*

Hasidic Lore

To be a good Jew. R. Samuel Shinaver visited R. Bunam for the first time and introduced himself. R. Bunam said, 'If it is your wish to be a good Jew, your coming was for nought; but if you wish to *learn* to be a good Jew, it is well that you have come to me'.

(ז) רַבִּי צָדוֹק אוֹמֵר אַל תִּפְרוֹשׁ מִן הַצִּבּוּר וְאַל תַּעַשׂ עַצְמְךָ כְּעוֹרְכֵי הַדַּיָּנִין וְאַל תַּעֲשֶׂהָ עֲטָרָה לְהִתְגַּדֵּל בָּהּ וְלֹא קַרְדּוֹם לַחְפּוֹר בָּהֶם. וְכַךְ הָיָה הִלֵּל אוֹמֵר וּדְאִשְׁתַּמֵּשׁ בְּתָגָא חֲלָף. הָא לָמַדְתָּ כָּל הַנֶּהֱנֶה מִדִּבְרֵי תוֹרָה נוֹטֵל חַיָּיו מִן הָעוֹלָם:

Mishnah Seven.

R. Zadok says: Do not separate yourself from the community and do not make yourself as they who prepare the judges and do not make it a crown where-with to magnify yourself nor a spade to dig with, and so Hillel used to say, 'And he who makes a servile use of the crown, wastes away'. Here you learn that anyone who makes profit from the words of Torah, removes his life from the world.

R. Zadok was a pious Sage who spent forty years in fasting and praying to avert the destruction of the Temple. Though he belonged to the school of Shammai, he followed the decisions of Hillel, on whom he patterned his own life, thus he quotes Hillel to confirm his statement. He was a personal friend of Rabban Gamliel and was an influential member of his Bet Din.

For the interpretation of the first clause, see 2:5, and on other clauses 1:8 and 1:13.

Do not make (the Torah) a crown wherewith to magnify yourself. Some interpret this statement as an elaboration of the previous Mishnah; one should not learn Torah for self-glorification or use the title of Rabbi for personal pride. The crown, which is the symbol of authority, belongs to the Torah and not to the person. For this reason we often have the words *Keter Torah*,the Crown of the Law, emblazoned on the curtain of the Ark and on the mantle of the Scrolls of the Law.

Nor a spade to dig with. This refers to a person who uses the Torah for his own selfish ends. Digging with a spade is the first operation leading to sowing and planting; we first break up and soften the earth. If we remember that the soil belongs to God and the spade is merely an instrument to produce food for the sake of man, we shall approach food-production inspired with the fear of God, and not as a means to enrich ourselves unduly at the expense of the poor. When there is a glut of a particular produce, tons of wholesome, staple food have been deliberately destroyed, rather than reduce the price to the consumer to make it available to all, This wanton devastation of God's food is abominable and a condemnation of the society in which we live. As God's food belongs to all, so does the Torah which was given in the wilderness, belong to all; no one should enrich himself through the teachings of the Torah, as R. Zadok states, 'Anyone who profits from the words of the Torah, removes his life from the world'.

This introduces us to a problem which has often been discussed by the Rabbis in the talmudic period. Rabbis were either craftsmen or engaged in business and the professions. To them, the teaching of Torah was a labour of love, for which they would never accept financial reward. The Sifre affirms, 'A man must not say, 'I will study the Torah in order that I may become rich by it, or that I may be rewarded by it in the world to come; he must study for love's sake. The Talmud (Ned. 37a) elaborates, 'It is written, 'Behold I have taught you statutes and ordinances even as the Lord my God commanded me' (Deut. 4:5). Even as I have taught you gratuitously, so should you teach others gratuitously'. On the other hand, the Talmud also states, 'Let a man devote himself to the study of Torah and to the Commandments even if it be for an ulterior purpose, because whaterver the motive may be, he will eventually arrive at the purpose' (Sanh. 105b).

Maimonides, who maintained his family through the practise of medicine, believed that it was essential for every person to have a vocation, and he castigates those who earn their livelihood by teaching Torah. However, Joseph Karo, the author of the Shulhan Arukh, disagrees with Maimonides' strictures. He rules that specialisation is essential to attain good results and that the full-time Rabbi or teacher should be paid. Another Rabbi states that a distinguished person needed by a community, may receive compensation, as it is permitted to be honoured. When the Torah is honoured, this is not an example of exploiting the Torah for one's personal advantage, for the honouring of a scholar is the honouring of the Torah (Duran).

It should be noted that in the pre-expulsion period in England the office of Rabbis was sponsored by the king and was held by a distinguished Jew known, not only for his scholarship and learning, but also favoured by the gentiles for his administrative qualities. Thus, the Rabbi was often a wealthy Jew and was generally called the 'Arch-Presbyter', who was not salaried but held the title in the same manner as the Exilarch, or *Resh*

Galuta, in Babylonia and *Nagid* in Egypt. The salaried Rabbi as the official of a community did not make his appearance until the fourteenth century.

Hasidic Lore

Function of a Rabbi., The Gerer Rabbi declared before Passover: I am not a professional Rabbi; I need neither more money nor more fame than I now possess. All I wish is to bend the hearts of Jews towards heaven that truth may enter into those who come to me for health, wealth or offspring- in these matters there are others to visit. But if a man feels he is unable to serve the Lord properly because he lacks health, wealth or offspring, then he may come to me. I shall strive to help him in his effort to remove the hindrance.

(ח) רַבִּי יוֹסֵי אוֹמֵר כָּל הַמְכַבֵּד אֶת הַתּוֹרָה גּוּפוֹ מְכֻבָּד עַל הַבְּרִיּוֹת. וְכָל הַמְחַלֵּל אֶת הַתּוֹרָה גּוּפוֹ מְחֻלָּל עַל הַבְּרִיּוֹת:

Mishnah Eight.

R. Jose says: Anyone who honours the Torah is himself honoured by mankind, but anyone who dishonours the Torah is himself dishonoured by mankind.

R. Jose is Jose Ben Halafta of Sepphoris. He learned Torah from his father and from the wise men of Javneh, but his main teacher was R. Akiva. He was well known and is mentioned three hundred times in the Mishnah and Tosefta. Jose was blessed with five sons who all became great scholars. His own standing in Halakhah can be gauged from the fact that Rabban Simeon Ben Gamliel explicitly followed Jose in all his halakhic decisions.

Anyone who honours the Torah ... Some commentators interpret 'Torah' here to refer specifically to the Sefer Torah, whilst others understand the word Torah to incorporate the whole body of Jewish law and precept. We shall deal with the claims of the Sefer Torah, which is our most cherished possesion. The Scroll of the Law is an essential element in Jewish worship; without it, no statutory service can be held. It is placed in a cabinet, or Ark, on the eastern wall facing Jerusalem. In front of the Ark hangs the *Ner Tamid*, the continual lamp, symbolic of the eternal flame of light emanating from the words of the Torah. The Scroll of the Law must be written (Deut. 31:9) by a *Sofer*, a professional scribe, using parchment made from the skin of a kosher animal, and black indelible ink. Before commencing to copy the text, the scribe recites, 'I am about to write this book as a sacred Scroll of the Law'. Every time he copies the Divine Name, he declares,'I am writing this word as the Sacred Name'. There are many rules which regulate the writing of a Sefer Torah. For instance, each line has a definite number of letters; some are permitted to be elongated in order to fill the line. The number of lines, as well as columns, are also regulated. All Scrolls are exactly alike and no vowels, points or marks are used. Everything in connection with the writing of the Scroll is of great antiquity and sanctity. It should be remembered that even a *pasul*, invalid, Sefer Torah still retains its full sanctity. Indeed, even if the greater number of letters are erased, as long as eighty five letters are fully formed, the Scroll retains its sanctity and it may be rescued from a fire even on the Sabbath.

Such is the uniqueness of the Scroll that it was in no way affected by the introduction of printing, which revolutionised the world. We now realise the unrivalled nature of the Sefer Torah, for it is the only Book which has retained its pristine glory and has in no way been affected by modern usage, nor is it mass-produced. This Scroll, therefore, must be honoured and revered. 'When a man sets out on a journey, he should not place the Scroll of the Torah in a sack upon an ass which he rides, but he should hold it in his lap' (Ber. 18a). 'They also prohibited sitting on a couch on which a Scroll of the Law is placed' (M.K. 25a) and it is not permitted to throw about copies of sacred Scriptures' (Er. 98a).

We now revert to the second interpretation that Torah signifies all Jewish teaching and observance. Whichever interpretation we follow, one common denominator governs both, the importance of reverence. We are asked to revere and honour the Torah and all it stands for. In schools our children are taught to count, measure, weigh and play, but how often, if ever, are they taught to revere? In Judaism every mitzvah expresses reverence. It is forbidden to study Torah in the midst of unclean surroundings (Shab. 10a). Judaism has always respected old age, 'Before the hoary head you shall rise and you shall honour the face of the aged' (Lev. 19:32). The Rabbis apply the words, 'He honours them that fear the Lord' (Ps. 15:4) to Jehoshaphat, King of Judah, of whom it is said that whenever he saw a learned man he rose from his throne, embraced and kissed him and called him 'My master, my teacher' (Ket. 103b). One must also honour the Synagogue and House of Study. Whatever one may not do in the place of a king, one may not do in a Syangogue. All mitzvot express veneration for God and man. One Rabbi honoured the Sabbath by wearing homespun garments on the day before the Sabbath but fine clothes on the Sabbath day (Shab. 119a). Similarly, we eat little food on a Friday afternoon as contrasted with a festive meal on Friday evening (Erev Shabbat).

Gufo. We have translated this word as 'he himself', but it literally means 'his body'. This word may appear to be superfluous; however, Judaism recognises not only the spiritual but also the physical side of man. A person who afflicts himself unnecessarily by fasting, is considered to be a sinner and the Nazirite brings a sacrifice because he abstains from drinking wine. We are enjoined to respect the body in life and in death; therefore, we are forbidden to practise cremation which we claim is disrespectful to the body of man, which is created in the image of God. Indeed, we must show deference even to the body of a criminal after death. Furthermore, our body is so closely linked with Jewish Law and practice that the six hundred and thirteen positive and negative commandments correspond to the joints and the arteries of the body which, it is claimed, possesses two hundred and forty eight joints and three hundred and sixty five veins and arteries. Thus the body of man is honoured through the observance of the mitzvot.

We should also underline the use of the word *beriot*, creatures, which refers to all people. It is generally conceded that the Jew who genuinely respects his religion in belief and practice is respected by the non-Jew. Conversely, the Jew who brazenly mocks and sneers at his religion, brings shame and mistrust upon himself from the non-Jewish world.

Hasidic Lore

The Scroll of the Law. The Berditchever said: When a Scroll of the Law is sewn together it becomes holy and it is forbidden to erase a letter in it, but when it is still in several parts it is permissible to make an erasure in it. The letters represent the souls of Israel - when united none may be blotted out.

Love without reverence. The personality of the honourable Jew is praised; the personality of the dishounourable Jew is frowned upon and disrespected. He who loves God but has no proper sense of reverence for Him, is likely to forget himself and become careless in the performance of God's commandments (Meseritz).

(ט) רַבִּי יִשְׁמָעֵאל בְּנוֹ אוֹמֵר הַחוֹשֵׂךְ עַצְמוֹ מִן הַדִּין פּוֹרֵק מִמֶּנּוּ אֵיבָה וְגָזֵל וּשְׁבוּעַת שָׁוְא. וְהַגַּס לִבּוֹ בְּהוֹרָאָה שׁוֹטֶה רָשָׁע וְגַס רוּחַ׃

Mishnah Nine.

R. Ishmael, his son says: He who refrains from judgment rids himself of hatred, robbery and false swearing, but he who is presumptuous in rendering decisions is a fool, wicked and arrogant.

R. Ishmael was one of the five sons of R. Jose mentioned in the previous Mishnah. His absolute integrity and honesty as a judge is mentioned in the Talmud, and he did not shrink from bringing before the Roman authorities a Jewish criminal (B.M. 84a).

The judge (judgment). From a cursory reading of the Mishnah it would seem that the judge, at the outset, would be reluctant to accept the responsibility of a position which demands decisions of such consequence. However, the appointment of judges is specifically mentioned in the Torah and is a positive mitzvah, as it is written, 'Judges and officers shall you appoint for you in all your gates, and they shall judge the people with just judgment' (Deut. 16:18).

This apparent contradiction is removed when we realise that the injunction in Deut. 16 is addressed, not to the judge, but to the community whose responsibility it is to appoint a *Bet Din*, a court of Law, in every town. One may argue that the difficulty still remains; how can the community appoint judges if they refrain from taking office? We must therefore interpret the Mishnah to mean that the community must look for a man who possesses the right qualifications, and the judge himself should accept office for the correct reasons. He should not be motivated by the honour and glory attached to the office; these he must shun. Not only should he be scrupulously honest, but he must be humble and modest, while at the same time he should be fearless and courageous in his decisions. The approach and attitude of the judge is given in a statement made by a Rabbi who, when called upon to act as judge, would exclaim, 'Here I go to my death ..... would that in the end I will be no worse off than in the beginning' (Sanh.7b).

The same caution and fear implanted in the heart of the judge is expressed in the following statement, 'A judge should always imagine that a sword is pointed at his heart and Gehinnom yawns at his feet' (Sanh. 7a). Such is the heavy responsibility that devolves upon him that the judge who administers justice equitably causes the *Shekhinah* to alight upon Israel ..... and a judge who does not adminster justice equitably causes the *Shekhinah* to depart from Israel (Sanh. 7a).

We can well understand the fear engendered in the heart of a judge when we ponder on this passage in the Talmud, 'If you see a generation afflicted with many troubles, go and scrutinise the judges of Israel, because all the adversities that come upon the world are only due to the judges in Israel, as it is said, 'Hear this I pray you, ye heads of the House of Jacob and rulers of the House of Israel, that abhor judgment and pervert all equity' (Micah 3:9). They are wicked and yet put their trust in Him. Accordingly, the Holy One blessed be He brings upon them three punishments corresponding to the three transgressions of which they are guilty, as it is said, 'Therefore shall Zion, for your sake, be ploughed as a field, and Jerusalem shall become heaps, and the mountain of the house as the high places of the forest' (Ibid verse 12). Moreover, God does not cause his *Shekhinah* to alight upon Israel until the evil judges and officials are exterminated from Israel, as it is said, 'I will turn My hand upon you and thoroughly purge away your dross as with lye and will take away your alloy: and I will restore your judges as at first and your counsellors as at the beginning; afterwards you shall be called the city of righteousness, the faithful city' (Is. 1:25) (Shab. 139a).

Regarding the personal qualities a judge should possess, we are told 'He should be appointed a judge in his city who is wise, humble, sin-fearing, of good repute and popular with his fellow-men'. On the other hand, 'One who appoints a man as judge who is unfitted, is as though he has set up an idolatrous image in Israel' (Sanh. 7b). In addition to the qualities mentioned above, a judge should be tender-hearted and compassionate, as we learn from this statement, 'We do not appoint to a Sanhedrin an old man, a eunuch or a childless man; R. Judah adds, 'One who is hard-hearted' (Sanh. 36b). We should also remember that judges were not paid officials; 'He who takes a fee to adjudicate, his verdicts are invalid' (Bekh. 4:6).

The stringent impartiality and integrity of the judge is illustrated in the Talmud. Once R. Samuel was crossing a bridge when a man approached him to offer his arm as support. When Samuel asked why he had done this, the man replied, 'I have a law-suit to submit to you'. Samuel then said, 'In that case, I am disqualified from adjudicating your law-suit'. Again, Ishmael the son of R. Jose had a tenant-gardener who customarily brought him a basket filled with fruit every Friday. However, on one occasion he presented the gift on a Thursday. When asked the reason for the change, the gardener replied, 'I have a law-suit and decided that at the same time, I might bring the fruit to the master'. Ishmael refused the offering and said, 'I am disqualified to act as your judge'. He thereupon appointed two Rabbis to adjudicate. As he was arranging the matter, he suddenly thought, 'If he wished, he could plead thus, or if he preferred, he might plead otherwise'. He then soliloquised, 'Oh the despair that awaits those who take bribes: If I who have not accepted the fruit, which in any case would have been my own, am in such a state of mind - how much worse would be the state of mind of those who accept bribes' (Ket. 105b).

So far we have interpreted the Mishnah to refer specifically to the judge. However, this can also apply to the litigants who are advised to refrain from taking legal action, but should settle their differences through arbitration; in this manner they would rid themselves of enmity and false swearing. This interpretation has Pentateuchal authority, 'Judges and officers shall you appoint to you in all your gates.' (Deut. 16:18).The word *Lekha*, to you, seems redundant, and our teachers read into this word an added meaning. 'Judges and officers shall you appoint to you' is not addressed to the judge, but to YOU; every person must judge himself and not hasten to the law courts. This would save much bitterness of spirit which inevitably folllows every law-suit. In the light of this interpretation, how do we explain the words 'in all your gates'? Our moralists expound these words to stand for the eyes, the mouth and the ears, These are the gates, the openings, which should be guarded. We should station a judge and an officer at our eyes that they look not at anything which is unseemly or improper; a judge and an officer should be placed at our mouth to guard our speech so that we utter the truth, and a judge and an officer should be set at our ears so that we do not listen to tale-bearing and mischievous gossip. When a person judges himself by guarding his eyes, mouth and ears, he will go a long way toward establishing justice, righteousness and peace of mind.

Hasidic Lore

Charity in judgment. R. David Leikes lived for more than a hundred years. He was esteemed as an authority in the civil law of the Talmud and his decisions, were admired by all the Dayanim. Once a very complicated case arose when the aged Rabbi was on his death bed and his demise was expected hourly. The Dayanim hoped that the Rabbi's mind might still be sufficiently clear to aid them perhaps for the last time. They visited his home and stated their request. The Rabbi's children protested vigorously and argued against troubling him lest thereby his end be hastened. Suddenly the door opened and the Rabbi entered. 'Do you know' he said, 'That we are taught in the Talmud (Shab. 10a) that one who judges a case correctly becomes God's partner? Yet you wish to deprive me of this opportunity'. He gave his decision in the difficult case in a manner so remarkable that it left no doubt of its correctness; he returned to his bed with the help of his children, and after a short while he died.

(י) הוּא הָיָה אוֹמֵר אַל תְּהִי דָן יְחִידִי שֶׁאֵין דָּן יְחִידִי אֶלָּא אֶחָד. וְאַל תֹּאמַר קַבְּלוּ דַעְתִּי שֶׁהֵן רַשָּׁאִין וְלֹא אָתָּה:

Mishnah Ten.

He used to say: Judge not alone for none except One judges alone, and say not, 'Accept my view', for they (the colleagues) may say it, but not you.

This Mishnah is a corrolary of the previous one and deals again with the concept of justice, which is central to the Jewish faith. Indeed, the Hebrew word for 'State' is *medinah* which is connected with *din*, law and justice. Also one of the names for the New Year is *Yom Hadin*, the day of Judgment, when God judges His people and forgives them for their sins.

Justice. Hebrew law introduced equality and combined the concept of justice together with liberty and the freedom of the individual. In addition, a covenant was needed for the establishment of the Torah to confirm the acceptance and consent of the people. Justice also pervades the spirit of prayer; *Lehitpalel*, to pray, really means to judge oneself; before we can commune with the Almighty we must judge ourselves, and so be prepared to petition God. We see, therefore, that justice embraces not only the State and government, but also every aspect of Jewish life. We can now direct our attention to the words of the Mishnah.

Judge not alone. The smaller Court of Law consisted of three judges. As justice is of the highest calibre, for God Himself is sanctified through justice, it is proper that the judge should consult with colleagues before arriving at the truth. The implications of a miscarriage of justice are very serious and far-reaching for if the judge wrongfully commits one to the death penalty he not only judges the person before him, but also those unborn generations that would have issued from him. 'Judge not alone' is therefore a warning to the judge that he is not passing sentence on a single person, but on all that come after him.

This maxim can be interpreted in another vein. In Jewish teaching the word justice rarely appears alone; it is often preceded by the word *tzedakah*, righteousness. Indeed, the first instance in which justice is mentioned in the Torah, it is accompanied by *tzedakah*, 'For I have known him (Abraham) so that he will command his children and his household after him, and they will keep the way of the Lord to do righteousness and justice' (Gen. 18:19). *Tzedakah*, righteousness, can also mean charity; the Talmud (Sanh.6) comments on the verse, 'And David executed *mishpat* and *tzedakah* towards all his people' (2 Sam. 8:15). How did David execute both at the same time? One Rabbi interpreted the verse literally as meaning that when David realised that the condemned man was poor, he himself undertook to pay the fine. In this manner, David dispensed justice with charity. Moreover, justice should always be tempered with charitableness, kindness and mercy. When we place the *retzuah*, strap of the Tefillin, round the middle finger, we recite the following words from Hosea 2:21, 'And I will betroth you unto Me for ever; I will betroth you unto Me in righteousness and judgment and in lovingkindness and compassion and I will betroth you unto Me in faithfulness'. Here we symbolically attach ourselves to God not only in *tzedek* and *misphat*, but also in *hesed*, kindness, and *rahamim*, mercy. Justice is not executed alone; it is surrounded by three other virtues, charity, kindness and mercy.

In the eleventh benediction of the week-day Amidah which is repeated three times daily, God is introduced to us as 'The King who loves righteousness and justice'. Thus justice is not alone, but is combined with and based upon righteousness.

Hasidic Lore

A case in judgment. A terrible famine once occurred in Ukraine and the poor could buy no bread. The Rabbis assembled at the home of the Spoler Grandfather for a session of the rabbinical court. The Spoler said to them, 'According to rabbinical law, a master who buys a Jewish serf for a designated time (six years or until the Jubilee year) must support not only him, but also his family (Kid. 22a). Now the Lord bought us in Egypt as His serfs, as it is written, 'For to Me are the sons of Israel serfs' (Lev. 25:55) and the Prophet Ezekiel declared that even in exile, Israel is the slave of God. Therefore, O Lord, I ask that Thou abide by the Law and support judgment in favour of the Spoler rabbi. In a few days a large shipment of grain arrived from Siberia and bread was available to the poor.

(יא) רַבִּי יוֹנָתָן אוֹמֵר כָּל הַמְקַיֵּם אֶת הַתּוֹרָה מֵעֹנִי סוֹפוֹ לְקַיְּמָהּ מֵעֹשֶׁר. וְכָל הַמְבַטֵּל אֶת הַתּוֹרָה מֵעֹשֶׁר סוֹפוֹ לְבַטְּלָהּ מֵעֹנִי:

Mishnah Eleven

R. Jonathan says: He who fulfils the Torah in poverty will in the end fulfil it in wealth, but he who annuls the Torah in wealth will in the end annul it in poverty.

R. Jonathan lived in the middle of the second century C.E. He was a pupil and devoted follower of R. Ishmael. Due to the Hadrianic persecutions he fled from Palestine, but because of his love and attachment to the Holy Land, he returned.

He who fulfils the Torah in poverty. Torah embraces every aspect of life, including poverty as well as riches. This is portrayed in the following extract. 'A poor man and a rich man presented themselves before the Heavenly Tribunal. The poor man was asked, 'Why did you not occupy yourself with the Torah?' If he replies that he was poverty stricken and worried about his livelihood, he is then asked, 'Were you poorer than Hillel?'

It is related of Hillel that for his work he earned only half of a denarius per day, half of which he paid to the doorkeeper of the House of Study for admission, and the remainder was all he had for the upkeep of himself and his family. On one occasion he had no work and earned no money, consequently the doorkeeper refused to admit him. In desperation, he climbed up to the roof and sat by the skylight to hear the words of the living God expounded by Shemaiah and Avtalion. According to tradition, this occurred on the eve of the Sabbath during winter and snow was falling heavily at break of dawn. Shemaiah said to Avtalion, 'My colleague, on every day this house is light and today it is dark, it is perhaps a cloudy day'. They looked up and saw the form of a man in the window. They found him covered by three cubits of snow. They released him from his position, washed and rubbed him and placed him before the fire and said, 'This man deserves that the Sabbath be profaned on his behalf' (Yoma 35b).

The rich man is asked, 'Why did you not occupy yourself with the Torah?' If he answers that he was rich and concerned about his possessions, he is asked 'Were you more wealthy than R. Eleazar Ben Harsum?' It was reported about R. Eleazar Ben Harsum that his father bequeathed to him a thousand cities and a corresponding fleet of a thousand ships, yet every day he flung a bag of flour over his shoulders, and went from city to city and from province to province in order to learn Torah. On one occasion, his servants who had not met him personally, seized him for forced labour. He said to them, 'I implore you, set me free to go and study Torah'. They answered, 'By the life of R. Eleazar Ben Harsum, we will not let you go'. Although they were employed by him, he had never seen them, for he sat day and night engrossed in the study of the Torah (Ibid).

A similar thought is expressed by the *Baal Haturim* who, in expounding the verse, 'And he dreamed and behold a ladder stood on the ground and the top of it reached to heaven' (Gen. 28:12), points out that *sulam* (ladder) is spelt deficiently minus a vav and has the numerical value of Sinai, one hundred and thirty, and *zeh kisei hakavod*, this is the Throne of Glory, is also equal to one hundred and thirty. However, *sulam* spelt with a vav has the numerical value of *mammon*, money, and *ani*, poverty, each of which is equal to one hundred and thirty six. Thus, if a man ascends the ladder of success and finds time and energy for the study and observance of Torah, he will reach the summit of Sinai and preserve Jewish tradition. If, however, he is so engrossed in the acquisition of *mammon*, money, at the expense of Torah, he will eventually become *ani*, impoverished spiritually and culturally and will estrange himself from the Jewish way of life.

He who fulfils .... This includes both learning and practising the study of Torah and observance of mitzvot. A bookworm is one who fills his mind with learning but does not necessarily practise what he learns. This can do harm, as is evident from a conversation between Moses and the rebel Korah, who asked Moses, 'If one's house is full of Scrolls of the Law, copies of the Bible and Talmud, must that home be adorned with a mezuzah? (Nu. R. 18) 'Moses' answer was in the affirmative. Korah imagined that a house or library filled with sacred writings did not require a mezuzah; and that book learning alone was sufficient. However, Moses warns us to add practise to learning; we should take the learning outside the home and perform the mitzvah for all to see. Thus the call of the Mishnah is not 'he who learns' but 'he who fulfils', he who combines learning with the performance of the mitzvot.

He who annuls the Torah in wealth. In the Jewish view all wealth belongs to God; we are only the stewards of our wealth. If a rich man disregards Torah and mitzvot he will obviously rebel against God should he fall upon bad times.

Hasidic Lore

Wealth versus poverty. The Rimanover Rabbi dreamed that he ascended to heaven and heard an angel pleading with the Lord to grant Israel wealth, saying, 'Behold how pious they are in poverty. Bestow upon them riches and they will be many times as pious'. The Rabbi enquired the name of the angel and was told he was called Satan. The Rabbi then exclaimed, 'Leave us in poverty, O Lord; safeguard us from the favours of Satan'.

(יב) רַבִּי מֵאִיר אוֹמֵר הֱוֵי מְמַעֵט בְּעֵסֶק וַעֲסוֹק בַּתּוֹרָה וֶהֱוֵי שְׁפַל רוּחַ בִּפְנֵי כָל אָדָם. וְאִם בָּטַלְתָּ מִן הַתּוֹרָה יֵשׁ לְךָ בְּטֵלִים הַרְבֵּה כְּנֶגְדְּךָ וְאִם עָמַלְתָּ בַּתּוֹרָה יֵשׁ לוֹ שָׂכָר הַרְבֵּה לִיתֵּן לָךְ:

Mishnah Twelve.

R. Meir says: Do little in business and be busy with the Torah and be of humble spirit before all men. If you have neglected the Torah you shall have many who bring you to neglect it, but if you have toiled at the study of Torah there is much reward to be given to you.

R. Meir was the brilliant pupil of R. Akiva. R. Judah Ha-Nasi, the redactor of the Mishnah, admitted that he owed much to R. Meir who facilitated his task. In addition to being a master of Halakhah and Aggadah, he was an outstanding preacher and attracted large congregations who were spellbound by his eloquence. He held the learning of Torah in such high esteem that he likened even a heathen who was engaged in the study of Torah, to a High Priest (B.K. 38a). His love for Israel is exemplified by a number of sayings, - for instance, 'Even the stones of Jerusalem are holy' and 'He who lives in Israel will be forgiven his sins'. He earned his livelihood as a scribe, a holy task in which he excelled.

Do little in business. The word *asak* used here for business is also common in modern Hebrew, but is not found in the Bible. Originally we were an agricultural people; we came from the village, not from the city. In the Hebrew language there are ten words, all synonyms for rain, whereas we have no word which precisely expresses business or commerce. The Bible is a history of a shepherd people; indeed, the word shepherd is found in the Bible more than two hundred times. Is. 40:11, Jer. 31:10, and Ez. 34:22, all refer to the shepherd and his flock, whilst the language of Ps. 23 has become universally popular. The landscape of the Bible is replete with green pastures, cornfields, vineyards and orchards. There are a number of words in the Bible which are connected with trading and merchants, but they do not specifically deal with business.

In Gen. 34:21 and 42:34 the word *veyisharu* is rendered 'and they shall trade'. This word is followed by the accusative *ota*, it, whereas one would expect 'in it' or 'with it'. The root *sahar* means 'to go round', thus a more correct translation would be 'and they shall move around freely', and this would fit in admirably with the words of the verse, 'Behold, the land is large enough before them'; that is, there is plenty of room for them to move around without restricting them in one neighbourhood. This version is also applicable to the text of 42:34, see Rashi.

Another word used for 'merchant' is *Canaan*, in Zeph. 1:11. The Canaanites, especially the Phoenicians, were early traders, compare Ez. 16:29, where *Eretz Canaan* is translated as 'the land of traffic' which seems to have an evil connotation. We are, however, forcibly enjoined to conduct ourselves honourably in all matters of buying and selling, see Lev. 25:16-17 and Deut. 25:13-15. Included in the ethics of commerce is Lev. 19:14, 'You shall not put a stumbling-block before the blind'. This does not refer only to those physically blind, but to the masses who are disadvantaged (penalised) by the vested interests of the racketeers who charge exorbitant prices for their wares. This would also include the drawing up of false balance sheets to blind the government tax collectors.

Furthermore, we can safely assume that there is no evidence of a class of financiers in the biblical era. However, we know that King Solomon developed extensive foreign trade and set up the caravan routes into Asia; nevertheless by the beginning of the Greek era, Jews lost the art of business enterprise. Josephus testifies that 'they have no taste for commerce'.

R. Meir is realistic; he does not entirely rule out business, for how would man maintain himself? This very question is discussed in the Talmud, 'And you shall gather in your corn' (Deut. 11:14). What has this to tell us? Since it is written, 'This book of the Torah shall not depart out of your mouth but you shall meditate therein day and night' (Jos. 1:8), it is possible to presume that these words are to be understood literally. Therefore there is a teaching to say, 'And you shall gather in your corn', that is, conduct at the same time a worldly occupation. These are the words of R. Ishmael. R. Simeon Bar Yohai says, 'Is it possible for a man to plough at the time of ploughing, sow at seed time, reap at harvest time, thresh at the time of threshing, and winnow at the time of wind - what is to become of Torah? But when Israel performs the will of God, their work is done by others, as it is said, 'And strangers shall stand and feed your flocks' (Is. 61:5): and at the time when Israel does not perform the will of God, their work has to be done by themselves, as it is said, 'And you shall gather in your corn.' Rava said to his disciples, 'I beg of you not to appear before me during the days of Nisan and Tishri, so that you may not be concerned about your maintenance the whole year' (Ber. 35b). Further on, the Talmud sums up the position with these words, 'Come and see that the later generations are not like the former generations. The former generations made the Torah their principal concern and their work only occasional, and both flourished in their hand; whereas the later generations made work their principal concern and their Torah only occasional, and neither flourished in their hand' (ibid).

This close association between work or business and the study of Torah is mirrored in the question that man is asked in the Hereafter: Have you dealt honourably in business? Have you fixed definitive times for the study of Torah? These two questions cannot be divorced one from the other; they are interdependent. It is the will of God that we pursue our worldly occupation or business parallel with the study of Torah.

Be of humble spirit before all men. We show our subservience to God in prayer and humble ourselves in His presence when we perform mitzvot, but do we practise the same humility in all our affiliations with men in business and in our social contacts? R. Meir cautions us to be modest, not only before God, but also before all men whatever their level in life, learned or ignorant, rich or poor.

Is there a possible connection between the first two sayings? The man of learning may combine scholarship with refinement of character and a humble spirit, whereas the unlearned could be coarse, rude and aggressive.

If you have neglected Torah. You are ignoring not only the basic teachings of Judaism, but your character is adversely affected. If, however, you labour in the Torah, you not only gain knowledge but you reap the reward of a richer and fuller life, for learning often leads to deeds and the performance of more mitzvot.

If you have toiled .... Two different verbs are used here - *asak*, to be engaged in learning and *amal*, to labour in learning. There are some who are fortunate to possess the ability to learn and study with ease; they have either a photographic memory or a special aptitude for Torah. For this group we use the word *asak*, to be engaged in Torah. These have the capacity to imbibe much learning without difficulty. However, others have to toil hard *(amal)* in order to master the intricacies of rabbinic wisdom; they have to labour and concentrate all their energies and mental powers to grasp some of the abstruse subjects of the Talmud. This group deserves to enjoy much reward, for they have suffered and persevered in order to acquire their learning.

Hasidic Lore

Torah and business. A man came to the Kosmirer Rabbi to ask his blessing in a financial enterprise. The Rabbi turned away his face and refused to listen to the petitioner. A few months later another hasid spoke with the Rabbi regarding a business venture and received his blessing. The first man was grieved and asked the Rabbi why he was refused a hearing, whilst a blessing was granted to the other man. The Rabbi answered, 'I shall explain my attitude by a parable.' A merchant came to a market town and entered a wholesale warehouse to make the necessary purchases. He became so interested in the stock that he remained there until late in the evening. When he was ready to leave, he noticed that the axle of his wagon was broken and it was too late to secure one. He told the wholesaler who offered him an extra axle reserved for his own use. Another person in a similar predicament asked whether he could purchase an axle, but he was refused by the wholesaler who replied, 'Do you think I sell axles? The other man purchased various materials from me so I helped him, but you are not my customer'. In the same way, continued the Kosmirer, 'The hasid to whom I gave my blessing learned from me Torah and ethics therefore I helped him in his business affairs as well, but as you have never come to me for instruction in any matter, why should I help you in purely business matters?'

(יג) רַבִּי אֱלִיעֶזֶר בֶּן יַעֲקֹב אוֹמֵר הָעוֹשֶׂה מִצְוָה אַחַת קוֹנֶה לוֹ פְּרַקְלִיט אֶחָד וְהָעוֹבֵר עֲבֵרָה אַחַת קוֹנֶה לוֹ קַטֵּגוֹר אֶחָד תְּשׁוּבָה וּמַעֲשִׂים טוֹבִים כִּתְרִיס בִּפְנֵי הַפּוּרְעָנוּת:

Mishnah Thirteen.

R. Eliezer Ben Jacob says: He who does one mitzvah acquires for himself one advocate, and he who commits one transgression acquires for himself one accuser. Repentance and good deeds are as a shield against punishment.

R. Eliezer Ben Jacob. There are two teachers bearing this name. One lived in the time of the Temple and the other was one of the last disciples of R. Akiva and was included amongst those who gathered at Usha after the Bar Kokhba revolt. According to some authorities the author of our Mishnah belongs to the latter category and not the former.

He who does one mitzvah.... It should be noted that the mitzvah is preceded by the word *asah*, to do, whilst the transgression, *averah*, is preceded, by *avar*, to transgress, both words derived from the same root. The mitzvah, from the root *tsivah*, to command, is a timely response to the will of God and involves activity.

It is inadequate to contemplate the performing of a mitzvah or a charitable act - it is essential to take resolute action promptly. A good deed is not borne in mind; it must be practised to be effective. The potential transgressor does not plunge directly into wrongdoing; he merely slips into a course of action which inevitably leads him into the vortex of sin; furthermore, *avar* means to pass or cross over. The transgressor simply crosses over the line of demarcation or he takes one false step and he is in the grip of sin. We practise good deeds, but commit a felony.

One mitzvah. The Mishnah emphasises the word 'one' advisedly, as a mitzvah should never be treated lightly. One mitzvah performed consistently and enthusiastically can achieve *olam haba*, the world to come. Conversely, one transgression committed regularly can deprive a person of his *olam haba*.

Peraklit - an advocate or intercessor. The Targum on Job. 33:23 translates the word *melitz*, intercessor, as *peraklit* which is synonymous with *saneigor*, advocate, and is usually opposed to *kateigor*, accuser. In legal language, the counsel for defence, and the counsel for prosecution vie with each other in argument and counter argument for their respective clients. Here we are not dealing with a human court of law, but with the divine Court of Law, over which God presides. The counsel for defence and for prosecution are the *mitzvah* and the *averah*. That the mitzvah is an angel of mercy is a beautiful thought and should encourage us to pursue mitzvot throughout our sojourn on earth.

The advocate and the accuser are portrayed in the hymn *Omnan Keyn* recited in the Kol Nidrei Service and was written by R. Yomtov Ben Isaac of York who in 1190 encouraged his co-religionists to die as martyrs, rather than fall into the hands of the wild mob who were intent on forcibly baptising them. In a couplet filled with pathos, the prayer cries out 'Silence the accuser and let the advocate take his place, and be Thou, O Lord, his support and say, 'I have forgiven'.

Repentance and good deeds. *Teshuvah*, repentance, is one of the saving graces of Judaism and is highlighted throughout the Ten Days of Penitence from Rosh Hashanah to Yom Kippur, but it is not restricted to these ten days alone. The world was created on Rosh Hashanah, and at this same period repentance came into being. *Teshuvah* is thus as old as the world. This would explain the comment on the words, 'And it was evening, and it was morning, one day' - this is the Day of Atonement. As repentance brings atonement, they were both created on one day. *Teshuvah* literally means return, which is more meaningful than repentance. God is always ready to accept the Jew who returns. No one is ever rejected, nor is it ever too late to return, declared Maimonides.

'Let no returnee to God imagine that he is too distant from the level of the righteous on account of his past sins and transgressions; this is not so. Beloved and dear is he before the Creator as though he never sinned. Not only that, but his reward is even greater for he tasted of transgression and turned away from it, mastering his evil inclination.' Our Sages said that in the place that a *baal teshuvah* stands, even the perfectly righteous cannot stand. In other words, his spiritual level is even greater than that of those who have never sinned ..... All the Prophets called for repentance, and the final redemption of Israel will only come about through repentance. (Hilkhot Teshuvah). So vital is the concept of *teshuvah* that it is first and foremost in the plaintive cry when we pray on Rosh Hashannah and Yom Kippur.

'*Teshuvah Tefillah u'Tzedakah...* repentance, prayer and charity avert the evil decree'. In addition to meaning repentance, *teshuvah* also means response, as is evident from the Responsa Literature, questions and answers which clarify the Halakhah in every age. We are too preoccupied with the material pursuits of life which stultify our heart and mind. We should rather practise *teshuvah* and answer the call of conscience which is latent in all people and is ready to serve us.

Teris, a shield. Every mitzvah is a shield and a protection. The head-Tefillin shields the brain from impure thoughts. The hand-Tefillin shields the hand from striking a person - rather is it sanctified to perform good deeds, such as assistance to the needy. We envelop ourselves with the *Tallit*, another shield, to shut out all evil designs and to concentrate prayerfully on service to God and the world. The Mezuzah on the doorpost shields and protects the family within to be loyal and truthful to one another. This lesson of shielding and protecting comes home to us forcibly in Israel where every home is buttressed on the outside with *trissim*, shutters, which keep out the rain, wind, sand and the dry heat (sharav) which are rife in the Middle East.

Hasidic Lore

Repentance. The Stretiner was discussing the meaning of repentance. He said, 'The Kabbalah teaches us allegorically that there are fifty regions of holiness above and fifty regions of impurity below. When a wicked man has descended to a low region in the section of impurity, and there repents sincerely, he is lifted up to the region bearing the same number in the section of holiness. The deeper he has fallen, the higher he ascends through repentance,as we say in the New Year Hymn, 'Our return from afar causes us to ascend His holy mountain'.

The celebration of a mitzvah. Rabbi Mordekhai Tzernobiler said: The banquet which we Jews give to celebrate a mitzvah is more worthy than the mitzvah itself. A parable illustrates this.

The Satan brought many serious accusations against the Jews, and their defender the Archangel Michael knew of no arguments in their behalf.

After a while he bethought himself and said, 'The few mitzvot which Jews perform offset their many transgressions. When a Jew performs a circumcision he gives a banquet because he is overjoyed at having observed a mitzvah. Have you ever seen a Jew, however, celebrating when he transgresses? This demonstrates that he feels no joy in his offence and only succumbs because of weakness. In the mitzvah, he feels intense happiness'. This defence before the Heavenly Tribunal proved successful. 'Hence you see', continued the Tzernobiler, 'How important is the celebration of a mitzvah'.

(יד) רַבִּי יוֹחָנָן הַסַּנְדְּלָר אוֹמֵר כָּל כְּנֵסִיָּה שֶׁהִיא לְשֵׁם שָׁמַיִם סוֹפָהּ לְהִתְקַיֵּם וְשֶׁאֵינָהּ לְשֵׁם שָׁמַיִם אֵין סוֹפָהּ לְהִתְקַיֵּם:

Mishnah Fourteen.

R. Johanan Ha-Sandelar says: Every assembly which is for the sake of Heaven will in the end be established, but one which is not for the sake of Heaven will not in the end be established.

R. Johanan the shoe-maker was a pupil of R. Akiva. We have already referred to the fact that many of the Rabbis of the talmudic era combined learning with a trade or vocation; here the trade is mentioned after the name. To illustrate how wide and varied were the occupations ascribed to the Rabbis, we shall mention R. Isaac Nappaha the blacksmith, R. Avin Naggara the carpenter, R. Nahum Halavlar the scribe, R. Simeon Hashazuri the weaver, etc.

Kenesiya. *Kenesiya* is a gathering or assembly of people and is closely allied to *Kenesset - Anshei Kenesset Hagedolah* - the Men of the Great Assembly or Synagogue. This group helped to strengthen and popularise the institution of the Synagogue, which is known by three different names; Bet Haknesset, Bet Hamidrash and Bet Hatefillah. As the Synagogue is primarily a house of prayer it should be called *Bet Hatefillah*, but it is generally referred to as Bet Haknesset. It would seem, therefore, that the *Kenesiya*, the gathering of people is employed not only for prayer but as a multi-purpose venue.

This is historically correct; the Synagogue was the first school and the centre of all communal and private activity. Indeed, it was referred to as *Bet Am*, the House of the People. The Synagogue was also used to foster political activity. Jewish tribunals sat in the Synagogue to judge and mete out punishment. In this connection, we should remember that certain offenders used the Synagogue as a right of asylum. In addition, charity was dispensed there and lost articles could be reclaimed in the Synagogue. Thus it will be readily seen that the Synagogue was more than a house of worship, and so rightly earned the title of *Kenesset* or *Kenesiya* which housed a variety of people and served manifold purposes.

Every assembly which is for the sake of Heaven. Commentators point to the Revelation on Mount Sinai as a gathering for the sake of Heaven. At Mount Sinai six hundred thousand Jews heard the Almighty declaim the Ten Commandments. Here the will of God manifested itself in a unique experience which will never again be repeated. It was not only a revelation, but also a revolution in the history of religion. This cataclysmic event proved that the Torah was not given by man, but was divine. Hence this assembly was called together *leshem Shamayim*, in the name of Heaven, and consequently will in the end be established and endure for ever.

On the other hand, the assembly of the generation of the Dispersion (Gen. chapter 11) is an example of a gathering which is not for the sake of Heaven. The generation of the Tower of Babel was the first of its kind to be recorded in the Torah. Here we are introduced to a gathering of people who conspired against God. This assembly endeavoured to build a tower to reach Heaven in order to oust God. Such a venture was at the outset foredoomed, for it was based on lies. The Revelation on Mount Sinai however resulted in a Torah of truth, *Torat Emet*, the Law of truth. The distinction is explicit in the two words, *sheker* and *emet*. *Sheker*, falsehood, can be found in the plural, *shekarim*, but *emet* as a noun has no plural form. Truth, the seal of the Almighty is indivisible, so every assembly rooted in Torah should be united to perform the will of God.

Commenting on this Mishnah, the Meiri states: A person's relationship with his fellow-man must not be based on the desire to triumph over him; this ruins the whole relationship and is the undoing of truth. When a person has in mind only the mastery over his fellow,he strives to establish his own point of view or his own wish, regardless whether it is true or false. When in any group, victory is the motive, one person does not listen to the other and controversy takes place.

An assembly which is not for the sake of Heaven will in the end not be an established operation. The first step towards wrongdoing may seem a harmless and innocent exercise, but it never stops there; it invariably leads to an ignominious end. To arrest this, the end should loom large on the horizon. The opening verse of the Psalms strikes the right note; it warns us to be cautious and wary of the ungodly, for the end can be disastrous. 'Happy is the man that has not walked in the counsel of the wicked, nor stood in the way of sinners, nor sat in the seat of the scornful.' We witness here the retrogression from walking to standing, and finally sitting and associating with undesirable company. The innocent passer-by may be irresistibly drawn into the circle of scoffers. Happy, therefore, is the man who resists such temptation, and wise is he who foresees the fruit of an action.

Hasidic Lore

The right assembly. R. Judah Zevi of Stretin declared: We say, 'And mayest Thou assemble the dispersed as one assembles grain stalks'. Why do we not say, 'As one assembles pearls?' The reason is that when we gather assembled pearls , we cleanse them of all impurities and select only those that are pure. Had we, therefore, said, 'Assemble us as pearls out of the dispersion', it would imply that we asked only for the redemption of the pure *tzaddikim* (righteous). But he who gathers grain stalks does so with hay clinging to them. We, likewise, petition that we may all be redeemed; the grain ears with the hay stalks, the tzaddikim with the ordinary Jews.

(טו) רַבִּי אֶלְעָזָר בֶּן שַׁמּוּעַ אוֹמֵר יְהִי כְבוֹד תַּלְמִידְךָ חָבִיב עָלֶיךָ כְּשֶׁלָּךְ וּכְבוֹד חֲבֵרְךָ כְּמוֹרָא רַבָּךְ וּמוֹרָא רַבָּךְ כְּמוֹרָא שָׁמָיִם:

Mishnah Fifteen.

R. Eleazar Ben Shammua says: Let the honour of your disciple be as dear to you as your own, and the fear of your associate as the fear of your master, and the fear of your master as the fear of Heaven.

R. Eleazar Ben Shammua HaCohen is often referred to as R. Eleazar. He was one of the pupils of R. Akiva who was ordained by R. Judah Ben Bava. He was a very lovable character and kindly disposed to all people. One authority states that he lived to the ripe old age of one hundred and five years.

Let the honour of your disciple ... It is our duty and privilege to show honour to our fellow-man at all times, for we are all equal in the sight of God. This is especially true of the relationship between teacher and pupil. The love of learning is innate in our people and it is therefore not surprising that a strong bond of respect and love existed between master and disciple. Indeed, the *derekh eretz* shown by the disciple towards his master was equal to, if not greater than, the honour afforded to parents by their children. This deference and regard was mutual and not one-sided. If the pupil owed much to the teacher, the teacher admitted that he was also indebted to his pupil, as is evident in the Talmud, 'Much have I learned from my teachers, more from my fellow-students, most from my disciples' (Ta. 7a).

Naturally, this mutual appreciation was built upon the firm foundations of sincerity and honesty of purpose. In early times the priest was the teacher and Malakhi rightly exalts him in these glowing terms, 'The priest's lips shall keep knowledge and they shall seek the law at his mouth, for he is the messenger of the Lord of Hosts' (2:7). R. Johanan commented on these words saying, 'If the teacher is like the messenger of the Lord, that is, he leads a pure life in the service of God, then people shall seek instruction at his mouth; if not, they cannot be instructed by him in the Law' (Yalkut).

If the teacher earned respect through his integrity, so did the student win the affection of his master through his conscientious approach to learning. In talmudic and geonic times the student often came from a poor background. He did not enjoy any comforts and subsisted mainly on fruits and vegetables. As an itinerant he wandered from place to place and endured many hardships in order to sit and learn at the feet of a great master whom he adored. Thus, on seeing a teacher at a distance, he would rise and not resume his seat until the teacher was out of sight (Kid. 33a). He would not occupy the teacher's seat (Nu. R. 15:13) nor would he call him by name (Sanh. 100a), nor would he interrupt or contradict him in public (Nu. R. 15:13). The pupil also attended to the personal needs of the master, but not in any menial sense. He would dress him and carry a torch before him in the dark streets (Pesikta de Rav Kahana, Beshallah). If the teacher was somewhat strict in public, in private, he was very kindly disposed towards his pupil (Ket. 103b). We see, therefore, that there was a healthy relationship between master and disciple; the pupil would not only listen to the master in the lecture hall, but would meet him face to face and be in close contact with him at his home. Many students were poor and this upholds the view of our Sages that we are beholden to the poor student, for Torah comes from him (Ned. 81b). The Mesillat Yesharim sums up the position in these words: As it is characteristic for the wicked to show contempt, so is it characteristic for the righteous to show respect, for honour always abides with them. Indeed, it never departs from them, as we read, 'Before His elders shall be honour' (Is. 24:23).

Let the fear of your associate be as dear to you as your own. For scriptural confirmation see Ex. 17:9 where we learn that Moses our Master said to Joshua, 'Choose us out men'. We should expect 'Choose me out men'. From this verse we deduce that Moses the Master regarded Joshua his pupil as his equal.

What is the proof-text for assuming that the fear of an associate should be as dear to him as the fear of his master? In Nu. 12:11 we read, 'And Aaron said to Moses, 'O my lord...'. In the first place, Aaron and Moses are brothers, yet Aaron addresses Moses as 'My lord, that is as his master. Secondly, Moses was younger, yet Aaron treated him as his master. That the honour of one's master is as dear as the honour of Heaven, we learn from Nu. 11:28, 'And Joshua the son of Nun, the minister of Moses from his youth, answered and said, 'My lord Moses, shut them in'. Joshua treated Moses as the equal of the *Shekhinah*, the divine presence (ARN 27).

Haver. The associate or comrade is the superior student who helps the less learned to revise again and again what the master taught. Constant revision is the key to the acquisition of knowledge. Of one student it is said that he repeated each lesson a hundred and one times (Ha. 9b) and of another student it is reported that he revised each lesson four hundred times (Er. 64b). From this we realise why the utmost respect of an associate should be held as high as the fear and respect of a teacher. Finally, as we have faith in God the Architect of Heaven and Earth, so should we place trust and confidence in the faithful teacher, for his expositions and interpretations of Torah bring us closer to God.

Hasidic Lore

Concern for a student. The Lizensker visited R. Schmelke at Nikolsburg. Passing a house he heard, through the open window, a student (later to become Rabbi Benet of Nikolsburg) devoting himself to the Torah with great zeal. He went over to him and said, 'Repent, my brother, repent!' R. Benet met R. Schmelke and told him of the Lizensker's mysterious injunction. R. Schmelke looked hard at his companion and said, 'You look as if you indulge in severe fasting; this is a grave sin for a man blessed with so remarkable an intellect for the study of the Torah; fasting weakens you and forms a serious obstacle to your study'.

(Here we find a typical example of real concern of a master for the health of a disciple).

(טז) רַבִּי יְהוּדָה אוֹמֵר הֱוֵי זָהִיר בְּתַלְמוּד שֶׁשִּׁגְגַת תַּלְמוּד עוֹלָה זָדוֹן:

Mishnah Sixteen.

R. Judah says: Be careful in teaching, for an error in teaching can amount to intentional sin.

R. Judah Bar Ilai was known as 'the first among the speakers', a title he earned because he was a brilliant expounder of the Law. He was known for his piety and abstinence, eschewing all comforts and pleasures of life, and he lived in abject poverty. He studied under R. Akiva, and Judah Ha-Nasi was amongst his pupils.

Be careful in teaching. This is a call to the teacher to be cautious and selective in the preparation and presentation of the lesson. Any errors committed through negligence or incompetence can mislead the disciple and cause irreparable harm to the mind and outlook of the innocent child and bring him to presumptuous sin. As a people we have always worshipped education and many parents will spare no effort to obtain for their children an all-embracing knowledge of Jewish learning. However, for a variety of reasons, the teaching imparted to our young is not necessarily of a high calibre. As far as the heder system and private school are concerned we have been bedevilled by a paucity of expert pedagogues, and this has contributed to a lowering of standards.

It is to be hoped that the founding of more Jewish day schools will help to bring about better results. Would that we could rise to the heights of enthusiasm which inspired the talmudic teacher, expressed in the answer of R. Akiva, who was in prison, to Simeon Bar Yohai, 'My son, more than the calf wishes to suck, does the cow yearn to suckle' (Pes. 112a). The importance of teaching is stressed in the following extract: R. Simeon Bar Yohai taught, 'If you see towns which have been uprooted, know that it is the result of not engaging and supporting teachers and scholars, as it is said, 'Wherefore is the land perished and laid waste like a wilderness? Because they have forsaken My Law which I set before them' (Jer. 9:11-12) (Y.Ha. 1:7).

Whilst commentators translate *Talmud* as study or teaching, we shall plough a lonely furrow and translate the word as 'The Talmud'. The meaning is therefore - be cautious in regard to the Talmud, do not treat it lightly. The Torah consists of the Written Law and the Oral Law. The Talmud is the Oral Law which is the complement of the Written Law. Throughout Jewish history we have had a number of reactionary movements which have rejected the Oral Law, the Talmud. For example, in the early centuries of our era the Sadducees, in the eighth century the Karaites and in modern times the Liberal and Reform Jews are all movements which may have started in error, but eventually they broke away from traditional Judaism, and in some cases they opted out of the Faith through intermarriage and apostasy.

In the non-Jewish world the Talmud was always suspected of heresy; thus Hadrian (117-138 C.E.) was determined to destroy the Talmud, and Justinian (553) forbade all Jewish interpretation and exposition of the Scriptures on Sabbath in the Synagogues. The early Persian kings were relentless in the persecution of Jews and closed the talmudical colleges of Sura and Pumbedita, the Jewish Oxford and Cambridge of antiquity. A number of Popes issued edicts and bulls to the heads of the Churches in various countries to confiscate all copies of the Talmud, and in 1242 twenty four cart-loads of the Talmud were publicly burned in Paris; this was the first official burning of the Talmud. Later, such burnings took place at frequent intervals.

To return to our Mishnah, it is possible to interpret the words of R. Judah to be a prophetic cry to Jews in all ages to resist our reactionaries who belittle the Talmud. On the contrary, we should strengthen our hold on the Talmud so that more of our youth are introduced to its teachings which are the life-line of Judaism and the repository of Jewish wisdom, thought and practice. 'Some of the greatest Talmudists in the Middle Ages were also devoted to science and philosophy in the technical sense of these terms, but there were masses of Jews who knew no other intellectual interest than the Talmud and its allied literature; the Talmud saved them from stagnation' (Israel Abrahams).

Hasidic Lore

What to study. The Hasidim came to R. Phineas of Frankfurt with this question, 'Master, who, if anyone, is to study the 'Guide to the Perplexed'?

The master replied: Know that the Guide is like an apothecary's shop. The chemist dwelling within prepares many useful remedies for many ills, being licenced as a man of skill. But he who has no learning of remedies and diseases, let him beware how he meddles with the contents of the shop. The smallest error may kill a man and any mistake entails loss of reputation.

(יז) רַבִּי שִׁמְעוֹן אוֹמֵר שְׁלשָׁה כְתָרִים הֵן כֶּתֶר תּוֹרָה וְכֶתֶר כְּהֻנָּה וְכֶתֶר מַלְכוּת וְכֶתֶר שֵׁם טוֹב עוֹלֶה עַל גַּבֵּיהֶן׃

Mishnah Seventeen.

R. Simeon says: There are three crowns, the crown of Torah, the crown of priesthood and the crown of royalty, and the crown of a good name accompanies them.

R. Simeon here is recognised to be Simeon Ben Yohai, the father-in-law of Pinhas Ben Jair, and the supposed author of the Zohar. It is reported that in his old age he was succesful in obtaining concessions from Emperor Marcus Aurelius to repeal some of the edicts previously enacted against Jewish Law and custom, see 3:9.

The crown of the Torah. Though the crown is usually connected with royalty alone, in Judaism the crown of the Torah is the proud possession of every Jew. Indeed, one of the titles by which God is known is 'The King of Kings'. Hence we commence with the crown of the Torah given by God to Moses on Mount Sinai. The crown is symbolic of authority, and the Torah, which is our charter, is our authority. It is binding on us, and to it we owe our whole-hearted loyalty and devotion. It is understandable, therefore, why the crown of Torah should head our Mishnah.

The crown of priesthood. The priests were the first teachers of Israel. They taught the Torah and were the first guardians of the Law. They were humble and modest and did not glorify in their trusteeship. The character of the priest is delineated for us by Malakhi 2:6. In spite of the exalted status, the priest was not even included in the line of Jewish tradition, as can be seen from the first Mishnah of Avot. They were never an autonomous body who ruled with power and authority. How very different was the priesthood of other religions of antiquity! Many were autocratic and exeedingly wealthy. In Judaism the priests could not become rich as they were not permitted to possess land (Deut. 18:1).

The crown of royalty. In ancient Egypt the Pharaohs were regarded as divine and demanded that sacrifices be offered to them. The Jewish king was never deified; his powers were limited and his authority came from God. The kings could not dictate; on the contrary, they were dictated to by the Prophets who fearlessly and courageously denounced them if they took the law into their own hands or wished to act tyrannically. In Greece there was constant class warfare, and the commoner had no rights or privileges. The Roman Emperors misused their dictatorial powers and sucked the life-blood of their subjects. In Israel, the king was to be guided by a code of honour as expressed in Deut. 17:14-20. He was commanded to write his own Sefer Torah, which he was expected to study every day. This is what we mean by the crown of the Torah which is embroidered on the curtain of the

Ark and on the mantle of the Torah Scroll, uniting us all as loyal subjects of the 'King of Kings' whom we salute at all times. The crown of the Torah is also in a category apart, for the priesthood and royalty are hereditary whereas the Torah is accessible to all without distinction. Every Jew is eligible to wear the crown of the Torah whatever his station in life.

The crown of a good name. The climax of the Mishnah is the possession of a good name. A person of reputable character is prepared to make sacrifices to acquire a good name. Commenting on Ec. 7:1, 'A good name is better than precious oil', the Rabbis explain that every man has three names; one given to him by his father and mother, one by which others call him, and one which he earns for himself (Ec. R.) 'What is in a name?' is an expression which is not rooted in Jewish life. In rabbinic literature a name has meaning and purpose and is treasured by all good people. To demonstrate this truth we shall analyse, in the light of Jewish tradition, the names of four great biblical heroes who each received the divine call in a similar manner. Their names were repeated in Gen. 22:11, 'Abraham, Abraham'; Gen. 46:2, 'Jacob, Jacob'; Ex. 3:4, 'Moses, Moses and I Sam. 3:10, 'Samuel, Samuel'. This repetition of each name expresses divine endearment, love and friendship. See Rashi on Ex. 3:4. We should add that when the Hebrew letters of the name Moshe, mem, shin, hei, are reversed, we get the name of God, *Ha-Shem* (Lekah Tov on Ex. 3:14).

There are different interpretation for the repetition of the names Abraham, Jacob, Moses and Samuel. For instance, Tosefta Ber. 1:14 comments, 'They were the same in their righteousness whilst they had not yet entered on their greatness'.

R. Eleazar Ben Jacob said, 'The first mention of the name Abraham is the call unto Abraham himself; the second mention of the name Abraham is an exhortation unto his descendants. Similarly, in the case of Jacob, Moses and Samuel ..... there is no generation which has not the duty laid upon it of trying to emulate the example of the four great figures who received their call by the repetition of their names' (Gen. R. 56:7).

Yet another interpretation given by R. Abba Bar Kahanah is, 'All whose names were repeated when called have their portion in two worlds, in this world and in the world to come' (Gen. R. 30:4, Ex .R.2:6).

The names of our great heroes were so beloved that we even read them into the words of our liturgy. When we take the initial Hebrew letters of our four biblical heroes in reverse,we formulate the word *Shemaya* which means Heaven. Such is the force of Jewish tradition that when we hark back to our progenitors Samuel, Moses, Jacob and Abraham, we obtain a glimpse of the celestial heights above,which inspire us to emulate the lives of our great teachers of the past. Thus, in our prayers on Sabbath morning at the commencement of the Musaph service we recite, '*Yekum Purkan Min Shemaya*, which can be rendered, 'May salvation come from Shemuel, Moshe Yaacov and Avraham'. In this lengthy excursus we have only one example of rabbinic exposition on names of great Jews who have worn the crown of a good name.

We shall now interpret the last clause of the Mishnah, *Oleh al gabayhen*. Most commentators translate these words as follows - 'And the crown of a good name excels them all'. We find this translation incorrect and untenable for it infers that a good name is superior and preferable to the acquisition of Torah. We cannot accept the thesis that Torah should be denigrated and that a good name by itself should be elevated. We prefer to follow the literal translation of the words *oleh al gebayhen* which means 'it goes up (alights) on their backs'. A thorough knowledge of Torah is desirable, but the *ben Torah*, the Jewish scholar, should also enjoy a good reputation and possess an honourable name. If a Torah scholar befouls the fair name of Judaism, he is dragging the crown of the Torah into the mire. The Talmud asserts that if the teacher is like an angel of the Lord, then seek Torah at his mouth, but if his relationship with human beings is bad, he is guilty of profaning the name of God, and if he is guilty of misconduct he is worse than an *am haaretz*, an ignoramus (M.K.17a). The scholar must carry with him, at all times, the crown of a good name. The authentic Jew is one who enjoys both sound scholarship and an excellent name. Similarly with priesthood and royalty, a good name should accompany them and be borne with dignity.

Hasidic Lore

The crown of the Lord. Whilst reciting the Selihot prayers, the Sassover Rabbi exclaimed: O Lord, consider that Thou must need Israel to sin for the fulfilment of Thy attributes which are like thirteen gems in Thy crown, otherwise Thou wouldst lack some of the most precious gems, long-suffering and forgiving iniquity (Ex. 34.7), and Thy crown would lose much of its glory. Thus even by their sins the Children of Israel contribute to Thy glory and they deserve to be treated with clemency.

(יח) רַבִּי נְהוֹרַאי אוֹמֵר הֱוֵי גוֹלֶה לִמְקוֹם תּוֹרָה וְאַל תֹּאמַר שֶׁהִיא תָבוֹא אַחֲרֶיךָ שֶׁחֲבֵרֶיךָ יְקַיְּמוּהָ בְיָדֶךָ וְאֶל בִּינָתְךָ אַל תִּשָּׁעֵן׃

Mishnah Eighteen.

R. Nehorai says: Wander to a place of Torah and do not say it will come after you, or your associates will fulfil it through you; and do not rely on your own understanding.

R. Nehorai. There is some doubt as to his identity; he has been connected with R. Nehemiah and R. Eleazar Ben Arakh. The word *nehorai* is Aramaic for enlightenment and was eventually used as a name or title for a number of distinguished people.

Wander to a place of Torah. The Hebrew word *goleh* is derived from a root which means 'to leave home' or 'to go into exile'. Here we are advised how best to acquire the learning of Torah. As the study of the Law is all-absorbing and requires our whole-hearted and undivided attention, we are recommended to leave home where there are many distractions, and go into exile far removed from home comforts. For this reason the Yeshivah was often situated, not in a busy city or town characterised by its noise and bustle, but in a secluded area 'away from the madding crowd', which can offer facilities for contemplation, meditation and tranquillity. Historically it is true that the Torah preserves Israel throughout its dispersion. On the verse, 'And yet for all that when they are in the land of their enemies, I will not reject them neither will I abhor them to destroy them utterly' (Lev. 26:44) the Rabbis ask, 'Was there anything left with Israel to keep them from being abhorred and rejected? Were all their precious gifts and possessions not taken away from them when they went into exile? It was through the existence of the Torah that Israel has survived and preserved its national integrity' (Sifra Behukosai).

The advice offered by our Mishnah that students should leave home and travel from place to place in order to equip themselves with a thorough knowledge of Torah is referred to in a number of instances in rabbinic literature. Commenting on Deut. 33:3, 'And they are cut at Thy feet', R. Joseph inferred that 'These are the students of the Torah who cut their feet in going from town to town and from country to country to learn the Torah' (B.B.8a). In another context the Rabbis expound the words in Jud.

5:10, 'You who ride on white asses', as referring to the learned men who travel from town to town and from province to province to study the Torah; whilst in Kid. 29b (Tosafot) we are told that the Babylonians went to Palestine and the Palestinians went to Babylonia to learn at the respective academies of both lands.

An allusion to the opening words of our Mishnah is recorded by the Baal Haturim which he deduces from the juxtaposition of the two verses in Deut. 4:43-45:

Bezer in the wilderness, in the table-land, for the Reubenites; and Ramot in Gilead, for the Gadites; and Golan in Bashan, for the Manassites... And this is the law which Moses set before the Children of Israel; these are the testimonies and the statutes and the ordinances, which Moses spoke unto the children of Israel when they came forth from Egypt....

An interesting interpretation of our Mishnah is afforded by R. David Ha-Nagid, the grandson of Maimonides, who says that if a man endows a large sum of money to build an institution of Torah, he is still obligated to learn Torah for himself. This seems to run counter to the generally accepted principle that those who are wealthy should maintain others who sacrifice everything in order to study Torah. According to R. David Ha-Nagid, no person is excused from learning Torah. In the same manner that we cannot delegate the mitzvah of Tefillin which devolves upon every man, so we cannot rid ourselves of the paramount duty which is enforced upon every Jew, rich or poor, to spend time in the pursuit of Torah, even if it entails leaving one's home or going into exile. As our national exile was followed by redemption, so our voluntary exile to a house of learning must lead to a spiritual redemption. In addition to learning Torah, the Mishnah underlines the significance of the environment of Torah, *the place of Torah*. At a Yeshivah, Torah is not only studied, it is also practised and lived.

Do not rely on your own understanding.... This is only a part of the verse which is preceded by, 'Trust in the Lord with all your heart and lean not.... (Prov. 3:5). Every person, however wise, needs advice on some of the manifold problems which arise. No one can rely solely on his own judgment. Those who trust in God will always lean on Him; thus the religious Jew will seek the guidance of Sages and scholars, whose rich experience, mature wisdom and ripe counsel befit them to offer advice.

Many are the stories told of the Rabbis of every generation who have helped their followers by counselling them aright.

The biographer (M.M. Yoshar) in his book entitled 'Saint and Sage' relates that a merchant, a former Yeshivah student, bought a lottery ticket and decided to visit the Hafez Hayyim to request a blessing that he be successful. However, on the advice of a friend who was convinced that the saintly Rabbi would disapprove of gambling, he did not mention the real motive behind his request. The Rabbi blessed him that he be granted children who would grow up to be loyal and faithful Jews, but this blessing did not altogether satisfy the disciple, who decided to remain for another day in order to receive a further blessing. The Hafez Hayyim repeated the same blessing, but the merchant looked worried and did not leave the presence of the Rabbi. The Hafez Hayyim noted that the visitor was dissatisfied and, thinking aloud, gave utterance to these words: Some people who are asked how they are, answer 'Quite well, but it could be better'. Now, how can they know that it could be better? Surely the Almighty knows the requirements and desires of every individual. Many people come to me for advice, but what they really expect is that I should agree with their wishes, and that I cannot always do.

The Rabbi then arose, and putting his hand on the man's shoulder he continued, 'There came to me a young man who wanted to win a lottery; but if the Almighty wishes to grant him good children, who are the greatest treasure on earth, wealth can only interfere with their education. Therefore be content with what you have and do not aspire to more'. Amazed at the foresight of the Rabbi, the young man returned home happy and content.

Hasidic Lore

Understanding. On Understanding, the Bratzlaver said: Lack of understanding lies in the heart. Perfection of understanding is possible only to the man who keeps his five senses holy. Holy inspiration and enlargement of the mind's powers may be attained thereby.

He who thinks holy thoughts in the Torah and in Divine Service is rewarded by the ability to understand more and more. This means that a man allows himself to be influenced by the Universal Mind which immediately surrounds him, and this may continue even unto his death. As he observes and imbibes more of the Universal Mind, he is able to attain a higher degree in the world to come, whereas others must be content with a lesser degree. Such understanding warms the soul, as garments warm the body.

(יט) רַבִּי יַנַּאי אוֹמֵר אֵין בְּיָדֵינוּ לֹא מִשַּׁלְוַת הָרְשָׁעִים וְאַף לֹא מִיִּסּוּרֵי הַצַּדִּיקִים:

Mishnah Nineteen.

R. Jannai says: It is not in our power (to explain) either the contentment of the wicked or the suffering of the righteous.

R. Jannai was a teacher of the fourth or fifth generation. He is possibly the father of R. Dostai ben Jannai and R. Eleazar Ben Jannai. Throughout the Pirkei Avot this is the only statement recorded in his name.

Here is enunciated the principle of 'Theodicy', the prosperity of the wicked and the suffering of the righteous. Philosophers and thinkers of every creed have struggled with this problem. At the outset, we must understand what we mean by the terms wicked and righteous. Do we really know who is wicked and who is righteous? Ecclesiastes reminds us, 'There is none righteous upon the earth who does only good and does not sin' (7:20). God alone knows; human beings are apt to judge man harshly.

It is possible that this is implied in the unusual expression with which this Mishnah begins, *ein beyadenu*. This is an idiomatic phrase which we translate 'It is not in our power', but literally means, 'It is not in our hands'. The hand, which is an external limb, is symbolic of action which is visible. Jannai warns us not to look at the hands of the wicked or of the righteous; we may be misled by their outward actions. God can see into the inner recesses of the heart and mind, which are hidden from the gaze of man. Even the wicked may have redeeming features which merit reward on earth.

Shalvah, ease or contentment. The wicked may ostensibly give the impression that they are happy, but do they really enjoy *shalvah*, peace of mind, tranquillity of spirit and an inner serenity? Their conscience must torment them in the stillness of the night.

Suffering. Regarding the suffering of the righteous, we should acknowledge the fact that suffering in some form is the lot of mankind. Suffering can ennoble, purify and refine the character of man. The truly righteous accept suffering as 'chastisements of love' and will submit and resign themselves to the will of God, for punishment is not necessarily inflicted on man on account of his sins. 'Yet it pleased the Lord to crush him by disease to see if his soul would offer itself by restitution that he will see descendants and live long and the desire of the Lord will prosper in his hand' (Is. 53:10).

The Book of Job is dedicated to this very problem. Job lost everything he possessed and suffered much, but he never lost his confidence in, or ever doubted God. At times we forget that we are enjoined to bless God, not only for our joys, but also for our afflictions. This we record at every Burial Service, and it should not surprise us to learn that it is derived from the Book of Job, 'The Lord gave and He has taken away, blessed be the name of the Lord' (1:21). We bless God when He gives and when He takes away life as witnessed by the countless martyrs who willingly sacrificed their lives for the sanctification of the Name of God. Although the problem in our Mishnah is seemingly an intractable one, the Rabbis offer an answer: The potter does not test cracked vessels for he need only knock upon them once and they break, but if he tests sound vessels he can knock upon them many times without breaking them. Similarly, the Holy One blessed be He does not try the wicked, but the righteous, as it is said, 'The Lord tries the righteous' (Ps. 11:5); and it is written, 'God did test Abraham' (Gen. R. 32:3). Finally, we should record the accepted teaching which asks, 'Which is the way which leads a man to the world to come?' The answer is 'The way of suffering' (Mekhilta to Ex. 20:23).

Hasidic Lore

Suffering. Boundless was the Apter's love for Israel. Once he broke down and wept for half a day. On this particular day R. Sussya of Anipol visited him and asked the reason for his excessive weeping, adding, 'Has not the Besht commanded us to be always cheerful? The Apter cast a mournful glance at his friend and cried, 'Sussya, what will befall you, do you not feel the dreadful suffering and bitter persecutions to which the people of Israel are subjected?' R. Sussya answered, 'I feel them, but it is written in the Book of Zohar that God inflicts upon mankind as much suffering as it can endure'.

During the last three years of his life R. Yehuda Zevi was afflicted with a terrible disease which caused painful ulcers to break out all over his body. The doctors said that from what they knew of human fortitude it was impossible for a man to bear such pain. When one of the Rabbi's close friends asked him about this, he said, 'When I was young and one who was sick came to me, I would pray with all the force of my soul that his suffering might be taken from him. Later the strength of my prayer flagged and all I could do was to take the suffering upon myself. And so now I bear it'.

(כ)רַבִּי מַתְּתְיָה בֶּן חָרָשׁ אוֹמֵר הֱוֵי מַקְדִּים בִּשְׁלוֹם כָּל אָדָם וֶהֱוֵי זָנָב לָאֲרָיוֹת וְאַל תְּהִי רֹאשׁ לַשֻּׁעָלִים:

Mishnah Twenty

R. Mattityah Ben Heresh says: Be first in greeting every man and be a tail to lions and not a head to foxes.

R. Mattityah of the second century was born in Judea. His teachers were R. Eliezer Ben Hyrcanus and R. Eleazar Ben Azaryah. Because of the persecutions by Hadrian he left for Rome, where he established a Yeshivah.

Be first in greeting every man. The Jewish greeting is *Shalom*, peace. Generally speaking, peace or war is part of the programme of the government of the day. The ordinary man in the street can do precious little either to promote peace or initiate a war. Both peace and war belong to the political vocabulary of mankind. Judaism endeavours to remove peace from the political arena and to introduce it as one of the social graces. By greeting every person with *Shalom* we may sow the seeds of peace in the hearts of all mankind. We should always think and speak in terms of peace, that elusive quality for which we all pray and yearn. For this reason we attach great importance to the Jewish greeting, and the Rabbis, with hindsight, have surrounded it with a number of rules which have established it as a significant section of Jewish teaching.

Greeting a person is the first step towards understanding, equality of status, and friendship. Indeed, it is a charitable act of the highest order (Yalkut Shimoni 201). However, refusing to respond to a greeting is an act of robbery. 'He who was usually saluted with *Shalom* by his friend first, shall extend *Shalom* first... yet if he greeted his friend who did not reply, that refusal is regarded as an act of violence' (Ber. 6b). On the other hand, one should not greet a mourner whose mind is perturbed with his personal loss, as he is not at peace with himself and is in need of something other than a formal greeting. 'He who is at peace with himself may bring a peace offering, except a mourner; he cannot bring a peace offering. It is also forbidden to greet a mourner, as it is said, 'Your sighing be mute' (Ez. 24:17), (M.K. 15a-b).

Furthermore, we do not treat the greeting as an ordinary social habit; it is a form of blessing and prayer. 'When visiting the sick, R. Eleazar used to say, 'May God remember you for peace', or 'The Merciful One may remember you for peace' (Shab. 12b). In this connection we should note that it has been suggested that the Jewish greeting *Shalom* owes its origin to the Priestly Benediction which closes with the word *Shalom* (Nu. 6:24). This would elevate our every-day greeting to the exalted heights of a prayerful blessing from God, and the fact that *Shalom* is one of the names of God would strengthen our thesis. However, it affords us a great educational lesson. Too many think of God as an impersonal Being who resides in the heavens above, or who blesses man only in the Synagogue during Divine Service in the awe-inspiring Priestly Benediction. This is denied by the Jewish greeting *Shalom* which contains overtones of God's blessing on earth, in the street, on all occasions and in all circumstances. This would invest the greeting with an added sanctity.

That the name of God was originally part of the Jewish greeting can be traced to the oft repeated phrase, '*has veshalom*', God forbid; this is an abbreviation of 'God spare you and give you peace' (Lev. R. 5:4). As the name of God is not to be taken in vain, it was dropped from all forms of greeting. The Jewish greeting does not apply to individuals only, but also to groups of people. Thus the workers of Jerusalem would salute the pilgrims (Mishnah Bik. 3:3) and the guards leaving the Temple greeted with Shalom those who entered (Ber. 12a).

So vital was the concept of peace that we are asked to greet all men, even the heathen. This is the interpretation of our Mishnah and is contained in the favourite saying of Abbaye, 'A man should always increase... peace with his brethren and relatives and with all men, even the heathen in the street, so that he may be beloved above and popular on earth and acceptable to his fellow creatures. They say of Rabban Johanan Ben Zakkai that no person ever greeted him first, not even the heathen in the street (Ber. 17a).

It now remains to explain why we reverse the greeting in reply to *Shalom aleikhem*, which is used when meeting a friend after a lapse of time, to '*Aleikhem shalom*'. We have already indicated that it is considered to be an act of violence not to reply to a greeting. If a person repeats the same formula, he might give the impression that he has not suitably replied and so be guilty of ignoring the greeting. He therefore reverses it, leaving no doubt in the mind of his friend. The plural form *aleikhem* is used to indicate that we offer peace both to the physical, as well as the spiritual nature of man.

In conclusion we should compare the Jewish form of greeting, with the non-Jewish greeting, 'hello', which is universally used. According to the dictionary 'hello' is equivalent to 'hollo' which means to shout, to excite dogs to chase, to shout 'hello' to animals to urge them on. From this reference to animals, we can now proceed to the latter part of the Mishnah.

Be a tail to lions... This proverbial saying is found in the Jerusalem Talmud in reverse, 'Be the head among foxes rather than the tail among lions' (Sanh. 4:10). Commenting on this one writer says, 'The proverb is mere worldly wisdom, the child of practical sense. The mind of the Rabbi, on the other hand, is fixed upon the ethical purpose. He, therefore, desires above all, association with his superiors in however modest a capacity. The proverb gives preference to leadership, though exercised among inferiors' (M. Lazarus).

The lion is recognised as the king of beasts. He is the head of his family and was used as a symbol for the princely tribe of Judah (Gen. 49:9). The lion is crowned with a massive mane and has a stupendous roar, which inspires terror. The hope for the Messianic Peace is closely connected with the lion (Is. 11:6). The fox is noted for its sly and cunning nature but is also considered to be a foolish animal. To interpret the proverbial saying of the Mishnah we should remember that it is the nature of the lion to lift up its tail towards its head, whereas the fox lowers its head to the ground. Similarly, man should not aspire through cunning, sly and dishonest means to become a leader, and in the process bring ruin and destruction on himself and on those who put their trust in him. Rather be a tail to the lion and become a loyal and true follower; co-operate with your leader to whom you owe allegiance, and do not aspire to reach the shaky height of a cunning and corrupt leader.

There appears to be no logical connection between the two sections of the Mishnah. We can but hazard a guess. We must cultivate the peaceful greeting and inculcate the ideal of peace into the hearts of our young and old. Prayerfully, this may lead us to the Messianic Era, when 'The lion shall eat straw like an ox and the sucking child shall play on the hole of the asp' (Is. 11:11). Is it possible that the Tanna of the Mishnah connected our formal greeting of peace, with the most exalted form of peace depicted by Isaiah in chapter 11, where he introduces us to the animal kingdom? When the wolf dwells with the lamb and we follow the tail of the lion, we shall attain the durable peace for which we all pray.

Hasidic Lore

Greeting. The Lizensker met a group of Jews who were travelling to Warsaw. 'Greet my father, please', requested the Rabbi. 'Who is he?' the Rabbi was asked. 'He is mine and yours — our Father in Heaven', replied the Lizensker.

(כא) רַבִּי יַעֲקֹב אוֹמֵר הָעוֹלָם הַזֶּה דּוֹמֶה לִפְרוֹזְדוֹר בִּפְנֵי הָעוֹלָם הַבָּא הַתְקֵן עַצְמְךָ בִּפְרוֹזְדוֹר כְּדֵי שֶׁתִּכָּנֵס לִטְרַקְלִין:

Mishnah Twenty One

R. Jacob says: This world is like a vestibule before the world to come; prepare yourself in the vestibule so that you may enter the banqueting hall.

(כב) הוּא הָיָה אוֹמֵר יָפָה שָׁעָה אַחַת בִּתְשׁוּבָה וּמַעֲשִׂים טוֹבִים בָּעוֹלָם הַזֶּה מִכֹּל חַיֵּי הָעוֹלָם הַבָּא וְיָפָה שָׁעָה אַחַת שֶׁל קוֹרַת רוּחַ בָּעוֹלָם הַבָּא מִכֹּל חַיֵּי הָעוֹלָם הַזֶּה:

Mishnah Twenty Two

He used to say: Better is one hour of repentance and good deeds in this world than all the life of the world to come; and better is one hour of calmness of spirit in the world to come than all the life of this world.

These two statements deal with the same subject and in some editions they are treated as one Mishnah.

R. Jacob Ben Kurshai has been referred to in 3:9. According to talmudic sources (Kid. 39a; Hul. 142a) he was the grandson of Elisha Ben Avuya, the former scholar who strayed from the path of Judaism on account of a traumatic experience which changed his outlook and shook his faith. The Torah mentions two laws, the performance of which merit a long and good life. One is the honouring of parents, and the second is the sending away of the mother bird contingent on keeping the young or the eggs (Deut. 22:6).

It is reported that a father once directed his son to climb a tree where a bird was nesting and to perform the mitzvah of *shiluah hakan*, sending away the mother bird. As the lad descended, the ladder collapsed and he fell to his death. This incident led to the apostasy of Elisha, who subsequently became known as *Aher*, the other one. R. Jacob was deeply troubled by this change of heart on the part of his grandfather and was determined to plumb the depths of the temporal life of this world and the eternal life of the world to come. He it was who formulated what later became a basic tenet of Jewish theology, namely, that 'there is no material reward for the fulfilment of God's commandments in this world' (Kid. 39b). He interpreted the words 'length of days' to refer, not to this world, but to the world to come. Similarly, 'And it shall be well with you', does not apply to this world but to the Hereafter, which is a life of eternal bliss.

Prepare yourself. We distinguish between this world, the vestibule, verandah or ante-chamber and the world to come, the banqueting hall. This world is one of action, deeds and responsibilities. In the world of the future there is no activity; heavenly bliss and tranquillity prevail. 'In the world to come there is no eating, no drinking, no business, no sensual pleasure, but the righteous sit with their crowns adorning their heads and enjoy the splendour of the Divine Presence' (Ber. 17a). However, we must prepare ourselves in this world in order to enjoy the bliss of the future world. Here, we have the means to form, fashion and build our personality and to refine our nature through Torah study and observance of the precepts. These spiritual exercises will create in us a sensitive soul which will prepare us for the future life. Whereas the body is a frame which is discarded at death and it disintegrates, decomposes and returns to the earth from which it came, the soul is eternal and never dies; it returns to God who gave it. Every morning we recite in our prayers, 'O my God, the soul which Thou gavest me is pure, Thou didst create it, Thou didst form it and Thou didst breathe it into me, Thou preservest it within me and Thou wilt take it from me'. Cherishing and treasuring the soul is the art of religion. It is the soul which is immortal and passes from the vestibule to the banqueting hall in the presence of the Shekhinah.

Yafah. It is interesting that whilst we translate this word as 'better', it literally means beautiful. One writer states that the author of this Mishnah was familiar with Hellenic culture and mode of speech, as the Greeks worshipped beauty (M. Lazarus).

One hour of repentance and good deeds .... Judaism, unlike Christianity, is not an other-worldly religion. We are not to become engrossed in the workings of the future life. 'The heavens belong to God, but the earth belongs to the sons of man' (Ps. 19). We are cautioned not to dabble in necromancy or spiritualism. The Torah forbids all speculations into the future but stresses this life, repentance and good deeds. There is much constructive work to be done on this earth. Thus the Law-giver clearly states, 'Keep My statutes and ordinances which, if a man do, he shall live by them' (Lev. 18:5). These words obviously refer to this world as the Rabbis underline by commenting, 'He shall not die by them'. This is what the Mishnah wishes to convey — one hour of repentance and good deeds on earth is richer than all the life in the world to come, for the simple reason that one is unable to repent or to perform good deeds in the world to come; this is reserved only for this world. However, one hour of serenity in the world to come is better (more beautiful) than all the life in this world, which is referred to as *olam d'shikra*, a world of lies, envy, suspicion, jealousy, strife and war. The Hereafter is known as *olam haemet*, the world of truth, which is the seal of God Almighty. There, celestial bliss and perfect peace hold sway. This is vouchsafed for all, as we read in the opening words of Pirkei Avot, 'All Israel have a share in the world to come'.

H. Loewe writes: The final quotation in this Mishnah is a great favourite of mine yet we must not analyse its exact meaning too closely. The paradox seems to indicate, with a wonderful yearning and graciousness, that there may be a blissful experience in this world which not even the glories of the world to come can rival, but that the fulness in the world to come is far beyond the best experience which life in this world can offer.

Hasidic Lore

The two impulses, good and evil. The Lizensker interpreted Gen. 3;22-24, 'And the Lord said, 'Behold the man is become as one of us, to know good and evil'. He acquired the power to think and desire both good and evil, just as in the world of divinity there are holy and unholy spirits. 'And now lest he put forth his hand and take also of the tree of life and eat and live for ever'. Man became endowed with the ability to do evil and thereby to die; on the other hand he is able to do good and gain immortality for his soul by partaking of the tree of life, namely, by obedience to the Lord's instruction. 'Therefore the Lord God sent him forth from the Garden of Eden to till the ground whence he was taken'. Since good deeds cannot be performed and self-improvement cannot be achieved in Paradise where there are no evil impulses, the Lord sent him forth from the state of primitive happiness to labour in the world of strife and impulse. 'So He drove out the man and He placed at the Garden of Eden the cherubim and the flaming sword, which turned every way to keep the way of the Tree of Life'. Therefore, the Lord placed within man the quest for pleasure and the evil desire that revolves continuously in his brain inflaming his heart with its intensity and urgent power. They guard the way and force man to battle with them. He must gain victory over them before he can perform the will of God and thereby gain the right to immortality.

(כג) רַבִּי שִׁמְעוֹן בֶּן אֶלְעָזָר אוֹמֵר אַל תְּרַצֶּה אֶת חֲבֵרְךָ בִּשְׁעַת כַּעֲסוֹ וְאַל תְּנַחֲמֵהוּ בְּשָׁעָה שֶׁמֵּתוֹ מֻטָּל לְפָנָיו וְאַל תִּשְׁאַל לוֹ בִּשְׁעַת נִדְרוֹ וְאַל תִּשְׁתַּדֵּל לִרְאוֹתוֹ בִּשְׁעַת קַלְקָלָתוֹ:

Mishnah Twenty Three

R. Simeon Ben Eleazar says: Do not appease your fellow in his hour of anger; do not comfort him whilst his dead is laid out before him; do not question him in the hour of his vow and do not strive to see him in his hour of disgrace.

R. Simeon Ben Eleazar was a disciple of R. Meir whom he quotes frequently. He was well versed in both Halakhah and Aggadah and he is often mentioned in the Talmud. Tractate Kiddushin ends with one of his sayings, 'If those (animals) who were created only to serve me are sustained without trouble; how much more so should I who was created to serve my Maker'.

Do not appease... The Talmud rightly remarks, 'Even as a man is commanded to speak up when his words will be listened to, so he is commanded to hold his peace at moments when he will not be listened to' (Yev. 65b). In the hour of anger, death, vow or disgrace, one is not in the frame of mind to listen; in all such circumstances it is preferable to be silent. The following extract from the Midrash will illustrate that silence can prove to be as eloquent and powerful as speech. 'Two advocates stood before Hadrian, the Roman Emperor. One of them pleaded the cause of speech, the other the cause of silence. The spokesman for speech explained that speech was essential in order to communicate with people in all circumstances. When the counsel for silence commenced to state his claim, he was attacked by the counsel for speech who objected to him using the weapons of speech which he reserved for himself alone' (Yalkut Shimoni Behaalotekha). In other words, there are occasions as stipulated in our Mishnah when silence can prove to be more efficacious than speech.

Anger. Anger is to be avoided, for it is a natural weakness which affects all people. Even Moses gave way to anger on three occasions (Lev. 10:16, Nu. 20:10 and 31:14). We are therefore advised not to placate a man in his hour of anger, but to wait until it subsides. It is related of the Sefat Emet that on travelling abroad, he was accompanied by a number of his followers. One, who was quick tempered, asked the Rabbi for a blessing before departure. The Rabbi explained that the locomotive has the power to draw all the carriages along with it because the steam within it is controlled. So should man control his anger from within. The Talmud recognises this human weakness as reflected in the popular adage in the name of R. Ilai, 'By three things may a person's character be determined — *bekiso*, by his pocket, *bekoso*, by his drink, and *bekaaso*, by his anger (Er. 65b).

Do not comfort him whilst his dead is laid out. In Jewish Law it is considered wrong to pacify a person whilst his dead is before him; this is not the appropriate occasion for comforting. *Nihum avelim*, comforting the mourners, has its appointed time during *shiva*, the seven days of mourning which commence immediately after the funeral, when relatives and friends are encouraged to fulfil this great mitzvah. However, prior to the funeral, when the hearts of the mourners are seared with intense grief and abject sorrow, comfort is misplaced. Consequently, mourners should be allowed to express their emotions vocally without restraint. This is sound and healthy advice. Modern psychiatry and psychology warn us not to repress our feelings in the presence of death, but to give vent to them and thus avoid neuroses and other psychological disturbances which are liable to ensue if emotions are forcibly controlled.

Do not question him in the hour of his vow. We are advised not to treat the vow lightly. Pious Jews refrain from taking a vow; indeed, they feel compelled to add the expression *beli neder*, without a vow, thus invalidating any wish or promise they may be unable to fulfil.

Some people give an undertaking under desperate or extreme conditions and this is not the opportune moment to question them about their vow. An interregnum period should be allowed before counselling them on the implication of their vow. Rashi explains that the vow here refers to the giving of charity. If a person vows to donate a sum of money to a worthy cause, we should not question him or demand immediate payment as this may prompt the donor to change his mind and not to redeem the pledge he has taken.

Do not strive to see him in his hour of disgrace. See 3:15.

When a person feels ashamed because he has committed a wrongdoing it is not tactful to present yourself before him for, by doing so, you may add to his indignity. Before you undertake to assist the wrongdoer, he should be given time to help himself through repentance and the study of the Torah. This may explain the order of the words of the Psalmist, 'Depart from evil and do good' (34:15). In the first place man should depart from evil and strive to correct himself. Once he takes this initiative, others are able to encourage him to do good. See also Ps. 37:27 and Is. 1:16.

Moses would not publicly reprove Israel by putting them to shame. He merely alluded to their sins by mentioning the names of the places where they provoked God. Moses went to these lengths in order to save the dignity of Israel; he did not strive to see them in their disgrace. In this manner Rashi explains the first verse of the Book of Deuteronomy.

It should be remembered that the imprecatory Psalms are not found in the Synagogue liturgy, with one exception; even that does not apply to the

Ashkenazi rite. Thus Psalm 137 is recited by Sephardim prior to the evening service on Tisha B'Av.

Hasidic Lore

Anger: R. Pinhas once said to a hasid: If a man wishes to guide the people in his house the right way, he must not grow angry with them, for anger does not only make one's soul impure; it transfers impurity to the souls of those with whom one is angry.

On another occassion he said: Since I have tamed my anger, I keep it in my pocket. When I need it, I take it out.

Do not see him in the hour of his disgrace. Said the Besht: A prince was banished from his father's realm. Two servants were assigned to him and were commissioned to report on his conduct. One servant made a dry report of facts unfavourable to the prince. The other made a similar report, but added that the youth's misconduct was the result of his exile and his sense of disgrace and melancholy. The father took compassion on his son, restored him to the palace, and rewarded the loyal servant. In the same manner, when a Sage or preacher reproves Israel, let him always employ the method of the second servant. It is in this way that he will surely please our Father in Heaven.

(כד) שְׁמוּאֵל הַקָּטָן אוֹמֵר בִּנְפוֹל אוֹיִבְךָ אַל תִּשְׂמָח וּבִכָּשְׁלוֹ אַל יָגֵל לִבֶּךָ פֶּן יִרְאֶה יְהֹוָה וְרַע בְּעֵינָיו וְהֵשִׁיב מֵעָלָיו אַפּוֹ:

Mishnah Twenty Four

Samuel the Small says: Rejoice not when your enemy falls, and let not your heart be glad when he stumbles, lest the Lord see it and it displeases Him and He turn away His wrath from him (unto you) Prov. 24:14-18.

Samuel the Small was so called because of his modesty and humility. He made himself small in the presence of others. The Palestinian Talmud (So. 9:13) says, 'He earned his name because he was second to Samuel the Prophet'. It is recorded in the Talmud (Ber. 28b) that he formulated the twelfth paragraph of the Amidah, which is directed against the *minim*, the heretics. The above interpretation of Samuel's name brings to mind the biblical name Joktan (Gen. 10:25) which is also connected with the word *katan*, small. Indeed, the Midrash interprets Joktan to convey the thought that he belittled himself and his affairs (Gen. R. 34:4).

It is unusual for a Mishnah to consist only of a citation from Tanakh (Prov. 24:17-18). Obviously Samuel was deeply influenced by these words which he uses as his text, and the editor of Avot found them worthy to be included amongst the gems of rabbinic ethics and he has highlighted a teaching which is generally overlooked.

Rejoice not when your enemy falls. In addition to the text in our Mishnah we have ample scriptural authority to uphold this noble teaching. Thus we read, 'If your enemy be hungry give him bread to eat, and if he be thirsty give him water to drink' (Prov. 25:21). The Mosaic legislation unequivocally states, 'If you meet your enemy's ox or his ass going astray, you shall surely bring it back to him again; if you see the ass of him who hates you lying under its burden you shall forbear to pass by him, you shall surely release it with him' (Ex. 23:4-5). We must not penalise our enemy; strict justice demands that we should not turn aside but actively assist him in every possible manner.

The late Chief Rabbi Dr. Hertz in his commentary on the Pentateuch (P. 316) quotes the New Testament which states, 'You have heard that it was said that you shall love your neighbour as yourself and hate your enemy' and adds that this partisan statement is absolutely baseless. The latter half of this verse is a wicked distortion of the truth. Not only is it found nowhere in the Torah but, as we have seen, we are enjoined explicitly not to rejoice at the downfall of an enemy. Rabbinic teaching on this subject is patently clear; for instance, we are advised, 'Let him curse, but you bless; be of those that when insulted, do not insult; hearing their reproach, give no answer, for such an act will shine like the noon-day sun which sheds its brilliant light upon good and bad alike' (Git. 36b). Commenting on Ps. 104:35, 'Let the sins be consumed out of the earth, and let the wicked be no more', the Rabbis point out that the text does not refer to 'sinners' but to 'sins'. Thus with the eradication of sins, there will be no wicked on earth. For this reason R. Meir says, 'One should not pray for the death of the wicked but that they should turn their hearts to God and repent of their wickedness' (Ber. 10a).

The specific Jewish insight into the treatment of enemies has even permeated the Synagogue service and our liturgy. R. Johanan expressed the view that God does not rejoice in the downfall of the wicked. The ministering angels wished to sing a hymn at the destruction of the Egyptians in the waters of the Red Sea but God said, 'My children are drowning in the sea and you would sing Psalms?' (Meg. 10b). In the Musaf of the Rosh Hashanah Service we pray, 'As Thy Name is merciful, so is Thy praiseworthy character, with difficulty excited to wrath but easily reconciled, for Thou desirest not the death of the sinner but that he return from his evil way and live'. Again, when we read the Book of Esther on Purim which is obligatory on women as well as men, on reaching the passage recording the execution of the ten sons of Haman, their names are rushed through in one breath, not to emphasise or dilate an unpleasant episode in Jewish history. Similarly, during the Passover Seder Service, we spill a little wine from the goblet at the mention of each of the ten plagues. The salutary thought of showing regard to an enemy was also extended by the Rabbis to include the greeting of *Shalom*. Thus, if a person is being cursed, he should reply with, 'Shalom' and he is obliged to say to the offender, 'May the Torah forgive you for what you did unto me' (Kallah Rabbah III).

Some point to the apparent contradiction between Prov. 24:17 (the text of the Mishnah) and Prov. 11:10 which reads as follows, 'And when the wicked perish, there is joy'. Here we must underline the word *oyivekha*, your enemy. When the enmity is directed against you personally, you should forgive your enemy and not rejoice over his defeat. But when persecution and destruction are directed against the people of Israel collectively, there is naturally rejoicing on their deliverance from such brutality. To continue with Prov. 24:17, 'And He turn away His anger from him', we follow the Bartinaro who points out that the word used is not *veshav* but *veheishiv* (in the hifil). The Bartinaro paraphrases the verse as follows, 'He will transfer the anger from your enemy and will place it upon you'. Rashi also understands it in the same sense.

This lofty thought, which proscribes vengeance or vindictiveness of any kind, is also expressed in another verse of the same chapter (24:29). 'Say not I will do so to him as he has done to me; I will render to the man according to his work'. On the contrary, we are told not to be vindictive but to show true forgiveness. This summarises Jewish Ethics at its highest level. It should be noted that in Prov. 11:10 the Hebrew word *rinah* is used.

Though translated as 'song', it does not signify joy or happiness in the physical sense. *Rinah* is synonymous with prayer; compare I K. 8:28, *Lishmoa el harinah ve'el hatefilah*, to listen to the song and prayer, which is the popular refrain at the Selihot Service. In the Midrash Rabbah on Vaethanan (Deut. 3) we learn that there are ten expressions which indicate prayer; *rinah* is one of them. To paraphrase the verse, we should therefore render it as follows — when the wicked perish, sing a song of praise to God. We thank the Almighty for rescuing us from the wicked who plan to destroy us, the people of Israel. This is a very far cry from rejoicing at the downfall of our enemies.

Hasidic Lore

Love all mankind. R. Benjamin Halevy and R. Raphael Bershider were engaged in a disputation. The latter declared that one must love even the wicked, and the former argued that it is incumbent upon us to pray for their downfall. When R. Benjamin departed from the Synagogue he said to a friend, 'Rabbi Raphael, to be sure, was right and it is truly a praiseworthy attribute to love all Israel. However, before the multitude, it is desirable to preach that evil-doers will receive their punishment speedily. Moreover, it is a trait which few people possess. My master (the Koretzer) told me that Raphael has the unique quality of loving even coarse doers of evil'. He further declared, 'When Raphael comes to me I surrender to him my desk and my table, yet I know I have not done my full duty to him'.

(כה) אֱלִישָׁע בֶּן אֲבוּיָה אוֹמֵר הַלּוֹמֵד יֶלֶד לְמָה הוּא דוֹמֶה לִדְיוֹ כְתוּבָה עַל נְיָר חָדָשׁ. וְהַלּוֹמֵד זָקֵן לְמָה הוּא דוֹמֶה לִדְיוֹ כְתוּבָה עַל נְיָר מָחוּק:

Mishnah Twenty Five

Elisha Ben Avuya says: He who learns when a youth, to what is he like? To ink written on new paper; and he who learns when old, to what is he like? To ink written on blotted paper.

We have referred to Elisha Ben Avuya in connection with his grandson R. Jacob. We should add that it is possible that Elisha was influenced by the Greek philosophy and mystical speculation. We have evidence in the

Talmud (Ha. 14b) where we read that four entered the *Pardes*, the garden of mysticism, and Elisha was one of them. In the words of the Rabbis, 'He mutilated the shoots', that is he became an apostate. All his friends left him with one exception, his pupil R. Meir who, when chided for associating with one who discarded Judaism, retorted, 'I eat the kernel after I cast away the shell'. It is remarkable that R. Meir did not lose faith in his master until the end, hoping that he would repent. When R. Meir visited Elisha on his death-bed, R. Meir re-affirmed that it was not too late to repent, and it is recorded that Elisha wept. R. Meir interpreted the weeping before death as a sign of repentance. Other scholars question this interpretation.

Clean and blotted paper. It should be remembered that we are dealing with the age before printing and in those early days all writing was recorded on leaves of papyrus. This material was expensive, and the writing would be erased with a stone in order to make it possible to write again on the same surface. The result was that the new writing was blurred, whereas the original words were still faintly visible.

We are advised that the best time to learn is when one is young. In youth one is comparatively healthy and virile, free from the cares and anxieties of making a livelihood; the mind is retentive and, like a sponge, absorbs all that is taught easily and quickly. During youth, the brain is like a clean sheet of paper and instruction during that period can influence and leave an indelible impression on the mind. Wisely did the Rabbis extol *girsa d'yankuta*, learning acquired in early youth is more abiding (Shab. 21b). The teaching of the young was always considered to be a sacred and primary obligation which devolves on every parent. Therefore the *Shema* reminds us, 'You shall teach them diligently to your children' (Deut. 6:6).

It is not readily recognised that we were pioneers in establishing an elementary school system on a nation-wide scale, and it is interesting to record how this was evolved. 'Remember for good the man named Joshua Ben Gamla because were it not for him the Torah would have been forgotten from Israel. At first a child was taught by his father, and as a result the orphan was left uninstructed. It was thereupon resolved that teachers of children be appointed in Jerusalem and a father should bring his child there and have him taught, but again the orphan was ignored. Then it was resolved to appoint teachers for higher education in each district and boys of the age of sixteen or seventeen were placed under them. However, on occasion, when the master was angry with a pupil, the lad would rebel and leave. Finally, Joshua Ben Gamla instituted that teachers should be appointed in every province and in every city and all children from the age of six or seven were placed in their charge' (B.B. 21a).

It is true to say that the tuition of Jewish children is one of the first tasks undertaken by every Jewish community in the world. Such institutions were looked upon as natural outgrowths of every community and were referred to as either *heder* or *Talmud Torah*. The indispensability of Torah education for children was considered by parents to be vital for the continuity and preservation of Judaism, and consequently they were prepared to pay dearly for such instruction, often in the face of hardship and poverty.

We are generally guided by the good advice in Prov. 22:6. 'Train up a child in the way he should go, and even when he is old he will not depart from it,.'

This verse is particularly appropriate, for our Mishnah deals with both young and old. It is also fundamental to Jewish teaching because the first word of this verse, *hanokh*, is derived from the same Hebrew word for education, *hinukh*. Furthermore, the phrase *al pi darko*, literally 'according to his way', means, 'the way in which he is to pursue the course of life'. This demonstrates the fact that youth is the right period in which to sow the seeds of correct habits and formation of character which will sustain him in his mature years of manhood. This reminds us of another verse from Ec. 11:6, 'In the morning sow your seed and in the evening withhold not your hand.' Paraphrased, this verse can be rendered thus — From morning (youth) until evening (old age) we should fulfil our tasks and responsibilities with the same eagerness of mind and simplicity of purpose.

Old. When we discuss old age we again find that *zaken*, old, does not necessarily mean old in years, but old in experience and mature in counsel. Thus the Rabbis teach *zaken ze shekanah hakhmah* (Kid. 32b) 'old' means he who has acquired wisdom, even though he may be young in years. The classical reference to old age is found in Lev. 19:32, 'Before the hoary head you shall rise and you shall honour the face of the aged and you shall fear your God; I am the Lord'. Even here the Rabbis endeavoured to deduce the same lesson. Commenting on the words, 'Before the hoary head you shall rise', the Zohar interprets the word 'before', not 'in the presence of', but 'in sequence of time'. Thus the Zohar paraphrases this verse, 'Before you have grown old, *takum*, you should stand firmly rooted in your adherence to Jewish precept'. We are advised not to wait until old age creeps upon us, but long before that period we should stand up and be counted.

We shall now append a number of proverbial sayings on young and old in Jewish thought culled from the Talmud and post-talmudic literature.

'Touch not Mine anointed and do My prophets no harm (I Chron. 16:22). 'Mine anointed' are the school children; 'My prophets' are the scholars (Shab. 119b).

The world only exists through the breath of school children (ibid).

'The voice is the voice of Jacob and the hands are the hands of Esau' (Gen. 27:22) - when Jacob's voice is heard in the schoolhouse the hands of Esau are powerless (Gen. R. 65:20).

See how precious children are; The Shekhinah did not go with the Sanhedrin and priestly watches into exile, but it did go with the children (Lam. R. 1.6.33).

Honour the children of the ignorant, Torah may issue from them (Sanh. 96a).

Train children in their youth and they will not train you in your old age (Lazarov).

Little children do not lie till they are taught to do so (Saadiah). When you lead your sons and daughters in the good way, let your words be tender and caressing in terms when disciplining them and so win the heart's assent (Vilna Gaon).

Hasidic Lore

Learning when old. Commenting on this Mishnah the Koretzer asked, 'Why discourage the older man? But the passage may be understood thus — 'One who learns as a child, namely, as one who concentrates his thoughts on that which he is learning and has no foreign thoughts at the time, is like ink written on clean paper; his learning will be engraved upon his mind and in his heart'. Thus, even an old man may learn as a child if he displays the old requisite concentration.

(כו) רַבִּי יוֹסֵי בַּר יְהוּדָה אִישׁ כְּפַר הַבַּבְלִי אוֹמֵר הַלּוֹמֵד מִן הַקְּטַנִּים לְמָה הוּא דוֹמֶה לְאוֹכֵל עֲנָבִים קֵהוֹת וְשׁוֹתֶה יַיִן מִגִּתּוֹ. וְהַלּוֹמֵד מִן הַזְּקֵנִים לְמָה הוּא דוֹמֶה לְאוֹכֵל עֲנָבִים בְּשׁוּלוֹת וְשׁוֹתֶה יַיִן יָשָׁן:

Mishnah Twenty Six

R. Jose Bar Judah of K'far Habavli says: He who learns from the young, to what is he like? To one who eats unripe grapes and drinks wine from his vat; and he who learns from the old, to what is he like? To one who eats ripe grapes and drinks old wine.

R. Jose Bar Judah is not to be confused with R. Jose Bar Judah Ben Ilai. His identity and age are not known.

He who learns from the young. Though the Mishnah, by implication, denigrates the young teacher because of his inexperience and immaturity, we cannot entirely eliminate him from the educational scence. Jewish learning is a religious duty incumbent upon all, young and old. The fact that the Mishnah explicitly refers to 'learning from the young' is proof that young teachers were not unknown. Indeed, we are not interested in the age of the teachers; the only criterion here is whether he possesses profound scholarship. This is his claim to fame.

Grapes. The poetic imagery here comparing learning with grapes and wine must be understood in the background of rabbinic language which equates clusters of grapes with learned men; for instance, 'The clusters from the days of Moses until the death of Jose Ben Joezer were as learned in the Law as Moses our teacher; thenceforth they were not as learned as he' (Tem. 15b). Again, 'How is it with the vine? It has both fresh and withered grapes, even so is it with Israel. There are amongst them men versed in the Scriptures, men learned in the Mishnah, in the Talmud and in the Aggadah' (Lev. R. 36:2). In the same context we read that the vine has both large and small clusters of grapes and the larger clusters appear to hang lower than the lighter clusters; even so is it with Israel. The more strenuously a person toils in the Torah and the more learned he is than his neighbour, the more humble is he. As grapes can refer to the scholar, so wine in its natural state and prepared form, represents the Law. Wine matures with age, so does knowledge of Torah improve with age (Job 12:25, Sifre Deut to 11:22).

There are still a number of difficulties facing us. Why should the Mishnah compare learning to a liquid and not to a solid food? Again, if it is a liquid, why wine and not any other liquid? Regarding food, it is true to say that a person can survive longer without food than without drink. As drink is indispensable, so is learning the life-line of our people. Also, food requires utensils such as spoons, forks, etc., whereas the intake of liquid is more simple and it can be digested more easily.

Why should learning be compared with wine? Because wine has a special benediction (Ber. 35b) and enjoys the unique distinction of introducing and concluding Sabbaths and Festivals with Kiddush and Havdallah. The Rabbis explicitly state *Zokhrayhu al hayayin,* (Pes. 106a) remember the Sabbath over wine, thus the Kiddush is obligatory upon every Jew (Nazir 3b, 44a). We recite Grace after Meals over a cup of wine at festive occasions. Wine plays a significant role at the wedding when the bride and groom drink from the same goblet, and at the Brit Milah. During the Passover Seder Service four cups of wine are the pivot of the ritual, and standing resplendent on the table is the cup of Elijah filled with wine. Apart from religious seasons, many social gatherings are enhanced by the partaking of wine.

Manifold are the scriptural verses and rabbinic aphorisms which extol wine. Malkhizedek brought out bread and wine when he blessed Abraham (Gen. 14:18); Isaac drank wine when he blessed Jacob (Gen. 27:25); Jacob blessed Judah with wine (Gen. 49:11-12); the Land of Israel is praised for its wine (Deut. 8:8); and 'Wine gladdens the heart of man' (Ps. 104:15).

On the other hand there are many deprecatory references to wine. The Rabbis ask why wine is called *yayin* and *tirosh. Yayin* brings lamentation into the world, and *tirosh* refers to one who becomes poor through over-indulgence (Yoma 76b). According to R. Meir, the tree from which Adam ate in the Garden of Eden was a vine (Sanh. 70a). Commenting on Gen. 9:21, 'And Noah began and planted a vineyard', Rashi interprets the word *vayahel,* and he began, to mean 'And he profaned and degraded himself; he should have planted anything but the vine'. Lot, too, sinned on account of wine (Gen. 19:31) and the Ten Tribes were exiled through wine (Amos 6:6).

However, there is no contradiction between the various statements cited. When wine is used for religious purposes, Kiddush, Havdallah or a Seudat Mitzvah, it is recognised as an act of sanctification because we are commanded by God to drink wine and recite a blessing. Under such circumstances there can be no harmful results. This explains why, on the whole, Jews are comparatively free from drunkenness. When, however, drink is indulged in to excess, it is robbed of its sanctifying effect and may cause much harm and distress. This must surely be the reason why we exclaim 'Lehaim' when we raise the cup of wine. We express the wish that the wine will be the source of happiness and gladness and bring LIFE to the person or state toasted at a *simhah*, and not misery and death which alcoholism can bring in its train.

We can now revert to our Mishnah. One who learns from the young, either an inexperienced teacher or one little in faith, is compared to unripe grapes and dregs from the wine, which can cause harm. Such learning can mislead the pupil and distort his mind. But he who learns, from old experienced and trusted teachers who are animated with the fear of God, he is compared to one who eats ripe grapes and drinks old mature wine, both of which are considered to be included amongst the 'clusters' the outstanding scholars of the future.

Hasidic Lore

The reason for saying 'Lehaim'. A hasid asked a zaddik, 'Why is it customary to say '*Lehaim*', for life, before reciting the benediction over a drink of wine? Is it not disrespectful to bless mortals before blessing the Immortal One.

In reply the zaddik pointed to the passage (Lev. 19:18) wherein we are enjoined to accept the mitzvah of loving our neighbour before accepting the mitzvah of loving God. The reason doubtless is that mortals need our love and sympathy more than God does.

(כז) רַבִּי מֵאִיר אוֹמֵר אַל תִּסְתַּכֵּל בְּקַנְקַן אֶלָּא בְּמַה שֶׁיֵּשׁ בּוֹ יֵשׁ קַנְקַן חָדָשׁ מָלֵא יָשָׁן וְיָשָׁן שֶׁאֲפִילוּ חָדָשׁ אֵין בּוֹ:

Mishnah Twenty Seven.

R. Meir says: Look not at the flask but at what it contains. There may be a new flask full of old wine and an old flask that has not even new wine in it.

We can interpret this Mishnah to follow logically our exposition of the first clause of the previous Mishnah. The argument would run along these lines — we should not regard the outward appearance of a flask but examine what it contains. Similarly, do not reject a teacher because of his outward youthful appearance. There are teachers who are *hadash*, new, young in years, but *maleh yashan*, they are thoroughly immersed in the old traditional Halakhah. On the other hand there are teachers who are old in years but convey no new, fresh or original interpretation to bear on the subject at hand.

Alternatively, we may interpret the Mishnah to refer to the merging of learning and conduct. Learning is old, rooted in the past and an on-going process; conduct is superficial and changes with the spirit of the age. There are teachers who are dressed in modern garb, *hadash*,, but still retain the old traditional love for scholarship and learning. These teachers judiciously synthesise the old and the new and so inspire and influence the youth. Others, however, refuse to merge the old with the new; they prefer to retain the old life-styles and mannerisms and eschew all things new. If we follow this interpretation, our Mishnah advises us not to be guided solely by outward appearances. Modern dress and conduct may be pleasing to the eye, but are ineffective without ripe and mature scholarship.

On the other hand we should not be deterred by the old fashioned teacher whose outward appearance may seem to be forbidding. Look inside the flask; the same teacher may possess sterling qualities of heart and mind which are unexcelled and unrivalled. The principle underlying the Mishnah is summed up by the Rabbis in two words — *tokho kebaro* (within as without) (Ber. 28a). This proverbial saying implies that one's outward behaviour should truthfully express one's inner thoughts and vice versa. It is unfortunate that too many divorce one from the other; they mislead people by concealing their true intentions. Rava said: Any scholar whose inside is not like his outside (who is insincere) is no scholar (Yoma 72b). Regarding the woman of virtue the Book of Proverbs says: Grace is false, beauty is vain (external appearance); but a woman who fears the Lord, she shall be praised' (31:30).

Concerning the authorship of this Mishnah, some texts introduce the name of R. Judah Ha-Nasi but others suggest that R. Meir is the author. The latter would add a new dimension to our interpretation and would reflect the philosophy of R. Meir who, as a pupil of Elisha (Aher) whom he befriended to the last, was of the opinion that one should accept learning from every source and not judge by 'the outside of the flask'. This exposition would obviously favour R. Meir to head our Mishnah, but many scholars still regard R. Judah Ha-Nasi as its author.

Hasidic Lore

The flask of old wine. An opponent of R. Schmelke wished to shame him in public and sent him a flask of very old wine on the day before Yom Kippur hoping that he would become intoxicated through drinking from it. The Rabbi tasted a little and perceived the sender's intention. When he was reciting Psalms after the Services, he repeated several times the verse (Ps. 41:12), 'By this I know that Thou delightest in me, that mine enemy does not triumph over me', and he translated it thus, 'By this I shall know that Thou art pleased with me, that those who wished to disgrace me receive no harm because of me'. R. Schmelke's adversary was moved by the Rabbi's prayer for his enemies, and begged him for forgivenes. R. Schmelke remarked, 'You would not have done me injury but only good if your plan had succeeded. The disgrace would have washed away many of my sins. I regret truly that awe of the Holy Day sobered me'.

(כח) רַבִּי אֶלְעָזָר הַקַּפָּר אוֹמֵר הַקִּנְאָה וְהַתַּאֲוָה וְהַכָּבוֹד מוֹצִיאִין אֶת הָאָדָם מִן הָעוֹלָם:

Mishnah Twenty Eight

R. Eleazar Ha-Kappar says: Envy, lust and hankering for glory drive a man out of the world.

R. Eleazar Ha-Kappar (second century) is the father of Eliezer Bar Kappara. Little is known of him. He is sometimes referred to as 'Beribi' and he lived in Lod. In the course of his sayings he often referred to the power of peace.

Envy. Envy is the manifestation of a malicious nature and a distorted mind. The envious person often has no justification for his jealousy, nor is envy restricted to one particular class of society. Poor and rich are envious of each other for different reasons. Envy causes 'the rottenness of the bones' (Prov. 14:30). The Rabbis were students of human nature and realised that some were envious of others who were succesful; especially is this true of members of the same profession. The Rabbis testify that 'men of the same calling hate each other' (Gen. R. 19:4). The Mesillat Yesharim reminds us that if men realised that no one may obtain even so much as a hair's breadth of that which is destined for his neighbour (Yoma 38b) and that every thing is ordained by God in accordance with His marvellous purpose and inscrutable wisdom, they would have no reason to resent their neighbour's good fortune. We pray for the day when 'The envy of Ephraim shall depart and they that harass Judah shall be cut off; Ephraim shall not envy Judah and Judah shall not vex Ephraim' (Is. 11:13).

Lust. Lust or cupidity flows from envy and is an inordinate desire to covet the wealth or possessions of another person. Our Sages have observed that 'no man dies with his desires even half fulfilled' (Ec.R. to 1:13).

Furthermore, Ecclesiastes reminds us that he who loves silver will not be satisfied with silver (5:9). *Taavah,* lust, also includes gluttony, drunkenness and lewdness. Cupidity of every form deters a man from studying Torah and performing the precepts, for these bring him no profit; on the contrary, they remove him from his gainful occupation.

Kavod. *Kavod* or hankering after glory is considered to be the most dangerous of the three traits mentioned in the Mishnah because envy and cupidity can be controlled, whereas personal glory is a weakness to which many of us succumb. One character who sought honours was Korah, the cause of whose rebellion was due to the fact that Elizaphan the son of Uzziel was made prince, an appointment which he coveted for himself (Nu. R. 18:2). It was the longing for honour which caused the spies to spread an evil report of the Holy Land and thus brought death upon themselves and that whole generation. They feared that when the Israelites would enter the land they would be deprived of their rank as princes and others would be appointed in their place (Zohar 2 on Nu. 13:3).

Again, it was the lust for honour that caused Saul to pursue David. We read, 'And the women sang one to another in their play and said, 'Saul has slain his thousands and David his tens of thousands'. Saul was very angry and this saying displeased him; and he said, 'They have ascribed unto David tens of thousands and to me they have ascribed but thousands; and all he lacks is the kingdom'. And Saul eyed David from that day and forward' (I Sam. 18:7-9). The Mesillat Yesharim sums up in these words: The lust for honour is more of an impelling force than all other longings and desires. Were it not for this lust a man would be willing to eat whatever he might get, to wear whatever might cover him, and to dwell under whatever roof which might protect him'.

The most remarkable lesson we derive from our Mishnah is the fact that only the abuse of jealousy, cupidity and honour put one out of the world. Basically, these traits are good and healthy. For instance, God is called a jealous God in the Ten Commanments (Ex. 20:5, Deut. 5:9). Again, Pinhas turned away the wrath of God because he was 'very jealous for My sake' (Nu. 25:11). In these instances commentators render jealous as 'zealous'. In the realms of the spirit jealousy is good because it is competitive. Thus the envy, *kinah*, of scholars increases wisdom (B.B. 22a). God said, 'Be zealous in My cause for were it not for envy, (kinah), life could not continue. A man would not build a house, plant a vineyard, or marry' (Shohar Tov 37).

Taavah and Kavod, cupidity, can also be transformed into a good quality as delineated by the Psalmist (38:10), 'Lord, all my desire, (taavah) is before Thee'. Of the three qualities *kavod*, honour, in its pure and unadulterated form, is the most ardent wish of all parents who long for the honour and respect of their children. 'Honour your father and mother so that your days may be long' is a universal prayer and in the Synagogue we pray for a life of prosperity and honour (Shabbat M'varkhim). Three times a day we recite the words, 'The majestic glory (kavod) of Thy splendour' (Ps. 145:5), and on Rosh Hashanah we pray, 'Give glory *(kavod)*, O Lord, unto Thy people' (Amidah). Solomon advises us, 'Honour the Lord with your substance and with the first fruits of all your increase' (Prov. 3:9), and the Psalmist declares, 'Thou wilt guide me with Thy counsel and afterward receive me with glory *(kavod)*' (73:24). We feel that the good uses to which we can channel envy, cupidity and honour were in the forefront of the mind of Eleazar Ha-Kappar who infers that we should elevate and exalt these qualities and not misuse them. Misrepresentation can place man outside the pale of society and thus remove him from the world.

Hasidic Lore

Envy. R. Yehiel Mihal of Zlotov said: I never require anything till I have it, for as long as I did not have it I was sure I did not need it.

The Bratzlaver said: When envy will cease, redemption will come. Envy is often the cause of destruction and murder. Envy of another man's property may cause derangement of the mind.

Cupidity. The Gerer was present at a function in the home of a wealthy hasid. The host wished to bestow a certain honour on his distinguished guest, but the Rabbi declined it. The host remarked, 'But Rabbi, the Talmud teaches that it is good manners for the guest not to contradict his host' (Pes. 86b). The Rabbi replied, 'But the Talmud adds the words, 'Except when he tells you to leave'. We are also taught that jealousy, desire and honour compel man to leave the world. Thus, when the host seeks to force honour upon his guest, the latter is entitled to decline it'.

(כט) הוּא הָיָה אוֹמֵר הַיִּלּוֹדִים לָמוּת וְהַמֵּתִים לְהֵחָיוֹת וְהַחַיִּים לִדּוֹן לֵידַע וּלְהוֹדִיעַ וּלְהִוָּדַע שֶׁהוּא אֵל הוּא הַיּוֹצֵר הוּא הַבּוֹרֵא הוּא הַמֵּבִין הוּא הַדַּיָּן הוּא הָעֵד הוּא בַּעַל דִּין הוּא עָתִיד לָדוּן. בָּרוּךְ הוּא שֶׁאֵין לְפָנָיו לֹא עַוְלָה וְלֹא שִׁכְחָה וְלֹא מַשּׂוֹא פָנִים וְלֹא מִקַּח שׁוֹחַד וְדַע שֶׁהַכֹּל לְפִי הַחֶשְׁבּוֹן וְאַל יַבְטִיחֲךָ יִצְרְךָ שֶׁהַשְּׁאוֹל בֵּית מָנוֹס לָךְ שֶׁעַל כָּרְחֲךָ אַתָּה נוֹצָר וְעַל כָּרְחֲךָ אַתָּה נוֹלָד וְעַל כָּרְחֲךָ אַתָּה חַי וְעַל כָּרְחֲךָ אַתָּה מֵת וְעַל כָּרְחֲךָ אַתָּה עָתִיד לִיתֵּן דִּין וְחֶשְׁבּוֹן לִפְנֵי מֶלֶךְ מַלְכֵי הַמְּלָכִים הַקָּדוֹשׁ בָּרוּךְ הוּא:

Mishnah Twenty Nine.

He used to say: Those who are born are for death and the dead are for life and those that live are to be judged, to know, to make known, and to be made aware that He is God, He is the Maker, He the Creator, He the Discerner, He the Judge, He the Witness, He the Accuser: He it is Who will be the future Judge, blessed be He, with Whom there is no unrighteousness nor forgetfulness, nor respect of persons, nor taking of bribes; and know that everything is according to the reckoning. Let not your imagination give you hope that the grave will be a place of refuge for you; for in spite of yourself you were formed, and in spite of yourself you were born, and in spite of yourself you live, and in spite of yourself you die, and in spite of yourself you will have to give just account and reckoning before the King of the King of Kings, the Holy One, blessed be He.

The concluding Mishnah of the chapter contains a brief summary of some of the important tenets of the Jewish faith.

Those who are born are for death. The Mishnah traverses the whole gamut of life from birth to death. Man is the crown of God's creation; he is created in the image of God and possesses a spark of the Divine. His pre-eminence in the world, however, should not mislead him; he must remember he is just a mortal being destined to die. This thought should make him humble and he should never lose an opportunity to serve God through the mitzvot, for this is the purpose and function of man.

The dead are for life. Here we have enunciated the principle of the resurrection of the dead, a belief which is rooted in the Torah and is the final article in Maimonides' Thirteen Principles of Faith incorporated in the Prayer Book. This teaching is clearly articulated in the second blessing of the daily Amidah of our liturgy, We read in Ez. 37:12, 'Behold I will open your graves and bring you up... and bring you to the Land of Israel', and now that we have returned to Israel it is no longer a dream. We have implicit faith in the Almighty and sincerely believe that those who died through persecution and martyrdom for the sanctification of the Name and all the dead will one day be physically resurrected in our Land. How this resurrection will take place we do not know.

This is a controversial issue amongst the giants of Jewish scholarship. However it is an essential ingredient in Jewish belief and thought. As we have indicated, our belief in the resurrection is based on the justice of God. This is borne out by the following phrase in the Mishnah, 'Those that live are to be judged'. But the justice of God is founded upon knowledge and learning. This is exemplified by the three-dimensional attitude towards knowledge; to know, make known, and be made aware that He is God.

The verb *yada*, to know, is used in the *kal*, *hiphil* and *niphal* conjugations. The *kal* is the simple,natural approach to knowledge which we imbibe from our parents and teachers. Our learning, however, must not be restricted; we must inspire others to learn, (hiphil), and pass on our knowledge to our disciples and friends. We are told that we learn most from our pupils, so that the dissemination of knowledge will make us fully aware of the justice of God. Some have read into *yada* an allusion to the world to come. 'To make known', they say, means that one teaches others in this world, and 'to be aware of knowledge' refers to the world to come when one will receive the knowledge by himself without the help of a teacher (Jer. 31:34); this reminds us that the *niphal* can also be reflexive.

At this juncture the Mishnah introduces us to some of the concepts which lead us to an appreciation of the Jewish idea of God.

'He is the Discerner', reminds us of Ps. 33:15, 'He fashions their hearts altogether; He has regard to all their works'.

'He is the Judge, the Witness' — compare Mal. 3:5, 'And I will come near to you to judgment; and I wil be a swift witness against the sorcerers and against the adulterers and against false swearers and against those that oppress the hireling in his wages, the widow and the fatherless and that turn aside the stranger from his right and fear not for Me, says the Lord of Hosts'.

Nor respect of persons, nor taking of bribes. Compare II Chron. 10:7. 'Take heed and act, for with the Lord our God there is no injustice, no respect for persons, nor taking of bribes'. Maimonides understands this verse to convey the meaning that a person cannot bribe God with good deeds and therefore expect his evil designs to be forgiven. A bad deed is not forgiven even by the practice of a hundred good actions, but punishment is meted out for the bad and a person is rewarded for the good he achieves. Thus, each action is judged entirely on its own merits. God is not a respecter of persons. He punished Moses for his action at Merivah; on the other hand the Almighty rewarded Esau for honouring his parents and Nebukhadnezzar for respecting Him.

In spite of yourself. Even as you were born in spite of yourself and continue to live in travail and vanity in spite of yourself - for many were the occasions that you have wished to die but were powerless to bring this to pass — or when the time to die came you were unable to escape or elude it — so, too, in the future you will have to give account and reckoning for every thing and for all you have done (Vitry).

Maimonides says: Take careful note of this statement which mentions things which come to pass by nature over which man has no choice. The Mishnah did not say 'In spite of yourself do you sin or transgress or walk or stand still and such matters.' These are within man's power and he is coerced into none of them.

To sum up — This Mishnah clearly highlights the justice of God in this world and in the world to come. The vocabulary employed categorically states that the Jewish God is primarily a God of justice. It is ironic that we who have underscored the pre-emincence of justice should be subjected in every age to such vile injustice by a hostile world. We shall rid the world of envy, suspicion, hatred and war when the Jewish ideal of a just God is enthroned in the councils of the capitals of the Universe.

Hasidic Lore

Purpose of life. A hasid once asked the Berditshever Rabbi to explain why the Lord did not provide man once a year with sufficient funds for his annual needs and thus free his mind for spiritual activities.

The Rabbi replied, 'We cannot comprehend God's reasons. Perhaps He desires to see what you will make of the life He has granted you, while you are burdened with the task of providing a livelihood for yourself.

When Abraham Mordekhai, the last remaining son of the Gerer Rabbi, died, a hasid sought to comfort him with the traditional words from Job (1:21): The Lord has given and the Lord has taken'. The Gerer responded, 'My grief comes not because I have lost my son to everlasting life, since this is God's will. My sorrow arises from the knowledge that I shall now lack the opportunity to perform the mitzvah, 'You shall teach them diligently unto your children" (Deut. 6:7).

Concluding Mishnah. Text, translation and commentary, see p. 71.

PEREK FIVE

Introductory Mishnah. Text, translation and commentary on p. 11.

פרק חמישי

(א) בַּעֲשָׂרָה מַאֲמָרוֹת נִבְרָא הָעוֹלָם וּמַה תַּלְמוּד לוֹמַר וַהֲלֹא בְּמַאֲמָר אֶחָד יָכוֹל לְהִבָּרְאוֹת אֶלָּא לְהִפָּרַע מִן הָרְשָׁעִים שֶׁמְּאַבְּדִין אֶת הָעוֹלָם שֶׁנִּבְרָא בַּעֲשָׂרָה מַאֲמָרוֹת. וְלִתֵּן שָׂכָר טוֹב לַצַּדִּיקִים שֶׁמְּקַיְּמִין אֶת הָעוֹלָם שֶׁנִּבְרָא בַּעֲשָׂרָה מַאֲמָרוֹת:

Mishnah One.

With ten sayings the world was created. What does this teach us ? Could it not have been created with one saying? It is to exact penalty from the wicked who destroy the world which was created by ten sayings and to give good reward to the righteous who preserve the world which was created by ten sayings.

At the outset we should note the difference in style and arrangement between this chapter and the previous four chapters. For instance, Mishnayot 1-22 are all anonymous. In addition 1-18 are arranged in numerical groups based on numbers ten, seven and four.

Ten. The figure ten is popular in Jewish thought and has religious overtones. Thus God created the world with ten sayings; we received the Ten Commandments on Sinai; the religious quorum in the Synagogue (minyan) is constituted of ten males; and the Priests pronounce their benediction in the Synagogue spreading out their ten fingers. Incidentally, we are reminded that a Cohen should not spread out his fingers except in prayer (Zohar 111. 145a).

The number ten is applied not only for good, but also for evil, to denote the wrath of God as exemplified by the Ten Plagues with which Egypt was smitten. Compare also Lev. 26:26, 'Ten women shall bake your bread in one oven'. As to the origin of the Hebrew word for ten, *eser*, some suggest that it is derived from the root *sarrar*, to act as a prince, to rule. Indeed, the figure ten does rule in our decimal system which the Bible uses. Both

Noah's Ark and The Sanctuary are built on measurements of multiples of ten.

Ten sayings. The expression 'And God said' occurs ten times in the opening chapter of Genesis, verses 3, 6, 11, 14, 20, 24, 26, 28 and 29. In the Talmud (R.H. 32a) the ten sayings are compounded of 'And God said' nine times in Gen 1, and the first word *Bereshit*, in the beginning, being the tenth saying. This is based on Ps. 33:6, 'By the word of the Lord were the heavens made'.

It is evident that the opening words of our Mishnah deal with the Creation and this presents a difficulty. Should not, therefore, *Avot* commence with this Mishnah and not with the receiving of the Torah at Sinai? Nahmanides asks this question in his introduction to the Decalogue where he suggests that a reference to the God of the Creation would be a fitting prologue to the Ten Commandments which enjoy universal application and are not a local reference to the God 'who brought you out of Egypt.' Nahmanides replied that the Children of Israel did not witness the Creation of the world, but they did witness the Exodus from Egypt. Similarly, we may add that *Avot* did not commence with the creation, for the ethical and philosophical foundations of the Creation are beyond the comprehension of *Kol Yisrael*, all Israel. We underline the importance of the giving of the Torah which is the fountain of all knowledge and the source of all life. After having discussed many aspects of Torah knowledge and understanding, we are here introduced to the ten utterances regarding the Creation. Could not the world have been created with one saying — Punish the wicked and reward the righteous?

Many commentators have grappled with the correct interpretation of this Mishnah. How are the wicked or righteous affected by the ten sayings of Genesis? The answer surely is in the word *maamar*, saying. Our Mishnah mentions nothing about the deeds or actions of the wicked or of the righteous, but it does underscore the saying, that God created the world with ten utterances.

Could not the good Lord have created the world with one saying? We on earth are to imitate God and utilise our words judiciously. The Psalmist said, 'The Heavens declare the glory of God and the firmament His handiwork, day unto day pours forth speech' (19:2). Such words should inspire us all to raise our sights heavenwards and tell of the wonders of the Almighty.

Words are the vehicles of our thoughts and the outlet of our ideas. Commenting on the words, 'And He breathed into his nostrils the breath of life' (Gen. 2:7), the Targum adds the words, 'The spirit of speech', thereby conveying the interpretation that speech is synonymous with the soul, the breath of life with which God has endowed every human creature. We should remember that the Ten Commandments are referred to in Hebrew as *Aseret Hadibrot*, the ten WORDS. The world can be destroyed by the wicked who scandalise and slander innocent individuals and nations by their foul words which the Rabbis call *lashon hara*, the wicked tongue. Domestic bliss can be ruined by a wrong or misplaced word, nations go to war on account of broken pledges or promises, and mischievous words can destroy friendships and wreck whole families. On the other hand, 'A word in due season, how good is it!' (Prov. 15:23). An encouraging word to a child by a parent or a teacher can work wonders; a helpful word of advice can alter a person's outlook on life, and a consoling and comforting word to a mourner can heal a bruised or seared heart. The spoken word is a divine gift; we must not misuse or profane it.

The terms *reshaim*, wicked and *zaddikim*, righteous, used in our Mishnah do not apply to those who abrogate or fulfil the mitzvot in general, but refer to those who destroy the world by their tale-bearing, or preserve the world by utilising the *maamar*, the saying of God. Those who are acquainted with theological terminology will know that the righteous person will punctuate his speech by a *maamar hazal*, an appropriate word or saying of the Rabbis. Such sayings, parables or maxims are woven into his speech and guide him in his every day life.

Maimonides interprets the Mishnah in these words: There was a separate utterance for each act of the Creation in order, to make known the greatness of every thing that exists and the beauty of its order so that he who wrecks it destroys a great thing, whilst he who improves it is establishing a great thing.

Hasidic Lore

The importance of the word. Rabbi Judah Zevi of Stretin said: One should keep his special piety hidden; otherwise he is guilty of pride. The word אני ani 'I' which denotes the proud and haughty person and אין

ein 'naught' which denotes the meek and humble one , have the same letters but in the first word the 'Yud' is on the outside while in the second word it is in the inside.

(ב) עֲשָׂרָה דוֹרוֹת מֵאָדָם וְעַד נֹחַ לְהוֹדִיעַ כַּמָּה אֶרֶךְ אַפַּיִם לְפָנָיו שֶׁכָּל הַדּוֹרוֹת הָיוּ מַכְעִיסִין וּבָאִין עַד שֶׁהֵבִיא עֲלֵיהֶם אֶת מֵי הַמַּבּוּל:

(ג) עֲשָׂרָה דוֹרוֹת מִנֹּחַ וְעַד אַבְרָהָם לְהוֹדִיעַ כַּמָּה אֶרֶךְ אַפַּיִם לְפָנָיו שֶׁכָּל הַדּוֹרוֹת הָיוּ מַכְעִיסִין וּבָאִין עַד שֶׁבָּא אַבְרָהָם אָבִינוּ וְקִבֵּל שְׂכַר כֻּלָּם:

Mishnah Two. and Three.

There were ten generations from Adam to Noah to make known how much long-suffering is before Him, for all the generations went on provoking Him until He brought upon them the waters of the flood.
There were ten generations from Noah to Abraham to make known how much long-suffering is before Him for all the generations went on provoking Him, until Abraham our father came and received the reward of all of them.

Dor generation, is derived from the root to live, dwell; a generation consists of a number of people who live in a certain period of time.

Ten generations The ten utterances of the previous Mishnah are followed by the ten generations from Adam to Noah. They are: Adam, Seth, Enokh, Kenan, Mahalalel, Jared, Enosh, Methuselah, Lemekh and Noah. Here we have the earliest recorded history in the annals of mankind. Some have questioned the advisability of including these Mishnayot in a treatise devoted to ethics. What ethical content do the ten generations possess? However, Judaism is a civilisation and more than a history of events recorded in time. Judaism presents us with a constant challenge to plant righteousness and justice in the world, to refine the character of man and to educate him to live in peace with his neighbour and God.

This historical and spiritual perspective was a legacy which Moses our teacher bequeathed to us in his last stirring sermon which he delivered to the Children of Israel before he left this mortal earth, 'Remember the days of old, consider the years of each generation' (Deut. 32:7). History is built on the foundations of remembering, understanding and learning from every generation. What can we learn from the ten generations between Adam and Noah? We had appeared on the horizon of this earth very early in the history of the world and in our peregrinations we have been in touch with many civilisations, but we still hark back to Adam, our first ancestor. We should remember that Adam was created after the other creatures were formed. This is one of the first concepts which Jewish history has taught us — that other creatures came before Adam. This should teach us to be humble. We are not the first in God's creation, but we do score over the animal, for God made man with His own hands. 'The body of man is a microcosm of the whole world in miniature and the world in turn is a reflex of man'. Man is a universal being. The first man is called Adam, a name which is derived from *adamah*, earth. We are told that the dust from which Adam was created was gathered from the four corners of the Earth and we also learn from the Midrash that the dust was of different colours - red, black, white and green. All men, of every colour, were created by the one God.

We have referred above to the word *dor*, a generation, but another word meaning generation is *toladah* derived from the root *yalad*, to give birth, to create. Both words suggest the creativity of life and the giving of an account of our ancestors and descendants; this is the essence of Jewish history. History is not the accumulation of dates or statistics, but a detailed account of the manner of life and how it should be lived. It is interesting to record that the word *dor*, a generation, is found at the end of the Pentateuch, whilst *toledot*, generations, appears at the beginning of the Humash, 'This is the book of the generations of Adam' (Gen. 5:1).

Incidentally the expression 'This is the book of the generations' appears ten times in Genesis. Ben Azzai translated this verse as 'This is the book of the generations of man'. Here at the commencement of Jewish history, the Torah emphasises the universalism and unity of man wherever and whoever he may be and thus the Torah had sown the seeds of world brotherhood under the Fatherhood of God. We see, therefore, that in Jewish history Adam plays a very significant role and we can understand what R. Simeon Ben Lakish wished to convey when he said, 'The Holy One blessed be He showed Adam each generation with its expositors, its sages and its leaders' (Sanh. 38b). The great spiritual teachings which Providence bestowed upon Adam were to pass from him to the teachers and leaders of every generation thus forging the links of a continuous chain of Jewish tradition.

Noah. In many respects Noah was a great man and comforter to his generation. Indeed, his other name was *Menahem*, the comforter. Tradition tells us that he invented and introduced a number of agricultural implements for cultivating the soil. However, his generation assailed all the ten utterances of the Lord and filled the earth with violence and robbery. Noah lacked the qualities essential for firm and strong leadership and was reluctant to reprove the people. This weakness of character has been read into the words '*tamim haya bedorotav*' (16:9) which have been paraphrased to mean that Noah was whole-hearted with every member of his generation. In other words, Noah never censured the rebels, therefore God brought a flood of waters which engulfed that wicked generation which was thenceforth known as *dor hamabul*, the generation of the flood.

We should note the long-suffering of God who waited for ten generations to pass before He destroyed them. *Erekh apayim*, slow to anger, is one of the thirteen attributes of God which form an important and vital section of the Festival liturgy in the Synagogue.

Abraham The Mishnah contrasts the character of Abraham with that of Noah who did not have the courage to reprove his people when criticism was called for. Abraham came and received the reward for all of them because, unlike Noah, he was a born leader. In the first place he was able to reason and argue with himself; he it was who discovered God and was thus fitted to become the father of Judaism and the friend of God. He first led himself and then applied the qualities of leadership towards other people. He was fearless in his denunciation of idolatry. He even remonstrated with his father and shattered the worthless gods of an idolatrous age, thus becoming an iconoclast fighting the battles of the Almighty.

Abraham was not concerned with himself alone but, together with his wife Sarah, endeavoured to convert the pagan world to a realisation of the existence of God. The Rabbis point out the different nuances of the word *tamim* in regard to Abraham. In 17:1 God says to Abraham, 'Walk before Me and be *tamim*' (perfect). Abraham was inflexible and unwavering in his relationship to God, but in his dealings with man he judiciously employed the qualities of true leadership. Abraham was the first Hebrew (Ivri), which is interpreted to mean 'my side'. 'Even if the whole world is against me' said

Abraham, 'I shall stay on my side and fight the cause of the Jew.' Little wonder that he received the reward at the hand of God.

ARN explains how Abraham practised charity and justice: When two litigants would come before Abraham for judgment and one would say of his fellow, 'He owed me a minah', Abraham our father would take out a minah of his own, give it to him and say to them, 'Draw up your claims before me' and each would stake his claim. In the event that the defendant was found owing the other a minah, Abraham would say to the one with the minah, 'Give the minah to your fellow'. But if it was not so, he would say to them, 'Divide the sum between you and depart in peace'.

Rashi on Gen. 37:1 sums up the qualities of Adam, Noah and Abraham in these words: You will find that in the case of the ten generations from Adam to Noah it states, 'So and so begat so and so'; but when it reaches Noah it deals with him at length. Similarly, of the ten generations from Noah to Abraham it gives but a brief account, but when it comes to Abraham it speaks of him more fully. It may be compared to the case of a jewel that falls into the sand — a man searches in the sand, sifts it in a sieve, until he finds the jewel. When he has found it he throws away the pebbles and keeps the jewel.

Hasidic Lore

Noah. Said the Berditchever: We read (Gen. 6:9), 'These are the generations of Noah. Noah was in his generation a man righteous and perfect (whole-hearted).' We learn from this verse that the good man's generations are his good acts, the means by which he is continually reborn as a better man.

Only this kind of man can be truly called 'born' as he seeks to be born again and again in an ever higher degree. We may thus explain the words of Rava in Mak. 17b, 'When birth is given, it should be given to one like R. Simeon Bar Yohai ...... Only an illustrious person like R. Simeon is properly called 'born'.

The Zaddik's grief. Said the Koretzer: We find that ten generations passed from the time of Adam to the flood who were not punished for their sins. Ten generations passed from the flood until the destruction of Sodom, during which Sodom was spared. Why? Because God is all-merciful and cares not how much the people sin against Him. But when a zaddik comes into the world and feels aggrieved at the contempt in which the people hold God, then the Lord restrains His mercy and punishes the wicked. The coming of Noah brought the flood; Abraham brought the destruction of Sodom; Moses, the drowning of the Egyptians. It is for this reason that the zaddikim feel impelled to offer prayers for the wicked.

(ד) עֲשָׂרָה נִסְיוֹנוֹת נִתְנַסָּה אַבְרָהָם אָבִינוּ וְעָמַד בְּכֻלָּם לְהוֹדִיעַ כַּמָּה חִבָּתוֹ שֶׁל אַבְרָהָם אָבִינוּ:

Mishnah Four.

With ten trials Abraham our father was tried and he withstood them all to make known how great was the love of Abraham our father.

Ten trials. Authorities differ as to the composition of the ten trials, but we can reckon them as follows:

1. Abraham's migration. (Gen. 12).
2. The famine in Canaan (12.10).
3. The seizing of Sarah by Pharaoh (12:15).
4. The battle with the four kings (Chapter 14).
5. Abraham's marriage with Hagar (16:2).
6. The circumcision of Abraham (17:10).
7. Sarah and Avimelekh, King of Gerar (20:2).
8. The banishment of Hagar (21:10).
9. The banishment of Ishmael (21:10).
10. Akedat Yizhak, the binding of Isaac (22:2).

We cannot deal with all the ten trials but shall concentrate on the climactic trial, the binding of Isaac, which is central to Jewish life and is incorporated in the Rosh Hashanah liturgy. Akedat Yitzhak literally means the binding and not the sacrifice of Isaac as the non-Jewish world labels it.

Nissayon, trial. We connect this word with the introductory word *nissah* of the story of the *Akedah* (22:1). A nissayon is a test which demands giving, sacrificing, surrendering one's talents, energies and even life, to the will of God. The question has been asked, why did God test Abraham? God is omniscient and knew that Abraham would heed His command. Abraham was put to the test in order that we should know how to respond to the trials and tribulations visited upon us throughout life. Abraham and Isaac walked together with one heart towards Moriah; so should we all accept our reverses and sufferings with equanimity and resignation. Such conduct as Abraham displayed should imbue us with spirituality, inspiration and edification. Why did God test Abraham? Because God tests the righteous. In the parable of the Midrash, if a farmer has a strong animal and a weak one, upon which of the two will he place the yoke? Will he not choose the stronger? So God tested the righteous Abraham (Gen.R. 55:2).

Another interpretation of *nissayon* may be seen in the verse quoted by the Midrash in its comment on the opening words of the *Akedah*. The Rabbis quote Ps. 60:6, '*Natata lireiekha nes lehitnoses mipnei koshet selah*' —'You have given a banner to them that fear You that it may be displayed, because of the truth selah'. The Rabbis connect *nissayon* with *nes*, a flag. Abraham's readiness to heed the call of God is as a banner fluttering nobly and courageously in the strong wind of change. We, as children of Abraham our father, are asked to emulate his example and hold the flag of Judaism aloft with pride and dignity and so perpetuate the survival of Judaism and the Jewish people.

The love of Abraham. This reminds us of the honoured title by which Abraham was known, for he was called 'friend of God' (Is. 41:8).

Hasidic Lore

We are all tested.

R. Joshua Belzer said: When a tribulation overtakes you, know that God wishes to put you to the test that He may learn how you will accept it. If you receive the blow with fortitude and repeat the words of Nahum Ish Gamzu, 'This also is for my good' (Ta. 21), your distress will vanish and there will be no need to try you further, as you will then perceive that the misfortune was truly for your good.

(ה) עֲשָׂרָה נִסִּים נַעֲשׂוּ לַאֲבוֹתֵינוּ בְּמִצְרַיִם וַעֲשָׂרָה עַל הַיָּם:

Mishnah Five.

Ten miracles were performed for our fathers in Egypt and ten by the sea.

Ten Miracles. These miracles correspond to the ten trials by which Abraham was tried and in all of them he was steadfast. They can also refer to the ten plagues visited upon the Egyptians and from which the Children of Israel escaped.

At the sea. The ten miracles at the Red Sea were:

1. The waters divided.
2. The waters were like a tent or a vault.
3. The sea-bed was dry and hard.
4. When the Egyptians trod upon it, it became muddy and slimy.
5. The sea was divided into twelve parts, one for each tribe.
6. The waters became as hard as stone.
7. The congealed waters appeared like blocks of stone.
8. The water was transparent in order that the tribes could see each other.
9. Fresh drinking water flowed from the congealed water.
10. After Israel had partaken of the drinking water, it immediately became congealed and did not wet the ground underfoot.

Miracles. There is an affinity between this Mishnah and the previous one as the first syllable of the word *nissayon*, reminds us of the Hebrew word *nes* which means miracle. Indeed, the miracle of the Akedah is reflected in the fact that Isaac was not sacrificed.

There are many definitions of a miracle, but it has rightly been said that it takes a miracle to prove a miracle. The Rabbis have often rationalised the miracles and read into them poetic and symbolic interpretations. Miracles are not isolated phenomena; they have a moral and spiritual sequence. The Book of Deuteronomy, Chapter 13, reminds us not to be misled by the so-called miracles of the false prophet. Maimonides strikes the right note when he writes, 'Moses our teacher was not believed by the Israelites because of the signs which he wrought. Whoever believes because of signs, has doubts in his heart'.

Hasidic Lore

Miracles The Medzibozer said:The Lord is sparing of miracles in order to give wider opportunity to man's exercise of his free-will. Were miracles common, man's fear of God's power would remove his free-will to choose for himself between evil and good.

The Rabbi of Kobryn said: We paid no attention to the miracles our teachers worked, and when sometimes a miracle did not come to pass, their reputations increased in our eyes.

The Rabbi of Kotzk was told of a wonder-worker who was versed in the secret art of making a robot. 'That is unimportant', he said. 'But does he know the secret art of making a hasid?'

(ו) עֶשֶׂר מַכּוֹת הֵבִיא הַקָּדוֹשׁ בָּרוּךְ הוּא עַל הַמִּצְרִיִּים בְּמִצְרַיִם וְעֶשֶׂר עַל הַיָּם:

Mishnah Six.

Ten plagues did the Holy One blessed be He bring upon the Egyptions in Egypt and ten by the sea.

Ten Plagues.

1. Blood. (Ex. 7:17).
2. Frogs. (Ex. 7:27).
3. Lice (Ex. 8:12).
4. Swarms (Ex. 8: 17).
5. Murrain (Ex. 9:3).
6. Boils (Ex. 9:8).
7. Hail (Ex. 9:18).
8. Locusts (Ex. 10:4).
9. Darkness (Ex. 10:21).
10. Death of the firstborn (Ex. 11:4).

To the question, 'Why did God select just these plagues to inflict upon the Egyptians', the Rabbis replied that, 'It was measure for measure' (Ex. R. 9:9). They conveyed the lesson that the punishments inflicted upon the Egyptians fitted the crimes they deliberately pursued. Egypt was formerly the mistress of her own destiny; she boasted of a highly scientific and technical civilisation. Now, however, she enslaved her people and deprived them of the elementary principles of justice, liberty and freedom. Because of this flagrant denial of human rights, God sent the ten plagues which were not specifically miracles, but the natural outcome of their own wicked and lustful devices. The decline and fall of the Egyptian Empire was inevitable and the ten plagues helped to bring it about.

Each year on Pesah we gather round the Seder table and in the course of reading the Haggadah we solemnly recite the ten plagues. What significance do they posses for us today?

Blood. Egypt does not enjoy a regular season of rainfall. She is sustained by the waters of the Nile which fill the rivers and canals of the country. These productive waters were transformed into blood. These waters were drenched with the blood of innocent Jewish infants following the harsh decree of Pharaoh. Therefore, measure for measure; the waters of the Nile were turned to blood. It should be noted that God told Moses to ask Aaron to strike the waters with the rod in order to produce blood. Why Aaron and not Moses? Because Moses was delivered from the waters of the Nile, therefore it would be unethical for him to strike the waters which saved him. 'Cast no stone into a well from which you once drank' (B.K.92b). The same principle operated in the second and third plagues; the dust and the earth assisted Moses when he hid the Egyptian.

Frogs. The same waters which were polluted with human blood were filled with frogs which entered in immense numbers into the homes of the Egyptians and made life intolerable. We learn much from the animal kingdom. An old Midrash tells us that when David concluded writing the Book of Psalms he felt elated when suddenly a frog appeared and humbled David saying that it also praised God and sacrificed its life with many others when they heeded the call of the Almighty to leave the waters of the Nile and find their way into the homes of the Egyptians and to enter the ovens where they perished in the flames — all this they accomplished to praise the Creator of the Universe.

Lice. The magicians of Egypt were unable to use their magic arts and exclaimed, 'It is the finger of God'. It is interesting to record that 'the finger of God' is referred to on three different occasions. In connection with the writing of the Ten Commandments (Ex. 31:18) we read, 'The tables of stone written with the finger of God'. Again, the Psalmist praises God with the words, 'When I behold Thy heavens, the work of Thy fingers, the moon and the stars which Thou hast established' (8:4), and here in connection with the plague of lice, the finger of God is mentioned a third time. Understandably there was justification for employing the expression 'The finger of God' in reference to the Ten Commandments and the heavenly spheres because they speak of the lofty heights of divine Providence, but the plague of lice brings us down to earth. However, this is not accidental, but deliberate. God does not reside only in the heavens above; He also created the earth and everything in it including the vermin. As to the ethical implication of this plague, we would add that those who trample human beings underfoot are themselves smitten by the dust of the earth.

Swarms (of flies) and beetles. It is well to note that the Egyptian Standard bore the emblem of a fly, whilst the beetle was sacred and regarded as the emblem of the sun-god. This plague was a protest against the heathen and pagan gods of antiquity.

Murrain. This plague was directed not against man, but against the cattle in the field: thus the true God could distinguish between man and animal.

Boils. Moses and Aaron took the soot of the furnace, threw it heavenward, and the result was the outbreak of boils on man and beast. Here we have a typical example of the relevance of the plagues we bring upon ourselves, even today. The soot of our furnaces in industrial areas can pollute the air, thus causing the outbreak of a variety of diseases.

Hail. In Ex. 9:19 the people of Egypt were explicitly warned to take their cattle and remain in their homes. Those who disregarded the warning were smitten with hail and died. God had mercy on man and beast in order to save the sinners and deliver them from death (Nahmanides). It was this justice of God which prompted Pharaoh to say, 'I have sinned this time, the Lord is righteous and I and my people are wicked' (9:27).

Locusts. Locusts are frequently found in the Middle East. It was the immensity of the clouds of locusts which filled 'the whole air to twelve or even eighteen feet above the ground' which caused havoc and devastated the earth.

Darkness. This plague differed from the others all of which were preceded by warnings of the impending disaster. Here there was no warning. The Torah clearly depicts the essence of this plague. 'They saw not one another, neither rose any from his place' (21:23). The depravity of the Egyptian civilisation resulted from utter selfishness which reigned supreme. The Egyptians refused to recognise the needs of other people. This self-indulgence was so ingrained in their character that they would not heed any warning; self-love and self-involvement were too entrenched in their nature.

The Rabbis ask from where did the darkness emanate? R. Judah says, 'From above', whereas R. Nehemiah says that it emerged from below (Gen. R. 45:2).The Rabbis were obviously anxious to ascertain who were responsible for the spiritual darkness which enveloped Egyptian society. One said that it came from below: from the masses, the common herd who were inured to a life of degradation and humiliation. The other Rabbi insisted that it came from above, from the upper strata of society, the priests, teachers and nobility. When the top echelons of society are demoralised they bring doom and destruction to the whole nation. Through this plague the Egyptians began to discern the honesty and integrity of the Israelites who, unaffected by the darkness, could easily have robbed the Egyptians of all their treasures, but true to their religion they refrained from doing so.

Lastly came the climactic plague of the slaying of the firstborn which, unlike the previous plagues, was irrevocable.

Ten at the sea. These are read into the words of Chapter 15 of Exodus, which is incorporated into the Prayer Book and recited every morning of the year.

They are enumerated as follows:
The horse (1) and his rider (2) has He thrown into the sea (15:1).
Pharaoh's chariots (3) and his host (4) has He cast into the sea (15:4).
And his chosen captains (5) are sunk in the Red Sea (15:4).
Thou overthrowest (6) them that rise against Thee (15:7).

Thou sendest (7) forth Thy wrath (15:7).
They sank (8) as lead in the mighty waters (15:10).
And with the blast of Thy nostrils (9 and 10) the waters were piled up (15:8) ARN.

Hasidic Lore

The Lord helps. The Yud said:All commentators on the Torah ask, 'Why is it written, 'For I am the Lord that healed you' (Ex. 15:26) when it is said before this, 'I will put none of the diseases upon you'. Since there will be no diseases, what need is there of healing? The answer is as follows. Previously the plagues of Egypt served to heal the souls of Israel through their fear of punishment similar to the trials of the Egyptians. Now, after the exodus, if Israel obeys the Lord He need no longer enforce their obedience and loyalty through fear of penalties, but He will heal their souls by demonstrating through His Providence that He is the Lord.

(ז) עֲשָׂרָה נִסְיוֹנוֹת נִסּוּ אֲבוֹתֵינוּ אֶת הַקָּדוֹשׁ בָּרוּךְ הוּא בַּמִּדְבָּר. שֶׁנֶּאֱמַר וַיְנַסּוּ אֹתִי זֶה עֶשֶׂר פְּעָמִים וְלֹא שָׁמְעוּ בְּקוֹלִי:

Mishnah Seven.

With ten tests our ancestors tried God the Holy One blessed be He in the wilderness, as it is said: And they tried Me these ten times and hearkened not to My voice (Nu. 14:22).

Ten tests. This refers to the wilderness at Aravah over against Suph in the neighbourhood of Paran (Deut. 1:1) and in the wilderness where they made the golden calf, as it is said, 'They made a calf in Horeb' (Ps. 106:19) at Aravah where they clamoured for water, as it is said, 'And the people thirsted there for water' (Ex. 17:3). Some say that this refers to the idol of Micah (Jud. 18:24) and is a reference to their being rebellious over against Suph at the Red Sea. R. Judah says that they were rebellious at the sea, as it is said, 'But they were rebellious at the sea, even in the Red Sea, (Ps. 106:7). 'In the neighbourhood of Paran' refers to the incident of the spies, as it is said, 'And Moses sent them from the wilderness of Paran' (Nu. 13:3). 'And

Tophel' refers to the slanderous words which were uttered over the manna. 'And Lavan' refers to the controversy of Korah. 'And Hazerot' refers to the incident of the quails. These are seven, and elsewhere it says, 'And at Taverah and at Massah and at Kivrot-hattaavah you made the Lord angry (Deut. 9:22). 'And Di-zahav' — Aaron said to them, 'Enough for you the sin of the gold which you brought for the calf'. R. Eliezer Ben Jacob says, 'For this iniquity there is enough to punish Israel from now until the dead are resurrected' (ARN Chapter 34).

The Mishnah here emphasises how the people of Israel tested God in the wilderness, whereas in the proof text quoted here (Nu, 14:22) the verse explicitly states that Israel saw the glory and signs of God 'in Egypt and in the wilderness'. However, as the previous Mishnah enumerates the ten plagues from which Israel were miraculously delivered, this Mishnah underlines how Israel tested God in the wilderness.

Even more significant is the differentiation the Tanna of the Mishnah makes between Egypt (not mentioned here) and the wilderness. The children of Israel enjoyed the fleshpots of Egypt, but the wilderness was a veritable waste ground lacking all the features of a highly civilised society of which Egypt boasted. The wilderness had no attraction for the people of Israel; they even found the manna unpalatable. Here, Israel was close to nature; they were to be weaned away from the cult of Egyptianism. They were no longer slaves of Pharaoh; they now enjoyed freedom and liberty and were being prepared to accept the yoke of the kingdom of Heaven. Yet in spite of all the new experiences and divine manifestations visited upon them, 'They tempted Me ten times and did not listen to My voice' (Nu. 14:22).

We must now refer to an important and glaring distinction between the previous Mishnah and the one we are dealing with. In the previous Mishnah we are reminded of ten occasions when God tested man. Here it is the reverse; we learn that man tested God ten times. That God should test man is understandable, for this is His inalienable right as Creator of the universe; but on what grounds can man reserve for himself the right to test God? How long-suffering and patient the Almighty must be towards His creatures and their human failings and weaknesses? After He favoured us with His manifold blessings and miracles, we test Him with our petty foibles and intransigence. This Mishnah should serve as a constant challenge to man not to put God to the test, but that we should willingly submit ourselves to His will and crave protection under the wings of the Divine Presence.

Hasidic Lore

The fiftieth gate — testing God. Without telling his teacher anything of what he was doing, a disciple of R. Barukh had enquired into the nature of God, and in his thinking had penetrated further and further until he was tangled in doubts, and what had been certain up to this time became uncertain. When R. Barukh noticed that the young man no longer came to him as usual he went to the city where he lived, entered his room unexpectedly, and said to him, 'I know what is hidden in your heart. You have passed through the fifty gates of reason. You begin with a question and think, and think up an answer — and the first gate opens to a new question. And again you plumb it, find the solution, fling open the second gate — and look into a new question. On and on like this, deeper and deeper, until you have forced open the fiftieth gate. There you stare at a question whose answer no man has ever found, for if there were one who knew it, there would no longer be freedom of choice. But if you dare to probe still further, you plunge into the abyss'. 'So I should go back all the way, to the very beginning?' cried the disciple.

'If you turn you will not be going back', said R. Barukh. 'You will be standing beyond the last gate; you will stand in faith'.

(ח) עֲשָׂרָה נִסִּים נַעֲשׂוּ לַאֲבוֹתֵינוּ בְּבֵית הַמִּקְדָּשׁ. לֹא הִפִּילָה אִשָּׁה מֵרֵיחַ בְּשַׂר הַקֹּדֶשׁ. וְלֹא הִסְרִיחַ בְּשַׂר הַקֹּדֶשׁ מֵעוֹלָם. וְלֹא נִרְאָה זְבוּב בְּבֵית הַמִּטְבְּחַיִם. וְלֹא אֵירַע קֶרִי לְכֹהֵן גָּדוֹל בְּיוֹם הַכִּפּוּרִים. וְלֹא כִבּוּ הַגְּשָׁמִים אֵשׁ שֶׁל עֲצֵי הַמַּעֲרָכָה. וְלֹא נִצְּחָה הָרוּחַ אֶת עַמּוּד הֶעָשָׁן. וְלֹא נִמְצָא פְסוּל בָּעוֹמֶר וּבִשְׁתֵּי הַלֶּחֶם וּבְלֶחֶם הַפָּנִים. עוֹמְדִים צְפוּפִים וּמִשְׁתַּחֲוִים רְוָחִים. וְלֹא הִזִּיק נָחָשׁ וְעַקְרָב בִּירוּשָׁלַיִם מֵעוֹלָם. וְלֹא אָמַר אָדָם לַחֲבֵרוֹ צַר לִי הַמָּקוֹם שֶׁאָלִין בִּירוּשָׁלָיִם:

Mishnah Eight.

Ten miracles were wrought for our ancestors in the Temple, no woman miscarried because of the smell of the sacred meat, and the sacred meat never became putrid. Never was a fly seen in the slaughter house and no uncleanness befell the High Priest on the Day of Atonement, and no rain extinguished the fire of the wood pile of the Altar; and no wind overcame the pillar of smoke and no defect was found in the omer or in the two loaves or in the shewbread. The people stood pressed together but had room to prostrate themselves. No serpent or scorpion did harm anyone in Jerusalem, and no one said to his fellow, 'The place is too narrow for me to lodge in Jerusalem.'

Bet Hamikdash. The Temple contained two elements. It was a house not located in the heavens above for angels, but rooted in the ground for human beings. It was also a residence of holiness and drew towards it families from every direction who would be united by bonds of love. If the Bible is holiness in words and teachings, the Temple is holiness in families and people. Other religions have holy places; we alone aspire to become a holy people, 'A kingdom of priests and a holy nation'. In accordance with biblical injunction, we made pilgrimages to the Temple in Jerusalem three times a year, hence Pesah, Shavuot and Sukkot are called Pilgrim Festivals, *Shalosh Regalim*. The Temple was the cynosure of all eyes. Solomon, in his prayer of dedication, included also the non-Jew, and in this manner united all people in a spirit of brotherhood. The Temple was unique, for whilst we have thousands of Synagogues, the Temple always stood alone in its day. The first Temple was destroyed by Nebukhadnezzar in 586 B.C.E.

and the Second Temple was destroyed by Titus in 70 C.E. The Western Wall, the *Kotel Maaravi*, is today a relic of the Temple of old. In spite of the destruction of the Temple, this wall stands as a silent sentinel proclaiming to Jews throughout the world that the holiness of the Temple still exists and unites us in prayer as one people. It is therefore not surprising that many miracles occurred in the Temple. Here the Mishnah enumerates the ten miracles.

No woman miscarried. In connection with the talmudic ruling (Yoma 82a) that if a woman with child had a craving for food on Yom Kippur, her craving should be met, our Mishnah records here the first miracle in the Temple, namely, that no woman with child was ever affected by the smell of food in the Temple, thus avoiding a miscarriage.

The sacred meat never became putrid and a fly was not seen in the slaughterhouse. If we take into consideration the excessive heat that obtains in the Middle East together with the fact that there was no refrigeration such as we enjoy today, it was surely a miracle that the sacred meat which at times lay for two days and a night, never became putrid nor was a fly ever seen in the slaughterhouse. This miracle affords added confirmation to the classic maxim that 'cleanliness is next to godliness'. We derive an ethical lesson from the Talmud (Ber. 61a) where we learn that, 'The evil impulse is like a fly and dwells between the two entrances of the heart'. This is a reminder that we should master the evil inclination so that it does not contaminate the soul, the temple of man.

No uncleanness befell the High Priest on Yom Kippur. An exception to this was R. Ishmael Ben Kimhit. We are told that he went out to converse with a certain general, and spittle fell from the general's mouth and settled on Ishmael's clothes thus disqualifying him temporarily. Resulting from this his brother served as High Priest in his place. Their mother therefore enjoyed the unique experience of witnessing her two sons acting as High Priests on the same day. When the Sages saw her they asked, 'What merit is thine?' She replied, 'Never did the rafters of my house see the hair of my head' (ARN). This lesson is specifically directed towards the spiritual leader to be above suspicion and to possess 'clean hands and a pure heart', for he is the cynosure of all eyes and is able to influence, for good or for evil, the many people under his authority.

No rain extinguished the fire of the wood pile. The Altar stood in the centre of the roofless Temple hall, but it was never affected by the rain. Similarly, the spark of religious enthusiasm in our hearts should be strong enough to withstand the storms of temptation and assimilation which assail us every day.

No wind overcame the pillar of smoke. Here we have a further simile portraying uprightness of character and integrity of purpose. As the pillar of smoke ascended towards heaven, unmoved by the wind, so should we aspire to walk uprightly, unaffected by the winds of change which mislead and misdirect many people into alien and undesirable paths.

No defect was found in the omer or in the two loaves or in the shewbread. On the second day of Pesah an offering was brought of 'the beginning of the harvest'; it consisted of an omer of barley (Lev. 23:9).

The two loaves were brought on the Festival of Shavuot (Lev. 23:17).

Regarding the shewbread, see Lev. 24:8. Every Sabbath twelve loaves of bread were placed on a table in the Sanctuary to serve as a reminder to the twelve tribes that their place was before the Altar of God. These three miracles are classed together as one.

The Rabbis in the Talmud (R.H.16a) ask, 'Why did the Torah enjoin us to offer an omer on Pesah? Because Pesah is the season of produce. Therefore the Holy One blessed be He said, 'Bring before Me an omer on Pesah so that your produce in the fields may be blessed. Why did the Torah enjoin us to bring two loaves on Shavuot? Because Shavuot is the season for the fruit on the tree. Therefore, the Holy One blessed be He said, 'Bring before Me two loaves on Shavuot so that the fruit of your trees may be blessed (the first fruits were not brought to the Temple before Shavuot).

The Zohar observes that the shewbread was symbolic of the staff of life which would be plentiful, and the Rabbis remind us that the shewbread was as fresh on the day it was removed from the table as on the day it was first placed there; compare I Sam. 21:7. It will thus be readily comprehended why these three miracles are grouped together, for they refer to the different foods, of the fields, trees, and the ground, which God in His bounty provides for us throughout the seasons of the year.

The people stood pressed together but had room to prostrate themserlves. On the occasion when Israel went up to worship, whilst they were sitting they were crowded so closely together that no one could force a finger between them, yet when they bowed down there was sufficient room.... Rabban Simeon Ben Gamliel says, 'In the future, Jerusalem will be the gathering place of all the nations and all the kingdoms, as it is said, 'And all the nations shall be gathered unto it to the name of the Lord to Jerusalem' (Jer. 3:17). Now elsewhere it says, 'Let the waters under the heaven be gathered unto one place' (Gen. 1:9). Even as the gathering spoken of in the latter instance refers to the assembling of all the waters of God's creation in one place, so the gathering spoken of here refers to the assembling of all the nations and kingdoms in one place, as it is said, 'And all the nations shall be gathered unto it' (ARN).

No serpent or scorpion ..... Although Jerusalem was surrounded by mountains where snakes abound, such was the holiness and purity of the Temple that no one was harmed by a snake. Indeed, it is said that whoever would meet with an accident outside Jerusalem would be healed as soon as he saw the walls of Jerusalem.

No man said to his fellow ..... No payment for a bed was accepted there. R. Judah says: Not even payment for beds and coverings. The hides of the sacrificial beasts were not for sale there. What was done with them? Rabban Simeon Ben Gamliel says, 'They were given to the innkeepers. The guests would stay indoors and the innkeepers out of doors. The guests resorted to an evasion by buying painted sheep whose hides were worth four to five selaim, and these were left as compensation for the men of Jerusalem' (ARN).

No man ever said to his fellow, 'I am pressed for time' or 'I have not sufficient means and I am unable to remain or lodge in Jerusalem', for the Holy One provides with a livelihood all those who dwell in Jerusalem so that they need not leave it ..... but the statement actually refers to the Pilgrim Festivals when all Israel gathered in Jerusalem, and the upkeep was enormous ..... and no man spoke ever to his fellow, as people on such occasion are wont to complain and grumble that 'the place is too crowded for me to spend the night here' either because a night's lodging was not available or because one could not get what he needed in the city' (Vitry).

Jerusalem. It is assumed that David chose Jerusalem as his residence because it belonged neither to Judah nor to Israel, but was situated on the border of both. One of David's first actions after he settled in Jerusalem was to bring up the Ark of the Covenant, so establishing it as a religious centre.

Geographically and strategically Jerusalem was suited to become the capital and it was bounded on three sides by walls and was almost impregnable. Jerusalem was conquered from the Jebusites through a subterranean passage which had been dug in order to convey water from the only nearby spring to the centre of the city. This passage was stormed by Joab, the son of David's sister. He overcame the Jebusites by initiating a swift and unforeseen attack. Even at that early period, Jerusalem was an important junction linking the principal highways of the country. On account of its religious character, Jerusalem became the political and religious centre of the land and in addition was also one of the strongest fortresses of the country.

Hasidic Lore

Jerusalem Said the Ropshitzer: By our service to God we will build Jerusalem daily. One of us adds a row, another only a brick. When Jerusalem is completed the Redemption will come.

The Shepser Rabbi wrote: It is the duty of every Jew either to migrate to Eretz Yisrael, or to help support the colonists. The holiness of the Land is broadened as the number of Jews increases. In the Talmud (Ket. 111a) we are taught that one who demonstrates his yearning for Eretz Yisrael by aiding its Jews contributes to the broadening of its holiness, just as if he himself went to reside there. We are also taught that the Lord says, 'I shall not enter the upper Jerusalem — of the truly pious — until they shall come to the lower Jerusalem (Ta. 5a) — they, meaning the people who are enjoined to perform their daily labour.

G.G. Scholem writes, 'I have had occasion in Jerusalem to meet men who to this day adhere to the practice of mystical meditation in prayer, as Luria taught it, for among the eighty thousand Jews of Jerusalem there are still thirty or fifty masters of mystical prayer who practise it after years of spiritual training. I am bound to say that in the majority of cases a glance is sufficient to recognise the mystical character of their devotion'.

(ט) עֲשָׂרָה דְבָרִים נִבְרְאוּ בְּעֶרֶב שַׁבָּת בֵּין הַשְּׁמָשׁוֹת וְאֵלּוּ הֵן. פִּי הָאָרֶץ. פִּי הַבְּאֵר. פִּי הָאָתוֹן. הַקֶּשֶׁת. וְהַמָּן. וְהַמַּטֶּה. וְהַשָּׁמִיר. הַכְּתָב. וְהַמִּכְתָּב. וְהַלֻּחוֹת. וְיֵשׁ אוֹמְרִים אַף הַמַּזִּיקִין וּקְבוּרָתוֹ שֶׁל מֹשֶׁה וְאֵילוֹ שֶׁל אַבְרָהָם אָבִינוּ. וְיֵשׁ אוֹמְרִים אַף צְבַת בִּצְבַת עֲשׂוּיָה:

Mishnah Nine.

Ten things were created on the eve of the Sabbath at twilight, and these they are: The mouth of the earth, the mouth of the well, the mouth of the ass, the rainbow, the manna, the rod, the shamir, the text and the writing and the tables (of the Commandments); some say also the evil spirits and the grave of Moses and the ram of Abraham our father, and some say tongs also made with tongs.

Ten things were created. Many imagine that the miracle is outside the natural order of things, but our Mishnah affirms that there is nothing new under the sun (Ec. 1:9) nor is anything accidental. Every thing was preordained and created between the end of *maase bereshit*, the work of the Creation, and the eve of the Sabbath. Every miracle has its assigned purpose and function and is produced at a definite period in history. Here ten such miracles are enumerated, but in the Talmud (Pes. 54a) other additional miracles are included.

At twilight. This is the doubtful period which is neither day nor night. This teaches us to resolve our doubts and difficulties prior to the Sabbath rest. When we reach the age of reason and are assailed by doubt and vacillation, we should buttress our faith with an implicit belief in Divine Providence which manifests itself in the constant interplay of the miraculous workings of God throughout life.

The mouth of the earth. Compare Nu. 16:32, 'And the earth opened her mouth and swallowed them up and their households and all the men that appertained to Korah and all their goods'.

All the miracles are rooted in ethical considerations. This is a warning not to slander or rebel against divinely ordained leadership. To lead a life without resorting to tale-bearing is in itself a miracle. At the creation — at birth — we should prepare ourselves to avoid Korah-like *mahloket*, (quarrelling).

The mouth of the well. This can refer either to the mouth of the well in the rock which Moses struck (Nu. 20:7-11) or the mouth of the well of Miriam which followed the Children of Israel in the wilderness (Nu. 21:16) or the well of which Israel sang, 'Spring up, O Well' (Nu. 22:17). In Jewish tradition water is often compared to Torah; we draw our spiritual sustenance from the wells of salvation.

The mouth of the ass of Balaam. (Nu. 22:28) This emphasises the power of speech which in this instance is ascribed to the animal 'who cries out against the injustice meted out to her'. Rabbinic literature is replete with instances warning us not to be cruel to dumb animals. Commenting on the words, 'Wherefore have you smitten your ass?', the Midrash remarks, I have been commissioned to demand restitution from you for the injustice you have meted out to the ass', and Maimonides adds, 'There is a rule laid down by our Sages that it is directly prohibited in the Torah to cause pain to an animal and that the rule is based on the words, 'Wherefore have you smitten your ass?' (Nu. 22:32).

The rainbow. As it is said, 'I have set My bow in the cloud' (Gen. 9:13). As the rainbow unites the variegated colours within its compass, so we pray that the different segments of world Jewry will be united and will reflect the glory of God on earth.

The manna. (Ex. 16:4). This was a heavenly substance which sustained the Children of Israel in the wilderness. This miracle teaches us to trust in God at all times and under all circumstances. Compare the statement of R. Eleazar of Modiin: He who created the day, created also its requisite sustenance, and he who has enough to eat for today and says, 'What shall I have to eat tomorrow?' - such a person belongs to those who lack perfect trust in God (Mekhilta Vayisa 3).

The rod, or staff. With this rod Moses split the Red Sea. There was nothing like it in the world, for on the rod was engraved the Ineffable Name of God. This rod Adam handed on to Seth, and it was passed down from one generation to another until Jacob went down to Egypt and handed it to Joseph. When Joseph died, Pharaoh's servants searched his house and deposited the rod in Pharaoh's treasury. In Pharaoh's household Jethro, the father-in-law of Moses, was interested in astrology through which science he perceived the intrinsic importance of the rod, which he planted in his garden where it took root. By means of astrology, Jethro discovered that whosoever would be able to uproot this rod would become the saviour of Israel. He therefore put people to the test, and when Moses arrived and succeeded in uprooting the rod, Jethro threw him into the dungeon which was at the rear of his house. There, Zipporah, the daughter of Jethro, saw him and became enamoured with him and requested that her father give him permission to marry her and this was granted.

Another interpretation is presented to us in Nu. 17:23 where we read that, '... Moses went into the tent of the testimony; and behold, the rod of Aaron for the house of Levi was budded, and put forth buds, and bloomed blossoms, and bore ripe almonds', and it was decreed that by means of the rod Moses would achieve all the signs and wonders (Vitry).

The shamir. The shamir was a kind of legendary worm which cut through the stones of the Ephod and Breastplate of the High-Priest and miraculously engraved the names of the Tribes of Israel, as explained in the Talmud (Git. 68a; So. 48 b). Tradition affirms that it also split the stones of the Temple of Solomon in conformity with the biblical command, 'If you make Me an altar of stone you shall not build it of hewn stones, for if you lift your tool upon it you have profaned it' (Ex. 20:22). See also I K. 6:7, where we learn that no tool was heard during the building of Solomon's Temple. The Mishnah in Middot 3:4 enlightens us that 'Iron is created to shorten man's life, but the altar was created to prolong man's life'.

The text. *The writing and the tables of stone.* Compare, 'And the Lord said unto Moses, 'Come up to Me into the Mount and I will give you the tables of stone and the Law and the Commandments which I have written' (Ex. 24:12). This implies that God had already written the Law before He called Moses into the Mount. 'The shape of the written characters on the tables which were held to have been of unique nature in that the letters, having been cut through the stone, were not only equally readable on both sides, but a letter such as the ancient *ayin* which was O-shaped could, in such circumstances, have been possible only by a miracle (Shab. 104a). This belief was based on Ex. 32:15, 'Tables that were written on both their sides, on the one side and on the other were written' (Avot, Soncino edition).

The writing. The Hebrew alphabet is one of the oldest in the world and the art of writing revolutionised early society. In this respect we are unique in that the Scroll of the Law from which we read in the Synagogue must be written by a scribe. Hebrew is known as *lashon hakodesh*, the Holy Tongue, as it is the language of the Holy Scriptures. Any ancient writings which were not in the original Hebrew were excluded from the canon of the Bible but formed part of the Apocrypha.

The grave of Moses. It is written, 'And no man knows of his sepulchre unto this day' (Deut. 34:6). Judaism did not allow the grave of Moses to be turned into a shrine; the Law of Moses is *Torat Hayyim*, a Law of Life, which is relevant in every age.

The ram. The ram was offered up as a sacrifice by Abraham, as it is said, 'And behold, behind him a ram caught in the thicket by its horns' (Gen. 22:13). It was ordained on the eve of the first Sabbath at twilight that a certain ram, during the life-time of Abraham, should be *hefker*, ownerless, so that when Abraham should require one as a surprise substitute for Isaac he might find it ready at hand and so rightfully appropriate it without robbing any person.

The evil spirits. These are the evil forces which are constantly at work from birth and which must be resisted.

Tongs also made with tongs. Compare this with the saying in Tosefta Eruvin; 'Tongs are made with tongs but how was the first pair made? It could only have been a creation of God'. According to Pes. 54a, the first tongs could have been cast in a mould.

When compared with the previous nine things, this one appears to be irrelevant. With the exception of the evil spirits, the other items are specifically historical and based on scriptural authority. Why then are the 'tongs' mentioned? We believe that this is a rightful climax to the ten 'things' created by God. The operative word is 'created', *nivreu*. We are partners with God in the creation and preservation of the universe. The tongs are the means whereby vessels or articles which are shaped and patterned to our liking, are made. This is a utilitarian and indispensable function of man. As God is creative, so is man. 'When you eat the toil of your hands, happy are you and it is well with you' (Ps. 128:2). The Mishnah aptly concludes with a conspicuous reference to the dignity of labour, which the Rabbis have consistently upheld. Furthermore, the tongs too, were created on the eve of Sabbath at twilight as a constant reminder to man that work and industry must be followed by the Sabbath rest which completes the week with the divine imprimatur.

Hasidic Lore

Ram of Abraham. Said the Sassover: Abraham was not commanded to offer up a ram instead of his son Isaac. But he was a prophet and he foresaw that his children would worship a calf and he therefore offered up a ram as an atonement for them in advance. Some have perceived this interpretation from the words in Gen. 22:13, 'And behold, behind him a ram caught in the thicket'. The Hebrew word for 'thicket' is composed of the letters samekh, bet and kaph; the letters following each of these respectively in the alphabet are, ayin, gimel, and lamed, which form the Hebrew word *egel,* calf.

(י) שִׁבְעָה דְבָרִים בְּגוֹלֶם וְשִׁבְעָה בְּחָכָם. חָכָם אֵינוֹ מְדַבֵּר לִפְנֵי מִי שֶׁגָּדוֹל מִמֶּנּוּ בְּחָכְמָה וּבְמִנְיָן. וְאֵינוֹ נִכְנָס לְתוֹךְ דִּבְרֵי חֲבֵרוֹ. וְאֵינוֹ נִבְהָל לְהָשִׁיב. שׁוֹאֵל כְּעִנְיָן וּמֵשִׁיב כַּהֲלָכָה. וְאוֹמֵר עַל רִאשׁוֹן רִאשׁוֹן וְעַל אַחֲרוֹן אַחֲרוֹן. וְעַל מַה שֶּׁלֹּא שָׁמַע אוֹמֵר לֹא שָׁמַעְתִּי. וּמוֹדֶה עַל הָאֱמֶת. וְחִלּוּפֵיהֶן בְּגוֹלֶם:

Mishnah Ten.

Seven signs are in an uncultured person and seven concerning a wise man. A wise person does not speak in the presence of one who is greater than he in wisdom, and does not interrupt the words of his fellow, and does not hasten to reply. He questions according to the subject and answers according to rule. He speaks of the first things first and of the last things last, and concerning what he has not heard, he says, 'I have not heard' and he acknowledges the truth. The reverse of these is in the uncultured person.

Seven. The number seven is often found in the Bible. The Hebrew *sheva* is connected with *sava,* full, satisfied and complete. Compare Deut. 33:23, 'Naphtali is satisfied with favour and full of the blessing of the Lord'. In pre-Masoretic Hebrew the letters *shin* and *sin* looked alike. Thus the week is full and complete with seven days; the marriage is complete with the recital of the seven blessings, *sheva berakhot*, and the observance of the seven days of festivities, whilst the male child enters the Convenant of Abraham and is considered to be a full and complete Jew soon after seven days have elapsed. At the other end of the scale, when death takes its toll seven days of mourning are observed which complete the first period of the mourning rites, *shivah*. That the number seven denotes completeness is evident in the Bible- Gen. 4:15, Lev. 26:18, Deut. 28:7, etc.

However, *sheva* can also mean to swear. If, as it seems apparent, all the three words, seven, completeness, and swearing, are traced to the same root, how do we equate swearing with completeness? Now we know that heaven and earth are invoked to act as witnesses to a covenant between God and man, as in Deut. 31:28, 32:1, Is, 1:2 and Ps. 1:4. As we call upon heaven and earth to act as witnesses, we can readily comprehend that the completion of a covenant or contract is accompanied by the taking of an oath which finalises and fulfils an agreement.

Golem. Golem is a shapeless or lifeless substance. When referring to a person it is an uncultured and uneducated being, one who has not fulfilled himself in life nor used to the full the talents and abilities with which he is endowed. This word has been immortalised by the exalted R. Judah Loewe of Prague (1513-1609) who, inspired by heavenly voices and dreams, created a Golem from a clod of earth and invested it with the Ineffable Name of God.

The Golem performed miracles and waged war against the tormentors of Jews who falsely accused them of the so-called blood libel. A full and fascinating story of the Rabbi and the uses he made of the Golem are narrated in 'The Golem Legends in the Ghetto of Prague' by Chaim Bloch.

A wise man. The Rabbis endeavoured to trace each of the seven qualities of the wise to the Torah, which is the source book of all ethical and moral virtues. Thus the wise man does not speak before him who is greater than he is in wisdom; this refers to Moses. We read, 'And Aaron spoke all the words which the Lord had spoken unto Moses ....' (Ex. 4:30). It was Moses who heard those words from the mouth of God, yet Aaron spoke them. Moses, the wise man, preferred that his older brother should give utterance to the words, and he remained silent.

He does not interrupt the words of his fellow. This refers to

Aaron, as it is written, 'And Aaron spoke unto Moses, 'Behold, this day have they offered their sin-offering and their burnt-offering ..... and there have befallen me such things as these' (Lev.10:19). Aaron remained silent until Moses had concluded his words. Only after Moses had spoken did he say, 'Behold, this day they have offered their offerings.....' Furthermore, when Abraham was praying on behalf of the men of Sodom, God said to him, 'If I find in Sodom fifty righteous ..... then I will forgive all the place for their sake' (Gen. 18:21). It was obvious that if there had been even three or five righteous men no harm would have befallen Sodom, yet God waited until Abraham had finished what he wanted to say and only then answered him, as it is said, 'And the Lord went His way when He had left off speaking to Abraham' (Gen. 18:33). If God, the Master of the Universe, did not wish to interrupt Abraham, how much more so should man not interrupt the speech of his fellow.

He does not hasten to reply. This refers to Elihu the son of Barakhel the Buzite, as it is said, 'I am young and you are very old; wherefore I held back and dare not declare you my opinion. I said, 'Days should speak and multitude of years should teach wisdom' (Job 32:6-7). This teaches that Job's friends sat and remained quiet in his presence. They followed him in every move he made; eventually he asked their permission and spoke, as it is said, 'After this Job opened his mouth and cursed his day...' (Job 3:1).

How do we know that they did not respond out of turn? It is said, 'Then Job answered and said' (Job 3:4); 'Then answered Eliphaz the Temanite and said' (Job 4:1); 'Then answered Bildad the Shuhite and said' (Job 8:1); 'Then answered Zophar the Naamathite and said (Job 11:1); 'And Elihu the son of Barakhel the Buzite answered and said' (Job 32:6). 'Scripture arranged them one by one in order to make known to all the inhabitants of the world that the wise man does not speak before him who is greater than he is in wisdom; he does not interrupt his fellow's speech and is not in a hurry to reply' (ARN).

He questions according to the subject. Such was Judah who said, 'I will be surety for him' (Gen. 43:9). Asking what is not relevant was Reuben, for it is said, 'And Reuben said unto his father, 'You may slay my two sons' (Gen. 42:37).

He speaks of the first things first. Such was Rebekah the daughter of Betuel, as it is said, 'Whose daughter are you? Tell me I pray you, Is there room in your fathers's house for us to lodge in?' And she said unto him, 'I am the daughter of Betuel the son of Milcah whom she bore unto Nahor'. She said moreover unto him, 'We have both straw and provender enough and room to lodge' (Gen. 24:23-5).

Concerning what he has not heard.... He is not ashamed to say, 'I have not heard'. Such a person was Moses, as it is said, 'And Moses said unto him, 'Stay that I may hear what the Lord will command concerning you' (Nu. 9:8). In the words of the Talmud (Ber. 4a), 'Teach your tongue to say, 'I do not know', lest you be caught in error' (ARN).

When a person has not heard something from his teacher, let him say, 'The following view I have not heard from my teacher'. If he has an opinion of his own in the matter let him give it, but let him add, 'So it seems to me' (R. Jonah).

He acknowledges the truth. Such was Moses, as it is said, 'And the Lord said to me 'They have well said that which they have spoken' (Deut. 18:17). So, too, God acknowledged what is true, as it is said, 'And the Lord spoke unto Moses saying, 'The daughters of Zelaphhad speak right (Nu. 27:6).

The reverse of these is in the uncultived person ..... He is in a hurry to speak, he interrupts his fellow's speech, he speaks in the presence of those who are greater than he, he hastens to reply, he asks what is not proper and replies irrelevantly; of things that are first he says they are last and of last things that they are first. He does not acknowledge the truth, he is ashamed to learn and ashamed to say, 'I have not heard' (ARN).

Hasidic Lore

The wise man. Said R. Bunam: The Psalm (107) enumerates various misfortunes which God may send upon man and concludes with the verse, 'Whoso is wise, let him observe these things and let him consider the mercies of the Lord' (Ps. 107:43). From this we learn never to lose hope in the midst of misfortune but to believe that it is truly meant for good. Let us have fortitude and patience to await better days and we shall perceive that all was a sign of God's mercies.

(יא) שִׁבְעָה מִינֵי פוּרְעָנִיּוֹת בָּאִים לָעוֹלָם עַל שִׁבְעָה גוּפֵי עֲבֵרָה. מִקְצָתָן מְעַשְּׂרִין וּמִקְצָתָן אֵינָן מְעַשְּׂרִין רָעָב שֶׁל בַּצּוֹרֶת בָּא מִקְצָתָן רְעֵבִים וּמִקְצָתָן שְׂבֵעִים. גָּמְרוּ שֶׁלֹּא לְעַשֵּׂר רָעָב שֶׁל מְהוּמָה וְשֶׁל בַּצּוֹרֶת בָּא. וְשֶׁלֹּא לִטּוֹל אֶת הַחַלָּה רָעָב שֶׁל כְּלָיָה בָּא. דֶּבֶר בָּא לָעוֹלָם עַל מִיתוֹת הָאֲמוּרוֹת בַּתּוֹרָה שֶׁלֹּא נִמְסְרוּ לְבֵית דִּין וְעַל פֵּרוֹת שְׁבִיעִית. חֶרֶב בָּאָה לָעוֹלָם עַל עִנּוּי הַדִּין וְעַל עִוּוּת הַדִּין וְעַל הַמּוֹרִים בַּתּוֹרָה שֶׁלֹּא כַהֲלָכָה. חַיָּה רָעָה בָּאָה לָעוֹלָם עַל שְׁבוּעַת שָׁוְא וְעַל חִלּוּל הַשֵּׁם. גָּלוּת בָּאָה לָעוֹלָם עַל עֲבוֹדַת כּוֹכָבִים וְעַל גִּלּוּי עֲרָיוֹת וְעַל שְׁפִיכוּת דָּמִים וְעַל שְׁמִטַּת הָאָרֶץ:

Mishnah Eleven.

Seven kinds of calamity came upon the world for seven chief transgressions. When some give tithes and some do not, famine through drought comes; some go hungry and some are full. If (all) have decided not to give tithes, famine through tumult and drought comes, and if (they have decided) not to give hallah the dough offering an all-consuming famine comes. Pestilence comes to the world for crimes punishable by death according to the Torah and do not come under the jurisdiction of the court (Bet Din), also for fruits of the seventh year. The sword comes to the world for the delay of justice, for the perversion of justice, and because of those who teach the Torah not in accordance with the Halakhah. Evil beasts come to the world on account of false swearing and profaning the Name. Exile comes to the world on account of idolatry, incest and bloodshed and (neglect) of the year of release of the land.

Calamity. We are asked to scrutinise continuously our actions and consider any calamity to be a punishment from heaven.

Gufei averah, chief trangressions. Some emphasise the word *guf*, body, to remind us that the soul is pure and that we sin through the body.

Tithing. The Talmud (Shab. 32b) warns us that if we neglect to give heave-offerings and tithes the heavens will withhold dew and rain. This may explain why the second blessing of the Amidah is called *Gevurot* and refers to the rain. Man must acknowledge the power and might of the

Creator who sustains us with the rain which helps to produce the food we eat. It is His power and strength (Gevurot) and not the ingenuity of man which supplies us with the bounty of nature, therefore *Mashiv haruah umorid hageshem,* You cause the wind to blow and the rain to fall, is preceded by *Ata gibor,* You are mighty. We now comprehend why neglecting to give tithes is tantamount to robbing God and denying His sovereignty over the earth.

Hallah, the dough offering. In the same manner that *terumah,* the heave-offering, represents God's blessing in the field, so *hallah* represents God's blessing in the home. *Hallah* is one of the three mitzvot which devolve on the woman and, as the home is of paramount importance, the law of *hallah* (Nu. 15:21) should not be treated lightly. It should be remembered that *hallah* is taken from the dough (flour and water). At this early stage we must recognise the handiwork of God in nature. The ears of corn ripen in the fields through the rain and sun which descend from heaven. Recognising this,a piece of dough is removed with the recital of a blessing, and so the home is hallowed through the domestic duties of the mistress of the home. This is a refreshing and revitalising thought and should help to strengthen the ramparts of the Jewish home which is built on the firm foundations of faith, belief and practice. On the other hand, those who disregard the law of *hallah* weaken the Jewish home, bringing famine and drought both in the physical and spiritual sense.

R. Eleazar Ben R. Judah said: Because of this neglect of *hallah* there is no blessing in what is stored, a curse is sent upon prices (what is stored, grain, wine, oil, etc. does not keep, with the result that prices rise) and seed is sown and others consume it (Shab. 32b).

Pestilence comes to the world. This applies to the time 'when the courts have not sentenced a person with the death penalty he deserved; this is a form of 'measure for measure'. In this penalty is included he who is guilty of neglecting the law regarding the earth's fruits in the sabbatical year, that is, he does not make such fruits free to all, and this is the cause of death to the poor who have nothing to eat; for in the seventh year men have not sown and the poor are therefore deprived of tithes or poor man's gifts. For this reason pestilence comes upon the world' (Meiri).

Delay of justice. *Inui* means suffering or oppression. but when used together with the word *din*, judgment, it means a delay in the administration of justice which in itself brings unnecessary suffering on the convicted person. This is a timely warning to those governments who unmercifully cast innocent people into prison, where they languish for long periods of time without trial. Such action must lead to perversion of justice and brings the sword of death to the prisoner. The Talmud (B.K.119a) affirms: He who robs his fellow has taken his soul from him, and the perverter of justice is he who takes the wealth of one person and gives it to another unjustly.

To teach the Torah not in accordance with Halakhah. This refers to one who pronounces forbidden that which is pemitted, and permits that which is forbidden.

Evil beasts. Compare Lev. 26:6 where God promises, 'I will cause wild beasts to disappear from the land, neither shall the sword go through your land', with Lev. 26:22 where we are told, 'And I will let the wild beasts of the open loose against you'. How do we reconcile the two verses? In Gen. 1:28 man, who bears the image of God, was to rule over the beasts of the field; but if man discards his divine image by swearing falsely and profanes the Name of God he automatically loses his mastery over the wild beasts.

Exile comes upon the world for idolatry. See Lev. 26:30-33, 'And I will destroy your high places ..... and you will I scatter among the nations..

An interesting passage regarding exile is found in the Tana Dbei Eliyahu: He said to me, 'Twice did Israel go into exile; for the first exile a time for return was given, but for the second, none. Why?' I said, 'Though the men of the First Temple practised idolatry, yet there was proper behaviour, *derech eretz*, amongst them. And what was this *derekh eretz?* Almsgiving and deeds of loving-kindness'.

Incest. R. Ishmael the son of R. Jose said: As long as Israel abandon themselves to unchastity, the *Shekhinah* withdraws from their midst, as it is said, 'That He sees no unseemly thing in you and turn away from you' (Deut. 23:15) (ARN).

Bloodshed. See Nu. 35:33, 'You shall not pollute the land wherein you are, for blood pollutes the land and no expiation can be made for the land for the blood that is shed therein'.

Neglect of the year of release of the land. See Lev. 26:34. 'Then shall the land be paid her Sabbaths'. God said to Israel, 'Since you did not release the land, it will release you; the number of months which you did not release it will release itself' (ARN).

The three commandments against idolatry, incest and murder are in a category of their own. If one is told that his life will be spared if he commits a transgression, he may do so; but this does not apply to these three commands which he must resist even at the risk of his life. These three commands are included in the Noahide Laws.

Hasidic Lore

Exile. Said the Belzer: There are three kinds of exile — exile among the nations; exile among Jews; and exile among one's own desires. The first is the easiest to bear. The nations may be influenced by gifts and goodwill, and respite may thereby be gained.

More difficult is the exile of a Jew among Jews. His Jewish adversary knows every wile used by the Jews and will oppress his fellow-Jew until he has gained everything the latter can give.

The worst exile is the exile from peace of mind. It is suffered by him who is overpowered by his evil desires at the same time that he is aware of their wickedness. This person needs redemption most urgently, as it is said, 'With him is plenteous redemption, and He will redeem Israel from all his iniquities' (Ps. 130:7-8).

(יב) בְּאַרְבָּעָה פְרָקִים הַדֶּבֶר מִתְרַבֶּה. בָּרְבִיעִית וּבַשְּׁבִיעִית וּבְמוֹצָאֵי שְׁבִיעִית וּבְמוֹצָאֵי הֶחָג שֶׁבְּכָל שָׁנָה וְשָׁנָה. בָּרְבִיעִית מִפְּנֵי מַעֲשַׂר עָנִי שֶׁבַּשְּׁלִישִׁית. בַּשְּׁבִיעִית מִפְּנֵי מַעֲשַׂר עָנִי שֶׁבַּשִּׁשִּׁית. בְּמוֹצָאֵי שְׁבִיעִית מִפְּנֵי פֵּירוֹת שְׁבִיעִית. בְּמוֹצָאֵי הֶחָג שֶׁבְּכָל שָׁנָה וְשָׁנָה מִפְּנֵי גֶזֶל מַתְּנוֹת עֲנִיִּים:

Mishnah Twelve.

At four periods pestilence increases; in the fourth year, in the seventh, at the departure of the seventh, and annually at the departure of the Feast (Tabernacles). In the fourth because of the tithe for the poor in the third; in the seventh because of the tithe for the poor in the sixth; at the departure of the seventh year because of the fruits of the seventh; annually at the departure of the Feast, for robbing the poor of their gifts.

Four. This number has a universal application as it reminds us of the four directions of the compass — north, south, east and west. The universalistic character of Judaism is strikingly expressed in our daily morning prayers through this number when we recite the beautiful prayer *Ahavah rabbah*, which emphasises the abounding love of God for Israel. At the mention of the words, 'Bring us in peace from the four corners of the earth', the Jew gathers together the four fringes of his *tallit* thus symbolising his attachment and loyalty to Jews scattered throughout the world. In this manner we bind ourselves with the four fringes, and are tied together by bonds of unity, love, kindness and peace.

Incidentally, the expression 'four corners of the earth' is not to be understood literally that we believe the world is square. This is denied by Isaiah (40:22) where we read of the 'circle of the earth'. As the four corners denote vastness and completeness, so Ezekiel refers to the four winds, 'Come from the four winds, O breath, and breathe upon these slain that they may live' (37:9). Job, too, refers to the four-fold division of the heavens, 'Who makes the Bear, Orion and Pleiades and the chambers of the south' (9:9).

The number four occurs often in the Bible. The river Eden is parted into four heads to embrace the whole earth (Gen. 2:10), and Nehemiah's enemies are sent to him four times (Neh. 6:4). What is particularly interesting so far as our Mishnah is concerned, is the reference to the four kinds of pestilence or judgments sent by God in Ez. 14:21, 'For thus says the Lord God; 'How much more when I send my four sore judgments against Jerusalem, the sword and the famine and the evil beasts and the pestilence, to cut off from it man and beast'.

Our interpretation of the universalism underlying the number four is borne out by the subject matter of all the Mishnayot (14-18) dealing with categories of four. While these specifically refer to Jewish life they could easily be directed towards mankind in general. For instance, our Mishnah upholds the rights of the poor; they must not be robbed of the gifts due to them. Similarly, the poor of the world should not be deprived of their rights and privileges; this, too, is Jewish doctrine. With even greater force does the spirit of universalism breathe in Mishnayot 14-18 which deal with a variety of characteristics found not only in the Jew, but in all people. Thus we have four types of men, four types of temperament, four different approaches towards study and education, and four types of 'brain'. All these distinctive features apply equally well to Jews and non-Jews.

Pestilence increases. The Talmud (B.K.119a) quotes the verses in Proverbs (22:22-23), 'Rob not the impoverished because he is impoverished neither crush the poor in the gate, for the Lord will plead their cause and despoil of life those that despoil them'. These verses refer to the gifts due to the poor man, and to what do the words, 'And despoil of life those that despoil them' refer? To the robber's own life; the grasping hands of the robber condemn him to death.

The fourth year. The Torah says, 'At the end of every three years, even in the same year,you shall bring forth all the tithe of your increase and you shall lay it up within your gates, and the Levite, because he has no portion or inheritance with you, and the stranger and the fatherless and the widow that are within your gates, shall come and eat and be satisfied' (Deut. 14:28-29). This is the order for the giving of tithes — in the first and second years (of the Sabbatical cycle) the first tithe is given to the Levite, and the second tithe is set aside to be eaten in Jerusalem. In the third year the first, and the poor man's tithe are set aside; and so too in the fourth and fifth years, the first and second tithes are set aside; in the sixth year the first and poor man's tithes are set aside.

Annually at the departure of the Feast. The Feast refers to the

Festival of Tabernacles. Sukkot is known by a variety of names; for our purpose, we shall concentrate on the title, The Feast of the Ingathering, *Hag Haasif*. Sukkot was celebrated at the season of the year when the barns and wine-presses were laden with the products of the earth, when the farmer was blessed with God's bounty. This is also the season of our rejoicing, *Zeman Simhatenu*, we rejoice with our possessions, but our happiness must not be one-sided and selfish. We must share our comforts with others, with the poor, the needy, the orphan, the widow and the stranger. The keynote of the Festival is expressed in Deut. 16:15, 'And you shall be altogether joyful'.

The spiritual joy of the Jew manifests itself when his happiness is hallowed and dignified, when he is with his family and people, and when he makes the heart of the poor also joyful. This is what we mean by '*akh sameah*,' altogether joyful; when we are altogether, united to do the bidding of the Almighty, we serve the Lord with gladness. This is the message of our Mishnah. Sukkot is a happy Festival, when we do not rob the poor of the gifts due to them but rejoice with them. If we deny the poor these gifts we bring pestilence into the world. It is significant that whilst Pesah and Shavuoth are always qualified by their specific names, Sukkot alone is not always labelled by its full name but is recognised as *Hahag*, The Festival. See Nu. 29:12; IK. 8:2; Ezek. 45:25; Neh. 8:14; and II Chron. 5:3, 7:8. The Haftarah for the first day of the Festival predicts that in the Messianic Era the Festival will be celebrated by all the nations of the world. Here we have another echo of the spirit of universalism which is mentioned above.

Hasidic Lore

Sukkot. A hasid asked the Dzikover Rabbi before Sukkot to grant him a blessing so that he might have an exceptionally fine palm branch, *etrog*, myrtle twigs and willows of the brook for the Festival. The Rabbi replied: What you need for Sukkot is a kind heart, a humble spirit, a truthful mind, and the will to perfect yourself. After you have attained these it will be proper to concern yourself regarding an exceptionally fine set of symbols for Sukkot.

(יג) אַרְבַּע מִדּוֹת בָּאָדָם. הָאוֹמֵר שֶׁלִּי שֶׁלִּי וְשֶׁלְּךָ שֶׁלְּךָ זוֹ מִדָּה בֵינוֹנִית וְיֵשׁ אוֹמְרִים זוֹ מִדַּת סְדוֹם. שֶׁלִּי שֶׁלָּךְ וְשֶׁלְּךָ שֶׁלִּי עַם הָאָרֶץ. שֶׁלִּי שֶׁלָּךְ וְשֶׁלְּךָ שֶׁלָּךְ חָסִיד. שֶׁלְּךָ שֶׁלִּי וְשֶׁלִּי שֶׁלִּי רָשָׁע:

Mishnah Thirteen.

There are four types of men: One who says, What is mine is mine and what is yours is yours, he is a neutral type, some say, this is a Sodom type; (he who says) What is mine is yours and yours is mine, is an am haaretz; (he who says) Mine is yours and yours is yours, is a saint; (he who says) Mine is mine, and yours is mine, is the wicked type.

We are presented here with four points of view regarding our approach to 'mine' and 'yours'. The first is the neutral rule of conduct which can be summarised by the philosophy that every person lives for himself. The second is the *am haaretz* who wishes to share with his wealthy or talented neighbour but is ready to give very little in return. The third is the saint who is prepared to surrender all he possesses without expecting or receiving anything. The fourth is the wicked person who covets the property of his neighbour without attempting to offer anything in return.

Mine is mine. The Mishnah offers two different statements regarding the first type. One is the neutral who does not wish to become involved in any way with his fellow-man. He believes that every person should live his own life. Superficially there appears to be nothing inherently wrong with this attitude of mind which claims that what is mine is mine and what is yours is yours. There are mitigating factors; he does not rob his neighbour of his deserts, nor does he interfere with or hurt him. He wishes to be left alone.

Sodom. The second and alternative view of the first statement goes much further. It gives the neutral character a specific name — a follower of Sodom. We know that 'the men of Sodom were evil and very sinful towards God' (Gen. 13:13). Is this perhaps too harsh a pronouncement to be levelled against those who believe that mine is mine and yours is yours? We learn from the Prophet Ezekiel that the men of Sodom would not allow any poor man to benefit from their possessions, 'Behold, this was the iniquity of your sister Sodom, pride, fulness of bread, and careless ease, was in her and her daughters; neither did she strengthen the hand of the poor and needy' (16:49). When Isaiah denounced those who were outwardly religious and inwardly corrupt he called them 'Rulers of Sodom' (1:10).

It is wrong to consider neutrality as harmless; it is hypocritical to parade one's religiosity and at the same time refuse to become involved in the spiritual growth of the community. There are occasions when one must be committed to a positive course of action, to help the poor and the needy and to work for the betterment of mankind. To say 'Yours is yours' and do nothing constructive to bring this to fruition is reminiscent of the life of the men of Sodom. There are times when we must rise and actively defend that which belongs to our neighbour and even to fight for his legitimate rights and privileges. We must not be smugly satisfied with 'what is mine' and oblivious to 'what is yours'. 'A person who does not allow anyone to enjoy that which he has, will eventually disallow him to enjoy even that which costs him nothing' (Duran).

In this connection it may be of interest to point out that some underline the use of the word *omrim*, they 'say'.They merely 'say': they pay lip-service to the philosophy of 'mine is mine' and 'yours is yours', but they secretly harbour the intention to confiscate that which belongs to others. This is a 'Sodom' approach, for the men of Sodom had ample resources of land, wealth and industry, but cruelly refused to assist the needy or entertain any guest.

A further distinction between the neutral and Sodom-type can be ascertained if we detect the difference in the language of the Mishnah. Regarding the neutral type, the Mishnah uses the singular 'mine', but in the alternative view the plural is used, 'there are those who say', *yesh omrim*. An individual who adopts the policy of 'mine' is not a danger to society, but when a number of people follow this selfish attitude the consequences prove disastrous, with the result that the poor and needy will die from hunger.

Mine is yours and yours is mine. The *am haaretz* or boor, expects much from others. He is prepared to concede that 'mine is yours', but this is conditional; he hopes to receive in return far more than what he gives. 'Such a person, whilst not so wicked as to rob and indulge in violence, is nevertheles lacking in character. This deficiency will lead him to covet the wealth of others even though he does not intend to rob since he is not entirely wicked. However, because of his covetousness he is always thinking in his heart that his neighbour's wealth is greater than his own. How many people are haunted by this affliction? It is difficult to find even two brothers or two partners who, after having taken their respective share, will not be jealous of each other's position' (Aknin).

Before we pass on to the second half of the Mishnah, we should examine again the first two views in the context of our political systems today. The first view which makes a distinction between 'mine and yours' seems to point to a divisiveness, an echo of the class warfare which has waged for centuries between the rich and the poor, the bourgeois and the common people in modern political terminology, the rise of capitalism which distinguished between the nobility and aristocracy on the one hand, and the downtrodden labourer on the other hand. The second view, 'mine is yours and yours is mine', seems to reflect the rise of communism which allegedly authorises the equal distribution of all wealth in order to serve the needs of the proletariat. Judaism steers clear from all extremes, favouring neither capitalism nor communism but a system based on social justice.

Mine is yours and yours is yours. This characterises the saint, who is always ready to give freely of his possesions, talents and energy, without thought of payment or honours. The word *hasid*, saint, is similar to *hesed*, kind. Kindness is the language which the deaf can hear, the dumb can understand, and the blind can see. The saintly person is constantly engaged in performing benevolent actions and kindly deeds. He dedicates his entire life to the service of God and man. The *hasid* is the embodiment of true religion because he inherits in good measure an abundance of God's grace, and lovingkindness.

The hasid is to be found in every age and is not relegated to any particular sect. This is not to denigrate the work of Hasidism which, since the eighteenth century, has inspired many Jews to join the ranks of traditional Judaism. The outstanding success of the Lubavitcher hasidim, for example, is due to their kindliness, *hesed*, to all people, their warmhearted approach to the problems of the day, and to their absolute love for all Jews. It is certainly not easy to cultivate the saintly approach towards life, but it should always be in the forefront of our minds and we should aspire to reach the exalted heights of the *hasid*.

The wicked. It is interesting to note that in the first three types depicted in the Mishnah the introductory word is *sheli* (mine), whereas the fourth, the wicked, is *shelakh*, yours. It is characteristic of the wicked to be ever eager to seize that which belongs to another person. This contributed to the downfall of Korah as testified in the Torah, 'And Korah took' (Nu. 16:1). Korah took from others (yours) and gave nothing in return. The wicked despise the ethical and moral tone of the Torah; in the scramble for wealth or honour they will stoop to any depths to aggrandise themselves at the expense of others.

Hasidic Lore

The ignorant man. The Alexanderer Rabbi commenting on the Mishnah said that we are taught by our Rabbis that everything is in the hands of Heaven except the fear of Heaven. Hence, if one says, 'For my fear of Heaven I depend upon Thee, O Lord, to grant it to me, whereas for my worldly gains I can depend upon my own diligence and ability', he is an ignorant man. It is the very opposite which is true.

יד) אַרְבַּע מִדּוֹת בַּדֵּעוֹת. נוֹחַ לִכְעוֹס וְנוֹחַ לִרְצוֹת יָצָא הֶפְסֵדוֹ בִּשְׂכָרוֹ. קָשֶׁה לִכְעוֹס וְקָשֶׁה לִרְצוֹת יָצָא שְׂכָרוֹ בְּהֶפְסֵדוֹ. קָשֶׁה לִכְעוֹס וְנוֹחַ לִרְצוֹת חָסִיד. נוֹחַ לִכְעוֹס וְקָשֶׁה לִרְצוֹת רָשָׁע:

Mishnah Fourteen.

There are four kinds of temperaments: He whom it is easy to provoke and easy to pacify, his loss disappears in his gain. He whom it is hard to provoke and hard to pacify, his gain disappears in his loss. He whom it is hard to provoke and easy to pacify is a saint. He whom it is easy to provoke and hard to pacify is a wicked man.

Here we have another list of four traits of character. The operative word is *bedayot* which we translate by temperament, but literally means 'tendency of the mind' or 'by reason of the intellect'. The Mishnah deals specifically with two qualities inherent in every human being, namely anger and appeasement or conciliation.

Anger. No individual is completely free from anger, but it is the duty of every person to control his anger so that it does not breed a greater measure of anger in our neighbour. Anger in itself is an evil trait which should be avoided; it can lead to vice and strife. King Solomon warns us, 'An angry man stirs up strife, and the wrathful man abounds in transgression' (Prov. 29:21). The Talmud adds, 'It is certain that the iniquities of the angry man outweigh his merits' (Ned. 22b). Anger, however, is implanted in the heart of man and there are occasions when one should exercise it.

Pinhas, a descendant of Aaron the High Priest, averted a catastrophy by exercising his holy anger against Zimri and Cosbi (Nu. 26). On the other hand we learn of another example of righteous indignation which is not rewarded, but cursed. When the Patriarch Jacob was on his death bed he castigated his sons Simeon and Levi with these words, 'Cursed be their anger for it was fierce, and their wrath for it was cruel' (Gen. 49:7). Here the anger was cursed because it was fierce and uncontrolled and the wrath was cruel and unwarranted. Anger must not reach the wild proportions which Simeon and Levi visited upon the men of Shekhem. In the words of the Rabbis, 'Even when Jacob was reproving them, he did not curse them, but their anger' (Gen.R.99).

Here we return to the force and application of the qualifying word of every section of our Mishnah, *bedayot*, to which we referred above. Anger should be employed judiciously with reason and intellect; it must never be allowed to explode to its fullest extent in our dealings with our fellow-man. See 2:15.

Similarly with appeasement or pacification; this, too, should be limited and not allowed to become unrestrained. Appeasement is an admirable quality and we should train ourselves to apply it but, again, with reason, and we should be mindful of the maxim, 'Do not be over sweet lest you be swallowed up'.

Hard to provoke and easy to pacify. Maimonides cites this section of the Mishnah to bring home the potency of repentance, 'It is prohibited for a man to be hard-hearted and to refuse his forgiveness; but he should be 'hard to provoke and easy to pacify'. When the sinner seeks pardon he must forgive with a perfect heart and a willing mind. Even though one has oppressed him and sinned against him greatly, he shall not be vengeful nor bear a grudge; for this is the way of the seed of Israel and those whose heart is right, but the heathens of uncircumcised heart are not so, for they retain their anger for ever' (Laws of Repentance ii, 10).

Hard to provoke. The Mishnah advisedly employs the word 'hard' and not 'impossible', for there are occasions when it is essential to exercise one's anger. Angels cannot be provoked, but human beings should find it 'hard' to be provoked. Even the great Moses, who was meek and humble, was provoked to anger.

In the light of what we have written we should refer briefly to an outstanding problem, the anger and wrath of God. If anger is deplored in man, why does the Torah speak of the anger and wrath of God? Our concept of God stresses the fact that God is incorporeal; He has no body, no passions or impulses; yet we read that the anger of God is kindled against man. However, we should remember that the Torah speaks in the language of man. We are to imitate God; as He is long-suffering, so should we be slow to anger. God is presented to us with human emotions in order to educate us to realise that anger is a sacred quality and should be utilised with great care.

Anger is not the opposite of mercy; both are the essence of God's nature. Thus the Prophet Habakkuk understood this when he prayed, 'In wrath remember mercy' (3:2). We are to learn God's ways, but man is very different from God, as the Midrash on Ps. 30:6 explains, 'It is the nature of a mortal that when he is in a state of anger he is not at the same time in a state of conciliation, and when he is in a state of conciliation he is not at the same time in a state of anger. However, the Holy One blessed be He, when He is angry He is ready for conciliation in the midst of His anger, as it is said, 'For His anger is but for a moment, His favour is for a lifetime'.

The Prophets never thought that anger is something that cannot be accounted for, upredictable or irrational. It is never a spontaneous outburst but a reaction occasioned by the conduct of man. 'The anger of God is not a blind explosive force operating without reference to the behaviour of man, but rather voluntary and purposeful, motivated by concern for right and wrong' (Heschel).

Hasid The saintly person is not necessarily one who is completely free from anger, but one whom it is hard to provoke to anger. His saintliness is founded as much on his ability to appease with ease, as on his persistent desire to find it hard to be provoked. The person who can remain silent in the midst of a quarrel and is not provoked to reply, is praised by the Rabbis

(Hul. 89a). Said R. Ilai, 'The world exists on account of him who restrains himself (keeps silent) in strife'.

Rasha. The wicked person is an obstinate individual; he is easily provoked, for he is not at peace with himself. He also stubbornly refuses to be appeased. He harbours vengeance in his heart and makes no allowances for the frailties of human nature. 'He who gives vent to anger commits as grave a sin as though he worshipped idols' (Shab. 105b).

Hasidic Lore

Anger. The Stanislaver Rabbi was accustomed to be awakened every morning by the warden in order to be punctual at divine worship. One morning the warden failed to call the Rabbi who therefore arrived late at the Synagogue. The Rabbi, who was quick tempered, struck the warden twice on the cheek. Immediately, he regretted his hasty action and resolved to make atonement by leaving the town and wandering about as a beggar for a year. When the year ended he returned to Stanislav, but his ragged garments and uncut hair and beard made him unrecognisable. He came to the Synagogue and stood near the door among other poor tramps. At the conclusion of the Services he was invited to the president's home for the Sabbath meal. His behaviour pleased his host and he was invited to remain for the night. The disguised beggar awoke early and began quietly to recite Psalms.

Soon after, the warden came to awaken the president, and finding him still asleep he stole the silver candlesticks from the dining-room table. Hiding them beneath his cloak, the warden knocked at the president's bedroom door. When the latter emerged, he immediately noted that the candlesticks were missing and asked the warden whether he had seen any stranger in the vicinity. The warden expressed the opinion that the tramp had stolen the candlesticks, whereupon the Rabbi asked the warden, 'Will you take an oath that I stole them?' This query so enraged the warden that he slapped the Rabbi's face twice and when he was about to do so a third time the Rabbi exclaimed, 'You owe me two blows only; return the candlesticks to their place and announce to the congregation that the Rabbi has returned'.

Pacification. The Ropshitzer said, 'Moses led the life of a hermit and established his tent outside the camp, and promptly his critics condemned him for exclusiveness and aloofness. Aaron, on the other hand, took pains to pacify all who quarrelled and mixed freely amongst the people. He was, in his turn, condemned for being too democratic and unmindful of his high position. The opponents of a good man will blame him no matter what his behaviour is'.

(טו) אַרְבַּע מִדּוֹת בְּתַלְמִידִים. מָהִיר לִשְׁמוֹעַ וּמָהִיר לְאַבֵּד יָצָא שְׂכָרוֹ בְּהֶפְסֵדוֹ. קָשֶׁה לִשְׁמוֹעַ וְקָשֶׁה לְאַבֵּד יָצָא הֶפְסֵדוֹ בִּשְׂכָרוֹ. מָהִיר לִשְׁמוֹעַ וְקָשֶׁה לְאַבֵּד זֶה חֵלֶק טוֹב. קָשֶׁה לִשְׁמוֹעַ וּמָהִיר לְאַבֵּד זֶה חֵלֶק רַע:

Mishnah Fifteen.

There are four qualities in disciples: He who is quick to learn and quick to lose (forget); his gain disappears in his loss. He who learns with difficulty and loses (forgets) with difficulty; his loss disappears in his gain. He who is quick to learn and loses (forgets) with difficulty; this is a good portion. He who learns with difficulty and is quick to lose (forget); this is an evil portion.

Torah education was always highly rated, and there was such a close affinity between teacher and disciple that the teacher constantly weighed up the qualities and weaknesses of the student. The bright pupil was praised for his powers of concentration and comprehension, whilst the less intelligent was guided and encouraged to continue his learning in spite of his inability to remember his studies. As the Rabbis speak of the 'sea of the Talmud', they compare the student to the fish which abound in the sea. It was their hope and prayer that disciples will multiply as the fish of the sea.

Thus Rabban Gamliel the Elder spoke of four kinds of fish — the unclean fish, the clean fish, the fish from the Jordan, and the fish from the Great Sea. The unclean fish he compared to a poor youth who studied Scripture, Mishnah, Halakhah and Aggadah, but is without understanding. The clean fish is comparable to the rich youth who studies Scripture, Mishnah, Halakha and Aggadah, and has understanding. The fish from the Jordan is likened to the scholar who studies Scripture, Mishnah, Halakhah and Aggadah, and lacks the skill of logical disputation. The fish from the

Great Sea are compared to the scholar who studies Scripture, Mishnah, Halakhah and Aggadah, and has the talent for dialectics.

Another passage from the ARN depicts four types of students with the following definitions: One desires that he might study and that others would emulate his example; he is a liberal student. One desires that he alone should study to the exclusion of others; he is the grudging student. One who expects others to study but not he; he is the commonplace type and some add that this is the Sodom type. One who desires that neither he nor others should study; he is the wicked student.

Mahir lishmoa. Literally this expression means quick to listen, but the correct interpretation can be ascertained only in the context of the conditions and circumstances which obtained in the ancient Academies of Learning. It was very different from the modern University where the student takes notes of the lecture given and with the aid of a variety of text books equips himself with the required knowledge demanded of him. Not so with the student of the mishnaic and talmudic period. In the age before printing, the student had no text books to assist him apart from the basic works, the Bible, Mishnah and Talmud; nor did he write notes. The discussions in the ancient lecture hall resembled those of a modern parliamentary session. The head of the Academy, the Nasi, would himself deliver a lecture or invite an ordained Rabbi to do so. The discussion was then thrown open to all those present, masters and disciples, and through question and answer the subject at issue was probed and examined by a variety of speakers, each one elucidating the topic in accordance with his own theory of interpretation. The students relied on their memory and ability to expound.

In the light of this background we can understand the purpose of this Mishnah. *Mahir lishmoa* is therefore a valid description of the student whose perception and analytical mind are keen and penetrating. He is quick to listen, sagacious, and mentally alert; he will not allow anything to pass unnoticed. His weakness lies in his memory which does not retain the knowledge acquired. On the other hand, the second type, *kashe lishmoa*, the student who finds it difficult to listen, is not necessarily hard of hearing but is unable to comprehend the depth of that which is imparted. His reactions are not as sharp as those of the first type, but he is compensated by possessing a retentive memory.

Commentators point out that the bright and intelligent pupil is not referred to as a saint, because we are dealing here with intellectual ability and not with moral or ethical behaviour. He has a good portion; he is fortunate to possess a clear perception and an excellent memory. Again, the person who finds it difficult to comprehend his learning is not wicked. He has an evil or unfortunate portion and the Talmud offers him this advice: What must a man do that he may become wise? Let him engage much in study and little in business. Did not many, they said, do so and it was of no avail to them? Rather let them pray for mercy, for from Him is the wisdom, as it is said, (Prov. 2:6), 'For the Lord gives wisdom, out of His mouth comes knowledge and discernment' (Nid. 70b).

Hasidic Lore

The diligent pupil. The Kobriner visited the Slonimer Rabbi and asked him, 'Have your teachers left any writings as a heritage?' 'Yes', replied the Slonimer. 'Are they printed or are they still in manuscript?' asked the Kobriner. 'Neither', said the Slonimer. 'They are inscribed in the hearts of their disciples.'

(טז) אַרְבַּע מִדּוֹת בְּנוֹתְנֵי צְדָקָה. הָרוֹצֶה שֶׁיִּתֵּן וְלֹא יִתְּנוּ אֲחֵרִים עֵינוֹ רָעָה בְּשֶׁל אֲחֵרִים. יִתְּנוּ אֲחֵרִים וְהוּא לֹא יִתֵּן עֵינוֹ רָעָה בְּשֶׁלוֹ. יִתֵּן וְיִתְּנוּ אֲחֵרִים חָסִיד. לֹא יִתֵּן וְלֹא יִתְּנוּ אֲחֵרִים רָשָׁע:

Mishnah Sixteen.

There are four dispositions regarding givers of charity: He who desires to give but that others should not give, his eye is evil towards that which appertains to others. He who desires that others should give but will not give himself, his eye is evil against that which is his own. He who gives and wishes that others should give is a saint. He who will not give and does not wish that others should give is a wicked person.

Whilst there is no chronological order in arranging the sequence of the Mishnah, one is tempted to see an affinity between Mishnah fifteen and Mishnah sixteen. Students of the period of the Mishnah and Talmud were generally poor. Thus we read that at one period six students had to share only one blanket with which to cover themselves throughout the winter months (Sanh. 20a). We also learn that two students covered themselves with the same garment because of poverty (So. 49a) and there are many other references which depict the plight of students. It is therefore possible that Mishnah sixteen was placed here in order to remind us at all times to be charitably disposed towards students of Yeshivot and Academies of learning to enable them to study with peace of mind. It should also be remembered that the *am-haaretz* looked down on the student and refused to help him materially (Pes. 49b) thus rendering the call for philanthropic endeavour more urgent.

Charity, or in its broader sense philanthropy, has always been a favourite theme of the Rabbis, and it is not surprising that a Mishnah has been assigned to the significance of almsgiving.

Tsedakah, charity is based primarily on the principle that we are the stewards of all wealth, which belongs to God. We are not donating our own money, but merely returning a portion of it to those of our brethren who are stricken with poverty, or to those institutions which are maintained through public funds. 'Honour the Lord with your substance' (Prov. 3:9) is translated by the Rabbis to mean, 'Honour the Lord with what He has graciously given to you' (Pesikta Rabbati) and 'You are My steward, give Me of My own' (ibid. 126b).

Givers of charity. Some suggest that the word *benotnei*, givers of, is superfluous. However, the Mishnah emphasises the 'giving' of charity advisedly. There are those who maintain that they are charitably minded, yet rarely if ever do they actually give charity. Others publicly promise a donation to a worthy cause, yet fail to redeem their promise. These are not givers of charity, but pseudo-givers. The Mishnah therefore makes it patently clear that we are dealing with genuine givers of charity.

Another form of giving, which is not encouraged, is presented by the person who promises to leave a leagacy for charity to be donated after his death. It is possible that the Mishnah implies that charity should be given during a person's life-time in order that the beneficiary could enjoy the benefits of the legacy as early as possible. We cannot give charity after death; it is then taken away from us. Indeed, many charities have suffered because of the tardiness and vacillation of the 'giver' who might die intestate, in which case the State often confiscates the money.

The story is told of a Rabbi who had a premonition in a dream that his nephews would be denied a large fortune by the Roman government. He immediately requested that his nephews should give the greater part of their fortune to charity and so avoid the confiscation of it by the Romans, but he did not divulge his dream. When eventually the nephews learned of their uncle's dream, they asked him why he had kept it a secret. He replied, 'My purpose was to have you perform the good deed for its own sake' (B.B. 10a).

On the other hand we have known of cases where the will of a testator has been contested and a goodly portion of the fortune has been dissipated in legal fees as the proceedings were unnecessarily drawn out for a period of years. If the money had been distributed to worthy causes during the life of the person, much wrangling and bitterness of spirit could have been avoided. The mitzvah of *tsedakah* is performed when it is given, and this should not be delayed. This, incidentally, will explain the reason why we do not recite a blessing prior to the giving of charity. Help should be offered as soon as it is needed; procrastination in the giving of charity may result in the loss of life.

Four dispositions. The first type mentioned in the Mishnah gives charity grudgingly. He is pressured to donate because of his social contacts, and once he has given he casts an evil eye against others and does not desire that they should imitate him. He thus deprives them of the blessing which attends the giver. He wishes to reserve the honours for himself alone.

The second type wishes to be freed from the responsibility of giving but desires that others should fulfil the mitzvah of charity.

The third type appreciates the importance of *tsedakah*. He takes the initiative and hopes that others will emulate his example. This agrees with the talmudic maxim, 'Greater is he who causes others to do good than he who only himself does good' (B.B. 9a); this is a sign of piety.

The fourth type is completely disinterested in and indifferent to the fate of his fellow-man; he is prepared to see him suffer from malnutrition; this is wicked.

The Mishnah is summarised by ARN in these words: Three things were said of men — One gives charity, may blessing come upon him. Superior to him is one who lends his money (free of interest). Superior to all is one who forms a partnership with the poor in terms of one half of the profits for each, or on terms of sharing what remains.

One commentator, obviously basing himself on Ex. 25:3 where we read that the offerings to the Sanctuary consisted of gold, silver and brass, classifies three types of givers; those who give charity like gold, silver and brass. Charity that is like gold is that of a person who donates in secret. Charity that is like silver is hardly a credit to a man. It is the charity a man gives when he is in trouble, or when a favourite son is sick, or when his wife is giving birth with difficulty, or when he is on board ship and a storm rages. Charity that is like brass is donated by the man who is totally hostile to giving; he begrudges parting with his money. But when he imagines that his end is near and he must leave this mortal earth, he orders the members of his household to use his wealth for charitable purposes hoping that the charity will deliver him from death (David Hanagid).

Hasidic Lore

Regarding the uncharitable. On this Mishnah the Besht remarks:The last person appears to have no connection with alms-giving, hence there may be only three dispositions. Why are four, mentioned? Light is known to exist because there is darkness; wisdom, because of folly; righteousness because of wickedness; pleasure, because of pain; memory, because of forgetfulness. One is the chair upon which the other sits. One is like the man who holds an object in his upraised hand, and the other is like the object thus held. In the same way the uncharitable man is the chair upon which the charitable one sits, or the hand which raises up the uncharitable.

(יז) אַרְבַּע מִדּוֹת בְּהוֹלְכֵי לְבֵית הַמִּדְרָשׁ. הוֹלֵךְ וְאֵינוֹ עֹשֶׂה שְׂכַר הֲלִיכָה בְּיָדוֹ. עֹשֶׂה וְאֵינוֹ הוֹלֵךְ שְׂכַר מַעֲשֶׂה בְּיָדוֹ. הוֹלֵךְ וְעֹשֶׂה חָסִיד. לֹא הוֹלֵךְ וְלֹא עֹשֶׂה רָשָׁע:

Mishnah Seventeen.

There are four characteristics amongst those who attend the House of Study: He who goes and does not practise, secures the reward for going. He who practises but does not go, secures the reward for practising. He who goes and practises is a saint. He who neither goes nor practises is wicked.

Mishnah fifteen dealt primarily with the student and his intellectual attainment. This Mishnah discusses the attitude of the rank and file of the community towards the House of Study.

Bet Hamidrash, House of Study. The *Bet Haknesset*, Synagogue, is reserved expressly for divine worship and the House of Study is set aside for the study of the Bible, Mishnah, Talmud and cognate literature. The origin of the Bet Hamidrash is considerably older than the Synagogue and was founded by Shem and Eber before the period of the Patriarchs. Commenting on Gen. 25:22, 'The children struggled within her', Rashi quotes the Midrash, 'Whenever she (Rebekah) passed by the doors of the Torah, that is the school of Shem and Eber, Jacob moved convulsively in his efforts to come to birth'. Again, when the Patriach Jacob heard that Joseph was alive in Egypt, 'He sent Judah before him unto Joseph to direct him unto Goshen' (Gen. 46:28). Rashi comments, quoting the Midrash, 'That there might be teaching before him — to establish for him a House of Study from which teaching might go forth' (Gen. R. 95).

The Prophet Samuel had his own House of Study for the sons of the Prophets. The influence of the House of Study was perhaps most effective in the Days of Hezekiah. It is reported in the name of R. Isaac the Smith that the yoke of Sennaherib was destroyed on account of the oil of Hezekiah which burnt in the Synagogue and Houses of Study. Search was made from Dan to Beersheba and no ignoramus was found ... no boy or girl, man or woman, was found who was not thoroughly versed in the laws of cleanliness and impurity (Sanh. 94b).

Finally, the Talmud (Ber. 64a) declares that he who goes out from the Synagogue and enters the House of Study to occupy himself with Torah is worthy to receive the Presence of the *Shekhinah*, as it is said, 'They go from strength to strength, every one of them appears before God in Zion' (Ps. 84:8). How many of our every-day expressions of speech are derived from the Bible? Here, the words 'from strength to strength' originally refer to the movement from one institution to another, in the period when the Synagogue and the House of Study were separated from each other. Today we often house both institutions in the same precinct. It is interesting to record that those who attended the House of Study considered themselves to be superior to the *amei haaretz*, as we learn from the prayer which they recited: I thank Thee O Lord, that Thou hast given my lot among those that sit in the Bet Hamidrash and not with them that sit at street corners. We both rise early; I for the words of Torah, they for vain things. I toil, they toil; I receive reward, they do not. I run, they run; I run to eternal life, they to the pit of destruction (Ber. 28b).

From the historical point of view, we have records of the existence of the House of Study during the period of the Second Temple in Palestine. The Bet Hamidrash was also a haven of refuge for the Jew in all the vicissitudes of our martyred history. There, the Jew would find comfort and solace listening to the Maggid, preacher, or Rabbi expound the Torah, and for a while he would forget the anguish and torment of a cruel world. The Bet Hamidrash attracted not only the scholar, but also the masses who were unlearned , but loved the atmosphere and warmth of the House of Study.

He who goes and does not practise secures the reward for going. The Jew is rewarded for wending his way to the Bet Hamidrash, though he does not practise all the minutiae of Jewish Law. He is commended for joining his brethren and thus helping to make the House of Study a beehive of Jewish activity. The rendering of the word *oseh*, doing or practising, is open to more than one interpretation. As it is associated with the House of Study, practice can refer to the revision of the learning imparted by the teacher. The Mishnah informs us that attendance alone without revising the lesson taught there, is also a rewarding exercise; he is helping to form a minyan, no mean achievement.

On the other hand *oseh* may refer to the practising of deeds of goodness or the performing of mitzvot. This translation reminds us of a discussion in the Talmud (Kid. 40b) where the Rabbis ask which is of greater value, active benevolence or the study of Torah. The conclusion arrived at is, 'Great is Talmud (Study) in that it brings one to *maaseh*, deeds'. In the light of this decision the Mishnah stresses that going to the Bet Hamidrash is a worthy act even if the person in question does not practise deeds of benevolence or mitzvot. The Mishnah implies that listening to an exposition of Torah will eventually lead to the performance of mitzvot. The Rabbis often emphasise the significance of listening to words of Torah. Thus, one Rabbi declares that when a scholar expounds Torah and the people sit and listen, God forgives them their sins. Rashi augments this translation of *oseh* to refer to one who listens but does not master what is taught.

He who practises but does not go. This may refer to the scholar who has mastered the intricacies and subtleties of Jewish law and studies at home. He enjoys the reward of practising, learning and revising Torah for his enrichment, but by implication he forfeits the reward for attendance because he absents himself from the House of Study. The Mishnah apparently echoes the principle that even those who are learned in Jewish Law should humble themselves and attend the Bet Hamidrash and so encourage others to follow their example and in this manner they will strengthen and help to preserve the House of Study to become the pivot of Jewish life.

The word, *oseh* may also refer to the communal worker who is engaged in maintaining the House of Study in good repair and administering to the financial needs of the institution, but does not attend regularly the Services and lessons that operate there. He enjoys the reward of *maaseh* because he renders practical service which is essential for the preservation of the study of Torah.

Hasid, saint. The hasid is one who attends and practises. Some authorities question the advisability of referring to a hasid as a saint; he is performing the normal duties incumbent upon every Jew. However, we have hinted at this above. There are those who consider themselves intellectually and morally superior to their co-religionists and consequently refrain from mixing freely with the multitude and do not attend the Bet Hamidrash. They do not hear the sermons or lectures of the Rabbis and therefore create divisiveness. More praiseworthy and meritorious is the conduct of the scholar who, in spite of his knowledge presents himself at the House of

Study and listens to the discourse of the Rabbi. Such understanding bespeaks humility and meekness, and such a person is worthy of the title *hasid*, saint.

Wicked. The *rasha* deliberately divorces himself from all religious practice. He dissociates himself spiritually, intellectually, culturally and morally from all contacts with Judaism. He closes the door to any possible influence that might bring him back to his people and his heritage; as the *rasha*, one of the four sons mentioned in the Haggadah, he excludes himself from the community of Israel.

Hasidic Lore

Builders. R. Isaac of Lentzner related the following story: In my youth I was accustomed to study all night in the Bet Hamidrash, and to snatch a little sleep after sunrise. Once I became so engrossed in a subject that I did not lie down to rest until a short time before Sevice. I awoke, but had not time to change from my sleeping robe and a worshipper admonished me for appearing at Service in so unseemly a garment. I replied as follows, 'We recite in the evening service for Sabbath, 'Read not here *banayikh*, Thy children, but *bonayikh*, Thy builders, namely Thy students'. When the general public call at a palace they must be garbed in fitting dress, but when builders enter to do repairs they appear in their working clothes.

(יח) אַרְבַּע מִדּוֹת בְּיוֹשְׁבִים לִפְנֵי חֲכָמִים. סְפוֹג וּמַשְׁפֵּךְ מְשַׁמֶּרֶת וְנָפָה. סְפוֹג שֶׁהוּא סוֹפֵג אֶת הַכֹּל. וּמַשְׁפֵּךְ שֶׁמַּכְנִיס בְּזוֹ וּמוֹצִיא בְזוֹ. מְשַׁמֶּרֶת שֶׁמּוֹצִיאָה אֶת הַיַּיִן וְקוֹלֶטֶת אֶת הַשְּׁמָרִים. וְנָפָה שֶׁמּוֹצִיאָה אֶת הַקֶּמַח וְקוֹלֶטֶת אֶת הַסּוֹלֶת:

Mishnah Eighteen.

There are four types among those who sit in the presence of the Sages: a sponge, a funnel, a strainer and a sieve. A sponge, because it sucks up everything. A funnel, because it takes in at one end and lets out at the other. A strainer, because it lets out the wine and keeps back the dregs. A sieve, because it lets out the coarse meal and keeps the fine flour.

Here we have another classification of students who are perhaps more advanced than those mentioned in Mishnah fifteen, for these sit in the presence of the Sages. Here the four types are introduced by comparing them to different objects or utensils in every Jewish home, especially in the days when families made their own wine and baked their own bread.

Sponge. This is porous and easily absorbs all kinds of liquid, clean and unclean. Similarly, the first type of disciple absorbs all things indiscriminately, the good and the bad; he does not distinguish between the essential and non-essential.

Funnel. This vessel accepts everything but also emits it at the same time. This student will imbibe much knowledge, but will soon forget all he has learnt.

Strainer. As the strainer retains only the dregs of the wine, so the student will remember only the false and misleading interpretations of what he has learnt and will allow the good wine, that is the correct and traditional exposition, to filter through and evaporate into thin air.

Sieve. This refers to a scholar who retains the best teachings, the fine flour, and casts away the inferior teachings, the *kemah*, or coarse flour. The sieve in mishnaic times was different from that used today. 'The sieve referred to is one which retains the fine flour in a receptacle attached to the machine and is so constructed that the coarse grain passes out at the end of the sieve' (Charles Taylor). It is interesting to note that the Talmud (Men. 76b) describes *solet* to be inner (best) kernel which, by being sieved repeatedly, is freed from the inferior *kemah* which passes through the sieve as superfine dust. It should be noted that whilst the dregs are useless, the coarse meal does not come under the same category as it can be utilised.

The four types of students are characterised in a different manner by a number of commentators. They compare the first to a simpleton, the second to a fool, the third as having an evil portion and the fourth as wise (Aknin). 'Like the strainer there are disciples who retain the dregs, that is to say such interpretations, traditions and legends (of a playful kind) that they forget what is of chief importance. This is characteristic of the mass of people .... Like the sieve there are disciples who study and retain the heart of the matter and forget the chaff; this is the best kind of disciple. Such a person is called learned and acute. In ARN a disciple of this kind is described as 'mighty and armed' and it is of such disciples that it is said that they are fit to render decisions on all matters' (Meiri).

Hasidic Lore

The dregs. Said the Besht: When a man squeezes wine grapes into a vessel he must first use a sieve with large holes to strain it; later, he uses a cheese cloth. But however often he will strain it, some sediment will still remain. It is the same with the zaddik. He must rid himself of his evil inclinations and continue to do so throughout his entire life; but a few dregs always remain.

(יט) כָּל אַהֲבָה שֶׁהִיא תְלוּיָה בְדָבָר בָּטֵל דָּבָר בְּטֵלָה אַהֲבָה. וְשֶׁאֵינָהּ תְּלוּיָה בְדָבָר אֵינָהּ בְּטֵלָה לְעוֹלָם. אֵיזוֹ הִיא אַהֲבָה שֶׁהִיא תְלוּיָה בְדָבָר זוֹ אַהֲבַת אַמְנוֹן וְתָמָר. וְשֶׁאֵינָהּ תְּלוּיָה בְדָבָר זוֹ אַהֲבַת דָּוִד וִיהוֹנָתָן:

Mishnah Nineteen.

Whenever love depends upon some material cause, with the passing away of that cause the love, too, passes away. But if love is not dependent upon such a cause, it will never pass away. Which love was that which depended upon a material cause? Such was the love of Amnon and Tamar. And that which depended upon no such cause? Such was the love of David and Jonathan.

With Mishnah nineteen we cease to pursue the numerical classification of objects and characters to which we have been treated until now. We here deal with the subject of love in its relationship between man and woman, and man and man. The wrong approach to love is that which is based on a material cause, *davar*.

An object or thing is transient and changeable, consequently a love which depends on an impermanent thing will eventually break down. Such was the so-called love of Amnon and Tamar; it was a momentary gratification of the flesh, and the love was very soon transformed into bitter hatred. This is testified by the verse, 'Then Amnon hated her with exceeding great hatred; for the hatred wherewith he hated her was greater than the love wherewith he had loved her' (II Sam. 13:15). True love is unselfish and unmotivated by any material cause. A successful marriage is founded on loyalty and faithfulness, which are permanent and sacred. For this reason Hebrew marriage is called *Kiddushin*, sanctification. True love leads to a holy bond which unites both partners with ties of affection and steadfastness, which cannot be rent asunder. The Zohar expresses it in this manner: God splits each soul into two parts, male and female. Thus divided, they descend to earth and the early parts of their respective lives are spent in search for completion. When they succeed, that is if they are worthy, there is true mating.

The second type of love mentioned in the Mishnah is that of David and Jonathan. This is a love which is not dependent on a transient thing, but was rooted in an idealistic friendship which knitted their souls together as one harmonious love. This absolute love has been idolized by writers and dramatists throughout the ages as one of the most sublime friendships ever recorded in the literature of the world.

Jonathan's love for David was not the outcome of an ordinary friendship. Jonathan made great sacrifices in order to win the love of his friend David. This we learn from the command which Saul addressed to his son Jonathan. 'For as long as the son of Jesse lives upon the earth, you shall not be established nor your kingdom. Now send and fetch him unto me, for he deserves to die' (I Sam. 20:31). The love of Jonathan for David was pure and unselfish; his aim was to benefit David, even at the cost of injuring himself and his future. 'Jonathan's greatness was manifested in the clash of duty between his loyalty to his father and his love of David ..... he fails in neither' (Hertz).

The reader of the Mishnah is struck by an obvious omission. The act of Amnon and Tamar is not characterised as shameful, nor is the friendship of David and Jonathan hailed as extraordinary. The Mishnah neither castigates the one nor praises the other. The failure of the one and the success of the other rests on our approach to God and man. Do we love God? Do we love our fellow-man? This is the burden of our Mishnah. The love of God is the highest degree which man can attain. This we learn from Abraham who received from God the title of 'My friend' (Is. 41:8) at a very late stage in his life, after the incident of the *Akedah* when he was prepared to sacrifice his son Isaac. It was then that Abraham was told, 'Now I know that you are a God-fearing man' (Gen. 22:12). It is interesting to remember that the same Abraham first discovered the concept of the oneness of God, which is the foundation of all Jewish belief and practice.

Monotheism is not a vague theological abstraction, nor is it unrelated to man and impersonal. On the contrary, Monotheism leads to the love of God. This is the essence of the *Shema*, the great rallying call of Judaism, 'Hear O Israel, the Lord is our God, the Lord is one'. This is followed by *veahavta*, 'and you shall love the Lord your God with all your heart and with all your soul and with all your might' (Deut. 6:5). God is not a nebulous idea detached from the world; He is near to all who call upon Him in truth. He is a personal God who is concerned with our welfare and it is therefore our duty and privilege to love Him. How does the Torah characterise God? He is passionately and intensely interested in the poor, the widow, the orphan and the stranger. He is not concerned with Himself, but with man. We are to love God because God loves us. In antiquity the pagans and heathens were terrified of the gods, who quarrelled with each other. Judaism was the first religion which taught man to love God with a three-dimensional love of heart, soul and might. In rabbinic interpretation we are to love God whole-heartedly, ready to sacrifice the whole of our life and the whole of our wealth.

As for the love of man to man, this is summarised in the great fundamental principle, 'You shall love your neigbour as yourself' (Lev. 19:18). It has been said that the love of man can operate only in the context of justice and righteousness. 'Whereas justice would be impossible did man give no acknowledgement whatever to the law of love, it would be unnecessary did the law of love prevail in the relation of men in society' (W. Herberg). The love we owe to our fellow-man should be spontaneous and unmotivated. As God is One, our love should be one and undivided; nor should we discriminate between Jew and non-Jew, for we are all created in the image of God. However, we should qualify this statement by adding that our neighbour, whoever he may be, must be a rational and decent human being. If he is susceptible to criminal or violent behaviour, he becomes a danger to society. He, too, needs the love and understanding of a doctor, psychiatrist or psychologist. We should also remember that the word *rea*, which we translated as neighbour, strictly means companion, a fellow-man, who is ready to play his rightful part in society. Indeed, Judaism was the first religion to create the concept of the brotherhood of man and the Fatherhood of God, which is echoed in the well known words of Malakhi, 'Have we not all one father? Has not one God created us? (2:10).

The depth and intensity of our love for man is best exemplified in the Pentateuch where special emphasis is laid on the love we owe to the stranger, 'The stranger who dwells with you shall be unto you as one born among you and you shall love him as yourself' (Lev. 19:34). This sensitive love of the stranger of another country and creed is proof positive that *rea* in the golden rule cannot possibly refer, as out ill-wishers have maliciously suggested, only to one of our own faith. The Torah makes no distinction between man and man; in the eyes of God all are alike. 'One law and one ordinance shall be for you and for the stranger that sojourns with you' (Nu. 15:16).

In the light of the foregoing, we can understand fully the implications of our Mishnah. All love flows from God and it manifests itself in a variety of ways, the love between a lover and his spouse, the master and his disciple, the employer and the employee, or the love regulating the parent-child relationship. A selfish love drags one down to the mire, but a disinterested love can raise both the lover and the beloved to supreme heights of spiritual ecstasy.

It is not accidental that the beautiful story of David and Jonathan (I Sam. 20:18-42) is introduced into the Synagogue,as it forms the Haftarah on *Mahar Hodesh*, that is when Rosh Hodesh falls on a Sunday, the morrow after the Sabbath. The happy story enjoys an appropriate name and place in the Jewish calendar, *Mahar Hodesh*, tomorrow is new. We avidly await the morrow, when a new order and a new spirit will reign in the hearts of mankind and when the love and friendship between David and Jonathan will overtake us speedily in our days.

Hasidic Lore

Love your neighbour. The Radziviller Rabbi said: The commandment to love our fellow-men as ourselves does not necessarily imply that if one buys himself a garment, he must buy one also for another person. Most of us cannot afford to do so and the Torah does not contain a command that only the wealthy are in a position to observe. What we are capable of doing, rich and poor alike, is to participate in a fellow-man's joys or griefs. If we hear that another person is prospering and successful, we should rejoice with him and treat his good fortune as our personal victory. If, on the other hand, our neighbour is in distress, we should actively share with him in his grief as though the misfortune were our own. This is the essence of brotherly love.

(כ) כָּל מַחֲלוֹקֶת שֶׁהִיא לְשֵׁם שָׁמַיִם סוֹפָהּ לְהִתְקַיֵּם וְשֶׁאֵינָהּ לְשֵׁם שָׁמַיִם אֵין סוֹפָהּ לְהִתְקַיֵּם. אֵיזוֹ הִיא מַחֲלוֹקֶת שֶׁהִיא לְשֵׁם שָׁמַיִם זוֹ מַחֲלוֹקֶת הִלֵּל וְשַׁמַּאי. וְשֶׁאֵינָהּ לְשֵׁם שָׁמַיִם זוֹ מַחֲלוֹקֶת קֹרַח וְכָל עֲדָתוֹ:

Mishnah Twenty.

Every controversy that is in the name of Heaven shall in the end lead to a permanent result, but every controversy that is not in the name of Heaven shall not lead to a permanent result. Which controversy was that which was in the name of Heaven? Such was the controversy of Hillel and Shammai. And that which was not in the name of Heaven? Such was the controversy of Korah and all his congregation.

Following a discussion on love (Mishnah 19) we are here introduced to the subject of controversy which is presented in two forms. One is dedicated to the cause of truth and Godliness, in the name of Heaven; the other to division and strife. One culminates in peace and unity; the other degenerates into dissention and rebellion against the Establishment. Throughout our chequered history we have had many controversies like those of Hillel and Shammai, who were engaged in the search for truth. They argued and debated passionately, but there were no hostile feelings of bitterness of spirit between them; they treated one another with mutual respect. In the words of ARN, 'They who sat and occupied themselves with Torah were zealous in argument against each other; but when they parted they were as though they had been lifelong friends'. However, those who, like Korah, were engaged in controversies which were directed against their superiors or rivals and stooped to base ingratitude and dishonourable depths in order to aggrandize themselves, in the end met their doom in ignominy, because their motives were not in the name of Heaven.

Commentators point to the wording of the Mishnah which appears to be inconsistent. On the one hand we have Hillel and Shammai, the two disputants, but in contradistinction we do not mention Korah and Moses, the other two disputants, but Korah and his congregation. Indeed, this is the essence of the message of the Mishnah. Hillel and Shammai differed and argued on a point of the Law; they both searched and plumbed the depths of Jewish interpretation. However, their differing views would never lead to an abrogation of Jewish Law. Hillel and Shammai were therefore linked together; their argumentation and striving were in the name of Heaven. However, Korah and Moses were antithetical; it would be incongruous to class them together. The first step Korah took in his opposition to Moses was to form his own congregation. Instead of striving for unity and peace within the camp of Israel, Korah chose to secede and form his own community. This has been the pattern of all controversialists who, motivated by personal honour, have broken away from traditional Judaism and formed separate sects and schisms.

This fragmentation of Jewish belief and practice has unfortunately been a recurring theme in Jewish history. Already in the days of Ezra when the canon of the Bible was being finalised, the Samaritans refused to accept any books of the Bible outside the Pentateuch, which alone was sacred to them; nor did they recognise Jerusalem, but Mount Gerizim, because it was situated in their territory. This was followed by another controversy between the Pharisees and the Sadducees. The Pharisees were the forerunners and founders of rabbinical Judaism. They believed in the unbroken chain of Jewish tradition which merged the Written Law and the Oral Law into one homogeneous entity. The Sadducees, however, rejected the Oral Law which, to them, was not as authoritative as the Written Law. The next major religious conflict occurred in the eighth century when the Talmud, our mentor and guide to this day, experienced its first official challenge by the Karaites. The story is told that Anan Ben David was overlooked in the appointment of Exilarch, the secular head of Babylonian Jewry, and as a consequence he introduced the religion of Karaism.

So far we have mentioned in our brief historical analysis controversies which were waged, not in the name of Heaven, and which in the words of the Mishnah 'in the end they will not be established'. This prophecy has been realised. The Samaritans are a small insignificant sect which plays no vital role in the future of Judaism, nor are the Sadducees or Karaites heard of today. The orthodox Jew is the heir of Pharisaical Judaism, which reigns supreme; 'it is established' because it is 'in the name of Heaven'.

We shall now add two examples of Jewish religious conflicts which were undertaken 'in the name of Heaven'. Both sides spoke in the name of the living God, but differed from each other in the interpretation and application of Jewish Law. From the ninth century, Greek philosophical thought was in the ascendant. Maimonides, for the first time, introduced in his 'Guide to the Perplexed' some philosophical concepts which were considered dangerous by other scholars who maintained that philosophy was irreconcilable with Judaism. Maimonides stressed the application of reason and attempted to rationalise the miracles, whilst others were sceptical of reason and feared that it might adversely affect the Revelation of Torah which to them was supreme. This resulted in a bitter controversy between Maimunists and anti-Maimunists. Kimhi, the famous commentator, sided with Maimonides, but Nahmanides, equally famous, opposed Maimonides. Both protagonists argued and debated 'in the name of Heaven' and it is needless to add that the differences were resolved and that Maimonides is today universally acclaimed as the authority who has judiciously merged belief and reason into a seasoned philosophy which guides us till this day.

Another dispute of the faithful is that of the Vilna Gaon and his battle against Hasidism. The Gaon staunchly upheld the enthronement and nobility of Halakhah and Jewish learning, whilst Hasidim were rooted in prayer, piety and good deeds. One emphasised the intellectual strivings of the mind, and the other devotions of the heart; but Judaism is all-embracing and can therefore synthesise the two strands of thought into one spiritual exercise. This *mahloket*, controversy, also ended in a peaceful solution. Hasidism, which afforded status to the ordinary layman, is happily with us and is exerting a meaningful influence in many quarters, whilst the spirit of the Vilna Gaon hovers over every institution and home where Jewish learning flourishes. The end justifies the means because it was a controversy 'in the name of Heaven'.

We shall now touch upon another controversy which was not of our making, but was cruelly forced upon us by the Christian world. Throughout the Middle Ages public disputations were inflicted upon us with a view to forcing us to adopt baptism and conversion to the dominant faith. The disputations were often held in the presence of royalty, and the masses were encouraged to jeer and abuse our spiritual leaders who were submitted to a gruelling test to admit to blasphemous charges allegedly made against Christianity in the Talmud. Jews were excellent debaters, but their prowess only served to inflame the Church and consequently they burnt cartloads of copies of the Talmud and persecuted whole Jewish communities. The disputations were often initiated by apostates who used their learning to distort statements in the Talmud which they maintained denigrated the authority of the Church.

On the dangers of *mahloket*, Israel Abrahams includes in his 'Ethical Wills' the following extract attributed to Maimonides: Make not your souls abominable by dissension, which wastes body and soul and substance, and what else remains? I have seen the white become black, the high of station brought low, families smitten sore, princes humiliated from their position, great cities ruined, assemblies dispersed, the pious destroyed, men of faith have perished and the honourable held in light esteem — all because of contention. Prophets have prophesied, Sages have spoken wise words, philosophers have probed, all have dilated on the evils of faction without exhausting the subject. Therefore hate dissension and flee from it; keep aloof from its lovers, its supporters and its admirers.

Hasidic Lore

Controversy for the sake of Heaven. The Rabbi of Rizin said: When the hasidim see one Rabbi carrying on a controversy with another, they too begin to argue with one another. But in reality only the zaddikim are permitted to carry on a controversy, for it is a controversy for the sake of Heaven. That is why it says in the Talmud, 'Which controversy was for the sake of Heaven? That of Hillel and Shammai'. It does not say 'Of the school of Shammai and the school of Hillel', for a controversy for the sake of Heaven can be waged only by the teachers, not by their disciples.

(כא) כָּל הַמְזַכֶּה אֶת הָרַבִּים אֵין חֵטְא בָּא עַל יָדוֹ. וְכָל הַמַּחֲטִיא אֶת הָרַבִּים אֵין מַסְפִּיקִין בְּיָדוֹ לַעֲשׂוֹת תְּשׁוּבָה. מֹשֶׁה זָכָה וְזִכָּה אֶת הָרַבִּים זְכוּת הָרַבִּים תָּלוּי בּוֹ שֶׁנֶּאֱמַר צִדְקַת יְהֹוָה עָשָׂה וּמִשְׁפָּטָיו עִם יִשְׂרָאֵל. **יָרָבְעָם** בֶּן נְבָט חָטָא וְהֶחֱטִיא אֶת הָרַבִּים חֵטְא הָרַבִּים תָּלוּי בּוֹ שֶׁנֶּאֱמַר עַל חַטֹּאת יָרָבְעָם אֲשֶׁר חָטָא וַאֲשֶׁר הֶחֱטִיא אֶת יִשְׂרָאֵל:

Mishnah Twenty One.

Whoever leads the multitude to virtue, through him shall sin not come; but whoever causes the multitude to sin shall be given no opportunity to repent. Moses was virtuous and led the multitude to virtue therefore the merit of the many is linked to him, as it is said, 'He achieved the righteousness of the Lord and His ordinances are with Israel' (Deut. 33:21). Jeroboam, the son of Nevat, sinned and caused the multitude to sin; therefore the sin of the many is linked to him, as it is said, 'For the sins of Jeroboam which he sinned and wherewith he made Israel sin' (I K. 15:30).

Before proceeding to discuss the main item of the Mishnah, the doctrine of merit, we the multitude, should take cognisance of the word *harabim*, the multitude. Judaism always encouraged mass education. The *am haaretz*, it is said, could never become pious or virtuous. From the dawn of history, we stressed the education of the multitude rather than the specialisation of the few. This is reflected at the Revelation of the Law at Sinai. The uniqueness of the Revelation lies in the fact that it was witnessed by all the people of Israel. The Torah was received, not by an exclusive sect, but by the broad masses. No individual, however great, may enjoy a monopoly of virtue or righteousness; it is the heritage of the nation. Israel was to become a kingdom of priests and a holy nation.

Moreover, the Rabbis declared that the Decalogue does not belong to any one nation, but to all mankind. The Divine voice, they said, divided itself into seventy languages, so that all the multitudes of the earth would understand its universal message. This, too, explains why the Torah expresses itself in simple language for all to understand. At Sinai, all the people accepted the Law and in unison cried, 'We will do and obey'. Since Sinai, it has been the avowed aim of Judaism to produce an educated laity and an enlightened multitude dedicated to preserve the Torah in every age. This leads us to the doctrine of merit, *zekhut*, which is enunciated in our Mishnah.

Zekhut. The doctrine of merit is a theological concept of some importance and dates back to the Patriarchs. Hence in the opening benediction in the Amidah we invoke the God of our fathers Abraham, Isaac and Jacob ..... who remembers the pious deeds of the Patriarchs. To this day we recall to mind the merits of the Patriarchs three times each day. This principle is even more forcibly emphasised in the Musaf of the New Year liturgy. As every building rests on its firm and solid foundations, so the fabric of Judaism rests upon and is sustained by its spiritual foundations, the Patriarchs and the Matriarchs. 'If you find that the *zekhut* of the fathers and the mothers are on the decline, hope for the grace of God' (Y. Sanh. 27d; Lev.R. 36). Nor is *zekhut* limited to ancestral piety; it can also include a pious contemporary, as we learn from the bold manner in which Abraham pleads with God to spare the cities of Sodom and Gomorrah — 'If there be found ten righteous people there' (Gen. 18:32).

Moses. The Mishnah naturally cites Moses as the greatest exponent of the doctrine of merit. The Law is known as *Torat Moshe*. Moses was divinely inspired; he received the Torah from the hands of God and transmitted it to us. Those who study and observe the Torah add to the *zekhut* of Moshe Rabbenu, whose timeless message inspires and preserves us. Moses was not motivated by self-interest, but lived and strove for the multitude. The art of prophecy was reserved only for the select few, chosen by God; but Moses, in his exceeding humility and abounding mercy, prayed, 'Would that all the Lord's people were prophets' (Nu. 11:29). Moses was virtuous, and because of this redeeming quality he led the multitude to virtue.

The proof text adduced to underline the virtue inherent in Moses can thus be paraphrased: Because Moses himself achieved the righteousness of God, he was in a position to impart the ordinances to Israel. The teacher can inspire others to become virtuous only if he himself is virtuous.

Parallel with ancestral and contemporary *zekhut*, we have ancestral and contemporary sin. The cumulative effect of sinfulness, which is more infectious than goodness, can destroy whole generations and even deny the perpetrator the opportunity of repenting, which is one of the saving graces of Judaism. This apparent denial of man's free-will is discussed by Maimonides in his 'Shemoneh Perakim' (chapter 7), 'Just as some of man's undertakings which are ordinarily subject to his own free will are frustrated by way of punishment, as, for instance, a man's hand can be prevented from working so that he can do nothing with it, as was the case of Jeroboam the son of Nevat, or a man's eyes from seeing, as happened to the Sodomites who had assembled about Lot, so does God withhold man's ability to use his own free will in regard to repentance so that it never occurs to him to repent and he thus finally perishes in his own wickedness'.

We are guided by the supreme principle that all Israel are a surety for one another (Sanh. 27b). The Rabbis have compared this to one sailing in a ship and who is totally oblivious of what is around him. He bores a hole under his seat and when the others protest he naively retorts that it is his seat and he is entitled to act as he wishes. The others answer, 'But will not the water come up through this hole and flood the vessel?' The sin of one can therefore endanger the whole community (Tanna dbe Elijahu page 56; Lev. R. 4).

Jeroboam. Concerning Jeroboam, this name has been interpreted to mean, 'he made strife with the people', see Sanh. 101b, 'Three kings have no portion in the world to come, Jeroboam, Ahab, and Manasseh'. The question was raised by commentators as to why Jeroboam alone of the three kings was singled out as an inveterate sinner. Indeed, the Talmud asks this very question, 'Why does Scripture make Jeroboam the exemplar of sin?' The answer given is two fold. In the first place, God pleaded with Jeroboam to retract from his evil way and repent but he obstinately refused. To spurn and openly reject the invitation of the Almighty to repent, is unpardonable. Jeroboam was also the first to corrupt his generation, and therefore 'the sin of the multitude was linked with his name'.

Hasidic Lore

Merit. It was the habit of R. David Talner to spend half an hour early each morning reading his mail in his private room. An intimate friend asked why he did this before prayers, which should have priority. The Rabbi answered, 'I wish to commence the day aright. As you know, the more important a man is, the more difficult are his struggles against his evil thoughts since the Satan strives hardest to tempt him. Hence, when I look over my letters and read in the salutation that I am called a *zaddik*, a leader, a holy man, and the like, I pray to the Lord, 'Thou knowest and I know that I do not merit these titles of honour. But since so many good men believe them to be true in all sincerity, I beseech Thee to aid me to avoid the snares of Satan so that people may not feel shame'.

(כב) כָּל מִי שֶׁיֵּשׁ בּוֹ שְׁלֹשָׁה דְבָרִים הַלָּלוּ הוּא מִתַּלְמִידָיו שֶׁל אַבְרָהָם אָבִינוּ. וּשְׁלֹשָׁה דְבָרִים אֲחֵרִים הוּא מִתַּלְמִידָיו שֶׁל בִּלְעָם הָרָשָׁע. עַיִן טוֹבָה וְרוּחַ נְמוּכָה וְנֶפֶשׁ שְׁפָלָה מִתַּלְמִידָיו שֶׁל אַבְרָהָם אָבִינוּ. עַיִן רָעָה וְרוּחַ גְּבוֹהָה וְנֶפֶשׁ רְחָבָה מִתַּלְמִידָיו שֶׁל בִּלְעָם הָרָשָׁע. מַה בֵּין תַּלְמִידָיו שֶׁל אַבְרָהָם אָבִינוּ לְתַלְמִידָיו שֶׁל בִּלְעָם הָרָשָׁע. תַּלְמִידָיו שֶׁל אַבְרָהָם אָבִינוּ אוֹכְלִין בָּעוֹלָם הַזֶּה וְנוֹחֲלִין הָעוֹלָם הַבָּא שֶׁנֶּאֱמַר לְהַנְחִיל אֹהֲבַי יֵשׁ וְאוֹצְרוֹתֵיהֶם אֲמַלֵּא. אֲבָל תַּלְמִידָיו שֶׁל בִּלְעָם הָרָשָׁע יוֹרְשִׁין גֵּיהִנֹּם וְיוֹרְדִין לִבְאֵר שַׁחַת שֶׁנֶּאֱמַר וְאַתָּה אֱלֹהִים תּוֹרִידֵם לִבְאֵר שַׁחַת אַנְשֵׁי דָמִים וּמִרְמָה לֹא יֶחֱצוּ יְמֵיהֶם וַאֲנִי אֶבְטַח בָּךְ:

Mishnah Twenty Two.

Whoever possesses these three qualities, he is of the disciples of Abraham our father; and whoever possesses three other qualities, he is of the disciples of Balaam the wicked. The disciples of Abraham our father possess a good eye, a humble spirit, and a lowly soul. The disciples of Balaam the wicked possess an evil eye, a haughty spirit, and a proud soul. What is the difference between the disciples of Abraham our father and the disciples of Balaam the wicked? The disciples of Abraham our father enjoy their share in this world and inherit the world to come, as it is said, 'That I may cause those that love Me to inherit substance and that I may fill their treasuries' (Prov, 8:21). But the disciples of Balaam the wicked inherit Gehinnom and descend into the pit of destruction, as it is said, 'But Thou, O God, will bring them down to the pit of destruction: men of blood and deceit shall not live out half their days, but as for me I will trust in Thee' (Ps. 55.24).

We distinguish between the disciples of Abraham and the false disciples of Balaam, each of whom is characterised by three attributes.

Disciples of Abraham. In the Bible and rabbinical literature we often meet the expression 'the seed of Abraham'. It is well to note the difference between these two expressions. The 'seed of Abraham' indicates the inherited characteristics, only those which come from intensive study of the personality of Abraham. 'The seed of Abraham' suggest that we take pride in our ancestor and that we bask in the reflected glory of our pedigree. This in itself is commendable, but it is inadequate. To glorify in our forefathers falls short of our duty. We can only become committed to our faith if we are disciples of Abraham and learn to study the origins of our ancestral faith, which are rooted in Abraham.

To be disciples of Abraham also means to follow him and pattern our lives in conformity with the life of the founder of Judaism by exhibiting the same moral courage and self-sacrificing zeal in order to do the bidding of God. Abraham did not inherit his quest for God from Terah the idolator. He made an original contribution to the basic truths of Judaism. To be disciples of Abraham implies that we are not passive onlookers, but active progatonists of the vibrant faith founded by Abraham our father. It should also be remembered that in a sense all mankind are disciples of Abraham.

Abraham and Sarah proselytized the pagan and for this very reason, our Mishnah does not speak of the disciples of Moses, for to be disciples of Moses we must observe the laws and mitzvot of the Torah — this is reserved for Jews alone. Abraham is the father of the universalistic doctrine of a good eye, a humble spirit, and a lowly soul. Would that mankind were permeated with these admirable qualities, which are the basis of a good life.

Where in the life of Abraham do we find the three universal qualities enumerated here? In Gen. 18:6 we read, 'And Abraham ran unto the herd and fetched a calf, tender and good'. The Rabbis interpret these words as follows; a calf, two years old, good, is an animal a year old. Although Abraham initially suggested that he would bring 'a morsel of bread', his love and concern for complete strangers was such that he prepared a lavish feast. Hospitality of such proportions is the result of 'a good eye', a universal trait we could emulate.

How do we know that Abraham was possessed of a humble spirit? The Torah informs us that Abraham said, 'I am a stranger and sojourner with you' (Gen. 23:4). Here the great Abraham, a prince of God, stands humbly before the children of Het as an alien and stranger pleading, not for landed property, but for a grave for Sarah. That Abraham was a lowly soul we learn from (Gen. 18:27), when Abraham refers to himself as being but 'dust and ashes'.

We should add that there is a fine distinction between a humble spirit which may operate only outwardly, and a lowly soul which asserts itself quietly and unobtrusively in one's own privacy. The genius of Abraham the master is reflected in his disciples who, by possessing a good eye, a humble spirit, and a lowly soul, 'eat in this world and inherit the world to come'. As a way of life, Judaism stresses that our eating habits, that is our physical and material pursuits on earth, should be elevated and hallowed to such a degree that we should be worthy to inherit the world to come and so perpetuate the Abrahamic covenant for all times.

This is borne out by the proof text from Prov. 8:21, 'That I may cause those that love Me to inherit substance'. This verse refers to Abraham, who alone is considered the friend of God; compare Is. 41:8, 'The seed of Abraham who loves Me'. God's love is all-embracing. Judaism is not confined to a number of theological abstractions; all who live a good, clean and honourable life are loved by God and qualify to enjoy the title 'Disciples of Abraham'.

Balaam. The heathen prophet Balaam is here contrasted with Abraham. At first glance we question the propriety of this contrast, but on closer scrutiny we realise that the Mishnah deliberately juxtaposes these two men to point out that whilst both were world-renowned we respect the one for his idealism and become his disciples, whereas we shun the other for being an opportunist. Abraham shattered the idols of sorcery, magic and divination and converted the heathen to the pure faith of the One God; Balaam led people to believe in superstition. Abraham was consistent, truthful and humble; Balaam was haughty, arrogant, erratic and unpredictable. At one period Balaam readily accepted a commission from Balak the King of Moab to curse Israel, but inexplicably changed the curse to a blessing. It is little wonder that thinkers and writers have been baffled by the enigmatic personality of Balaam.

For a true appraisal of the character of Balaam as well as of the heathen prophets, we quote the Midrash: See the difference between the Prophets of

Israel and the Prophets of the gentiles. The Israelite Prophets warned the people against transgressions, as it is said, 'Son of man, I have made you a watchman' (Ez. 3:17), but the Prophet who rose from the peoples, Balaam, initiated licentiousness to destroy his fellow-men from the world. Not only that, but the Prophets of Israel were moved with compassion for their own people and also for the gentiles; as Jeremiah said, 'My heart does sound for Moab like pipes' (48:36), and Ezekiel was told, 'Take up a lamentation for Tyre' (27:2). This cruel one (Balaam) on the other hand, aimed at uprooting an entire nation (Israel) without cause. For this reason, the section about Balaam is included in the Scriptures to inform us why the Holy One blessed be He removed the holy spirit from the heathen peoples since this one arose among them and He saw what he did (Nu. R. 20:1).

It would appear from the above Midrash that the prohecy among the gentiles which God graciously bestowed upon them, actually ceased on account of Balaam.

The proof text (Ps. 55:24) cited by the Mishnah seems to confirm the evil character imputed to Balaam for it brands him, by implication, a murderer and a deceiver, 'men of blood and deceit'. Balaam was directly responsible for the death of twenty four thousand Israelites (Nu. 25:9). Furthermore, the Talmud (Sanh. 105b) asks what is the meaning of the verse, 'Faithful are the wounds of a friend, but the kisses of an enemy are importunate' (Prov. 27:6). This implies that the curse uttered by Ahijah the Shilonite against Israel was better than the blessing offered to them by the wicked Balaam'.

These and other uncomplimentary remarks about Balaam raise a pertinent question. It is true that Balaam uttered a very sublime and spiritual pronouncement, 'How goodly are your tents, O Jacob, your dwelling places, O Israel' (Nu. 24:5). *Ma Tovu*, at the head of our Prayer Book, takes pride of place over other beautiful and meaningful verses. Initially it is more than difficult to understand why this verse, attributed to Balaam the wicked one, should be recited and sung to a variety of melodies at so many independent services in the Synagogue. Indeed, the outstanding Halakhist of the sixteenth century, R. Solomon Luria, the Maharshal, wrote in his Responsa (number 16), 'I begin with the second verse and omit *Ma Tovu* which was composed by Balaam and was intended as a curse'. The Jewish world did not follow the Maharshal and retained *Ma Tovu* to teach us that a blessing can be wrung out of a curse, a phenomenon which has manifested itself often in Jewish history; in our age we have extracted from the curse of the Holocaust, the blessing of the State of Israel. However, it should be noted that the author of our Mishnah does not differentiate between Abraham and Balaam, but more specifically between the disciples of Abraham and the disciples of Balaam. The Maharshal adopts the principle that the story of Balaam as recorded in the Torah has a telling message, that we should not trust the sweet and honeyed words of a Balaam, and there it should rest. We are not to become disciples of Balaam by perpetuating his name in our Siddur, nor should we emblazon *Ma Tovu* on the curtain of the Ark in the Synagogue. Whilst the vox populi have won the day and *Ma Tovu* enjoys the approbation of the majority of Jews, the Maharshal and those who subscribe to his view may be correct, and perhaps we should play down the continued popularity of *Ma Tovu* and rely only on the story in the Torah.

In contrast to the sentiments expressed by the Maharshal, a spirited defence for the retention of the *Ma Tovu* at the head of the Siddur is upheld by R. Tsevi Hirsh Ferber in his 'Siah Tsevi', a commentary on the Siddur. R. Ferber elicits the support of the Talmud (B.B.14b). The reference to Balaam is seemingly superfluous, as this portion is a section of the 'Book of Moses' (The Pentateuch). However, the talmudic statement wishes to convey the thought that Moses wrote the whole of the Pentateuch including the portion of Balaam, who was not directly responsible for *Ma Tovu.* Balaam mouthed *Ma Tovu,* but did not write it. Consequently, no objection can be raised to the honoured position it enjoys at the beginning of the Siddur. On the contrary, *Ma Tovu* is a part of *Torat Moshe* and owes its origin to Divine Providence.

Indeed, this thought has scriptural authority. On his own admission Balaam contends that he is merely a tool in the hands of the Almighty and can give utterance only to the words which God places in his mouth. 'And Balaam said unto Balak, 'Behold I am come unto you; have I now any power at all to speak anything? The word that God puts into my mouth, that shall I speak' (Nu. 22:38). Thus we see that there is good reason for the continued popularity of the *Ma Tovu* in the Siddur and above the Ark in the Synagogue. The striking language and the beautiful spiritual and moral idealism underlying the *Ma Tovu* were the creation of Moses our Teacher.

Hasidic Lore

Humility. 'To walk in true humility is the first duty of every hasid. It is said in Avot 5:22, A good eye, an humble mind and a lowly spirit are the tokens of the disciples of our father Abraham'. R. Joshua ben Levi set humility above all else as the surest means of guarding against the evil tongue. The Law abides only with the meek. 'Be not, like the ceiling, out of reach, but like the threshold that is trodden upon by everyone without stirring'. If offended, seek not satisfaction but bear with offence in silent humility. Our Ancients said, 'If all the world proclaims you a *zaddik*, think of yourself as one of the wicked' (Nid. 30b). Thus, says the Zohar, 'Whoever thinks of himself as of small account in this world will be one of the great in the world to come'. R. Elimelekh of Lizensk said, 'The top of the ladder leading to perfection is humility. He who has it, has everything else'.

R. Aaron of Starasola was once asked, 'How can man attain humility?' Said he, 'By the fulfilment of the commandments', and added a parable. A tree rich in fruit is dragged to earth by its fruits and its branches hang downward. But a branch that is barren and withered stands upright, without bending.

'Humility', said the Besht, 'leads to love of man and love of God, for the truly humble in heart does not feel it a hardship to love one of the wicked, for in all his wickedness he is better than I am'.

It is told of R. Meir of Premislan that a hasid once came to him, boasting in his pride of being on the way to the Holy Land. The Rabbi chided him, saying, 'What, impudence of face, will you take precedence of the Messiah?' And thus he plucked the root of haughtiness out of his heart.

Balaam Said the Pulnoer: Balaam showered praises upon Israel, while the Prophets rained reproofs upon them. Who was the better friend? The ultimate intention of each gives the answer. Balaam intended to persuade the Israelites that they had already attained perfection and need not improve themselves. Had they accepted his counsel, they would have deteriorated and become like other nations. The Prophets, however, intended to spur Israel into attaining a state of higher purity and goodness. They, therefore, rebuked them for minor sins and did not hesitate to exaggerate their shortcomings.

(כג) יְהוּדָה בֶּן תֵּימָא אוֹמֵר הֱוֵי עַז כַּנָּמֵר וְקַל כַּנֶּשֶׁר רָץ כַּצְּבִי וְגִבּוֹר כָּאֲרִי לַעֲשׂוֹת רְצוֹן אָבִיךָ שֶׁבַּשָּׁמַיִם. הוּא הָיָה אוֹמֵר עַז פָּנִים לְגֵיהִנֹּם וּבוֹשֶׁת פָּנִים לְגַן עֵדֶן: יְהִי רָצוֹן מִלְּפָנֶיךָ יְהֹוָה אֱלֹהֵינוּ וֵאלֹהֵי אֲבוֹתֵינוּ שֶׁיִּבָּנֶה בֵּית הַמִּקְדָּשׁ בִּמְהֵרָה בְיָמֵינוּ וְתֵן חֶלְקֵנוּ בְּתוֹרָתֶךָ:

Mishnah Twenty Three

Judah Ben Tema says: 'Be bold as the leopard, swift as the eagle, fleet as the gazelle, and strong as the lion, to do the will of your Father who is in Heaven'. He used to say, 'The bold-faced is for Gehinnom and the shame-faced for the Garden of Eden. May it be Thy will, O Lord our God, to rebuild Thy city speedily in our days and grant our portion in Thy Torah.

Judah Ben Tema. This is the only reference to Judah Ben Tema in the Mishnah, but we meet him several times in the Baraita. The exact period in which he lived is uncertain (Ha. 14a). He is included among the 'Masters of the Mishnah', of whom there were six or seven hundred.

This Mishnah introduces us to the animal kingdom. The Bible is one of the oldest sources we possess which delineates some of the habits and characteristics of the animal world. The Talmud abounds with proverbial sayings, parables, anecdotes, and practical observations of the life of the animal world in nature. But all the observations were inspired by one thought, that the dumb creature owes its existence to God, and we must therefore show kindness and considerateness to the animal.

In ancient Egypt and Assyria, as well as amongst the Greeks and Romans, a few selected animals were deified whilst the remainder were totally ignored. Judaism, with its introduction of monotheism and prohibition of idolatry, gave the animal world a new humane charter. The animal was to serve man, but it also possessed rights which had to be respected. The gladiatorial fights in the Roman arenas were a favourite entertainment, but such animal sport was not the prerogative of the ancient world. Blood sports are popular even today in many countries. We witness bull fights, cock fights and hunting with the hounds which, in England, is patronised by royalty and the aristocracy. Judaism denounces all forms of blood sports. Indeed, one of the specific reasons underlying the function of Shehitah is the avoidance of pain to the animal. This the Rabbis have called *tsar baalei hayim* which, literally paraphrased, means 'pain to owners of life'. As the human being is an owner of property or possessions, so the animal too is an owner of life, In short, we are not to treat animals cruelly, but mercifully, for they too are creatures of God.

Kindness to animals is emphasised in the Pentateuch ; 'You shall not muzzle the ox when it threshes the corn' (Deut. 25:4). 'You shall not plough with an ox and ass together' (Deut. 22.10). In the Talmud the story is told of R. Judah Hanasi that a calf was being taken to the slaughterer, when it broke away and hid its head in terror under the Rabbi's cloak. The Rabbi said, 'Go, for this you were created'. At that moment a heavenly voice cried out, 'Since he has no pity, let us bring suffering upon him', and the Rabbi accepted his ill-fortune for thirteen years. One day the housemaid was sweeping the floors of the Rabbi's home and on seeing a litter of new born kittens, attempted to sweep them away. The Rabbi said, 'Leave them, for it is written, 'His tender mercies are over all His works' (Ps. 145:9). Thereupon the voice from heaven declared, 'Since he is compassionate, let us be compassionate towards him' (B.M.85a).

According to Cecil Roth, until the nineteenth century cruelty to animals was nowhere illegal except in Jewish Law. These undeniable facts underline the message of our Mishnah. It should be noted that of the four animals mentioned by Judah Ben Tema, three are predatory animals and have cruel and rapacious tendencies, yet we are told to emulate the audacity of the leopard, the untiring energy of the eagle, and the bravery of the lion, and thereby perform the will of God.

Be bold as a leopard. By nature the leopard is unabashed, but daring and bold. Man, too, should be unashamed but bold to do the bidding of God. The Prophet Jeremiah asks, 'Can the Ethiopian change his skin or the leopard his spots, then may you also do good, that you are accustomed to do evil' (13:23). The spots of the leopard symbolise the evil impulse which clings to man naturally, but should be subdued. Some think that the expression 'bold as a leopard' points to the pursuit of the study of Torah. If a student does not comprehend an exposition, he should be bold and daring and have the courage to ask for clarification. 'If a leopard, a creature of no intelligence, uses all his daring to seize his prey to get food, how much more should man, a creature of intelligence, use all his daring to acquire life for his soul in the world to come' (Aknin).

Swift as an eagle. The eagle is considered to be the mightiest of all birds, the king of the skies. It builds its nest in the highest parts of the loftiest rocks. It flies higher than any other bird and with its large eyes and keen sight it can see from the heights above the whole landscape below and in this manner it swiftly falls upon its prey. 'The image of the eagle is to teach us that even as the eagle soars higher and higher but swoops down, so should scholars act. Though they be brilliant, they should not be conceited in the presence of their teachers, but listen humbly so that they may learn from them' (Aknin).

Another characteristic of the eagle is that it flies with its young on its back, and this serves a dual purpose. The eagle teaches its young to fly at a tender age, but it also shows gentleness and concern for its young by protecting it from the arrows of missiles. Compare Deut. 32:11, 'As an eagle that stirs up her nest hovers over her young, spreads abroad her wings, takes them, bears them on her pinions'. Here we have a striking simile. The eagle carries its young above its wings so that no harm befall it. It is questionable whether we carry our young with such care and devotion! In the education of their young, parents should carry their children with them to the highest possible rung of the spiritual ladder connecting heaven and earth.

Fleet as a gazelle. Of the four animals mentioned in this Mishnah, only the gazelle is kasher. It runs faster than any other animal on account of the slenderness of its legs, compare II Sam. 2:18, 'And Asahel was as light on foot as one of the gazelles that are in the field'. It is also known as the roe (or roebuck.) The gazelle is symbolic of grace and beauty, see Cant. 2:9, 'My beloved is like a gazelle or a young hart'.

In the midrashic comment on this verse, the gazelle leaps from place to place and from fence to fence and from tree to tree, so God jumps and leaps from Synagogue to Synagogue to bless the Children of Israel (Nu.R. 11:2). A further interesting reference to this animal is found in a comment on a different verse in Cant. 8:14, 'Be thou like a gazelle'. The Rabbis add, 'As the gazelle, when it sleeps, has one eye open and one eye closed, so when Israel fulfils the will of God He looks on them with two eyes, but when they do not fulfil the will of God He looks on them with one eye'. This animal is not only beautiful to look at with its delicate legs and sturdy body; its meat, too, is very tasty and was served at the tables of King Solomon (I K.

5:3).The grace and beauty of the gazelle has passed into the Hebrew vocabulary where the word *tsevi*, beautiful, is widely used in the Bible when referring to the products of the soil of Israel, Jerusalem and the Temple. *Tsevi* is also a very popular Hebrew name, the feminine of which is Tsivia or Tsvia (Cant. 4:5)

R. Jonah interprets the expression 'fleet as a gazelle' in this manner, 'Let men hasten like the gazelle and not grow weary. In general when people run they get tired, but if they run in order to carry out a commandment, they will not tire'.

Strong as a lion. As the eagle is the king of the birds, so the lion is the king of the beasts. The lion is often mentioned in the Bible and Talmud. His popularity is gauged by the fact that he is referred to by a number of names: *Aryeh* is a lion of adult age (Gen. 49:7); *Kefir*, is a young lion (Jud. 14:5), *Shahal*, a fierce lion (Job 4:10); *Lavee*, a huge, old lion (Job 4:11); *Shahatz*, a lion advanced in age (Job 28:8); *Laish*, an old but weak lion (Is. 30:6) and *Gur*, a cub (Gen. 49:7).

The lion possesses a number of features which make it conspicuous. The head and neck are covered with a thick, long and shaggy mane, considered by some as a crown. His great strength, thunderous roar and majestic appearance, inspire his enemies with dread. The lion will devour when he is hungry but he is not naturally cruel. He will aid weaker animals and procure food for them, and is known to spare human beings. He will not chase his prey, but will wait patiently and time his attack.

As the lion triumphs over his enemies, so will Judah. 'Not in the fighting and in the thick of the fray does Judah's greatness lie ..... even when he is quietly resting, he remains a lion' (S.R. Hirsch). In this strain, Hirsch translates the verse (Gen. 49:9). 'A young old lion is Judah; above plunder, my son, are you risen; he kneels down, he rests like a lion, and who would rouse him up to an excited lion?' The pride of Judah was powerful — from this tribe kings were raised. The image of the lion has left a deep imprint on Jewish life. In spite of the prohibition to make graven images (Deut. 4:16), we find that on either side of the steps of Solomon's Temple thirteen lions were carved out. Moreover, the Lion of Judah is with us today in almost every Synagogue. It is embroidered on the *parokhet*, the curtain of the Ark, and on the mantle covering the Scroll of the Law; it is engraved on the silver ornaments hanging on the Scroll and is also carved on the reading desk.

This Mishnah has probably been responsible to some extent in popularising the Lion of Judah.

The lessons of our Mishnah are summarised by Meiri as follows: With all your might and all your powers, strive to serve your Creator; in those matters where strength is needed a man should be strong as a leopard; where promptness is needed, he should be swift as the eagle; where a stout heart and courage are required, let him be brave as the lion and fleet as the gazelle to do the will of his Father in Heaven.

Finally, our Mishnah has received the approbation of R. Joseph Karo who has incorporated it with his introduction in the first chapter of his *Shulhan Arukh*, which is a digest of Jewish Law and is used as a text book on Judaism. He explains, 'Bold as a leopard' signifies that a person should not feel ashamed because people scoff at his religiosity. 'Light as an eagle' corresponds to the sight, for even beholding of evil can trigger off sin; for instance, the eye sees, the heart covets and the limbs of the body conclude the act. 'Fleet as a gazelle' refers to the feet, which should always run to do good. 'Mighty as a lion' is directed to the heart, for the service of God demands the heart; stregthen your heart to serve Him and prevail over the evil impulse as a mighty man prevails over his assailant by overcoming him and casting him to the ground.

Your Father who is in Heaven. This oft-repeated expression is characteristically Jewish and frequently used (Gen. 49:19; Ex. 4:22; Deut. 32:6; II Sam. 5:44; Ps. 89:27; Is. 63:16, 64:8 and Mal. 2:10). In the Mishnah we read, 'Who is purifying you? Your Father who is in Heaven' (Yoma 8:8). Again in So. 9:15, 'On whom have we to lean? On our Father who is in Heaven'. This expression is also frequently found in the Siddur.

The bold-faced. The expression *az panim*, fierceness of countenance, betokens a harshness of character which shows no consideration to young or old, compare Deut. 28:50 and Ec. 8:1. In modern vernacular it is the nearest equivalent to *hutzpah*. In our daily prayers we petition God that we be delivered from insolence or impudence and from arrogant people (Ber. 16b).

This Mishnaic statement is intended to counteract the previous section of the Mishnah where we are taught that in our relationship with God we should be bold and active to perform His will. However, in our relationship with our fellow-man we should avoid impudence, which drags one to Gehinnom. Rather should we elevate ourselves and aspire to the heights of

Gan Eden by being shame-faced, timid and reticent. It is one of the distinguishing signs of the seed of Abraham that they are bashful merciful and benevolent (Yev. 79a).

ARN sums up this section of the Mishnah as follows: If you have done your fellow a slight wrong, it shall be a serious matter in your eyes; but if you have done your fellow much good, it shall be a trifle in your eyes. If your fellow has done you a slight favour, consider it to be a great thing in your eyes, but if your fellow has done you a great evil, let it be a small matter in your eyes.

May it be Thy will O Lord our God. This familiar prayer which concludes every Amidah in the Prayer Book suggests that originally Pirkei Avot ended here with this appropriate entreaty. Indeed, the text of Pirkei Avot in the Mahzor Vitry does conclude here. It would seem that the passages following this Mishnah were added by different authors, and not by R. Judah Ha-Nasi who edited the Mishnah.

Hasidic Lore

Animals. The Koretzer said, 'It is preferable to eat sparingly, thereby a man tends to lengthen his life. We find among animals and reptiles that those which eat the least, live the longest'.

Once R. David went to Lublin with his disciple R. Yitzhak in order to spend the New Year with his teacher the Seer, as he did year after year. On New Year's Day, before the blowing of the ram's horn, the Seer looked around and noticed that R. David was not there. Yitzhak immediately ran to the inn to look for him. He found R. David standing in front of the gate to the house, holding out his cap full of barley to the horses which their driver, in his hurry to get to the House of Prayer, had left behind unfed. When R. David, having finished feeding the horses, came to the House of Prayer, the Seer said, 'That was a fine blowing of the ram's horn R. David treated us to'.

One Friday afternoon R. David was on a journey when suddenly the horse stopped and refused to go on. The driver beat the horse, but the zaddik objected. 'Rabbi,' cried the driver, 'The sun will soon be setting and the Sabbath is almost here'. 'You are quite right' answered R. David, 'but what you have to do is to make the animal understand you, otherwise it will some day summon you to court in Heaven, and that will not be to your honour'.

The bold-faced and the shame-faced. Our Sages say, 'The bold-faced go to hell, the shame-faced to paradise'. R. Sussya, expounded these words as follows, 'Whoever is bold in his holiness, may descend to hell in order to raise what is base. He may roam about in alleys and market-places and need not fear evil. But he who is shame-faced, who lacks boldness, must keep to the heights of paradise, to studying and praying. He must beware of coming in contact with evil'.

(כד) הוּא הָיָה אוֹמֵר בֶּן חָמֵשׁ שָׁנִים לַמִּקְרָא. בֶּן עֶשֶׂר שָׁנִים לַמִּשְׁנָה. בֶּן שְׁלֹשׁ עֶשְׂרֵה לַמִּצְוֹת. בֶּן חֲמֵשׁ עֶשְׂרֵה לַגְּמָרָא. בֶּן שְׁמוֹנֶה עֶשְׂרֵה לַחוּפָּה. בֶּן עֶשְׂרִים לִרְדּוֹף. בֶּן שְׁלֹשִׁים לַכֹּחַ. בֶּן אַרְבָּעִים לַבִּינָה. בֶּן חֲמִשִּׁים לָעֵצָה. בֶּן שִׁשִּׁים לְזִקְנָה. בֶּן שִׁבְעִים לְשֵׂיבָה. בֶּן שְׁמוֹנִים לִגְבוּרָה. בֶּן תִּשְׁעִים לָשׁוּחַ. בֶּן מֵאָה כְּאִלּוּ מֵת וְעָבַר וּבָטֵל מִן הָעוֹלָם:

Mishnah Twenty Four.

He used to say: Five is the age for Scripture, ten for Mishnah, thirteen for Commandments, fifteen for Talmud, eighteen for marriage, twenty for pursuing, thirty for strength, forty for understanding, fifty for counsel, sixty for old age, seventy for a hoary head, eighty for (special) strength, ninety a bent (figure), a hundred, as though he were dead, passed away and faded from the world.

This Mishnah demonstrates two primary concepts:

1. The Jewish attitude towards age.
2. The Jewish attitude towards education.

1. The Jewish attitude towards age is reflected in the word *ben*, a son or a child which prefaces each of the fourteen stages in life. When a child attains its first birthday, we say he is a year old. Surely the word 'old' is incongruous in this context. In Hebrew we express age by the use of the word *ben*, for example, a male child is circumcised at the age of eight days, in Hebrew *Ben shemonat yamim* (Gen. 17:12). We shall take this discussion a step further. We call the owner of a house a *baal habayit*, and a craftsman a *baal melakhah*. However, a *ben Torah* is one who is well versed in Torah scholarship; *a ben bayit* is one who frequents one's home. Why

should we employ *baal* in one instance and *ben* in the other? Ownership of a home and the possession of a craft both belong to the world of materialism.

Baal, too, has overtones of idolatrous worship. Indeed, undue emphasis on the material things of life can lead to idolatry. There are occasions when our ownership, *baalut*, is temporarily suspended. On every Shabbat and Yom Tov we do not handle money; we neither add to nor subtract from our wealth. Once every seventh year and during every Jubilee Year the earth enjoys a respite and we renounce all ownership of land. However, the title of *ben* is never renounced. We are always Bnei Yisrael, Children of Israel. We honour our parents in life and death. Whenever we are called to the Reading of the Law we are named, for example, Yaacov ben Avraham. There is no generation gap; 'ben' links father and son together and we retain this sonship even after the parent has passed away.

The word *ben* signifies humaneness, whereas *baal* denotes a harsh and demanding character. *Ben* reminds us of the family — tenderness, kindness and consideration; *baal* refers to the individual and may denote selfishness. Torah is the spiritual possession of all, rich and poor, young and old; we therefore speak of a *ben Torah*, He who loves and lives for the Torah is a child of God and should love and live for his parents. Again, a *ben bayit* is not a stranger; he is treated as a member of the family. Indeed, he is loved and respected and earns the name of *ben*. He owns nothing belonging to the house, but gives friendship, loyalty and service. Similarly, the *ben Torah* is characterised, not by ownership, but by achievement and scholarship.

Moreover, the *ben* is a child of God, 'You are children *(banim)* of the Lord your God (Deut. 14:1). A home can be sold, a vocation can be changed, but God never disowns a human being who is always a loving child in His sight, this also obtains in the family. A son or daughter who is already married and has children, is still called a child by the aged parent. We all owe allegiance to our Father in Heaven who cares for us. In His service we are eternally young. Even at an advanced age we are referred to as *ben;* such is the optimism of Judaism.

Finally, we shall discuss briefly the Jewish attitude to old age. In antiquity some nations ignored the old and decrepit, and even exposed them to an ignoble death. Our opproach is clearly enunciated in the Pentateuch; 'You shall rise up before the hoary head and honour the face of the old man' (Lev. 19:32). The Rabbis add that he who welcomes an old man is as if he welcomed the *Shekhinah* (Gen. R. 63:6).

R. Judah said, 'Be careful to honour an old man who has forgotten his learning involuntarily, for both the second Tables and the fragments (of the first) were placed in the Ark' (Ber. 8b). When R. Meir saw even an old *am haaretz*, illiterate man, he would rise up for, he said, 'It is not for nothing that his days are prolonged' (Y. Bik. III).

2. The Jewish attitude towards education.

Jewish education is a vital and significant adjunct of Jewish life. There are numerous passages in Bible and Talmud exalting Jewish education. The author of our Mishnah introduces education as a 'design for living'. Here we have a tabulated chart which includes every stage in life. As the mariner sails the high seas with the aid of a compass, so a loyal Jew will travel on the road of life with the compass of the Torah which will guide him through the stormy seas of life. The Mishnah warns us not to drift aimlessly, but to plan intelligently and methodically a Jewish programme based on a sound Jewish education.

The business or professional man will introduce order and careful planning into his financial transactions or professional duties, but will often ignore his spiritual responsibilities. Judah Ben Tema reminds us that a full Jewish life must be founded on a Torah prescription as outlined briefly here and which affects us during every period throughout life; a pre-arranged order is mapped out for us. Judaism is well ordered from morning to night, week to week, month to month and year to year. The religious Jew is governed by the Prayer Book, the *Siddur*, which means order. Every Sabbath he reads the *Sidrah*, order for the week. Halakhically, he is guided by the *Shass*, which stands for *shisha sedarim*, the six orders of the Talmud. In the home, the most meaningful meal of the year designed for young and old, is the Seder (order) on Pesah night.

The ordering of a religious life is measured in different ways. Some belong to a *Hevra Tehillim* and love to chant Psalms to the adoration and praise of God. Others are attached to a *Hevra Mishnayot* and regularly study the Mishnah. Another section consists of members of a *Hevra Shass* or *Gemara* and undertakes to pursue an intensive study of a page of the Talmud each day, known as *daf yomi*. The common denominator underlying and linking the different types of faithful Jews is a consistent regular ordering of the mind, whether it be for the purpose of reciting Psalms, studying of Mishnah and Gemara, or any branch of Torah ideology.

It is noteworthy that we draw a line of demarcation between the reading of prayer and the study of Torah. One school of thought maintains that prayer should not be ordered or fixed, but should proceed spontaneously from the heart, compare 2:18, 'Do not regard prayer as a fixed mechanical task'. Study of Torah, however, is in a different category. We are encouraged to train our minds to enjoy fixed and methodical sessions devoted to the study of the Torah. Indeed, we have to give an account of this in the world to come. Thus, one of the questions facing every Jew in the Hereafter is, 'Did you fix times for learning Torah?' (Shab. 31a).

This is the burden of the Mishnah — to introduce order into our lives through education. Every day must have its programme and be counted. 'So teach us to number our days that we may get a heart of wisdom' (Ps. 90:12). The Jewish calendar is well ordered and is divided into months and years. Each month, as each year, brings its own challenges and opportunities to which we should respond with orderly minds. We normally translate *Rosh Hodesh* and *Rosh Hashanah* as New Month and New Year. More correctly, however, *Rosh Hodesh* means the Head of the Month, and Rosh Hashanah is the Head of the Year. With each month and year we enrich our minds intellectually, culturally and spiritually, with Torah ideology. We would do well to heed the words of our Mishnah, which are also reflected in the advice offered by Isaiah to King Hezekiah, 'Set your house in order' (38:1).

Five for Scripture. Authorities differ as to the age at which a child should commence to learn Torah. According to some, a child should learn the letters and vowels at the age of three. This is based on the Tanhuma on Lev. 19:23-4. Regarding the prohibition of the eating of the fruit of a tree in the first three years, the Midrash says, 'This is also the case with the child. In the first three years the child is unable to speak and is therefore exempted from every religious duty. However, in the fourth year, all the fruits shall be holy to praise the Lord, and the father is obliged to initiate the child in religious works'.

On the other hand, under the system introduced by Joshua Ben Gamla, the school age began at six. This is corroborated by the Talmud, 'Under the age of six we do not receive a child as a pupil; from six upwards, accept him and stuff him (with Torah) like an ox' (B.B.21a). The reference in our Mishnah to five years would obviously apply to the parents, upon whom devolved the responsibility of teaching the child at home. This is in accordance with the injunction in Deut. 6:7 which is part of the Shema, 'And you shall teach them diligently to your children'. The first teacher of the infant was the parent, who prepared the child before he was enrolled into the school.

Mikra. This word is derived from *kara*, to read, from the Bible; see Neh. 8:8. The Karaites took their name from *kara* because they believed in the Written Law, the Bible, but did not accept the Oral Law, the Talmud. *Mikra* also means convocation (Ex. 12:6).This was a holy gathering where the reading of the Law took place in the Synagogue.

Ten for Mishnah. From the study of the Bible to the study of the Mishnah there is a lapse of five years. This may be based upon a talmudic maxim which suggests that if a student sees no tangible result after a period of five years, he will not be succesful. We therefore allot to the student the full period of five years to prepare himself for the next stage in his education .

The word Mishnah is derived from a root meaning to repeat; compare *sheni*, second. Learning, in ancient times, involved memorising and continually repeating the text, 'The teacher must continue to repeat the lesson until the pupil has learnt it' (Er. 54b). We are also informed that 'He who repeats a lesson one hundred times is not like one who repeats it one hundred and one times' (Ha. 9b).

The Mishnah, the Oral Law, is a collection and codification of subjects based on the Written Law. The groundwork of the Mishnah was prepared by R. Akiva, but the final redaction was prepared by R. Judah Ha-Nasi. The Mishnah is divided into six orders covering every facet of Jewish life and they are designated as follows:
First order. *Zeraim*, Seeds, dealing with laws of agriculture.
Second order. *Moed*, Seasons, discussing laws on Sabbaths and Festivals.
Third order. *Nashim*, Women, laws on marriage and divorce.
Fourth order. *Nezikin*, Damages, civil and criminal law.
Fifth order. *Kadashim*, Holy Things, on the Sacrifices in the Temple.
Sixth order. *Taharot*, Purifications, on the distinction between clean and unclean.

Thirteen for mitzvot. The boy becomes a son of Commandment, *Bar Mitzvah*, at the age of thirteen when he matures to manhood, the age of puberty. One doctor has testified that 'At puberty there is often an intense period of religious fervour' (Chesser). That the age of thirteen was designated as an important period of religious awakening in the boy is attested to by Rashi on Gen. 25:27. 'As long as they (Esau and Jacob) were young, they could not be distinguished by what they did ..... but when they reached the age of thirteen one proceeded to the House of Learning and the other to the idolatrous temples'.

ARN attaches much importance to the age of thirteen and suggests that the good impulse, the *yetzer tov*, begins to influence the lad at this age. There is a dubious reference to Bar Mitzvah according to some in Soferim (18:5). In the thirteenth century the Rosh (R. Asher Ben Yehiel 1250-1328) was asked, 'Whence is it inferred that a boy at the age of thirteen is responsible for his actions and subject to punishment for his misdeeds?' He replied that this is *Halakhah l'Moshe MiSinai*, a law handed down orally to Moses at Mount Sinai (Teshuvot Harash 16). It is generally conceded that though the idea of Bar Mitzvah was known in early days, the ceremonial ritual and festivities which obtain today were not practised before the fourteenth century.

Fifteen for Talmud. The word Talmud basically means learning; some texts read in place of Talmud, *Gemara*, the Aramaic for Talmud. Gemara means completion and is a collection of the discussions and debates on the Mishnah. The word Talmud was later the title given to the Mishnah plus the Gemara and is found in two versions the Jerusalem and Babylonian Talmud.

Eighteen for marriage. Some cite Lev. 21:13, 'And he shall take a wife in her virginity'. The first word of this verse, *vehu*, has the numerical value of eighteen. Rashi remarks that the word *adam*, man, is found eighteen times in Gen. 1-2 prior to the words, 'She shall be called woman because she was taken out of man' Others refer to Deut. 24:5 where we read, 'When a man takes a new wife, he shall not go out to the army ..... he shall be free one year and he shall cheer his wife whom he has taken'. If he is to be ready to enlist for military service at the age of twenty (Nu. 1:3) he would be obliged to marry when he is eighteen years of age.

Twenty for pursuing. This is interpreted differently by a number of commentators. It can refer to military service as we have indicated, but many prefer to argue that *lirdof*, to pursue, suggests looking for and attaining a livelihood, which was always an arduous task. Some think that the word pursue might well point to the performance of mitzvot, good deeds and the continuation of the study of Talmud.

Thirty for strength. Some cite Nu. 4:47, 'From thirty years old and upward, every one that entered in to do the work of service and the work of bearing burdens in the Tent of Meeting'. The Levites commenced their heavy task of carrying the mobile Ark at the age of thirty when one's strength is at its highest peak. The Meiri remarks that a man has his full physical strength at the age of thirty and he should be particularly careful not to dissipate it, but to reserve it for the service of God.

Forty for understanding. The Talmud (A.Z.5b) cites the verse from Deut. 29:3, 'But the Lord has not given you a heart to know and eyes to see and ears to hear unto this day. And I have led you forty years in the wilderness'. Rava says, 'From this you can learn that it may take one forty years to know the mind of one's master'.

Fifty for advice. See Nu. 8:25. 'From the age of fifty years they (the Levites) shall return from the service of the work and shall serve no more but shall minister with their brethren'. From this verse we learn that the Levites retired from active work at the age of fifty and ministered to the needs of their brethren. Ministering is taken to mean counselling. The Meiri expresses a similar interpretation. 'Proper counsel depends on two things; first the man's natural intelligence, second the experience he has gained in the course of time .... by the time a man has reached his fiftieth year he has had many experiences, and at that age he is in full strength of his intelligence; that is, his thinking faculties have not begun to decline and his counsel then is tested on both scores.

Sixty for old age. Discussing ages from sixty to eighty, the Talmud (M.K. 28a) observes, 'If one dies at sixty, that is by the hand of heaven. What is the text for this? 'You shall come to your grave in ripe age' (Job. 5:26) and the numerical value of the word for 'in ripe age', *vekhelah*, yields sixty.

At seventy it is the death of the hoary head. At eighty it is the death of a vigorous old man, for it is written, 'The days of our years are three score and ten, or even by reason of strength, four score years' (Ps. 90:10) As the

Rabbis include in the same passage the statement that death between the ages of fifty and sixty is death by *karet*, that one is cut off in early life because of one's sins, the age of sixty which is beyond *karet* is referred to here as old age. Others understand *ziknah*, old age, as referring to *hakhmah*, wisdom, relying on the talmudic maxim in the name of R. Jose the Galilean who said, '*Zaken* means he who has acquired wisdom', reading *zaken* as an abbreviation (each letter representing a Hebrew word) — *zeh kanah (hakhmah)*, this one has acquired wisdom (Kid. 32b).

Ninety, a bent (figure). Some take the word *shuah* to mean 'bend, bow down'. Others connect the word with the noun *shuhah*, a pit or grave, compare Prov. 22:14, 'A deep pit'.

A hundred. The Soncino Talmud quotes the Vilna Gaon who cites Is. 65:20, 'There shall be no more thence an infant of days, nor an old man, that has not filled his days; for the youngest shall die a hundred years old'. The Gaon points out that the context there deduces that this is intended as a blessing. Thus the extreme limit up to which life is a blessing is a hundred years, and one who exceeds that limit is as one who no more belongs to the world.

Hasidic Lore

The age of man. The Dinover said: When men of impiety are being urged to change their ways and become God-fearing, many protest that the place where they reside makes it difficult for them to perform religious duties. Others declare that their wives are opposed to their pursuance of piety since it entails additional labour and stands in the path of many pleasures. Still others affirm that the age in which they live makes it arduous to be loyal servants of the Lord. It is to these three groups that our Sages addressed their teaching, 'How should you return unto God? In your place, with your wife, and in your AGE'. Every penitent meets with obstacles, hindrances and difficulties. It is the duty of the sincere Jew to overcome them, even as others have succeeded in doing.

(כה) בֶּן בַּג בַּג אוֹמֵר הֲפָךְ בָּהּ וַהֲפָךְ בָּהּ דְּכֹלָּא בָהּ וּבָהּ תֶּחֱזֵי וְסִיב וּבְלֵה בָהּ
וּמִנָּהּ לָא תָזוּעַ שֶׁאֵין לְךָ מִדָּה טוֹבָה הֵימֶנָּה:

Mishnah Twenty Five.

Ben Bag Bag says: Turn it and turn it for everything is in it, and look in it and grow grey and old in it and stir not from it, for there is no better rule for you than it.

Ben Bag Bag. The full name is Johanan Ben Bag Bag; he is mentioned in Kid. 10b. He was proselytised by Hillel the Elder and became a teacher in Israel. To understand the origin of his name we go to the Talmud Shab, 31a. There we learn that a heathen who was repulsed by Shammai came to Hillel and asked that he be proselytised on condition that he was taught only the Written Law and not the Oral Law. On the first day Hillel taught him Aleph, Bet, Gimmel and Dalet. The following day he reversed the letters and taught him Dalet, Gimmel, Bet and Aleph. The heathen protested, 'But yesterday you did not teach them to me thus'. 'Must you then not rely upon me? Then rely upon me with respect to the Oral Torah too' said Hillel. From this cryptic statement we learn that Hillel wished to impress upon the heathen that the Written Law and the Oral Law both enjoy equal status and both are rooted in Jewish tradition.

The letters in their alphabetical order represent the Written Law, and the letters transposed to form words represent the Oral Law. The Written Law by itself is incomplete and cannot be fully comprehended without the addition of the Oral Law. Hillel made it patently clear that he would accept the heathen as a proselyte only if he agreed to embrace both the Written and the Oral Law. The heathen was impressed with the argument and consented to follow the whole Torah, both the letters and the words. The new proselyte became known as Bet Gimmel, the first two hard letters of the alphabet. The story in the Talmud is immortalised by the name Bag Bag, who eventually became a true disciple of Hillel. Indeed, he it was who faithfully followed the dictum of his teacher to turn it (the alphabet of the Torah) and turn it again. Whether the letters Aleph, Bet, Gimmel and Dalet are in their usual order or reversed, we must continually turn the words and draw inspiration from them.

Some explain the name Ben Bag Bag as being the *notarikan* or abbrevation of the following words: Ben Ger, Ben Gioret — the son of a proselyte father and the son of a proselyte mother.

The Midrash Shmuel brings a tradition in the name of the Rashbam that the original names of Ben Bag Bag and Ben He He of the following Mishnah were withheld because of the *malshinim*, the slanderers, who would report their teachers to the Roman authorities and so, to avoid any dangerous repercussions, they concealed their original identities.

For everything is in it. Those who are ignorant of the Hebrew genius and its influence on modern thought consider Judaism to be primitive, obsolete, and out of touch with modern scientific thinking. It is therefore interesting to retrace our steps and to examine the Torah and see what it contains. The Tanakh does not claim to be a text book of science; this is not its function. However, it is amazing to discover how much of modern thought owes its origin to our Torah.

The observant Jew is very conscious of natural science and beauty. This is evident from the large variety of Blessings he recites in gratitude to God. There are different Blessings for vegetables, fruits, drinks and animal foods. We also have Blessings for pleasures enjoyed through the sense of smell and sight such as the smelling of fragrant woods, barks or spices, odorous plants and fruit. We also recite Blessings on seeing a tree blossoming the first time in the year, falling stars, lofty mountains or great deserts. Special Blessings and prayers are recited at the appearance of new moon each month and once every twenty-eight years on the sanctification of the sun. These Blessings and many others ordained by the Rabbis compel the Jew to be familiar with, and to differentiate between, a variety of plants and seasonal foods, and also to comprehend the courses of the heavenly hosts which bring him in touch with the variegated forms of nature.

The authentic Jew is not ignorant of general science; 'Your cattle you shall not let gender with a diverse kind' (Lev. 19:19). This law imposes on the Jew a study of biology and genetics. 'Your field shall you not sow with mingled seeds' (ibid). This requires expert knowledge of sowing so that each kind of seed has sufficient space below the ground to receive its nourishment separately. This necessitates knowledge of the science of botany. The Talmud Berakhot contains much useful information on a wide variety of trees, plants and flowers. The talmudic Sages were thoroughly conversant with many aspects of agricultural life.

The Jewish dietary laws demand a familiarity with biology and anatomy. Accurate biological knowledge was essential to recognise, for example, which birds have the requisite signs of kashrut and which animals and fish were permitted for Jewish consumption. This demanded a thorough comprehension of the different species of animals, including the various diseases which would render them *trefah*, unfit to be eaten. Thus the shohet, who slaughters the animal, must be cognisant of medical and veterinary science including bacteriology and anatomy.

In the field of preventive medicine, including infection and isolation, we can trace the laws of purification as dealt with in Lev. 12-15.
There is no doubt that the survival of the Jew to this day is, to a large extent, due to the unique and remarkable sanitary code of the Torah which laid down strict rules for frequent washing of the body and clothing and especially regulations for a clean water supply, which is one of the major discoveries of modern science. The Torah also provides explicit instructions regarding the disposal of sewage, thus avoiding typhoid fever, dysentery and other diseases. The Talmud asserts, that, within Jerusalem, rubbish heaps and dung hills should not be permitted, and the Valley of Hinnom was used as a public incinerator which helped to prevent infection (B.K. 82b). One writer (Wendle Short) remarks that these regulations put to shame many a town and village in England. The Italian expert in tropical medicine writes, 'No one can fail to be impressed by the careful hygienic precautions of the Mosaic period. The extremely stringent quarantine rules very likely did a great deal of good' (Castellani). Another scholar (Garrison) in his standard work on the History of Medicine quotes Neuberger as saying, 'The chief glory of biblical medicine lies in the institution of social hygiene as a science'.

The Jewish calendar is a remarkable feat of astronomical detail. To ascertain the commencement and termination of each Sabbath and Festival and estimate the *Molad*, the conjunction of the moon each month requires mathematical and geometrical understanding.

Hillel II (middle of 4th century) was responsible for fixing the dates of the Jewish calendar as we have it today. However, Saadiah Gaon (892-942) is considered to be the father and founder of the science of the calendar. The importance of our calendar is reflected in the words of a renowned non-Jewish scholar (Scaliger) who wrote, 'There is nothing more perfect than the calendar of the Jewish year'.

To comply with the laws on the Sabbath forbidding the carrying of burdens from the private premises to the public thoroughfare, the Jew must be familiar with town and country planning.

This is not the place to enlarge on the spiritual, moral and ethical foundations enshrined in the Sabbath, but as we commenced this section with a note on nature we shall conclude with a brief reference to the wonders of nature as they impinge on the Sabbath. Both the beginning and the end of the Sabbath are phenomena of natural beauty. The Sabbath commences prior to the setting of the sun. Great artists have portrayed the sunset on canvas, but this cannot be compared with the magnificence of a natural sunset. The termination of the Sabbath is also resplendent in glory with the appearance of three stars in the firmament. Thus the Sabbath is surrounded with surpassing beauty; we usher in, and bid farewell to, the Sabbath with sentiments of wonder, awe and glorification.

Finally, the vast Responsa Literature grapples and deals comprehensively with a large and varied number of modern problems such as artificial insemination, euthanasia, space travel, etc., all grounded in rabbinical literature. Nothing has escaped the penetrating minds of our Sages. We have touched only on the periphery of Jewish Law, but sufficient has been said to warrant the proud assertion of this Mishnah that 'everything is in it,' (the Torah). Indeed, there is nothing new under the sun.

Look. Normally, 'to look' is expressed by the word *raah* or *hibit*, here we have the root *hazah*, to see with vision; compare *hazon Yeshayahu*, the vision of Isaiah (Is. 1:1). In the Amidah we pray three times a day, *vetehezenah eineinu*, 'and may our eyes behold in mercy Thy return to Zion.' Our ancestors did not look into the future return to Zion with cold logic; they looked with prophetic vision and insight; they dreamt, yearned and prayed passionately; all this is expressed by the word *hazah*, Similarly we look at the Torah, not with ordinary sight, but with the vision of the seer. Consequently our hearts are stirred and our minds are quickened and we are inspired with the eternal truths we behold in the Torah.

Stir not from it. The words of the Torah are our constant companions; we must not veer away from them to the right or to the left. Compare Jos. 1:8, 'This Book of the Law shall not depart out of your mouth, but you shall meditate therein day and night'. A similar thought is expressed in the beautiful prayer *ahavat olam* immediately before the

Shema in Maariv, 'For they are our life and the length of our days and we will meditate on them day and night'.

Hasidic Lore

Perfection of Torah. The Koretzer said: We learn that the Torah is higher than all other sciences from the fact that he who is learned in Torah finds it easy to understand any other science; but he who has learned other sciences finds it difficult to understand Torah.

The Yud said: We read in the Selihot prayers, 'And nothing but this Torah was left us'. But since the Torah has been left to us, we have everything, for from the Torah we should be able to regain our former state of holiness.

(כו) בֶּן הֵא הֵא אוֹמֵר לְפוּם צַעֲרָא אַגְרָא:

Mishnah Twenty Six

Ben He He says: According to the suffering is the reward.

The concluding Mishnah follows the same pattern as the previous one. Indeed, in some editions they both constitute one Mishnah.

Ben He He. This name is also traced to the same source as that of the author of the previous Mishnah (Shab. 31a). The Talmud informs us that a heathen presented himself before Hillel and asked that he be converted on condition that he was taught the Torah whilst standing on one foot. Hillel accepted the challenge and crowned it with the dictum, 'What is hateful to you, do not to your fellow man; this is the whole Torah, the rest is explanation, go, learn it!'

It is possible to reconstruct this story and discover a clue to the unusual name of He He. The heathen , who later became a proselyte and a disciple of Hillel, demanded that he stand on one foot, that is on his five toes, while he concentrated on the advice offered by Hillel which was summarised in five Aramaic words — *dealakh senei lehavrakh lo saavid*, what is hateful to you do not to your fellow man. The latter half of Hillel's advice also consisted of five words — *veidakh perusha he zil gemor*, the rest is explanation, go and learn it.

In this story the number five plays an important role, and because of this the heathen became known as He He which is numerically equivalent to five and also represents the Five Books of Moses. The Hebrew letter He is also recognised to be the Name of God, and by his conversion the heathen accepted the yoke of *Hashem*, the Name of God. We should also note that the concluding word of Hillel's famous pronouncement is *gemor*, identical with *Gemara*, Talmud, which is the completion of the Written Law. In both instances (Mishnah 25-26) Hillel stresses the fundamental principle that one can understand the Written Law only in the light of the Oral Law. Here Hillel seems to remind the new proselyte that whilst he may repeat the five-worded maxim standing on one foot, he must walk with two feet and complete the task by immersing himself in the *Yam Hatalmud*, the sea of the Talmud, where he will study and endeavour to absorb the unfathomable depths of the Gemara.

To return to the name He He and the significance of the letter *He* in Hebrew, we know that the original names of the first Patriarch and Matriarch were Abram and Sarai (Gen. 17:5, 15). The change in the names is explained in an interesting passage: Rav Huna said in the name of Rav Aha, 'The *yod* (equal to ten) which the Holy One blessed be He removed from the name of Sarai which later became Sarah the first Mother of Israel, He divided into two halves; the one *he*, (five) He gave to Abram, who thus became Abraham, and the second *he* (five) he gave to Sarai to form her new name, Sarah' (Y. Sanh. 1, 20c; Lev. R. 19:2).

From this statement we see that there is a direct link between the letter *he* and the process of proselytising, for Abraham and Sarah were intensely active in proselytising the heathen. Commenting on, 'The souls they (Abraham and Sarah) had gotten made in Haran' (Gen. 12:5), Rashi remarks, 'The souls which he had brought beneath the sheltering wings of the Shekhinah, Abraham converted the men and Sarah converted the women, and Scripture accounts it unto them as if they had made them'.

We also have an explicit reference to Ben He He in Tosafot on Ha. 9b where we read that Bar (Ben) He He was a proselyte, and a son of Abraham and Sarah; incidentally, the name Bag of the previous Mishnah is also equivalent to the number five.

As the Talmud (Shab. 31a) records three separate incidents of Hillel and his success with converts, we are prompted to inquire whether there were any special circumstances in the life of Hillel which attracted him to the welfare of proselytes. Indeed, this is so. We are familiar with the account recorded in the Talmud how Hillel, in his passionate desire to hear the words of Torah from his teachers Shemaiah and Avtalion, climbed on to the roof of the Bet Hamidrash and was completely covered with a layer of three cubits of snow. Were it not for the prompt action of Shemaiah and Avtalion who revived the frozen Hillel with oil and warmth, he might have died (Yoma 38b). Hillel was deeply indebted to his masters; they saved him and rescued him from death, but they also taught him much and were partly responsible for the building of his character. However, the overriding factor which must have influenced Hillel throughout his life was that Shemaiah and Avtalion were themselves proselytes and were descended from Sennaherib (Git. 57b). Notwithstanding their heathen origin, they rose to the highest pinnacle of Jewish scholarship and are mentioned as one of the 'pairs' in the chain of Jewish tradition (1:10).

It is possible that the kindness and consideration shown to Hillel by his teachers, the proselytes, left a deep imprint on his mind and he felt that he would show his appreciation to his masters by being particularly attentive to any would-be proselytes who approached him. Perhaps Hillel imagined that he might be responsible for producing another Shemaiah or Avtalion. This deep-seated appreciation which Hillel nurtured in his heart toward his teachers might also have affected Judah Ha-Nasi, the editor of Pirkei Avot, for he was the sixth direct descendant of Hillel, and he, too, was indebted to the proselytes Shemaiah and Avtalion. What better and more fitting conclusion to the five chapters of Pirkei Avot than the two sayings recorded by Ben Bag Bag and Ben He He, both proselytised by Hillel. In this manner Judah Ha-Nasi honoured both Shemaiah and Avtalion as well as Hillel, an appropriate climax to the Mishnah and a literary and spiritual monument to their collective memory.

According to the suffering is the reward. This may well refer to the proselytes Schemaiah and Avtalion themselves. To uproot one's heritage and adopt an entirely new mode of life by embracing a despised and persecuted faith was a revolutionary step which would have entailed much anguish and suffering. In addition to overthrowing their former behavioural pattern, the two proselytes had to undergo a very intensive course of study of Jewish Law and custom. Initially, this must have been a painful and traumatic experience, but their painstaking labours led to their reward when they eventually became recognised and respected teachers in Israel.

In general terms, too, the truth of this proverbial saying manifests itself in life from birth to death. The pangs of childbirth which the mother suffers melt away the moment she holds her infant in her arms. This is her reward. So it is in every area of life; pain is often followed by reward. In school or university, in the profession or business, the result will be proportionate to the pain expended. 'They who sow in tears will reap in joy' (Ps. 126:5). Nothing of permanent value has been won without sustained effort and pain. The Hafetz Hayyim, commenting on the verse, 'Also unto Thee, O Lord, belongs mercy, for Thou dost render to every man according to his work'. (Ps. 62:13) asks a pertinent question, if God pays a man only according to his work, where is His mercy? However, the key word is 'work'. Human beings pay for the end product; they are not concerned with the labour of the craftsman. God, in His mercy, rewards a man according to his efforts irrespective of the finished product; if we are to reap the reward of a vibrant Jewish faith, we must experience painful sacrifices at every level in life.

Before we leave this chapter, there is one brief comment we would add and this refers to the language of the last two passages which are couched in Aramaic, which was the popular language of the masses; it was also the language of Babylonia, from which Hillel descended. Two other sayings of Hillel are presented in Aramaic, 1:13 and 2:7.

Hasidic Lore

According to the suffering is the reward. R. Bunam said: One who devotes himself to the study of the Torah but neglects the service of the Lord, is like a book-case containing learned tomes. The book-case stands by itself and the books stand by themselves, entirely without connection. A zealous reader is required, and this demands sacrifice.

Concluding Mishnah. Text, translation and commentary, see p. 71.

PEREK SIX

Introductory Mishnah. Text, translation and commentary on p. 11.

פרק ששי

(א) **שָׁנוּ** חֲכָמִים בִּלְשׁוֹן הַמִּשְׁנָה בָּרוּךְ שֶׁבָּחַר בָּהֶם וּבְמִשְׁנָתָם. רַבִּי מֵאִיר אוֹמֵר כָּל הָעוֹסֵק בַּתּוֹרָה לִשְׁמָהּ זוֹכֶה לִדְבָרִים הַרְבֵּה וְלֹא עוֹד אֶלָּא שֶׁכָּל הָעוֹלָם כֻּלּוֹ כְּדַאי הוּא לוֹ. נִקְרָא רֵעַ אָהוּב אוֹהֵב אֶת הַמָּקוֹם אוֹהֵב אֶת הַבְּרִיּוֹת וּמַלְבַּשְׁתּוֹ עֲנָוָה וְיִרְאָה וּמַכְשַׁרְתּוֹ לִהְיוֹת צַדִּיק חָסִיד יָשָׁר וְנֶאֱמָן וּמְרַחַקְתּוֹ מִן הַחֵטְא וּמְקָרַבְתּוֹ לִידֵי זְכוּת וְנֶהֱנִין מִמֶּנּוּ עֵצָה וְתוּשִׁיָּה בִּינָה וּגְבוּרָה. שֶׁנֶּאֱמַר לִי עֵצָה וְתוּשִׁיָּה אֲנִי בִינָה לִי גְבוּרָה וְנוֹתֶנֶת לוֹ מַלְכוּת וּמֶמְשָׁלָה וְחִקּוּר דִּין וּמְגַלִּין לוֹ רָזֵי תוֹרָה וְנַעֲשֶׂה כְּמַעְיָן הַמִּתְגַּבֵּר וּכְנָהָר שֶׁאֵינוֹ פּוֹסֵק וְהֹוֶה צָנוּעַ וְאֶרֶךְ רוּחַ וּמוֹחֵל עַל עֶלְבּוֹנוֹ וּמְגַדַּלְתּוֹ וּמְרוֹמַמְתּוֹ עַל כָּל הַמַּעֲשִׂים:

Baraita One

The Sages have taught in the style of the Mishnah: Blessed be he who chose them and their Mishnah.

R. Meir says: Every one who is occupied with the Torah for its own sake merits many things; and not only so, but the whole world is indebted to him. He is called friend, beloved, one who loves the All-Present, a lover of mankind and it clothes him with humility and fear and fits him to be righteous, pious, upright and faithful; it also keeps him far from sin and brings him near to virtue; through him (men) enjoy counsel and sound knowledge; understanding and strength as it is said: Counsel is mine and sound knowledge; I am understanding; I have strength (Prov. 8:14); and it gives him sovereignty and dominion and discerning judgment; to him the secrets of the Torah are revealed; he is made like a never failing fountain and like a river that flows on with ever sustained vigour, and he becomes modest, long-suffering and forgiving of insult, and it makes him great and exalts him above all things.

As we have stated above, Pirkei Avot originally closed with chapter five. Traditionally, a chapter was read every Shabbat Afternoon commencing on the first Shabbat after Pesah. As there are six Sabbaths between Pesah and Shavuot a sixth chapter, appropriately called Kinyan Torah, the acquisition of the Torah because it exalted and glorified Torah above all things, was added and read on the Shabbat before Shavuot which commemorates *Matan Torah*, the giving of the Torah on Mount Sinai. This chapter is also known as Perek R. Meir, the chapter of R. Meir; or alternatively Baraita de R. Meir, the external teaching of R. Meir, because the opening statement is attributed to the name of R. Meir.

The Sages have taught... This introductory paragraph implies that the first five chapters are a section of the Mishnah edited by R. Judah Ha-Nasi. This chapter is strictly outside the purview of the Mishnah. It is a Baraita, an external teaching; none the less it is written in the language and idiom of the Mishnah and contains the traditions and opinions of authorities on the Mishnah not specifically embodied in the Mishnah of R. Judah Ha-Nasi. There is thus an affinity between this annexed chapter and the previous one. Another possible connection between chapters five and six is the fact that the last two passages in chapter five are recorded in the name of proselytes, and the first statement in chapter six commences with the name of R. Meir who, it was presumed, was also a proselyte and could trace his descent to Nero, the Roman Emperor, who according to Jewish legend became an all-embracing convert to Judaism (Git. 56a).

Blessed be he... Here tribute is paid to the authors and their teachings. Because they practised what they preached they were able to influence others. When an author is meticulously honest with himself, he is chosen by God. This interpretation would favour the translation offered by some that the words 'blessed be he' refer to God.

Rabbi Meir, see 4:12.

Lishmah. This word literally means for its own sake or name. At the outset we should differentiate between *lishmah* and *lishmo*, which means for his own sake, and constitutes a selfish attitude. *Lishmah* is a word which plays a prominent role in rabbinic literature. In this context it means that the study of Torah should be pure and unadulterated by mixed motives. Such study of Torah can produce good and lasting results. It is indeed a high and noble ideal and the Rabbis were tolerant to realise that it was difficult to attain. This can be detected from a prayer offered up by a Rabbi, 'May it be Thy will to bring peace... among those students who are occupied with the study of Torah, both who do it for its own sake and those who do not do it for its own sake, and that these latter may ultimately come to occupy themselves with it for its own sake' (Ber. 17a). The reward promised to him who does occupy himself with the study of Torah for its own sake is explicitly mentioned in our Baraita, 'He merits many things'. Because of his undivided devotion to the study of Torah he even enjoys the reward of many mitzvot which do not apply to him and which he cannot possibly perform.

Some interpret 'many things' in a different vein. The Torah-true scholar will be introduced to many subjects far removed from his immediate scope. This accounts for the fact that outstanding Rabbis have been intensely interested in a variety of subjects outside their own field, such as astronomy, mathematics, medicine and philosophy. A mind richly endowed with Torah will respond to new vistas of knowledge. This, in turn, explains why the world is indebted to the genuine Torah scholar whose vast erudition and mature experience single him out to speak with authority on a number of diverse subjects. Moreover, the performance of a mitzvah is not only good in itself; it also nurtures and sustains the world.

He merits. The influence of Torah study for its own sake is so far-reaching that the Torah becomes the personal possession of the individual. This observation is strikingly made by the Rabbis in their interpretation of Ps. 1:2, 'But his delight is in the law of the Lord; and in His law does he meditate day and night'. Rava said that one should always study that part of the Torah which is his heart's desire, as it is said, 'But whose desire is in the law of the Lord'. Rava also said, 'At the beginning of this verse the Torah is assigned to the Holy One blessed be He, but at the end it is assigned to him who studies it, for it is said, 'Whose desire is in the law of the Lord and in his own law does he meditate day and night' (A.Z. 19b).

The whole world is indebted to him. Commenting on Ec. 12;13, 'The end of the matter, all having been heard, fear God and keep His commandments, for this is the whole of man', the Talmud asks, 'What means - this is the whole of man?' R. Eliezer answered, 'The Holy One blessed be He said, 'The whole universe was only created for his sake'. Abba Bar Kahana said, 'Such a man is equal in worth to the whole world'. R.

Simeon Ben Azzai said, 'The whole world has only been created to be subservient to him' (Ber. 6b).

Friend, rea. Compare Ps. 139:17. 'How precious are your thoughts (friends) to me, O God'. The righteous scholars who are steeped in Torah are friends of God. A similar thought is expressed by the Rabbis in their interpretation of the verse, 'This is the book of the generations of Adam' (Gen. 5:1). God showed Adam every coming generation with its expositors, every generation with its sages, every generation with its leaders. When he reached the generation of R. Akiva, he rejoiced at his teaching but was grieved about his death and said, 'How precious are your thoughts (friends) unto me, O God' (A.Z. 5a).

Beloved. Compare Prov. 8:17, 'I love them that love me'. We are also reminded of the beautiful expression which is incorporated in the prayer addressed to the bride and groom in the Seven Blessings, *Reim haahuvim*, the beloved companions. Friendship must not be motivated. The true friend is he who displays a goodly measure of loyalty and love reminiscent of the love between husband and wife.'Friendship is one heart in two bodies' (Zabara).

One who loves the All-Present, a lover of mankind. Judaism cannot envisage one without the other; they are interdependent. 'You shall love your neighbour as yourself' is immediately followed and qualified by, 'I am the Lord' (Lev. 19:18). If the love for man is divorced from the love for God, or vice versa, we do justice neither to man nor to God. Abraham, the friend of God, prayed for the sinful men of Sodom, whom he loved. On the other hand, dictators generally detest God and any who criticise their policy; for example, godless Russia today proscribes all religious education and stifles all opposition with dire punishment.

Clothes him with humility and fear. Compare Prov. 22:4, 'The reward of humility is the fear of the Lord'. It is interesting to note that both in this Baraita and in the above verse humility precedes the fear of God. Humility is the pre-requisite of fear of God; without humility there can be no true reverence for God. This may explain the function of the word 'clothe'. We naturally cover our bodies with garments; similarly should we clothe ourselves with humility which should be the very foundation stone of our character-building. Religion without humility produces harmful results.

Fits him to be righteous. The Hebrew word *makhsharto*, fits him, reminds us of the regulations in Jewish Law whereby a treifah vessel can lose its impurities by being scoured or rinsed in boiling hot water or undergoing a process of burning. This kashering of vessels can apply to man metaphorically. The impurities which cling to a person can be removed through kashering by immersing himself in the waters of the Torah, which is a 'fiery law' (Deut. 33:2). In this manner, man cleanses and purifies himself to prepare and adjust him for a life of righteousness and piety. One who successfully passes through the crucible of fire of Jewish Law and Custom is qualified to earn the title of a *zaddik*, (righteous) *hasid*, (pious) *yashar* (upright) and *neeman* (faithful).

Some understand the word *yashar* to be an adjective qualifying *hasid* and explain that *hasid yashar* is to be differentiated from *hasid shoteh*, a foolish hasid. The Rabbis explain that a foolish pietist is one who looks on whilst a woman is drowning because he is afraid to touch a strange female (Sot. 21b). The Torah Jew is an upright hasid who will render assistance and rescue a person in all circumstances.

Keeps him far from sin and brings him near to virtue. The word *zekhut* which we translate as virtue is preceded by *yedei* and literally means 'the hands of zekhut'. We welcome the Torah student by holding out both hands; in this manner we become a near relative to Torah.

Counsel, Compare Is. 28:20, 'Wonderful is His counsel and great His wisdom' and Solomon says: Where there is no wise guidance people must fail: but salvation is through the multitude of counsellors (Prov. 11:14).

Tushiyah. This word is usually translated, 'sound wisdom' which represents the Torah. The Talmud (Sanh. 26b) discusses this word and offers a variety of interpretations such as, 'The Torah is called *Tushiyah* because it weakens, *mateshet*, the strength of man through constant and intense study'. Another interpretation suggests that the Torah was given to Moses in secret (bahashai) because of Satan who opposed the deliverance of the Law on Mount Sinai.

In reply to one Sage who said that anxiety adversely affects one's learning, Rabbah said that if scholars study Torah for its own sake, anxiety has no adverse effects and he cites Prov. 19:21, 'There are many thoughts in man's heart, but the counsel of the Lord, that shall stand'.

Understanding. Understanding is to be applied to all the mitzvot which should be explored in depth as to their meaning and interpretation.

Gevurah. *Gevurah*, might, is to be directed against the evil impulse which one must master with spiritual strength. The proof text is in Prov. 8:14. All the qualities mentioned in this verse proceed from God; we should therefore accept His advice, wisdom, understanding and power, without question. As God's messengers on earth it behoves us to pass on these divine qualities from which the entire world will benefit.

Sovereignty and dominion and discerning judgment. The Torah scholar is compared to a king. As a monarch reigns over his dominion, so the scholar should reign over and master his learning. Compare, 'By me (Torah)kings reign and princes decree justice' (Prov. 8:15).

The secrets of the Torah. This heading includes a number of themes in Torah, especially the account of the creation in Genesis, the chariot theme in Ezekiel and the *Sefer Yezirah*, the Book of Creation (Vitry). Compare also Ps. 119:18, 'Open my eyes that I may behold wondrous things out of Thy Law' and Ps. 25:14, 'The secret of the Lord is with them that fear Him and His covenant to make them know it' and 'He has revealed His secrets to His servants and Prophets' (Amos 3:7).

A never-failing fountain. Compare note on 2:10. See also Prov. 5:16, 'Let your springs be dispersed abroad and courses of water in the streets'.

Modesty. Though he is famed for his knowledge of Torah, the scholar remains humble for he is clothed with humility. Torah studies which are permeated with modesty will not be forgotten says the Talmud (Y. Berakhot 5:1) and Rashi on (Ex. 34:3) quotes the Tanhuma to the effect that the first Commandments were broken because they were given amidst a fanfare of trumpets but the second endured because they were received in modesty.

Long-suffering. Compare Prov. 19:11. 'It is the discretion of a man to be slow to anger'. Learning should restrain a man from becoming angry. See also Prov. 14:29. 'He who is slow to anger is of great understanding, but he who is hasty of spirit exalts folly'. Some distinguish between *erekh apayim* and *erekh ruah*; the former is slow to anger, but eventually he displays his wrath; the latter is of a higher calibre as he controls his anger and will not allow himself to be provoked.

Forgiving of insult. Compare the talmudic dictum, 'Those who are insulted but do not insult, hear themselves reviled without answering, act through love and rejoice in suffering, of them Scripture says, 'But they who love Him are as the sun when he goes forth in his might' (Jud. 5:31), (Shab. 88b). It should be noted that the Baraita goes beyond the Talmuḍ, for in addition to not replying to the insult cast at him, the student of Torah also forgives the person who insulted him.

Makes him great and exalts him. The *piel* participle *megadel*, making great, does not connote bigness. Compare the growth of a tree, which has roots deep down in the earth and these roots nourish the tree, similarly the true Torah scholar is sustained by the roots of Jewish tradition which help him to grow sturdy and strong. In this manner he becomes exalted in stature and progresses spiritually ethically and morally.

We can also interpret the word to mean that man is the crown of creation; he is above all things. As the Psalmist says, 'Thou hast made him to have dominion over the works of Thy hands, Thou hast put all things under his feet' (8:7). The pre-eminence of man, who is great and exalted, manifests itself in every age. It is even possible for him to change the course of nature. Joshua issued the command, 'Sun stand still upon Gibeon and thou, moon, in the valley of Aijalon' (10:12), and Elijah and Elisha resuscitated the dead (IK. 17:21, II K.4:34).

In tractate Taanit we learn how Honi Hamaagal and Nakdimon Ben Gurion brought down rain (19a, 20a). The potentialities for good inherent in man are inexhaustible. The Baraita concludes with the healthy advice that man and nation should combine greatness with exaltation. When we harness our inventiveness and ingenuity to benefit mankind, we achieve greatness and exaltation; but when we employ, for example, atomic and nuclear energy to destroy whole continents, we aim for domination which is neither great nor exalting.

Hasidic Lore

As Perek Six is entitled 'Acquisition of Torah', we devote the first extract of Hasidic Lore to the subject

'How we should learn'. The disciples of R. Barukh asked him, 'How can a man ever learn the Talmud adequately? For there we find that Abbaye said one thing and Rava another. It is just as if Abbaye were of one world and Rava of quite another. How is it possible to understand and learn both at the same time?'.

The zaddik replied, 'He who wants to understand Abbaye's words must link his soul to the soul of Abbaye; then he will learn the true meaning of the words as Abbaye himself utters them. And after that, if he wants to understand Rava's words he must link his soul to the soul of Rava. That is what is meant in the Talmud (Sanh. 90b) where we read, that if a halakhah is said in any person's name in this world, his lips speak in the grave, as it is written: Moving gently the lips of those that are asleep to speak (Cant. 7:10).

Love for fellow-man. R. Schmelke's pupil, Moshe Leib Sassover, sat at the bedside of sick boys of his city, nursing and tending them. Once he said, 'He who cannot suck the matter from the boils of a child sick with the plague, has not yet gone half way up the height of love for his fellow-men.

Forgiving of insults. R. Moshe Sassover said, 'To hear yourself insulted and not make reply, is worthier than self-chastisement'.

(ב) אָמַר רַבִּי יְהוֹשֻׁעַ בֶּן לֵוִי בְּכָל יוֹם וָיוֹם בַּת קוֹל יוֹצֵאת מֵהַר חוֹרֵב וּמַכְרֶזֶת וְאוֹמֶרֶת אוֹי לָהֶם לַבְּרִיּוֹת מֵעֶלְבּוֹנָהּ שֶׁל תּוֹרָה שֶׁכָּל מִי שֶׁאֵינוֹ עוֹסֵק בַּתּוֹרָה נִקְרָא נָזוּף שֶׁנֶּאֱמַר נֶזֶם זָהָב בְּאַף חֲזִיר אִשָּׁה יָפָה וְסָרַת טָעַם. וְאוֹמֵר וְהַלֻּחֹת מַעֲשֵׂה אֱלֹהִים הֵמָּה וְהַמִּכְתָּב מִכְתַּב אֱלֹהִים הוּא חָרוּת עַל הַלֻּחֹת. אַל תִּקְרָא חָרוּת אֶלָּא חֵרוּת שֶׁאֵין לְךָ בֶּן חוֹרִין אֶלָּא מִי שֶׁעוֹסֵק בְּתַלְמוּד תּוֹרָה וְכָל מִי שֶׁעוֹסֵק בְּתַלְמוּד תּוֹרָה הֲרֵי זֶה מִתְעַלֶּה שֶׁנֶּאֱמַר וּמִמַּתָּנָה נַחֲלִיאֵל וּמִנַּחֲלִיאֵל בָּמוֹת:

Baraita Two

R. Joshua the son of Levi said: Every day a Bat Kol goes forth from Mount Horeb and proclaims and says, 'Woe to mankind because of their contempt of the Torah, for whoever occupies himself not with Torah is called reprobate, as it is said, 'As a ring of gold in a swine's snout, so is a fair woman that turns aside from discretion' (Prov. 11:22). And it says (Ex. 32:6) 'And the tables were the work of God and the writing was the writing of God graven upon the tables. Read not *harut*, graven, but *herut*, freedom, for you have no free man but he who occupies himself with the study of the Torah; and whoever occupies himself with the study of the Torah, he is exalted; as it is said, 'And from Mattanah to Nahaliel and from Nahaliel to Bamot' (Nu. 21:19).

R. Joshua the son of Levi was one of the early Palestinian Amoraim who lived in the middle of the third century. He was foremost in Aggadah, but he was also recognised in Halakhah. R. Joshua was known as a miracle worker and was respected for his piety. He was a man of peace and most tolerant towards all people. This is reflected in his belief that immortality was vouchsafed not for Israel alone but for mankind (Gen. R.26). His mystical tendencies are apparent in the legends that have circulated about him, especially the journey he made to Paradise and the detailed report he brought back (Derekh eretz zuta).

Bat Kol. Literally a daughter voice. This is a contracted form of the fuller expression *Bat Kol min Hashamayim* and indicates that it is a heavenly voice expressing the will of God and addressing itself to individuals or nations. Only those who are attuned to hear the celestial message will receive it. With the advent of radio and television, thousands of messages reverberate through the ether, but only those who are tuned in will hear or see the message. Every person possesses a divine spark, for we are all created in the image of God, but only those whose spiritual 'batteries' are charged are able to receive the *bat kol* emanating from Sinai.

Rashi in his commentary on the opening words of the Book of Leviticus hints at the function of the heavenly voice. The first word of the Book, *Vayikra*, is not immediately followed by the Name of God and there is no apparent subject. Who then called Moses? Rashi senses this difficulty and explains that the voice of God went on its way and eventually reached his (Moses') ears. Through repentance and good deeds we should regulate our lives so that the divine voice reaches our ears.

The author of our Baraita deliberately addresses himself to *beriot*, ordinary creatures, in the hope that they, too, can train themselves to receive the *bat kol*. In our biographical details of R. Joshua we remarked on his universalistic tendencies to include the non-Jewish world in the belief of immortality. It is possible that the author advisedly used the word *beriot* to include mankind. If this assumption is correct, the author spreads his net wide and reminds the world not to despise Torah, for its ethical and moral code applies equally well to Jew and non-Jew alike.

The Talmud contains a number of anecdotes in which a *bat kol* was heard and we shall quote one which is pertinent to our Baraita as it refers to the study of Torah. The Talmud (Ta. 21a) relates that Ilfa and R. Johanan were concerned about their poverty and decided to enter the world of business. They then sat down under a ruined wall and, whilst eating, R. Johanan heard one angel saying to the other, 'Let us throw down the wall upon them for they are about to neglect the study of the Torah and to occupy themselves with the life of the moment'. However, the other angel advised, 'Leave them alone, for one of them has a great future before him'.

R. Johanan turned to Ilfa and asked if he had heard anything. When the reply was in the negative, R. Johanan intuitively sensed that he must be the one with a great future before him and consequently decided to return to the study of Torah. By the time Ilfa reached the city, R. Johanan had been appointed as head of the Academy, and the people of the town remarked that had he remained and devoted himself to the study of Torah, he, Ilfa, would have been appointed as head of the Academy. From a discussion on this passage it would appear that Ilfa was intellectually more brilliant than his colleague R. Johanan, but he sacrificed his future in Torah scholarship because he did not hear the heavenly voice and was already preoccupied with more mundane affairs.

The Midrash Shemuel interprets the dictum of the Mishnah in these words, 'As the Torah was given at Mount Horeb, that is Sinai, and it was there that all Israel took an oath to observe the Torah, the mountain registers its disappointment and protests against those who hold the Torah in contempt.'

Nazuf. *Nazuf*, reprobate, is an abbreviation consisting of the letters of the words *nezem zahav b'af (hazir)*, a ring of gold in a swine's snout. The verb *nazaf* means to rebuke, chide, and the participle passive used here, *nazuf*, can mean reprimanded, placed under the ban of excommunication; see Tanhuma Ki Sissa 16.

This verse from Proverbs highlights and contrasts two dissimilar objects which are deliberately juxtaposed to underline the message. In antiquity the nose-ring was a recognised female adornment (Gen. 24:22, Is. 3:21). The swine was not only an unclean animal, but was abhorred by Jews. Many who do not observe the Jewish dietary laws will nevertheless abstain from eating the flesh of pig. In this verse the ring is placed in the swine's snout, whilst the expression 'fair woman' represents Torah. The general tenor of this verse is interpreted by the Rabbis to refer to the student. 'If a person places a golden ornament into the nose of a pig, he will make it filthy with mud and refuse; so is the student of Torah, if he abandons himself to immorality, he defiles the Torah' (Yalkut).

Read not... but... This is a recognised formula of rabbinic interpretation. It is not a mere juggling of letters and certainly not a tampering with Holy Writ. The Rabbis love every word and letter of the Torah and would readily transpose them if a telling message could be deduced therefrom.

Harut and herut. If we examine Ex. 32:16 carefully we shall detect the reason for the change in the vocalization from *harut*, graven, to *herut*, freedom as explained in the following paragraphs. The writing on the tables of the Law was not an ordinary secular script such as we use today.

The tables were the work of God and the writing the writing of God. The writing appeared miraculously and legibly on both sides of the tables of stone. Now let us scrutinise the words *harut* and *herut* according to S.R. Hirsch. The root common to both words may be *hor*, which means a hole, an aperture, which is free, and in our context unhindered by the background of stone. It is possible that this free space subsequently came to mean freedom, free from restriction. We thus see that both translations, graven and free, can be traced to the one word, *herut*. Indeed, there is a close affinity between *harut* and *herut*, not only in the pronunciation, but also in the spiritual concepts we derive from both these words. *Herut*, freedom, reminds us of Pesah, *zeman herutenu*, the time of our freedom. But this is only the commencement of our physical freedom. From Pesah we count forty nine days which lead to Shavuot, *zeman matan Toratenu*, the time of the giving of our Law on Sinai. On Pesah we were released from our physical slavery in Egypt; on Shavuot we received our spiritual freedom from Sinai, which is the foundation of Jewish tradition. Thus Shavuot is the complement of Pesah. The Torah can be engraved on the hearts of all Jews and we can receive spiritual redemption inherent in the Torah only if we release ourselves from the slavish subjection of Egyptianism which rules and masters us in every age. This timeless message is contained in the logical conclusion of the Baraita, 'No man is free but he who labours in the Torah'.

At all levels of life we actively strive and passionately fight for freedom of action and freedom of expression, but too often the hard-won freedom degenerates into license, and we then abuse the very freedom for which we made such superhuman sacrifices. Throughout our history, some Jews have sold their precious heritage for a mess of pottage in order to attain social, political or intellectual preferment, but this new apparent freedom had not saved them from persecution. The Holocaust in Germany had no compassion for half-Jews. The loyal and devoted Jew is spiritually free when he retains his own code of Law, as enshrined in the Torah. To return to Pesah, our ancestors were released from the shackles of slavery, they were freed from a cruel tyranny, they were delivered from degradation and humiliation, but they were still not free until they stood at the foot of Mount Sinai and in unison exclaimed that they accepted the Law; as the Psalmist declares, 'I will walk at liberty, for I have sought Thy precepts' (119:45). Compare, R. Jeremiah said to R. Zeera: Whoever makes himself a slave for the Torah in this world will be free in the world to come (B. M. 85b).

Religion may impose certain restraints on our human liberty, but what we imagine we have lost is actually gained by acquiring a spiritual liberty which teaches us to distinguish between right and wrong, to follow the old tested morality and to shun the so-called new morality which is playing havoc with our modern society. We should opt rather for a spiritual subservience to the higher will of God than debase ourselves by pandering freely to our uncontrolled and selfish desires. This has been summed up in the classical phrase *avdut betokh herut*, which paraphrased means that we should be servile to God, rather than free under the dominion of man.

Whoever occupies himself with the study of Torah exalts himself. The study of Torah must lead to exaltation, and not overweening pride.

The proof text from Nu. 21:19 mentions the names of three encampments of the Israelites in the Wilderness, and these names are homiletically interpreted to refer to three stages in the life of the Jewish people. In the first stage, we recognise the Torah as a gift from God, *Mattanah*. When we treat the Torah, not as a burden, but as a priceless endowment from the Almighty, it eventually becomes our heritage, *Nahaliel*. Moses commanded for us a Law, an inheritance of the congregation of Jacob (Deut. 32:4). When we transmit this heritage faithfully from generation to generation we reach the highest stage, that of spiritual exaltation, *Bamot*, heights.

Hasidic Lore

The Lord is my shepherd. The Radomsker Rabbi said: We read in Cant. 1:4, 'O draw me; we run after Thee'. A shepherd employs either of two methods to draw his sheep to him. He whistles and they come, or he drives them with his staff and they move forward. In the first instance, they follow him; in the second, he follows them. We petition that the Lord shall draw us near unto Him by His voice and we promise to follow after Him, but we do not desire that He should drive us to godliness with the staff of misfortune.

(ג) הַלּוֹמֵד מֵחֲבֵרוֹ פֶּרֶק אֶחָד אוֹ הֲלָכָה אֶחָת אוֹ פָּסוּק אֶחָד אוֹ דִבּוּר אֶחָד אוֹ אֲפִילוּ אוֹת אֶחָת צָרִיךְ לִנְהָג בּוֹ כָּבוֹד. שֶׁכֵּן מָצִינוּ בְּדָוִד מֶלֶךְ יִשְׂרָאֵל שֶׁלֹּא לָמַד מֵאֲחִיתוֹפֶל אֶלָּא שְׁנֵי דְבָרִים בִּלְבָד קְרָאוֹ רַבּוֹ אַלּוּפוֹ וּמְיֻדָּעוֹ שֶׁנֶּאֱמַר וְאַתָּה אֱנוֹשׁ כְּעֶרְכִּי אַלּוּפִי וּמְיֻדָּעִי. וַהֲלֹא דְבָרִים קַל וָחוֹמֶר וּמַה דָּוִד מֶלֶךְ יִשְׂרָאֵל שֶׁלֹּא לָמַד מֵאֲחִיתוֹפֶל אֶלָּא שְׁנֵי דְבָרִים בִּלְבָד קְרָאוֹ רַבּוֹ אַלּוּפוֹ וּמְיֻדָּעוֹ הַלּוֹמֵד מֵחֲבֵרוֹ פֶּרֶק אֶחָד אוֹ הֲלָכָה אֶחָת אוֹ פָּסוּק אֶחָד אוֹ דִבּוּר אֶחָד אוֹ אֲפִילוּ אוֹת אֶחָת עַל אַחַת כַּמָּה וְכַמָּה שֶׁצָּרִיךְ לִנְהָג בּוֹ כָּבוֹד. וְאֵין כָּבוֹד אֶלָּא תוֹרָה שֶׁנֶּאֱמַר כָּבוֹד חֲכָמִים יִנְחָלוּ וּתְמִימִים יִנְחֲלוּ טוֹב. וְאֵין טוֹב אֶלָּא תוֹרָה שֶׁנֶּאֱמַר כִּי לֶקַח טוֹב נָתַתִּי לָכֶם תּוֹרָתִי אַל תַּעֲזֹבוּ:

Baraita Three

He who learns from his fellow one chapter or one law or one verse or one expression or one letter, is obliged to treat him with honour; for so we find with David, King of Israel. He learnt from Ahitophel only two things, yet he called him his master, his companion and his familiar friend, as it is said, 'But it was you, a man mine equal, my companion and my familiar friend' (Ps. 55:14). Now is there not an inference to be drawn from this? If David, King of Israel, who learnt from Ahitophel only two things yet he called him his master, his companion, his familiar friend, all the more must he who learns from his companion one chapter, one law or one verse or one expression or even one letter, treat him with honour? And honour means nothing but Torah, as it is said, 'The wise shall inherit honour (Prov. 3:35) and (ibid. 28:10), 'The perfect shall inherit good' and good is nothing but Torah, as it is said, 'For I give you good doctrine, forsake not My Torah' (ibid. 4:2).

This Baraita deals with two themes, the learning of Torah and the honouring of our fellow man. These have been discussed in previous passages; here we merge the two and extend the honour due to our fellow man even if we learn only a single letter from him.

The emphasis here on honouring our fellow men, because of the little we learn from them, may be an additional qualification to the message of the previous Baraita where we are warned not to insult the Torah, which is a negative approach. Our Baraita complements the previous one and teaches us a positive lesson; not only should we refrain from despising Torah, but we should honour the person from whom we learn even one single letter. In this manner we honour not only our fellow man, but more so the Torah. This lesson can be deduced from the statement of Rav who said, 'He who loves scholars, will have sons who are scholars; he who respects them, will have scholarly sons-in-law. He who reveres scholars will become a scholar himself, and if he is fit for this his words will at least be respected like those of an ordained scholar' (Shab. 23b).

Perek. In talmudic Hebrew this word can mean both chapter and lesson. It is therefore suggested that the actual lessons imparted by Judah Ha-Nasi, the editor of the Mishnah, to his students, were afterwards utilised by him as the bases for the subdivisions of the tractates into chapters.

Halakhah. This word is derived from the root *halakh*, to walk. Compare Gen. 17:1, 'Walk before Me and be whole-hearted'. See also Ps. 119:1, 'Happy are they who are upright in the way, who walk in the Law of the Lord'. Judaism is a way of life and all who traverse this road uprightly are followers of the Jewish way. As there are many laws and customs regulating the life of the Jew, we have divided them into *Halakhah* and *Aggadah*, the legal rabbinic injunctions, and the non-legal; this is an ongoing process. In every age we walk with the Halakhah, and where it is possible, we solve many an intricate problem by probing and adapting the teachings in the ancient Halakhah to serve our needs and requirements in modern times. The Halakhah has been called the 'science of deeds'.

Pasuk. This is derived from the root *pasak*, to divide, and applies to the verses in the Tanakh. According to tradition, the division of verses is traced back to the time of Moses, as we learn from a talmudic discussion between Rav and Samuel. Rav is of the opinion that we must not divide any verse that has not been divided by Moses. Samuel averred that it was permitted to do so. Here the Talmud employs the word *pasak*, to divide, and *pasuka*, the Aramaic of *pasuk*, to refer to a biblical verse (Ta. 27b).

Dibbur. This is an expression relating to Torah which, according to Rashi, is full of scund reasoning. In other words, we are indebted to any person who may utter even one expression which reasonably interprets any teaching of the Torah.

Dibbur can also mean divine speech, revelation. See Cant. R. to 3:4, 'Of the various expressions for prophecy, *dibbur* is the severest'.

Letter. *Ot* is a mark, sign or letter of the alphabet. Initially, one wonders why we should be indebted to a person from whom we have learnt a single letter. However, Hebrew is a rich language and every letter has a purposeful meaning Thus the first letter of the alphabet, *aleph*, is connected with a root meaning 'to learn or teach', compare Prov. 22:25 and Job 25:11.

Most interesting and instructive is the description of the letters of the alphabet by the Rabbis in the Talmud, (Shab. 104a). 'The Rabbis told Joshua ben Levi, 'Children have come to the Bet Hamidrash and made statements the like of which was not said even in the days of Joshua the son of Nun. Thus *aleph bet* means learn wisdom *(aleph binah); gimmel dalet* signifies kindness to the poor *(gemol dallim)*. Why is the foot of the *gimmel* stretched toward the *dalet*? Because it is fitting for the benevolent to pursue the poor...

Shin stands for *sheker*, falsehood; *tav* for *emet*, truth; why are the letters of *sheker, shin, kuph, resh*, close together, whilst those of *emet, aleph, mem, tav*, are far apart? Falsehood is frequent, truth is rare. And why does falsehood stand on one foot, whilst truth has a brick-like foundation? Truth can stand, falsehood cannot stand.'

The above curtailed passage is remarkable and illuminating in more senses than one. The study of the alphabet, which is normally a dull and unattractive subject, is here introduced to the child in an original and interesting manner. It conveys not only the form and meaning of letters of the alphabet, but also the fundamental principles of ethical and moral religion. Moreover, it contains pedagogical exercises for the adult.

A still more fascinating and gripping account of the letters of the alphabet is found in the Midrash where they are challenged by Abraham not to testify against Israel. The *aleph* commenced to testify and Abraham said to her, 'Aleph, you come to witness against Israel in the day of their affliction? Remember the day when God revealed Himself upon Mount Sinai and began with you, 'Anokhi... I am the Lord your God'. Yet no nation or tongue received you except God's children, and have you then decided to give evidence against them? The Aleph immediately stood aside and did not testify against them. Then the *bet* came forward to witness against Israel, and Abraham said to her, 'My daughter, have you come to attest against God's children who diligently keep the five books of the Law, at the beginning of which you are placed, as it is written, 'In the beginning, *Bereshit...?*' Immediately the bet stood aside and did not speak against Israel.

Then the *gimmel* came forward to testify against Israel, and Abraham said to her, '*Gimmel*, have you come to witness against Israel that they have transgressed the Law? Is there any nation in the world that upholds the precept of *Tzizit* at the head of which you are placed, as it is written, 'Fringes, *gedilim*, shall you make for yourselves?' (Deut. 22:12). Forthwith the *gimmel* stood to one side and did not utter a word. When the other letters perceived how Abraham had silenced them, they felt ashamed and refrained from testifying against Israel (Pesikta Lamentations).

Furthermore, the significance of the Hebrew letter manifests itself in the transcription of the text of the Tanakh by the scribes who were meticulously careful not to alter the original Hebrew text. In those cases where it was found necessary to add to or delete from a word in the text, the Masorites draw our attention in the margin to the *Keri* (how the word is read) and *Ketiv* (how the word is written). In many instances the alteration denotes one single letter which changes the meaning of the word. Finally, in the writing of a Sepher Torah we have the beautiful ceremony of filling in the concluding letters in order that other co-religionists apart from the Scribe may participate, to a small extent, in the mitzvah of writing a Scroll of the Law, which devolves upon every Jew. It will be readily seen from the foregoing that every single letter is pregnant with meaningful interpretation.

King David. David was a colourful personality. He began as a shepherd and reached the highest pinnacle in the monarchy of Israel. He was very talented and holds a unique position in the gallery of biblical heroes, for he excelled in composing religious poetry, in musical talent, in statesmanship, military strategy and kingship. David has been referred to as the supreme field-marshal of the biblical period, and modern generals have linked his name with Hannibal, Frederick the Great and Napoleon. David conquered Jerusalem and established the city as the religious and national capital of Israel.

In uniting the kingdoms of Judah and Israel, David displayed his unique qualities of military leadership. There were few rivals to the House of David, which reigned continuously from father to son for four hundred years. David withstood all attempts directed against him. His tolerance and magnanimity were manifested when he spared the life of King Saul who relentlessly pursued him in order to kill him, but when Saul was at his mercy David refused to harm the anointed of the Lord. Indeed, David was motivated by religious zeal. His organisational ability in the field of religion is emphasised in the Book of Chronicles, where we learn that he initiated the Levitical and Priestly courses. However, his religious piety manifests itself fully in the Book of Psalms which he dedicated to the world. The Midrash informs us that Moses gave Israel the Five Books of the Torah and correspondingly David bequeathed to Israel the Five Books of the Psalms. This similarity between Moses and David is illustrated by another passage which portrays God as saying, 'David understands how to pasture sheep, therefore he shall become the shepherd of My flock, Israel' (Midrash Tehillim 78:70, Ex. R. 2:2).

Because the Psalms are human documents and mirror the vicissitudes of life they are prized by mankind, Jew and non-Jew alike. Indeed, the Psalter is not only the basis of our liturgy in the Synagogue, but it also constitutes the greater part of the service in the Church. David's Psalms have given comfort and consolation to millions of people in every age and clime. His love for and devotion to Torah was so great, that he was satisfied with only sixty breaths of sleep (Suk. 26b). Notwithstanding his greatness, he was sufficiently humble to consult his teachers Ira of Jair and Mephiboshet regarding decisions in ritual questions (Ber. 4a). This thought naturally guides us to the lesson of our Baraita, that the king was ready and willing to learn from a commoner, Ahitophel.

Ahitophel. Like Balaam, he was an enigmatic personality. He was endowed with great wisdom, had a penetrating mind, was an astute politician, but possessed a complex character. His insight into the mysteries of the Holy Name and his intimate knowledge of astronomy led him to believe that he was destined to become king of Israel. However, he died by self-strangulation at the early age of thirty three.

He learnt from Ahitophel only two things. The extracanonical treatise (Kallah) refers to the two lessons imparted by Ahitophel to David. The first is based on the principle that it is preferable to study Torah not alone, but together with colleagues. David acknowledges this when he asserts, 'We took sweet counsel together' (Ps. 55:15), with emphasis on the word 'together', thereby learning Torah becomes sweet.

The second teaching emerges from an occasion when Ahitophel met David walking alone to the Bet Hamidrash at a leisurely pace. He asked, 'What are you doing? Is it not written, 'In the multitude of people is the king's glory'? (Prov. 14:28). Thereupon David asked what he should do and Ahitophel replied, 'To the House of God let us walk with eagerness' (Ps. 55:15). The word *beragesh* which is normally translated as 'with the throng', can also mean 'with eagerness or enthusiasm'.

The Yalkut Shemuel (142) offers two different teachings. Dr. Hertz suggests that the two Hebrew words *shenei devarim* should be read as one word, *shenidbarim*; it would then mean that they conversed together.

Kal vahomer. This is one of the norms of biblical interpretation; literally from the light (less important) to the heavy (more important) and vice versa. The argument would then be as follows — if David, King of Israel, learnt only two things from Ahitophel who was not his teacher, and yet he felt beholden to him and called him master, companion, faithful friend, how much more so should we ordinary folk and not of royal blood, show deference and honour to him from whom we have learnt even one letter.

K'erki aluphi. 'Mine equal', literally 'as my valuation'. 'My companion' is the usual translation, but the Baraita understands the word *aluph* to be derived from the root *aleph* meaning 'to learn', and is used as an epithet for teacher or chief, as in Gen. 36:15-21, 29-30.

Honour means nothing but Torah. The Baraita here wishes to underline a significant lesson. *Kavod*, honour, by itself may corrupt a person and degenerate into false pride; this we must avoid. The honour which we receive we reserve not for ourselves, but only for Torah.

To understand aright the intrinsic import of the proof text from Prov. 3:35, we quote it in full: 'The wise shall inherit honour, but as for fools, they carry away shame'. Only the wise, and not the fools, appreciate the fact that all honour due to us belongs to Torah, consequently the wise man is personally unaffected by the honour lavished upon him.

The sequence to this is the second proof text from Prov. 28:10, which again we quote in full. 'Whoever causes the upright to go astray in an evil way, he shall fall himself into his own pit; but the whole-hearted shall inherit good'. The true scholar will not be corrupted by honour, he will inherit 'good'; and 'good' stands for Torah, 'For I give you good doctrine, forsake not My Torah' (ibid. 4:2). *Lekah* is derived from the root *lakah*, to take or receive, and is synonymous with the Torah which we received traditionally from Sinai. Whilst we leave behind us all our wealth and possessions, we take with us the Torah we have learnt.

Hasidic Lore

The sacredness of every letter of the alphabet. The Besht said: If you speak, bear in mind that your power of speech comes from your soul, which is part of God. When you hear, bear in mind that your power of hearing comes from your soul. Thus you will be able to unite your soul with the Shekhinah. Bear also in mind that your profane words are composed of the same letters of the alphabet as your sacred words. Therefore, in the former, too, there is holiness; bring them to their Source.

(ד) כַּךְ הִיא דַּרְכָּהּ שֶׁל תּוֹרָה. פַּת בַּמֶּלַח תֹּאכֵל וּמַיִם בַּמְּשׂוּרָה תִּשְׁתֶּה וְעַל הָאָרֶץ תִּישָׁן וְחַיֵּי צַעַר תִּחְיֶה וּבַתּוֹרָה אַתָּה עָמֵל אִם אַתָּה עֹשֶׂה כֵּן אַשְׁרֶיךָ וְטוֹב לָךְ אַשְׁרֶיךָ בָּעוֹלָם הַזֶּה וְטוֹב לָךְ לָעוֹלָם הַבָּא:

Baraita Four

This is the way of Torah: A morsel of bread with salt shall you eat and water by measure shall you drink and upon the ground shall you sleep and live a life of trouble and toil in the Torah. If you do this, 'Happy shall you be and it shall be well with you'. (Ps. 128:2); happy in this world and well with you in the world to come.

The previous Baraita concludes with the thought that the Torah is synonymous with 'good'. To avoid any misinterpretation of the word 'good', our Baraita promptly adds a rider to the effect that good does not imply specifically the good things in life, namely luxury and comfort; on the contrary, those who wish to master Torah must at times deprive themselves of extravagances and adopt an austere regimen of bread and salt, a limited amount of drink, and a hard bed.

In terms of education, our Baraita has a vibrant message for the modern world, that learning entails strenuous work. This chapter is devoted to the acquisition of Torah, and here we are told how to acquire it. In one passage the Rabbis seemingly express themselves rather harshly. The Torah, they say, can be mastered only by him who is prepared to 'kill himself', that is, he denies himself all enjoyment (Ber. 63b).

Some university students combine learning with enjoyment and entertainment. They crave for change and adventure and consequently are liable to become addicted to drugs and lead a dissolute life. The Torah student realises that he will not attain the desired results without pain and suffering.

There are three things, say the Rabbis, which can be achieved only through *yissurim*, suffering; they are *Olam Haba*, the world to come, Eretz Yisrael and Torah (Ber. 5b). To gain proficiency in Torah learning, the student should leave the comforts of his home and wander from one Yeshivah to another and forego the amenities and pleasures of life.

This Baraita, however, does not imply that a student should become an ascetic; it is generally conceded that whilst asceticism is not entirely unknown in Jewish life, it is not encouraged. Indeed, it is frowned upon. Hinduism and Buddhism profess a form of self-mortification and encourage the life of a hermit detached from the stream of normal existence. Christianity is an other worldly religion which boasts of its monasteries and nunneries, whilst the Roman Catholic Church demands that its clergy live a life of celibacy; all these institutions are alien to the spirit of Judaism. Not one of the six hundred and thirteen mitzvot directs us to renounce the legitimate pleasures of this world. The Nazarite, who abstains from drinking wine, is termed a sinner, and the Rabbis deduce that if the man who denies himself wine only is designated a sinner, how much more so is he who denies himself the enjoyments of life (Ta. 11a). Nor do we encourage fasting for its own sake. Rabbi Samuel intimated that he who fasts for the sake of self-affliction is called a sinner (ibid), whilst Mar Zutra observed that the merit of a fast day lies in the charity dispensed (Ber. 6b).

Regarding celibacy, we should add that the first commandment in the Torah obligates us to 'be fruitful and multiply' (Gen. 1:28). A man who has no wife is not a complete man, for it is said, 'Male and female He created them' (Gen. 1:27) (Yev. 63a). Throughout the talmudic period there was only one Rabbi who was unmarried because of his intense and passionate love for the study of Torah, Ben Azzai.

The balanced and proper tone was set by the poet-philosopher Judah Halevi in his Kuzari, where we read, 'Know that our Torah is constituted of the three psychological drives; fear, love and joy. By each of these you may be brought into communion with your God. Your contriteness in the day of fasting does not bring you nearer to God than your joy on the Shabbat and Festival, provided that your joy emanates from a devotional and perfect heart. As prayer requires devotion and thought, so does joy... Consider the Festivals as if you were the guest of God invited to His table and bounty, and thank Him for it inwardly and outwardly. If your joy in God excites you even to the degree of singing and dancing, it is a service to God, keeping you attached to Him. But the Torah did not leave these developments to our arbitrary will, but put them all under control'.

We shall now proceed to the wording of the Baraita.

This is the way of Torah. Rashi suggests that the anonymous author is addressing himself to the poor who should not blame their lack of learning on their poverty and the inability to earn a livelihood. On the contrary, the poor should concentrate on learning in spite of their frugal conditions. Ease and luxury are not conducive to Torah learning. Moses foresaw this and warned Israel that the temptation of wealth will alienate a Jew from Torah, 'And Yeshurun waxed fat and kicked... and he forsook God who made him' (Deut. 32:15). We would add that the Baraita has a message for the wealthy also. Physicians remind us that rich and luscious food and fine beverages can be injurious to health. Those who indulge in an extravagant diet would do well to act on the advice in our Baraita and, at times, subsist on a simple diet of bread, salt, and a limited amount of water.

Toil in the Torah. In the Talmud, the word *amal*, to toil, is used of students who study Torah industriously, but in biblical Hebrew the word *amal* is used of toil or labour in general, and Job intimates that toil is the natural bent of man, 'But man is born unto toil' (5:7). Indolence can lead to mischief and a host of evils, but the dignity of labour is often praised. 'When you eat the labour of your hands, happy shall you be and it shall be well with you' (Ps. 128:2). We thus compare the toil in Torah with the toil of one's hands; as honest toil with one's hands can be productive so toil in Torah is creative and brings happiness.

The word employed here for happiness, *esher*, (connected here with *yashar*, upright) is the opening utterance in the Book of Psalms. This aptly chosen word does not designate a physical pleasure, excitement or adventure. It is an inward satisfaction, an exalted and spiritual happiness which transcends the prosaic pleasures of man. *Ashrei* is not found in the singular, and this, too, helps us to understand the application of this expression in the context of our Baraita. *Ashrekha*, happy are you if you toil in the Torah; you are happy with the Torah, and the Torah is happy with you. You are happy because you are contented with your lot, even if it be bread with salt, for whatever God does is for a good purpose (Ber. 60b).

Commentators point out that the word *atta*, you, preceding *amal* and *oseh* should be underlined. If you toil in the Torah and adopt this course of action and deprive yourself of the comforts of life in order to toil wholeheartedly in the Torah, happy are you in this choice, but you cannot impose this way of life on others. *Atta*, you alone, with the help of God, will enjoy the fruits of your labours in this world and in the Hereafter.

We can interpret the function of the word *atta* here in another vein. We are asked to differentiate between the physical and spiritual urges of man. The body demands the intake of food and drink; one cannot exist without them. Sleep, too, is essential; some need more, some less. The body must be refuelled with food and drink; the body, too, must be refreshed with sleep. However, man will still live, even if his soul is starved of spiritual nourishment. Regarding Torah, our spiritual food, we are told *atta ameil*, you alone must toil and strive to feed the soul with Torah. This exercise will not be realised without personal effort. You must exert yourself to acquire Torah. If you are fortunate enough to be inspired with this inward love and devotion for Torah, happy will you be in this world for you are contented with your lot, and it will be well with you in the world to come, for you will have done your duty to God and man.

Hasidic Lore

How to overcome suffering. On Yom Kippur eve the Tzidnover Maggid called in R. Samuel of Kaminka and, showing him his sick granddaughter, said, 'Is not the new dress she wears very beautiful, and does it not become her greatly?' R. Samuel also complimented the girl on her new gown and for a few moments she forgot about her incurable illness. When they had left the room the Tzidnover said, 'I know that we gave her only a few moments of gladness, but even these few are pleasing in the eyes of the Lord since we have done all we can for her. We are taught in the Ethics of the Fathers, 'This is the way that is becoming for the study of the Torah: a morsel of bread with salt you shall eat and water by measure you shall drink; you shall sleep upon the ground and live a life of trouble whilst you toil in the Torah'. Hence, it is not sufficient for you to eat nothing but bread and sleep upon the ground, but in addition you must also feel the troubles of all living creatures and you must seek to minimise them as much as possible.

(ה) אַל תְּבַקֵּשׁ גְּדֻלָּה לְעַצְמְךָ. וְאַל תַּחְמוֹד כָּבוֹד. יוֹתֵר מִלִּמּוּדְךָ עֲשֵׂה. וְאַל תִּתְאַוֶּה לְשֻׁלְחָנָם שֶׁל מְלָכִים שֶׁשֻּׁלְחָנְךָ גָּדוֹל מִשֻּׁלְחָנָם וְכִתְרְךָ גָּדוֹל מִכִּתְרָם וְנֶאֱמָן הוּא בַּעַל מְלַאכְתְּךָ שֶׁיְּשַׁלֶּם לְךָ שְׂכַר פְּעֻלָּתֶךָ:

Baraita Five

Do not seek greatness for yourself and covet not honour; practise more than you learn and desire not the table of kings, for your table is greater than theirs and your crown greater than theirs and your Employer is faithful to pay you the reward of your labour.

Greatness. The Hebrew word *gadol*, great, has religious overtones. Other nations use the title great or greatness in every area of life and the word often denotes worldly success. We reserve this word 'great' to convey, not personal advancement, but spiritual exaltation. God is described as Great in Deut. 10:17. Indeed, the attributes of God recorded in this verse are included in the first paragraph of the daily Amidah in the Siddur. See I Chron. 29:11, repeated in the Shaharit service.

The august body of scribes, elders and scholars, who are responsible for many of our traditional practices, is termed 'The Men of the Great Synagogue'. In the Grace after Meals the additional paragraph to be read on Shabbat refers to the great and holy Shabbat, whilst the Shabbat prior to Passover is termed *Shabbat Hagadol*. The Temple, too, is designated as the great and holy house. It should also be remembered that *gadol*, great, is the title which is applied to a rabbinic scholar who is outstanding in Torah learning, and pre-eminent in his age.

The first statement in our Baraita, therefore, stresses the fact that as greatness has religious connotations, we should seek it not for ourselves but for Torah. True greatness must emanate from others, not from oneself, and should be attributed to those accredited to be worthy. Moses was a unique personality, but it was God who raised him to greatness. We also learn that if King Uzziah (II Chron. 26:16) who did not intend to magnify himself and did not seek his own honour but that of his Creator was yet so heavily punished, how much more will he be punished who intends to magnify himself and seek his own honour and not the honour of the Creator (Sifre Nu. Behaalotekha). It is in the spirit of the above that we must stress the operative word *leatzmekha*, for yourself.

Do not seek greatness for yourself. Seek greatness and honour for Torah; this is desirable and commendable, but seek it not for yourself. A good example of greatness is recorded of Mordekhai in the concluding words of the Book of Esther (10:2). 'For Mordekhai the Jew was next unto King Ahazuerus and great among the Jews and accepted of the multitude of his brethren; seeking the good of his people and speaking peace to all his seed'.

In the privacy of his home a man should be unassuming and peaceable, but in the presence of a multitude, congregation or assembly, circumstances may demand that one should be vocal and strive for the greatness and honour of Torah. This lesson is forcibly expressed in the concluding words of the Pentateuch, *l'einei kol Yisrael*, in the sight of all Israel. This phrase is followed and qualified by the familiar exhortation, *hazak, hazak, venithazek*, be strong, be strong, and we shall be strong; in the sight of all Israel, we must be resolute.

Some interpret the word *atzmekha* to be derived from the word *etzem*, bone, representing the physical nature of man. Do not seek greatness in your ambitions at the expense of your spiritual life. We should ascribe greatness and honour to our soul, to the religious potentialities inherent in every person.

Covet not honour. The Hebre root *hamad* can be utilised in either a good or bad sense. In the Grace after Meals the Land of Israel is characterised as *eretz hemdah*, a desirable land, compare also Gen. 2:9, and Ps. 68:17. In the Ten Commandments covetousness is the source of all evil and we are here warned not to crave or even entertain an inward desire to obtain honour. Maimonides rules that he who lusts after any acquirable object of his neighbour by incessant importuning through friends or by any other means until he possesses it, even if he pays him a high price, transgresses the injunction, 'You shall not covet'.

If we interpret our passage in this spirit, we see how corrupt society has become for many do not merit the honours they receive and so undermine the quality of life. We would point out that contrary to the direct negative of the Ten Commandments, *lo*, the author here uses the milder and persuasive word *al*, requesting us not to covet honour. This pernicious lust for honour can transform an individual beyond all recognition. The intended meaning of the tenth Commandment is summed up by Abarbanel,

'The sequence of ideas in the latter five Commandments is: Do not injure your fellow men by action (murder, adultery or theft); by word (lying and falsehood), or even by thought (covetousness).

Albo states that it is not sufficient to refrain from injuring a neighbour in his body, property or through his wife; care must be taken not to harm him by word, or even by thought.

It is interesting to find that in the second version of the Decalogue (Deut. 5:18) *lo tahmod* is followed by *lo titaveh*, as used here. Hirsch quotes the Mekhilta which differentiates between *hemdah* and *taavah*. Whereas the latter indicates only inner longing or lust, the former includes a longing which proceeds to action. Hirsch continues, 'In general the Torah prohibits specifically both *hemdah* and *taavah; hemdah* so that you do not think that provided that the intention is to acquire the object legally, you may covet it, and *taavah* so that you do not think that the sin only commences with the deed. He who wishes not to be embroiled in sin must stifle the lust at its inception, for even the desire itself is a sinful urge.'

Your table is greater than theirs. See 3:4.

Here we are introduced to another form of greatness, that of the table in the Jewish home. The table epitomises some of the most essential features of Jewish life. We may arrange the table with our hands but God prepares the table, as portrayed by the Psalmist, 'Thou preparest a table before me (23:5).

The Jewish home may lack the luxurious and varied foods of a rich table, but we still treat our table as royal because the spirit of the King of Kings, the Holy One blessed be He, hovers over the humblest table of the faithful and devoted Jewish family who are content with their lot, study Torah and sing praises of God with gratitude and love. Such a table is the barometer of the Jewish home and sets the tone for a peaceful, harmonious and ideal home life. It also carries the invisible crown of Torah which adorns every loyal Jew, 'Thou hast crowned him with glory and honour' (Ps. 8:6). Thus the crown of Torah is reserved, not for royalty, the nobility or the privileged few, but every commoner can also qualify for this distinction. Such is the democratic attitude of Judaism.

Hasidic Lore

True greatness. The Zakilkover Rabbi in his work *Likkutei Maharil* said: Some persons, when visiting a great man, observe closely his outward actions and believe that these display his greatness. This is false. To know a man's greatness one must observe the creative powers of his inner spirit. Do we not read, 'And all the people perceived the thunderings and the lightnings and the voice of the horn and the mountain smoking; and when the people saw it they trembled and stood afar off.... But Moses drew near unto the thick darkness where God was' (Ex. 20:15, 18). The people saw only the outward signs, hence they were far from knowing God. Moses, however, went into the inner region and there he found God.

(ו) גְּדוֹלָה תּוֹרָה יוֹתֵר מִן הַכְּהוּנָּה וּמִן הַמַּלְכוּת. שֶׁהַמַּלְכוּת נִקְנֵית בִּשְׁלֹשִׁים מַעֲלוֹת. וְהַכְּהֻנָּה בְּעֶשְׂרִים וְאַרְבַּע. וְהַתּוֹרָה נִקְנֵית בְּאַרְבָּעִים וּשְׁמוֹנֶה דְבָרִים וְאֵלוּ הֵן. בְּתַלְמוּד. בִּשְׁמִיעַת הָאֹזֶן. בַּעֲרִיכַת שְׂפָתָיִם. בְּבִינַת הַלֵּב. בְּאֵימָה. בְּיִרְאָה. בַּעֲנָוָה. בְּשִׂמְחָה. בְּטָהֳרָה. בְּשִׁמּוּשׁ חֲכָמִים. בְּדִקְדּוּק חֲבֵרִים. בְּפִלְפּוּל הַתַּלְמִידִים. בְּיִשּׁוּב. בְּמִקְרָא. בְּמִשְׁנָה. בְּמִעוּט סְחוֹרָה. בְּמִעוּט דֶּרֶךְ אֶרֶץ. בְּמִעוּט תַּעֲנוּג. בְּמִעוּט שֵׁנָה. בְּמִעוּט שִׂיחָה. בְּמִעוּט שְׂחוֹק. בְּאֶרֶךְ אַפַּיִם. בְּלֵב טוֹב. בֶּאֱמוּנַת חֲכָמִים. בְּקַבָּלַת הַיִּסּוּרִין. הַמַּכִּיר אֶת מְקוֹמוֹ. וְהַשָּׂמֵחַ בְּחֶלְקוֹ. וְהָעוֹשֶׂה סְיָג לִדְבָרָיו. וְאֵינוֹ מַחֲזִיק טוֹבָה לְעַצְמוֹ. אָהוּב. אוֹהֵב אֶת הַמָּקוֹם. אוֹהֵב אֶת הַבְּרִיּוֹת. אוֹהֵב אֶת הַצְּדָקוֹת. אוֹהֵב אֶת הַמֵּישָׁרִים. אוֹהֵב אֶת הַתּוֹכָחוֹת. וּמִתְרַחֵק מִן הַכָּבוֹד. וְלֹא מֵגִיס לִבּוֹ בְּתַלְמוּדוֹ. וְאֵינוֹ שָׂמֵחַ בְּהוֹרָאָה. נוֹשֵׂא בְעֹל עִם חֲבֵרוֹ. וּמַכְרִיעוֹ לְכַף זְכוּת. וּמַעֲמִידוֹ עַל הָאֱמֶת. וּמַעֲמִידוֹ עַל הַשָּׁלוֹם. וּמִתְיַשֵּׁב לִבּוֹ בְּתַלְמוּדוֹ. שׁוֹאֵל וּמֵשִׁיב. שׁוֹמֵעַ וּמוֹסִיף. הַלּוֹמֵד עַל מְנָת לְלַמֵּד. וְהַלּוֹמֵד עַל מְנָת לַעֲשׂוֹת. הַמַּחְכִּים אֶת רַבּוֹ. וְהַמְכַוֵּן אֶת שְׁמוּעָתוֹ. וְהָאוֹמֵר דָּבָר בְּשֵׁם אוֹמְרוֹ. הָא לָמַדְתָּ כָּל הָאוֹמֵר דָּבָר בְּשֵׁם אוֹמְרוֹ מֵבִיא גְאֻלָּה לָעוֹלָם שֶׁנֶּאֱמַר וַתֹּאמֶר אֶסְתֵּר לַמֶּלֶךְ בְּשֵׁם מָרְדֳּכָי:

Baraita Six

The Torah is greater than the priesthood and kingship, seeing that kingship is acquired by thirty distinctions and the priesthood by twenty-four, but the Torah is acquired by forty-eight qualities. And these are: by study, by a listening ear, by distinct pronunciation, by understanding and discernment of the heart, by awe, by fear, by humility, by cheerfulness, by purity, by ministering to the Sages, by attaching oneself to colleagues, by discussion with disciples, by sedateness, by knowledge of the Scripture and Mishnah, by moderation in business, by moderation in worldly intercourse, by moderation in pleasure, by moderation in sleep, by moderation in conversation, by moderation in laughter, by long-suffering, by a good heart, by faith in the wise, by acceptance of the chastisements, recognising his place and rejoicing in his portion, putting a fence to his words, claiming no merit to himself, being beloved, loving the All-Present, loving mankind, loving just courses, loving rectitude, loving reproofs and keeping himself far from honour and does not boast of his learning and does not delight in giving legal decisions, bearing the yoke with his fellow, judging him in the scale of merit, leading him to truth and peace, he composes himself at his study, he asks and answers, he listens and adds (to his knowledge), he learns in order to teach and he learns in order to practise, he makes his teacher wiser, he fixes attention upon his discourse and reports a word in the name of one who said it. So you have learned: Whoever reports a word in the name of one who said it brings redemption into the world, as it is said, 'And Esther told the king in the name of Mordekhai...' (Esth. 2:22).

One of the titles given to this chapter, The acquisition of Torah, is probably due to the teaching contained in this Baraita where we learn that Torah is acquired by forty eight qualities, superseding that of priesthood and kingship. Whilst the priesthood was given to Aaron and his seed, and the kingship to David and his offspring where it remained uninterruptedly for four hundred years, the Torah was given to every Jew individually. Our ancestors received and accepted the Torah at Mount Sinai for all times. 'Moses commanded us a Torah, an inheritance of the congregation of Jacob' (Deut. 32:4).

Kingship is acquired by thirty distinctions. Some of these are listed in the Torah (Deut. 17:15, I Sam. 8:11) also in the Talmud, (Sanh. 18a).

The twenty-four distinctions of Priesthood. These distinctions correspond to the twenty-four emoluments of the Priests which are recounted in B.K. 110b. Some of the distinctions here mentioned are — holiness, purity, fine linen clothing, trimming of the hair of the head and beard every thirty days and of the High Priest every seven days. The remainder are found in Leviticus chapter 21.

Maalot. We should note that whilst the priesthood and kingship are governed by *maalot*, degrees, the Torah is acquired by *devarim*, words. *Maalot* can mean steps, degrees, advantages, qualifications or distinctions. The offices of the Priest and the King are limited and restricted to a selected number of persons who are privileged to serve the people. They are set aside and are somewhat apart from the multitudes. Even their robes and headgear are distinctive and different from the rest of the nation. They therefore enjoy *maalot*, certain degrees or advantages which place them above others. The Torah, however, is not the prerogative of any particular section of the Jewish people, but belongs to all. The Torah consists of the Written Law, the written word, also the Oral Law, the spoken word. The Book of Deuteronomy which recapitulates the essence of the first four books of the Pentateuch is known as *Devarim*, words, or *Mishneh Torah*, repetition of the Law. In the Haftarah for Shabbat Shuvah the prophet Hosea invites Israel to take with them 'words, and return to the Lord' (14:3). In the opening passage of this chapter R. Meir taught that he who is engaged in the study of Torah for its own sake merits *devarim harbeh*, many words, subjects or things. The *devar Torah*, the word of Torah, accompanies us at all times; we include a *devar Torah* even in our ordinary conversation.

Study. The first of the forty-eight qualities of the Torah is study, learning. The Jew is the eternal student; he never ceases to learn. Even if he has acquired much *hakhmah*, he is still a *talmid*, disciple. One commentator suggests that it is preferable to learn from a teacher than from the reading of books (Nahmias).

A listening ear. Compare Prov. 22:17, 'Incline your ear and hear the words of the wise'. This may well qualify the first stage in the study of Talmud. Not every student has the patience or ability to digest the contents of a learned book; some find it simpler to listen to a pedagogue who is an expert in the art of exposition. The attentive ear of a student complements the work of the research scholar. Furthermore, a good listener can achieve better results than a voracious reader who quickly skims the surface but does not imbibe the essence of a book. A bookworm is not necessarily a scholar.

Distinct pronunciation, literally 'arrangement of the lips'. The movement of the lips has always acted as an aid to the memory. This pedagogic rule was recommended in the Talmud, 'Open your mouth and read the Scriptures, open your mouth and learn the Talmud, that your studies may be retained' (Er. 54a). The lips play an important part in study and prayer. We introduce the Amidah each day with an entreaty, 'O Lord, open my lips and my mouth shall declare your praise'. When Hannah poured out her heart in prayer at the Temple in Shiloh, 'Only her lips moved but her voice could not be heard' (I Sam. 1:13). The word *arikhah*, which means arrangement, suggests that the words of study or prayer should not be chosen haphazardly but carefully and orderly arranged. As the Shulhan Arukh is a digest of law systematically arranged, so should our thoughts and words of prayer be assiduously formulated. In this connection, it is interesting to refer to the Shulhan Arukh which enjoins us to read the Shema attentively and to articulate every letter clearly. For instance, the letter zayin should be pronounced correctly in the word *tizkeru*, you shall remember, in order that it should not sound like *tishkeru*, connected with drunkenness. In Hebrew the mispronunciation of a single letter can alter the meaning of a word. To avoid the slurring of words one should use the lips and distinctly enunciate every letter.

Understanding and discernment of the heart. This may well apply to a Cantor who, in rendering the prayers, may be unduly enamoured with the musical composition before him rather than with the true import of the words which should stir and inspire the heart. This interpretation would logically follow the exposition of the previous expression which refers to prayer. The Tiferet Yisrael distinguishes between the two expressions and holds that understanding applies to the sense of deriving conclusions by means of logical processes while discernment refers to deep insights into the hidden meaning of the Torah.

Awe, fear. The disciple should be inspired with awe and fear in the presence of his teacher. The Talmud advises the instructor to be a strict disciplinarian and suggests that he should 'cast bile amongst the students'

(Ket. 103b). Commenting on the verse in Deut. 4:9, 'You shall make them known unto your children and your children's children .... the day that you stood before the Lord your God in Horeb', the Rabbis remark that as the Israelites stood at Horeb with dread, fear, trembling and shaking, so here, when teaching Torah, it should be accompanied by dread, fear, trembling and shaking (Ber. 22a).

Humility. Compare the talmudic dictum of R. Jeremiah who said to R. Zeera, 'It says in Job of Sheol (3:19), 'Small and great are there alike and the servant is free from his master'. Is it not obvious that small and great are there? It means that he who for the sake of the words of the Torah makes himself small in this world will be great in the world to come, (B.M.85b).

Cheerfulness. To the uninitiated Torah or Law is encircled by an austere, burdensome and rigid set of customs. The loyal Jew, however, revels in the observance of the precepts and rejoices in the learning of the Law. The precept to him is a *simhah shel mitzvah*; the joy of the mitzvah is not a mere slogan but a living reality. He rejoices in the Torah not only on Simhat Torah but whenever he is in contact with Jewish Law and custom, and he brings to them a zest and enthusiasm which inspire and gratify him. 'Let man fulfil the commandments of the Torah with joy and then they will be counted to him as righteousness' (Mekhilta 66b). The Talmud categorically states that the Divine Presence rests on man neither through gloom nor through sloth save through a matter of joy in connection with a precept' (Shab. 30b).

Purity. Purity is omitted in some editions of Pirkei Avot. Purity of thought and action is one of the great moral virtues in Judaism. At the outset of the Yom Kippur Service we stress that atonement is effective if we purify ourselves. 'For on this day he (the High Priest) will atone for you to purify you, so that you may be pure from all your sins before the Lord'. An instructive passage from 'Hebrew Ideals' by J. Strachan throws some light on the concept of purity, 'The Hebrews had the highest conceivable sanction of virtue because the God whom they adored, being Himself morally beautiful, was the archetype of purity, righteousness, truth and love. Among pagan races theology was not less strikingly divorced from morality than among the Hebrews, it was conjoined therewith. Jupiter, the highest god of the Greeks, was notoriously adulterous. Krishna, the favourite god of the Hindus, is the incarnation of abandoned immorality. But it is impossible to think of the God of the Hebrews as other than spotlessly pure'. The biblical idea of purity as freedom from sin is expressed by R. Jose the Galilean. 'Why did God speak to Moses out of the bush? Because the bush is pure and the gentiles worship it not as an idol' (Mekhilta on Ex. 3:1).

Ministering to the Sages. *Shimush* is the practical application of study and service. Joshua the successor to Moses, is introduced to us in these words: And he (Moses) would return into the camp, but his minister Joshua the son of Nun, a young man, departed not out of the Tent (Ex. 33:11). The young aspirant to the rabbinate must learn not only the theory of Torah, but also the practical application of Torah, from his master with whom he is in constant touch. As the Rabbis state, 'Greater is the service of Torah than its study; as it is said, 'Elisha the son of Shaphat is here, who poured water on the hands of Elijah' (II K. 3:11). The text does not mention that he studied with Elijah, but that he poured water. This teaches us that service is greater than study' (Ber. 7b). Again, we learn that even if one has studied Torah and Mishnah but has not ministered to the disciples of the wise, he is an *am haaretz* (Ber. 47b).

Attaching oneself to colleagues. *Havruta*, attaching oneself to a scholar or friend for the purpose of studying Torah, is a recognised exercise at every Yeshivah. To indicate the purpose of this practice the Rabbis explain that as a small piece of wood can set on fire a big log, so minor scholars sharpen the minds of greater ones (Ta. 7b).

A variant reading of the above term is *dikduk haverim* which would signify the fine points discussed among scholars. *Dikduk* also means to particularise; in this sense, the expression would be a warning to choose one's friends or associates judiciously. Indeed, the Rabbis explicitly state that the fair-minded Jerusalemites used to act in this manner. They would not sign a deed without knowing who would countersign their signature; they would not sit in judgment unless they knew who was to sit with them, and they would not sit at a table without knowing who their fellow diners would be (Sanh. 23a).

Discussion with disciples. *Pilpel* means pepper, and as pepper has a sharp pungent taste, the word *pilpul* eventually took on the meaning of fine acute argumentation amongst scholars. A master in dialectics is referred to as a *baal pilpul.*

Yishuv. Generally *yishuv* means public or social welfare. Rashi suggests that it stands for *yishuv hadaat,* meaning ease of mind or composure. As we are dealing here with the various stages leading to the acquisition of Torah it is natural to connect *Yishuv* with *Yeshivah,* especially as both words are derived from *yashav,* to sit or dwell. The atmosphere of the Yeshivah is far removed from the hustle and bustle of every-day life. There the student sits and concentrates on the large tomes of the Talmud, and with peace of mind he analyses and ponders on the great issues discussed by the Tannaim and Amoraim, which include the moral, ethical and philosophical problems of Jewish life. We thus see that there is an affinity between *yishuv hadaat* and Yeshivah. If we follow this interpretation of *yishuv* the following two stages, knowledge of Scripture and Mishnah, automatically fall into line. Scipture and Mishnah represent the Written Law and the Oral Law respectively. In this connection see Rashi on Ex. 32:18, where he remarks that a scholar should be thoroughly versed in the contents of the twenty-four books of Tanakh.

Moderation in business. The Rabbis were practical men; they did not advise that we should shun business but that we should restrain our business activities. In the opinion of R. Joshua, this moderation is interpreted very generously. Learn a little morning and evening and you may pursue your business interests for the remainder of the day, for R. Joshua claims, 'If a man learns two *Halakhot* in the morning and two in the evening and he is occupied with his work all the day, the Rabbis account it to him as if he had fulfilled the whole Law' (Mekhilta Beshallah). On the other hand, Rashi quotes the talmudic maxim to the effect that Torah is not found among travelling merchants (Er. 55a). Whenever the Rabbis use the word *miut,* moderation, they imply that it is dangerous to indulge in any material pursuit to excess, for this would alienate one from the study of Torah.

Worldly intercourse. *Derekh eretz* is a phrase which we have often discussed. Rashi's comment here is that people should not loiter in the street, implying that by doing so precious time is wasted and the study of Torah is neglected. This may be the 'way of the world', *derekh eretz,* but should not be indulged in by us.

Moderation in pleasure. The Rabbis were not kill-joys and looked upon those who denied themselves the legitimate pleasures of life with disfavour. 'Man will have to give a reckoning and account for all which his eye sees...'. Pleasure is often self-indulgent and should therefore be restricted.

Moderation in sleep. Sleep is essential and healthy; 'Sleeping at dawn is like a steel edge to iron' (Ber. 62b), but over-indulgence tends to make one lazy. Solomon reminds us, 'Love not sleep lest you come to poverty' (Prov. 20:13).

The story is told in the Talmud (Er. 65a) that the daughter of R. Hisda once asked him, 'Would not the master like to sleep a little?', to which he replied, 'There will soon come days that are long and short, and we shall have time to sleep long'. He referred to the sleep in the grave. See note on 3:10.

Moderation in conversation. Precious time is frittered away in idle gossip. Regarding the injunction in the Shema, 'And you shall speak of them', one commentator emphasises that we should speak words of Torah, but not idle words. See note on 1:5.

Moderation in laughter. Discussing the effect of laughter the Talmud (Ber. 31a) records: It is forbidden for a man's mouth to be filled with laughter in this world because it is written, 'Then will our mouth be filled with laughter and our tongue with singing' (Ps. 126:2). When? At the time when, 'They will say among the nations, 'The Lord has done great things with these' (ibid). It was said of R. Simeon Ben Lakish that never again was his mouth full of laughter in this world after hearing this teaching from his master R. Johanan. More in keeping with the spirit of our Baraita was the custom adopted by Rabbah who would introduce his discourse with a humorous anecdote in order to amuse his disciples (Pes. 117a). This is laughter in moderation, and incidentally this is a fine example of pedagogic psychology. See also note on 3:17.

Long-suffering. Long suffering, or slow to anger, is a divine attribute which man should emulate. See Ex. 34:6 and Nu. 14:18. R. Josiah said, 'For three reasons God is long-suffering to the wicked. Maybe they will repent or perhaps they will fulfil some commands the reward of which He may pay to them in this world, or perhaps some righteous sons may issue from them as Josiah of Amon, Hezekiah of Ahaz and Mordekhai of Shimei' (Ec.R.7).

Long-suffering has also been the subject of discussion between God and Moses. 'And Moses bowed down and worshipped' (Ex. 34:8). What did Moses see? R. Hanina said that Moses saw the attribute of long-suffering; the Rabbis maintained that he saw truth. In accordance with the former view it is taught that when Moses went up to the mountain, he found God sitting and writing the word 'long-suffering'. Moses asked, 'Long-suffering to the righteous?' God replied, 'Also to the wicked'. Moses said, 'May the wicked perish!' God said, 'You shall see what you have asked'. When the Israelites sinned, God said, 'Did you not say to Me long-suffering to the righteous?' Moses retorted, 'But didst Thou not assure me that long-suffering was also for the wicked?' (Sanh. 111a).

A good heart. See note on 2:13.

Faith in the wise or the faith of the wise. Both translations complement one another. The implicit faith of the Sages inspired us to have faith in them and their words. Our whole-hearted belief in the conscientiousness of the Sages led to the saying that even their profane talk was raised to the level of Torah.

Acceptance of the chastisements. The faithful Jew will not blaspheme or criticise God for the sufferings inflicted upon him; he will accept the sufferings without demur and even regard them as 'chastisements of love'. Commenting on Gen. 1:3, 'God saw everything that He had made', the Midrash observes that even death and suffering contributed to the welfare of the human race (Gen. R. 9:5). Furthermore, there are occasions when sufferings are preferable to happiness, as we see in this extract: Let a man rejoice in sufferings more than in happiness; for if a man has lived all his life in happiness and has never shown any remorse for sins he has committed, he will never be pardoned. Beloved are sufferings, for just as the sacrifices secured acceptance, so do sufferings secure acceptance. Nay, sufferings bring even greater acceptance since sacrifices entail money only, whereas suffering affects his body' (Sifre Deut. 73b). Buchler in his 'Sin and Atonement' devotes a whole chapter to 'The right attitude towards suffering'.

Recognising his place. This statement has been interpreted in a variety of ways. We shall commence with the inner structure of the Torah

Academy of old. In Horayot 13b we have a detailed account of the seating arrangements of the Sages and students. We learn that scholars should not be disturbed and that every one has his recognised place. Commenting on Cant. 4:1, 'Your eyes are as doves behind your veil', the Midrash remarks that as the dove recognises its dove-cote, so should every student recognise his proper place.

This expression can also apply to every individual, rich or poor, learned or ignorant. Every person has his alloted place in life and he should not act under a false guise. Man should recognise his limitations in every sphere of activity.

If we apply this expression to Synagogue attendance, it can provide a telling message. Those who attend Synagogue only on Rosh Hashannah and Yom Kippur will not easily recognise their seats, whereas regular worshippers will not be faced with this problem.

Finally, a man should recognise *mekomo*, his last resting place, the grave. This sober thought should spur him on to study Torah and observe the precepts in order that he may accumulate a goodly number of mitzvot for the world-to-come.

Rejoicing in his portion. In this context, these words specifically refer to the student who is happy with his portion of Torah, in which he is absorbed each day. 'The precepts of the Lord are right, rejoicing the heart' (Ps. 19:19). The Rabbis assure us that every day the Torah is endeared to those who study it as on the day it was given on Mount Sinai (Ber. 3b).

Putting a fence to his words. Compare 1.1, here we are dealing with words of Torah. A person should be precise and limit himself to the subject at hand and should not have recourse to vague generalisations. In this spirit the Talmud warns us, 'Thus far you have permission to speak; beyond this you have not permission to speak, for so it is written in the Book of Ben Sira (Ecclesiasticus 3:21), 'Seek not things that are too difficult for you and search not out things that are hidden from you. The things that have been permitted, you think thereon; you have no business with the things that are secret' (Ha. 13a).

The Midrash clearly enunciates this principle in the name of Ben Azzai who states, 'Set a border (seyag) to your words in the same manner as God sets a border to His words' (Deut. R. 99). The Rabbis elaborate this thesis and remind us that the unclean animals mentioned in the Torah are more numerous than the clean, therefore the Torah speaks only of the clean animals. However, the reverse is true of the fowl, therefore the Torah speaks of the unclean fowl. From this we learn that one should limit or spare one's words in teaching Torah, which has no room for verbosity.

Claiming no merit to himself. See 2:8.

If we are fortunate to be blessed with health, wealth, wisdom or understanding, we should not boast of our good fortune. Everything proceeds from the Almighty, the source of all, and we should be eternally grateful to Him for having bestowed upon us so generously and graciously the gifts of mind and heart, body and soul.

Being beloved, loving the All-Present, loving mankind. The love for people is stressed by the Rabbis. An incident recorded in the Talmud (Ber. 10a) illustrates the truth of this teaching. Beruriah the wife of R. Meir once heard her husband curse some neighbours who had vexed him. She suggested that he should rather pray that they amend their ways and quoted the verse in Ps. 104:35 not in its original form, but she slightly changed the vowels so that it read, 'Let sins be consumed out of the earth and then the wicked will be no more'. She continued, 'Rather should you pray that they repent and be no more wicked'. R. Meir complied with her request which produced the required result. To correct people's wrong-doing by love and consideration is a noble and ethical ideal, and we salute the memory of Beruriah for underlining and discussing this essential teaching. A similar incident is recorded of R. Joshua Ben Levi who was plagued by a heretic and it was his intention to reproach him. However, the opportune moment did not arise and he thanked God by quoting Ps. 145:9, 'His tender mercies are over all His works'.

It should be noted that loving the All-Present is buttressed on either side by 'being loved' and 'loving mankind' respectively. This is the essence of true religion, which should never lead to hatred but to inspired love. As this love of God is universal and not restricted to any one nation, so this love of man should be universal and not limited to the adherents of any one religion.

Loving just courses. Compare Ps. 11:7, 'For the Lord is righteous, He loves acts of righteousness (tzedakot). The Midrash on Ps. 17:15 points out that even wicked people who are bereft of mitzvot, if charitable, are eligible to receive the presence of the Shekhinah.

Loving rectitude. The word *meisharim* is connected with *yashar*, straight, correct, upright. When imbibing knowledge of the Torah the student requires the straight, simple interpretation; and in his general behaviour we pray that he be reliable, trustworthy and honourable.

Loving reproof and keeping far from honour. We can find a connection between loving rectitude and loving reproof from the following extract in the Talmud. Rabbi said, 'Which is the straight or the right way which a man should choose? Let him love reproof' (Tamid 28a). To reprove a neighbour is a positive command and the sensible person will welcome such reproof with love and understanding. This is emphasised by the Rabbis who comment on Prov. 9:8, 'Reprove a wise man and he will love you'. R. Jose Ben Hanina said: A love without reproof is no love. Resh Lakish said: Reproof leads to peace; a peace where there has been no reproof is no peace (Gen. R. Vayera 54).

Reproof, as we have seen, is an important ingredient in Jewish life. However, it should be exercised with care and tact; one must not put a person to shame in the process of reproving, for this in itself would be sinful. Thus R. Johanan asked, 'What did Jeroboam do to deserve kingship? He reproved Solomon. And why was he punished? Because he reproved him in public thus putting him to shame' (Sanh. 101b).

The word *tokhahot* appears in the plural because it was felt that one reproof is insufficient and it is on record that outstanding Rabbis have requested that they be reproved from time to time. This may be due to the statement of R. Hanina who observed that Jerusalem was destroyed only because none reproved his fellow-man (Arakhin 16b). From this we learn that we should invite genuine and constructive criticism and reproof; such a course of action will keep us far from seeking honour and self-esteem and for this reason we have joined these two expressions, for one is the outcome of the other.

Mitrahek. It should be noted that the form *mitrahek* is reflexive, meaning that he removed himself outwardly and inwardly from coveting honour. Man is the final arbiter of his own destiny, and he alone must resolve to shun every vestige of honour.

He does not boast of his learning. This follows the previous expression logically and qualifies the injunction to keep far from honour. Judaism underscores learning to such an exalted degree that it was necessary to remind some people not to boast of their intellectual ability but to exercise it in the interest of humanity. Rav Judah said in the name of Rav, 'If any learned man is boastful, his learning is removed from him; and from a boastful prophet, his prophecy departs from him'. So it was in the case of Hillel. He once rebuked his disciples with boastful words and then had to admit, 'This law I once knew but I have now forgotten it' (Pes. 66b). In another passage King David is chided for his boastfulness. 'Some righteous men boast how well they fulfil the Commandments, then God weakens their strength. So David said, 'Thy statutes are to me as songs' (Ps. 119:54), as if to say they were as easy and light to him as songs. So God said, 'One day you will err in a matter which children know'. When Uzzah was killed because he touched the Ark, and David was angry (II Sam. 6:3, 8) God said, 'Did you not say, 'Thy statutes are to me as songs?' Have you not learnt that the service of the Sanctuary belongs to the sons of Kehat, that they should bear the Ark upon their shoulders?' (Nu. 7:9, Nu. R. Pinhas 21).

Does not delight in giving legal decisions. In the light of what the Rabbis say concerning the office of the judge and the grave responsibilities that devolve on him because it is his duty to pass sentence, this statement of our Baraita comes as no surprise. See full note on 4:9.

Bearing the yoke with his fellow. If we understand the word *ol* to refer to the yoke of Torah as it often does, we are here reminded to help our fellow-man and make it possible for him to bear the yoke of Torah. *Ol*, however, can also refer to the responsibilities man owes to his neighbour. In this manner the Mesillat Yesharim explains this expression, 'bearing the yoke', in these words: With regard to moral conduct, the principle that a man must always act benevolently towards his neighbour and never cause him harm, applies to his neighbour's body, possessions and feelings. Regarding the body, a man should strive to be of as much help as possible to those who are weighed down with some burden. 'Bearing the yoke with his fellow is to prevent his neighbour from suffering bodily injury' (Chapter 18).

The Vitry follows this train of thought when he comments, 'Even in such matters as royal imposts, although he personally may be exempt'. See Lev. 25:35, 'If your brother be poor and his means fail with you, then you shall uphold him'.

Judging him in the scale of merit. If you are in doubt, judge your fellow lightly in the scale of merit. See 1:6.

Leading him to truth and peace. In Judaism these two essential qualities are often linked together. Making peace between man and man is one of those exercises which has no fixed measure. See 1:18.

He composes himself at his study. This signifies that he studies in depth; he concentrates on his subject and is anxious to master it thoroughly in a leisurely manner. Only a balanced and composed mind can produce beneficial results.

He asks and answers. The disciple expects from his teacher the solutions to the difficult problems which face him, but only he himself can deal with the questions asked of him by others. Because he is intensely interested, he listens attentively and is in a position to add his own interpretation. Alternatively, we can presume that he is so keen to learn from his teacher that he repeats the lesson which he revises again and again, and by means of question and answer he adds to his store of knowledge.

He learns in order to teach. Learning is commendable, but should be imparted to others. This is graphically explained by the Rabbis who ask, 'To what may a scholar be compared? To a flask of poliatum (a fragrant ointment). When it is opened its odour is diffused, but if it remains covered its odour does not diffuse (A.Z. 35b). In other words, the true scholar is he who allows the fragrance of the Torah to be dispersed so that it reaches his disciples. This illustrates the expression — he learns in order to teach. Moreover, through learning, his preceptive and analytical powers are sharpened and consequently even the hidden and secret laws are revealed to him. This, too, is elaborated by the Rabbis in their comment on Prov. 27:17, 'Iron sharpens iron, so a man sharpens the countenance of his friend'. The Talmud remarks, 'As one piece of iron sharpens the other, so do scholars sharpen one another's minds in the study of Torah' (Ta. 7a).

He learns in order to practise. See 4:5. Compare Deut. 5:1, 'Hear O Israel the statutes and the ordinances which I speak in your ears this day, that you may learn them and observe to do them'. Compare also Deut. 6:3, 'Hear therefore, O Israel, and observe to do it'.

He makes his teacher wiser. The teacher must of necessity be well prepared to cope with the intricate questions asked by some of his bright disciples. This gave rise to the proverbial saying that 'the teacher learns most from his disciples'.

He fixes attention upon his discourse. This denotes that the pupil is most meticulous not to add to the statement he has received nor to subtract from it (Vitry and Rashi). Others understand this to mean that the student notes with precision what he has heard in order to compare it with the exposition of the same text by another teacher; this may shed new light and understanding on the subject. Indeed, this method of learning is encouraged by the Rabbis who inform us that the words of Torah are poor in one place, and rich in interpretation in another place (Y.R.H. chapter 3). By comparing the two texts the erudite student will glean added knowledge. This approach to learning clarifies another statement in ARN (end of chapter 23) which says, 'Let the words of the Torah be distinctly marked one from the other, and let them be distinctly marked one beside the other'.

He reports a word in the name of one who said it. A cursory glance at any page of the Talmud or rabbinical writings will testify to the truth of this statement. The Rabbis were intellectually honest and most meticulous in reporting every teaching in the name of the author. Thus R. Hiyya maintained that if a disciple is unaccustomed to repeat a lesson in the name of his teacher, he will promptly forget it (Lev. R. 2). Another Rabbi went further and claimed that this maxim is derived from Sinaitic tradition. R. Tanhum the Scribe declared that he received the tradition from the Elders that this was an Halakhah which emanated from Sinai; that is, anyone who does not report a word in the name of one who said it — of him the verse says, 'Rob not the weak because he is weak' (Prov. 22:20, Tanhuma Nu. 27). The verse from Proverbs implies that failing to report a statement in the name of the author is tantamount to stealing.

According to the Oxford Dictionary the word 'plagiarism' was first introduced in 1621. However, the principle underlying plagiarism was first formulated in the Torah and is found in the Book of Esther 2:22, as quoted in this Baraita. By acknowledging the authority of every statement we truly acquire Torah. This may explain the inclusion of this saying amongst the forty eight qualities leading to the acquisition of Torah. In other words, if we do not acknowledge the source of our teaching, we cannot acquire Torah; on the contrary, we are stealing it from its rightful owner, and this is prohibited. In Jewish thought stealing is not restricted to money, goods or possessions, but applies equally to ideas, thoughts and words. See following note.

Brings redemption into the world. Our God is not a tribal God; He governs the whole world and is concerned with the fate of every human being. God is not only the Creator; He is also the Redeemer of the universe. Initially, there seems to be no logical connection between recording a correct statement and world redemption. However, on closer scrutiny of Jewish history, we detect a positive relationship between the two. Much of the religious antisemitism which arose in the early years of the Church and which persists until this day is the result of deliberate falsification of the textual sources of our Tanakh. Thus the cardinal principle of Jewish ethical behaviour, 'Love your neighbour as yourself', (Lev. 19:18) has often been quoted from the New Testament, and many other Jewish virtues are claimed to have their origin in Christianity. This is a travesty of historical truth. If the world at large had recognised and acknowledged the eternal verities in our Tanakh we would have been spared the vilification,and slanderous abuse, which have been foisted upon us throughout the ages. Would that the non-Jewish world had spoken *beshem omro*, in the name of him who recorded the statement. Indeed, this would have brought world redemption, and not world hatred and suspicion.

Closely allied to religious antisemitism is political antisemitism which is even more insidious in its blatant propaganda, because it reaches the whole of mankind. World opinion is largely fashioned by the news media which are, in the main, biased and prejudiced against Jews in general and the State of Israel in particular. The news media very often distorts views and facts about the Jewish people. Rarely, if ever, do they speak in the name or the spirit of our people. If we add to all this the base and wicked allegations directed against everything Jewish as portrayed in a large number of publications, both fiction and non-fiction, which contain half truths and malicious lies, we realise the enormity of the problem and appreciate the prophetic spirit underlying the climactic maxim of our Baraita.

We now revert to the correct interpretation of the word *beshem*, in the name. It seems strange that the mere repetition of the name of the author can, in itself, bring redemption to the world. Many irreligious people quote the Bible or rabbinical teachings in the name of the author; do they, too, bring redemption? We are therefore compelled to translate *beshem omro* as in the spirit of him who said it. The mention of the name is inadequate; we should also repeat the saying in the spirit of the writer, who speaks in the name of God. The word *shem* often refers to God. Many quote Scripture to suit their own purpose. Under the guise of Torah they introduce newfangled ideas which have no source in Jewish tradition. Although they mention the Torah they act against the spirit of the Torah, thereby undermining traditional Judaism. In this respect we should remind all who follow the so-called progressive forms of Judaism and who have seceded from traditional Jewish thought that they should ponder on the implications of *beshem omro* and refrain from quoting Torah sources which are divorced from their true spiritual import. Misleading the public is a grievous sin.

Esther told the king in the name of Mordekhai. In the light of what we have said, Esther spoke to the king in the spirit of Mordekhai. She did not simply repeat what Mordekhai had told her in his name. There was the fear that Esther might forget the plight of her people, for she was residing in the luxurious quarters of the palace surrounded by pomp and ceremony. As the story unfolds itself in the Megillah we see that Esther had indomitable faith and courage, and with self-sacrificing zeal she prepared herself to plead the cause of her people. She fasted and prayed for three days and eventually presented herself to the king and spoke in the name and spirit of the commoner, Mordekhai. In this moving episode we have the embodiment of the lesson that it is essential to report faithfully in the name and spirit of the person who initiated the statement.

Hasidic Lore

Reproof. R. Sussya interpreted the verse, 'You shall surely reprove your neighbour' to mean that ther reprover should in the first instance chide himself for the fault imputed to his neighbour. R. Susya put this to the test. In his travels he would ask for a night's lodging at a home. At midnight he would arise and read the *Tikun Hatzot* (an anthology of prayers recited at midnight) with fervour, and would add a number of sins of which he felt that his host was guilty. Moved by this spontaneous act of remorse, the host would implore his visitor to intercede on his behalf and pray for his forgiveness. The Rabbi went further and implored the other members of the household to be included in the prayers and in this manner many people atoned for their sins, amended their ways, and were brought nearer to God.

(ז) גְּדוֹלָה תוֹרָה שֶׁהִיא נוֹתֶנֶת חַיִּים לְעֹשֶׂיהָ בָּעוֹלָם הַזֶּה וּבָעוֹלָם הַבָּא. שֶׁנֶּאֱמַר כִּי חַיִּים הֵם לְמוֹצְאֵיהֶם וּלְכָל בְּשָׂרוֹ מַרְפֵּא. וְאוֹמֵר רִפְאוּת תְּהִי לְשָׁרֶךָ וְשִׁקּוּי לְעַצְמוֹתֶיךָ. וְאוֹמֵר עֵץ חַיִּים הִיא לַמַּחֲזִיקִים בָּהּ וְתוֹמְכֶיהָ מְאֻשָּׁר. וְאוֹמֵר כִּי לִוְיַת חֵן הֵם לְרֹאשֶׁךָ וַעֲנָקִים לְגַרְגְּרֹתֶיךָ. וְאוֹמֵר תִּתֵּן לְרֹאשְׁךָ לִוְיַת חֵן עֲטֶרֶת תִּפְאֶרֶת תְּמַגְּנֶךָּ. וְאוֹמֵר כִּי בִי יִרְבּוּ יָמֶיךָ וְיוֹסִיפוּ לְךָ שְׁנוֹת חַיִּים. וְאוֹמֵר אֹרֶךְ יָמִים בִּימִינָהּ בִּשְׂמֹאלָהּ עֹשֶׁר וְכָבוֹד. וְאוֹמֵר כִּי אֹרֶךְ יָמִים וּשְׁנוֹת חַיִּים וְשָׁלוֹם יוֹסִיפוּ לָךְ:

Baraita Seven

Great is Torah, for it gives life to those that practise it in this world and in the world-to-come, as it is said (Prov. 4:22), 'For they are life unto those that find them and health to all their flesh'. And it says (Prov. 3:8), 'It shall be health to your navel and marrow to your bones'. And it says (ibid. 3:18), 'She is a tree of life to those who grasp her and of those who uphold her everyone is rendered happy'. And it says, 'For they shall be a chaplet of grace unto your head and chains about your neck' (ibid 1:9). And it says, 'She will give to your head a chaplet of grace; a crown of glory will she bestow on you' (ibid 4:9). And it says, 'For by me your days shall be multiplied and the years of your life shall be increased' (ibid. 9:11). And it says, 'Length of days is in her right hand; in her left hand are riches and honour' (ibid. 3:16). And it says, 'For length of days and years of life, and peace shall they add to you' (ibid. 3:2).

This Baraita can serve as a postscript to the previous passage. After detailing the large number of qualities leading to Torah the Baraita here informs us that Torah is synonymous with life. Torah is the totality of Judaism; we cannot envisage life without Torah. Everyone is empowered to live a Torah-centred life; we cannot delegate it to another person. Those who are not imbued with a love and understanding of Torah may succumb to the crushing weight of continuous suffering, and in some cases they will reject life and commit suicide which is sinful in Jewish Law. Such a person not only cuts his life short in this world, but also forfeits all claims to any portion in the world-to-come. However, the Torah-true Jew will accept his sufferings with resignation and even with love. Through repentance and good deeds the Torah will give him a new incentive to amend his ways and live a full Jewish life.

Hayyim. In the nineteenth Benediction of the morning Amidah we thank God for having blessed us with *Torat Hayyim*, the Torah of life. Torah and life are linked together; they co-exist as one entity. On Rosh Hashanah and Yom Kippur we entreat God to remember us for life and inscribe us in the Book of Life. Here life is a blessing which emanates from God who delights in life, and His Torah which is the Book of Life. In the eyes of God life is precious. It is significant that the Hebrew word for life, hayyim, is in the plural form. This teaches us that in the Jewish mind one cannot live for himself alone. True life involves others with their problems and anxieties.

A further interpretation points to the spiritual and physical side of life. A full Jewish life demands a recognition of the claims both of the soul as well as the body. Whichever interpretation we follow, life is not restricted to any one aspect of Jewishness. The Patriarchs are not introduced to us as learned, charitable, or even good men. When God made a covenant with Abraham, God said to him, 'Walk before Me and be whole-hearted, *tamim*' (Gen. 17:1). The same word is used with regard to Jacob, who is portrayed as *ish tam* (Gen. 25:27), a whole-hearted man. In the words of Rashi, 'As his heart, so was his mouth'. Such a life, which is governed by Torah is not departmentalised but is all-embracing and covers every facet of Jewish existence.

It should also be noted that the word introducing *hayyim*, life, is in the present tense, *notenet*, giving. Torah is not static; it grows and becomes more meaningful as we advance in years and it colours all our actions. Thus the Baraita uses the word *leoseha*, to those who do it, and not *lelomdeha*, to those who learn it. The ben-Torah should be an active participant in all the happenings of life, and not a passive onlooker. As we have remarked, the learned man must also practise, observe, and do good. Commenting on, 'You shall diligently guard these commandments to do them' (Deut. 6:17, 11:22), the Rabbis declare, 'Lest a man might suppose that if he guards the words of the Law, he can sit quietly and need not do them', the verse explicitly states, 'to do them'. 'If a man learns the words of the Torah he fulfils one command; if he learns and guards them, he has fulfilled two; if he learns and guards and does them, there is no one greater than he' (Sifre Deut. Ekev). So penetrating are the life-properties of Torah that they extend beyond this world and accompany the Jew in the world-to-come; so far-reaching is the influence of the Torah. The pre-eminence of Torah and its close inter-relationship with 'life' is amply testified in our passage, for it is followed by the unusual large number of eight proof texts, four of which contain explicit references to life.

To understand the full implication of the proof texts vis-a-vis the Torah and life, we enlist the aid of the Talmud where they are expounded. 'Samuel said to Rav, 'Open your mouth and read the Scripture, open your mouth and learn the Talmud, that your studies may be retained and that you may live long, since it is said, 'For they are life unto those that find them and health to all their flesh' (Prov. 4:22). Read not, 'to those that find them', but 'to him who utters them with his mouth' (Er. 54a). The Rabbis here trace the word *motzeihem* not to the root *matza*, to find, but to the root *yatza*, to go out. Here we see that the words of study proceed from the mouth. Continuing with the next verse, R. Joshua Ben Levi said, 'If a man is on a journey and he has no company, let him occupy himself with the study of the Torah, since it is said, 'For they shall be a chaplet of grace unto your head' (Prov. 1:9). If he feels a pain in his throat let him engage in the study of Torah, since it is said, 'And chains about your neck'. If he feels pain in his bowels let him engage in the study of Torah, since it is said, 'It shall be health to your navel' (Prov. 3:8). If he feels pain in his bones let him engage in the study of Torah, since it is said, 'And health to all their flesh' (Prov. 4:22).

The Talmud proceeds to distinguish between man and God. 'The dispensation of mortals is not like that of the Holy One blessed be He. In the dispensation of mortals, when a man administers a drug to a fellow, it may be beneficial to one limb but injurious to another; but with God it is not so. He gave the Torah to Israel and it is a medicine of life to all his body, as it is said, 'And health to all their flesh' (ibid.).

The Torah is compared to a drug or medicine in the following parable: Like a king who inflicted a severe wound on his son and he put a plaster on the wound. He said, 'My son, as long as this plaster is on your wound eat and drink what you like and wash in cold or warm water and you will suffer no harm; but if you remove it you will get a bad boil'. So God says to the Israelites, 'I created within you the evil inclination, but I created the Law as a medicine. As long as you occupy yourselves with the Law the inclination will not rule over you, but if you do not occupy yourselves with Torah, then you will be delivered into the power of the evil inclination and all its activity will be against you' (Sifre Deut. Ekev).

The lesson of the parable is based upon the Shema where in Deut. 11:18 it says, 'And you shall set, *ve-sam-tem*, these my words upon your heart'. By a change of a vowel in *ve-sam-tem* to *ve-sam-tam* the verse means, 'And a perfect medicine (sam-tam) shall these my words be on your heart'. A similar lesson is taught by R. Benaah who said, 'If one studies the Torah for its own sake it becomes to him an elixir of life, *sam hayyim*, for it is said, 'She is a tree of life to them that lay hold on her' (Prov. 3:18), and it is further said, 'It shall be health to your navel', and again it is said, 'For they are life unto those that find them' (Prov. 4:22); but if one studies the Torah not for its own sake it becomes to him a deadly poison, *sam hamavet*' (Ta. 7a).

In Tanakh and talmudic literature the tree very often represents the Torah. R. Nahman Bar Isaac said, 'Why are the words of the Torah likened to a tree? As it is said, 'She is a tree of life to them who lay hold on her'. In order to tell you that as a small tree sets fire to the large one, so do young scholars set on fire the minds of old scholars; hence the saying of R. Hanina, 'Much have I learned from my teachers, more from my companions, most from my disciples' (Ta. 7a).

Length of days is in her right hand. Some question the veracity of these words, for many martyrs have died in their early years for the Jewish cause. The Rabbis, however, interpret the verse in this manner: The words of Torah have potentialities for life or death. Thus Rav said, 'To those who go to the right hand (that is they employ the Torah rightly) the Torah is a medicine of life; to those who go to the left (who use the Torah wrongly) the Torah is a deadly poison' (Shab. 88b). In the Talmud (Shab. 63a) a question is asked regarding our proof text. 'Is there in her right hand length of days only, but not riches and honour?' The answer given is, 'To those who go to the right hand thereof there is length of days and riches and honour a fortiori; but for those who go to the left hand thereof there are riches and honour, but not length of days'. Rashi interprets the above passage as follows — 'To the right hand means that they study with intent as the right hand is the stronger for work; alternatively, it refers to those who study the Torah for its own sake'.

Length of days and years of life and peace. How do we distinguish between length of days and years of life? Longevity in itself is no blessing; it may amount to an accumulation of days which are unproductive. Methuselah lived for nine hundred and sixty nine years. What did he bequeath to humanity? After recording his fabulous age, the Torah adds one word, *vayamot*, and he died. On the other hand, King David lived for seventy years but he produced one hundred and fifty Psalms which have comforted and inspired untold millions of Jews and non-Jews. Samuel the Prophet died at the age of fifty two, nevertheless he enriched the Tanakh with two books named after him, the First and Second Book of Samuel. Length of days becomes a boon only when translated into years of purposeful life, years of fruitful activity devoted to God and man. It is right and proper that the final quality of life mentioned in our Baraita should be *shalom*, peace, which is the supreme blessing of life for which we all pray and yearn.

The Midrash Shemuel explains that length of days refers to the life in this world, and years of life to eternal bliss in the world to come where the soul enjoys everlasting peace.

Hasidic Lore

Jewish Life. When Moshe Leib visited R. Elimelekh for the first time, his host honoured him at the Sabbath meal by asking him to say Torah. Now on this particular Sabbath the passage of the Scriptures to be read dealt with God's smiting the Egyptians and passing over the houses of the Israelites. Moshe Leib said, 'This cannot possibly mean that God passed over a certain place, because there is no place where He is not. But when He passed through the Egyptians' houses and saw the corruption of their souls and then came to a house full of piety and goodness, He was overjoyed and cried, 'A Jew lives here!'.

When R. Elimelekh heard this explanation he jumped on the table, danced upon it, and sang over and over, 'A Jew lives here, a Jew lives here!'

(ח) רַבִּי שִׁמְעוֹן בֶּן יְהוּדָה מִשּׁוּם רַבִּי שִׁמְעוֹן בֶּן יוֹחַאי אוֹמֵר הַנּוֹי וְהַכֹּחַ וְהָעוֹשֶׁר וְהַכָּבוֹד וְהַחָכְמָה וְהַזִּקְנָה וְהַשֵּׂיבָה וְהַבָּנִים נָאֶה לַצַּדִּיקִים וְנָאֶה לָעוֹלָם. שֶׁנֶּאֱמַר עֲטֶרֶת תִּפְאֶרֶת שֵׂיבָה בְּדֶרֶךְ צְדָקָה תִּמָּצֵא. וְאוֹמֵר תִּפְאֶרֶת בַּחוּרִים כּוֹחָם וַהֲדַר זְקֵנִים שֵׂיבָה. וְאוֹמֵר עֲטֶרֶת חֲכָמִים עָשְׁרָם. וְאוֹמֵר עֲטֶרֶת זְקֵנִים בְּנֵי בָנִים וְתִפְאֶרֶת בָּנִים אֲבוֹתָם. וְאוֹמֵר וְחָפְרָה הַלְּבָנָה וּבוֹשָׁה הַחַמָּה כִּי מָלַךְ יְהוָה צְבָאוֹת בְּהַר צִיּוֹן וּבִירוּשָׁלַיִם וְנֶגֶד זְקֵנָיו כָּבוֹד. רַבִּי שִׁמְעוֹן בֶּן מְנַסְיָא אוֹמֵר אֵלּוּ שֶׁבַע מִדּוֹת שֶׁמָּנוּ חֲכָמִים לַצַּדִּיקִים כֻּלָּם נִתְקַיְּמוּ בְּרַבִּי וּבְבָנָיו:

Baraita Eight

R. Simeon Ben Judah says in the name of R. Simeon Ben Yohai: Beauty, strength, riches, honour, wisdom, old age, a hoary head and children are becoming to the righteous and becoming to the world, as it is said (Prov. 16:31), 'The hoary head is a crown of glory, it is found in the way of righteousness', and it says (ibid 20:29), 'The glory of young men is their strength and the beauty of old men is the hoary head' and it says, (ibid 17:6), 'Children's children are the crown of old men and the glory of children are their fathers', and it says (Is. 24:23), 'Then the moon shall be confounded and the sun ashamed, for the Lord of Hosts shall reign in Mount Zion and in Jerusalem, and before His elders shall be glory'. R. Simeon Ben Menasya says, 'These seven qualities which the Sages have enumerated as becoming to the righteous were all of them realised in Rabbi (Judah Hanasi)and his sons'.

R. Simeon Ben Judah, Tanna of the fourth to the fifth generation, was a native of Acco and he is referred to as Ish Kfar Acco. He was the distinguished disciple of R. Simeon Ben Yohai in whose name he transmitted thirty sayings, all in the Tosefta. He is mentioned alone only twice, once in Mekhilta Beshallah on Ex. 14:15, and a second time in Sifre on Deut. 32:6.

Our Baraita is fundamentally an extension and elaboration of the previous passage, which taught that Torah gives life. Here life is spelled out for us in the listing of seven or eight qualities which are meaningful only if they are built on the firm foundation of Torah. Without Torah these same qualities can produce evil and destruction to the individual and to the world.

Beauty, or comeliness. As the qualities here have their source in God and Torah, beauty is a spiritual and moral quality which the righteous exude in their imitation of the Divine.

Rashi uses this identical word, *noy*, in his comment on Ex. 15:12 where we read, 'This is my God and I will glorify Him'. He adds that the last word has the sense of *noy*, beauty. The Jewish mind was trained to see 'beauty in holiness and holiness in beauty', consequently we recite a blessing on seeing the beauties of nature. R. Ishmael interpreted the same verse by asking a pertinent question whether man can beautify the Creator, to which he replied, 'I will make myself beautiful to Him through a beautiful Lulav, a beautiful Sukkah, beautiful Fringes, beautiful Tefillin... beautiful Scrolls of the Law written in beautiful ink with a beautiful quill by the hand of practised Scribes, enwrapped in beautiful silk' (Mekhilta Beshallah, Shab. 112b). A similar and even more extended passage is found in Cant. R. 1.

The Vitry suggests that one possessed of a beautiful face can look angelic but such external beauty has its dangers, and the Rabbis warn us to channel this beauty in the right direction. 'If you are handsome, do not go astray after lewdness but honour your Creator; fear and praise Him with the beauty which He has given you' (Pesikta Rabbati 125). In this respect we should add that Joseph was called 'hazaddik', the righteous because he resisted the advances of Potiphar's wife who was attracted by the beauty of his countenance. That the Jewish approach to beauty was different from that of classical Greece is stressed by those who render the name *Japhet* (Gen. 9:27) as 'beauty'. In the words of Hertz, 'The Rabbis conceived of beauty under the category of purity, and longed for Japhet, that is the beauty of Greece, to dwell in the tents of Shem'. The Greeks worshipped external beauty and even appeared naked in their athletic games. Judaism worshipped the inner beauty of character and fought heroically against the intrusion of hellenistic thought and practice in antiquity.

Strength. The Rabbis testify that the mental strain of studying Torah can weaken man. This may have given rise to the statement of one Rabbi who affirms that a scholar is not allowed to impose fasts upon himself which might lessen his heavenly work (Ta. 11b). It is interesting to note that the mighty Samson, who was born a Nazirite, drew his super-human strength from God and whilst he was under the Nazirite vow no one could overcome him. However, as soon as he broke the Nazirite vow and the locks of his head were shaven, the spirit of God departed from him, his strength waned and he was reduced to submission (Jud. 16:15).

Riches. Compare the maxim of R. Johanan who observed that the Holy One blessed be He caused His divine presence to rest only upon him who is strong, wealthy, wise and meek (Ned. 38a). The inclusion of wealth in this saying, as in our Baraita, may seem strange but the Rabbis were practical men. Poverty was not upgraded as a virtue, nor was wealth downgraded or considered sinful, so long as it was acquired honourably. An average community has an amalgam of poverty and riches. Amongst the Rabbis of the talmudic era, some were poor and others were rich.

Honour, kavod. This word has undergone a complete metamorphosis throughout the ages. The Psalmist observes that the heavens declare the glory, *kavod* of God. *Kavod* often represents the very presence of God, which we mortals are expected to introduce on earth in our relationship with parents, teachers, elders and fellow-men. However, we have often transformed this celestial gift into a petty and sordid self-glorification, thus denuding *kavod* of all its pristine glory, nobility and grandeur. When *kavod* is subservient to and allied with Torah it can reach majestic heights, but when it is alienated from Torah it degenerates into meanness and debases a person.

Wisdom, old age, and a hoary head. These terms are often grouped together as is evident from this passage in the Talmud, 'It is written, 'You shall rise up before the hoary head and honour the face of the old man and fear your God, I am the Lord' (Lev. 19:32). One might surmise that this implies the necessity to honour an aged man who is sinful, we should therefore remember that *zaken*, an old man, is a wise sage, as it says,

'Gather ye to Me seventy men of the elders of Israel' (Nu. 11:16). R. Jose the Galilean says, '*Zaken* means only he who has acquired wisdom' (Kid. 32b). The link between wisdom and old age is apparent in Tanakh (Job 12:12) where Rashi and Ibn Ezra render the verse as follows, 'With the ancient is wisdom, and understanding in length of days'. The significant role of the elders is expressed in Ex. R.83 where we learn that the elders helped to preserve Israel, as it says, 'And all Israel and their elders and officers and their judges stood on this side of the Ark and on that side' (Jos. 8:32). When does Israel stand? When they have elders, and any person who takes advice from elders will not stumble, as we learn from I.K. 20:7, 'Then the king of Israel called all the elders of the land', which means that he consulted with the elders.

Children. In Deut. 32:46 Moses said, 'Set your heart unto all the words wherewith I testify against you this day; that you may charge your children therewith to observe and do all the words of this law'. The Rabbis comment that Moses said to them, 'I give you credit that you will fulfil the Torah after me; you, too, must give credit to your children that they will fulfil the Torah after you' (Sifre Haazinu). At the death of a parent a surviving child can preserve life and assure continuity of tradition. This is reflected in the following scriptural text, 'And when Hadad heard in Egypt that David slept with his fathers and that Joab the captain of the host was dead' (IK. 11:21). The Talmud (B.B. 116a) asks, 'Why was the expression of 'sleeping' used in the case of David, and that of 'death' in the case of Joab?' 'Sleeping' was used in the case of David because he left a son; 'death' was used in the case of Joab because he did not leave a son who would observe the commandments.

In the Torah and rabbinic literature children are portrayed as our most cherished possession. They are the guardians of our cities and towns and are designated as the 'Messiahs of mankind'.

The proof texts. The subjects that are highlighted in these verses are the children and the aged. It is possible that the Baraita records the scriptural authority to these two themes because they embrace the whole of life, the morning, youth, and the evening, old age, of our earthly existence. What is even more striking is the fact that whilst every quality is mentioned in the proof texts, at least by word, the only exception is *noy*, beauty, which is omitted. This seeming difficulty is tied up with another problem introduced by R. Simeon Ben Menasya who informs us that seven qualities are enumerated in our Baraita, whereas there are actually eight.

This apparent difficulty is solved by one authority who ingeniously suggests that *noy*, beauty, is not to be counted among the qualifications but is to be regarded as a superscription governing all the qualities that follow and which, by implication, are rooted in beauty. This would reduce the number to seven and explain why *noy* is not explicitly mentioned in any of the verses quoted. Moreover, this theory seems to solve yet another problem. The clause, 'Becoming to the righteous and becoming to the world', which summarises the qualities preceding it, is introduced by the word *naeh* which is akin to *noy*. If this clause were to refer to and conclude the qualities specified, it would commence with the plural form, *naim*. The singular, *naeh*, definitely points to the general title *noy*, and not to the individual subjects mentioned in the Baraita.

'The hoary head is a crown of glory if it is found in the way of righteousness' (Prov. 16:31). Judaism can be proud of its record toward the aged. We have always shown respect and consideration for old age, which is designated as 'A crown of glory'.

'The glory of young men is their strength and the beauty of old men is the hoary head' (ibid 20:29). In the glory of youth lies its ability to ward off with moral strength the evil impulse which attempts to wean away our young from their traditional moorings. Very apt is the talmudic aphorism, 'Happy is our youth when it does not put to shame our old age' (Sukkah 53a).

'Children's children are the crown of old men; the glory of children are their fathers' (ibid 17:6). Here we have the outline of a glorious picture of family life covering three generations, all linked by Torah. The Rabbis observe that when Torah is sustained for three generations, it will not depart (B.M.85a). The verse adduced in support of this is derived from Is. 59:21 and is recited in our daily morning prayers. 'And as for Me, this is My covenant with them, says the Lord; My spirit that is upon you and My words which I have put in your mouth shall not depart out of your mouth, nor out of the mouth of your seed, nor out of the mouth of your seeds' seed, says the Lord, from henceforth and for ever'. The narrowing of the generation gap and the merging and reconciliation between the old and the new is beautifully portrayed by Mal. 3:24, 'And he shall turn the heart of the fathers to the children, and the heart of the children to their fathers'.

'Then the moon shall be confounded and the sun ashamed; for the Lord of Hosts will reign in Mount Zion and in Jerusalem, and before His elders shall be glory' (Is. 24:23). This verse refers to the Messianic era when the natural light emanating from the moon and the sun will be superseded by the effulgence of the rays of Divine light which will illumine the face of the earth. This is predicted by the prophet Isaiah, 'The sun shall be no more your light by day neither for brightness shall the moon give light unto you; but the Lord shall be unto you an everlasting light, and your God, your glory. Your sun shall no more go down, neither shall your moon withdraw itself; for the Lord shall be your everlasting light' (Is. 60:19-20).

R. Simeon Ben Menasya, Tanna of the fourth to fifth generation, was a contemporary of R. Judah Ha-Nasi. He and Jose Ben Meshullam formed a distinctive group known as *Kehillah Kedoshah*, Holy Congregation, because the group set aside a third of each day to the study of Torah, one third to prayer, and the other third to work.

Hasidic Lore

Attaining perfection through beauty. Said the Lizensker, 'We read (Gen. 6.10), 'And Noah begat three sons, Shem, Ham and Japhet'. We may give to this verse an allegorical interpretation. Noah means the pleasing one, hence the good man; he begat three sons, three degrees of perfection. *Shem* is 'the Name'; the first degree is to sanctify the Holy Name within ourself through repentance of those sins which make a flaw in our holiness. *Ham* means warmth; the second step is to be warm in our worship by battling against the return of our former faults. *Japhet* means beautifying or perfecting; this is the third step; to offer to the Lord perfect devotion, a love that burns within us.

Youth and Old Age. A youthful prodigy visited the Kosnitzer Maggid and began to exhibit his profound learning before the disciples. The middle-aged adherents of the Maggid jokingly belittled his talents. When the youth returned home he complained to his father-in-law. The latter, who took immense pride in his son-in-law, laid the affair before the Maggid saying that 'those that do not reach to his knees' in learning dared ridicule the remarkable youth.

The Maggid replied: Let me relate to you this fable. A lioness instructed her cub saying to him, 'You need fear no living being except the man'. The young lion saw an old man, bent with age, and enquired from the mother, 'Is he dangerous?' 'No', retorted the mother, 'He was a man.'

The cub soon after saw a child and repeated the same query. 'No', answered the mother lion, 'He will be a man'. Then a hunter, tall and powerful, appeared. 'This is the dangerous being' exclaimed the lioness and ran with the cub to their den. In the same fashion your son-in-law is yet to be a man, whilst the disciples are men now. 'It was unseemly for a youth to display his knowledge vaingloriously before his elders as if he were superior. Modesty becomes the young'.

(ט) אָמַר רַבִּי יוֹסֵי בֶּן קִסְמָא. פַּעַם אַחַת הָיִיתִי מְהַלֵּךְ בַּדֶּרֶךְ וּפָּגַע בִּי אָדָם אֶחָד וְנָתַן לִי שָׁלוֹם וְהֶחֱזַרְתִּי לוֹ שָׁלוֹם. אָמַר לִי רַבִּי מֵאֵיזֶה מָקוֹם אָתָּה. אָמַרְתִּי לוֹ מֵעִיר גְּדוֹלָה שֶׁל חֲכָמִים וְשֶׁל סוֹפְרִים אָנִי. אָמַר לִי רַבִּי רְצוֹנְךָ שֶׁתָּדוּר עִמָּנוּ בִּמְקוֹמֵנוּ וַאֲנִי אֶתֵּן לְךָ אֶלֶף אֲלָפִים דִּנְרֵי זָהָב וַאֲבָנִים טוֹבוֹת וּמַרְגָּלִיּוֹת. אָמַרְתִּי לוֹ אִם אַתָּה נוֹתֵן לִי כָּל כֶּסֶף וְזָהָב וַאֲבָנִים טוֹבוֹת וּמַרְגָּלִיּוֹת שֶׁבָּעוֹלָם אֵינִי דָר אֶלָּא בִּמְקוֹם תּוֹרָה. וְכֵן כָּתוּב בְּסֵפֶר תְּהִלִּים עַל יְדֵי דָוִד מֶלֶךְ יִשְׂרָאֵל טוֹב לִי תוֹרַת פִּיךָ מֵאַלְפֵי זָהָב וָכָסֶף. וְלֹא עוֹד אֶלָּא שֶׁבִּשְׁעַת פְּטִירָתוֹ שֶׁל אָדָם אֵין מְלַוִּין לוֹ לְאָדָם לֹא כֶסֶף וְלֹא זָהָב וְלֹא אֲבָנִים טוֹבוֹת וּמַרְגָּלִיּוֹת אֶלָּא תּוֹרָה וּמַעֲשִׂים טוֹבִים בִּלְבָד שֶׁנֶּאֱמַר בְּהִתְהַלֶּכְךָ תַּנְחֶה אוֹתָךְ בְּשָׁכְבְּךָ תִּשְׁמוֹר עָלֶיךָ וַהֲקִיצוֹתָ הִיא תְשִׂיחֶךָ. בְּהִתְהַלֶּכְךָ תַּנְחֶה אֹתָךְ בָּעוֹלָם הַזֶּה. בְּשָׁכְבְּךָ תִּשְׁמוֹר עָלֶיךָ בַּקָּבֶר. וַהֲקִיצוֹתָ הִיא תְשִׂיחֶךָ לָעוֹלָם הַבָּא. וְאוֹמֵר לִי הַכֶּסֶף וְלִי הַזָּהָב נְאֻם יְהוָה צְבָאוֹת:

Baraita Nine

R. Jose Ben Kisma said: Once I was walking by the way when a man met me and gave me (the salutation of) peace and I returned him (the salutation of) peace. He said to me, 'Rabbi, from what place are you?' I said to him, 'From a great city of sages and scribes am I'. He said to me, 'If it is your wish to dwell with us in our place I will give you a thousand thousand denarii and precious stones and pearls'. I said to him, 'If you were to give me all the silver and gold and precious stones and pearls that are in the world, I would not dwell except in a place of Torah and thus it is written in the Book of Psalms by the hand of David, King of Israel (Ps. 119:72), 'The Torah of Thy mouth is better to me than thousands of gold and silver'; and not only so, but in the hour of man's death it is neither silver nor gold nor precious stones nor pearls which accompany him, but Torah and good deeds only, as it is said (Prov. 6:22), 'When you walk it shall lead you in this world; when you lie down it shall watch over you in the grave; when you wake it shall talk with you in the world-to-come'. And it says (Hag. 2:8) 'The silver is Mine and the gold is Mine, says the Lord of Hosts'.

R. Jose Ben Kisma was a learned Sage and an outstanding leader in Caesarea. He was greatly respected by the Roman authorities and it is reported that, 'All the great men of Rome went to his burial and made great lamentations for him' (A.Z. 18a). He was a personal friend of R. Hanina Ben Teradyon who was martyred by the Romans (ibid).

Walking by the way. The ordinary Jew will treat the road as a public thoroughfare and divest himself of all mitzvot, but the pious Jew will not reserve his religion for the Synagogue or the home, but will take his religion with him along the road of life. This is in conformity with the familiar words of the Shema, 'And you shall speak of them when you sit in your house and when you walk by the way'. *Paga* followed by a *bet* means to come in contact with, but it does not signify a chance meeting; it is rather an occasion when one makes an impression upon another. Thus here the individual must have been struck by the informality of the Rabbi who was probably clad in Tallit and Tefillin and perhaps studying a religious tract. He must have looked and behaved as a Sage. Furthermore, the Rabbi was so preoccupied with his prayers or studies that he did not notice the individual, otherwise he would have anticipated the stranger and greeted him first, as is the custom of pious Jews. Compare (Ber. 17a) where it is said of R. Johanan Ben Zakkai that no one greeted him first, not even the heathen in the street. R. Helbo said, 'Whoever is in the habit of greeting his neighbour and omits to do so a single day transgresses the injunction, 'Seek peace and pursue it' (Ps. 34:15), (ibid 6b).

Shalom We notice that the Rabbi replied to the greeting by saying, 'Shalom', but we generally reply, 'Aleikhem shalom'. This formula which gives credit to the one who anticipated the greeting with 'Shalom' is correct in a public thoroughfare where people are passing to and fro; but in a solitary place the greeting 'Shalom' is adequate. This is hinted at in the Talmud (Meg. 3a) where R. Joshua Ben Levi observed that it is forbidden to greet a stranger by night, for fear that he may be a demon. Tosafot qualifies this statement and adds that it is only forbidden to greet one at night outside the city if one is in an empty open space, but if it is frequented by people it is permitted. Here the Rabbi was alone and he followed talmudic precedent and replied, 'Shalom'. On 'Greetings in Jewish Life', see 4:20.

A great city of Sages and scribes. The stranger asked the Rabbi the name of the place in which he lived, but the Rabbi ignored this query and replied that he came from a great city of Sages and scribes. Why did the Rabbi not mention the name of the city? We can only surmise that the Rabbi presumed that the stranger was not a scholar; for instance, he did not contribute a *devar Torah*, a word of Torah, but concentrated only on such items as money and precious jewellery. This person may not even have been acquainted with the names of important centres of Jewish learning. The Rabbi therefore replied that he came from a city which boasted of great scholars. The Rabbi's intention was to underline the significance of Torah, intimating in advance that he was not interested in the material things of life.

I will give. When the stranger coaxed the Rabbi to leave his place of Torah, he added, 'I will give you a thousand thousand...'. We should emphasise the word 'I'. He did not promise that the community would reimburse him, but simply said, 'I will give'. This has been a perennial problem with the rabbinate. The salary of the Rabbi has too often been dependent upon the whim of an individual who consequently has the power to override the authority of the spiritual leader.

In reply to the invitation from the stranger the Rabbi stated, 'If *YOU* were to give me...', thus emphasising the point that even if he were offered an overwhelming monetary inducement he would not consider such an invitation because it emanated not from the general body, but from an individual person.

Denarius, or dinar. The accurate value of ancient currency cannot be precisely determined, but some suggest that a denarius was the normal wage for a day's labour of a field worker. In antiquity a thousand thousand denarii must have been a very large amount of money. There were two types of denarius, silver and gold; the silver denarius was equal to one twenty-fourth of the value of a golden denarius.

Gold and silver. The possible and inherent dangers of these precious metals are alluded to by the Rabbis who warn us that gold and silver remove a man from this world and from the world to come, but the Torah leads one to eternal life (Sifre Nu. Korah). In early days gold was used for ornamental and decorative purposes. There were seven types of gold which were extensively used in the Tabernacle and Temple. Although the word *kesef* specifically means silver, it is the generic term for money.

Place of Torah. We learn that the Rabbi wished to reside only in a place of Torah. One is tempted to ask how the Rabbi knew that the position offered to him was not a place of Torah. It is generally conceded that the great Sages in every age lived frugally and were not surrounded by wealth. We are reminded that to acquire learning one should be exiled to a place of Torah where scholarship reigns supreme and riches are not sought. As the vast sum of one million denarii was offered, the Rabbi surmised that the stranger represented, not a place of Torah, but a prosperous community where Torah played an insignificant role.

Proof text. The full import of the proof text emerges when it is read with the previous verse, 'It is good for me that I have been afflicted in order that I might learn Thy statutes' (Ps. 119:72). The pious man will submit to sufferings which he accepts with faith, and will spurn wealth and the comforts of life in order to devote all his efforts to the study of Torah and its precepts.

In the hour of a man's death. The Rabbis declare that a human being is born with his hands clenched to imply that he grasps everything, but he dies with his hands open to indicate that he departs from the world without any possessions (Ec. R.5). Compare Ec. 5:14, 'As he came forth of his mother's womb, naked shall he go back as he came, and shall take nothing for his labour, which he may carry away in his hand'.

David, King of Israel. The Midrash Shemuel queries the need for the full title of David King of Israel, in addition to the mention of the Book of Psalms. He suggests that this was deliberate and teaches us that we cannot compare the giving of charity and the pursuit of justice on earth with the study of Torah, which far exceeds every mitzvah. This we learn from the life of David, King of Israel. No one distributed charity and dispensed justice more than David. Thus we read, 'And David reigned over all his people' (II Sam. 8:15). But in spite of this he boldly declared, 'The law of Thy mouth is better unto me than thousands of gold and silver' (Ps. 119:72). This affirmation of David that Torah outweighs all money expended on earth is even more forcibly manifest when we take into account the vast sums of money he collected towards the building of the Temple, as we read in I Chron. 22:14, 'Now behold in my straits I have prepared for the House of the Lord a hundred thousand talents of gold and a thousand thousand talents of silver...'.

The proof text from Prov. 6:22 exalts the Torah way of life in three dimensions, in walking, sleeping and waking. Before proceeding to apply the interpretation of the verse to the Baraita we should comprehend its full implication. We note that the first word of the verse is not presented in the simple *kal* form, but in the reflexive, *behitalekhakha*, meaning walking hither and thither. This manner of movement is an aid to the student of Torah, who thereby finds it easier to concentrate and plumb the depths of Torah learning.

Torah will guard and protect one during sleeping hours, compare the first paragraph of the *Hamappil* prayer recited before retiring at night.

On waking in the morning the mind of the Torah student is filled with prayerful thoughts and the sayings of the Sages.

Whilst we have attributed the three daily exercises of man — walking, sleeping and waking to refer to this world, the Baraita rightly interprets walking alone to include the activities of man in this world, but sleeping to the sleep of death in the grave, and waking to the resurrection of the spirit in the world to come. In this manner the Baraita encompasses both worlds, *olam hazeh*, this world, and *olam haba*, the world to come.

The last quotation from Haggai 2:8 is a fitting conclusion to a Baraita which teaches that money should not be worshipped for its own sake, for it all belongs to God who loans it to us. Money can be a source of blessing only if it is acquired and expended in the service of Torah and mitzvot.

Hasidic Lore

The purity of prayer. The Berditchever walked over to a group of his hasidim in the congregation when they had concluded the Amidah, shook hands with them, greeting them with the words *shalom aleikhem*. They were greatly surprised at such an unexpected salutation inasmuch as they had not left the city and were not guests, who are usually greeted thus. The Rabbi noted their surprise and explained himself as follows: The reason for this salutation is that I could read in your faces whilst you were reciting the Amidah that you did not have in mind the meaning of the prayers, but were thinking of the grain market in Odessa, or the woollen market in Lodz. Now that you have returned from so long a voyage, it is appropriate for me to extend to you a welcome home.

The use of money. The Premislaner said: It is true that a Jew often concentrates most earnestly on those prayers which plead for a livelihood and for money. But to what purpose does he use the money? He keeps God's commandments therewith; he donates it to charities; he engages a teacher to instruct his children in the Torah; he spends it on meals appropriate to the Sabbath; he contributes it to the support of students of the Talmud. Is it improper, then, for him to pray for money?

(י) חֲמִשָּׁה קִנְיָנִים קָנָה לוֹ הַקָּדוֹשׁ בָּרוּךְ הוּא בְּעוֹלָמוֹ. וְאֵלּוּ הֵן. תּוֹרָה קִנְיָן אֶחָד. שָׁמַיִם וָאָרֶץ קִנְיָן אֶחָד. אַבְרָהָם קִנְיָן אֶחָד. יִשְׂרָאֵל קִנְיָן אֶחָד. בֵּית הַמִּקְדָּשׁ קִנְיָן אֶחָד. תּוֹרָה מִנַּיִן דִּכְתִיב יְהוָֹה קָנָנִי רֵאשִׁית דַּרְכּוֹ קֶדֶם מִפְעָלָיו מֵאָז. שָׁמַיִם וָאָרֶץ מִנַּיִן דִּכְתִיב כֹּה אָמַר יְהוָֹה הַשָּׁמַיִם כִּסְאִי וְהָאָרֶץ הֲדֹם רַגְלָי אֵי זֶה בַיִת אֲשֶׁר תִּבְנוּ לִי וְאֵי זֶה מָקוֹם מְנוּחָתִי. וְאוֹמֵר מָה רַבּוּ מַעֲשֶׂיךָ יְהוָֹה כֻּלָּם בְּחָכְמָה עָשִׂיתָ מָלְאָה הָאָרֶץ קִנְיָנֶךָ. אַבְרָהָם מִנַּיִן דִּכְתִיב וַיְבָרְכֵהוּ וַיֹּאמַר בָּרוּךְ אַבְרָם לְאֵל עֶלְיוֹן קוֹנֵה שָׁמַיִם וָאָרֶץ. יִשְׂרָאֵל מִנַּיִן דִּכְתִיב עַד יַעֲבֹר עַמְּךָ יְהוָֹה עַד יַעֲבוֹר עַם זוּ קָנִיתָ. וְאוֹמֵר לִקְדוֹשִׁים אֲשֶׁר בָּאָרֶץ הֵמָּה וְאַדִּירֵי כָּל חֶפְצִי בָם. בֵּית הַמִּקְדָּשׁ מִנַּיִן דִּכְתִיב מָכוֹן לְשִׁבְתְּךָ פָּעַלְתָּ יְהוָֹה מִקְּדָשׁ אֲדֹנָי כּוֹנְנוּ יָדֶיךָ. וְאוֹמֵר וַיְבִיאֵם אֶל גְּבוּל קָדְשׁוֹ הַר זֶה קָנְתָה יְמִינוֹ:

Baraita Ten

Five possessions has the Holy One blessed be He acquired in His world, and these are they, Torah is one possession, heaven and earth are one possession, Abraham is one possession, Israel is one possession, and the Temple is one possession. How do we know that the Torah is one possession? Since it is written (Prov. 8:22), 'The Lord possessed me in the beginning of His way before His works of old'. How do we know that heaven and earth are one of His possessions? Since it is written (Is. 66:1), 'Thus says the Lord, The heavens are My throne and the earth is My footstool. What manner of house will you build for Me and what place is My rest?' And it says (Ps. 104:24), 'How manifold are Thy works, O Lord? In wisdom hast Thou made them all; the earth is full of Thy possessions'. How do we know that Abraham is one of His possessions? Since it is written (Gen. 14:19), 'And He blessed him and said, 'Blessed be Abram of God Most High, Possessor of heaven and earth'. How do we know that Israel is one of His possessions? Since it is written (Ex. 15:16), 'Till Thy people pass over, O Lord, till this people pass over which Thou hast possessed'. And it says (Ps. 16:3), 'As for the saints that are in the earth, they are the excellent ones in whom is all My delight'. How do we know that the Temple is one of His possessions? Since it is written (Ex. 15:17), 'The place, O Lord, which Thou hast made to dwell in; the Sanctuary, O Lord, which Thy hands have prepared'. And it says (Ps. 78:5), 'And He brought them to the border of His Sanctuary, this mountain which His right hand has possessed'.

This passage is strictly an extension of Baraita six where we learnt that the Torah was acquired by forty eight qualities. Here we are told that God acquired the world by means of five special purchases or possessions.

Five. The five subjects enumerated here are also found in a number of texts, including the Tanna Dbe Eliyahu 17, but in the Mekhilta on Beshallah and in the Talmud (Pes. 87b) only four are mentioned, whereas the Sifre on Deut. 32 refers to three only — Torah, Israel and the Temple.

Kinyan. The right of possession or purchase is a recognised procedure in Jewish Law. It is based on Ruth 4:7, and it is discussed in the Talmud (B.M. 47a). *Kinyan*, however, is not restricted to monetary considerations; it is also found in a spiritual sense. One of the titles of this chapter is 'Kinyan Torah'. Torah can be purchased and metaphorically treated as a high-graded commodity.

It was very familiar to Jewish mothers of former days who would, whilst rocking the cradle, sing the lullaby, 'Die Torah is die beste sehorah', Torah is the finest merchandise. We have seen (1:6) how the vocabulary of the commercial world was drawn upon to propagate the study of Torah — 'Buy for yourself a companion' (to study the Torah). Indeed, God himself is designated as *konei hakol*, the Possessor of all, as we read in the first paragraph of the Amidah. Underlying this concept of God as *konei* is the great ethical principle of Imitatio Dei, to imitate God. If God, the Creator and Sovereign of the universe, deems it essential to acquire the rights of certain objects, how much more so does it devolve upon us, ordinary mortal beings, to acquire the right of possession of everything we claim to own. However, it should be remembered that if we steal from an individual, we also steal from God.

The five possessions. It is noteworthy that the five possessions are not grouped together here, but each one is particularised by the same phrase, *kinyan ehad*, one possession. This obviously points to the significance and individuality of each possession. Moreover, it teaches us that it is essential to strive and work for each possession. Nothing exists of its own accord; this is the essence of *kinyan* which differs from *yerushah*, a legacy or heritage. One may inherit a legacy without any conscious effort whatsoever on the part of the legatee. On the other hand a *kinyan*, a possession, is acquired after a person has expended time, energy and money. Whereas the legacy or bequest may at times be squandered and frittered away, the *kinyan* is often treasured and cherished. These and similar sentiments inspire us to strive for these five possessions and translate them into our daily lives.

Torah. Torah is the first divine possession we acquire at birth. On account of its celestial origin it is the miracle of our continued survival in every age. The Torah sustains and maintains us in spite of all the hardships and sufferings inflicted upon us. There is no greater possession than the Torah. This was forcibly expressed by R. Nehorai who said, 'I abandon every trade in the world and teach my son Torah only, for man enjoys the reward thereof in this world, while the principal remains to him in the world to come. But all other professions are not so, for when a man suffers sickness or old age or misfortune and cannot engage in his craft he dies of starvation, whereas the Torah guards him from all evil in his youth and gives him a future and hope in old age' (Kid. 82a). Torah is timeless and ageless and is not dependent upon the whims of any mortal ruler; it is God's possession and creation and is therefore immortal.

Kinyan ehad, one possession. We have already remarked on the meaning of this expression in general. We now deal with it specifically with regard to Torah. Torah has too often been labelled as orthodox, conservative, reform or liberal. It has been fragmentised into a variety of philosophical systems of thought unrecognised by the authentic Jew. We are here assured that Torah is an acquisition which is *ehad*, one, unique, and indivisible. This was formulated by Maimonides in his Thirteen Articles of Faith — 'I believe with a perfect faith that this Law will not be changed and that there will never be any other Law from the Creator, blessed be His Name'.

The proof text for Torah is Prov. 8:22, 'The Lord possessed me as the beginning of His way, the first of His works of old'. From this verse we learn that Torah, which is here personified by wisdom, was created and acquired by God even before the creation of the world (the first of His works). Indeed, through the medium of the Torah, the blue-print of the universe, God created the world. This thought is beautifully portrayed in the Yalkut Shimoni, an early Midrash on Gen. 1:1 which places these words in the mouth of the Torah, 'I was the architectural instrument of the Holy One blessed be He. It is customary that when a human king erects a palace he does not build it according to his own ideas, but according to the plans submitted by an architect. The architect likewise does not depend entirely upon the thoughts in his mind but requires parchments and tablets to enable him to plan the rooms and entrances. So did the Holy One blessed be He look into the Torah and He created the universe accordingly'. God, the universal Architect, therefore acquired the Torah which is unique and very different from any other constitutional law. The laws of the nations are dependent on time and space; they can be altered by the ruler or the government of the day; but Torah is everlasting. Torah is not dependent on any mortal ruler; it is God's possession and creation and is therefore everlasting and indestructible.

Heaven and earth. Having commenced with Torah, which is all-embracing, the Baraita proceeds to particularise and mentions the second possession, the two main constituents of the Universe heaven and earth. R. Eleazar said (Pes. 68b), 'But for the Torah heaven and earth would not endure, for it is said, 'If not for My covenant by day and by night, I had not appointed the ordinances of heaven and earth' (Jer. 33:25). This signifies that heaven and earth exist on account of the Torah which is studied day and night.

There are some who draw a line of demarcation between heaven and earth and divide them into watertight compartments. They maintain that God resides in His high heavens and is completely disinterested in the affairs of mankind on earth. This is blasphemous. The universe is round;

there are no sharp corners and heaven and earth are twin sections of one vast circle. Heaven and earth merge and intertwine with each other. The heavenly, the spiritual, coalesces with the earthly, the mundane. They are both *kinyan ehad*, one possession. The one God encircles and rules over both heaven and earth. 'Know this day and lay it to your heart, that the Lord, He is God in heaven above and upon the earth beneath; there is none else' (Deut. 4:39).

Proof texts. The above identical thought is expressed in the proof text Is. 66:1, 'The heavens are My throne and the earth is My footstool'. As the throne and footstool are one, so are heaven and earth one entity. God's rule and authority stretch from His throne in the heavens to the footstool on earth. To correct a false impression that the earth is somewhat denigrated by comparing it to a footstool, another verse is quoted which does more justice to the claims of the earth, 'The earth is full of Thy possessions' (Ps. 104:24). The earth is sated with God's products which feed and nourish mankind.

Abraham. The third possession is one specific personality in the world singled out as the foremost emissary of God on earth. It is not surprising that the choice should fall on Abraham, who is called the father of Judaism. He is the head of the three Patriarchs who are considered to be the foundation pillars of the fabric of Judaism and are therefore invoked three times a day in the first paragraph of the Amidah. A possible connection between Abraham and heaven and earth is found in the midrashic interpretation of Gen. 2:4, 'These are the generations of heaven and earth when they were created'. The word *behibaram*, when they were created, contains the Hebrew letters of Abraham, and the Rabbis suggest that the heaven and earth were created through the merit, *zekhut* of Abraham (Gen. R. 12).

The proof text is Gen. 14:18, 'And he (Melkhizedek) blessed him and said, 'Blessed be Abram of the Most High God, possessor of heaven and earth'. This verse establishes a vital principle. Abraham was profusely blessed by the priest Melkhizedek because he (Abraham) was the first person on earth who recognised that God was the Creator and Master of heaven and earth. Indeed, Abraham was ready to sacrifice all his spiritual and material gifts and powers in the service of God, the Possessor of heaven and earth.

Abraham was 'one possession' because he was the first to discover the Oneness of God. He also qualifies to be *kinyan ehad* because he converted many heathens who embraced Judaism and so introduced Monotheism into the world.

Israel. Israel is the fourth possession. If Abraham is the father of Judaism, Jacob or Israel is the father of our nation or people, and this explains our function in life. The name Israel was first given to Jacob by the angel of God with whom he wrestled... 'Your name shall be called no more Jacob, but Israel, for you have striven with God and with man and you have prevailed' (Gen. 32:29). The etymology of the Hebrew name *Yisrael* has been variously interpreted to mean *Yisra El*, he will strive for God; he who sees God and he who walks straight with God. Whatever the derivation be, the word *Yisrael* is in the future tense. This signifies that the name Israel was not reserved for an isolated historical occurrence, but was to be used in the future for all time. Indeed, since 1948 when the Jewish State was proclaimed it is known not as Palestine, but as Israel.

That the transition from Jacob to Israel was not to be treated lightly is evident from this dictum which is transmitted to us in the name of Bar Kappara: He who calls Jacob by the name Jacob and not Israel, violates a positive command (Gen. R. 78), whilst another Rabbi states that Israel may also be called Jacob, but Jacob must always be the *tafel*, the less important, whilst the name Israel must be the *ikkar*, his principal distinction (ibid). Our mission in life is to fight for God and act as a prince of God, *Sar El*, ever mindful of the historic title we possess for all time.

The proof text Ex. 15:16 underlines this positive fact, *am zu kanita*, 'You have acquired this people'. Israel is the possession of God. 'Therein lies the whole of Israel's destiny, by all that Thou hast done for this people, it belongs with every fibre of its being to Thee' (Hirsch). Commentators question the need for the second verse, Ps. 16:3, especially as it does not seem to have any overt reference to 'possession'. It would appear that the writer of this passage understands *Kedoshim* to refer to the people of Israel who are a 'Holy Nation', and 'My delight' is taken to mean 'that which I desire to possess'; compare Mal. 3:2. Others suggest that this additional verse is included to emphasise the universal love of God towards every section of the Jewish people, even those who are not faithful to God. We survive and flourish through this merit of the saints, *Kedoshim*, that live in every age; and in this manner Israel is a true posession of God.

Israel was *kinyan ehad*, for God chose Israel alone from all the nations to be His peculiar people.

Temple. The fifth possession is reserved for an institution, which was the holiest and greatest edifice in the Jewish world. The Temple served as a unifying factor because to it flocked Jews from every corner of the world. Pilgrimages were made to the Temple three times a year. 'The influence of the Temple must have been far-reaching and intensive, for through its well-ordered ritual it possessed the power to release certain spiritual energies which, if directed aright, were capable of enhancing the whole social and moral order of the community' (I. Epstein). Since the destruction of the Temple in 70 C.E. we have inherited a rich spiritual legacy which manifests itself in the Synagogue, the miniature Sanctuary, having substituted prayer for sacrifice, and the *Bimah*, central platform, for the Altar.

The proof text is derived from the Song of Moses and underlines the holiness and inner spirituality of the Temple as a House of God. The word 'possession' is not explicitly recorded, but it is evident because the Sanctuary was erected and established with God's own hands as His dwelling place. 'The Home prepared for Thy habitation which Thou, O Lord, hast made for Thee to dwell in, the Sanctuary which Thy hands have established'. This indeed constitutes a veritable possession.

The second verse is mentioned because it has a definite reference to the possession of the Temple Mount. Now that the first half of this verse has been fulfilled, for the Western Wall which is a relic of the ancient Temple is once again in our hands and we have reached the 'border' of the Temple area, we hope and pray that the second half of the verse will also be realised and that we shall reach the 'Mountain (the whole of the Temple area) which His right hand has possessed'.

The Temple was *kinyan ehad* because there was only one of its kind at any one period of time.

Hasidic Lore

Heaven and earth. Said the Alexanderer Rabbi: The expression in Ps. 115:16, 'The heavens are the heavens of the Lord, but the earth has He given to the children of men' means, 'The heavens are already heavenly, but the earth has the Lord given unto men that they may inject a heavenly spirit into it'.

Abraham and Israel. The Kosmirer Rabbi said: The Lord gave Canaan to Abraham on the condition that his heirs should follow in his footsteps. When Ishmael did not adhere fully to his father's teaching, Isaac received the inheritance. When Esau did not comply with the true tradition, Israel was given the heritage. When Israel became habitually delinquent, his heirloom reverted to Esau (the name given to Rome in Hebrew literature). When Esau's followers degenerated, they were compelled to surrender Canaan to Ishmael (the Moslems). At the present the process is reversing itself; the land was lost by Ishmael to Edom (Esau) and will shortly be given up by Edom to its rightful owner — Israel.

Thoughts on the Temple. The Bratzlaver said: He who influences others for good erects a Holy Temple unto the Lord, and builds an altar whereon is offered unto God the goodness which has been awakened.

The Ropshitzer used to say during the three weeks before the ninth of Av, 'It is not fitting that we should deplore the loss of the Holy Temple with our entire heart, for the Lord, who endowed this edifice with holiness, is with us in exile. We should mingle mourning with joy because our Lord is present among us.

Said the Koretzer: We read, 'Like the scarlet thread are your lips' (Cant. 4:3). As the scarlet thread hung at the Temple on Yom Kippur showed by its miraculous change into white the forgiveness of sins (Mishnah Yoma 6:8), your sins now will be forgiven if you are able to change your everyday prayers and study, (adulterated as they are with foreign thoughts) into pure worship and concentrated study'.

(יא) כָּל מַה שֶּׁבָּרָא הַקָּדוֹשׁ בָּרוּךְ הוּא בְּעוֹלָמוֹ לֹא בְרָאוֹ אֶלָּא לִכְבוֹדוֹ שֶׁנֶּאֱמַר כֹּל הַנִּקְרָא בִשְׁמִי וְלִכְבוֹדִי בְּרָאתִיו יְצַרְתִּיו אַף עֲשִׂיתִיו. וְאוֹמֵר יְהוָֹה יִמְלֹךְ לְעֹלָם וָעֶד:

Baraita Eleven

Whatever the Holy One blessed be He created in His world, He created but for His glory, as it is said (Is. 43:7), 'Everything that is called by My name and that I have created for My glory, I have formed it, yea, I have made it'; and it says (Ex. 15:18), 'The Lord shall reign for ever and ever'.

Whereas the previous Baraita particularises and enumerates the five possessions with which God created the world, here we learn that everything in the world is created for the glory of God. This universalism of God's power and influence is a fitting climax to the collection of sayings we call *Pirkei Avot.*

His glory. The glory of God manifests itself throughout the whole universe and is popularly known as the *Shekhinah*, His Divine Presence. Some imagine that it is the prerogative of the ministering angels in heaven to give glory to God. Thus the Psalmist exclaims, 'The heavens declare the glory of God' (19:2) and Isaiah enters his ministry hearing the Seraphim cry, 'Holy, Holy, Holy is the Lord of Hosts, the whole earth is full of His glory' (6:3). The Baraita teaches us that the purpose of life is to give glory to God. This is not reserved for the angels above; it is the duty of man to live a life dedicated to the glory of God who is near to all who call upon Him in truth. God is not a transcendental Being far removed from us. He is not ensconced in the celestial heights. He walks with us on earth. Thus we read in Lev. 26:12, 'And I shall walk among you and will be your God and you shall be My people'. Rashi explains as follows, 'I shall promenade in the Garden of Eden like one of you and you shall not be frightened of Me'. God is not unapproachable; He lives in our midst. Indeed, the Midrash records a conversation between God and the angels. God said to Israel, 'Make Me a dwelling (Ex. 25:8, 26:1) for I desire to dwell amid My sons'. When the ministering angels heard this they said to God, 'Why wilt Thou abandon the creatures above and descend to those below? It is Thy glory that Thou shouldst be in heaven, O Lord our God, who has set Thy majesty in the heavens' (Ps. 8:2) But God said, 'See how greatly I love the creatures below that I shall descend and dwell beneath the goat's hair'. Hence it says, 'Make curtains of goat's hair for the Tabernacle' (Ex. 26:7) (Tanchuma Terumah). God wishes to associate with man. The perennial question. however, is whether man wishes to associate with God. In rabbinic thought man is a co-partner with God in the creation of the world but man, who is presumably a little lower than the angels, does not always rise to his full stature, hence the existence of much evil on earth and the abandonment of God's glory.

It is the will of God that man should utilise his talents and gifts of mind to promote the well-being of the human race and this would redound to His glory and honour, but man, God's co-worker, has not always exercised the divine spark latent in him. Instead, man employs his intellect and wisdom to plan and manufacture destructive machines of war which threaten to engulf whole continents. The glory of God has been blasphemously transformed into the self-glorification of man. With prophetic insight Ecclesiastes foresaw this rebellious spirit inherent in man. 'Behold, this only have I found, that God made man upright but they have sought out many inventions' (7:29). Would that all the inventions of our scientists in every field of endeavour were employed only for the glory of God on earth.

The purpose and quality of life and man's duty on earth are discussed in the opening chapter of Mesillat Yesharim. 'This world has been created for man's use; this is why the fate of the world depends upon man's conduct. If a man is allured by the things of this world and is estranged from his Creator, not only is it he who is corrupted, but the whole world is corrupted with him. But if he exercises self-control, cleaves to his Creator, and makes use of this world only in so far as it helps him to serve his Creator, he himself rises to a higher order of being and he carries the world along with him. All created things are transfigured when they are made to serve the perfect man who reflects the holiness of God'.

In the proof text the purpose of life and the goal which man should aspire to attain are delineated for us by Isaiah who said, 'Everything that is created by My name and that I have created for My glory, I have formed it, yea I have made it' (43:7). We should note the sequence of the three verbs which follow in quick succession. The omnipotence of God manifests itself in three dimensions — God creates, God designs or forms, and God acts.

We recognise and appreciate the glory of God if we fully comprehend these three nuances.

God creates. The verb *bara* signifies the principle of *yesh meayyin*, something out of nothing. The world did not come into existence by chance. It was created by the will of God through a divine fiat.

God designs or forms. The verb *yazar* is first used in the Torah in connection with the creation of man who was formed, so to speak, with the hand of God (2:7).

God is active. The verb *asa* here implies an ongoing and continuous process of creation by God in the world. We are reminded of the morning prayer, 'And in His goodness He renews the creation every day continuously'. Commenting on Gen. 2:3 where we find the words *bara* and *asa* in close proximity, Hertz says, 'The work of creation continues and the world is still in the process of creation as long as the process of good and evil remain undecided. Ethically, the world is thus still unfinished and it is man's glorious privilege to help finish it. He can, by his life, hasten the triumph of the forces of good in the universe'.

The Lord shall reign for ever and ever. (Ex. 15:18). The final proof text to this Baraita and to the whole of Pirkei Avot is well chosen. In spite of all the trials and tribulations to which we have been subjected by a hostile world,we conclude on an optimistic and universalistic note. The verse is derived from the Song of Moses which we recite each morning in our prayers. With a song on our lips we look forward to the days when the Lord will reign gloriously not for one generation, but for ever and ever, and He will plant on earth righteousness, justice, truth and peace.

Hasidic Lore

Glory of God. Rabbi Bunam was once asked if he would care to change places with Abraham. Would he not be happy to know that he was Abraham? He replied, 'If I were Abraham and Abraham were Bunam, there would still be in the world only one Abraham and one Bunam. Does it matter whether I contribute the Bunam share of the glory of God or the Abraham share? Is not the important fact that ultimately the Almighty has the glory given by an Abraham and the lesser glory given by a Bunam?'

Concluding Mishnah. Text, translation and commentary, see page 71.

INDEX

NAMES AND SUBJECTS

About the Author

Shlomo P. Toperoff was born in London in 1907 and after studying for several years at Eitz Hayim Yeshiva, won a scholarship to Jews' College and graduated from University College, London, with a B.A. in Semitics. He was later ordained as a rabbi by the London Beth Din. He served as a minister to the Sunderland community and then as regional rabbi to Newcastle Upon Tyne until his retirement. During these years he was very active in Jewish education and was well-known as a broadcaster, lecturer, and an exponent of the Jewish cause among non-Jews. Rabbi Toperoff is the author of the following books: *Eternal Life, A Handbook for the Mourner; Ehad Mi Yodea, Questions and Answers on Jewish Life; The Animal Kingdom in Jewish Thought*, and *Bishop Henson and the Jewish Problem.* He is currently enjoying his retirement in Israel with his wife, three children, ten grandchildren, and twenty-four great-grandchildren.